Human Behavior Recognition Technologies:

Intelligent Applications for Monitoring and Security

Hans W. Guesgen
Massey University, New Zealand

Stephen Marsland
Massey University, New Zealand

Information Science
REFERENCE

Managing Director:	Lindsay Johnston
Editorial Director:	Joel Gamon
Book Production Manager:	Jennifer Yoder
Publishing Systems Analyst:	Adrienne Freeland
Development Editor:	Austin DeMarco
Assistant Acquisitions Editor:	Kayla Wolfe
Typesetter:	Alyson Zerbe
Cover Design:	Jason Mull

Published in the United States of America by
 Information Science Reference (an imprint of IGI Global)
 701 E. Chocolate Avenue
 Hershey PA 17033
 Tel: 717-533-8845
 Fax: 717-533-8661
 E-mail: cust@igi-global.com
 Web site: http://www.igi-global.com

Library of Congress Cataloging-in-Publication Data

Human behavior recognition technologies : intelligent applications for monitoring and security / Hans Guesgen and Stephen Marsland, editors.
       pages cm
 Includes bibliographical references and index.
  Summary: "This book takes an insightful glance into the applications and dependability of behavior detection and looks into the social, ethical, and legal implications of these areas"--Provided by publisher.
  ISBN 978-1-4666-3682-8 (hardcover) -- ISBN 978-1-4666-3683-5 (ebook) -- ISBN 978-1-4666-3684-2 (print & perpetual access) 1. Human activity recognition. 2. Home automation. I. G?sgen, Hans Werner, 1959- II. Marsland, Stephen.
  TK7882.P7H86 2013
  681'.25--dc23
                                      2012045192

British Cataloguing in Publication Data
A Cataloguing in Publication record for this book is available from the British Library.

List of Reviewers

Alexander Artikis, *NCSR Demokritos, Greece*
Juan Carlos Augusto, *University of Ulster, UK*
Asier Aztiria, *University of Mondragon, Spain*
Debraj Basu, *Massey University, New Zealand*
Wilfried Bohlken, *University of Hamburg, Germany*
Liangliang Cao, *IBM T.J. Watson Research Center, USA*
Chao Chen, *Washington State University, USA*
Sook-Ling Chua, *Massey University, New Zealand*
Diane J. Cook, *Washington State University, USA*
Aaron S. Crandall, *Washington State University, USA*
Anuroop Gaddam, *Massey University, New Zealand*
Björn Gottfried, *University of Bremen, Germany*
Gourab Sen Gupta, *Massey University, New Zealand*
Ayesha Hakim, *Massey University, New Zealand*
Joachim Hertzberg, *University of Osnabrück, Germany*
Wen-Chen Hu, *University of North Dakota, USA*
Sajid Hussain, *Fisk University, USA*
Patrick Koopmann, *University of Hamburg, Germany*
Zicheng Liu, *Microsoft Research, USA*
Fulvio Mastrogiovanni, *University of Genova, Italy*
Subhas Chandra Mukhopadhyay, *Massey University, New Zealand*
Bernd Neumann, *University of Hamburg, Germany*
Bolutife J. Ogunjobi, *Fisk University, USA*
Fabian N. Okeke, *Fisk University, USA*
Georgios Paliouras, *NCSR Demokritos, Greece*
Ute Schmid, *University of Bamberg, Germany*
Marek Sergot, *Imperial College, UK*
Antonio Sgorbissa, *University of Genova, Italy*
Weihua Sheng, *Oklahoma State University, USA*
Gita Sukthankar, *University of Central Florida, USA*
YingLi Tian, *The City College, USA*
An Cong Tran, *Massey University, New Zealand*

Table of Contents

Detailed Table of Contents

Chapter 1

> *Alexander Artikis, NCSR Demokritos, Greece*
> *Marek Sergot, Imperial College, UK*
> *Georgios Paliouras, NSCR Demokritos, Greece*

Artikis, Sergot, and Paliouras present a logic-based approach to behaviour recognition. They introduce a system for recognising human activities based on symbolic representations of video data. They define long-term activities as spatio-temporal combinations of short-term activities and use constraints on short-term activities to recognise long-term activities from short-term activities. These constraints are expressed in a dialect of the event calculus.

Chapter 2

> *Asier Aztiria, University of Mondragon, Spain*
> *Juan Carlos Augusto, University of Ulster, UK*

Aztiria and Augusto link behaviour recognition with context awareness to assist the user in their daily activities. Their focus is on behaviours that happen frequently and therefore lend themselves towards automatic support. The multi-layer system that they introduce uses rules that are learned on the basis of sensor data.

Chapter 3

> *Wilfried Bohlken, University of Hamburg, Germany*
> *Patrick Koopmann, University of Hamburg, Germany*
> *Lothar Hotz, University of Hamburg, Germany*
> *Bernd Neumann, University of Hamburg, Germany*

Bohlken, Koopmann, Hotz, and Neumann aim at real-time behaviour interpretation. Their chapter describes a generic framework for model-based behaviour interpretation, using OWL-DL for concept definition and SWRL for constraints. The conceptual models are automatically converted into an operational scene interpretation system. This system is used to monitor aircraft service activities.

Chen and Cook look at novelty detection in human behaviour. Instead of interpreting sensor data from a smart home, they analyse the energy consumption in the home. They demonstrate that energy consumption and human activities are related. By looking at outliers in the energy consumption, they are able to identify novelties in human behaviour.

Chua, Marsland, and Guesgen investigate how unlabelled sensor data can be used to train a behaviour recogniser. After describing a general setting for behaviour recognition and discussing some issues that arise when performing this task, they introduce an unsupervised learning algorithm based on text compression. Their idea is to use the dictionary produced by the Lempel-Ziv-Welch compression algorithm as a basis and to modify this dictionary so that it contains typical entries that represent typical behaviours.

Crandall and Cook introduce a tracking system for multiple smart home residents. Their system uses a Bayesian updating method for tracking individuals through the space of a smart home. Unlike other approaches, their approach does not employ a carried wireless device or an imaging system, and therefore poses less social problems when deployed over long periods of time.

Gaddam, Sen Gupta, and Mukhopadhyay discuss different sensors for smart homes, using criteria such as availability, cost, installation, and performance. They then describe a case study that shows how some of these sensors can be used in a smart home monitoring system. The system includes units for monitoring electrical appliances, movements and locations in beds, and water usage in showers, baths, toilets, washing machines, dishwashers, etc.

Gottfried defines a framework for the design and analysis of behaviour monitoring and interpretation systems that consists of five layers with different levels of abstraction. As an example scenario, he presents a pedestrian navigation and service tool, which guides the user navigating around a city by providing instructions through a hearing-aid similar device.

Han and Pereira present a coherent framework for decision-making based on logic programming, which extends their previous work on evolution prospection for decision-making. They demonstrate the usefulness of the system with several examples in different application domains, including moral reasoning, ambient intelligence, elder care, and game theory.

Nunes, Rebelo, Abreu, Gamboa, and Fred introduce a time series clustering algorithm for human behaviour recognition that uses biosignals as input and captures the general morphology of the signal's cycles in one mean wave. In their validation tests, they demonstrate that the algorithm has a high accuracy level and outperforms other algorithms.

Odella describes the sociological perspective of technologies for monitoring behaviour and debates implications from both the scientific and ethical point of view. She uses a number of specific implementations of technologies for this, ranging from healthcare automated assistance to mobile communication devices, RFID and smart-meter technology.

Tian, Cao, Liu, and Zhang discuss an approach for detecting behaviours in crowds by analysing video data. They combine hierarchically filtered motion with spatiotemporal interest point features to overcome the problem of detecting behaviours in cluttered videos. Their approach uses a combination of Gaussian mixture models and branch-and-bound search.

Wernsdorfer and Schmid show a way from streams of observations to knowledge-level productive predictions of sequences of actions. They present an approach that combines sequence abstraction networks with inductive generalisation of recursive rule sets. The underlying assumption is that the benefits of ambient assisted living systems depend on the successful recognition of human intentions.

Zhao, Wang, and Sukthankar introduce two techniques for improving supervised learning of human behaviours from motion data. One is an active learning framework to reduce the number of samples required to segment motion traces. The other is an intelligent feature selection technique that both improves classification performance and reduces training time.

Zhu and Sheng discuss an approach for behaviour recognition in smart homes that combines motion data and location information. As one of its components, the system uses an inertial sensor to be worn by the inhabitant. This sensor provides motion data to the system, while a motion capture component is used to record the location of the inhabitant. The combination has the advantage of significantly reducing the obtrusiveness to the inhabitant while maintaining a high accuracy of recognition.

Preface

In recent years there has been a move in information technology and computer science from a machine-centred approach to a human-centred and knowledge-based approach. Keywords such as ubiquitous computing, ambient intelligence, and cloud computing are used more and more to describe tomorrow's paradigm of computing. In these systems, interacting with the user is often done in an implicit way, by reacting to the user's behaviour. Examples of such systems are smart environments in which the user's behaviour is perceived through sensors such as video cameras, motion sensors, RFID tags, etc., and then used to perform an action that adequately responds to that behaviour. The applications for this are widespread, ranging from behavioural monitoring for biosecurity and homeland security to market research and to monitoring the elderly in their own homes so that they can continue to live independently for longer.

Behaviour recognition has a multitude of facets. From the computational point of view, there is the question of how to detect human behaviour reliably from the sensor data that is available. The data is often noisy, and therefore, probabilistic approaches such as hidden Markov models seem to have an advantage over rule-based approaches that use predefined conditions to recognise the behaviour. On the other hand, the latter are usually easier to verify by a human, which facilitates validation of the system. A second question is where, when, and how can a behaviour occur. Consecutive behaviours carried out by one individual are easier to recognise than interleaved behaviours conducted by a group of individuals.

The second facet of behaviour recognition is concerned with the applications that it is used in. Some applications are more critical than others, and therefore less tolerant to errors in the recognition process. Behaviour recognition in a smart environment with the purpose of delivering the most appropriate environmental conditions (warm and cosy for less physically demanding activities such as reading a book versus fresh air and a cooler temperature in the case of the daily workout) can cope more easily with false positives than behaviour recognition at the airport to detect terrorists: reading a book in a room that is slightly too cold is generally less disturbing than spending a night in prison because of a false accusation.

Application-oriented aspects of behaviour recognition are closely related to the third facet of research in this area: the social, ethical, and legal implications. Monitoring people in their own homes is generally only acceptable if it is done in a non-obtrusive way and if the information gathered is only passed on to a very select group of people (like the carers of the people living in the smart home). This severely restricts the means by which we can collect data in smart environments: while video cameras might be acceptable at airports, they are not usually a good idea in a person's private bathroom. As a result, it becomes more difficult to correctly recognise the behaviour, which might have ethical and legal implications: is it acceptable not to detect if something is wrong with the inhabitant of the home, and if as a result of this negligence the inhabitant is harmed, who is responsible?

As with any book that aims at covering different aspects of a research area, it is impossible to provide a thorough discussion of all of the aspects. As it turns out with this book, the bias is towards methods for behaviour recognition:

Artikis, Sergot, and Paliouras present a logic-based approach to behaviour recognition. They intoduce a system for recognising human activities based on symbolic representations of video data. They define long-term activities as spatio-temporal combinations of short-term activities, and use constraints on short-term activities to recognise long-term activities from short-term activities. These constraints are expressed in a dialect of the event calculus.

Aztiria and Augusto link behaviour recognition with context awareness to assist the user in their daily activities. Their focus is on behaviours that happen frequently and therefore lend themselves towards automatic support. The multi-layer system that they introduce uses rules that are learned on the basis of sensor data.

Bohlken, Koopmann, Hotz, and Neumann aim at real-time behaviour interpretation. Their chapter describes a generic framework for model-based behaviour interpretation, using OWL-DL for concept definition and SWRL for constraints. The conceptual models are automatically converted into an operational scene interpretation system. This system is used to monitor aircraft service activities.

Chen and Cook look at novelty detection in human behaviour. Instead of interpreting sensor data from a smart home, they analyse the energy consumption in the home. They demonstrate that energy consumption and human activities are related. By looking at outliers in the energy consumption, they are able to identify novelties in human behaviour.

Chua, Marsland, and Guesgen investigate how unlabelled sensor data can be used to train a behaviour recogniser. After describing a general setting for behaviour recognition and discussing some issues that arise when performing this task, they introduce an unsupervised learning algorithm based on text compression. Their idea is to use the dictionary produced by the Lempel-Ziv-Welch compression algorithm as a basis and to modify this dictionary so that it contains typical entries that represent typical behaviours.

Crandall and Cook introduce a tracking system for multiple smart home residents. Their system uses a Bayesian updating method for tracking individuals through the space of a smart home. Unlike other approaches, their approach does not employ a carried wireless device or an imaging system, and therefore poses less social problems when deployed over long periods of time.

Gaddam, Sen Gupta, and Mukhopadhyay discuss different sensors for smart homes, using criteria such as availability, cost, installation, and performance. They then describe a case study that shows how some of these sensors can be used in a smart home monitoring system. The system includes units for monitoring electrical appliances, movements and locations in beds, and water usage in showers, baths, toilets, washing machines, dishwashers, etc.

Gottfried defines a framework for the design and analysis of behaviour monitoring and interpretation systems, which consists of five layers with different levels of abstraction. As an example scenario, he presents a pedestrian navigation and service tool, which guides the user navigating around a city by providing instructions through a hearing-aid similar device.

Han and Pereira present a coherent framework for decision making based on logic programming, which extends their previous work on evolution prospection for decision making. They demonstrate the usefulness of the system with several examples in different application domains, including moral reasoning, ambient intelligence, elder care, and game theory.

Nunes, Rebelo, Abreu, Gamboa, and Fred introduce a time series clustering algorithm for human behaviour recognition, which uses biosignals as input and captures the general morphology of the signal's cycles in one mean wave. In their validation tests, they demonstrate that the algorithm has a high accuracy level and outperforms other algorithms.

Odella describes the sociological perspective of technologies for monitoring behaviour and debates implications from both the scientific and ethical point of view. She uses a number of specific implementations of technologies for this, ranging from healthcare automated assistance to mobile communication devices, RFID, and smart-meter technology.

Tian, Cao, Liu, and Zhang discuss an approach for detecting behaviours in crowds by analysing video data. They combine hierarchically filtered motion with spatiotemporal interest point features to overcome the problem of detecting behaviours in cluttered videos. Their approach uses a combination of Gaussian mixture models and branch-and-bound search.

Wernsdorfer and Schmid show a way from streams of observations to knowledge-level productive predictions of sequences of actions. They present an approach that combines sequence abstraction networks with inductive generalisation of recursive rule sets. The underlying assumption is that the benefits of ambient assisted living systems depend on the successful recognition of human intentions.

Zhao, Wang, and Sukthankar introduce two techniques for improving supervised learning of human behaviours from motion data. One is an active learning framework to reduce the number of samples required to segment motion traces. The other is an intelligent feature selection technique that both improves classification performance and reduces training time.

Zhu and Sheng discuss an approach for behaviour recognition in smart homes that combines motion data and location information. As one of its components, the system uses an inertial sensor to be worn by the inhabitant. This sensor provides motion data to the system, while a motion capture component is used to record the location of the inhabitant. The combination has the advantage of significantly reducing the obtrusiveness to the inhabitant while maintaining a high accuracy of recognition.

Hans W. Guesgen
Massey University, New Zealand

Stephen Marsland
Massey University, New Zealand

Chapter 1
A Logic–Based Approach
to Activity Recognition

Alexander Artikis
NCSR Demokritos, Greece

Marek Sergot
Imperial College, UK

Georgios Paliouras
NSCR Demokritos, Greece

ABSTRACT

The authors have been developing a system for recognising human activities given a symbolic representation of video content. The input of the system is a stream of time-stamped short-term activities detected on video frames. The output of the system is a set of recognised long-term activities, which are pre-defined spatio-temporal combinations of short-term activities. The constraints on the short-term activities that, if satisfied, lead to the recognition of a long-term activity, are expressed using a dialect of the Event Calculus. The authors illustrate the expressiveness of the dialect by showing the representation of several typical complex activities. Furthermore, they present a detailed evaluation of the system through experimentation on a benchmark dataset of surveillance videos.

1. INTRODUCTION

A common approach to human activity recognition separates low-level from high-level recognition. The output of the former type of recognition is a set of activities taking place in a short period of time: 'short-term activities'. The output of the latter type of recognition is a set of 'long-term activities', that is, pre-defined spatio-temporal combinations of short-term activities. We focus on high-level recognition.

We define the set of long-term activities of interest, such as 'fighting' and 'meeting', as combinations of short-term activities - for example, 'walking', 'running', and 'inactive' (standing still) - using a logic programming implementation of the Event Calculus (Kowalski & Sergot, 1986; Artikis & Sergot, 2010). More precisely, we

DOI: 10.4018/978-1-4666-3682-8.ch001

employ the Event Calculus to express the temporal (and other) constraints on a set of short-term activities that, if satisfied, lead to the recognition of a long-term activity.

In this chapter we extend our previous work on activity recognition (Artikis & Paliouras, 2009) in the following ways. First, we use a more efficient Event Calculus dialect and implementation to compute the intervals of long-term activities. Second, we illustrate the expressiveness of the proposed Event Calculus dialect by presenting several complex activity definitions. We are able to construct much more succinct representations of activity definitions for video surveillance than we had in our earlier work. Third, we present a more detailed and informative evaluation of the Event Calculus on activity recognition. We show through experimentation how incomplete short-term activity narratives, inconsistent annotation of short-term and long-term activities, and a limited dictionary of short-term activities and context variables affect recognition accuracy. Fourth, we evaluate our approach on a dataset with a refined dictionary of short-term activities, in order to validate experimentally our intuition that a finer classification of short-term activities increases, under certain circumstances, the accuracy of long-term activity recognition. Indeed, the refined dictionary of short-term activities—which can be provided by state-of-the-art short-term activity recognition systems—together with the updated long-term activity definitions presented in this chapter, lead to much higher Precision and Recall rates.

The remainder of the chapter is organised as follows. First, we present the Event Calculus dialect that we employ to formalise activity definitions. Second, we describe the dataset of short-term activities on which we perform long-term activity recognition. Third, we present our knowledge base of long-term activity definitions. Fourth, we present our experimental results. Finally, we discuss related work and outline directions for further research.

2. THE EVENT CALCULUS

Our Long-Term Activity Recognition (LTAR) system consists of a logic programming (Prolog) implementation of an Event Calculus dialect. The Event Calculus, introduced by Kowalski and Sergot (1986), is a many-sorted, first-order predicate calculus for representing and reasoning about events and their effects. For the dialect used here, hereafter LTAR-EC (event calculus for long-term activity recognition), the time model is linear and it may include real numbers or integers. Where F is a *fluent* – a property that is allowed to have different values at different points in time - the term $F = V$ denotes that fluent F has value V. Boolean fluents are a special case in which the possible values are true and false. Informally, $F = V$ holds at a particular time-point if $F = V$ has been *initiated* by an event at some earlier time-point, and not *terminated* by another event in the meantime.

An *event description* in LTAR-EC includes axioms that define, among other things, the event occurrences (with the use of the happensAt and happensFor predicates), the effects of events (with the use of the initiatedAt and terminatedAt predicates), and the values of the fluents (with the use of the initially, holdsAt and holdsFor predicates). Table 1 summarises the main predicates of LTAR-EC. Variables, starting with an upper-case letter, are assumed to be universally quantified unless otherwise indicated. Predicates, function symbols and constants start with a lower-case letter.

The domain-independent axioms for holdsAt and holdsFor are such that, for any fluent F, holdsAt($F = V$, T) if and only if time-point T belongs to one of the maximal intervals of I such that holdsFor($F = V$, I). However, for efficiency the implementation employs different procedures for these two tasks, and various indexing techniques to reduce search and improve efficiency further. Briefly, to compute holdsFor($F = V$, I), we find all time-points Ti in which $F = V$ is initiated, and then, for each Ti, we compute the first time-point after Ti in which $F = V$ is terminated.

Table 1. Main predicates of LTAR-EC

Predicate	Meaning
happensAt(E, T)	Event E is occurring at time T
happensFor(E, I)	I is the list of maximal intervals during which E takes place
initially(F = V)	The value of fluent F is V at time 0
holdsAt(F = V, T)	The value of fluent F is V at time T
holdsFor(F = V, I)	I is the list of maximal intervals for which F = V holds continuously
initiatedAt(F = V, T)	At time T a period of time for which F = V is initiated
terminatedAt(F = V, T)	At time T a period of time for which F = V is terminated

If the list of initiating time-points is generated in sorted order, which is easy to arrange, both steps can make effective use of indexing. In particular, if the list of initiating time-points contains an adjacent pair..., Ti, $Ti+1$,... then the terminating time-point corresponding to Ti must occur between Ti and $Ti+1$. In outline, the indexing works as follows.

The domain-independent axioms for holdsAt can be written in the following form:

$$\text{holdsAt}\left(F = V, T\right) \leftarrow$$
$$\text{initiatedAt}\left(F = V, Ts\right) \quad (1)$$
$$\text{not broken}\left(F = V, Ts, T\right)$$

$$\text{broken}\left(F = V, Ts, T\right) \leftarrow$$
$$\text{terminatedAt}\left(F = V, Tf\right) \quad (2)$$
$$Ts < Tf < T$$

$$\text{broken}\left(F = V1, Ts, T\right) \leftarrow$$
$$\text{initiatedAt}\left(F = V2, Tf\right)$$
$$V1 \neq V2 \quad (3)$$
$$Ts < Tf < T$$

The "not" in Rule 1 represents 'negation by failure', which provides a default form of persistence ('inertia') of fluents.

According to Rule 2, a period of time for which $F=V$ holds is broken at Tf if $F=V$ is terminated at time Tf. According to Rule 3, if $F=V2$ is initiated at Tf then effectively $F=V1$ is terminated at time Tf, for all other possible values $V1$ of F. Rule 3 ensures therefore that a fluent cannot have more than one value at any time.

Besides the general, domain-independent rule initiatedAt$(F=V,0)<$— initially$(F=V)$, the definitions of initiatedAt and terminatedAt are domain specific. One common form of rule for initiatedAt, for example, has the general form:

$$\text{initiatedAt}\left(F = V, T\right) \leftarrow$$
$$\text{happensAt}\left(Ev, T\right) \quad (4)$$
$$Conditions\left[T\right]$$

where *Conditions*[T] is some set of further conditions referring to time T. Concrete examples of initiatedAt rules are presented in the section that follows.

To explain what we mean by indexing, note that clauses 1, 2, and 3 can be written equivalently as follows:

$$\text{holdsAt}\left(F = V, T\right) \leftarrow$$
$$\text{initiatedAt}\left(F = V, 0, Ts, T\right) \quad (5)$$
$$\text{not broken}\left(F = V, Ts, T\right)$$

$$\text{broken}\left(F = V, T\min, T\max\right) \leftarrow$$
$$\text{terminatedAt}\left(F = V, T\min, Tf, T\max\right) \quad (6)$$

$$\text{broken}\left(F = V1, T\min, T\max\right) \leftarrow$$
$$\text{initiatedAt}\left(F = V2, T\min, Tf, T\max\right)$$
$$V1 \neq V2 \quad (7)$$

where every rule of (4) is transformed into the form:

$$\text{initiatedAt}\left(F = V, T\min, T, T\max\right) \leftarrow$$
$$\text{happensAt}\left(Ev, T\min, T, T\max\right) \quad (8)$$
$$Conditions\left[T\right]$$

The extra arguments in initiatedAt, terminatedAt, and happensAt specify the range of time-points *Tmin* and *Tmax* between which the time-point *T* of interest must occur. Thus happensAt(*Ev, Tmin, T, Tmax*) if and only if happensAt(*Ev, T*) and *Tmin* < *T* < *Tmax*.

Our implementation automatically transforms initiatedAt rules of the Form 4 into the Form 8 on compilation, in a process transparent to the user. The advantage is that in Prolog execution of holdsAt and holdsFor, when happensAt(*Ev, Tmin, T, Tmax*) is called, *Ev* is always ground (variable-free), which exploits Prolog's built-in indexing when searching for occurrences of event *Ev*. But much more importantly, *Tmin* and *Tmax* are also always ground which means that the storage of happensAt data can be indexed to exploit this and reduce search very significantly.

"terminatedAt" and other forms of "initiatedAt" rules are handled similarly. We omit these and other details for lack of space. The complete code for LTAR-EC is available upon request.

3. SHORT-TERM ACTIVITIES

Our Long-Term Activity Recognition system (LTAR) includes long-term activity definitions in LTAR-EC. The input to LTAR is a symbolic representation of short-term activities. The output of LTAR is a set of recognised long-term activities. In Artikis and Paliouras (2009), we used the first dataset of the CAVIAR project (http://homepages. inf.ed.ac.uk/rbf/CAVIARDATA1/) to perform long-term activity recognition. This dataset includes 28 surveillance videos of a public space.

The videos are staged—actors walk around, sit down, meet one another, leave objects behind, fight, and so on. Each video has been manually annotated in order to provide the ground truth for both short-term and long-term activities.

Our preliminary experiments with this dataset, however, showed that the limited dictionary of short-term activity types compromised the recognition of some long-term activities - it was often impossible to distinguish between certain long-term activities. To overcome this problem, in the context of this chapter we introduced in the CAVIAR dataset a short-term activity for 'abrupt motion': we manually edited the annotation of the CAVIAR videos by changing, when necessary, the label of a short-term activity to 'abrupt motion'. This is a form of short-term activity that is recognised by some state-of-the-art recognition systems, such as (Kosmopoulos, Antonakaki, Valasoulis, Kesidis, & Perantonis, 2008). A person is said to exhibit an 'abrupt motion' activity if he moves abruptly and his position in the global coordinate system does not change significantly—if it did then the short-term activity would be classified as 'running'. For this set of experiments, therefore, the input to LTAR is:

1. The short-term activities abrupt motion, walking, running, active (non-abrupt body movement in the same position) and inactive (standing still), together with their time-stamps, that is, the video frame in which that short-term activity took place. These activities are mutually exclusive. This type of input is represented by means of the happensAt predicate - for example, happensAt(*abrupt(id6), 15560*) expresses that *id6* moved abruptly at video frame (time-point) *15560*. Short-term activities are represented as events in the Event Calculus in order to use the initiatedAt and terminatedAt predicates for expressing the conditions in which these activities initiate and terminate a long-term activity.

2. The coordinates of the tracked people and objects as pixel positions at each time-point. The coordinates are represented with the use of the holdsAt predicate – for example, holdsAt(*coord(id2)= (14, 55), 10600*) expresses that the coordinates of *id2* are(*14, 55*) at time-point (frame number) *106000*.

3. The first and the last time a person or object is tracked ('appears'/'disappears'). This type of input is represented using the happensAt predicate. For example, happensAt(*appear(id10),300*) expresses that *id10* is first tracked at time-point (frame number) *300*.

Given this input, LTAR recognises the following long-term activities: a person leaving an object, a person being immobile, people meeting, moving together, or fighting. Long-term activities are represented as Event Calculus fluents in order to use the holdsFor predicate for computing the intervals of these activities. For example, holdsFor(*moving(id1, id3)=*true, *[(0,40), (340,380)]*) states that *id1* was moving together with *id3* in the intervals *(0,40)*, and *(340,380)*.

To recognise long-term activities, LTAR processes the input information as follows. First, given input type (i), that is, the short-term activities detected at each time-point and recorded using the happensAt predicate, LTAR computes the maximal duration of each short-term activity, and represents it using the happensFor predicate. For example, happensFor(*walking(id5), [(40, 400),(600, 720)]*) expresses that the maximal intervals for which *id5* was walking are *(40, 400)* and *(600, 720)*. *appear(A)* and *disappear(A)* are instantaneous events. (They occur at one time point.) Second, given input type (ii), LTAR computes the distance between two tracked entities and compares the distance with pre-defined thresholds. For example, holdsAt(*close(id3, id5, 30)=*true, *80*) expresses that *id3* is 'close' to *id5* at time *80* in the sense that their distance is at most *30* pixel positions. Further, LTAR computes the

maximal intervals for which two tracked entities are 'close' – for example, holdsFor(*close(id3, id5, 24)* = true, *[(40, 80)]*) states that *(40, 80)* is the maximal interval for which the distance between *id3* and *id5* is continuously at most *24* pixel positions.

Long-term activity recognition is based on a knowledge base of long-term activity definitions. Next we present example definition fragments of LTAR's knowledge base.

4. LONG-TERM ACTIVITY DEFINITIONS

The 'leaving an object' activity is defined as follows:

$$
\begin{aligned}
\text{initiatedAt}&\big(\textit{leaving\_object}\big(P,Obj\big) = \text{true}, T\big) \leftarrow \\
&\text{happensAt}\big(\textit{appear}\big(Obj\big), T\big) \\
&\text{happensAt}\big(\textit{inactive}\big(Obj\big), T\big) \\
&\text{holdsAt}\big(\textit{close}\big(P,Obj,30\big) = \text{true}, T\big) \\
&\text{holdsAt}\big(\textit{person}\big(P\big) = \text{true}, T\big) \\
&\text{happensAt}\big(\textit{appear}\big(P\big), T0\big) \\
&T0 < T
\end{aligned}
$$

(9)

$$
\begin{aligned}
\text{terminates}&\big(\textit{leaving\_object}\big(P,Obj\big) = \text{true}, T\big) \leftarrow \\
&\text{happensAt}\big(\textit{disappear}\big(Obj\big), T\big)
\end{aligned}
$$

(10)

In the CAVIAR videos an object carried by a person is not tracked - only the person that carries it is tracked. The object will be tracked, that is, 'appear', if and only if the person leaves it somewhere. Moreover, objects (as opposed to persons) can exhibit only inactive short-term activity. Accordingly, Axiom 9 expresses the conditions in which 'leaving an object' is recognised. The fluent recording this activity, *leaving_object(P, Obj)*, becomes true at time *T* if *Obj* 'appears' at *T*, its short-term activity at *T* is 'inactive', there is a person P 'close' to *Obj* at T, and P has 'appeared' at some time earlier than T. Recall that *appear(A)* is an event that takes place at the first time A is tracked and that the *close(A, B, D)* fluent is true when the distance between A and B is at most D pixel positions. The value of *30* pixel positions was determined from an empirical analysis of CAVIAR.

In CAVIAR there is no explicit information that a tracked entity is a person or an inanimate object. Therefore, in the activity definitions we try to deduce whether a tracked entity is a person or an object given, among others, the detected short-term activities. We defined the fluent *person(P)* to have value true if P has exhibited an active, walking, running or abrupt motion short-term activity since P 'appeared'. The value of *person(P)* is time-dependent because in CAVIAR, the identifier P of a tracked entity that 'disappears' (is no longer tracked) at some point may be used later to refer to another entity that 'appears' (becomes tracked), and that other entity may not necessarily be a person.

Unlike the specification of *person,* it is not clear from the CAVIAR data whether a tracked entity is an object, and for this reason we do not have a fluent explicitly representing that an entity is an object. *person(P)*=false does not necessarily imply that P is an object; it may be that P is not tracked, or that P is an inactive person. Note finally that Axiom 9 incorporates a (reasonable) simplifying assumption, that a person entity will never exhibit 'inactive' activity at the moment it first 'appears' (is tracked). If an entity is 'inactive' at the moment it 'appears' it can be assumed to be an object, as in the first two conditions of Axiom 9. (This assumption is adequate for CAVIAR. Removing it raises further issues we do not have space to discuss fully here.)

The lack of explicit information that a tracked entity is an inanimate object may compromise recognition accuracy in certain conditions. A discussion about the effects of the limitations of CAVIAR's dictionary on recognition accuracy will be presented in the next section.

Axiom 10 expresses the conditions in which a *leaving_object* activity ceases to be recognised. In brief, *leaving_object* is terminated when the object in question is picked up. An object that is picked up by someone is no longer tracked - it 'disappears' - terminating *leaving_object*.

The long-term activity *immobile* was defined in order to signify that a person is resting in a chair or on the floor, or has fallen on the floor (for example, fainted). Note that there is no short-term activity in the CAVIAR annotation for the motion of leaning towards the floor or a chair. The absence of such a short-term activity substantially complicates the definition of *immobile*, and, as discussed in the next section, sometimes reduces the accuracy of recognising *immobile*. Below is one of the axioms of the *immobile* definition:

$$\text{initiatedAt}\left(immobile\left(P\right) = \text{true}, T\right) \leftarrow$$
$$\text{happensFor}\left(inactive\left(P\right), Intervals\right)$$
$$\left(T, T1\right) \in Intervals$$
$$T1 > T + 54$$
$$\text{holdsAt}\left(person\left(P\right), \text{true}, T\right)$$
$$findall\left(S, shop\left(S\right), Shops\right)$$
$$\text{holdsAt}\left(farS\left(P, Shops, 24\right) = \text{true}, T\right)$$
(11)

The *immobile(P)* is recognised if the following conditions are satisfied. First, P stays inactive for more than *54* frames (see lines 2-4 of Axiom 11). We chose this number of frames, like all other numerical constraints of the definitions, based on empirical analysis of the CAVIAR dataset. Second, P is a person (see line 5 of Axiom 11). With the use of this constraint we distinguish between an inanimate object, which is inactive since it is first tracked, from an immobile person. Third, P is not 'close' to a shop (see lines 6-7 of Axiom 11). If P were 'close' to a shop then he would have to stay inactive much longer than *54* frames before *immobile* could be recognised. (Those conditions are specified in other axioms defining *immobile* not shown here.) In this way we avoid classifying the activity of browsing a shop as *immobile*. *farS(A, List, D)* is true when *A* is more than *D* pixel positions away from *every* element of the *List*.

The *immobile(P)* is terminated when *P* starts walking, running or 'disappears', that is, he is no longer tracked by the video cameras. The relevant axioms for terminatedAt are straightforward and are not shown here.

The *meeting* (of two persons *P1* and *P2*) is recognised when two people 'interact': at least one of them is active or inactive, the other is neither running nor moves abruptly, and the distance between them is at most *25* pixel positions. In the CAVIAR annotations, this interaction phase can be seen as some form of greeting (for example, a handshake). The rule below shows one set of conditions in which *meeting* is initiated:

$$
\begin{aligned}
\text{initiatedAt}&\left(meeting\left(P1,P2\right)=true,T\right) \leftarrow \\
&\text{holdsAt}\left(close\left(P1,P2,25\right)=true,T\right) \\
&\text{holdsAt}\left(person\left(P1\right)=\text{true},T\right) \\
&\text{happensAt}\left(inactive\left(P1\right),T\right) \\
&\text{holdsAt}\left(person\left(P2\right)=true,T\right) \\
&\text{not happensAt}\left(running\left(P2\right),T\right) \\
&\text{not happensAt}\left(abrupt\left(P2\right),T\right)
\end{aligned}
$$
(12)

The *meeting* is terminated when the two people walk away from each other, or one of them starts running, moves abruptly, or 'disappears'. The formalisation is straightforward and so omitted here.

The activity *moving* was defined in order to recognise whether two people are walking along together. This activity, like the activities presented so far, could be formalised in terms of initiatedAt/terminatedAt predicates to specify the conditions

in which *moving* starts/ceases to be recognised, and then using the domain-independent axioms of holdsFor to compute the maximal intervals of this activity: *moving* is initiated when two people are walking and are 'close' to each other, and terminated when the people walk away from each other, when they stop moving, that is, become active or inactive, when one of them starts running, moves abruptly, or 'disappears'.

A considerably more concise representation of *moving*, however, can be given directly in terms of holdsFor:

$$
\begin{aligned}
\text{holdsFor}&\left(moving\left(P1,P2\right)=\text{true},MovingI\right) \leftarrow \\
&\text{holdsFor}\left(close\left(P1,P2,34\right)=true,CloseI\right) \\
&\text{happensFor}\left(walking\left(P1\right)=WalkingI1\right) \\
&\text{happensFor}\left(walking\left(P2\right)=WalkingI2\right) \\
&\text{intersect\_all}\left(\begin{bmatrix} CloseI,WalkingI1, \\ WalkingI2 \end{bmatrix},MovingI\right)
\end{aligned}
$$
(13)

CloseI are the maximal intervals in which the distance between *P1* and *P2* is continuously at most *34* pixel positions. We compute these intervals using the recorded trajectories of *P1* and *P2* given as input to LTAR. intersect_all computes the intersection of a list of intervals. The implementation of intersect_all and other constructs manipulating intervals is available with the source code of LTAR-EC. According to Axiom 13, the maximal intervals in which *P1* and *P2* are *moving* together are produced by the intersection of the intervals in which *P1* is 'close' to *P2*, *P1* is walking and *P2* is walking.

As in the case for *moving*, we could also have formalised *leaving_object*, *immobile* and *meeting* directly in terms of holdsFor (as opposed to representing these activities in terms of initiatedAt and terminatedAt and then using the domain-independent axioms of holdsFor to compute their maximal intervals). However, formalising *leaving_obect*, *immobile* and *meeting* directly in terms of holdsFor is not more concise than formalising these activities in terms of initiatedAt and terminatedAt. For *leaving*, *immobile* and *meeting* it is much simpler to identify the conditions in which these activities are initiated and terminated, than identifying all possible conditions in which these activities hold.

The last definition of LTAR's knowledge base concerns the *fighting* activity:

$$
\begin{aligned}
holdsFor\left(fighting\left(P1, P2\right) = true, FightingI\right) \leftarrow \\
happensFor\left(abrupt\left(P1\right), AbruptI\right) \\
holdsFor\left(close\left(P1, P2, 24\right) = true, CloseI\right) \\
intersect\_all\left(inactive\left(P1\right), T\right) \\
holdsAt\left(\left[AbruptI, CloseI\right], AbruptCloseI\right) \\
happensFor\left(inactive\left(P2\right), InactiveI\right) \\
complement\begin{pmatrix} AbruptCloseI, \\ InactiveI, FIghtingI \end{pmatrix}
\end{aligned}
$$

$$(14)$$

The complement is an implementation of the complement operation. Two people are assumed to be *fighting* if at least one of them is moving abruptly, the other is not inactive, and the distance between them is at most *24* pixel positions. As in the case of *moving*, we expressed the definition of *fighting* directly in terms of holdsFor because expressing the conditions in which two people are fighting leads to a more succinct representation than expressing the conditions in which *fighting* is initiated and terminated.

5. EXPERIMENTAL RESULTS

We present experimental results on 28 surveillance videos of the CAVIAR dataset. These videos contain 26419 frames that were manually annotated by the CAVIAR team in order to provide the ground truth for short-term and long-term activities. We edited the original CAVIAR annotation by introducing a short-term activity for abrupt motion. Table 2 shows the performance of LTAR; it shows, for each long-term activity, the number of True Positives (TP), False Positives (FP) and False Negatives (FN), and the corresponding Recall and Precision values. Long-term activities are recognised with the use of the holdsFor Event Calculus predicate.

LTAR achieved high Recall and Precision rates, indicating that it may adequately represent complex activities. Perfect Recall and Precision rates were not achieved due to various reasons. One of these reasons concerns the fact that the narrative of short-term activities (produced by manual annotation, in the present experiments) is incomplete. For example, the single FN concerning *leaving_object* is due to the fact that in the video in question the object was left behind a chair and was not tracked. In other words, the left object never 'appeared', it never exhibited a short-term activity.

Another reason for having FP and FN is the lack of consistency in the annotation of the videos; for example, the long-term activity of people walking in the same direction while being 'close' to each other is not always classified as *moving*

Table 2. Experimental results

Behaviour	TP	FP	FN	Recall	Precision
leaving object	4	0	1	0.8	1
immobile	9	8	0	1	0.52
meeting	6	1	3	0.66	0.85
moving	15	3	2	0.88	0.83
fighting	6	0	0	1	1

(this type of inconsistency leads to FP concerning the recognition of *moving*), the short-term activity of people being active is sometimes classified as walking (for example, leading to FN in the recognition of *moving*), and so on.

The most important reason for not achieving perfect Recall and Precision in the CAVIAR dataset concerns the limited dictionary of short-term activities and context variables with which the tracked activity is represented. The recognition of *immobile*, for instance, would be much more accurate if there were a short-term activity for the motion of leaning towards the floor or a chair. In the absence of such an activity, the recognition of *immobile* is primarily based on how long a person is inactive. In the CAVIAR videos a person who falls on the floor or rests in a chair stays inactive for at least *54* frames. Consequently LTAR recognises *immobile* if, among other things, a person stays inactive for at least *54* frames. There are situations, however, in which a person stays inactive for more than *54* frames and has not fallen on the floor or sat in a chair: people watching a fight, or just staying inactive waiting for someone. It is in those situations that we have the FP concerning *immobile*.

For similar reasons we did not achieve perfect Recall and Precision in the recognition of *meeting*; it is impossible to define this activity precisely due to the absence of a short-term activity for 'greeting'.

A particular refinement of CAVIAR's dictionary—the introduction of a short-term activity for abrupt motion - considerably increased LTAR's recognition accuracy. More precisely, compared to our earlier results (Artikis & Paliouras, 2009), the introduction of abrupt motion reduced the number of FP regarding *moving* and *meeting*. In the original annotation of CAVIAR, the short-term activities of people *fighting* were sometimes classified as walking or active. In the first case LTAR incorrectly recognised *moving*, because two people were walking while being 'close' to each other, while in the second case LTAR incorrectly

recognised *meeting* (in addition to recognising *fighting*), because two people were active while being 'close' to each other. Labelling the short-term activities of people *fighting* as abrupt motion resolved this issue, because abrupt motion does not initiate *moving* or *meeting*.

In addition to increasing the recognition accuracy of *moving* and *meeting*, the introduction of abrupt motion eliminated FP and FN regarding *fighting*. Moreover, the introduction of abrupt motion did not increase FP or FN in the recognition of the other long-term activities.

Similar to introducing abrupt motion, we could have enhanced CAVIAR's dictionary by including activities for greeting a person, falling on the floor, etc, and variables explicitly representing that a tracked entity is an object. We did not do this because we are not aware of any short-term activity recognition systems that detect such activities and explicitly represent the aforementioned type of information. In contrast, there are systems that detect abrupt motion—for example, see Kosmopoulos, Antonakaki, Valasoulis, Kesidis, and Perantonis (2008). We expect that a finer classification of short-term activities and the addition of context variables such as the one mentioned above, will, under certain circumstances, increase the overall activity recognition accuracy, provided that the long-term activity definitions are updated accordingly.

We should like to point out that the issues identified above do not always compromise recognition accuracy. For example, the lack of explicit information that a tracked entity is an object did not the affect the recognition accuracy of *leaving_object* in the 28 CAVIAR videos. This lack of information would have led to FP in the recognition of *leaving_object* in certain conditions, but these conditions did not arise in the CAVIAR videos. Similarly, the lack of consistency in the annotation of activities, and the incompleteness of short-term activity narratives do not always lead to FP or FN.

Concerning recognition efficiency, we were able to recognise each long-term activity in less than 1 second CPU time, given as input around 1800 temporally sorted short-term activities representing, on average, a CAVIAR video, on an Intel Core i7 920@2.67GHz with 6 GB RAM running Linux Kernel 2.6.

6. DISCUSSION

Numerous recognition systems have been proposed in the literature (see Artikis, Skarlatidis, Portet, & Paliouras, 2012; Cugola & Margara, 2011, for two recent surveys). In this section we focus on long-term activity (high-level) recognition systems that, similar to our approach, exhibit a formal, declarative semantics.

A well-known system for activity recognition is the Chronicle Recognition System (CRS) (http://crs.elibel.tm.fr/). A 'chronicle' can be seen as a long-term activity - it is expressed in terms of a set of events (short-term activities in our example), linked together by time constraints, and, possibly, a set of context constraints. The language of CRS relies on a reified temporal logic, where propositional terms are related to time-points or other propositional terms. Time is considered as a linearly ordered discrete set of instants. The language includes predicates for persistence and event absence. Details about CRS may be found on the web page of the system and (Dousson & Maigat, 2007).

The CRS language does not allow mathematical operators in the constraints of atemporal variables. Consequently, the computation of the distance between two people/objects, which is of great interest in the domain of activity recognition, cannot be computed. CRS, therefore, cannot be directly used for activity recognition in video surveillance applications. More generally, CRS cannot be directly used for activity recognition in applications requiring any form of spatial reasoning, or any other type of atemporal reasoning. These

limitations could be overcome by developing a separate tool for atemporal reasoning that would be used by CRS whenever this form of reasoning was required. To the best of our knowledge, such extensions of CRS are not available. Clearly, the computational efficiency of CRS, which is one of the main advantages of using this system for activity recognition, would be compromised by the integration of an atemporal reasoner.

Hakeem and Shah (2007) have presented a hierarchical activity representation for analysing videos. The temporal relations between the subactivities of an activity definition are represented using the interval algebra of Allen and Ferguson (1994) and an extended form of the CASE representation (Fillmore, 1968), originally used for the syntactic analysis of natural languages.

In our approach to activity recognition, the availability of the full power of logic programming is one of the main attractions of employing the Event Calculus as the temporal formalism. It allows activity definitions to include not only complex temporal constraints—LTAR-EC is at least as expressive as the CRS language and the extended CASE representation with respect to temporal representation—but also complex atemporal constraints. Moreover, when necessary more expressive Event Calculus dialects may be adopted (see, for example, Miller & Shanahan, 2000).

Shet et al. have presented a logic programming approach to activity recognition. See Shet, Neumann, Ramesh, and Davis (2007) and Shet, Harwood, and Davis (2005) for two recent publications. These researchers have presented activity definitions concerning theft, entry violation, unattended packages, and so on. A distinguishing feature of our approach with respect to this line of work concerns the fact that we use the Event Calculus for temporal representation and reasoning. The temporal aspects of the definitions of Shet, Davis et al. are crudely represented—for example, there are no rules for computing the intervals in which a long-term activity takes place. In contrast, the Event Calculus has built-in axioms for complex temporal representation, including the formalisation of inertia, durative events, events with delayed effects, etc., which help considerably the system designer develop activity definitions.

Shet and colleagues have incorporated in their logic programming framework a mechanism for reasoning over rules and facts that have an uncertainty value attached. We aim to extend our work by allowing for uncertainty values in the rules of activity definitions as well as the short-term activities, in order to address, to a certain extent, the issues arising from incomplete short-term activity narratives, inconsistent annotation of short-term and long-term activities, a limited dictionary of short-term activities and context variables, as well as erroneous short-term activity detection. A first step towards this direction is presented in Katzouris, Skarlatidis, Filipou, Artikis, and Paliouras (2011).

Probabilistic graphical models, such as variants of Hidden Markov Models and Dynamic Bayesian Networks, have been successfully applied to activity recognition in various settings (Brand, Oliver, & Pentland, 1997; Hongeng & Nevatia, 2003; Nguyen, Phung, Venkatesh, & Bui, 2005; Shi, Bobick, & Essa, 2006; Xu & Shelton, 2008). Such models can naturally handle uncertainty. Their propositional structure, however, provides limited representation capabilities. Consequently, the definition of long-term activities becomes complicated and the integration of domain/background knowledge very hard.

Paschke et al. (2008) have also proposed the use of an Event Calculus dialect for activity recognition. This dialect and LTAR-EC have numerous differences. For example, unlike LTAR-EC, there is no support in the dialect of Paschke et al for multi-valued fluents - only Boolean fluents are considered. Moreover, the treatment of intervals is quite different. The Event Calculus dialect of Paschke and colleagues, for instance, does not include axioms for recognising an 'on-going' long-term activity, that is, a activity that started taking place at some earlier time-point and still

holds. There are also very significant differences in the implementations.

Apart from the numerous differences in expressiveness and implementation, a key contribution of the work presented here, as we see it, is that we have illustrated the expressiveness of the Event Calculus for complex activity recognition on a benchmark example, showed a range of different types of definition, and evaluated the adequacy of our representation empirically. We expect that the example itself will be a valuable resource in future uses of the Event Calculus for activity recognition.

The manual development of activity definitions is a tedious, time-consuming and error-prone process. Moreover, it is often necessary to update activity definitions during the recognition process, due to new information about the application under consideration. Consequently, methods for automatically generating and refining activity definitions from data are highly desirable. A logic programming approach to activity recognition has, among others, the advantage that machine learning techniques can be directly employed for developing/refining activity definitions. An area of current work is the use of abductive and inductive logic programming techniques for learning activity definitions. Details about this line of work are given in Artikis and Sergot (2010).

LTAR-EC does not currently store the outcome of query computation, that is, the intervals of the recognised activities. Consequently, LTAR-EC often performs unnecessary computations, re-computing activity intervals that it already computed but did not store. We are currently experimenting to find the most effective options for caching in LTAR-EC, including those presented in Chittaro and Montamari (1996).

ACKNOWLEDGMENT

This work was supported partly by the EU PRONTO Project (FP7-ICT 231738).

REFERENCES

Allen, J., & Ferguson, J. (1994). Actions and events in interval temporal logic. *Journal of Logic and Computation*, 4(5), 531–579. doi:10.1093/logcom/4.5.531

Artikis, A., & Paliouras, G. (2009). *Behaviour recognition using the event calculus. Artificial Intelligence Applications & Innovations*. Berlin, Germany: Springer Press.

Artikis, A., & Sergot, M. (2010). Executable specification of open multi-agent systems. *Logic Journal of IGPL*, 18(1), 31–65. doi:10.1093/jigpal/jzp071

Artikis, A., Skarlatidis, A., & Paliouras, G. (2010). Behaviour recognition from video content: A logic programming approach. *International Journal of Artificial Intelligence Tools*, 19(2), 193–209. doi:10.1142/S021821301000011X

Artikis, A., Skarlatidis, A., Portet, F., & Paliouras, G. (2012). Logic-based event recognition. *The Knowledge Engineering Review*. doi:10.1017/S0269888912000264

Brand, M., Oliver, N., & Pentland, A. (1997). Coupled hidden Markov models for complex action recognition. In *Proceedings of CVPR*, (pp. 994–999). IEEE Computer Society.

Chittaro, L., & Montamari, A. (1996). Efficient temporal reasoning in the cached event calculus. *Computational Intelligence*, 12(3), 359–382. doi:10.1111/j.1467-8640.1996.tb00267.x

Cugola, G., & Margara, A. (2011). *Processing flows of information: From data stream to complex event processing*. New York, NY: ACM Computing Surveys.

Dousson, C., & Maigat, P. L. (2007). *Chronicle recognition improvement using temporal focusing and hierarchisation*. Retrieved from http://www.ijcai.org/papers07/Papers/IJCAI07-050.pdf

Fillmore, C. (1968). The case for CASE. In Bach, E., & Harms, R. (Eds.), *Universals in Linguistic Theory* (pp. 97–135). Berlin, Germany: Holt, Rinehart, and Winston.

Hakeem, A., & Shah, M. (2007). Learning, detection and representation of multi-agent events in videos. *Artificial Intelligence*, 171(8-9), 586–605. doi:10.1016/j.artint.2007.04.002

Helaoui, R., Niepert, M., & Stuckenschmidt, H. (2011). Recognizing interleaved and concurrent activities: A statistical-relational approach. In *Proceedings of Pervasive Computing and Communications* (pp. 1–9). IEEE. doi:10.1109/PERCOM.2011.5767586

Hongeng, S., & Nevatia, R. (2003). Large-scale event detection using semi-hidden markov models. *Proceedings of* IEEE Computer Society. *ICCV*, 1455–1462.

Katzouris, N., Skarlatidis, A., Filipou, J., Artikis, A., & Paliouras, G. (2011). *First version of algorithms for learning event definitions*. Deliverable 4.3.1 of the EU-funded FP7 PRONTO project (FP7-ICT 231738). Available from the authors.

Kosmopoulos, D., Antonakaki, P., Valasoulis, K., Kesidis, A., & Perantonis, S. (2008). Human behavior classification using multiple views. *Lecture Notes in Artificial Intelligence, 5138*.

Kowalski, R., & Sergot, M. (1986). A logic-based calculus of events. *New Generation Computing*, 4(1), 67–96. doi:10.1007/BF03037383

Miller, R., & Shanahan, M. (2000). The event calculus in a classical logic. *Journal of Experimental & Theoretical Artificial Intelligence*, 4(16).

Nguyen, N. T., Phung, D. Q., Venkatesh, S., & Bui, H. H. (2005). Learning and detecting activities from movement trajectories using the hierarchical hidden Markov model. In *Proceedings of CVPR*, (pp. 955-960). IEEE Computer Society.

Paschke, A., & Bichler, M. (2008). Knowledge representation concepts for automated SLA management. *Decision Support Systems*, *46*(1), 187–205. doi:10.1016/j.dss.2008.06.008

Shet, V., Harwood, D., & Davis, L. (2005). Vid-MAP: Video monitoring of activity with prolog. In *Proceedings of Advanced Video and Signal Based Surveillance*. IEEE.

Shet, V., Neumann, J., Ramesh, V., & Davis, L. (2007). Billatice-based logical reasoning for human detection. In *Proceedings of Computer Vision and Pattern Recognition*. IEEE.

Shi, Y., Bobick, A. F., & Essa, I. A. (2006). Learning temporal sequence model from partially labeled data. *Proceedings of CVPR*, IEEE Computer Society. *2*, 1631–1638.

Xu, J., & Shelton, C. R. (2008). Continuous time Bayesian networks for host level network intrusion detection. In *Proceedings of ECML/PKDD*, (pp. 613-627). Springer.

Chapter 2
Context–Aware Discovery of Human Frequent Behaviours through Sensor Information Interpretation

Asier Aztiria
University of Mondragon, Spain

Juan Carlos Augusto
University of Ulster, UK

ABSTRACT

The ability of discovering frequent behaviours of the users allows an environment to act intelligently, for example automating some devices' activation. Moreover, such frequent behaviours could be used to understand and detect bad or unhealthy habits. Such a discovering process must be as unobtrusive and transparent as possible. In that sense, the ability of inferring interesting information from sensors installed in the environment plays an essential role in order to provide the discovering process with meaningful data. The importance of this system is clear due to the fact the process of discovering frequent behaviours will totally depend upon the actions/activities identified by such a system. This development reinforces the link between context-awareness and human behaviour understanding as it can perceive a current situation, compare it to typical behaviour, and differentiate between the two.

INTRODUCTION

Intelligent Environments (IEs) are "…digital environments that proactively, but sensibly, assist people in their daily lives" (Augusto et al. 2007). They offer an opportunity to blend a diversity of disciplines, from the more technical to those more human oriented, which at this point in history can be combined to help people in different environments, at home, in a car, in the classroom, shopping centre, etc.

One of the hidden and most important assumptions in IEs is that they are pioneering a transition from techno-centered systems to human-centered

DOI: 10.4018/978-1-4666-3682-8.ch002

systems. IEs suppose a change of roles in the relationships between humans and technology. Unlike current computing systems where the users have to learn how to use the technology, an IE adapts its behaviour to the users, even anticipating their needs, preferences or habits.

For that shift to take place, an environment should learn how to react to the actions and needs of the users, and this goal should be achieved in an unobtrusive and transparent way. In order to provide personalized and adapted services, the requirement of knowing the preferences and frequent habits of users is clear. Thus, the ability to learn patterns of behaviour becomes an essential aspect for the successful implementation of IEs, because knowing such patterns allows the environment to act intelligently and proactively. In IEs, learning means that the environment has to gain knowledge about the preferences, needs and habits of the user in order to better assist the user (Galushka et al. 2006; Leake et al. 2006).

IEs also assume that the process of acting intelligently over the user cannot disturb them. Otherwise, if a user is continuously disturbed, it could be a reason to reject the system (Liao et al. 2004; Pollack 2005). This requirement demands IEs to be conscious of the current situation in each moment (Ramos et al. 2006). Context aware environments are concerned with the unobtrusive acquisition of context (e.g., using sensors to perceive different situations), understanding of context (e.g., inferring the actions/activities the users are doing), and making decisions based on the recognized situation (e.g., automating the activation of a device).

Being aware of the importance of these two areas, it must be said that they are not independent areas but they must be combined to achieve a real intelligent environment. Taking the learning system as the base to provide the environment with intelligence, this chapter analyses the influence of context awareness in the learning process. For

that, using a real scenario, we identify the steps of the learning process where it is necessary to apply context awareness techniques to allow the environment to provide personalized and adapted services at the right time. Let us consider a scenario that illustrates an IE that makes the life of the users easier and safer.

Michael is a 60-year-old man who lives alone and enjoys an assistance system that makes his daily life easier. On weekdays, Michael's alarm goes off a few minutes after 08:00 a.m.; approximately 10-15 minutes later, he usually steps into the bathroom. At that moment, the lights are turned on automatically. On Tuesdays, Thursdays and Fridays, he usually takes a shower; Michael prefers the temperature of the water to be around 24-26 degrees Celsius in the winter and around 21-23 degrees Celsius in the summer. When he finishes taking a shower, the fan of the bathroom is turned on if the relative humidity level of the bathroom is high (in Michael's case >70%). Before he leaves the bathroom he turns off the fan and the lights. When he goes into the kitchen the radio turns on so that he can listen to the news while he prepares his breakfast. When he is preparing his breakfast the system reminds him that he has medicine to take. He leaves the house 15-20 minutes after having breakfast. At that moment, all the lights are turned off, and safety checks are performed in order to detect potentially hazardous situations in his absence (e.g., checking if the stove is turned on), and if needed, the house acts accordingly (e.g., turning the stove off).

The remainder of this chapter is organized as follows. Section 2 provides a literature review of related works. Section 3 introduces the architecture of the system that discovers frequent behaviours. Then, Section 4, 5, and 6, respectively define the different layers of such a system. Finally, conclusions and future research directions are identified.

RELATED WORK

IEs as a technological paradigm has attracted a significant number of researchers and many applications are already being deployed, with different degree of success. The complexity of these systems is due to the combination of hardware, software and networks which have to cooperate in an efficient and effective way to provide a suitable result to the user. Due to this complexity, up to now, each project has focused upon different aspects of such complex architectures. In that sense, it is understandable, and even logical in some way, that the first developments have been focused upon the needs associated with hardware and networking as supporting infrastructure. Many researchers have identified the learning and context awareness (Ramos et al. 2006; Friedwald et al. 2007; Augusto and Nugent, 2006) as key element to achieve real IEs.

Regarding the learning frequent behaviours different groups have used different techniques such as Artificial Neural Networks (Mozer et al. 1995; Chan et al. 1995; Campo et al. 2006), Classification techniques (Gal et al. 2001), Fuzzy rules (Hagras et al. 2004; Doctor et al. 2005), Sequence discovery (Cook and Das 2007; Jakkula et al. 2007) or Reinforcement learning (Mozer 2004; Zaidenberg et al. 2008). A survey can be found in (Aztiria et al. 2010a). Analyzing different applications, it seems clear that the use of different techniques is firmly conditioned by the specific needs of each environment or application. In that sense, the main objective of our system is to combine the strengths of different techniques in order to develop a domain independent learning system that provides comprehensible patterns taking into account all the particularities of IEs.

Context awareness has also been identified as necessary area in IEs. Many researchers have used Markov Models and extensions to recognize activities of the users (Philipose et al. 2004; Oliver et al. 2002; Modayil et al. 2008). In that sense, most of the activity recognition systems are based on supervised learning algorithms, so that they need large training data that are difficult to collect. Some groups have started using ontologies and statistical inference to address this problem (Riboni and Bettini 2009).

ARCHITECTURE

One of the main characteristics of IEs is the key role that the user plays as the focus of the entire process, from the beginning to the end. In other words, the process starts by collecting data about the user and the environment in which the user is situated, and it finishes by acting intelligently. The variety of user types that can be involved in each IE and the multitude of potential objectives of each particular environment, demands an exhaustive analysis of all components to be included.

The main objective of the architecture that we propose for the learning system is to distinguish those aspects of the learning process related to particular environments, in which, each particular environment requires a different treatment (environment-dependent), from those aspects that can be generalized for all types of environments (environment-independent). The system proposed in the current work, Learning Frequent Patterns of User Behaviour System (LFPUBS), is based on a three-layered architecture that takes into account all aspects related to the learning process. Figure 1 shows the global architecture of LFPUBS.

It can be said that the Transformation Layer fills the gap between the real environment and the system, whereas the Application Layer just fills the opposite gap, from the system to the real environment. Due to the fact that in both cases real environments are involved, they must take into account the particularities of them. On the contrary, the Learning Layer is exempt of any external influence.

Figure 1. Three-layered global architecture

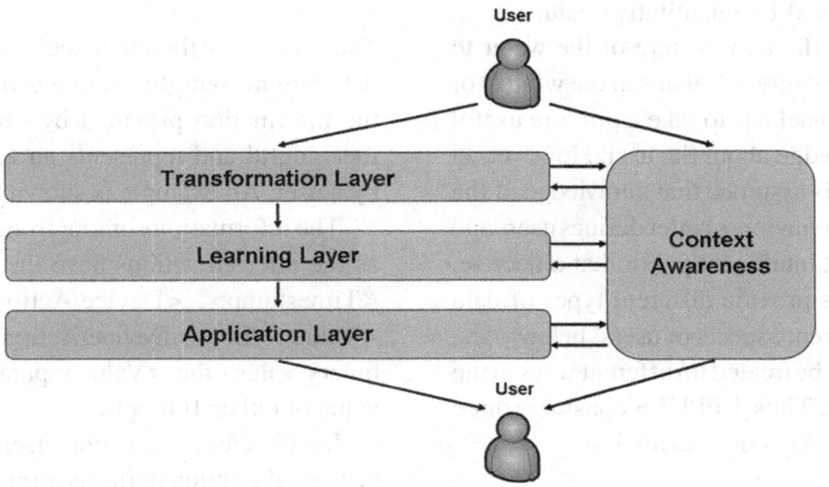

TRANSFORMATION LAYER

The objective of the first layer is to transform raw data, i.e., data collected from sensors, into meaningful information for the learning layer. In other words, to have conscience about the information represented by the collected data. We identify this layer as one of the layers where Context Awareness has a major impact, due to the fact that the process of providing with meaning the data collected by the sensors demands the use of Context Awareness techniques.

Most of the transformations to perform will be dependent of the particular environment they are being applied, because the objective and the sensors installed in a particular environment greatly influence such transformations. Even so, in most of the environments the objective of the transformations will be the same, so that the need of some transformations (e.g., activity recognition) can be generalized and even integrated in the learning system. Following, some of the most general transformations are identified, dividing those ones that are already integrated in the LFPUBS from those ones that are not yet.

Context Awareness Transformations Integrated in the LFPUBS

One of the most necessary transformations to be conscious of the situations defined by the collected data is the one that recognizes the users' actions and activities from the collected data. Its importance is enhanced due to the fact that the users' actions and activities are the base for the learning algorithm that discovers users' frequent behaviours (See 'Learning Layer' section for more details). Depending on the granularity of the information we want to infer, the recognition task will be focused on simple actions or activities.

The action/activity inference module integrated in LFPUBS works offline, i.e. once all data have been collected and are available. The main objective of this inference module is to recognize actions/activities showed by the collected data using predefined templates.

Nature of Data

A perfect learning system should gain knowledge about everything related to users that would help the environment act intelligently and proactively. Knowledge about users can cover types of information with very different natures. Users' preferences for devices defined by quantitative values (e.g., Michael prefers the temperature of the water to be around 24-26 degrees Celsius in the winter) or needs (e.g., Michael has to take a pill) are useful pieces of knowledge about the user. However, in this approach it is assumed that knowledge of the users' frequent behaviours better defines users and allows IEs to act intelligently. For that objective, different sensors provide different types of data that define different aspects of users' behaviours, so that they must be treated in different ways in the learning process. Thus, LFPUBS considers three main different groups of information:

- **Type A:** Information about the actions of the users. This information can be directly provided by sensors installed in objects (devices, furniture, domestic appliances etc.) or inferred by combining different pieces of information in the Transformation Layer (for further details see the previous Section).
- **Type C:** Context information. Some sensors provide information about context, but not about actions of the user. Temperature, light and smoke sensors are examples of type C sensors.
- **Type M:** Motion information. This information can be used to infer where the user is (in the bedroom, outside the house or elsewhere). This type of information is mainly used in the Transformation Layer to infer the actions of the user.

It is clear that other types of information already exist, such as those that indicate the health status of the user or alarm pendants, which could be interesting in IEs. The inclusion of other types of sensors is being considered for future versions of the system.

Recognizing Simple Actions

The objective of this inference is to translate the raw data into meaningful simple actions. Sometimes the information provided by sensors is already meaningful and represents an action performed by a user. An example is shown in Box 1.

The information coming from sensors, as well as the inferred actions have the same structure: <Timestamp>, <Device/Action>, <On/Off>, <Value>. If the Device/Action can only have binary values the <Value> parameter takes the value of either 100 or 0.

In this case, the action itself is meaningful because the action of the user (he switched on the light) can be directly inferred from it. However, there are other actions that are quite difficult to infer from the simple activation of a sensor. For example, the inference of the simple action 'Go into the Bathroom' is not possible from the activation of a simple sensor, so it must be inferred by combining different actions. The following example shows that there is a motion in the corridor, followed by the RFID tag installed in the door of the bathroom detecting the presence of Michael and finally there is motion in the bathroom. It can be inferred that Michael has entered the bathroom. Thus, the transformation of those three actions into only one meaningful action allows the addition of meaning to the sequence of raw data items. See Box 2.

The most basic way of inferring these actions is by means of templates. Templates define which actions must be combined as premises, as well as which constraints must be considered. The im-

Box 1.

from *2008-10-20T08:15:57, SwitchBathroomLights, on, 100* *it is inferred* *2008-10-20T08:15:57, BathroomLights, on, 100*

Box 2.

from
2008-10-20T08:15:54, Motion Corridor, on, 100
2008-10-20T08:15:55, Bathroom RFID, on, Michael
2008-10-20T08:15:55, Motion Bathroom, on, 100
it is inferred
2008-10-20T08:15:55, Bathroom, on, 100

portance of each action in the template is different, so that actions can be labeled either as mandatory or as optional. As far as constraints are concerned, they can affect the order of the actions or the duration. The template for the action 'Go into bathroom' is defined in Box 3.

The objective of these first transformations is to make all actions meaningful. It is clear that the definition of templates depends on particular environments because they are defined in terms of particular sensors installed in the environment and by the set of actions to be identified. This initial step of recognizing meaningful actions, is important because once such actions are identified the rest of the learning process will depend upon them.

Recognizing Activities

Once simple actions have been recognized, a similar process can be carried out in order to recognize activities such as 'Make coffee' or 'Take a pill'. This recognition process might be necessary because simple actions do not always represent the type of behaviours we want to analyse. As in recognizing simple actions, the most basic method for recognizing activities is the use of templates, with one difference. Whereas the former transformation combines raw data, recognizing activities combines simple actions. The 'Make coffee' action's template could be defined as in Box 4.

Combining different actions into only one activity does not make it impossible to define its frequent internal structure. For example, in retrieving all the cases labelled as 'Make coffee', a particular learning process can be carried out in order to detect if there is a pattern that defines how the user makes coffee.

Splitting Actions into Sequences

In IEs, data is generally collected in a continuous way from sensors, so that they will be represented as a string of actions with a temporal ordering but without any extra structure or organization. The aim of this transformation is to structure the data collected from sensors according to the meaning of the actions. Such an organization of the actions in sequences is essential for the learning layer.

In that sense, many different organizations can be suggested. The approach proposed here assumes that the user carries out actions in a sequenced way, and such actions are mainly influenced by prior and later actions. Thus, the string of actions

Box 3.

'Go into Bathroom (Bathroom, On, 100)'
Actions:
Motion Corridor (Mandatory)
RFID Detection (Mandatory)
Open Door (Optional if already open)
Motion Bathroom (Mandatory)
Constraints:
Order
Motion Corridor <RFID Detection <Open door <Motion Bathroom
Time
$T_{MotionBathroom} - T_{MotionCorridor} < 3seg.$

Box 4.

> *'Make Coffee (MakeCoffee, On, 100)'*
> *Actions:*
>   *Put Kettle on (Optional)*
>   *Open Cupboard (Optional)*
>   *Get Coffee (Mandatory)*
>   *Take a cup (Mandatory)*
>   *Open fridge (Optional)*
>   *Get Milk (Optional)*
> *Constraints:*
>   *Time*
> $$T_{FirstAction} - T_{LastAction} < 5min.$$

is split into sequences, but instead of using a quantitative window-width, a more flexible criteria that determines the end of one meaningful sequence and the beginning of a new one is used. For instance, going to bed and staying for more than 2 hours or going out and staying out for more than 30 minutes are considered as 'landmarks' that demarcate sequences.

This task is environment-dependent because different environments will demand different criteria. For example, a criterion defined for a Smart Home will not make sense in a Smart Car.

Other Context Awareness Transformations

Transformations integrated in the LFPUBS allow one to have conscience about the situations defined by the data. Other transformations, which are not integrated in the LFPUBS, have been identified as interesting for IEs.

Multiuser IEs, if patterns must be personalized, demand to identify the user that performs each action if discovered. Different approach can be analyzed for it, for example camera based or RFID based identification systems.

Regarding the recognition of actions and activities, previously trained recognition system could recognize actions/activities while it is recording the data. An approach to create such a system is based on a training period where different

participants carry out the same action/activities, allowing the system to model it, for example by means of a Markov Model.

LEARNING LAYER

The objective of this layer is to transform the information coming from the Transformation Layer into knowledge to be used by the Application Layer. This layer is the core of the system because it allows the environment to adapt to users. In addition to being the layer that allows the environment to discover users' frequent behaviour, the importance of this layer is enhanced because of its independence from particular environments.

As mentioned above, the Learning Layer is independent of particular environments and it considers all the possibilities that can take place in any environment. Although its design and develop is free of any external influence, the patterns that it discovers are totally influenced by the information provided by the Transformation Layer.

Architecture of the Learning Layer

Being an environment-independent layer, the architecture as well as different modules must be designed and developed taking into account all of the characteristics of the different environments. The architecture proposed for this layer is depicted in Figure 2.

The underlying idea is the separation of the representation of the discovered patterns from the process of discovering per se. The core of the representation module is a language (L_{LFPUBS}) that provides a standard conceptualisation of the patterns so that the environment is able to represent all type of patterns that can occur in the environment. On the other hand, the process of discovering is based on an algorithm (A_{LFPUBS}) that taking into account all of the characteristics of the IEs attempts to discover frequent patterns.

Figure 2. Architecture of the learning layer

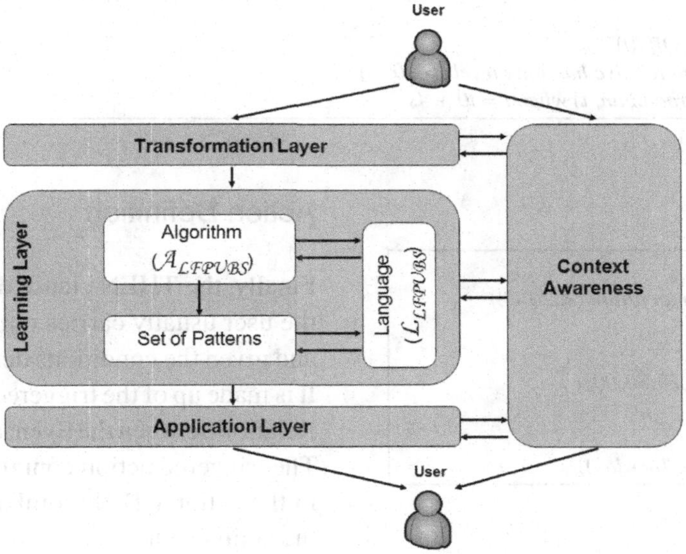

Representing Patterns with L_{LFPUBS}

Because of the complexity of IEs, defining a language that allows the environment to represent discovered patterns in a clear and unambiguous way is difficult but necessary. A frequent behaviour is defined by means of an *Action Map*, which contains all of the specific relations between actions. In other words, an Action Map is created relating actions in pairs, and each of those relations is called an *Action Pattern*, which are defined by means of ECA (Event-Condition-Action) rules (Augusto and Nugent 2004). Besides providing a standard way of representing patterns, it makes sure those patterns are clearly specified and enables other technologies to check their integrity. In the same way as ECA rules, L_{LFPUBS} basically relates two actions (defined by the ON and THEN clauses) and the specific conditions (defined by the IF clause) under which that relation occurs. Finally, unlike basic ECA rules, L_{LFPUBS} allows the environment to define the time relation between both actions. Considering Michael's behaviour of turning on the fan in the bathroom; using L_{LFPUBS} it would be represented as in Box 5.

Event Definition

The part of the pattern defined by the ON clause defines the event that occurs and triggers the relationship specified by the pattern. The components of the Event Definition are the device implied in the action ('Shower'), the nature of the action ('Off') and the timestamp of such an action ('t0'). As patterns relate users' behaviours, the ON event must be the effect of a user's action. In this case, such actions are collected by means of A-type sensors. In Michael's case, the Event Definition is defined as:

ON occurs (Shower, Off, t0)

Condition Definition

The IF clause defines the necessary conditions under which the action specified in the THEN clause is the appropriate reaction to the event listed in the ON clause. Because it is almost impossible for an Event-Action relation to be true under any condition, appropriate conditions are necessary to represent accurate patterns. In Box 6, some examples of conditions are provided.

Box 5.

(Action Pattern 0)
    ON occurs (Shower, Off,t0)
    IF context (Bathroom relative humidity level (>,70%))
    THEN do (On, BathroomFan, t) when t = t0 + 4s

Box 6.

(Condition 1)
IF context (Living room temperature (<,20ºC))

(Condition 2)
IF context (TimeOfDay (>,20:30:00))

(Condition 3)
IF context (DayOfWeek (=, Tuesday))

Conditions are defined by means of attribute-value pairs. Whereas the ON and THEN clauses define the actions of the user, the conditions must specify the status of the environment at that moment, such that the information involved in that clause must be related to the context. Thus, L_{LFPUBS} has two possible ways to define the conditions:

- Information coming from C-type sensors (e.g., 'Relative humidity level' (Action Pattern 0) or 'Temperature' (Condition 1))
- Calendar information (e.g., 'Time of Day' (Condition 2) or 'Day of Week' (Condition 3))

The possible values of such attributes depend on the nature of each attribute. In that sense, L_{LFPUBS} considers two types of values:

- Qualitative values (e.g., 'Tuesday' (Condition 3))
- Quantitative values (e.g., '20ºC' (Condition 1) or '20:30:00' (Condition 2))

Action Definition

Finally, the THEN clause defines the action that the user usually carries out given the ON clause and given the conditions defined in the IF clause. It is made up of the triggered action, and the Time Relation between the Event and Action situations. The triggered action contains the device implied in the action ('BathroomFan') and the nature of the action ('On').

The Time Relation can be either quantitative (Action 1) or qualitative (Action 2), with the usefulness of each type of relation being different. See Box 7.

Compared to qualitative relations, quantitative relations provide higher quality information because it is possible to use them for other purposes. One of those additional purposes is the automation of devices, which is possible with quantitative relations. Consider Michael's behaviour of turning on the fan 4 seconds after having a shower. If such a relation was defined by means of a qualitative term like 'after', the system would not be able to infer when it had to turn on the fan because it would not have known whether the time delay was 4 seconds, 5 minutes or 2 hours. However, using quantitative relations (4 seconds in Michael's case) allows the system to turn on the fan at the right time.

Box 7.

(Action 1)
THEN do (On, BathroomFan, t) when t = t0 + 4s

(Action 2)
THEN do (On, BathroomFan, t) when t is after t0

Learning Pattern with A_{LFPUBS}

Coupled with L_{LFPUBS}, an essential component in the Learning Layer is the algorithm (A_{LFPUBS}) that discovers the frequent behaviours of the users. In order to coordinate with L_{LFPUBS} and discover complete and unambiguous patterns, A_{LFPUBS} must consider all of the different aspects defined by the language.

The different steps to be performed by A_{LFPUBS} in order to discover the frequent behaviours of the users are depicted in Figure 3.

The same idea represented by means of a pseudo-algorithm is given in the A_{LFPUBS} Algorithm (Algorithm 1).

Below, each one of the steps is explained in more detail.

Identifying Frequent Sets of Actions

The objective of this step is to discover the sets of actions that frequently occur together (Frequent Sets). This task of identifying Frequent Sets is actually divided into three sub-tasks.

The underlying idea of this first sub-task is both simple and efficient. Defining a demanded minimum level (minimum confidence level), it discovers all those sets of actions that occur more times than the minimum level. These sets of actions are treated as Basic Frequent Sets. The set of Sequences in which the Basic Frequent Set is present is also identified. To discover Basic Frequent Sets in large amounts of data, the Apriori algorithm (Agrawal and Srikant 1995) is used.

Once the Basic Frequent Sets have been discovered, an aspect to consider for each Basic Frequent Set is whether there is any action that was not discovered as frequent taking into account all the Sequences, but it is frequent enough when considering only those Sequences where the Basic Frequent Set occurs. In other words, the goal of this task is to discover whether there are any Extra Actions that frequently happen in those particular Sequences. As in the previous sub-task, a minimum confidence level must be defined, and the process to discover such Extra Actions is the same. The only difference is that instead of all of the Sequences, only those Sequences in which the Basic Frequent Set is present are considered. The Frequent Sets are created by adding these Extra Actions to the respective Basic Frequent Sets.

Figure 3. Steps to be performed by the learning algorithm

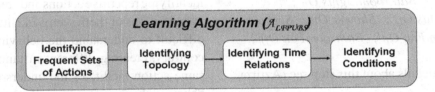

Algorithm 1. A_{LFPUBS}

```
Identify Frequent Sets of Actions
For each Frequent Set
    Identify the Topology
    For each Action Pattern
        Identify possible quantitative Time Relations
        Identify Specific Conditions using context/calendar information
Identify General Conditions (See Section)
```

For the following steps of A_{LFPUBS} (e.g., 'Identifying Topology'), it is essential to know in which Sequences a Frequent Set is present. Although initially considering only those Sequences identified in the task of 'Identifying Basic Frequent Sets' seems enough, other Sequences could also provide interesting information. There could be Sequences in which most of the actions of a Basic Frequent Set are present, but as they do not contain all of the actions, they are not considered. Being aware that small deviations could mean a loss of information, a strategy to reduce the impact of such deviations has been designed. It is based on a parameter (similarity level) that indicates (as a percentage) the minimum number of actions of a Basic Frequent Set to be included in a Sequence in order to consider such a Sequence interesting. Thus, not only those Sequences that have all of the actions (similarity level = 100%) of the Basic Frequent Set would be considered interesting, but also those Sequences in which the similarity level is over the demanded level.

In Michael's case, considering the first part of his morning behaviour, this step would discover a Frequent Set which would be made up of the following actions:

Frequent Set 1
Actions: 'Alarm On'; 'Bathroom On';
'Bathroom Off'; 'BathroomLights On';
'Bathroom-Lights Off'; 'Shower On'; 'Shower Off'; 'BathroomFan On'; 'BathroomFan Off';

For further details about this step see (Aztiria et al. 2009).

Identifying Topology

The step 'Identifying Frequent Sets of Actions' discovers which sets of actions frequently occur together. In order to properly model the user's behaviours defined by such sets of actions, it is necessary to define the order of such actions. That is the goal of this step, to discover the frequent order (defined as Topology) of the actions in the behaviour of the user. The actions involved in the behaviour and the Sequences that contain the information are provided by the previous step, 'Identifying Frequent Sets of Actions'.

In this context, representing the user's behaviours by means of Action Maps makes them easier to understand and makes it possible to use them in tasks such as prediction or automation of future actions. Even so, few groups have dealt with this problem in IEs. Because of this, other meaningful domains in which users' actions have been used to extract models of behaviour have been analysed. In that sense, one of the closest domains is the area of Workflow Mining in which process models are discovered from event logs. Both domains are equal, with the only difference being that instead of event logs, LFPUBS considers the actions of the user. Even so, because of the nature of IEs, some modifications to the Workflow Mining algorithm must be considered. Next, the different aspects that need to be considered are explained.

Unlike other domains in which an action is unique and there is no more than one occurrence of each action per Sequence, in IEs, there could be different occurrences of the same action. In fact, the nature of repetitive occurrences will probably be different because the user can do the same action with different purposes. Initially, identifying repetitive actions and creating different instantiations of them seems like it could make it difficult to understand the behaviour. Quite the contrary, creating different instantiations of the same action facilitates the understanding of the behaviour because they simplify the complexity of the Topology. Considering the possible existence of more than one instance of the same action, a methodology to automatically discover such situations has been developed. This methodology is based on the idea that the meaning, and by extension, the nature of an action is mainly defined by the previous and next actions. In other words, the occurrence of an action is related to the previous and next actions because the set of those actions will probably follow a specific objective. Thus, the nature of different actions is defined by creating groups of actions that take into account the similarities among the previous and next actions of their occurrences.

Other particularity of IEs is the occurrence of unordered subsets of actions, i.e. a set of actions in which it has not been possible to define an order for such actions. Although this idea is not considered by researchers of the Workflow Mining area, it representation is very similar to the idea of parallel subsets of actions considered in the Workflow Mining works. As in the parallel actions of Workflow mining cases, the representation of unordered sets of actions shows bidirectional relationships between such actions. To decide whether a bidirectional relationship (let us say between A and B) must be considered as an unordered set of actions, LFPUBS includes a set of parameters:

- **Minimum Level for Origin (%):** The percentage of occurrences of A followed by B out of the total occurrences of A must be higher than the demanded minimum level.

$$\frac{\left(A \rightarrow B\right)}{\left(Occurrences A\right)} > Minimum\ Level\ for\ Origin$$

- **Minimum Level for Destiny (%):** The percentage of occurrences of B followed by A out of the total occurrences of B must be higher than the demanded minimum level.

$$\frac{\left(B \rightarrow A\right)}{\left(Occurrences B\right)} > Minimum\ Level\ for\ Destiny$$

- **Minimum Balanced Level (%):** The percentage of occurrences of A followed by B out of the occurrences of B followed by A (and vice versa) must be higher than the demanded minimum level.

$$\frac{\left(A \rightarrow B\right)}{\left(B \rightarrow A\right)}\ \&$$
$$\frac{\left(B \rightarrow A\right)}{\left(A \rightarrow B\right)} > Minimum\ Balanced\ Level$$

Considering Michael's case and the Frequent Set discovered by the first step, the final topology of Michael's behaviour once repetitive actions as well as unordered subset of actions were identified it would be represented as shown in Figure 4 (For more details about this step see (Aztiria et al. 2010b).

Identifying Time Relations

Topologies define a first temporal representation of the frequent behaviour by means of qualitative relations (using the term 'after'). The objective of this step is to discover frequent quantitative Time Relations between the actions defined by each one of the relations defined by the topology, because they provide higher quality information because it is possible to use them for other purposes. One of those additional purposes is the automation of devices, which is possible with quantitative relations. Consider Michael's behaviour of turning on the fan 4 seconds after having a shower. If such a relation was defined by means of a qualitative term like 'after', the system would not be able to infer when it had to turn on the fan because it would not have known whether the time delay was 4 seconds, 5 minutes or 2 hours. However, using quantitative relations (4 seconds in Michael's case) allows the system to turn on the fan at the right time.

Before applying any algorithm, the first task is to collect the necessary data. The relations to study are already defined by the topology discovered in the previous step. Thus, for each relation the Time Distances between the actions involved in such a relation are retrieved.

Figure 4. Topology of the Michael's morning behavior

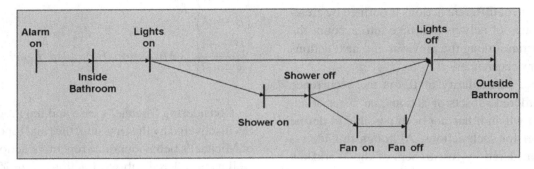

Once the Time Distances are collected, the next step is to identify possible quantitative time relations. For that purpose, LFPUBS includes two algorithms - the 'Basic Algorithm' and the 'EM Algorithm' - so that the user of the system may choose either of them to identify such quantitative relations. Both algorithms are based on the same idea of grouping occurrences by taking into account their similarity and deciding whether a group represents a quantitative Time Relation. The basic idea of the Basic Algorithm is to group Time Distances by taking into account the similarity between them. The process of creating groups is defined by Algorithm 2.

To determine whether a Time Distance falls within an existing group, each group has a range that defines what Time Distances it covers. Such a range is established by the following:

$$\left[min, max\right] = \overline{x} \pm \left(\overline{x} * tolerance\right)$$

where

$$\overline{x} = \frac{\Sigma_{i=1}^{n} a_i}{n}$$

Once the groups are created, it is clear that not all al the groups define interesting quantitative Time Relations. For this reason, a minimum confidence level must be established in this case too, so that only those groups that cover more instances than the minimum established by the confidence level define a quantitative Time Relation. In such cases, the mean value of the group is treated as the quantitative Time Relation.

Besides the 'Basic Algorithm', LFPUBS includes another algorithm that creates clusters of Time Distances based on the Expectation-Maximization (EM) algorithm. The basic idea of the EM algorithm is to estimate the maximum likelihood between parameters. An important advantage of this algorithm is that it automatically calculates the necessary number of groups and includes each occurrence in its corresponding group. Once groups are created by the EM algorithm, the process of deciding what groups

Algorithm 2. Basic algorithm for identifying time relations

Randomly select an initial Time Distance
Create a new group for that initial Time Distance
For each Time Distance
    Calculate if it is within any existing group (See below for further details)
    If it is, Then Include it in the group and recalculate the parameters of the group
    If it is not, Then Create a new group and calculate the parameters of the group

defines a quantitative Time Relation is he same as the 'Basic Algorithm'.

In Michael's case, and considering the Time Distances between the actions 'Shower Off' and 'BathroomFan On' are depicted in Figure 5, the 'Basic Algorithm' would create two groups ('group 0' and 'group 1') which would cover three and one occurrences, respectively. In order to extract quantitative Time Relations, the LFPUBS checks whether the confidence level of different groups is over the demanded one (let us say 50% in this case). It is clear that 'group 0' represents a quantitative Time

Relation because it covers 3 out of 4 occurrences (75%), whereas 'group 1' does not. Thus, in this case the mean value of 'group 0' (4 seconds) defines a quantitative Time Relation for such a relationship.

For further details about this step see (Aztiria et al. 2010c).

Identifying Conditions

Once Topology and Time Relations have been identified, user's behaviours are represented by means of Action Maps in a comprehensible way. Even so, a final step that identifies the Specific and General Conditions for each Action Map is necessary in order to create accurate representations of the behaviours of the user.

On one hand, it is clear that all of the relations represented in an Action Map are supported by a number of occurrences. In that sense, a particularity to treat could be the case in which an action is followed by two (or more) different actions. These situations indicate that after an action, the user sometimes carries out one action and other times he/she carries out some other action. In an Action Map, these situations are easily identified because these situations are represented as splitting points from which more than one relation is created. In those cases, it is necessary to identify under what conditions each of those relations is true.

On the other hand, it is necessary to define the general context in which an Action Map occurs. General Conditions refer to calendar and context information that allow the user of the system to understand under what conditions the whole Action Map occurs.

For the purpose of discovering specific conditions, two tables - *covered* and *non-covered* - are created. In the covered table, those occurrences that are correctly classified by the pattern appear, together with the calendar and context information collected when such occurrences happened. The same information for occurrences in which the patterns fails is registered in the non-covered table. Once the tables are created, separating both tables by using the information they contain allows one to discover conditions. In that sense, the task of separating can be solved by treating it as a classification problem. The JRip Algorithm (Witten and Frank 2005) was used to accomplish this task.

In Michael's case, after having a shower he sometimes turns on the fan of the bathroom and some other times he does not. Figure 6 shows the covered and non-covered tables created for that case, with their corresponding calendar and context information. Because these tables contain few instances, the covered and non-covered classes

Figure 5. Time distances between occurrences of 'shower off' and 'bathroom fan on'

	O1 (Sequence 1)	O2 (Sequence 5)	O3 (Sequence 6)	O4 (Sequence 8)
Shower Off				
BathroomFan On	00:00:04 (4s)	00:00:03 (3s)	00:05:34 (334s)	00:00:05 (5s)

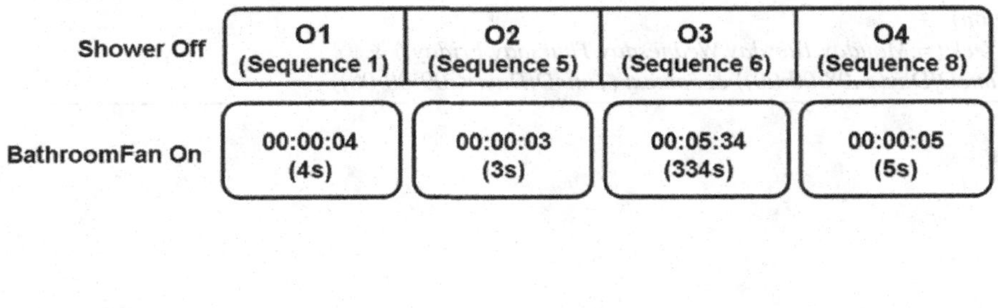

Figure 6. Covered and non-covered tables with calendar and context information

covered

	Sequence 1	Sequence 5	Sequence 6	Sequence 8
time of day	08:29:37	08:29:28	08:30:39	08:23:29
day of week	Monday	Friday	Monday	Wednesday
Temp. Bathroom	19	22	21	17
Hum. Bathroom	72	75	71	78

non-covered

	Sequence 3	Sequence 10
time of day	08:28:18	08:29:07
day of week	Wednesday	Friday
Temp. Bathroom	22	18
Hum. Bathroom	65	69

can be separated in many different manners. Even so, the most efficient manner is using the context information Bathroom relative humidity level. Thus, the condition obtained in this case is as follows:

IF context (Bathroom relative humidity level (>,70%))

Regarding the General Conditions only calendar information ('Time of Day' and 'Day of Week') has been considered. In order to identify General Conditions, a simple algorithm has been developed. It is based on identifying the period of time, both in terms of 'Time of Day' and 'Day of Week', that covers all of the occurrences of such an Action Map.

In Michael's case, it would discover that his behaviour occurs on weekdays and between 08 a.m. and 09 a.m., creating a General Condition such as in Box 8.

Once the process finished, Michael's behaviour would be represented as Figure 7.

Influence of Context Awareness in the Learning Layer

Although the Learning Layer is independent of the environment where the LFPUBS is applying, the learning process could be enriched if it considers other types of information.

When it comes to discovering Specific Conditions, information provided by all of the context sensors is considered equally, without considering the nature of each of them. Thus, it could happen that the discovered conditions correctly separate the different occurrences, but analysing the nature of the actions to be separated does not provide a meaningful explanation. For that, it would be interesting to add semantic information to both actions and context information so that, in the process of discovering conditions, only context

Box 8.

(General Condition)
context (DayOfWeek (=,Monday,Tuesday,Wednesday,Thursday,Friday)) &
    context (TimeOfDay(>,08:00:00)) & context (TimeOfDay(<:09:00:00))

Figure 7. Michael's morning behavior

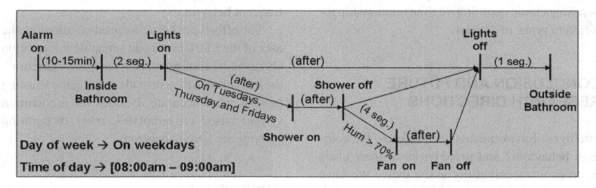

information that is related to the nature of the actions would be considered.

Extra information about the user could also help the learning process to discover more accurate patterns. Information about his/her agenda could be an example of it, so that knowing when the user goes on holiday or when he/she has got a meeting could allow the LFPUBS to learn more accurate patterns.

APPLICATION LAYER

Once pieces of knowledge about users' frequent behaviours have been learned, they can be used for different purposes. This use will be mainly influenced by the objectives of particular environments. Automating the activation of devices, issuing an alarm when bad habits are detected or saving energy are some of the applications that can be achieved using learned patterns.

Need of Context Awareness in the Application Layer

Besides discovering patterns that describe users' frequent behaviours, an IE should apply them at the right time. For that, it is necessary to be conscious of the current situation in each moment.

Learned patterns allow an IE to automate the activation/deactivation of different devices. For example in Michal's case, the IE knows that it should turn on the fan of the bathroom 4 seconds after he finishes taking a shower, if the relative humidity level is > 70% and it is a weekday between 8 a.m. and 9 a.m.. Thus, in order to apply such knowledge correctly, it must know if the current situation fulfills all the requirements.

Bad or unhealthy habits could also be identified in the learned patterns, and then, to issue alarms when such situations are detected in the behaviour of the user. In this case too, it is clear the need of being context awareness.

In general, it can be said that the application of the learned patterns demand to be conscious of the current situation and match it with the situations defined by such patterns. In that sense it is worth noting the importance of the L_{LFPUBS} because such a standard and comprehensible representation of patterns allows the translation of those patterns into any type of model, such as Markov models, set of rules or finite state machines which can be used to match different situations.

Apart from recognizing situations and matching them with the learned patterns, to be conscious of the current situation and the nature of the actions could allow the IE to adopt some approaches to solve undefined or ambiguous situations. If automation of devices is considered, relationships defined by the term 'after' could be an example of it. Problems caused by such undefined situations could be mitigate knowing the nature of the actions involved in such a relationships and for example defining a basic quantitative time relationship for different types of actions.

CONCLUSION AND FUTURE RESEARCH DIRECTIONS

Intelligent Environments need to know the common behaviours and preferences of their users in order to meaningfully assist them. We have developed a system called LFPUBS which aims precisely at supporting an Intelligent Environment in the important task of understanding what the frequent behaviours of the occupant are in a given environment.

LFPUBS is made up of three layers which objective is to separate those aspects that are dependent on the environment where the system is being applying from those ones that are not. In that sense, it was identified the need of being aware of the situations occurred in the environment, especially in the case of those layers that are directly related to the real environment.

On one hand, in the Transformation Layer the ability of inferring interesting information, i.e. recognizing actions/activities, from sensors installed in the environment plays an essential role in order to provide the discovering process with meaningful data. On other hand, Application Layer must know the current situation in order to apply the discovered knowledge correctly.

It is clear the need of integrating context awareness techniques in the learning process and the advantages it could involve. Thus, taking the learning process as the starting point, we have identified those situations of the learning process where context awareness techniques are necessary.

As future work, the objective should be to integrate the necessary context awareness techniques in the learning process, so that LFPUBS provides a holistic solution for the problem of learning and applying the knowledge about users' frequent behaviours.

The efforts are being focused on allowing the user of the LFPUBS to add semantic information about the data collected from sensors would enrich the information they provide making the learning process more accurate. Besides the recognition system based on templates, other recognition systems are being analyzed.

REFERENCES

Agrawal, R., & Srikant, R. (1995). Mining sequential patterns. In *Proceedings of the 11th International Conference on Data Engineering*, (pp. 3–14). IEEE.

Augusto, J. C. (2007). Ambient intelligence: The confluence of pervasive computing and artificial intelligence. In Schuster, A. (Ed.), *Intelligent Computing Everywhere* (pp. 213–234). Berlin, Germany: Springer. doi:10.1007/978-1-84628-943-9_11

Augusto, J. C., & Nugent, C. (2006). Smart homes can be smarter. In Augusto, J. C., & Nugent, C. D. (Eds.), *Designing Smart Homes: The Role of Artificial Intelligence* (pp. 1–15). Berlin, Germany: Springer. doi:10.1007/11788485_1

Augusto, J. C., & Nugent, C. D. (2004). The use of temporal reasoning and management of complex events in smart homes. In *Proccedings of European Conference on AI (ECAI 2004)*, (pp. 778–782). ECAI.

Aztiria, A., Augusto, J. C., Basagoiti, R., & Izaguirre, A. (2010c). Accurate temporal relationships in sequences of user behaviours in intelligent environments. In *Proceedings of the Ambient Intelligence and Future Trends-International Symposium on Ambient Intelligence (ISAmI 2010)*, (pp. 19-27). ISAmI.

Aztiria, A., Izaguirre, A., & Augusto, J. C. (2010a). Learning patterns in ambient intelligence environments: A survey. *Artificial Intelligence Review*, *34*(1), 35–51. doi:10.1007/s10462-010-9160-3

Aztiria, A., Izaguirre, A., Basagoiti, R., Augusto, J. C., & Cook, D. J. (2009). Discovering of frequent sets of actions in intelligent environments. In *Proceedings of the 5th International Conference on Intelligent Environments*, (pp. 153-160). IEEE.

Aztiria, A., Izaguirre, A., Basagoiti, R., Augusto, J. C., & Cook, D. J. (2010b). Automatic Modeling of frequent user behaviours in intelligent environments. In *Proceedings of the 6th International Conference on Intelligent Environments*. IEEE.

Campo, E., Bonhomme, S., Chan, M., & Esteve, D. (2006). Learning life habits and practices: An issue to the smart home. In C. Nugent & J. C. Augusto (Eds.), *International Conference on Smart Homes and health Telematic*, (pp. 355–358). Berlin, Germany: Springer.

Chan, M., Hariton, C., Ringeard, P., & Campo, E. (1995). Smart house automation system for the elderly and the disabled. In *Proceedings of the 1995 IEEE International Conference on Systems, Man and Cybernetics*, (pp. 1586–1589). IEEE Press.

Cook, D. J., & Das, S. K. (2007). How smart are our environments? An updated look at the state of the art. *Pervasive and Mobile Computing*, *3*, 53–73. doi:10.1016/j.pmcj.2006.12.001

Doctor, F., Hagras, H., & Callaghan, V. (2005). A fuzzy embedded agent-based approach for realizing ambient intelligence in intelligent inhabited environments. *IEEE Transactions on Systems, Man, and Cybernetics*, *35*, 55–65. doi:10.1109/TSMCA.2004.838488

Friedwald, M., Costa, O. M. D., Punie, Y., Ala-huhta, P., & Heinonen, S. (2005). Perspectives of ambient intelligence in the home environment. *Telematics and Informatics*, *22*, 221–238. doi:10.1016/j.tele.2004.11.001

Gal, C. L., Martin, J., Lux, A., & Crowley, J. L. (2001). Smartoffice: Design of an intelligent environment. *IEEE Intelligent Systems*, *16*(4), 60–66. doi:10.1109/5254.941359

Galushka, M., Patterson, D., & Rooney, N. (2006). Temporal data mining for smart homes. In Augusto, J. C., & Nugent, C. D. (Eds.), *Designing Smart Homes: The Role of Artificial Intelligence* (pp. 85–108). Berlin, Germany: Springer. doi:10.1007/11788485_6

Hagras, H., Callaghan, V., Colley, M., Clarke, G., Pounds-Cornish, A., & Duman, H. (2004). Creating an ambient-intelligence environment using embedded agents. *IEEE Intelligent Systems*, *19*(6), 12–20. doi:10.1109/MIS.2004.61

Jakkula, V. R., Crandall, A. S., & Cook, D. J. (2007). Knowledge discovery in entity based smart environment resident data using temporal relation based data mining. In *Proceedings of the 7th IEEE International Conference on DataMining*, (pp. 625–630). IEEE Press.

Leake, D., Maguitman, A., & Reichherzer, T. (2006). Cases, context, and comfort: Opportunities for case-based reasoning in smart homes. In Augusto, J. c., & Nugent, C. D. (Eds.), *Designing Smart Homes: The Role of Artificial Intelligence* (pp. 109–131). Berlin, Germany: Springer. doi:10.1007/11788485_7

Liao, L., Patterson, D., Fox, D., & Kautz, H. (2004). Behavior recognition in assisted cognition. In *Proceedings of the IAAA-04 Workshop on Supervisory Control of Learning and Adaptive Systems*, (pp. 41–42). IAAA.

Mozer, M. C. (2004). Lessons from an adaptive home. In Cook, D. J., & Das, S. K. (Eds.), *Smart Environments: Technology, Protocols and Applications* (pp. 273–298). New York, NY: Wiley-Interscience.

Mozer, M. C., Dodier, R. H., Anderson, M., Vidmar, L., Cruickshank, R. F., & Miller, D. (1995). The neural network house: An overview. In Niklasson, L., & Boden, M. (Eds.), *Current Trends in Connectionism* (pp. 371–380). Mahwah, NJ: Lawrence Erlbaum.

Oliver, N., Horvitz, E., & Garg, A. (2002). Layered representations for human activity recognition. In *Proceedings of the Fourth IEEE International Conference on Multimodal Interfaces,* (pp. 3–8). IEEE Press. Modayil, J., Bai, T., & Kautz, H. (2008). Improving the recognition of interleaved activities. In *Proceedings of ubiComp 2008.* ubiComp.

Philipose, M., Fishkin, K. P., Perkowitz, M., Patterson, D. J., Fox, D., Kautz, H., & Hähnel, D. (2004). Inferring activities from interactions with objects. In *Proceedings of IEEE Pervasive Computing,* (pp. 50–57). IEEE Press.

Pollack, M. E. (2005). Intelligent technology for an aging population: The use of ai to assist elders with cognitive impairment. *AI Magazine, 26*(2), 9–24.

Ramos, C., Augusto, J. C., & Shapiro, D. (2008). Ambient intelligence - The next step for artificial intelligence. *IEEE Intelligent Systems, 23*(2), 15–18. doi:10.1109/MIS.2008.19

Riboni, D., & Bettini, C. (2009). Context-aware activity recognition through a combination of ontological and statistical reasoning. In *Proceedings of Ubiquitous Intelligence and Computing* (pp. 39–53). IEEE. doi:10.1007/978-3-642-02830-4_5

Witten, I. H., & Frank, E. (2005). *Data mining: Practical machine learning tools and techniques* (2nd ed.). London, UK: Elsevier.

Zaidenberg, S., Reignier, P., & Crowley, J. L. (2008). Reinforcement learning of context models for a ubiquitous personal assistant. In *Proceedings of the 3rd Symposium of Ubiquitous Computing and Ambient Intelligence,* (pp. 254–264). IEEE.

Chapter 3
Towards Ontology–Based Realtime Behaviour Interpretation

Wilfried Bohlken
University of Hamburg, Germany

Lothar Hotz
University of Hamburg, Germany

Patrick Koopmann
University of Hamburg, Germany

Bernd Neumann
University of Hamburg, Germany

ABSTRACT

The authors describe a generic framework for model-based behaviour interpretation and its application to monitoring aircraft service activities. Behaviour models are represented in a standardised conceptual knowledge base using OWL-DL for concept definitions and the extension SWRL for constraints. The conceptual knowledge base is automatically converted into an operational scene interpretation system implemented in Java and JESS that accepts tracked objects as input and delivers high-level activity descriptions as output. The interpretation process employs Beam Search for exploring the interpretation space, guided by a probabilistic rating system. The probabilistic model cannot be efficiently represented in the ontology, but it has been designed to closely correspond to the compositional hierarchy of behaviour concepts. Experiments are described that demonstrate the system performance with real airport data.

1. INTRODUCTION

This chapter is about realtime monitoring of object behaviour in aircraft servicing scenes, such as arrival preparation, unloading, tanking, and others, based on video streams from several cameras[1]. The focus is on high-level interpretation of object tracks extracted from the video data. The term "high level interpretation" denotes meaning assignment above the level of individually recognised objects, typically involving temporal and spatial relations between several objects and qualitative behaviour descriptions corresponding to concepts used by humans. We prefer to use the term "scene interpretation" in order to avoid reference to a particular level structure. Scene interpretation is understood to include the recognition of multi-object structures (e.g. the facade of

DOI: 10.4018/978-1-4666-3682-8.ch003

a building) as well as the recognition of activities and occurrences (e.g. criminal acts). Regarding its scope, scene recognition can be compared to silent-movie understanding.

For aircraft servicing, scene interpretation has the goal to recognise the various servicing activities at the apron position of an aircraft, beginning with arrival preparation, passenger disembarking via a passenger bridge, unloading and loading operations involving several kinds of vehicles, refuelling, catering, and other activities. Real-time monitoring may serve several purposes. For one, delays in performing scheduled activities can be noticed and counteracted early. Secondly, predictions about the completion of a turnaround can be provided, alleviating planning. Thirdly, monitoring of service activities can be extended to include unrelated object behaviour, e.g. of vehicles not allowed in the proximity of the aircraft.

Our approach aims at developing a largely domain-independent scene interpretation framework, designed to be adaptable to changes and to be reusable for other applications. In fact, our basic approach of structuring the conceptual knowledge base in terms of compositional hierarchies and guiding the interpretation process accordingly has been used in other domains (Hotz & Neumann, 2006; Hotz, Neumann & Terzic, 2008) and by other authors (Rimey, 1993; Fusier, Valentin, Brémond, Thonnat, Borg, Thirde & Ferryman 2007; Mumford & Zhu 2007). In this introductory section we shortly discuss major contributions of past research which have influenced our current understanding of scene interpretation and our design decisions for a framework. We also compare with recent work on ontology-based scene interpretation.

Although scene interpretation has enjoyed much less attention in Computer Vision research than object recognition, there exists a considerable body of related work dating as far back as into the seventies. Badler (1975) was one of the first to derive high-level descriptions of simple traffic scenes represented by hand-drawn sketches for lack

of computer-generated low-level data about real scenes. He used spatial relations between pairs of objects, corresponding to spatial adverbials, to describe a snapshot of a scene, and changes of these relational structure to describe the temporal development. A temporal concept such as "across-motion" would be recognised by rules defined in terms of preconditions and postconditions. His work showed that spatial predicates form the bridge from quantitative low-level data to qualitative high-level descriptions.

A first systematic approach to motion analysis is due to Tsotsos, Mylopoulos, Covvey, and Zucker (1980) who introduced a taxonomy of motion types. Specific high-level motion events (in this case pathological human-heart motions) were described as a composition of elementary motions, thus also establishing a compositional hierarchy.

Structuring motion by taxonomical and compositional hierarchies, reflecting the logical structure of natural language terms, has played a significant part in most approaches to model scene interpretation, also in the early work of Neumann (1989) on natural-language description of traffic scenes. One of his additional achievements was the separation of behaviour models from control structures for behaviour recognition. Occurrences in street traffic were modelled as declarative aggregates enabling both bottom-up and top-down recognition. Temporal relations between occurrences were modelled by constraints and processed by a constraint system. As in earlier work, low-level image analysis had to be bypassed by manually providing input data in terms of a "Geometric Scene Description" (GSD) consisting of typed objects and quantitative object trajectories.

A first attempt of modelling scene interpretation in a logical framework is due to Reiter and Mackworth (1987). They showed that, for a finite domain, scene interpretation could be formulated as a logical model construction task, i.e. as a search for instantiations of the conceptual knowledge covering the domain, consistent with the factual evidence. This search could be implemented as constraint satisfaction.

Later, the model construction paradigm was extended to Description Logics (DLs) (Schroeder & Neumann, 1996; Neumann & Moeller, 2006). This was motivated by the attractive possibilities for object-centred concept representations offered by a DL and its guarantee for decidable reasoning processes. Unfortunately, it remains difficult to realise scene interpretation with a DL system. One of the reasons is the need to model the quantitative-qualitative mapping from sensory to symbolic data outside the logics. Also, a central reasoning service for scene interpretation, the incremental construction of a model, is not provided by existing systems.

A slightly different logical paraphrase of scene interpretation was given by Cohn, Magee, Galata, Hogg, and Hazarika (2003), and Shanahan (2005) in terms of abduction, i.e. as a search for high-level concepts whose instantiation would entail the evidence. Similar to logical model construction, experiments are difficult because few logical systems offer abduction services which can be used for scene interpretation. The pioneering work on multimedia interpretation in the group of Moeller (Gries, Moeller, Nafissi, Rosenfeld, Sokolski & Wessel, 2010) is a recent example for using a DL system for abduction. Here, the RacerPro reasoner has been extended by abduction facilities.

Several researchers propose ontology-based activity recognition in a customised logical framework which does not necessarily realise model construction or abduction. Chen and Nugent (2009) present an activity recognition procedure where conceptual descriptions constructed from evidence are tested for equivalence with ontological concepts using a DL reasoner.

An interesting approach to exploiting an OWL ontology using a DL reasoner has been reported in (Riboni & Bettini, 2011a). They use RacerPro to check the consistency of sensor data in the elderly-care domain with asserted interpretations. This procedure realises logical model construction for a fixed inventory of activities. It does not offer a solution for an incremental and multi-level interpretation process.

Irrespective of difficulties in using existing reasoners, the work on a logical formulation of scene interpretation has provided important clarifications, in particular that, from a logical perspective, scene interpretation is inherently ambiguous. The ambiguity is quite striking in temporal scenes where interpretations typically imply predictions about the future. For example, a driver assistance system has to interpret an observed scene with regard to its future development. Will the pedestrian enter the street or wait? As humans, we seem to exploit our experiences for such decisions and prefer the most likely or utile choice given all we know about the domain and the current scenario. Hence, it appears natural to provide a probabilistic model for the uncertainty of logically ambiguous choices.

The need for a preference measure is all the more evident when one considers the stepwise process which must be used when interpreting scenes with several objects and extending over time. As evidence is incorporated piece by piece, early and intermediate interpretation decisions may have to be made with poor context, i.e. in highly ambiguous interpretation situations.

Independently of the logically motivated need for a preference measure, probabilistic approaches to scene interpretation have been developed, motivated by the success of probabilistic methods in other areas of Computer Vision and Robotics, and the desire to develop a seamless integration of low-level image analysis with high-level scene interpretation. In early work (Binford, Levitt & Mann, 1989; Rimey, 1993), Bayesian Networks (BNs) were conceived isomorphic to the compositional structure of high-level concepts, i.e. with aggregates "causing" their parts. While this basic structure is intuitively plausible, it implies that parts are statistically independent given aggregate data. This is not the case in many applications, hence more general probabilistic structures have been developed. In (Koller & Pfeffer, 1997; Getoor & Taskar, 2007) BNs were extended in an object-oriented manner, introducing Probabilistic Relational Models. This way, crisp relational structures can be augmented with an arbitrary probabilistic dependency structure. To describe multiple levels of granularity, hierarchical BNs were proposed by Gyftodimos and Flach (2007). More recently, Markov Logic Networks have been employed for modelling events and activities (Murariu & Davis, 2011). While these contributions improve the expressive power of BNs or propose an alternative probabilistic framework, they do not adequately support compositional hierarchies of aggregates as required for scene interpretation. For this purpose, Bayesian Compositional Hierarchies (BCHs) have been developed (Neumann, 2008) which are also employed for the work in this chapter and will be described in detail in Section 4.

An interesting alternative approach to combining compositional hierarchies with BNs has been presented by Mumford and Zhu (2007). Here, a grammatical formalism takes the place of hierarchical knowledge representation, and (probabilistic) parsing algorithms are applied for scene interpretation, leading to efficient processing, but complicating the integration with large-scale knowledge representation.

Our approach, presented in the following sections, tries to build on the insights gained from past research, while simultaneously employing standardised or generally applicable formalisms as far as possible. We have chosen OWL DL[2], the standardised web ontology language, for the representation of the conceptual models for scene interpretation in general and for the specific application domain, this is presented in Section 2. The choice of OWL emphasises our interest in connecting to logic-based knowledge representation and reasoning services. But, as will be shown, we must make use of the SWRL extension of OWL to express crisp dependencies between concepts, and we must connect with components outside OWL for probabilistic modelling.

An important contribution of our work is the automatic translation of OWL concepts into an interpretation procedure in JESS, described in Section 3. The procedure realises a bottom-up, evidence-driven parallel Beam Search for all probable interpretations, guided by a Bayesian Compositional Hierarchy (BCH). One of the achievements is a decomposition of this process into independent subgoals which may provide evidence for several higher-level concepts.

The probabilistic model is described in detail in Section 4. It provides a rating for alternative interpretations given the evidence available so far, and also for predictions of future events. We use a BCH to model the temporal relationships of servicing activities and derive ratings using a very efficient probabilistic inference process.

In Section 5, we present results for interpreting aircraft turnarounds at the Toulouse Blagnac Airport. We demonstrate the predictive power of our probabilistic framework and show its effect when rating alternative interpretations.

We conclude with a summary of insights gained and an outlook on future work.

2. BEHAVIOUR MODELLING

In this section, we describe the representation of behaviour models in a formal ontology. Our main concern is the specification of aggregate models which can be used to describe an aircraft turnaround and its constituting activities.

2.1. Aggregate Representation

In a nutshell, an aggregate is a representational structure consisting of:

- A specification of aggregate properties,
- A specification of parts, and
- A specification of constraints between parts.

To illustrate the requirements for aggregate specifications, consider the aggregate Arrival-Preparation as an example. It has the parts GPU-Enters-GPU-Zone, GPU-Stopped-Inside-GPU-Zone, and Drop-Chocks (Figure 1).

The first part, GPU-Enters-GPU-Zone, marks the event when the GPU enters its designated standing area (GPU denotes Ground Power Unit). GPU-Stopped-Inside-GPU-Zone begins at the moment, the GPU has come to a stop, and ends when the GPU begins leaving the area much later in the turnaround. We use predefined zones for locations following the work of Fusier et al. (2007). The event Drop-Chocks marks the moment an operator has deposited the chocks where the airplane is expected to stop.

The example shows that behaviour concepts of different kinds play a role: some extend over a time interval, some mark a time point, some can be derived from tracking data, some require special image analysis procedures. Furthermore, all components of the aggregate Arrival-Preparation must obey certain temporal constraints for the model to be realistic. GPU-Enters-GPU-Zone typically precedes GPU-Stopped-Inside-GPU-Zone by less than a minute. After the GPU has been positioned, it may take up to 10 minutes until a person steps out and deposits the chocks. The duration of GPU-Stopped-Inside-GPU-Zone roughly corresponds to a complete turnaround, but does not matter for the definition of Arrival-Preparation.

As mentioned in the introduction, we have chosen the web ontology language OWL DL for defining aggregates and related concepts.

OWL DL is a standardised formalism with clear logical foundations and provides the chance for a smooth integration with large-scale knowledge representation. Furthermore, the object-centred style of concept definitions in OWL and its support by mature editors such as Protégé[3] promise transparency and scalability. Simple constraints can be represented with SWRL, the Semantic Web Rule Language, albeit not very elegantly, as will become apparent shortly.

The availability of DL reasoning systems such as Pellet or Racer may be considered an additional bonus, but—as pointed out in the introduction—incremental scene interpretation in terms of model-construction or abduction steps is not supported by current DL systems. Hence, in our application, the use of a commercial DL reasoner is limited to consistency checks of the conceptual knowledge base. The interpretation process is realised with our own framework called SCENIOR (SCENe Interpretation with Ontology-based Rules) which translates the OWL concepts into a search for instantiations, see Section 3.

In a DL setting, an aggregate has the generic structure displayed in Box 1.

Hence an aggregate with the class name Aggregate_Concept is defined by a taxonomical parent, by the parts to which it is related via has-PartRoles, and by conceptual constraints relating aggregate and parts to each other. The left-hand side implies the right-hand side, corresponding to an abductive framework. In our definition, the aggregate may name only a single taxonomical parent because of the intended mapping to single-

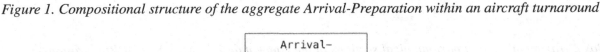

Figure 1. Compositional structure of the aggregate Arrival-Preparation within an aircraft turnaround

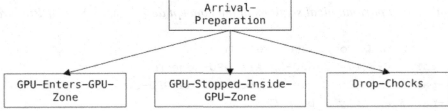

Box 1. Generic structure of an aggregate

```
Aggregate_Concept ⊑ Parent_Concept ⊓
        ∃_=1 hasPartRole_1.Part_Concept_1 ⊓ ... ⊓
        ∃_=1 hasPartRole_k.Part_Concept_k ⊓
        conceptual constraints
```

inheritance Java templates. Furthermore, the aggregate must have exactly one part for each hasPartRole. While the DL syntax would allow number restrictions for optional or multiple parts, we found it useful to have different aggregate names for different part configurations and a distinct hasPartRole for each part to simplify the definition of conceptual constraints.

Within the OWL ontology, conceptual constraints can be expressed using the Semantic Web Rule Language SWRL[4] which combines OWL with RuleML[5] (Rule Markup Language). It is well-known that SWRL rules may cause undecidability of the conceptual knowledge base unless they are restricted to be DL-safe, i.e. only applied to facts (to ABox content in DL terminology). This is the case during scene interpretation where rules are only applied to instances grounded in scene data. However, there exists no reasoner which evaluates SWRL rules for a consistency check of the conceptual knowledge base.

SWRL is supported by the Protégé editor, which guarantees that a certain amount of consistency is maintained. For example, it is not possible to define a rule with classes which are not defined in the knowledge base, or to use variables in the consequent which are not introduced in the antecedent.

For the aggregate Arrival-Preparation, the taxonomical and partonomical sections of the concept definition in Protégé read in Box 2.

The parent concept Composite-Event refers to a concept type defined in the Upper Model which will be discussed further down. We now discuss the SWRL section of the definition in Box 3.

The antecedent part of this rule has the single purpose to establish local variables (prefixed by a '?') for the constraints in the consequent part. The first two constraints (12, 13) relate the starting and finish time of the aggregate to specific time points of the parts. The next constraint (14) requires that the vehicles referred to in GPU-Enters-GPU-Zone and GPU-Stopped-Inside-GPU-Zone are the same. Finally, min-before checks whether the difference between the first and the second argument is less than the third argument. In this case, the gaps between consecutive events are constrained by 100 ms (14) and 1000 ms (15), respectively. When the ontology is translated into an interpretation procedure, all constraints of the consequent part are transformed into a temporal constraint system (TCN) which generates a conflict when a potential instantiation of the aggregate and its parts violates the constraints.

Box 2. Taxonomical and partonomical sections of the concept definition of Arrival-Preparation

```
Arrival-Preparation ⊑ Composite-Event ⊓
        has-part1 exactly 1 GPU-Enters-GPU-Zone ⊓
        has-part2 exactly 1 GPU-Stopped-Inside-GPU-Zone ⊓
        has-part3 exactly 1 Drop-Chocks
```

Note that a concept such as GPU-Stopped-Inside-GPU-Zone could have also been expressed by the more general concept Vehicle-Stopped-Inside-Zone, constrained by the predicates GPU(?veh-stopped-ag) and GPU-Zone(?veh-stopped-zn) in the SWRL section. In this case, ?veh-stopped-zn must have been introduced as a variable for the filler of the has-zone property. We have taken the design decision to provide specific concept names for all activities in a turnaround in order to establish a transparent correspondence to the probabilistic aggregate models which will be introduced in Section 4.

The complete ontology comprises a domain-independent Upper Model, shown in Figure 2, with concept types which are generally useful for scene interpretation, roughly corresponding to the Fluent Calculus (Russell & Norvig, 2010). The Domain Model with the specific concepts for aircraft servicing is shown in Table 1. We first describe the concepts of the Upper Model.

2.2. Upper Model

The root concept Thing (analogous to the OWL identifier owl:thing) represents every entity which is needed for scene interpretation (not only physical objects). A Conceptual-Object is used to represent a behaviour concept and may be either a State or an Event. A State is a predicate true over an interval and all its subintervals, a property which is often called "durative". A State may be a Composite-State with several states as parts, all of which must be true over the interval of the parent state. An Event is a non-durative Conceptual-Object, for example marking a transition from one state to another. A Composite Event may have states or events as parts and is used, for example, to describe a complete aircraft turnaround or the aggregate Arrival-Preparation presented above. Primitive states and events have no parts and thus constitute the leaves of the compositional hierarchy. Instances of primitives are typically determined

Box 3. SWRL section of the concept definition of Arrival-Preparation

```
Arrival-Preparation(?arr-prep)                                      1
∧  has-part1(?arr-prep, ?GPU-enters)                               2
∧  has-part2(?arr-prep, ?GPU-stopped)                              3
∧  has-part3(?arr-prep, ?drop)                                     4
∧  has-start-time(?arr-prep, ?arr-prep-st)                         5
∧  has-finish-time(?arr-prep, ?arr-prep-ft)                        6
∧  has-time-point(?GPU-enters, ?GPU-enters-tp)                     7
∧  has-agent(?GPU-enters, ?GPU-enters-ag)                          8
∧  has-start-time(?GPU-stopped, ?GPU-stopped-st)                   9
∧  has-agent(?GPU-stopped, ?GPU-stopped-ag)                       10
∧  has-time-point(?drop, ?drop-tp)                                11
→
   equal(?arr-prep-st, ?GPU-enters-tp)                            12
∧  equal(?arr-prep-ft, ?drop-tp)                                  13
∧  equal(?GPU-enters-ag, ?GPU-stopped-ag)                         14
∧  min-before(?GPU-stopped-st, ?arr-prep-st, 100)                 15
∧  min-before(?drop-tp, ?GPU-stopped-st, 1000)                    16
```

Figure 2. Upper model of the behaviour ontology for the aircraft-servicing domain

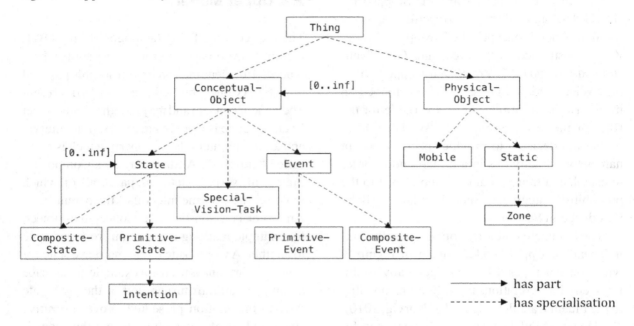

by lower-level processes which provide the input for scene interpretation.

The ontology also includes some unusual concepts which play a specific part in our work but are not further addressed in this contribution. With Intention we refer to the mental state of a person. An Intention is not observable, of course, but intentions can be made part of event models and may be inferred from observations.

While most primitives can be generated from object trajectories obtained from stationary wide-angle cameras, there are important events which require a dynamically controlled Pan-Tilt-Zoom (PTZ) camera and a special image analysis module, for example to recognise whether a pipe is attached to the airplane for refuelling. An event obtained this way is addressed as a Special-Vision-Task.

Another unusual concept is Zone which describes a qualitative location in the horizontal plane. Predefined zones on the apron play a significant part in event models for service activities, exemplified by the primitive event GPU-Enters-GPU-Zone and its property has-zone in the example above.

It may be surprising that the ontology does not include views or similar concepts related to the appearance of objects. In our work on structure recognition in the facade domain (Hotz et al., 2008), instances of 2D object views have been provided as input for high-level interpretation. Hence interpretation included object recognition based on appearances. In the work described here, however, the primitives entering high-level interpretation are recognised 3D entities without appearance properties.

2.3. Domain Model

The Domain Model comprises more than 50 behaviour concepts which are part of a compositional hierarchy with Turnaround as the roof concept (see Table 1). Activities difficult to recognise have been omitted here, such as Catering, Air-Conditioning, Waste-Removal, Replace-Drinking-Water etc. Note that some concepts occur as a part in more than one aggregate. For example, Loader-Enters-Right-AFT-LD-Zone is part of Unload-Right-AFT and Load-Right-AFT. This illustrates the ambi-

Table 1. Domain model with aggregates of the Turnaround hierarchy

```
Turnaround
         Arrival
                     Arrival-Preparation
                                 GPU-Enters-GPU-Zone
                                 GPU-Stopped-Inside-GPU-Zone
                                            GPU-Stopped
                                            GPU-Inside-GPU-Zone
                                 Drop-Chocks
                     Airplane-Enters-ERA
                     Airplane-Stopped-Inside-ERA
                                 Airplane-Stopped
                                 Airplane-Inside-ERA
         Services
                     Passenger-Activity
                                 Passenger-Stairs-Enters-PS-Zone
                                 Passenger-Stairs-Stopped-Inside-PS-Zone
                                            Passenger-Stairs-Stopped
                                            Passenger-Stairs-Inside-PS-Zone
                     Unload-Right
                                 Unload-Right-AFT
                                            Loader-Enters-Right-AFT-LD-Zone
                                            Transporter-Enters-Right-AFT-TS-Zone
                                            Unload-Motion-Right-AFT-Belt
                                            Transporter-Leaves-Right-AFT-TS-Zone
                                            Loader-Leaves-Right-AFT-LD-Zone
                                 Unload-Right-FWD
                                            Loader-Enters-Right-FWD-LD-Zone
                                            Transporter-Enters-Right-FWD-TS-Zone
                                            Unload-Motion-Right-FWD-Belt
                                            Transporter-Leaves-Right-FWD-TS-Zone
                                            Loader-Leaves-Right-FWD-LD-Zone
                     Refuelling
                                 Tanker-Enters-Tanking-Zone
                                 Tanker-Stopped-Inside-Tanking-Zone
                                            Tanker-Stopped
                                            Tanker-Inside-Tanking-Zone
                                 Pumping-Operation
                     Load-Right
                                 Load-Right-AFT
                                            Loader-Enters-Right-AFT-LD-Zone
                                            Transporter-Enters-Right-AFT-TS-Zone
                                            Load-Motion-Right-AFT-Belt
                                            Transporter-Leaves-Right-AFT-TS-Zone
                                            Loader-Leaves-Right-AFT-LD-Zone
                                 Load-Right-FWD
                                            Loader-Enters-Right-FWD-LD-Zone
                                            Transporter-Enters-Right-FWD-TS-Zone
                                            Load-Motion-Right-FWD-Belt
                                            Transporter-Leaves-Right-FWD-TS-Zone
                                            Loader-Leaves-Right-FWD-LD-Zone
Departure
         Start-Beacon
         Pushback
```

guities which may arise in bottom-up interpretation and the need for constraints provided by the established context.

In setting up a domain model, it may be useful to introduce abstract temporal behaviour patterns as a common parent for more specific models, so that inheritance can be exploited. For example,

Box 4. Taxonomical and partonomical sections of the concept definition of Visit

```
Visit ⊑ Composite-Event ⊓
        has-part1 exactly 1 Vehicle-Enters-Zone ⊓
        has-part2 exactly 1 Vehicle-Stopped-Inside-Zone
```

Box 5. SWRL section of the concept definition of a Visit

```
Visit(?vis)
        ∧  has-part1(?vis, ?veh-enters)
        ∧  has-part2(?vis, ?veh-stopped)
        ∧  has-start-time(?vis, ?vis-st)
        ∧  has-finish-time(?vis, ?vis-ft)
        ∧  has-time-point(?veh-enters, ?veh-enters-tp)
        ∧  has-agent(?veh-enters, ?veh-enters-ag)
        ∧  has-zone(?veh-enters, ?veh-enters-zn)
        ∧  has-start-time(?veh-stopped, ?veh-stopped-st)
        ∧  has-agent(?veh-stopped, ?veh-stopped-ag)
        ∧  has-zone(?veh-stopped, ?veh-stopped-zn)
        →
           equal(?vis-st, ?veh-enters-tp)
        ∧  equal(?vis-ft, ?veh-stopped-ft)
        ∧  equal(?veh-enters-ag, ?veh-stopped-ag)
        ∧  equal(?veh-enters-zn, ?veh-stopped-zn)
        ∧  min-before(?veh-enters-tp, ?veh-stopped-st, 10000)
```

Passenger-Activity and Refuelling each consist of two consecutive parts, the first a Vehicle-Enters-Zone, and the second a Vehicle-Stopped-Inside-Zone. This behaviour pattern could be defined as a Visit in Box 4.

The SWRL constraints (Box 5) define the start and finish time of a visit and ensure that (1) the agents of the two parts are the same, (2) the zones are the same, and (3) the first event happens before the second begins.

The definitions of Passenger-Activity and Refuelling could then simply read as shown in Box 6.

In addition to behaviour concepts, the domain ontology contains definitions of specific zones, specific mobile objects (Person or Vehicle) and refinements of Vehicle in terms of GPU, Loader, Tanker etc.

The temporal constraints specified for each aggregate provide only a crude model of temporal relationships in a turnaround. As the data of real turnarounds show, there are sometimes exceptions and unusual delays, hence tight crisp constraints may exclude valid interpretations, while overly loose constraints may spawn too many false positives. As pointed out in the introduction, we there-

Box 6. Simplified definitions of Passenger-Activity and Refuelling

```
Passenger-Activity ⊑ Visit ⊓
        has-part1 exactly 1 Passenger-Stairs-Enters-PS-Zone ⊓
        has-part2 exactly 1 Passenger-Stairs-Stopped-Inside-PS-Zone

Refuelling ⊑ Visit ⊓
        has-part1 exactly 1 Tanker-Enters-Tanking-Zone ⊓
        has-part2 exactly 1 Tanker-Stopped-Inside-Tanking-Zone
```

This way, additional SWRL constraints are not necessary

fore developed a probabilistic model for temporal relations. Conceptually, it should be part of the ontology, but unfortunately there is currently no way to efficiently connect probability distributions with OWL. Our probabilistic framework, described in Section 4, is therefore represented outside of OWL and connects to the interpretation system at runtime.

Key terms: Behaviour recognition, monitoring, event ontology, Beam Search, probabilistic guidance, Bayesian Compositional Hierarchy, prediction, aircraft servicing.

3. GENERATING A SCENE INTERPRETATION SYSTEM FROM THE ONTOLOGY

In this section, we describe the scene interpretation system SCENIOR which is automatically generated from the conceptual knowledge base represented in OWL and SWRL. We first give an overview and provide some motivation for design decisions. We then describe the tasks of the conversion process in detail, in particular generating rules for rule-based scene interpretation and generating a temporal constraint system (TCN) for the evaluation of SWRL constraints.

3.1. Motivation and System Overview

The design decisions which have led to SCENIOR are based on insights gained from past scene interpretation projects (Neumann & Weiss, 2003; Hotz & Neumann, 2005) and shared by many researchers in the field:

1. The interpretation system must be based on conceptual knowledge represented in a standardised way. This is a prerequisit for reusability of knowledge and for an economical development of application systems.
2. Interpretation can be viewed as a mixed bottom-up and top-down search for the best explanation of evidence in compositional and taxonomical hierarchies. Hence interpretation steps can be modelled with predefined generic patterns.
3. For stepwise scene interpretation, it is necessary to entertain several possible interpretations in parallel. A greedy interpretation strategy would be likely to fail, in general, and backtracking would cause high system complexity and inefficient performance.
4. In addition to a logic-based framework and crisp constraints, a probabilistic model is required to provide preferences among interpretation alternatives.

We have therefore chosen an approach where the conceptual knowledge base is converted into a rule-based system with rules realising both bottom-up and top-down processing, and parallel threads for processing alternative interpretations. Probabilistic guidance is provided by a probabilistic model homomorphic with compositional hierarchies of the conceptual knowledge base.

Concretely, SCENIOR is implemented as a Java application with JESS[6] (Java Expert System Shell) for rule-based processing. JESS is one of the fastest rule engines available, it can directly manipulate and reason about Java objects. Figure 3 shows the main components of the system.

In the initialisation phase of the system, a converter (which is also part of SCENIOR) loads the knowledge base and translates it into rules and templates in JESS format (see Subsection 3.2). The result is called *JESS conceptual knowledge base* (JCKB). The temporal constraints defined with SWRL rules are translated into temporal constraint nets (see Subsection 3.3). Then a JESS thread is created for each submodel of the com-

positional hierarchy and provided with a submodel hypothesis composed of Working Memory Elements (WMEs) for each expected instantiation for this submodel, and with a corresponding TCN. Now the system is ready to start the interpretation process (see Subsection 3.5).

SCENIOR expects real-time evidence about an evolving scene in the form of primitive symbolic activity tokens with attached quantitative temporal information and other useful properties as input. For aircraft servicing scenes, this evidence is provided in terms of primitive states or events generated by a tracking component and a simple-event detector developed by project partners.

The interpretation process, described in detail in Subsection 3.5, employs Beam Search to generate possible interpretations in parallel threads. In each thread, a JESS rule engine effects data-driven rule applications, and a Java constraint solver evaluates crisp temporal constraints and terminates a thread in the case of a conflict. In addition, a probabilistic inference engine for Bayesian Compositional Hierarchies (BCHs)

Figure 3. Main components of the scene interpretation system SCENIOR

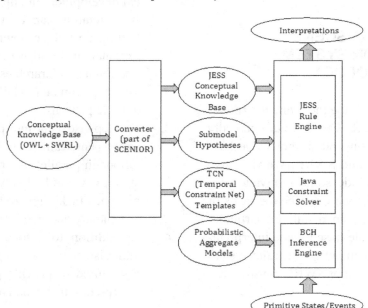

provides a rating of each partial interpretation to control the Beam Search.

3.2. Rule Generation from the Ontology

It has been shown by Neumann and Moeller (2006) that scene interpretation can be viewed as a search in the space of possible interpretations defined by taxonomical and compositional relations and controlled by constraints. Four kinds of interpretation steps are required to navigate in interpretation space and to construct interpretations:

- Aggregate instantiation (moving up a compositional hierarchy)
- Aggregate expansion (moving down a compositional hierarchy)
- Instance specialisation (moving down a taxonomical hierarchy)
- Instance merging (unifying instances obtained separately)

In our framework, we create rules for the first three steps, with some additional supporting rules. It will be shown that the step "instance merging" becomes expendable with the use of submodel hypotheses and parallel search.

Creating Templates and Slots

Before creating JESS rules, every concept of the OWL knowledge base is converted into a JESS *template* with the same name as the concept. Templates are the main structuring feature of the JESS rule language, they are analogous to Java classes. A template is defined by a name and a number of *slots*, which are comparable to the member variables of a Java class. Here, slots of a template are defined corresponding to the properties of the concept and complemented with an additional slot *name*, which will hold the name of a particular instance (e.g. vehicle_17). To preserve the taxonomical hierarchy of the OWL knowledge base, we use the inheritance mechanism of JESS, where templates can be defined as sub-templates which inherit the slots of the parent template. Our approach differs from the transformation of OWL and SWRL to JESS described in (Erikson, 2003), where the properties are modelled as *ordered facts* which are simply JESS lists, and the template structure is flat. This would have the effect that properties are decoupled from the concept template, and the taxonomy must be emulated by duplicating facts along the taxonomical hierarchy, destroying the object-centered structure of an aggregate and possibly leading to scalability problems.

Submodel Hypotheses

In the next step, a hypothesis structure is generated for each submodel identified in the conceptual knowledge base. A submodel hypothesis represents the compositional structure of the submodel, respecting the equality constraints described with SWRL rules, and provides placeholders for all expected instantiations. Each submodel hypothesis defines an independent interpretation goal. This facilitates evidence assignment and splitting of the search tree into several alternatives which are tracked in parallel. A submodel hypothesis can also be viewed as a structure for coherent expectations. During interpretation it can be used to "hallucinate" missing evidence and thus to continue a promising interpretation thread. Figure 4 shows a simplified submodel hypothesis for the submodel Arrival.

Rules

In the next step of the transformation process, the following rules are created fully automatically from the ontology:

- Evidence-assignment rules
- Aggregate-instantiation and hallucination rules
- Aggregate-expansion rules

Figure 4. Submodel hypothesis for the submodel Arrival

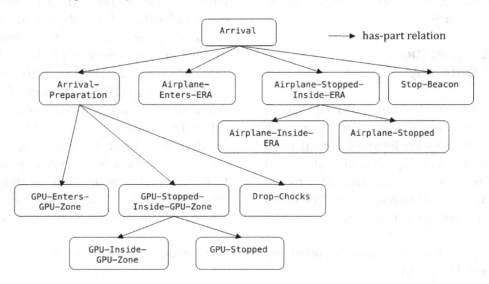

- Specialisation rules
- Time-update rules.

An *evidence-assignment rule* assigns evidence provided by lower-level processing to a hypothesis element which is the leaf of a submodel hypothesis. In the premise of the rule, the template corresponding to the aggregate is addressed (GPU-Enters-GPU-Zone in the example below), and the temporal constraints are checked with a test function (*test conditional element*). The processing of the temporal constraints is described in detail in the next subsection. In the action part of the rule, the status of the evidence is changed from evidence to assigned, and the status of the hypothesis element is changed from hypothesised to instantiated.

Figure 5 illustrates the generic pattern of an evidence-assignment rule.

An *aggregate-instantiation rule* instantiates an aggregate with status hypothesised if all its parts are instantiated or hallucinated. This is a bottom-up step in the compositional hierarchy and the backbone for the scene interpretation process. It is not necessary to check the temporal constraints here, because this has already been done in the evidence-assignment rules of the parts. A simplified example illustrating the generic pattern of an aggregate-instantiation rule is given in Figure 6.

A *specialisation rule* refines an instance to a more specialised instance. Unfortunately, the inbuilt JESS template structure only recognises if an instance of a concept satisfies a more general concept restriction, for example, an instance

Figure 5. Example illustrating the generic pattern of an evidence-assignment rule

```
(defrule GPU-Enters-GPU-Zone_ea_rule
    ?e-id <- (GPU-Enters-GPU-Zone
                (name ?gegz_17)
                (status evidence))
    ?h-id <- (GPU-Enters-GPU-Zone
                (name ?gegz_h)
                (status ?status_1))
    (test (or (eq ?status_1 hypothesised)
              (eq ?status_1 hallucinated)))
    ;; check temporal constraints
=>
    (modify ?e-id (status assigned))
    (modify ?h-id (status instantiated))
    ;; update temporal constraint net
)
```

Figure 6. Example illustrating the generic pattern of an aggregate-instantiation rule

```
(defrule Arrival-preparation_ai_rule
    ?h-id <- (Arrival-Preparation
             (name ?ap_h)
             (status hypothesised)
             (has-part-1 p1)
             (has-part-2 p2)
             (has-part-3 p3))
    (GPU-Enters-GPU-Zone
             (name ?p1)
             (status ?status_1))
    (test (or (eq ?status_1 instantiated)
              (eq ?status_1 hallucinated)))
    (GPU-Stopped-Inside-GPU-Zone
             (name ?p2)
             (status ?status_2))
    (test (or (eq ?status_2 instantiated)
              (eq ?status_2 hallucinated)))
    (Drop-Chocks
             (name ?p3)
             (status ?status_3))
    (test (or (eq ?status_3 instantiated)
              (eq ?status_3 hallucinated)))
    =>
    (modify ?h-id (status instantiated)))
```

Figure 7. Example illustrating the generic pattern of a specialisation rule

```
(defrule GPU-Enters-GPU-Zone_s_rule
    ?e-id <- (Vehicle-Enters-Zone
             (name ?vez_14)
             (status evidence)
             (has-agent ?a1)
             (has-location ?l1))
    (GPU (name ?a1))
    (GPU-Zone (name ?l1))
    (not (GPU-Enters-GPU-Zone (name ?vez_14)))
    =>
    (retract ?e-id))
    (assert (GPU-Enters-GPU-Zone
             (name ?vez_14)
             (status evidence)
             (has-agent ?a1)
             (has-location ?l1)))
```

Figure 8. Simplified generic pattern for an aggregate-expansion rule

```
(defrule Arrival-preparation_ae1_rule
    (Arrival-Preparation
             (name ?ap_h)
             (status hypothesised)
             (has-part ?p))
    ?p-id <- (GPU-Enters-GPU-Zone
             (name ?p)
             (status hypothesised))
    =>
    (modify ?p-id (status hallucinated)))
```

of GPU-Enters-GPU-Zone is recognised as a an instance of Vehicle-Enters-Zone. However, it is not recognised that an instance of Vehicle-Enters-Zone with has-agent GPU and has-location GPU-Zone is an instance of GPU-Enters-GPU-Zone. This classification could be easily performed by any DL reasoner, but we preferred a solution within the JESS system, hence the rules for specialisation. A simplified rule for this example is given in Figure 7.

An *aggregate-expansion rule* instantiates part of an aggregate if the aggregate itself is instantiated or hallucinated. This is a top-down step in the compositional hierarchy. A separate rule is created for every part of the aggregate. It will be invoked if a fact has not been asserted bottom-up but by other means, e.g. common-sense reasoning. Such facts receive the status hallucinated, alluding to a sentence attributed to Max Clowes (1971): "Vision is controlled hallucination". If an aggregate has the status hallucinated, aggregate-expansion rules will also hallucinate all its parts. If some of the parts have already been instantiated by an evidence-assignment rule or an aggregate-instantiation rule, then the corresponding rules will not fire; a mechanism for instance merging is not necessary.

In the current state of our interpretation system, an event (or state) will be hallucinated if (1) it is defined as *hallucinatable* in the ontology, and (2) it can be derived from the temporal constraint net that the event should have happened by now. This check is done in the Java background. For example, the event Drop-Chocks in an Arrival-Preparation is difficult to detect by an image processing module, so it could be defined as *hallucinatable*.

Figure 8 illustrates the generic pattern of an aggregate-expansion rule.

The *time-update rules* set the has-finished property of a primitive state to true and update the temporal constraint net. These rules are necessary, because a primitive state has a duration and is added as evidence to the working memory at the moment of its first occurrence in the input data stream. This is desirable so that other rules, like evidence-assignment rules and aggregate-instantiation rules, can fire before the primitive state has finished. For example, a Vehicle-Enters-Zone event can be inferred even though the primitive state Vehicle-Inside-Zone has not yet finished. If the update caused by a time-update rule leads to an inconsistency of the TCN, the thread representing this interpretation alternative will die.

Summarising rule generation, we note that format and flavour of the rules are noticeably influenced by the expressivity of a classical rule language like JESS, and may raise doubts regarding the verifiability of the intended behaviour. Generated from an OWL ontology, however, most of the drawbacks of large rule systems can be avoided, as will be explained in the following.

First, the ontology provides an unerring inventory of aggregate models organised below the Upper-Model node Conceptual-Object. Hence a rule generation process can be set up which is complete and non-redundant regarding all aggregate-related rules. Second, the taxonomical structure of the ontology specifies exactly, which specialisation inferences have to be provided by rules, supplementing the inbuilt inferences.

A commonly experienced drawback of rule systems is the intransparent flow of control, influenced by conflict resolution between multiple rules applicable to a processing state. Rule conflicts are not avoided in our framework, but they are resolved by giving every rule an equal chance in a separate interpretation thread, see Section 3.5. Furthermore, control decisions regarding termination of a thread are subject to declarative constraints and an independent rating scheme.

3.3. Temporal Constraints

The temporal constraints in the SWRL section of the ontology use expressions of the *convex time point algebra* (Vila, 1994). The *Allen temporal operators* used in the SWRLTemporalOntology[7] are not expressive enough for our purposes, because they only allow to model qualitative relations, whereas the complexity of our domain requires quantitative temporal models.

As the basic format of a temporal relation in the convex time point algebra, we use

$$t_2 - t_1 \leq c_{12} \qquad (1)$$

where t_1 and t_2 are range-valued variables for time points and c_{12} is a constant. A range is a unary constraint specifying the minimal value t_{min} and maximal value t_{max} which a time variable t may take. An event is described with a single time point, a state with a start and a finish time point. We use SWRL rules to express arbitrary linear-inequality relations between time points of different aggregates. This way, it is possible to model important features of the temporal structure of a scene.

Temporal constraint nets are generated for each aggregate of the ontology and then merged into a constraint net for each submodel. Figure 9 shows the temporal constraint net for the submodel Arrival introduced in Figure 4. The suffix "st" indicates a start time point and the suffix "ft" a finish time point of a state. The suffix "tp" indicates the time point of an event. A directed arc represents an inequality according to Equation 1, with the arrow pointing from t_1 to t_2 and the number at the arrow representing c_{12}. A double-ended arrow with the offset 0 indicates equality of the connected time points.

Initially the range of each time variable is open-ended, i.e. $[-\infty\ +\infty]$. When an evidence-assignment rule or a time-update rule fires, the corresponding variables will receive concrete values which are then propagated through the constraint net as follows (Neumann, 1989):

Figure 9. Temporal constraint net for the submodel Arrival

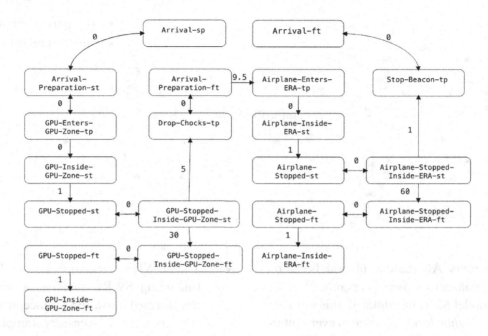

- Minima are propagated in edge direction:
$$t'_{2\min} = \max(t_{2\min}, t_{1\min} + c_{12}) \qquad (2)$$
- Maxima are propagated against edge direction: $t'_{1\max} = \min(t_{1\max}, t_{2\max} - c_{12}) \qquad (3)$

A TCN is consistent, if $t_{\max} \geq t_{\min}$ holds for all time variables. The TCN maintains the consistency of the crisp temporal constraints, while the scene is evolving. It is implemented procedurally in Java using *shadow facts* (Friedmann-Hill, 2003). This way, changes of the TCN are immediately visible to JESS and may effect rule activations.

3.4. Using Submodels

Usually, several models have to be considered in a scene interpretation task. One reason is the need to cope with several alternative variants of a scene model. In our domain of airport activity monitoring, for example, there are turnarounds with or without refuelling, with or without de-icing etc. One can easily imagine that there are similar situations in other domains, where alterna-

tive models exist that vary in some parts but are identical otherwise.

One way of coping with alternatives is to create separate complete models. This approach is illustrated with the abstract models M_1 and M_2 on the left-hand side of Figure 10. It has the obvious disadvantage of leading to redundancies in the interpretation process, since identical alternatives have to be maintained in parallel. A better approach is to decompose the alternative models into several submodels, as depicted on the right-hand side of Figure 10. This has the added advantage of allowing subgoals to be defined, each of which may be interesting for a monitoring task in its own right.

Subgoals lead to intermediate results which will not be discarded and can be used as "higher-level evidence" for other aggregates. In the OWL ontology, concepts corresponding to subgoals are marked as context-free, indicating that the conceptual definition is designed to be valid in several contexts. This is a signal for the transformation process to generate submodels with these

Figure 10. Decomposition of separate models into submodels

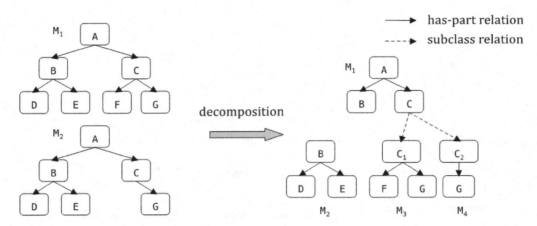

concepts as roots. Alternative submodels can be defined as variants of a common parent. If a root R of a submodel M_k is instantiated, this instance is offered as *higher-level evidence* to every interpretation thread with R or a superclass of R as a leaf.

On the right-hand side of Figure 10, the concepts B and C are marked as context-free. Furthermore, $C_1 \sqsubseteq C$ and $C_2 \sqsubseteq C$. For example, C_1 could stand for a Service with De-icing (F), and C_2 for a Service without De-icing. If C_1 or C_2 is recognised (instantiated), a corresponding higher-level evidence is provided for every interpretation thread containing a concept of type C as a leaf. In our example this could be M_1 modelling a Turnaround.

For the transformation process from OWL and SWRL to JESS rules, submodels cause separate threads to be created, and a separate temporal constraint net is generated for every submodel. Furthermore, evidence-assignment rules are generated not only for primitive but also for higher-level evidence.

3.5. Interpretation Process

We can now give an overview of the interpretation process with SCENIOR. In the initialisation phase the following steps are performed:

- The OWL conceptual knowledge base (including SWRL rules) is automatically transformed into a JESS conceptual knowledge base. All necessary templates and rules are generated.
- A separate interpretation thread is created for every submodel, equipped with a submodel hypothesis structure and a temporal constraint net. Each thread has its own independent JESS engine.

Now the system is ready to start the interpretation process. It receives primitive states and events as input, and feeds these as WMEs to every interpretation thread. Then the rules are applied and may eventually lead to instantiated aggregates, which again may cause higher-level aggregates to be instantiated. If there is more than one activation for an evidence-assignment rule within one thread (i.e. if multiple evidence assignments are possible), then this thread is cloned into several threads, one for each possible alternative assignment. A newly created thread is an exact copy of the original thread. Then each of the possible assignments is performed on a separate clone by forcing the corresponding rule to fire. This way, a search tree is established which examines all interpretation possibilities in parallel.

So far, we have not yet discussed how to deal with noise, which can either occur in terms of activities not modelled in the ontology, or as errors of low-level processing. Both kinds of noise are abundantly present in our aircraft servicing domain. Various kinds of vehicles not taking part in a service or performing some unknown task enter and leave the servicing area throughout a turnaround. Also, low-level processing in our application is difficult and not at all perfect, hence strange events not corresponding to real activities are delivered as input to SCENIOR.

We have therefore extended our scene model to include a noise model which allows anything not covered by the turnaround model to happen at any time. Naturally, this causes an exponential explosion of interpretation threads: For each evidence, the number of threads increases, reduced only by inconsistent threads.

As it turned out, SCENIOR can process up to ca. 150 threads in parallel and in real-time on an ordinary PC. Nevertheless, the number of interpretation threads required for all possibilities will exceed the capacity after a few steps. Clearly, a preference measure is required which allows to discard less promising threads even if they satisfy the scene model. To this end, we have developed a probabilistic scene model which will be presented in the next section.

4. A PROBABILISTIC PREFERENCE MODEL

As explained in the preceding section, scene interpretation can be controlled by a crisp constraint net, in our case the temporal constraint net TCN, such that only consistent interpretations survive in a parallel search. This approach has the advantage that the scene model can be completely represented in OWL and SWRL, and that the constraint solver can be realised efficiently. However, as pointed out before, constraints may not be tight, else correct interpretations may be missed. Hence the interpretation system may generate many false positives, depending on the discriminative qualities of the evidence.

We have therefore developed a probabilistic rating system to obtain a preference measure for consistent interpretations. By computing this rating for intermediate partial interpretations, the most promising ones can be kept, unlikely ones can be discarded. Applied to multiple consistent final interpretations, a single most likely interpretation can be selected.

We first formulate a general probabilistic model for scene interpretation and derive a rating for partial and final interpretations. We then present Bayesian Compositional Hierarchies (BCHs) which are special probabilistic models structured in congruence with the compositional hierarchy of the OWL ontology.

4.1. A General Probabilistic Model for Scene Interpretation

In a general form, probabilistic scene interpretation can be modelled as evidence-based reasoning with large Joint Probability Distributions (JPDs). In the context of a parallel search, the task is to determine which of M alternative models applies to a scene. A generative probabilistic model for a scene can be written as

$$P_{scene} = q_m P^{(m)}(\underline{X}_1^{(m)} \cdots \underline{X}_{N^{(m)}}^{(m)} \underline{Y}_1^{(m)} \cdots \underline{Y}_{K^{(m)}}^{(m)}) P_{clutter} \quad (4)$$

We assume that there are M competing models with priors q_m, m = 1 .. M. Each model is described by a JPD consisting of hidden variables $\underline{X} = [\underline{X}_1 .. \underline{X}_N]$ and observable variables $\underline{Y} = [\underline{Y}_1 .. \underline{Y}_K]$. The indices suggest distinct conceptual entities (for example aggregates), each described by a vector of random variables, indicated by the underline.

Values for observable variables are provided by evidence from low-level processing, values of hidden variables are determined by probabilistic inference. In our temporal model for the aircraft servicing domain, the observables correspond to time points marking a primitive event such as Vehicle-Stopped-Inside-Zone, whereas hidden variables could describe beginning and duration of higher-level activities such as Arrival-Preparation.

$P_{clutter}$ is a catch-all distribution for evidence not fitting a model. This could simply be a JPD modelling the occurrence of "unexplainable" evidence objects during a turnaround as independent events.

To guide the interpretation process, we are interested in ranking alternative partial interpretations given evidence $\underline{e}$. Alternatives do not only arise from the models 1 .. M but also from alternative assignments of evidence within a model. For example, a Vehicle-Enters-ERA event (ERA is the large Entrance Restricted Zone where all turnaround activities occur) can be part of many service activities of a turnaround, in particular, if the type of vehicle is uncertain or tracking errors have occurred. Alternative assignments cause additional competing interpretations. Further alternatives arise from assigning some of the evidence - say $\underline{e}_n^+$ - to the model and the rest - say $\underline{e}_n^-$ - to clutter, possibly different for each model. To simplify the notation, we enumerate all alternatives – due to competing models and alternative assignments - using the index n.

The ranking R_n of a scene model n is given by the probability that the model has generated $\underline{e}_n^+$ as part of the service model and $\underline{e}_n^-$ as clutter. This is captured by the following equation:

$$R_n = q_n P^{(n)}\left(e_n^+\right) P_{clutter}\left(\underline{e}_n^+\right) \qquad (5)$$

Equation (5) shows that alternative rankings can be determined from Equation (4) by marginalising the observables of each model n which have been chosen for evidence assignment, and computing the resulting probabilities.

To determine the final interpretation, one has to perform two maximisations. First, determine the highest-ranking model n*, and then determine the values $\underline{x}_n^*$ for hidden variables of this model which maximise its posterior probability. These steps are described by the following equations:

$$n^* = \arg\max_n \left(q_n P^{(n)}\left(\underline{e}_n^+\right) P_{clutter}\left(\underline{e}_n^-\right) \right) \qquad (6)$$

$$\left[X = x^*, Y = \underline{e}^+ \right]$$
$$= \arg\max_x \left(q_{n*} P^{(n*)}\left(\underline{x}, \underline{e}_{n*}^+\right) \right) \qquad (7)$$

Note that the probabilistic model given by Equation (4) does not explicitly account for missing evidence, for example due to occlusion or tracking limitations. To deal with this, the range of observables could be extended to include "missing evidence" as a possible "value", but an assignment and probabilistic appreciation will necessarily depend on the context. The issue of missing information will not be treated in the sequel.

If interpretation is performed in real-time, probabilistic models may be adapted to the progressing time. In our application, a scene model as given by Equation (4) will involve temporal random variables representing observable events on a quantitative time scale relative to some common reference event, for example relative to an initial observation. Real-time processing using such a model implies that we have a current time t_c which progresses as we observe a concrete scene, and that modelled events not observed so far are bound to happen at times $t > t_c$, if at all. This should influence our ranking of alternatives to the effect that reduced chances for an event cause a reduced ranking.

Let $\underline{e}$ be evidence assigned up to time t_c, and $\underline{T}_n \subseteq \underline{Y}$ be unassigned temporal observables of a model. Then the rank of model n at time t_c is given by

$$R_n\left(t_c\right) = q_n P^{(n)}\left(e_n^+, T_n > t_c\right) P_{clutter}\left(e_n^-\right) \qquad (8)$$

Equation (8) shows that the ranking of an alternative model changes according to its share in the probability space for the remaining temporal variables. This refines Equation (8) which implied that the complete probability space was left for unassigned variables. Note that real-time updating does not apply to hidden temporal variables for which values $t < t_c$ may be inferred.

4.2. Bayesian Compositional Hierarchies

In order to preserve the advantages of ontology-based scene models, it is useful to achieve a tight integration of the probabilistic model with a logic-based compositional hierarchy. As an important step towards integration, we present an approach for formulating probabilistic scene models in terms of probabilistic aggregate models complementing the aggregate definitions in OWL. Rimey (1993) modelled compositional hierarchies using tree-shaped Bayesian Networks (BNs). To ensure efficient processing, he had to assume that parts of an aggregate are statistically independent given the parent aggregate. In Neumann (2008), a more powerful hierarchical probabilistic model has been presented, called Bayesian Compositional Hierarchy (BCH). In the following, we briefly summarise the definition of a BCH for arbitrary probability distributions. Thereafter, we describe the structure of a Gaussian BCH which is the kind used for modelling the temporal structure of aircraft services in our work.

A BCH is a probabilistic model of a compositional hierarchy. It consists of aggregates, each modelled individually by an unrestricted JPD in an object-centered manner. The hierarchy is formed by using the aggregate headers as part descriptions in aggregates of the next hierarchical level, abstracting from details of parts at the lower level.

Figure 11 illustrates the schematic structure of a BCH. Each aggregate is described by a JPD $P(\underline{A}\,\underline{B}_1...\underline{B}_K\,\underline{C})$ where $\underline{A}$ is the aggregate header providing an external description to the next higher level, $\underline{B}_1...\underline{B}_K$ are descriptions of the parts, and $\underline{C}$ expresses conditions on the parts. The hierarchy is constructed by taking the aggregate headers at a lower level as part descriptions at the next higher level, hence $\underline{B}_1^{(1)} = \underline{A}^{(2)}$ etc.

In our aircraft servicing domain, for example, a Turnaround aggregate consists of a header which provides an external description of a turnaround in terms of its duration (abstracting from details about the parts), and an internal description of the temporal structure of the three parts Arrival, Services and Departure. The parts are also described as aggregates themselves, for example Arrival is an aggregate with parts Arrival-Preparation, Airplane-Enters-ERA and Stop-Beacon, compare with the hierarchy shown in Table 1.

In general, the JPD of a complete hierarchy is given by

$$P(\underline{A}^{(1)}..\ \underline{A}^{(N)}) = P(\underline{A}^{(1)}) \prod_{i=1..N} P(\underline{B}_1^{(i)}..\ \underline{B}_{K_i}^{(i)}\underline{C}^{(i)} \mid \underline{A}^{(i)})$$

$$(9)$$

This remarkable formula shows that the JPD of a BCH can be easily constructed from individual aggregate representations, and belief updates can be performed by propagation along the tree structure. Let $P'(B_i)$ be an update of $P(B_i)$, by evidence or propagation from its parts below. Then the updated aggregate JPD is

$$P'\left(\underline{A}\,\underline{B}_1..\,\underline{B}_K\underline{C}\right) = P\left(\underline{A}\,\underline{B}_1..\,\underline{B}_K\underline{C}\right) P'\left(\underline{B}_i\right) / P\left(\underline{B}_i\right)$$

$$(10)$$

A similar equation holds when $P(A)$ is updated by propagation from its parent above.

Storage and updating operations for large hierarchies can be computationally very expensive. We have therefore developed an implementation

Figure 11. Schematic structure of a BCH. Triangles represent aggregates, circles represent parts. Aggregate models overlap, their headers represent parts of aggregates at the next higher level.

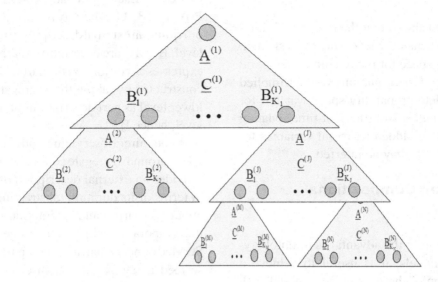

for aggregates with multivariate Gaussian distributions. Roughly symmetric, unimodal distributions can often be approximated by a Gaussian in a range corresponding to $-2\sigma .. +2\sigma$, where σ is the standard deviation. Multivariate Gaussian aggregate models can be compactly represented by their means and covariance matrices, and propagation in a BCH can be performed very efficiently by closed-form solutions, as shown in the following.

Let $G = [\underline{E}\ \underline{F}]$ be a vector of Gaussian random variables representing an aggregate. Let $\underline{F}$ be the subset whose distribution is changed by evidence or incoming propagation. $\underline{F}$ can be the aggregate header in the case of downward propagation or a part header in the case of upward propagation. We want to compute the effect of the changed distribution of $\underline{F}$ on $\underline{G}$. Before propagation, the distribution of $\underline{G}$ is $P(\underline{G}) = N(\underline{\mu}_G, \Sigma_G)$ where $\underline{\mu}_G$ is the mean vector and Σ_G the covariance matrix. The partitions corresponding to $\underline{E}$ and $\underline{F}$, respectively, are denoted as shown:

For a probability update, we assume that the distribution of $\underline{F}$ is changed to

$P'(\underline{F}) = N(\underline{\mu}_F{}', \Sigma_F{}')$. Then the new distribution of $\underline{G}$ is $P'(\underline{G}) = N(\underline{\mu}_G{}', \Sigma_G{}')$ with

$$\Sigma_E{}' = \Sigma_E - \Sigma_{EF}\Sigma_F^{-1}\Sigma_{EF}^T \\ + \Sigma_{EF}\Sigma_F^{-1}\Sigma_F{}'\Sigma_F^{-1}\Sigma_{EF}^T \tag{11}$$

$$\Sigma_{EF}{}' = \Sigma_{EF}\Sigma_F^{-1}\Sigma_F{}' \tag{12}$$

$$\underline{\mu}_E{}' = \underline{\mu}_E + \Sigma_{EF}\Sigma_F^{-1}\left(\underline{\mu}_F{}' - \underline{\mu}_F\right) \tag{13}$$

It is evident that both upward and downward propagation for an aggregate with random variables $\underline{A}\ \underline{B}_1 \ ... \ \underline{B}_K\ \underline{C}$ can be performed by fairly simple matrix computations.

Multivariate Gaussians are also very convenient for computing the ranking as described in Equation (5). The marginalisations required for ranking alternative interpretations are directly available from the aggregate covariances, and the final maximizing interpretation according to Equations (6) and (7) can be given in terms of the mean values of hidden variables.

There are, however, clear limitations of the applicability of multivariate Gaussian BCHs, for example in connection with discrete random variables, range-limited flat distributions or the truncated distributions arising in real-time updates according to Equation (8). In some cases it may be possible though to use Gaussians as approximations. This will be shown in the following for the temporal structure of aircraft services.

4.3. A Probabilistic Model for the Temporal Structure of Aircraft Services

To perform real-time interpretation of aircraft servicing operations, a BCH for all aggregates shown in Table 1 has been determined from the statistics of 52 turnaround records. For each aggregate, the temporal structure of its parts is specified in terms of correlated random variables for durations and delays. Figure 12 illustrates the structure of the aggregate Arrival-Preparation as an example. It is defined by the two random variables Delay1 and Delay2 which denote the delays between the point event GPU-Enters-GPU-Zone, the beginning of GPU-Stopped-Inside-GPU-Zone and the point event Drop-Chocks, respectively. The aggregate header is a random variable for the duration of Arrival-Preparation, its value is defined as the sum of Delay1 and Delay2.

Table 2 shows the means and the covariance matrix of the Gaussian JPD. Since the duration of Arrival-Preparation is determined by the sum of the random variables describing the parts, the covariance is singular, but this does not jeopardise the updating procedure. The positive correlation between the delays reflects the observation that activities in some turnarounds are generally faster than in others.

All aggregate models have a similar structure, with activities described by their durations and related to each other by delays. Gaussians are used with the understanding that only the range $-2\sigma \dots +2\sigma$ is valid in the model. To ensure that durations of activities take only positive values, their models are constrained by $\mu > 2\sigma$.

The reader may wonder how the probabilistic model relates to the crisp temporal constraints of the ontology. As a matter of fact, the crisp constraints have initially been the only means to express temporal relationships (Bohlken & Neumann, 2009), and experiments showed their

Table 2. Multivariate Gaussian JPD for Arrival-Preparation (units in minutes)

	Mean	Covariance		
Arrival-Preparation	6	29.3	2.25	27
Delay1	1	2.25	0.25	25
Delay2	5	27	2	25

Figure 12. Temporal structure of the aggregate Arrival-Preparation

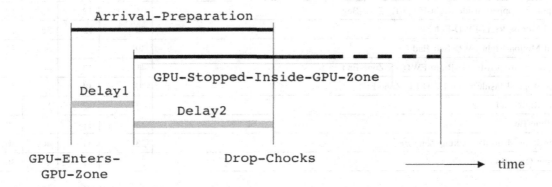

Table 3. Estimated timeline of a turnaround after an initial observation (Case 1) and after observations up to Airplane-Enters-ERA (Case 2). Columns show times T and uncertainties of estimates D (standard deviations) in minutes.

	Case 1		Case 2	
	T	**D**	**T**	**D**
Turnaround-Beg	**0**	0	**0**	0
Arrival-Beg	0	0	**0**	0
Arrival-Preparation-Beg	0	0	**0**	0
GPU-Enters-GPU-Zone-Eve	0	0	**0**	0
GPU-Stopped-Inside-GPU-Zone-Beg	1	0,5	**1**	0
Drop-Chocks-Eve	6	3	**6**	0
Arrival-Preparation-End	6	3	**6**	0
Airplane-Enters-ERA-Eve	9	6	**15**	0
Airplane-Stopped-Inside-ERA-Beg	9	6	15	0
Stop-Beacon-Eve	17	6	23	1
Arrival-End	17	6	23	2
Services-Beg	19	8	26	3
Passenger-Activity-Beg	19	8	26	3
Passenger-Stairs-stopped-Inside-PS-Zone-Beg	19	8	26	3
Passenger-Stairs-stopped-Inside-PS-Zone-End	55	16	62	15
Passenger-Activity-End	58	17	65	15
Unload-Right-Beg	23	9	30	5
Unload-Right-AFT-Beg	23	9	30	5
Loader-Stopped-Inside-Right-AFT-LD-Zone-Beg	23	9	30	5
Transporter-Stopped-Inside-Right-AFT-TS-Zone-Eve	25	9	32	5
Unload-Motion-Right-AFT-Belt-Beg	29	9	36	6
Unload-Motion-Right-AFT-Belt-End	39	10	46	7
Transporter-Stopped-Inside-Right-AFT-TS-Zone-End	41	10	48	7
Loader-Stopped-Inside-Right-AFT-LD-Zone-End	43	10	50	7
Unload-Right-AFT-End	43	10	50	7
Unload-Right-FWD-Beg	24	12	31	10
Loader-Stopped-Inside-Right-FWD-LD-Zone-Beg	24	12	31	10
Transporter-Stopped-Inside-Right-FWD-TS-Zone-Beg	25	12	33	10
Unload-Motion-Right-FWD-Belt-Beg	29	13	36	11
Unload-Motion-Right-FWD-Belt-End	39	13	46	11
Transporter-Stopped-Inside-Right-FWD-TS-Zone-End	41	13	48	11
Loader-Stopped-Inside-Right-FWD-LD-Zone-End	43	14	50	12
Unload-Right-End	43	13	50	11
Refuelling-Beg	33	31	40	30
Tanker-Stopped-Inside-Tanking-Zone-Beg	33	31	40	30
Pumping-Operation-Beg	36	31	43	30

continued on following page

Table 3. Continued

	Case 1		Case 2	
	T	**D**	**T**	**D**
Pumping-Operation-End	43	31	50	30
Tanker-Stopped-Inside-Tanking-Zone-End	47	31	54	30
Services-End	55	23	62	22
Departure-Beg	57	24	69	21
Start-Beacon	57	24	69	21
Pushback-Beg	58	25	70	22
Pushback-End	60	25	72	22
Departure-End	60	25	72	22
Turnaround-End	60	25	72	22

strengths and weaknesses. A carefully tailored probabilistic model with zero probabilities outside a specific range would make the crisp model dispensable, of course. But since we decided to employ a multivariate Gaussian model with tails which are not quite realistic, a combination of the two models, where the crisp constraints cut off the distributions outside their -2σ ... +2σ ranges, seems to be a good solution.

5. INTERPRETING AIRCRAFT TURNAROUNDS

In this section, we present results obtained in experiments with real turnaround data. First, we demonstrate the predictive power of the BCH and changes caused by partial evidence. To this end, the estimated timeline for turnaround events and the remaining uncertainty (measured in standard deviations) has been determined for two cases, (1) after observing the very first event, GPU-Enters-GPU-Zone, and (2) after observing all events up to a late Airplane-Enters-ERA, see Table 3.

Note that extended activities are marked with the suffix -Beg and -End indicating begin and end, respectively, while point events are marked with the suffix -Eve. It can be seen that observa-

tions in Case 2 significantly change the expectations of future events due to the correlations within aggregate models. Also, as to be expected, the uncertainty of estimates decreases with additional evidence.

Figure 13 illustrates the change of expectation for the Stop-Beacon event in terms of its probability density before and after the Airplane-Enters-ERA evidence. Note that the density values scale the rating; hence, the evidence will have a significant influence on controlling the Beam Search.

We now describe the initial phase of a concrete scene interpretation task to demonstrate the selective effect of the ranking provided by the BCH in a Beam Search. The input data have been obtained from one of the 80 turnarounds recorded at the Blagnac Airport in Toulouse by low-level processing of project partners in France and England.

To rate interpretations in this experiment, the probability density of clutter has been set to 0,01 which is less than the typical probability of a regular piece of evidence for a turnaround. Note that the probability density is taken to measure the "probability" of an event. A small constant factor Δt for a time span, over which a density must be integrated, is omitted for clarity. Since the ratings are naturally decreasing with each step and may reach very small numbers, the natural

Figure 13. Change of the probability density of Stop-Beacon caused by evidence for a late arrival

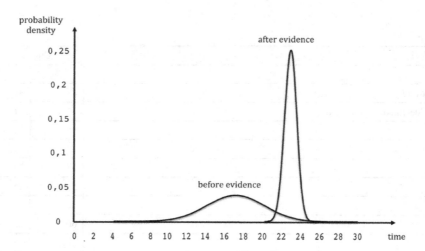

logarithm of a probability is taken, resulting in negative ratings.

Based on evidence up to the event Airplane-Enters-ERA, SCENIOR generates 8 alternative interpretations (one of which has already been disqualified), performing a complete search where every event could also be a clutter event. In Figures 14 and 15, we show two competing interpretations,

with boxes at the bottom for the evidence received so far, dark boxes for expected further events according to hypotheses trees, and other boxes representing instantiations. The Drop-Chocks event could not be observed and was inferred from the context as "hallucinated". The figures do not show any of the several clutter events which did not fit the partially instantiated models.

Figure 14. Interpretation alternative no. 4 generated by SCENIOR after 3 minutes real-time

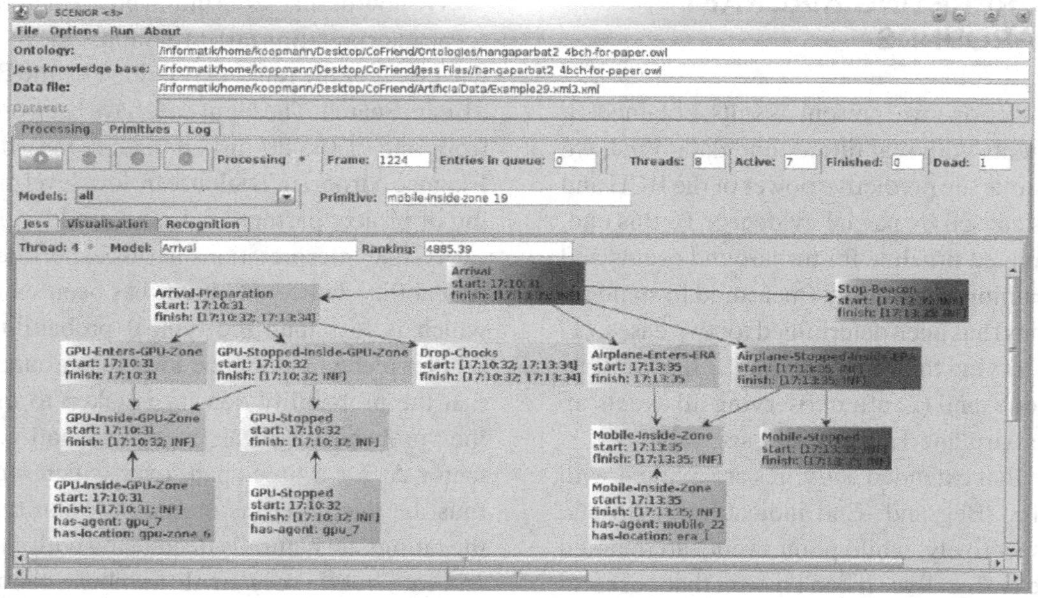

Figure 15. Interpretation alternative no. 5 generated by SCENIOR after 10 minutes

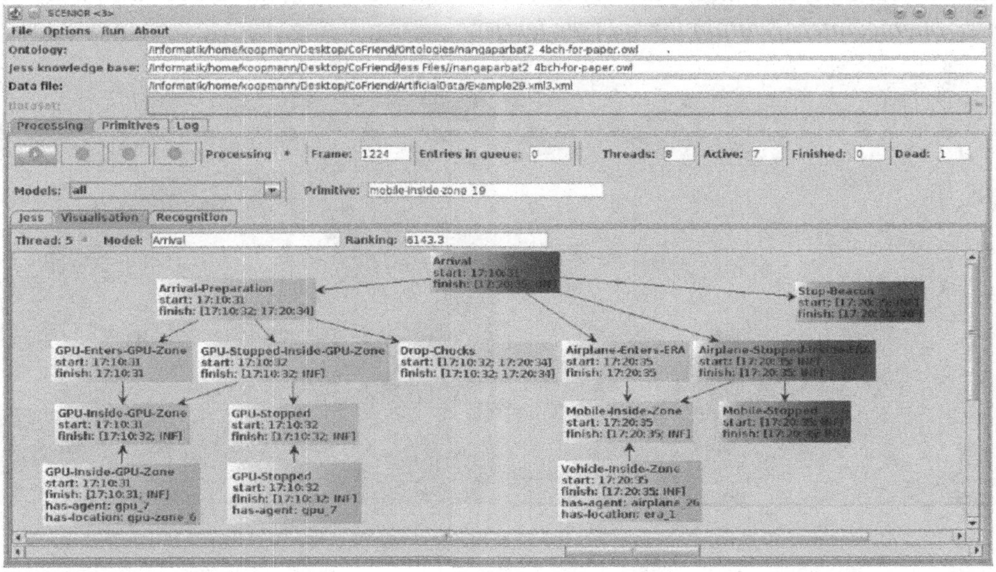

The main difference between the interpretations is an erroneous Airplane-Enters-ERA event generated by low-level processing for a tanker crossing the ERA shortly before the arrival of the airplane. Figure 16 shows the corresponding video frames taken by one of the eight cameras. The crossing tanker is visible in the far background of the image on the left.

The ratings for the partial interpretations of both alternatives are shown in Table 4. Interpretation 4 is the erroneous and Interpretation 5 is the correct one. Initially, the arrival of the GPU sets a context where a vehicle is expected to enter the ERA, hence the crossing tanker is a candidate. But as soon as the true airplane enters, an alternative arises and is favoured because the probabi-

Table 4. Initial ratings of the two alternative interpretations shown in Figures 14 and 15

Evidence	Time	Interpretation 4	Ranking 4	Interpretation 5	Ranking 5
e1	17:10:31	GPU-Enters..	0	GPU-Enters..	0
e2	17:10:32	GPU-Stopped..	-2.16	GPU-Stopped..	-2.16
e3	17:13:31	Airplane-Enters-ERA	-5.32	Clutter	-2.16
e4	17:20:35	Clutter	-5.32	Airplane-Enters-ERA	-5.09
est	≥17:13:35	Airplane-Stopped..	-6.24		
est	≥17:13:35	Stop-Beacon	-7.71		
est	≥17:20:35			Airplane-Stopped..	-6.01
est	≥17:28:35			Stop-Beacon	-7.48

e1=mobile-inside-zone-86
e2=mobile-stopped-90
e3=mobile-inside-zone-131
e4=mobile-inside-zone-155
est=estimated event

Figure 16. Snapshots of the ERA (entrance restricted area) after completing Arrival-Preparation. The GPU (ground power unit) and chocks are in place. The tanker crossing the ERA in the background (left) causes an erroneous interpretation thread (see text).

listic model expects an Airplane-Enters-ERA event 8 minutes after GPU-Enters-GPU-Zone, and the airplane's arrival is closer to that estimate than the tanker's. Note that clutter events not assigned to either of the two interpretations are not shown in the table.

The table also includes the estimated times of the next events Airplane-Stopped-Inside-ERA and Stop-Beacon together with the expected ratings of the competing interpretations. Note that estimated time windows may begin earlier than the actual time, allowing for hallucinated events in the past. Considering that Stop-Beacon will

Figure 17. Thread statistics for a typical interpretation process

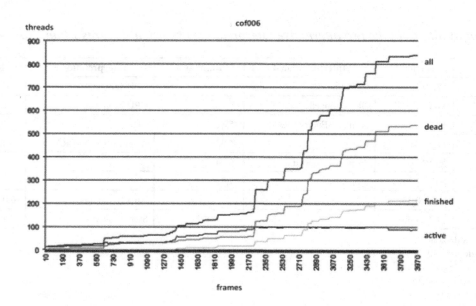

occur after the true aircraft arrival and not at the time expected in Interpretation 4, the rating of this interpretation will surely be much lower than the estimated value, further increasing the distance between the right and the wrong interpretation.

The performance of SCENIOR was evaluated for 20 annotated turnarounds, with primitive events provided by low-level image analysis of the project partners. The ontology and the probabilistic model were derived from 32 other turnarounds. Because of the noisy input data, it was necessary to interpret each evidence both as belonging to a turnaround (given that the constraints were satisfied) and as clutter. 17 of the 20 turnarounds resulted in complete interpretations. This was facilitated by Special Vision Tasks with controlled cameras for three crucial events, and by "hallucinations" for missing evidence in certain contexts. The three problematic sequences were highly irregular and did not match the conceptual model (e.g. GPU arrival after aircraft arrival). SCENIOR showed a reliable system performance with up to 100 parallel threads (limited by a preset beam width) for partial alternative interpretations, as shown in Figure 17. It can be seen that altogether more than 1000 partial interpretations have been initialised, many caused by the context-free submodels

which posed interpretation goals throughout the sequence.

The recognition rate of subactivities is shown in Table 5. It was limited to 75% because of the noisy low-level input data with missing crucial evidence.

6. CONCLUSION AND OUTLOOK

We have presented an approach to high-level scene interpretation with several novel features. First, the interpretation system is automatically generated from an ontology of behaviour concepts represented in the standardised language OWL-DL and its extension SWRL. Second, the interpretation process is organised as a Beam Search allowing several parallel interpretation threads. Third, a probabilistic model homomorphic to the compositional concept hierarchy provides a preference measure which rates competing interpretations and controls the Beam Search.

The approach is a step ahead on the way to a generic framework for scene interpretation, but it also shows current limitations regarding a standardised representation of behaviour models. Constraints, which are indispensable for object-centered aggregate representations, have

Table 5. Correctly recognised subactivities in 20 test sequences

Sequence	1	2	3	4	5	6	8	9	18	25	29	58	59	62	63	66
Arrival	1	1	1	1	1	1	1	1	1	1	1	1	1	1	1	1
Passenger-Boarding-Preparation	1	1	1	1	1	1	1	1	1	1	1	1	1	1	1	1
Unloading-Loading-AFT	1	1	1	0	1	0	1	1	1	1	0	0	0	0	0	0
Unloading-Loading-FWD				1		1	0	0				1	1		1	1
Refuelling			0	0	0			0		0		0		0		
Pushback-Arrival	1	0	0	0	0	0	0	1	0	0	0	0	0	1	0	0
Passenger-Bridge-Leaves-PBB-Zone	1	1	1	1	1	1	1	1	1	1	1	1	1	1	1	1
Departure	1	1	1	1	1	1	1	1	1	1	1	1	1	1	1	1

to be expressed with SWRL rules and cannot be included in a consistency check of the conceptual knowledge base. Unfortunately, this drawback prevails in OWL 2 (Riboni & Bettini, 2011b). Probabilistic relationships between properties, in our application time points marking the beginning and ending of activities, cannot be efficiently expressed in OWL or SWRL and must be represented separately. Also, we could not yet demonstrate the benefits of OWL regarding inference services by a DL reasoning system. As pointed out in the introduction, one reason is the need for incremental model construction which cannot be answered by the available DL systems. Another reason is the absence of large-scale knowledge bases to which scene interpretation might eventually be connected. We still believe that OWL (or its successors) may provide an attractive basis for such larger knowledge bases, hence justifying our OWL-based scene interpretation framework.

In the near future, our approach will be extended into several directions. One goal is to connect the rule system with common sense rules which can evaluate the interpretation context and determine dynamically whether missing evidence is "hallucinatable." Another goal is to extend quantitative constraints to also cover spatial information, refining the current representations based on "zones". To this end, a more powerful constraint system and an extended implementation of a BCH must be developed.

REFERENCES

Badler, N. I. (1975). *Temporal scene analysis: conceptual descriptions of object movements. Report TR 80*. Toronto, Canada: University of Toronto.

Binford, T. O., Levitt, T. S., & Mann, W. B. (1989). Bayesian inference in model-based machine vision. *Uncertainty in AI*, *3*, 73–96.

Bohlken, W., & Neumann, B. (2009). Generation of rules from ontologies for high-level scene interpretation. In Governatori, (Eds.), *Rule Interchange and Applications* (pp. 93–107). Berlin, Germany: Springer. doi:10.1007/978-3-642-04985-9_11

Chen, L., & Nugent, C. D. (2009). Ontology-based activity recognition in intelligent pervasive environments. *International Journal of Web Information Systems*, *5*(4), 410–430. doi:10.1108/17440080911006199

Cohn, A. G., Magee, D., Galata, A., Hogg, D., & Hazarika, S. (2003). Towards an architecture for cognitive vision using qualitative spatio-temporal representations and abduction. *Spatial Cognition*, *3*, 232–248. doi:10.1007/3-540-45004-1_14

Eriksson, H. (2003). Using JessTab to integrate Protégé and Jess. *IEEE Intelligent Systems*, *18*(2), 43–50. doi:10.1109/MIS.2003.1193656

Friedman-Hill, E. (2003). *Jess in action: Java rule-based systems*. Greenwich, CT: Manning.

Fusier, F., Valentin, V., Brémond, F., Thonnat, M., Borg, M., Thirde, D., & Ferryman, J. (2007). Video understanding for complex activity recognition. *Machine Vision and Applications*, *18*(3), 167–188. doi:10.1007/s00138-006-0054-y

Getoor, L., & Taskar, B. (Eds.). (2007). *Introduction to statistical relational learning*. Cambridge, MA: The MIT Press.

Gries, O., Moeller, R., Nafissi, A., Rosenfeld, M., Sokolski, K., & Wessel, M. (2010). A probabilistic abduction engine for media interpretation. In *Proceedings of the Fourth International Conference on Web Reasoning and Rule Systems*, (pp. 182-194). IEEE.

Gyftodimos, E., & Flach, P. A. (2002). Hierarchical Bayesian networks: A probabilistic reasoning model for structured domains. In E. de Jong & T. Oates (Eds.), *Proceedings of the Workshop on Development of Representations, ICML*, (pp. 23–30). ICML.

Hotz, L., & Neumann, B. (2005). Scene interpretation as a configuration task. *Kuenstliche Intelligenz, 3*, 59–65.

Hotz, L., Neumann, B., & Terzic, K. (2008). High-level expectations for low-level image processing. [Berlin, Germany: Springer.]. *Proceedings of, KI-2008*, 87–94.

Koller, D., & Pfeffer, A. (1997). Object-oriented Bayesian networks. In *Proceedings of the Thirteenth Annual Conference on Uncertainty in Artificial Intelligence*, (pp. 302–313). IEEE.

Morariu, V. I., & Davis, L. S. (2011). Multi-agent event recognition in structured scenarios. In *Proceedings of the IEEE Conference on Computer Vision and Pattern Recognition (CVPR), 2011*. CVPR.

Mumford, D., & Zhu, S.-C. (2007). *A stochastic grammar of images*. Now Publishers.

Neumann, B. (1989). Natural language description of time-varying scenes . In Waltz, D. (Ed.), *Semantic Structures* (pp. 167–206). Mahwah, NJ: Lawrence Erlbaum.

Neumann, B. (2008). *Bayesian compositional hierarchies - A probabilistic structure for scene interpretation. TR FBI-HH-B-282/08*. Hamburg, Germany: University of Hamburg.

Neumann, B., & Moeller, R. (2006). On scene interpretation with description logics . In Nagel, H.-H., & Christensen, H. (Eds.), *Cognitive Vision Systems* (pp. 247–275). Berlin, Germany: Springer. doi:10.1007/11414353_15

Neumann, B., & Weiss, T. (2003). Navigating through logic-based scene models for high-level scene interpretations. In *Proceedings of the 3rd International Conference on Computer Vision Systems (ICVS 2003)*, (pp. 212-222). Springer.

Reiter, R., & Mackworth, A. (1987). *The logic of depiction. TR 87-23*. Vancouver, Canada: University of British Columbia.

Riboni, D., & Bettini, C. (2011a). COSAR: Hybrid reasoning for context-aware activity recognition. *Personal and Ubiquitous Computing, 15*, 271–289. doi:10.1007/s00779-010-0331-7

Riboni, D., & Bettini, C. (2011b). OWL 2 modeling and reasoning with complex human activities. *Pervasive and Mobile Computing, 7*(3). doi:10.1016/j.pmcj.2011.02.001

Rimey, R. D. (1993). *Control of selective perception using Bayes nets and decision theory*. (Dissertation). University of Rochester. Rochester, NY.

Russell, S., & Norvig, P. (2010). *Artificial intelligence: A modern approach* (3rd ed.). Upper Saddle River, NJ: Pearson.

Schroeder, C., & Neumann, B. (1996). On the logics of image interpretation: Model-construction in a formal knowledge-representation framework. In *Proceedings of the International Conference on Image Processing (ICIP 1996)*, (vol. 2, pp. 785-788). IEEE Computer Society.

Shanahan, M. (2005). Perception as abduction: Turning sensor data into meaningful representation. *Cognitive Science, 29*, 103–134. doi:10.1207/s15516709cog2901_5

Shearer, R., Motik, B., & Horrocks, I. (2008). HermiT: A highly-efficient OWL reasoner. In *Proceedings of the 5th OWLED Workshop on OWL: Experiences and Directions*. OWL.

Tsotsos, J. K., Mylopoulos, J., Covvey, H. D., & Zucker, S. W. (1980). A framework for visual motion understanding. *IEEE Transactions on Pattern Analysis and Machine Intelligence, 2*, 563–573.

Vila, L. (1994). A survey on temporal reasoning in artificial intelligence. *AI Communications, 7*(1), 4–28.

ENDNOTES

[1]   This work was partially supported by EC Grant 214975, Project Co-Friend.

[2]   http://www.w3.org/TR/owl-semantics/

[3]   http://protege.stanford.edu/

[4]   http://www.w3.org/Submission/SWRL/

[5]   http://ruleml.org/

[6]   http://www.jessrules.com/

[7]   http://protege.cim3.net/cgi-bin/wiki.pl?SWRLTemporalOntology

Chapter 4
Novelty Detection in Human Behavior through Analysis of Energy Utilization

Chao Chen
Washington State University, USA

Diane J. Cook
Washington State University, USA

ABSTRACT

The value of smart environments in understanding and monitoring human behavior has become increasingly obvious in the past few years. Using data collected from sensors in these environments, scientists have been able to recognize activities that residents perform and use the information to provide context-aware services and information. However, less attention has been paid to monitoring and analyzing energy usage in smart homes, despite the fact that electricity consumption in homes has grown dramatically. In this chapter, the authors demonstrate how energy consumption relates to human activity through verifying that energy consumption can be predicted based on the activity that is being performed. The authors then automatically identify novelties in human behavior by recognizing outliers in energy consumption generated by the residents in a smart environment. To validate these approaches, they use real energy data collected in their CASAS smart apartment testbed and analyze the results for two different data sets collected in this smart home.

INTRODUCTION

Smart homes have become a very popular research area. One of the most exciting applications of this work is activity recognition and health monitoring for homes. Smart homes provide a forum for observing how these activities are performed, how they are affected by a variety of conditions, and for better understanding the nature of human behavior. Most of the analyzed sensors are used to identify the location of the environment residents as well as the objects with which they are interacting.

DOI: 10.4018/978-1-4666-3682-8.ch004

In this book chapter we focus on a different type of information that can be gathered and analyzed in smart environments. In particular, we gather and analyze electricity usage that is generated in a smart environment. By observing energy consumption in a smart environment we can perform novel types of analyses that correlate activity performance with energy consumption. We can also analyze energy consumption by itself to detect anomalies in the data and see if they correlate back to abnormalities in resident behavior.

The long-term vision for this project is to enhance understanding of human resource consumption and to provide resource efficiency in smart homes. We envision this as a three step process: 1) predict the energy that will be used to support specific daily activities, 2) analyze electricity usage to identify trends and anomalies, and 3) automate activity support in a more energy-efficient manner. This chapter addresses the first two steps in the process. We hypothesize that energy consumption is correlated with the type of activities that are performed and can therefore be predicted based on the automatically-recognized activities that occur in a smart environment. We further postulate that anomalies can be automatically detected and that these outliers can provide inside on novelties that occur in the behavior of residents in the space. We validate these hypotheses by implementing algorithms to perform these steps and evaluating the algorithms using data collected in the CASAS smart apartment testbed. The result of this work can be used to give smart home residents feedback on energy consumption.

In the next section of the chapter we summarize related work in the area of smart homes and energy analysis. In the following section we introduce our CASAS smart environment architecture and describe our data collection modules as well as the smart apartment testbed. We next describe our method of predicting energy consumption based on the activity that is performed in the smart environment and evaluate the algorithm using the CASAS datasets. After this, we describe the main statistical methods we utilize to detect outliers in energy usage and validate the approach using two different smart home energy data sets.

BACKGROUND

Given the recent progress in computing power, networking, and sensor technology, we are steadily moving into the world of ubiquitous computing where technology recedes into the background of our lives. Using sensor technology combined with the power of data mining and machine learning, many researchers are now working on smart environments which can discover and recognize residents' activities and respond to resident needs in a context-aware way.

A core technology component in this research is the ability to automatically recognize and identify activities performed by residents in smart environments. A variety of approaches have been used to achieve this goal. For example, Hu et al. (Hu, Pan, Zheng, Liu, & Yang, 2008) find common trends in Activities of Daily Living (ADLs) to see whether the inhabitants perform multiple concurrent and interleaved activities or single activities. Gao et al. (Gao, Hauptmann, Bharucha, & Wactlar, 2004) use hidden Markov models to characterize different stages in dining activities. The smart hospital project (Sánchez, Tentori, & Favela, 2008) develops a robust approach for recognizing user's activities and estimating hospital-staff activities by employing a hidden Markov model with contextual information in the smart hospital environment. The Georgia Tech Aware Home (Orr & Abowd, 2000) identifies people based on pressure sensors embedded into the smart floor in strategic locations. The CASAS smart home project (Singla, Cook, & Schmitter-Edgecombe, 2010) builds probabilistic models of activities and uses them to recognize activities in complex situations where multiple residents perform activities in parallel in the same environment. A new idea of transfer learning (Rashidi & Cook, 2010) is gaining popularity in smart home research due to its ability to use the knowledge gained from one domain to a different but related domain, making the learning problem more generalized for similar environments, activities, or inhabitants.

We note that these projects focus primarily on activity recognition using sensors for motion and object interaction. However, very few projects are expanding their scope to consider the resource utilization of smart home residents. Research (Perez-Lombard, Ortiz, & Pout, 2008) states that the primary energy consumption is increasing at a higher rate than population based on analyzing the world energy trend between 1973 and 2004. Another recent report (World Business Council for Sustainable Development, 2009) also points out the buildings are responsible for at least 40% of energy use in most countries. Furthermore, household consumption of electricity has been growing dramatically. Thus, the need to develop technologies that improve energy efficiency and monitor the energy usage of inhabitants in a household is emerging as a critical research area. The BeAware project (Beware, 2010) makes use of an iPhone application to give users alerts and to provide information on the energy consumption of the entire house. This mobile application can detect the electricity consumption of different devices and notify the user if the devices use more energy than expected. The PowerLine Positioning (PLP) indoor location system (Patel, Truong, & Abowd, 2006) is able to localize to sub-room level precision by using fingerprinting of the amplitude of tones produced by two modules installed in extreme locations of the home. Patel et al (Patel, Robertson, Kientz, Reynolds, & Abowd, 2007) records and analyzes electrical noise on the power line caused by the switching of significant electrical loads by a single, plug-in module, which can connect to a personal computer, then uses machine learning techniques to identify unique occurrences of switching events by tracking the patterns of electrical noise. The MITes platform (Tapia, Intille, & Larson, 2006)

monitors changes of various appliances in current electricity flow for the appliance, such as a switch from on to off by installing current sensors for each appliance. Another similar work (Bauer, Stockinger, & Lukowicz, 2009) also proposes several approaches to recognize the energy usage of electrical devices by the analysis of a power line current. These can detect whether the appliance is used and how it is used.

CASAS SMART ENVIRONMENT

The smart home environment testbed that we are using to recognize the status of each device is a three bedroom apartment located on the Washington State University campus. As shown in Figure 1, the smart home apartment testbed consists of three bedrooms, one bathroom, a kitchen, and a living/dining room. To track people's mobility, we use motion sensors placed on the ceilings. The circles in the figure stand for the positions of motion sensors. They facilitate tracking the residents who are moving through the space. In addition, the test bed also includes temperature sensors as well as custom-built analog sensors to provide temperature readings and hot water, cold water and stove burner use. A power meter records the amount of instantaneous power usage and the total amount of power which is used. An in-house sensor network captures all sensor events and stores them in a SQL database in real time.

The sensor data gathered for our SQL database is expressed by several features, summarized in Table 1. These four fields (Date, Time, Sensor, ID, and Message) are generated by the CASAS data collection system automatically.

To provide real training data, we have collected data while two students in good health were living in the smart apartment. Our training data was gathered during several months and more than 100,000 sensor events were generated during this time. Each student had a separate bedroom and shared the downstairs living areas in the smart

Figure 1. Three-bedroom smart apartment used for our data collection (motion [m], temperature [t], water [w], burner [b], telephone [p],and item [i])

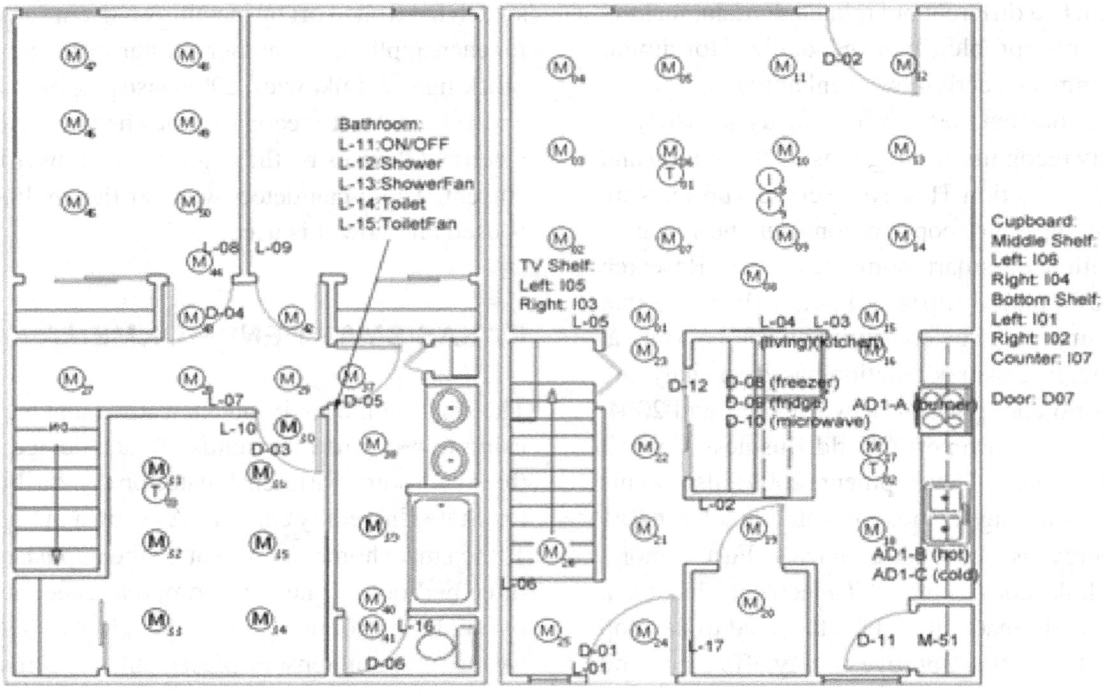

apartment. All of our experimental data are produced by the day to day lives of these students, which guarantee that the results of this analysis are real and useful.

After collecting data from the CASAS smart apartment, we annotated the sensor events with the corresponding activities that were being performed while the sensor events were generated. Because the annotated data is used to train the machine learning algorithms, the quality of the annotated data is very important for the performance of the learning algorithms. As a large number of sensor data events are generated in a smart home environment, it becomes difficult for researchers and users to convert sequence of sensor events into descriptions of resident activities (Szewcyzk, Dwan, Minor, Swedlove, & Cook, 2009) without the use of visualization tools.

To improve the quality of the annotated data, we built an open source Python-based sensor event visualizer, called PyViz, to graphically display the sensor events. Figure 2 shows a screenshot of PyViz as it shows sensor events occurring in the CASAS smart apartment. We also make use of PyViz's Annotation Visualizer to graph recognized resident activities, as shown in Figure 3.

With the help of PyViz, activity labels are optionally added to each sensor event, providing a label for the current activity. For our experiment, we selected six activities that the two volunteer participants regularly perform in the smart apart-

Table 1. Raw data from sensors

Date	Time	Sensor ID	Message
2009-02-06	17:17:36	M45	ON
2009-02-06	17:17:40	M45	OFF
2009-02-06	11:13:26	T004	21.5
2009-02-06	11:18:37	P001	747W
2009-02-09	21:15:28	P001	1.929kWh

Figure 2. PyViz visualizer

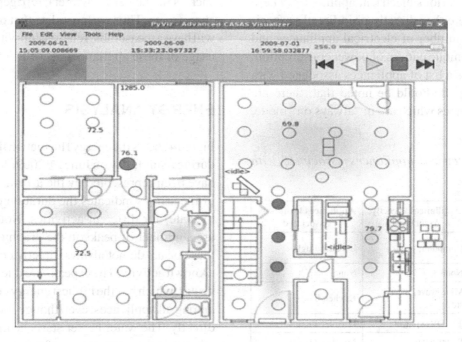

Figure 3. Visualizing activities in a smart home environment

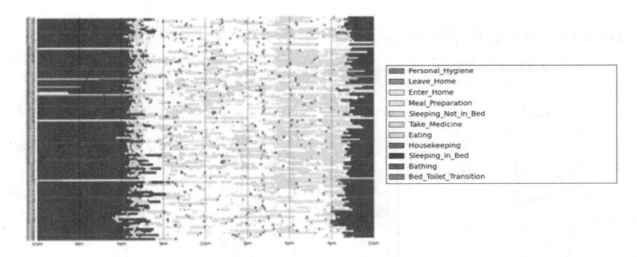

ment to predict energy use. These activities are as follows:

1. Work at computer
2. Sleep
3. Cook
4. Watch TV
5. Shower
6. Groom

All of the activities that the participants perform have some relationship with measurable features such as the time of day, the participants' movement patterns throughout the space, and the on/

off status of various electrical appliances. These activities are either directly or indirectly associated with a number of electrical appliances and thus have a unique pattern of power consumption. Table 2 gives a list of appliances associated with each activity. It should be noted that, there are some appliances which are in "always on" mode,

such as the heater (in winter), refrigerator, phone charger, etc. Thus, we postulate that the activities will have a measurable relationship with the energy usage of these appliances as well.

ENERGY ANALYSIS

Figure 4 shows the energy fluctuation that occurred during a single day on June 2nd 2009. The activities have been represented by the arrows. The length of the arrows indicates the duration of time (not to scale) for different activities. Note that there are a number of peaks in the graph even though these peaks do not always directly correspond to a known activity. These peaks are due to the water heater, which has the highest energy consumption among all appliances, even though it was not used directly. The water heater starts heating by itself whenever the temperature of water falls below a certain threshold.

Table 2. Electrical appliances associated with each activity

Activity	Appliances Directly Associated	Appliances Indirectly Associated
Work at computer	Computer, printer	Localized lights
Sleep	None	None
Cook	Microwave, oven, stove	Kitchen lights
Watch TV	TV, DVD player	Localized lights
Shower	Water heater	Localized lights
Groom	Blow drier	Localized lights

Figure 4. Energy usage for a single day

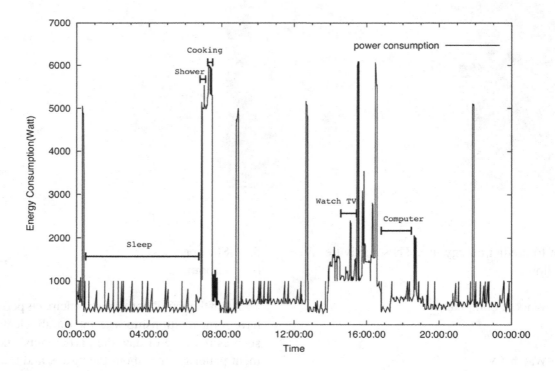

Figure 5 plots typical energy data for each activity together with the result of applying curve fitting to the data. Curve fitting (Coope, 1993) is the process of building a mathematical function model that can best fit to a series of data points. It serves as an aid for data visualization, to approximate the values when no data are available, and to express the relationships between different

Figure 5. Energy data curve fitting for each activity. There is a separate graph for each activity: A=shower, B=cook, C=work on computer, D=groom, E=sleep, and F=watch TV. The x axis in the graphs represents wattage and the y axis represents time of the activity in seconds.

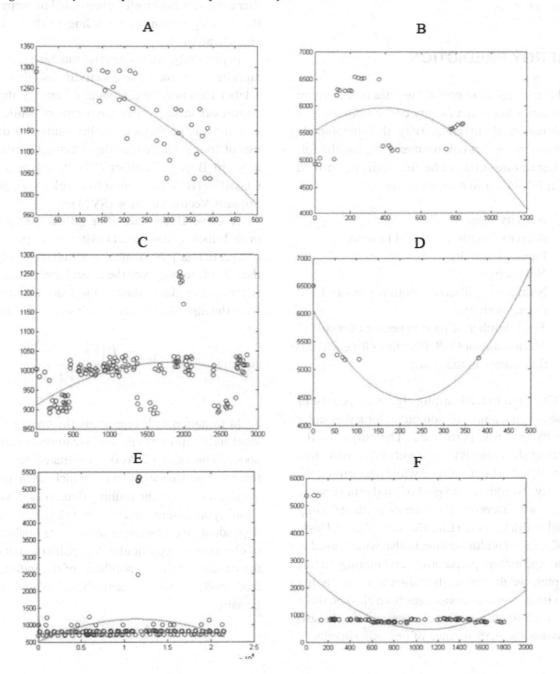

data points. From the figure, we see that each resident's activity generates different energy patterns. The "cook" activity consumes the highest energy because the participants may open the refrigerator and use the stove or microwave oven, which need a relatively high power. Meantime, when the participants were sleeping, the energy consumption was the lowest because most appliances were idle.

ENERGY PREDICTION

In the first step of our goal, we use machine learning techniques to predict energy consumption given information about an activity that inhabitants perform in a smart environment. We use the following features to describe an activity performed by an inhabitant in a smart home:

1. Activity label
2. Activity length, measured in seconds
3. Previous activity
4. Next activity
5. Number of different motion sensors fired during activity
6. Total number of motion sensor events
7. Motion sensor On/Off settings for each motion sensor in the space

The input to the learning algorithm is a list of these seven features as computed for a particular activity that was performed. The output of the learning algorithm is the amount of electricity that is predicted to be consumed while performing the activity. To address the goal of predicting energy usage, we discretize the energy readings using equal width binning (Liu, Hussain, Tan, & Dash, 2002). Equal width binning is also widely used in data exploration, preparation, and mining. In this chapter, we discretize the target average energy data into several interval sizes (two classes, three classes, four classes, five classes, and six classes) to assess the performance of our experiments.

A large number of features will be generated for energy prediction. However, some of these features are redundant or irrelevant, resulting in a drastic raise of computational complexity and classification errors (Bellman, 1961). In this chapter, we use the J48 Decision Tree classifier (Quinlan, 1986) which applies information gain to create a classification model, a statistical property that measures how well a given attribute separate the training examples according to their target classification.

In our study, we use several machine learning algorithms to map these activity features onto a label indicating the amount of energy that is consumed in the smart environment while the activity was performed. In this study, we make use of four popular machine learning methods: a Naïve Bayes Classifier (NBC), a Bayes Net Classifier (BNC), a Neural Network (NN), and a Support Vector Machine (SVM).

A naïve Bayes classifier (Rish, 2001) is a probabilistic classifier that assumes the presence of a particular input feature is unrelated to any of the other features given the target label. This classifier applies Bayes theorem to learn a mapping from the input features to the classification label.

$$\arg\max_{e_i \in E} P\left(e_i \mid F\right) = \frac{P\left(F \mid e_i\right) P\left(e_i\right)}{P\left(F\right)} \quad (1)$$

In Equation 1, E represents the energy class label and F represents the input features described above. The value of $P(e_i)$ is estimated based on the relative frequency with which each target value e_i occurs in the training data. Based on the simplifying assumption that feature values are independent given the target value, the probabilities of observing the particular data point (activity) is the product of the probabilities of the individual features describing the activity, calculated using Equation 2.

$$P\left(F\middle|e_j\right) = \Pi_i P\left(f_i\middle|e_j\right) \qquad (2)$$

Bayes belief networks (Pearl, 1988) belong to the family of probabilistic graphical models. They represent a set of conditional independence assumptions by a directed acyclic graph, whose nodes represent random variables and edges represent direct dependence among the variables and are drawn by arrows by the variable name. Unlike the naïve Bayes classifier, which assumes that the values of all the attributes are conditionally independent given the target value, Bayesian belief networks apply conditional independence assumptions only to the subset of the variables. They can be suitable for small and incomplete data sets and they incorporate knowledge from different sources. After the model is built, they can also provide fast responses to queries.

Artificial Neural Networks (ANNs) (Zornetzer, 1995) are abstract computational models based on the organizational structure of the human brain. ANNs provide a general and robust method to learn a target function from input examples. The most common learning method for ANNs, called Backpropagation, which performs a gradient descent within the solution's vector space to attempt to minimize the squared error between the network output values and the target values for these outputs. Although there is no guarantee that an ANN will find the global minimum and the learning procedure may be quite slow, ANNs can be applied to problems where the relationships are dynamic or non-linear and capture many kinds of relationships that may be difficult to model by other machine learning methods. In our experiment, we choose the Multilayer-Perceptron algorithm with Backpropagation to predict electricity usage.

Super Vector Machines (SVMs) (Boser, Guyon, & Vapnik, 1992) is a training algorithm for data classification, which maximizes the margin between the training examples and the class boundary. The SVM learns a hyperplane which separates instances from multiple activity classes with maximum margin. Each training data instance should contain one class label and several features. The goal of a SVM is to generate a hyperplane which provides a class label for each data point described by a set of feature values.

Experimental Results

We performed two series of energy prediction experiments. The first experiment uses the sensor data collected during two summer months in the testbed. In the second experiment, we collected data of three winter months in the testbed. The biggest difference between these two groups of data is that some high energy consuming devices like room heaters were only used during the winter, which are not directly controlled by the residents and are therefore difficult to monitor and predict. Using the Weka machine learning toolset (Witten & Frank, 2005), we assessed the classification accuracy of our four selected machine learning algorithms and reported the predictive accuracy results based on a 3-fold cross validation.

Figures 6 and 7 plot the accuracies of the two different group experiments, respectively. As shown in these two figures, the highest accuracy is around 90% for both datasets to predict the two-class energy usage and the lowest accuracy is around 60% for the six-class case in both datasets. These results also show that the higher accuracy will be found when the precision was lower because the accuracy of all four methods will drop from about 90% to around 60% with an increase in the number of energy class labels. From the figures we see that the Naïve Bayes Classifier performs worse than the other three classifiers. This is because it is based on the simplified assumption that the feature values are conditionally independent given the target value. On the contrary, the features that we use are not conditionally independent. For example, the motion sensors associated with an activity is used to find the total number of times motion sensor events were triggered and also the kinds of motion sensors involved.

Figure 6. Comparison of the accuracy for summer dataset

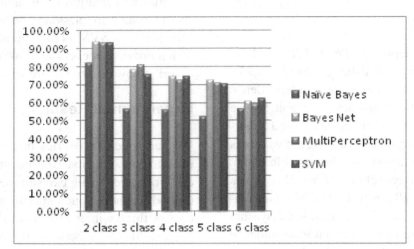

Figure 7. Comparison of the accuracy for winter dataset

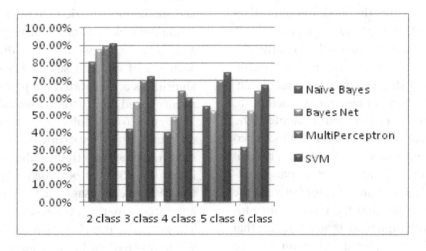

To analyze the effectiveness of decision tree feature selection, we apply the ANN algorithm to both datasets with and without feature selection. From Figure 8, we can see the time efficiency has been improved greatly using feature selection. The time for building the training model drops from around 13 seconds to 3 seconds after selecting the features with high information gain. However, as seen in Figure 9, the classification accuracy is almost the same or a slight better than the performance without feature selection. The use of feature selection can improve the time performance without reducing the accuracy performance in the original data set.

Figure 10 compares the performance of the ANN applied to the winter and summer data sets. From the graph, we see that the performance for the summer data set is shade better than the performance for the winter dataset. This is likely due to the fact that the room and floor heater appliances are used during the winter season, which consume a large amount of energy and are less predictable than the control of other electrical devices in the apartment.

Figure 8. Comparison of time efficiency (y-axis: second)

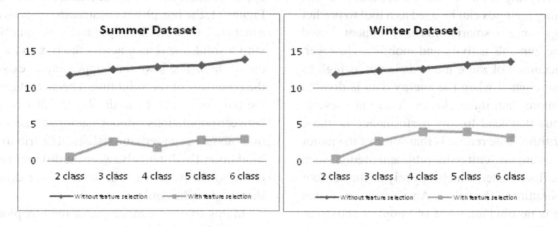

Figure 9. Comparison of prediction accuracy

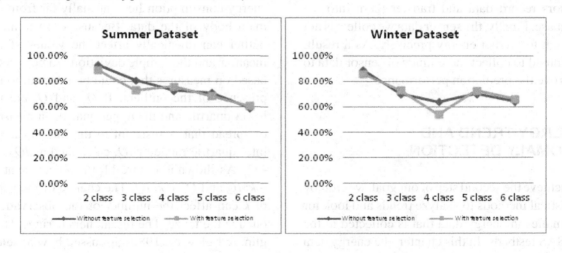

Figure 10. Comparison of the accuracy between two datasets

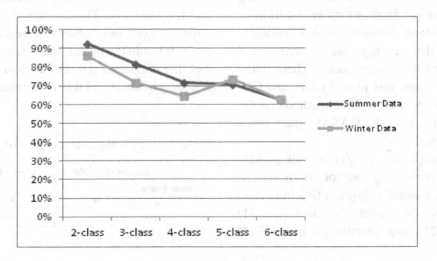

Analyzing these results, we see that machine learning methods can be used as a tool to predict energy usage in smart home environments based on the human's activity and mobility. However, the accuracy of these methods is not as high as we anticipated when the energy data is divided into more than three classes. There are several reasons that lead to low performance of these algorithms. One reason is that some of the major devices are difficult to monitor and predict, such as the floor heater, which may rely on the outdoor temperature of the house. Another reason is that there is no obvious cycle of people's activities. An additional factor we can't ignore is that there is some noise and perturbation motion when the sensors record data and transfer them into the database. Finally, the sensor data we collect is not enough to predict energy precisely. As a result, we intend to collect more kinds of sensor data to improve the prediction performance.

ENERGY TREND AND ANOMALY DETECTION

To achieve the second step of our goal, we employ statistical methods to analyze trends and look for anomalies in energy data that is collected in the CASAS testbeds. In this chapter, the energy data generated by smart environment residents is modeled as a random process with corresponding mean and variation. Here, we make use of three different statistical methods to automatically detect and analyze energy data anomalies and trends in smart home environments. These statistical approaches are: box plot, $\bar{x}$ chart, and CU-SUM chart. We test these three methods on energy data collected in the CASAS smart home apartment testbed.

The box plot (Tukey, 1977) is a quick graphic approach for examining one or more sets of data. A box plot usually displays five important parameters describing a set of numeric data: (1) lower fence, (2) lower quartile, (3) median, (4) upper quartile, and (5) upper fence. As shown in Figure 11, the box plot is constructed by drawing a rectangle between the upper and lower quartiles with a solid line drawn across the box to locate the median. The lower and upper fences exist at the boundary of the solid line. The advantage of the boxplot is that it can display the differences between populations without making any assumptions about the underlying statistical distribution. In addition, the distance between the different parts of the box helps indicate the degree of spread and skewness in the data set.

In this study, we make use of the box plot to identify the outliers in the collected energy data, which represent those periods of time where the energy consumption lies unusually far from the main body of the data. Because even a single outlier can drastically affect the values of the mean, $\bar{x}$ and the sample deviation s, a box plot is based on measures that could be resistant to the presence of the outliers. If Q_1 and Q_3 are the lower quartile and the upper quartile, a measure of spread that is resistant to the outliers is the inter-quartile range or IQ, calculated as $IQ = Q_3 - Q_1$. As shown in Figure 11, the fences lie at $Q_1 - k*IQ$ and $Q_3 + k*IQ$. The change of the value of k can affect the number of the observations outside the fence. The researchers (Frigge, Hoaglin, & Lglewicz, 1989) discussed how to select the value of k for the fence and pointed out the rule with $k = 1.5$ can be more acceptable by most of the situations. Thus, in this chapter, we chose the value of k as 1.5. Any sample data farther than $1.5*IQ$ from the closest quartile is an outlier. An outlier is extreme if it is more than $3*IQ$ from the nearest quartile and it is mild otherwise.

Figure 11. Configuration of a box plot

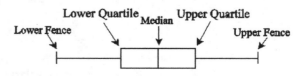

Statistical Process Control (SPC) (Deming, 1975) is the application of statistical charting techniques for detecting shifts in mean or variability of a process. While SPC is applied most commonly to controlling a product's quality, it encompasses a much broader scope of applications including: data and process analysis, experimental design and decision making. Here, energy usage data will be modeled as a random process whose mean and variance could be estimated by the sample data.

We will utilize two SPC techniques to identify abnormal energy usage data as follows. The first technique focuses on generating control charts. In statistical process control, control charts are particularly useful for monitoring quality and giving early warnings that a process may be going out of control. A typical control chart has control limits set at values such that if the process is in control, nearly all points will lie between the Upper Control Limit (UCL) and Lower Control Limit (LCL). Assume that for an in-control process, the data collection X follows a normal distribution with mean value, μ, and stand deviation, σ. If $\bar{X}$ denotes the sample mean for a random sample of size n selected at a particular time, the $\bar{x}$ chart for determining control limits first calculates the mean $E(\bar{X}) = \mu$ and standard deviation $\sigma_{\bar{X}} = \sigma / \sqrt{n}$ of the sample values. Next, upper and lower control limits are defined as $\{\mu + 3\sigma_{\bar{X}} / \sqrt{n}, \mu - 3\sigma_{\bar{X}} / \sqrt{n}, \}$. These control limits can be used to identify the outliers in energy data that occur in the specific monitoring time window. The plot of mean values associated with the control limits are used to determine when the process is "out of control." In the case of energy data analysis, when an important acute change has occurred, the $\bar{x}$ chart can identified the location of this change.

The disadvantage of a $\bar{x}$ control chart is its inability to detect a relatively small change in a process mean because the ability to judge the process as being out of control at a particular time depends only on the sample at that time, and not

the past history of the process. Cumulative sum (CUSUM) control charts (Thompson & Koronacki, 2002) have been designed to address this problem. The CUSUM chart works as follows: Let μ_0 denote a target value or goal for the process mean. The cumulative sums can then be calculated using Equation 3.

$$S_n = \sum_{i=1}^{n} (\bar{x}_i - \mu_0) \qquad (3)$$

As shown in Figure 12, these cumulative sums are plotted over various time windows and a V-shaped mask is superimposed on the graph of the cumulative sums. At any given time, the process is judged to be out of control if any of the plotted points lies outside the V-mask, either above the upper arm or below the lower arm. In the graph of Figure 12, an out-of-control situation has been identified by the V-mask because one point in the time window lies above the upper arm. The V-mask is calculated based on the lead distance d and the rise distance h. The parameter-defined variations in the shape of the V-mask will thus affect the type and number of outliers that are detected.

Experimental Results

We performed two series of experiments using the energy data collected during an entire year in our CASAS smart apartment testbed. The first experiment detects abnormal energy wattage during any single day. The second experiment looks for novelties in energy Kwh data consumed each week over the course of the entire year.

When we generate a $\bar{x}$ control chart, there is an assumption that the random process follows a normal distribution. Thus, we need to examine whether the energy data during different time windows fits the normal distribution. Based on the Central Limit Theorem (Rice, 1995), if a random sample of n observations is selected from any population, the sampling distribution will be

Figure 12. A sample v-mask demonstrating an out-of-control process

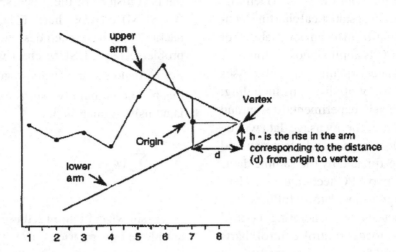

approximately normal. Unfortunately, the energy data for different time granularities in our smart home environment often demonstrate a positive skew. Thus, we use the lognormal distribution to describe the energy data distribution x. In this case, $\ln(x)$ should follow a normal distribution. As shown in Figures 13, 14, and 15, the plots on the left show how the original energy data x fits the lognormal distribution and the plots on the right describe how the normal curve simulates

the variation in log energy values. From the graphs, we see that the log of the energy data can basically fit the normal distribution very well. Thus, we can continue to use $\bar{x}$ charts for detecting energy data outliers.

For the first experiment we focus on energy wattage data collected for one day in the smart environment testbed. The purpose of this experiment is to detect the energy data outliers and determine possible reasons for the anomalies.

Figure 13. The lognormal and normal distribution of energy data (W) collected in the CASAS testbed over the course of one day

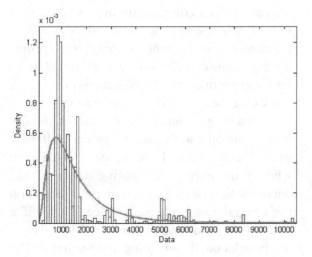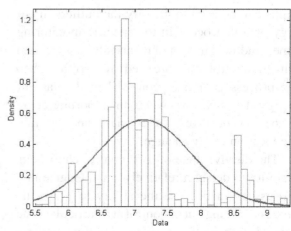

Figure 14. The lognormal and normal distribution of energy data (Kwh) for one day

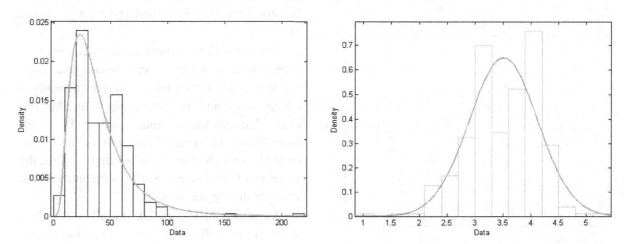

Figure 15. The lognormal and normal distribution of energy data (Kwh) for one week

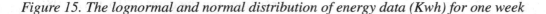

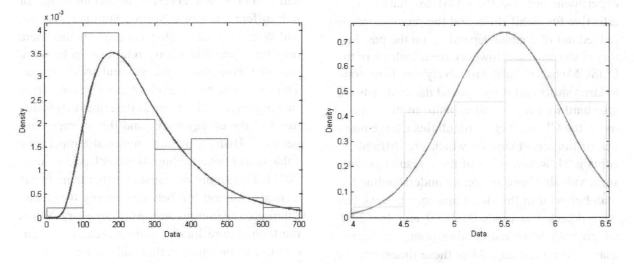

Figure 16 shows the box plot graph of the data. The points located on the right side represent the outliers. We examined those outliers in detail and found out these abnormal data occur during two main time intervals. The first set of anomalies was mainly concentrated at around midnight. One reasonable explanation is that all the heaters in our smart home worked at the same time because the temperature of that time is the lowest during the day. The outliers in the second group are located at the middle time of the day, which is the residents' cooking time and the large appliances are being used for cooking such as the microwave, the stove and the oven, all of which would give rise to dramatically increasing energy consumption.

For the $\bar{x}$ control chart shown in Figure 17, all the outliers fall below the lower control limit. All of these anomalies occurred between 01:00 am and 06:00 am, which is the common sleep time for the residents. And most of the appliances are idle during that time interval.

The CUSUM chart as described in Figure 18 detects some outliers not detected in the previous

Figure 16. Box plot of wattage energy data for one day

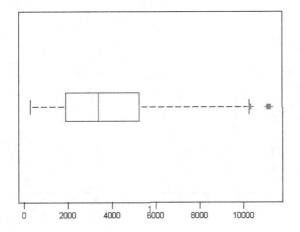

experiment because the CUSUM chart is very effective for small shifts and the process can be judged out of control depending on the past history of the process. However, the drawback of the CUSUM chart is that it is relatively slow to respond to large shifts and some special data patterns are also hard to analyze and explain. In this experiment, the CUSUM chart highlights a large number of outliers, many of which are difficult to explain. However, some of these results provide some valuable information for understanding human behavior in the smart apartment. Novelties were detected at times 00:31:07 and 16:12:50, which both represent turning points in energy usage during the day. After these times, energy

consumption decreased consistently, perhaps because some large electrical devices were turned off.

The second experiment analyzes energy consumption data (Kwh) by week over a year timeframe in order to look for the long term trends of energy usage and its relationship with other relevant elements like weather variation. However, from Figure 19, none of the outliers can be detected by box plots or $\bar{x}$ control charts. Thus, the variation of this dataset doesn't experience extreme changes during the year.

As shown in Figure 20, the CUSUM chart shows the periodic pattern of the cumulative sum. The CUSUM chart identifies four energy data abnormalities (on the dates 03/16, 05/25, 08/13, and 12/12), which represent the turning points of four different seasons (Spring, Summer, August, and Winter). That result gives us a cue that there may be a possible strong relationship between seasonal temperature changes and energy usage. Thus, we continue to explore this relationship as shown in Figure 21. Figure 21 describes the change trend of the energy usage and the average temperature. Historic average regional temperature values are obtained online (Weather Underground, 2010). This figure demonstrates that there exists a strong relationship between energy usage and external temperatures during the same time. When the temperature increases or decreases, the energy usage consumed by the residents will decrease

Figure 17. A $\bar{x}$ chart of energy wattage data for one day

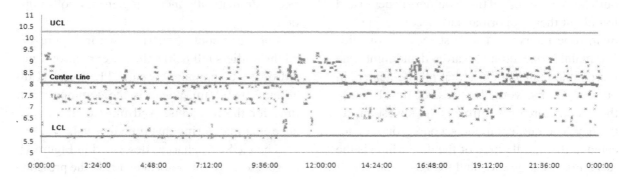

Figure 18. A CUSUM chart of energy wattage data for one day (d = 145.1, h = 30)

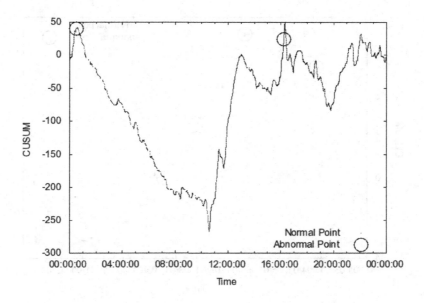

Figure 19. Bot plot chart (top) and $\bar{x}$ chart (bottom) of energy data (in Kwh) by week for one year

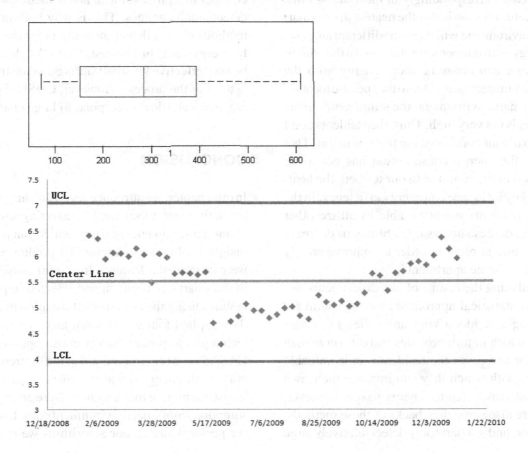

Figure 20. CUSUM chart of energy data (Kwh) by week during one year (d = 4.59, h = 0.95)

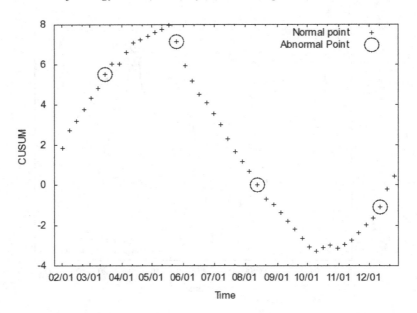

or increase correspondingly in most of the time. The likeliest reason is that the heaters in our smart home environment will consume different amounts of energy with temperature changes. In the winter, the heater can consume more energy with the temperature decreases. Due to the specific location of our smart environment, the temperature in the summer is not very high. Thus, the residents don't need to use air conditioner in the apartment. That is why the energy consumption has not a big variation in the summer. In our testbed, the heaters are key influences on energy efficiency. In the future, residents might be able to utilize other heating sources such as open blinds or decrease temperature at night in order to improve energy efficiency in the apartment.

Analyzing the results of our experiments, we see that statistical approaches can be useful for detecting and identifying anomalies in energy usage, which in turn provides insights on human behavior and gives the residents some valuable insights with which they can improve their own daily patterns to reduce energy usage. However, there are also some drawbacks of these methods. Box plots and $\bar{x}$ charts only detect relatively large

changes in a process mean and sometimes fail to detect small changes. This is why both of these methods did not detect the outliers for the weekly energy data. In contrast, CUSUM charts can be very effective for small shifts based on the past history of the process. However, CUSUM charts are relatively slow to respond to large changes.

CONCLUSION

In this chapter, we introduce several techniques for predicting energy usage and for detecting novelties, or anomalies, in energy usage which can provide insight on human behavior. To predict energy, we extracted the features from real sensor data in the smart environment and selected important features using the notion of information gain. We then applied four well-known machine learning techniques to predict energy consumption in our CASAS smart environment. To find the trends and outliers in energy usage, we introduced several statistical mining methods to analyze energy consumption from smart environment data. To assess the performance of our algorithms we provided

Figure 21. The comparison between mean temperature (top) and energy usage (bottom)

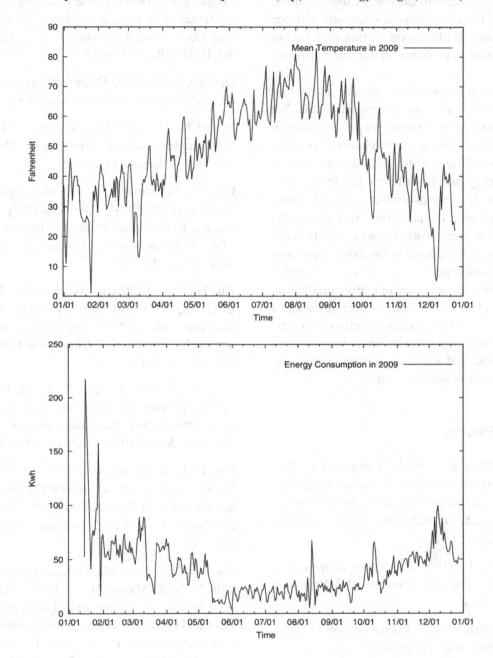

experimental results using real data collected in the CASAS smart environment testbeds.

The purpose of energy prediction is to validate our hypothesis that energy usage can be predicted based on the sensor data that can be generated by the residents in a smart home environment. The results of this work can be used to give residents feedback on energy consumption as it relates to various activities. In addition, predicted electricity use can form the basis for automating activities in a manner that consumes fewer resources including power usage. By detecting trends and anomalies, we can find some extreme energy usage values, which may indicate blackout situations, devices that were mistakenly left on, or that may lead to potential security problems in the smart environment.

In our ongoing work, we plan to investigate methods to detect a greater range of anomalies. We also plan to install more sensitive power meters in order to capture more accurate changes in energy consumption. To extend our existing work, we will predict energy during different lengths of time windows without the assumption that this usage is correlated with the activities. To improve the quality of discovered patterns, we continue to use data mining technique to explore existing patterns in energy consumption data, which may be helpful to improve the accuracy of energy prediction. Our future plans also include collecting data in a greater variety of households, which will allow us to determine whether energy predictions, energy usage trends, and energy anomalies exist and generalize across multiple settings.

REFERENCES

Bauer, G., Stockinger, K., & Lukowicz, P. (2009). Recognizing the use-mode of kitchen appliances from their current consumption. *Smart Sensing and Context*, *5741*, 163–176. doi:10.1007/978-3-642-04471-7_13

Bellman, R. E. (1961). *Adaptive control processes - A guided tour*. Princeton, NJ: Princeton University Press.

Beware. (2010). *Website*. Retrieved May 25, 2010, from http://www.energyawareness.eu/beaware

Boser, B. E., Guyon, I. M., & Vapnik, V. N. (1992). A training algorithm for optimal margin classifiers. In *Proceedings of the Fifth Annual Workshop on Computational Learning Theory*, (pp. 144–152). IEEE.

Coope, I. D. (1993). Circle fitting by linear and nonlinear least squares. *Journal of Optimization Theory and Applications*, *76*(2), 381–388. doi:10.1007/BF00939613

Deming, W. E. (1975). On probability as a basis for action. *The American Statistician*, *29*(4), 146–152.

Frigge, M., Hoaglin, D. C., & Iglewicz, B. (1989). Some implementations of the boxplot. *The American Statistician*, *43*(1), 50–54.

Gao, J., Hauptmann, A. G., Bharucha, A., & Wactlar, H. D. (2004). Dining activity analysis using a hidden markov model. In *Proceedings of the 17th International Conference on Pattern Recognition*. IEEE.

Hu, H., Pan, J., Zheng, W., Liu, N., & Yang, Q. (2008). Real world activity recognition with multiple goals. In *Proceedings of the 10th international Conference on Ubiquitous Computing*, (pp. 30–39). IEEE.

Liu, H., Hussain, F., Tan, C. L., & Dash, M. (2002). Discretization: An enabling technique. *Data Mining and Knowledge Discovery*, *6*(4), 393–423. doi:10.1023/A:1016304305535

Orr, R. J., & Abowd, G. D. (2000). The smart floor: A mechanism for natural user identification and tracking. In *Proceedings of the Conference on Human Factors in Computing Systems*, (pp. 275–276). IEEE.

Patel, S. N., Robertson, T., Kientz, J. A., Reynolds, M. S., & Abowd, G. D. (2007). At the flick of a switch: Detecting and classifying unique electrical events on the residential power line. In *Proceedings of the International Conference on Ubiquitous Computing*, (p. 271). IEEE.

Patel, S. N., Truong, K. N., & Abowd, G. D. (2006). Powerline positioning: A practical sub-room-level indoor location system for domestic. *Ubiquitous Computing*, *4206*, 441–458.

Pearl, J. (1988). *Probabilistic reasoning in intelligent systems: networks of plausible inference.* San Francisco, CA: Morgan Kaufmann.

Perez-Lombard, L., Ortiz, J., & Pout, C. (2008). A review on buildings energy consumption information. *Energy and Building*, *40*(3), 394–398. doi:10.1016/j.enbuild.2007.03.007

Quinlan, J. R. (1986). Induction of decision trees. *Machine Learning*, *1*(1), 81–106. doi:10.1007/BF00116251

Rashidi, P., & Cook, D. (2010). Multi home transfer learning for resident activity discovery and recognition. In *Proceedings of the International Workshop on Knowledge Discovery from Sensor Data.* IEEE.

Rice, J. (1995). *Mathematical statistics and data analysis.* New York, NY: Duxbury Press.

Rish, I. (2001). An empirical study of the naive Bayes classifier. In *Proceedings of the IJCAI Workshop on Empirical Methods in Artificial Intelligence,* (pp. 41–46). IJCAI.

Sánchez, D., Tentori, M., & Favela, J. (2008). Activity recognition for the smart hospital. *IEEE Intelligent Systems*, *23*(2), 50–57. doi:10.1109/MIS.2008.18

Singla, G., Cook, D. J., & Schmitter-Edgecombe, M. (2010). Recognizing independent and joint activities among multiple residents in smart environments. *Journal of Ambient Intelligence and Humanized Computing*, *1*(1), 57–63. doi:10.1007/s12652-009-0007-1

Szewcyzk, S., Dwan, K., Minor, B., Swedlove, B., & Cook, D. (2009). Annotating smart environment sensor data for activity learning. *Technology and Health Care*, *17*(3), 161–169.

Tapia, E., Intille, S., Lopez, L., & Larson, K. (2006). The design of a portable kit of wireless sensors for naturalistic data collection. In *Proceedings of Pervasive Computing* (pp. 117–134). IEEE. doi:10.1007/11748625_8

Thompson, J. R., & Koronacki, J. (2002). *Statistical process control: The Deming paradigm and beyond.* CRC Pr I Llc.

Tukey, J. W. (1977). *Exploratory data analysis.* Reading, MA: Addison-Wesley.

Weather Underground. (2010). *Website.* Retrieved June 26, 2010, from http://www.wunderground.com

Witten, I. H., & Frank, E. (2005). *Data mining: Practical machine learning tools and techniques.* San Francisco, CA: Morgan Kaufmann Publishing.

World Business Council for Sustainable Development. (2009). *Energy efficiency in buildings.* Retrievecd October 11, 2009, from http://www.wbcsd.org

Zornetzer, S. F. (1995). *An introduction to neural and electronic networks.* San Francisco, CA: Morgan Kaufmann.

Chapter 5
Towards Behaviour Recognition with Unlabelled Sensor Data:
As Much as Necessary, as Little as Possible

Sook-Ling Chua
Massey University, New Zealand

Stephen Marsland
Massey University, New Zealand

Hans W. Guesgen
Massey University, New Zealand

ABSTRACT

The problem of behaviour recognition based on data from sensors is essentially an inverse problem: given a set of sensor observations, identify the sequence of behaviours that gave rise to them. In a smart home, the behaviours are likely to be the standard human behaviours of living, and the observations will depend upon the sensors that the house is equipped with. There are two main approaches to identifying behaviours from the sensor stream. One is to use a symbolic approach, which explicitly models the recognition process. Another is to use a sub-symbolic approach to behaviour recognition, which is the focus in this chapter, using data mining and machine learning methods. While there have been many machine learning methods of identifying behaviours from the sensor stream, they have generally relied upon a labelled dataset, where a person has manually identified their behaviour at each time. This is particularly tedious to do, resulting in relatively small datasets, and is also prone to significant errors as people do not pinpoint the end of one behaviour and commencement of the next correctly. In this chapter, the authors consider methods to deal with unlabelled sensor data for behaviour recognition, and investigate their use. They then consider whether they are best used in isolation, or should be used as preprocessing to provide a training set for a supervised method.

DOI: 10.4018/978-1-4666-3682-8.ch005

1. INTRODUCTION

There are many reasons to want to recognise human behaviours, depending on the application, the particular scenario currently occurring, and the information that we can obtain from that scenario. This chapter views human behaviour recognition as the task of finding a mapping from a stream of sensor information to a sequence of recognised activities performed by the inhabitant of a smart home, with the aim of the home being to monitor their behaviour and detect illness or potentially dangerous behaviour. We aim for a general method of identifying the mapping that is independent of the particular sensors that are used, although obviously, precisely what information is available will change the potential behaviours that can be detected. For a smart home, the behaviour itself is performed by the inhabitant, and the sensors detect (potentially noisy) evidence of that behaviour. The task of human behaviour recognition is thus the inverse problem of identifying behaviours from sensors, and the properties of this inverse mapping

are of interest. In the ideal case, we would like to be able to map a sensor stream uniquely to a sequence of behaviours (as depicted in Figure 1a), but this is only possible if there is no ambiguity in the sensor stream, which is rather unlikely.

Ambiguity in the sensor information can have several causes. In the extreme case, in which we only have a simple motion sensor in the room where activities take place, we can only infer that some action is or is not happening in that room. In this 'burglar alarm' scenario, we would map sensor information either to the set of all possible behaviours, indicating that the inhabitant is involved in some activity, or to a 'null' behaviour, indicating that the inhabitant is not involved in an activity (Figure 1b). Although this might provide some valuable information (e.g., that the inhabitant is conscious), it is often not sufficient for the tasks that a monitoring smart home is supposed to fulfill. For example, we would not be able to determine whether the inhabitant has taken regular meals, has followed adequate hygiene routines, or has not put themselves in a dangerous situation

Figure 1. Different mappings between sensor information and behaviours

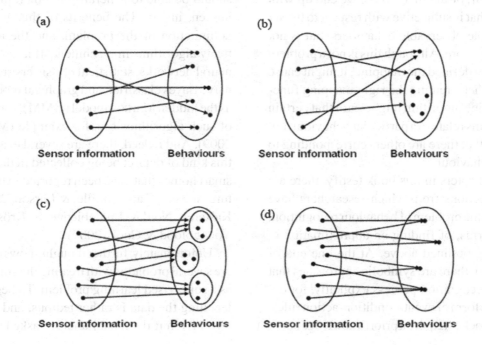

- all of which are typical tasks where a smart home has to support a carer in looking after an inhabitant with diminished physical or mental capabilities.

If the mapping of sensor information is able to distinguish between meaningful classes of behaviours, then the remaining ambiguity might be less significant (Figure 1c). Sensors placed in the kitchen in places, or on appliances, that are usually associated with preparing a meal (fridge door, stove, kitchen cupboard, etc.) might be able to provide us with the information that some meal-preparing event is going on, but we might not be able to distinguish what kind of meal it is. Similarly, we might be able to detect recreational activities, hygiene activities, house-cleaning activities, etc.

Another form of ambiguity is caused by the fact that a particular behaviour does not always trigger the same sensor events (Figure 1d). For example, there are various ways of making a meal, which might all be perfectly valid: some use the microwave, others the stove and oven, etc. Even if we were able to install a sufficient number of sensors to exactly determine which behaviour we are observing, we might end up over-specifying the behaviour, or in other words, we end up with a mapping that is subjective with respect to the set of all possible observable behaviours, but is not injective any more. Although this is not a problem once we have defined the mapping, it might cause problems when creating the right mapping function: a learning algorithm might learn that certain sensor streams relate to a particular behaviour, but might miss that there are others corresponding to the same behaviour.

As the chapters in this book testify, there are various directions from which researchers have approached the problem of behaviour recognition, or in our terms, of finding an approximation to the mapping outlined above. At the one end of the spectrum, there are symbolic approaches that model the recognition process explicitly, for example in the form of event-condition-action rules. These approaches require a priori knowledge about the environment, its inhabitants, and the possible behaviours that might occur. The approaches are relatively easy to verify and validate, but often suffer from "brittleness", as it is impossible to cover all possible behaviours. At the other end of the spectrum, we find sub-symbolic approaches, which try to approximate the mapping with data mining and machine learning methods. In this chapter we focus on methods at this latter end of the spectrum.

1.1. Supervised and Unsupervised Learning

There is one interesting issue that the learning of the mapping between sensor outputs and behaviours raises, which is training data. At first thought, it seems clear that behaviour recognition is a supervised learning problem, that is, the learning algorithm is presented with sets of exemplars of each behaviour that is to be learnt, with each exemplar labelled. The algorithm is then trained to minimise some error norm between the predicted output of the network and the target labels that are provided. In this way, it should be able to generalise to other, previously unseen, inputs. The benefits of this are a clear delimitation of the problem, and the access to many algorithms in machine learning, including neural networks, statistical classifiers such as the naïve Bayes classifier, and graphical models such as the hidden Markov model (HMM); for a review of such algorithms see, for example (Marsland, 2009). And indeed, there are several examples of this kind of dataset being collected in the various smart homes that have been reported in the literature, such as (Tapia, Intille, & Larson, 2004; van Kasteren, Noulas, Englebienne, & Kröse, 2008; Youngblood & Cook, 2007).

Unfortunately, further thought shows that there are several problems with treating the smart home as a supervised learning problem. To begin with, labelling the data is rather tedious, and prone to error. Even if the inhabitants are asked to keep a journal of what tasks they are engaged in at a very detailed level (and given facilities to help such as a smart phone or personal organiser), actually doing it accurately is very hard to remember, and irritating to perform. Certainly, it is not possible to imagine that anybody who ever wishes to live in a smart home would willingly go through several weeks of this before the home started to work! There are other problems, too: people rarely engage in one task and take it to completion before starting something else (for example, while cooking dinner the telephone may ring, the person may require a trip to the toilet, or the cat may demand to be fed); we term this as the interleaving of behaviours, and care needs to be taken to ensure that we do not end up with two short and hard-to-recognise parts of a behaviour interrupted by some other activity. When labelling their actions, people may also present different labels for the same task: 'making a beverage' for one person could be 'making tea', or even 'cooking' for another. Another limitation of human labelling is that the labelling only works for the subject under study and does not generalise to other inhabitants in different home settings. This means that that re-labelling is needed for different inhabitants, since different people have variations in their activities. Additionally, sensors are noisy and may provide spurious outputs, or no output when certain events have occurred.

Considerations such as these have led us to the conclusion that unsupervised learning may be a more sensible learning paradigm. In this approach, the algorithm is asked to identify structure within the inputs without any benefit of data labels. Thus, the algorithm tries to categorise the data into similar classes that exhibit some form of commonality. The challenge is to ensure that the algorithm identifies the structures that we want it to find. To see how this can be done it is worth considering what exactly a behaviour is. The basic idea that we want to stress is that the only reason why a set of activities form a behaviour is because they are

repeated, albeit with variation, over time. So making a hot drink is a behaviour, since it might well be repeated several times a day, and sleeping is a behaviour, because it is probably repeated daily. However, for most people, receiving a phone call while cooking dinner is not a behaviour, since it does not happen frequently. Based on this statement, it seems clear that—given enough data—an unsupervised learning algorithm should be able to identify behaviours as those things that are seen repeatedly in data.

The challenge then is to bias the behaviours to be as long as possible, since there are sub-behaviours that will be seen more frequently than any individual behaviour, such as boiling the kettle, which could be involved in making hot drinks, cooking, or possibly a few other things such as filling a hot water bottle.

One challenge of unsupervised learning is that there is no guarantee that the identified behaviour will match precisely what a human, with their knowledge of behaviours, would assign as labels. For example, if a person always has a shower before going to bed, an algorithm may well decide that there is only one behaviour here. Another challenge is that some behaviours may include other behaviours and care must be taken to differentiate them. For example, making breakfast may include making coffee, while 'making coffee' does not necessary means that the inhabitant is making breakfast. These can make the testing and interpretation of the outputs of an algorithm slightly harder than they would be otherwise.

In this chapter, we give an overview of behaviour recognition for unlabelled sensor data, which is not a problem that has received wide interest yet, but which we consider to be very important. We start by discussing the form in which we expect the data to appear, since this affects which methods are suitable. We then present three alternative approaches to the problem and discuss how they might best be used.

2. TOKENS: A REPRESENTATION OF SENSOR OUTPUT

There are many different types of sensor that could be involved in behaviour recognition in the home, from video cameras and microphones to touch and motion sensors, and RFID tags. Obviously, the degree of preprocessing required to analyse the output of the different sensors, the amount of information that can be obtained, and the amount of privacy intrusion, varies depending which sensors are fitted into the house. While these are all important considerations, and this is an area of ongoing debate, it is not something that we wish to consider in this chapter. We therefore suggest that a useful abstraction from the sensor properties is to assume that activity in the house is presented to the learning system as a set of 'tokens', which arrive in a sequence over time. Depending upon the particular sensor, a token could be the direct representation of the current sensor states being triggered (i.e., kitchen light is turned off, heater is switched on, bathroom door is closed, etc.) or some preprocessed interpretation (e.g., person is standing with their arms in the air).

An example of the input that the smart home receives could then be in the form of a timestamp and a sensor token:

- 2011-05-15, 20:22:19, B
- 2011-05-15, 20:22:47, X
- 2011-05-15, 21:08:32, Y
- 2011-05-15, 21:09:03, H
- ...

where the particular tokens could signify B: living room light on, X: sit on settee, Y: get off settee, H: leave living room, and would suggest that somebody spent some time in the evening sitting in their living room.

For this chapter we will ignore the timestamp part of the data and simply consider the set of sensor tokens 'B, X, Y, H' in the example above. While this seems to be rather naïve, timing is not necessarily as helpful as it seems at first. For example, in the above example there is a relatively long gap between tokens 'X' and 'Y', but that is not because there is a behaviour change there, just that the particular behaviour can take an arbitrarily long time without sensor activation.

Based on the token abstraction, the behaviour recognition problem consists of identifying 'words' within the token sequence that are seen repeatedly, either completely or with certain variations, such as the ordering, or certain tokens being additionally present or absent. We now describe three different approaches to the problem of behaviour recognition in our unlabelled data stream.

3. EXTRACTING BEHAVIOURS FROM UNLABELLED TOKEN SEQUENCES

The three approaches that we discuss are conceptually rather different from each other. They have not all been applied to problems of behaviour recognition, but we believe that they offer some potential in this area. All three take only the unannotated token stream as input, but from there the methods differ markedly. In the first, this information is extended with additional information from another source, namely the internet, gained through data mining. The second approach is to use traditional machine learning methods for unsupervised learning, such as the k-means algorithm or Self-Organising Map, to identify structure in the data. Finally, we present a method that exploits repetition in the data, arguing that repeated segments are 'redundant' in the compression sense, and therefore detectable.

3.1. Mining from the Web

As a source of data the World Wide Web has obvious benefits: there is a vast amount of information readily available through search engines, and obvious disadvantages: getting the information that is actually wanted is far from trivial, and what information there is can be contradictory.

The application of machine learning methods to extract meaningful knowledge from the web is called 'web mining'. There are three commonly identified subproblems in web mining (Borges & Levene, 2000):

- **Web *usage* mining:** Tracks the analysis of user behavioural patterns, i.e. user usage patterns on the web. Web usage mining keeps track on user behaviours when the user surfs the web. The web logs, user registration data, cookies or even mouse clicks can provide useful information where machine learning algorithms (such as clustering, association rules, classification, etc.) can be applied for knowledge discovery. Works in this category are often targeted for personalisation, system improvement, business intelligence and usage characterisation (Jaideep, Robert, Mukund, & Pang-Ning, 2000).
- **Web *structure* mining:** Tracks the structure of the web document hyperlinks at inter-document level. It aims to discover the relationships between web pages by identifying the hyperlinks reference to the page (Schenker, Bunke, Last, & Kandel, 2005). Graph models are often used for web structure mining by representing nodes in the graph as web pages and edges as hyperlinks between pages.
- **Web *content* mining:** Concerns the identification of structure within the web documents based on user queries (Kosala & Blockeel, 2000). This involves information discovery, document categorisation and clustering, and information extraction from the web pages. Unlike web structure mining, web content mining discovers structure within the Web documents at the intra-document level.

Clearly, it is the last of these that we are interested in for behaviour recognition, although we note that in fact the first is itself an example of behaviour recognition. The idea is that by extracting information from the web, parts of the token sequence could be separated out and automatically labelled. Of course, this would require knowing the mapping between sensor tokens and objects. An example of a website that might then be useful is http://ehow.com, which helpfully illustrates not only the sequence of steps involved to perform an activity (such as making coffee), but also the objects used (e.g., coffee machine, coffee beans, cup) involved (Perkowitz, Philipose, Fishkin, & Patterson, 2004). For example, suppose that token 'K' appears in the sequence, and that this is a token representing 'kettle is switched on.' By searching for the word 'kettle', various websites are found that include mention of tea making. However, there are also lots of other websites, and the different possibilities from these web sites need to be selected between, for example by using weights. This is what the web will find for us such as that the relation between kettle and tea making has higher weight than the relation between kettle and doing laundry. If 'K' is followed by 'P', which represents 'fridge opened,' then there can be extra information added to the search. Of course, bridging the gap between the website and the token evidence is far from trivial, and could involve interesting challenges in natural language recognition and image analysis as well as web mining itself.

The information that is mined from the web can be used to train any supervised machine learning algorithm, such as the HMM (Perkowitz et al., 2004) or a dynamic Bayesian network (Wyatt, Philipose, & Choudhury, 2005). It would be possible to add common-sense information in the reasoning about the human state (e.g. 'the inhabitant is in the kitchen making tea') (Pentney, Popescu, Wang, Kautz, & Philipose, 2006).

The web can also be a useful resource to learn similar behaviours that share some commonality (Zheng, Hu, & Yang, 2009). For example, suppose that there are labelled examples of 'sweeping the floor', but not other cleaning activities. In this case, web mining can try to extract similar tasks such as 'vacuuming' or 'doing laundry' and give those as possible behaviours to be identified. Various similarity functions (such as the cosine similarity metric, maximum mean discrepancy, Kullback-Leibler divergence) can be employed on the extracted web pages to measure the similarity between two different activities.

3.2. Clustering

The second method that we present is to use the standard machine learning approaches to unsupervised learning, namely the k-means algorithm and Self-Organising Map (SOM) (Kohonen, 1990). Both algorithms have the same aim, which is to identify structure in unlabelled data, such as clusters of similar patterns. If the input to the algorithm is a subset of the token sequence, such as the last 5 tokens, then when similar subsets are seen repeatedly, they will be recognised.

The k-means algorithm attempts to identify a set of k centroids or cluster centres that best represent the data, where k is a parameter that is chosen in advance. The positions of the centroids are initially chosen randomly, and then an update algorithm iterates until the centroid locations stop moving, whereupon each datapoint is represented by its closest centroid. For behaviour recognition, the centroid would represent the 'idealised' behaviour. Among the works that have used the k-means algorithm to recognise high-level activities are Hein and Kirste (2008), Huynh and Schiele (2005), and Rao and Cook (2004). Nguyen, Moore, and McCowan (2007) employ the k-means method to separate out the common and unusual events from sensor information.

The SOM algorithm has the benefit of being less reliant on the choice of the size (k for the k-means algorithm) and randomly chosen initial condition. It produces a representation of the input in a low dimensional (often 2D) set of map nodes or neurons, which are activated proportional to the distance between their weights and the input. The learning process is competitive in the sense that neurons with high activation are trained, while those with low activation are ignored. The algorithm modifies these weights in such a way that, after training, the outputs are arranged in a topological order so that neurons that are closer to one another represent similar features. During learning, the weights are iteratively adjusted along with the neighbouring weights until the maximum number of iterations is reached. The learning rate in SOM determines how the input weights are tuned.

In the smart home context, the inputs to the SOM could be a set of tokens that represent particular behaviours. When a new sequence is presented to the SOM, the output can be either the entire pattern of neuronal activations, or just the index of the most active node (as in the k-means algorithm), which can be used to represent the behaviour (Zheng, Wang, & Black, 2008; Kim, Song, & Kim, 2007). In the work of both Laerhoven (Laerhoven, 2001) and Krause et al. (Krause, Siewiorek, Smailagic, & Farringdon, 2003), they first apply the Kohonen self-organising map to reduce the number of dimensions of sensor data and further perform k-means clustering for behaviour classification. An example of a SOM is shown on the left of Figure 2, while the right side of the figure shows a way that different activations in the SOM could be interpreted as behaviours.

For both of these algorithms, the size of the input vector is chosen in advance. For behaviour recognition this means that the number of tokens that are presented is preset, and therefore the maximum number in a behaviour is preset and constant, which is rather unlikely in practice. An experiment is conducted to demonstrate the applicability of SOM to identify behaviours from sensors. The experiment is performed on a dataset collected from a real smart home, which is described in Section 5.

Figure 2. Left: A schematic of the self-organising map. Inputs (in grey) are fed to each neuron (in black) using weighted connections. There are connections between neurons in a local neighbourhood to ensure that neurons that are close together represent similar inputs. Learning consists of modifying the weights. Right: A possible way that neurons in the map could be mapped into particular behaviours. Note that the labels would be added after training to provide a human representation of the data.

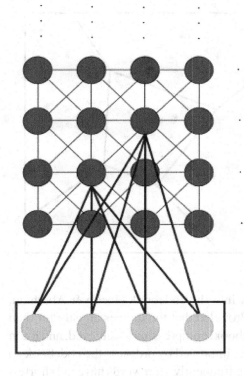 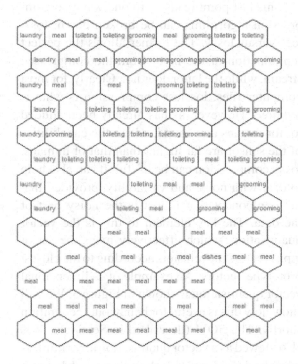

3.3. Compression and Text Analysis

The final approach that we present in this chapter is our method of choice, both for its simplicity and accuracy. It exploits the fact that a behaviour is a pattern that is a repeated set of tokens, and can thus be identified using any algorithm that looks to exploit redundancy in the input stream, i.e., a compression algorithm. There are two general types of compression: lossless and lossy. In order to allow similar, but not identical, patterns to be identified in the input stream, a lossy algorithm is more suited to our problem. We present a brief overview of compression before demonstrating how it can be used for the purposes of unlabelled behaviour recognition.

Compression has been a topic of interest in information storage for a very long time, since using less space for storage and reducing transmission times are obviously useful. Work on computerised compression began with the birth of information theory in the work of Shannon (1948), who identified the concepts of entropy and redundancy in a data stream. Most compression algorithms work by building a dictionary of codewords, with shorter codewords being used for frequent words and longer codewords for words that are less frequently used. Many compression algorithms aim to be general, in that they require no prior knowledge about the input data stream, but process it without a priori knowledge. Exceptions are often concerned with images (such as jpeg), sound (mp3), or the combination of both in video (mpeg), where knowledge of the type of data to be stored and the capabilities of humans to process their sight and sound stimuli enables more compression to be achieved by suppressing data that would not be detected by humans anyway, such as very high frequencies in sound recording.

This last point leads us to one way that compression algorithms can be broken down: lossless versus lossy. The former allows the perfect reproduction of the input from the compressed stream, while the latter does not. Clearly, for most computer files, lossless compression is what is required. However, as has already been alluded to, for images and sound, where the capabilities of the sensor are far higher than that of humans, lossy compression can be useful. It can also help to deal with noise and variability, provided that the component that is lost is the noisy part of the data. The key element to this is the vector quantisation, which effectively maps the set of input vectors into clusters according to the closest prototype vectors. An example of 2-dimensional vector quantisation is shown in Figure 3. We will show how this is useful for behaviour recognition shortly. The SOM (described in Section 3.2) is also viewed as a vector quantisation algorithm, as it can be considered to be building a codebook of prototype vectors. The learning vector quantisation in SOM finds the similarity between the input vectors and codebook vectors by minimising the Euclidean distance (Kohonen et al., 1996).

Lossless compression algorithms can be broken down by whether they are dictionary based or statistically based. Statistical methods predict the occurrence of the next symbol based on the symbols that precede it in the sensor stream (Cleary & Witten, 1984), and aim to learn this mapping so that many symbols do not need to be stored, as they can be predicted accurately. These methods tend to work best where the data is fairly regular. By contrast, dictionary methods adaptively build a codebook of commonly seen words, and then replace each incidence of the word with

Figure 3. An example of prototype vectors in 2-dimensional space. The asterisks are input vectors and circles represent the prototype vectors. A codebook is the set of prototype vectors. Input vectors are clustered according to the closest prototype vectors.

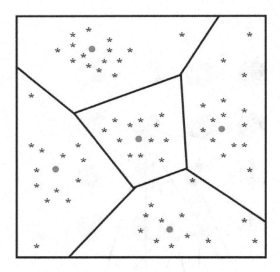

an index into the codebook (Jacob & Abraham, 1978). Provided that the indices are shorter than the codebook, compression is achieved, and it can be further improved by ordering the codebook so that more frequently seen words have the shortest index terms. The most common lossless compression algorithm, and the one that we will use, is the Lempel-Ziv-Welch (LZW) algorithm (Welch, 1984). In the form that we shall use it, the steps of the algorithm are shown in Algorithm 1.

We now need to identify how to use a compression algorithm for behaviour recognition. As was mentioned previously, the central idea is that a pattern that repeats is a potential behaviour. This is exactly what compression will find for us, as it is looking for such 'redundant' sequences. However, there are two challenges: as can be seen from the description of the algorithm, LZW produces many examples of each potential dictionary string, as it builds them incrementally, starting with single characters and then adding extended sequences in over time, starting from the last letter

Algorithm 1. Lempel-Ziv-Welch (LZW) compression algorithm (Welch, 1984)

Input: token stream

Initialisation: initialise dictionary to contain single character strings

ω = get first input character

while not end of token stream **do**

    K = get next input character

    if ω + K exists in the dictionary **then**

      ω = ω + K

    else

      output code for ω

      add ω + K to dictionary with new code

      ω = K

    end if

end while

output the code for ω

---

of the string that has just been added. As an example, the second time the phrase 'mo' is seen in the token sequence 'mousemousemousemouse...', it will take the index of 'mo' found in the dictionary and extend the phrase by concatenating it with the next character from the sequence to form a new phrase ('mou'), which is later added to the dictionary. The search then continues from the token 'u.'

Figure 4 shows an example. Suppose that token 'm' signifies that the kitchen door was opened, 'o' that the kettle was switched on, 'u' could be that the fridge was opened and the word 'mouse' basically represents the tea making behaviour. If the word 'mouse' is the tea making behaviour and is repeated in the token stream, then it makes sense to have the dictionary contain only the word 'mouse' rather than having 'mo' or 'use' separately in the dictionary. This means that the dictionary needs to be quantised so that it is biased towards the longest common words that represent behaviours (in this example, the word 'mouse'). This also has another benefit, which is that LZW tends to produce large dictionaries, since they include everything learnt during training, including all the single characters and all the substrings of each dictionary word, many of which are superfluous.

Another issue is that behaviours often do not repeat perfectly: we still want to identify tea making if the milk is put in before the hot water, rather than after, or even if milk is not added at all. We hence want to recognise variations on the behaviours. This leads us to the use of lossy compression: we do not want to reproduce the exact sequence of sensory tokens that occurred, but an idealised one that shows the exemplar behaviours.

In fact, by choosing the way that we do the lossy compression appropriately, we can use it to compress the dictionary as well. We have chosen to use the Levenshtein edit distance (Levenshtein, 1966), commonly known just as the edit distance. This is the minimum number of edits (insertions, deletions, and alterations) required to transfer one word into the other. It is the basis of spell checkers and a simple example of dynamic programming. The edit distance to turn a string p with word length m to string q with word length n is shown in Algorithm 2.

Figure 4. Illustration of using lossless and lossy compression on an unlabelled sensory stream by exploiting repeated subsequences that represent behaviours (token 'm' could be a sensor event showing that the kitchen door was opened, 'o' that the kettle was switched on, etc. and the word 'mouse' represents a tea making behaviour). Lossless compression (namely the Lempel-Ziv-Welch method) is first performed on the unlabelled sensor stream generating a list of phrases in the dictionary. Lossy compression further quantises the dictionary so that the dictionary only contains the phrase 'mouse', which represents a complete tea making behaviour rather than having 'mo' and 'use' separately in the dictionary.

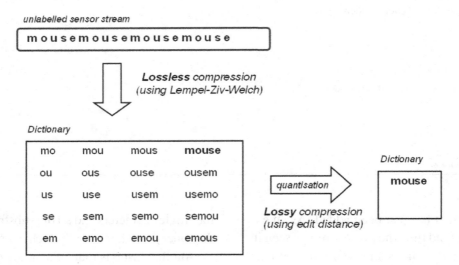

The edit distance can be used to reduce the size of the dictionary by picking a word from the dictionary, and looking for all its 'neighbouring' (i.e., edit distance one away) words. The word from this list with the highest frequency can be picked as the exemplar for this set, and the process iterated until the set of words does not change.

The SOM finds the similarity between the input vectors and the codebook vectors by minimising the Euclidian distance while our method minimises the edit distance between the input vectors and the 'words' in the dictionary.

Once the dictionary is quantised, the next step is segment the token stream into behaviours according to the words in the quantised dictionary. To see how this works, suppose that the word 'mouse' is in the dictionary as an exemplar for the tea making behaviour. While traversing the token sequence, the string 'mose' is found (making a tea without milk), and then later 'myouse', where another event occurs during the tea making

(either noise, or something else happening, such as the kitchen light being turned on). Rather than being identified as new behaviours, both of these examples should be identified as instances of the 'mouse' tea making behaviour. Figure 5 shows an example of this.

The edit distance can be used to identify the matches between the strings ('mose' and 'myouse') from the token sequence and the word 'mouse' in the dictionary. A match is determined when a low edit distance score is found. The starting point of the word boundary can be identified by traversing the distance matrix backward using dynamic programming to find the minimum distance of $\min(dist[i-1;j-1]; \quad dist[i-1;j]; \quad dist[i;j-1];)$. The highlighted areas shown in Figure 5 represent the paths that backward traversal follows to identify the starting point of the word boundary so that the token stream can be segmented into behaviours according to the behaviours in the dictionary after quantisation.

Algorithm 2. Edit distance algorithm (Levenshtein, 1966)

Input: p, q

Initialisation: m = length of p, n = length of q, $dist = [0..m, 0..n]$

  for $i=1$ to m **do**

    $dist\,[i.0] = i$

  end for

  for $j=1$ to n **do**

    $dist\,[0.j] = j$

  end for

  for $i=1$ to m **do**

    for $j=1$ to n **do**

      if $p[i] == q[j]$ **then**

$dist\,[i,j] = \min(dist\left[i-1, j\right] + 0;\, dist\left[i, j-1\right] + 1;\, dist\left[i-1, j-1\right] + 1)$

      else

$dist\,[i,j] = \min(dist\left[i-1, j\right] + 1;\, dist\left[i, j-1\right] + 1;\, dist\left[i-1, j-1\right] + 1)$

      end if

    end for

  end for

Figure 5. An example showing the mapping of token sequence ('mosexyzaamyousebb') to the word in the quantised dictionary ('mouse') using edit distance. The letters inbetween 'mose' and 'myouse' are just random noise added to the token sequence.

		m	o	s	e	x	y	z	a	a	m	y	o	u	s	e	b	b
Quantised Dictionary	m	0	1	1	1	1	1	1	1	1	0	1	1	1	1	1	1	1
	o	1	0	1	2	2	2	2	2	2	1	1	1	2	2	2	2	2
	u	2	1	1	2	3	3	3	3	3	2	2	2	1	2	3	3	3
	s	3	2	1	2	3	4	4	4	4	3	3	3	2	1	2	3	4
	e	4	3	2	1	2	3	4	5	5	4	4	4	3	2	1	2	3

(Token Sequence)

Among the works that have used edit distance for classification are those by Fihl, Holte and Moeslund (2007), and Hatun and Duygulu (2008). They apply the edit distance to find similarity between action sequences in videos. Shaw, Parui and Shridhar (2008) use edit distance for word recognition. They transform word images into strings of pseudocharacters and use edit distance to find the best matching word in a set of trained vocabulary.

A similar approach is taken by Wilson and Philipose (2005). They use edit distance to rate the performance of daily activities by finding the similarity between an activity trace and a set of rated activity exemplars. A threshold is used to control how much variation is allowed between activity traces. When a rating of a given activity trace falls below a threshold, the system provides a justification of the rate by correcting the activity trace according to the original activity. This differs from our approach, as we attempt to recognise behaviours from the token stream by mapping the token stream according to the 'words' in the quantised dictionary.

4. ADDING SUPERVISED LEARNING

In the previous section we have seen three different potential ways to take a sequence of unlabelled sensory tokens and extract repeat—or near repeat—patterns from it as potential behaviours. It is an interesting question what to do with this output. There are two different options. One is simply to use the system as is, since it will essentially report which behaviour is identified at each time. By adding a human label to each of the behaviours, which should be relatively simple, it is then possible to see what the inhabitant of the house is doing at each time. However, this might not always be sufficient, depending upon what the aim of the smart home is. For example, suppose that we wish to add other information, such as context (Guesgen & Marsland, 2010), or to detect abnormal behaviour. Neither of these would be easy to do using only the unsupervised learning approaches that we have identified.

An alternative is to use the unsupervised learning approach as a way to provide labels to training data for a supervised algorithm in a bootstrap approach to learning. This supervised algorithm can then be used to recognise behaviours from that point onwards. We will now briefly review some potential methods by which this supervised learning can be achieved.

Research in behaviour recognition on supervised data has led to a variety of solutions based on graphical models such as hidden Markov models (Chua, Marsland, & Guesgen, 2009), conditional random fields (Hu & Yang, 2008; Vail & Veloso, 2008), dynamic Bayesian network (Liao, Patterson, Fox, & Kautz, 2007) and the naïve Bayes classifier (Tapia et al., 2004). Graphical models are a useful framework in which to view many different machine learning algorithms. They take the form of a graph where the nodes represent the variable and the edges represent the conditional dependencies between the variables, where the lack of an edge signifies conditional independence between two nodes. The graph can be directed or undirected (this latter case is known as a Markov random field). For more on graphical models, see a standard machine learning textbook such as (Marsland, 2009), or a more specialist work such as (Koller & Friedman, 2009).

It is our experience that the Hidden Markov Model (HMM), which is the simplest dynamic Bayesian network, and which admits tractable algorithms for learning and prediction, is a very useful model for learning behaviours from labelled data (Chua, Marsland, & Guesgen, 2009). Figure 6 shows a representation of a HMM.

To illustrate the HMM, we consider the example of a clown who has three bags of different number of coloured balls in each of them. In the demonstration, he will blindfold himself and pick a ball from a bag that he randomly chooses, and repeat the process three times. His main task is to identify which particular bags he has chosen from, given the sequence of coloured balls that he has picked. Before he begins the demonstration, a volunteer from the audiences is called upon to help by writing down the coloured balls that he has picked. The first ball that he took was a red ball. Then he repeats the process by randomly choosing a bag, and picks a ball from it. The

Figure 6. Representation of a hidden Markov model. The nodes represent the variables (top three nodes are the hidden states and the bottom three nodes are the observations) and the edges (arrows) represent the conditional dependencies: the solid line represents the conditional dependencies between states, $P(S_t \mid S_{t-1})$ and the dashed line represents the conditional dependencies of the observation on the hidden states, $P(O_t \mid S_t)$.

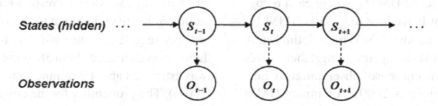

second ball was blue. He continues the process and the third ball chosen was again blue. His next task is to make guesses about which particular bags he has drawn the balls from. The only information he has, is the sequence of coloured balls (i.e. red, blue, blue). In this illustration, the bags are the states which are not directly visible (i.e. the bags are hidden from the clown), but can only be inferred through the sequence of coloured balls. This is where the word *'hidden'* in the hidden Markov model comes from. Based on this simple illustration, the main idea behind the HMM is basically to estimate the probabilities of the unobserved events (i.e. the bags) given a sequence of observable coloured balls. For details of the algorithm, see Rabiner (1989).

In the context of smart home, the observations are the tokens from the sensors. For example, the token could be that the shower tap is turned on, and the possible states would then be that somebody is showering or cleaning. HMMs are more successful than look-up tables of sensor readings because they allow for variation in the activity, such as different orders of sensor activation and the fact that certain sensor activations can be shared by multiple behaviours. They also deal well with noise since they are probabilistic.

Within smart home research it is also common to use more complicated variants of the HMM, such as the Hierarchical Hidden Markov Model (N. T. Nguyen, Phung, Venkatesh, & Bui, 2005)

and the Switching Hidden Semi-Markov Model (Duong, Bui, Phung, & Venkatesh, 2005). In both of these models, a top-level representation of behaviours (e.g., cooking or making coffee) is built up from a set of recognised activities that arise from the individual sensor values. This means that each state has its own HMM. Figure 7 shows an example of the hierarchical HMM.

Figure 7. The hierarchical HMM. One example is the tea making behaviour $\left(S_2^2\right)$ which can be broken down to represent the movement of the use of kitchen objects such as the cupboard $\left(S_1^3\right)$, drawer $\left(S_2^3\right)$ and the fridge $\left(S_3^3\right)$. Subscript 'e' means that a final state is reached where the child state returns the control to its parent state. For details on this algorithm, see Fine et al. (1998).

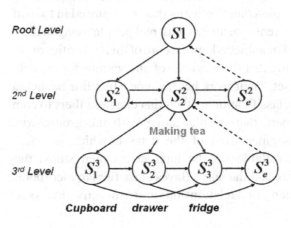

As these models attempt to represent a complete model of behaviours arising from sensor observations, they require more data for training and have higher computational complexity, which often becomes intractable for learning. Another variation is to use a set of HMMs, where each recognises a different behaviour (e.g., one HMM for preparing meal, another HMM for toileting, etc.), where these HMMs compete amongst themselves to explain the current sensor observations (Chua, Marsland, & Guesgen, 2009). A winning HMM is chosen based on the HMM that best recognises the sensor observations. An illustration of this method is shown in Figure 8.

Another variation to the methods pointed out above is the naïve Bayes classifier, which has shown a number of successes in machine learning applications such as text classification (McCallum & Nigam, 1998; Lewis & Ringuette, 1994) and spam filtering (Sahami, Dumais, Heckerman, & Horvitz, 1998; Metsis, 2006). The naïvety in the classifier is that all the features are assumed to be independent of each other, and the classifier then selects the class with the maximum likelihood based on the data. Figure 9 shows an example of a generic naïve Bayes classifier as a graphical model. The class node is the parent to its feature nodes.

Among the early work that used the naïve Bayes classifiers in behaviour recognition is the work of MIT PlaceLab (Tapia et al., 2004). They designed a system based on a set of simply installed state-change sensors that were placed in two different apartments with real people living in them. The subjects kept a record of their activities meaning that there is a set of annotations for the dataset. Their work has become a baseline behaviour classification method that enables others to compare their results along with the ground-truth segmentation of the dataset, which are made available via the internet. In their study, they extend the naïve Bayes classifiers to incorporate temporal relationships in sensor activations (such as whether token 'a' activated within some time interval and whether token 'a' activated before token 'b') to recognise activities. In order to recognise behaviours, they used a set feature windows, each represents one activity. The length of each feature window corresponds to the average duration that the inhabitant took to carry out that activity (e.g. the feature window for 'preparing lunch' was estimated about 38 minutes, 'toileting' was estimated about 7 minutes, etc. (Tapia et al., 2004)). The probability for the current activity is calculated by shifting the feature window over the sensor sequences (with an increment of three minutes). The probability reaches the maximum when the window aligns with the duration of the activity from the sensor readings, where the best match is found when the activity is ending.

Other machine learning methods that could potentially used for behaviour recognition include support vector machine (Ravi, Dandekar, Mysore, & Littman, 2005), decision tree (Bao & Intille, 2004; Logan, Healey, Philipose, Tapia, & Intille, 2007) and topic model (Huynh, Fritz, & Schiele, 2008). These methods are not covered in this chapter. However, interested readers could refer to (Hsu, Chang, & Lin, 2003; Blei, Ng, & Jordan, 2003; Marsland, 2009) for details of these methods.

The main idea of using unsupervised learning methods (discussed in Section 3) is to extract sensors that are related to the activities. However, relating the clusters of tokens to the activities is difficult since different people have their own ways of performing activities and it is not easy to identify potentially dangerous events (such as the microwave oven being used for too long or the stovetop being left on) using any of the unsupervised methods described in this chapter. One way to address this is to use the output of the unsupervised learning method to train a supervised method. Several supervised methods have already been described in this section. We will experiment in the next section how supervised learning can be achieved.

Figure 8. Illustration showing how behaviour recognition and segmentation are performed using the idea of competition between HMMs with the forward algorithm. In this example the window size is 10. $O_1, O_2, ..., O_t$ is the observation sequence. The solid arrow above the observation sequence represents the ground truth information ($O_1, O_2, ..., O_5$ labelled as preparing meal and $O_6, O_7, ..., O_9$ as tea making behaviour). In the competition among all the trained HMMs, 'preparing meal' is chosen as the winning behaviour. The forward algorithm is used to calculate the likelihood of $O_1, O_2, ..., O_{10}$ based on the model of the winning behaviour. To simplify the illustration, the α_t value is quantised into the set $\{0,1\}$. When the $\alpha = 1$, it means that the likelihood of the observation is high based on the winning HMM and 0 otherwise. When a drop in α is observed at O_6, it suggests that the behaviour has changed. We can therefore classify $O_1, O_2, ..., O_5$ as belonging to the winning behaviour. Competition is rerun by taking the next 10 observations (i.e. $O_6, O_7, ..., O_{15}$).

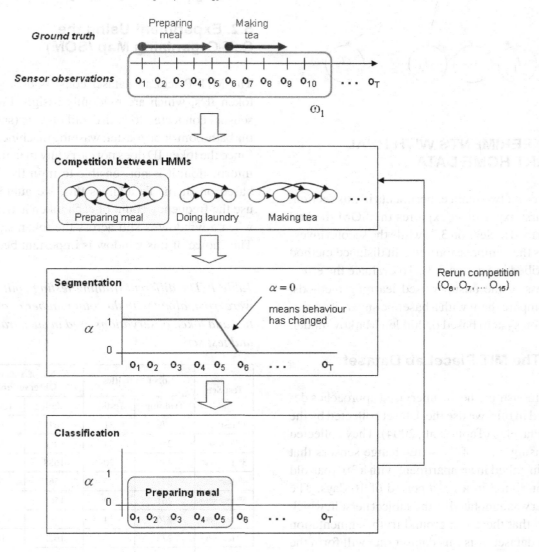

Figure 9. A graphical representation of a naïve Bayes classifier where the features $\left(a_1, a_2, a_3, ..., a_k\right)$ *are independent given the class node. In the context of smart home, the class node is basically the activity (such as toileting, preparing meal, doing laundry, etc), while the features could be the tokens that give rise to the activity such as flush toilet, toaster, washing machine, etc.*

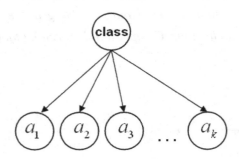

5. EXPERIMENTS WITH REAL SMART HOME DATA

We present two main experiments in this section. The first experiment explores the SOM method (described in Section 3.2) while the second investigates the compression and edit distance method (described in Section 3.3). To evaluate the effectiveness of the unsupervised learning methods, we compare them with a baseline supervised recognition system based on hidden Markov model.

5.1. The MIT PlaceLab Dataset

To demonstrate the unsupervised approaches described in this, we use the dataset collected by the MIT Placelab (Tapia et al., 2004). They collected data using a set of 77 state-change sensors that were installed in an apartment with a 30-year-old woman living in it for a period of 16 days. The dataset was annotated by the subject herself, which means that there is a ground truth segmentation of the dataset. It is this dataset that will form the basis for the experiments reported here.

We used a leave-two-out cross validation method for each evaluation in order to calculate the confusion matrix and measure the recognition accuracy. From the total of 16 days, we used 14 days for training and the remaining two days for testing. Table 1 shows the different training/testing splits along with the number of activities and tokens that we used for training and testing. We considered 5 different behaviours, i.e. toileting/showering, grooming/dressing, preparing meal/snack/beverages, washing/putting away dishes, and doing/putting away laundry.

5.2. Experiment Using the Self-Organising Map (SOM)

The MIT PlaceLab dataset consists of a set of token IDs, which are randomly assigned to the sensors connected to household objects (such as the bathroom door, toaster, washing machine, etc). Since the token ID does not carry any meaningful information, it is not sensible to train the SOM based on them. To address this, we attempt to use the frequency count of each token activation when a window is slid across the token stream. The choice of this window is important because

Table 1. The different training/testing splits that were tried, along with the total number of activities and token observations used in each training and test set

Test Sets	No. of Activities		No. of Token Observations	
	Training	Testing	Training	Testing
1st test set	279	31	1672	133
2nd test set	256	54	1456	349
3rd test set	290	20	1688	117
4th test set	277	33	1561	244
5th test set	261	49	1563	242
6th test set	276	34	1592	213
7th test set	273	37	1625	180
8th test set	258	52	1478	327

it is unlikely that the activities in the sequence belong to one behaviour. In our experiment, a smaller window size is preferred so that it can subsume sequences of behaviours that are longer in length. We determine the window size by taking the average number of sensor observations (i.e. the sensor activations) that describe the behaviours. On average, 3 sensor observations gave rise to a behaviour, and thus the window size is set to 3. The window is shifted with an increment of 1 observation.

We trained the SOM with 24 input token variables using the SOM Toolbox (Kohonen, Hynninen, Kangas & Laaksonen, 1996). The training of the SOM was in batch mode, the learning rate was set to 0.05 and neighbourhood size was 2. The output is the 7 x 7 map shown in Figure 10. Looking at the figure, we can see a few behaviours that form different clusters in the map. For example, 'toileting' behaviour forms a cluster at the right-top, the 'grooming' behaviour towards the right-bottom and the 'meal' behaviour towards the left-bottom in the map.

Not all nodes in the map fired during training. One problem with this is that when these nodes fire when data from the test set is presented, there is no way to determine which behaviours these

nodes belong to (in the figure, we labelled these as 'unknown behaviour'). Recognition accuracy is calculated by determining the nodes that are the best match according to the behaviours in the map. The results are presented in Table 2.

5.3. Experiment using the Compression and Edit Distance

In this experiment, we demonstrate our new method i.e. using the compression and edit distance method described in Section 3.3. First, we exploit the redundancy in the token stream using the LZW algorithm by building a dictionary of commonly seen words. We then perform lossy compression to quantise the dictionary. Within this experiment, we also investigate using the output of compression and edit distance to train a supervised machine learning method (i.e. the HMM) in a bootstrap approach to learning. These methods are compared to a baseline supervised recognition system, where we trained the HMM directly from the ground truth data and using the trained HMM to recognise behaviours from the token stream. Figure 11 illustrates how the three experiments are conducted.

Figure 10. The SOM output of the clusters representing the five different behaviours (left: training set; right: test set)

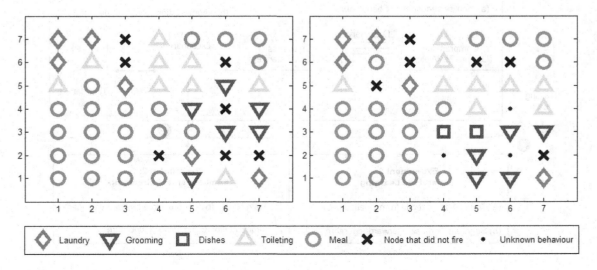

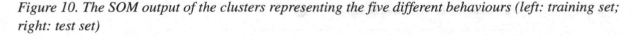

Table 2. Comparison results between two unsupervised learning methods: (1) the proposed method based on compression and edit distance and (2) the self-organising map (SOM). The second column of the table is the total number of activities used in each test set. The third column refers to the total number of activities correctly identified by the compression and edit distance method while the fourth column is the total number of activities that could not be identified by the compression and edit distance method. The recognition accuracy is the ratio of the total number of activities correctly identified by the algorithm over the total number activities used for testing.

Test Set	Compression and Edit Distance Method				SOM
	No. of Activities	No. of Activities Correctly Identified	Unidentified Activities	Recognition Accuracy	Recognition Accuracy
1st test set	31	25	2	81%	56%
2nd test set	54	41	7	76%	57%
3rd test set	20	18	0	90%	69%
4th test set	33	30	0	91%	56%
5th test set	49	41	3	84%	57%
6th test set	34	27	2	79%	64%
7th test set	37	32	2	86%	75%
8th test set	52	41	3	79%	47%
Average				83%	60%

Figure 11. Illustration of how three sub-experiments are conducted within the second experiment. The first experiment uses the LZW algorithm and edit distance to identify and recognise patterns from the unlabelled token stream. The second experiment uses the output from the first experiment (i.e. compression and edit distance) to train a supervised classifier (the HMM) and perform segmentation using the forward algorithm. The third experiment trains the HMM directly from the ground truth data, with the aim of obtaining a baseline recognition system.

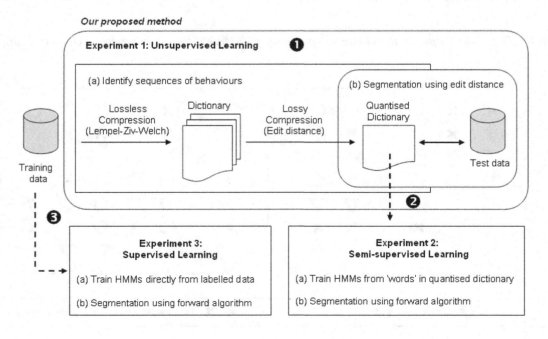

5.3.1. Experiment 1: Unsupervised Learning

We use the annotation in the training set only to attach a recognisable label to the words (behaviours) in the quantised dictionary, and used the annotation of the test set as a ground truth. Segmentation is performed by identifying matches between the token sequence in the test set and the dictionary. The tokens that have been segmented into behaviours are validated against the ground truth annotations on the test set. The recognition accuracy is the ratio of the total number of activities correctly identified by the algorithm over the total number activities used for testing. The results are presented in Table 2 and Figure 12.

Although our approach shows promise, it is still instructive to see if there are consistent reasons for the misclassifications that did occur. Some behaviours were too rare and compression simply could not be achieved, which results in some behaviours (such as 'doing/putting away laundry' and 'washing/putting away dishes') not being identified when building the dictionary. This is shown as 'unidentified activities' in Table 2. There are three places where this can be a problem. Firstly, instances in these behaviours vary from

the usual norm. Secondly, the behaviour is often interrupted by another event or noise from other sensors and thirdly, a combination of these two. These will result in a high value in the edit distance, which is above the value of the threshold, and so our algorithm could not identify the words.

Since the SOM is also an unsupervised learning method that builds a codebook of prototype vectors, we compared the compression and edit distance method with the SOM. The results are presented in Table 2, which shows that the compression and edit distance method has a higher recognition accuracy than the SOM. Our method did well because it can deal with codewords of different lengths, while for the SOM, as mentioned before, the size of input vector is constant for all behaviours. This means that the algorithm needs to be adaptive to learn new behaviour or additional information to describe current learned behaviours.

5.3.2. Experiment 2: Semi-Supervised Learning

We next train a supervised machine learning algorithm using the output from the unsupervised learning method. This can be seen as using the

Figure 12. Visualisation of the output of the ground truth (top) and the proposed method (bottom). The lower case letters on the x-axis show the sensor readings, while the y-axis shows the potential behaviours (which corresponds to the top-right of the figure). The notation 'W6' refers to one of the words in the quantised dictionary (shown on the bottom-right of the figure). The example is based on 5 activity instances on the 3rd test set.

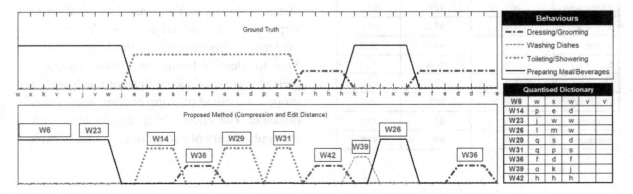

unsupervised learning method as a way to provide labels to training data in a bootstrap approach to learning.

We follow the method described in (Chua, Marsland, & Guesgen, 2009), where we train a set of HMMs from the pool of 'words' in the quantised dictionary. We used the same training/ testing settings as in the previous experiment (see Table 1). For the HMM, the observations are the tokens from the sensors and the hidden states are the events that arise from the observations. We trained the HMMs using the standard Expectation-Maximisation (EM) algorithm (Rabiner, 1989). The results are shown in Table 3. The performance of the semi-supervised method with an average recognition accuracy of 89% is slightly better than that of unsupervised learning. We believe that by adding additional contextual information (such as time or spatial information), it could improve the accuracy of the system. This could be useful to recognise behaviour that is not typical.

Table 3. A comparison results between unsupervised (compression and edit distance), semi-supervised (compression and edit distance with HMM) and supervised learning (HMM) methods based on different training/testing splits

Test Sets	Recognition Accuracy		
	Unsupervised Learning	Semi-Supervised Learning	Supervised Learning
1st test set	81%	84%	90%
2nd test set	76%	87%	91%
3rd test set	90%	95%	95%
4th test set	91%	94%	91%
5th test set	84%	90%	92%
6th test set	79%	88%	91%
7th test set	86%	92%	95%
8th test set	79%	83%	85%
Average	**83%**	**89%**	**91%**

5.3.3. Experiment 3: Supervised Learning

A comparison between these methods can only be made if a baseline classifier is obtained. We follow the same method described in (Chua, Marsland, & Guesgen, 2009), where we train a set of HMMs directly from the ground truth. Table 3 shows the comparison between these three different methods based on different training/testing splits. The results of unsupervised method with the recognition accuracy of 83% are comparable to the supervised method with an accuracy of 91%, considering that it works on unannotated data streams. This means that the unsupervised learning of approach based on compression and edit distance presented works effectively to identify behaviours from the unlabelled data stream. Our results are promising since our method does not need any prior annotations, which is likely to be the aim of any smart home, where the smart home can learn from scratch without any built-in prior knowledge when the sensors are installed in the home.

6. CONCLUSION

In this chapter, we have considered the task of recognising behaviours from two different directions: using supervised learning on annotated streams of sensor tokens and unsupervised learning on unannotated ones. We have presented a new method, based on compression and edit distance that maps the sensor information to a sequence of recognised activities. We have also explored another approach, the Self-Organising Map to identify behaviours from sensors and present a comparison of this approach with our proposed method of using compression and edit distance. The encouraging results have shown the applicability of using compression to exploit the regularities in the token stream, without any prior labelling of the sensors. One of the limitations of the proposed method is that compression cannot be achieved when the behaviours are too rare, which will results some behaviours not being identified (such as mowing the grass that happens every few weeks).

We have also discussed whether it is best to consider using only unsupervised method to identify behaviours from the unannotated token stream, or whether to use the output from unsupervised learning to train a supervised method for behaviour recognition. We compared the unsupervised method with a baseline supervised method, based on the hidden Markov model, to see how effective the system can be made. The results of using the unsupervised method are encouraging and we are continuing our work to look for 'informative' sensors from the sensor stream.

Regardless of the method chosen, by not using annotated token streams in the first place, we believe that a smart home can be built that starts from *tabula rasa*, meaning that the recognition system can learn from scratch without any built-in or prior knowledge when the sensors are installed in the home.

ACKNOWLEDGMENT

We acknowledge the support of the other members of the Massey University Smart Environments (MUSE) group (http://muse.massey.ac.nz).

REFERENCES

Bao, L., & Intille, S. S. (2004). Activity recognition from user-annotated acceleration data. In *Proceedings of the 2nd International Conference on Pervasive Computing*, (Vol. 3001, pp. 1-17). Springer.

Blei, D. M., Ng, A. Y., & Jordan, M. I. (2003). Latent Dirichlet allocation. *Journal of Machine Learning Research*, *3*, 993–1022.

Borges, J., & Levene, M. (2000). Data mining of user navigation patterns. In *Revised Papers from the International Workshop on Web Usage Analysis and User Profiling*, (pp. 92-111). London, UK: Springer-Verlag.

Chua, S.-L., Marsland, S., & Guesgen, H. W. (2009). Behaviour recognition from sensory streams in smart environments. In *Proceedings of the Australasian Conference on Artificial Intelligence*, (Vol. 5866, pp. 666-675). Springer.

Cleary, J. G., & Witten, I. H. (1984). Data compression using adaptive coding and partial string matching. *IEEE Transactions on Communications*, *32*, 396–402. doi:10.1109/TCOM.1984.1096090

Duong, T. V., Bui, H. H., Phung, D. Q., & Venkatesh, S. (2005). Activity recognition and abnormality detection with the switching hidden semi-Markov model. In *Proceedings of the 2005 IEEE Computer Society Conference on Computer Vision and Pattern Recognition*, (vol. 1, pp. 838-845). IEEE Computer Society.

Fihl, P., Holte, M. B., & Moeslund, T. B. (2007). Motion primitives and probabilistic edit distance for action recognition. *Proceedings of Gesture-Based Human-Computer Interaction and Simulation*, *5085*, 24–35. Springer-Verlag. doi:10.1007/978-3-540-92865-2_3

Fine, S., Singer, Y., & Tishby, N. (1998). The hierarchical hidden Markov model: Analysis and applications. *Machine Learning*, *32*(1), 41–62. doi:10.1023/A:1007469218079

Guesgen, H. W., & Marsland, S. (2010). Spatio-temporal reasoning and context awareness. In *Handbook of Ambient Intelligence and Smart Environments* (pp. 609–634). Berlin, Germany: Springer. doi:10.1007/978-0-387-93808-0_23

Hatun, K., & Duygulu, P. (2008). Pose sentences: A new representation for action recognition using sequence of pose words. In *Proceedings of the 19th International Conference on Pattern Recognition (ICPR)*, (pp. 1-4). Tampa, FL: IEEE.

Hein, A., & Kirste, T. (2008). Towards recognizing abstract activities: An unsupervised approach. In *Proceedings of the 2nd Workshop on Behaviour Monitoring and Interpretation, BMI 2008*, (pp. 102-114). CEUR-WS.org.

Hsu, C.-W., Chang, C.-C., & Lin, C.-J. (2003). *A practical guide to support vector classification*. Tech. Rep. National Taiwan University.

Hu, D. H., & Yang, Q. (2008). Cigar: Concurrent and interleaving goal and activity recognition. In *Proceedings of the 23rd Conference on Artificial Intelligence*, (pp. 1363-1368). AAAI Press.

Huynh, T., Fritz, M., & Schiele, B. (2008). Discovery of activity patterns using topic models. In *Proceedings of the 10th International Conference on Ubiquitous Computing*, (pp. 10-19). New York, NY: ACM.

Huynh, T., & Schiele, B. (2005). Analyzing features for activity recognition. In *Proceedings of the 2005 Joint Conference on Smart Objects and Ambient Intelligence*, (pp. 159-163). New York, NY: ACM.

Jacob, Z., & Abraham, L. (1978). Compression of individual sequences via variable-rate coding. *IEEE Transactions on Information Theory, 24*(5), 530–536. doi:10.1109/TIT.1978.1055934

Jaideep, S., Robert, C., Mukund, D., & Pang-Ning, T. (2000). Web usage mining: discovery and applications of usage patterns from web data. *SIGKDD Explorations Newsletter, 1*(2), 12–23.

Kim, D., Song, J., & Kim, D. (2007). Simultaneous gesture segmentation and recognition based on forward spotting accumulative HMMs. *Pattern Recognition, 40*(11), 3012–3026. doi:10.1016/j.patcog.2007.02.010

Kohonen, T. (1990). The self-organising map. *Proceedings of the IEEE, 78*(9), 1464–1480. doi:10.1109/5.58325

Kohonen, T., Hynninen, J., Kangas, J., & Laaksonen, J. (1996). *SOM_PAK: The self-organising map program package*. Helsinki, Finland: Helsinki University of Technology.

Kohonen, T., Hynninen, J., Kangas, J., Laaksonen, J., & Torkkola, K. (1996). *LVQ_PAK: The learning vector quantization program package. Tech. Rep*. Helsinki, Finland: Helsinki University of Technology.

Koller, D., & Friedman, N. (2009). *Probabilistic graphical models*. Cambridge, MA: MIT Press.

Kosala, R., & Blockeel, H. (2000). Web mining research: A survey. *SIGKDD Explorations, 2*, 1–15. doi:10.1145/360402.360406

Krause, A., Siewiorek, D. P., Smailagic, A., & Farringdon, J. (2003). Unsupervised, dynamic identification of physiological and activity context in wearable computing. In *Proceedings of the 7th IEEE International Symposium on Wearable Computers*, (p. 88). Washington, DC: IEEE Computer Society.

Laerhoven, K. V. (2001). Combining the self-organizing map and k-means clustering for online classification of sensor data. In *Proceedings of the International Conference on Artificial Neural Networks*, (pp. 464-469). London, UK: Springer-Verlag.

Levenshtein, V. (1966). Binary codes capable of correcting deletions, insertions and reversals. *Soviet Physics, Doklady, 10*, 707.

Lewis, D. D., & Ringuette, M. (1994). A comparison of two learning algorithms for text categorization. In *Proceedings of the Third Annual Symposium on Document Analysis and Information Retrieval*, (pp. 81-93). IEEE.

Liao, L., Patterson, D. J., Fox, D., & Kautz, H. (2007). Learning and inferring transportation routines. *Artificial Intelligence, 171*(5-6), 311–331. doi:10.1016/j.artint.2007.01.006

Logan, B., Healey, J., Philipose, M., Tapia, E. M., & Intille, S. S. (2007). A long-term evaluation of sensing modalities for activity recognition. In *Proceedings of the 9th International Conference on Ubiquitous Computing,* (pp. 483-500). Springer.

Marsland, S. (2009). *Machine learning: An algorithmic introduction.* Mahwah, NJ: CRC Press.

McCallum, A., & Nigam, K. (1998). A comparison of event models for naïve Bayes text classification. In *Proceedings of AAAI-98 - Workshop on Learning for Text Categorization,* (pp. 41-48). AAAI Press.

Metsis, V., Androutsopoulos, I., & Paliouras, G. (2006). Spam filtering with naïve Bayes - Which naive Bayes? In *Proceedings of the Third Conference on Email and Anti-Spam (CEAS).* CEAS.

Nguyen, A., Moore, D., & McCowan, I. (2007). Unsupervised clustering of free-living human activities using ambulatory accelerometry. In *Proceedings of the Annual International Conference of the IEEE Engineering in Medicine and Biology Society,* (pp. 4895-4898). IEEE Press.

Nguyen, N. T., Phung, D. Q., Venkatesh, S., & Bui, H. H. (2005). Learning and detecting activities from movement trajectories using the hierarchical hidden Markov model. *IEEE Computer Society Conference on Computer Vision and Pattern Recognition, 2,* 955-960.

Pentney, W., Popescu, A.-M., Wang, S., Kautz, H., & Philipose, M. (2006). Sensor-based understanding of daily life via large-scale use of common sense. In *Proceedings of the 21st National Conference on Artificial Intelligence,* (pp. 906-912). AAAI Press.

Perkowitz, M., Philipose, M., Fishkin, K., & Patterson, D. J. (2004). Mining models of human activities from the web. In *Proceedings of the 13th International Conference on World Wide Web,* (pp. 573-582). New York, NY: ACM.

Rabiner, L. (1989). A tutorial on hidden Markov models and selected applications in speech recognition. *Proceedings of the IEEE, 77*(2), 257–286. doi:10.1109/5.18626

Rao, S. P., & Cook, D. J. (2004). Predicting inhabitant action using action and task models with application to smart homes. *International Journal of Artificial Intelligence Tools, 13,* 81–100. doi:10.1142/S0218213004001533

Ravi, N., Dandekar, N., Mysore, P., & Littman, M. (2005). Activity recognition from accelerometer data. In *Proceedings of the 17th Conference on Innovative Applications of Artificial Intelligence,* (pp. 1541-1546). AAAI Press.

Sahami, M., Dumais, S., Heckerman, D., & Horvitz, E. (1998). A Bayesian approach to filtering junk e-mail. In *Learning for Text Categorization: Papers from the 1998 Workshop.* Madison, WI: AAAI Press.

Schenker, A., Bunke, H., Last, M., & Kandel, A. (2005). *Graph-theoretic techniques for web content mining.* Singapore, Singapore: World Scientific.

Shannon, C. E. (1948). A mathematical theory of communication. *The Bell System Technical Journal, 27,* 379–423, 625–656.

Shaw, B., Parui, S. K., & Shridhar, M. (2008). A segmentation based approach to offline handwritten devanagari word recognition. In *Proceedings of the 19th International Conference on Pattern Recognition (ICPR),* (pp. 1-4). Tampa, FL: IEEE.

Tapia, E. M., Intille, S. S., & Larson, K. (2004). Activity recognition in the home using simple and ubiquitous sensors. In *Proceedings of Pervasive* (pp. 158–175). IEEE. doi:10.1007/978-3-540-24646-6_10

Vail, D. L., & Veloso, M. M. (2008). Feature selection for activity recognition in multi-robot domains. In *Proceedings of the 23rd Conference on Artificial Intelligence,* (pp. 1415-1420). AAAI Press.

van Kasteren, T., Noulas, A., Englebienne, G., & Kröse, B. (2008). Accurate activity recognition in a home setting. In *Proceedings of the 10th International Conference on Ubiquitous Computing,* (pp. 1-9). New York, NY: ACM.

Wilson, D. H., & Matthai, P. (2005). Maximum a posteriori path estimation with input trace perturbation: Algorithms and application to credible rating of human routines. In *Proceedings of the 19th International Joint Conference on Artificial Intelligence,* (pp. 895-901). San Francisco, CA: Morgan Kaufmann Publishers Inc.

Wyatt, D., Philipose, M., & Choudhury, T. (2005). Unsupervised activity recognition using automatically mined common sense. In *Proceedings of the 20th Conference on Artificial Intelligence,* (pp. 21-27). AAAI Press.

Youngblood, G. M., & Cook, D. J. (2007). Data mining for hierarchical model creation. *IEEE Transactions on Systems, Man, and Cybernetics. Part C, 37*(4), 561–572.

Zheng, H., Wang, H., & Black, N. D. (2008). Human activity detection in smart home environment with self-adaptive neural networks. In *Proceedings of IEEE International Conference on Networking, Sensing and Control,* (pp. 1505-1510). IEEE.

Zheng, V. W., Hu, D. H., & Yang, Q. (2009). Cross-domain activity recognition. In *Proceedings of the 11th International Conference on Ubiquitous Computing,* (pp. 61-70). ACM.

KEY TERMS AND DEFINITIONS

Behaviour Recognition: A task of finding a mapping from a stream of sensor information to a sequence of recognised activities performed by the inhabitant of a smart home.

Edit Distance: Measures the similarity between pairs of strings. It works by computing the minimum number of actions (i.e., insertion, deletion, and substitution) required to transfer on string into another.

Lempel-Ziv-Welch Algorithm: A dictionary method which adaptively builds a codebook of commonly seen words and then replaces each incidence of the word with an index into the codebook.

Lossless Compression: Lossless compression allows the perfect reproduction of the inputs from the compressed stream.

Semi-Supervised Learning: In semi-supervised learning, the algorithm tries to build a classifier from a set of partially labelled examples and using the unlabelled examples to help training the classifier.

Supervised Learning: In supervised learning, the algorithm is presented with a set of inputs and their correspondence outputs (targets). The algorithm is then trained to minimise some error norm between the predicted output of the network and the target labels that are provided.

Unsupervised Learning: Unsupervised learning tries to identify similarities between the inputs and categorise the inputs into similar classes that share some commonality, without any data labelling.

Chapter 6
Tracking Systems for Multiple Smart Home Residents

Aaron S. Crandall
Washington State University, USA

Diane J. Cook
Washington State University, USA

ABSTRACT

Once a smart home system moves to a multi-resident situation, it becomes significantly more important that individuals are tracked in some manner. By tracking individuals, the events received from the sensor platform can then be separated into different streams and acted on independently by other tools within the smart home system. This process improves activity detection, history building, and personalized interaction with the intelligent space. Historically, tracking has been primarily approached through a carried wireless device or an imaging system, such as video cameras. These are complicated approaches and still do not always effectively address the problem. Additionally, both of these solutions pose social problems to implement in private homes over long periods of time. This chapter introduces and explores a Bayesian Updating method of tracking individuals through the space that leverages the Center for Advanced Studies in Adaptive Systems (CASAS) technology platform of pervasive and passive sensors. This approach does not require the residents to maintain a wireless device, nor does it incorporate rich sensors with the social privacy issues.

1. INTRODUCTION

Smart homes are providing an ever more important suite of tools for home care. From simple assistive tools to complex contextually aware interactive personas, smart home technology has penetrated many parts of the medical community. These tools rely on various sensors, artificial intelligence al-gorithms and human intelligence to operate. Most often the tools are geared towards recognizing the Activities of Daily Living (ADLs), with the purpose of providing historical and instantaneous feedback about the residents' behavior. Any improvements to these tools in recognizing ADLs is welcomed by care practitioners and the residents themselves because it gives them a more accurate

DOI: 10.4018/978-1-4666-3682-8.ch006

day to day picture of the residents' situation (Skubic, Alexander, Popescu, Rantz, & Keller, 2009).

Currently, the latest in smart home technology has trouble operating with low profile, privacy aware sensor platforms. These sensor platforms are designed to minimize effort on the part of the resident while maximizing privacy at the cost of sensor granularity. The goal of research in this area is to make use of this reduced sensor information to still build systems capable of providing quality assistive technologies.

As an added hurdle, the smart homes are often deployed where there is more than one resident dwelling in the space. Even visitors and care providers make it difficult for the smart home system to determine which person currently in the space caused a given event and attribute it appropriately. Without that ability, ADLs become much more difficult to detect through the noise in the data and individual histories are impossible to obtain.

The tools used to follow an individual through the space are commonly called tracking systems. A tracking system's goal is to determine the current number and location of individuals, as well as their identity if possible. This information is invaluable when dealing with multi-resident situations to provide the computer a method of attributing events to individuals. There are three main strategies for tracking people in smart homes:

1. Carried devices or tags
2. Video biometrics
3. Entity detection via dividing events spatially and temporally

Carried devices or tags are commonly done via RFID (Cook & Das, 2007; Naeem & Bigham, 2009; Choi, Lee, Elmasri, & Engels, 2009) or a wireless device carried on ones person (Hightower & Borriello, 2001; Luo & Chen, 2009; Navarro-Alvarez & Siller, 2009; Diaz, Maues, Soares, Nakamura, & Figueiredo, 2010). The device or a base station of some sort reports the current location of the device to the central system. This

has been accomplished using PDAs, cell phones, actigraphs, custom built RF devices, etc. While these kinds of systems work, it does require that every individual in the space keep and maintain their personal device at all times. It is easy for the residents to forget their device, have the batteries run down or not even want to have it. Additionally, guests need to be issued a device whenever they are in the space to ensure they are accounted for. In many environments this is a feasible solution, given the manpower to maintain it. For example, hospitals and full time care facilities are often able to make use of such systems. In private homes or understaffed situations, it becomes a less feasible solution.

For video biometrics, one or more cameras are placed around the monitored space. These cameras capture the current residents for tracking and processing (Libal, Ramabhadran, Mana, Pianesi, Chippendale, Lanz, & Potamianos, 2009; Menon, Jayaraman, & Govindaraju, 2010). The goal is to interpret the video data to identify individuals, detect ADLs and give more context to item interaction. While these tools are often very good at meeting these goals, they bear the overhead of expensive cameras and the privacy concerns of the residents. Asking individuals to have 24 hour video monitoring in the homes can be difficult. While some may be willing to accept such an intrusion, many others will not (Demiris, Hensel, Skubic, & Rantz, 2008; Klasnja, Consolvo, Choudhury, Beckwith, & Hightower, 2009).

The last solution, doing Entity Detection by interpreting the sensor network data directly, strives to remove the effort of carried devices and the privacy concerns of cameras in exchange for more complexity in the tracking algorithm (Woodman & Harle, 2008; Srinivasan, Stankovic, & Whitehouse, 2010). Many smart homes are very sensor rich. By exploiting the physical locality of the sensors with the timing and general behavior of the residents, tools can be developed to determine how many residents there are and attribute events accordingly. This approach is a much more classical artificial intelligence one, and one that will likely get a probabilistic result. Whether or not it is good enough to support the other tools, such as ADL detection, is the question.

The researchers at Washington State University's Center for Advanced Studies in Adaptive Systems (CASAS) have built a set of smart home testbeds to support research into assistive care technologies. After working with the systems and the residents it was hypothesized that an algorithm could be devised to take the full event stream from anonymous residents and exploit the spatial and temporal features to make a tracking system without a carried device or rich sensors such as cameras. This approach was chosen from the outset because of known privacy and acceptance issues with smart home monitoring systems. People are often wary of having a monitoring system in their home, especially older adults who are still living independently. By working with a system that does not require cameras, microphones or a carried wireless device, more people are accepting of having such a system in their home.

This work introduces two algorithms that would be considered entity detection and tracking tools. They are used to divide the events generated by the sensor system into different sets. Each set represents a person currently in the space, and the events they caused on the sensor network. These sets can then be used to identify individuals, detect ADLs and give a much better sense of the behaviors occurring within the smart home. The result is a tracking system that uses passive and unobtrusive sensors to track people as they go about their day within the smart home space.

2. SENSOR PLATFORM AND DATA

The Center for Advanced Studies in Artificial Systems has constructed a number of smart home testbeds. These testbeds are used to record sensor information from the activities of the residents, both in scripted and unscripted situations. The

testbeds were designed to support the detection of resident activities and track individuals in a passive manner. Unto these ends, a number of sensor types have been introduced:

1. Passive Infra-Red (PIR) motion detectors
2. Temperature sensors
3. Power meters
4. Door open/close sensors
5. Item presence platforms
6. Light switch monitors
7. Water flow meters
8. Phone use

The primary role of these sensors is to aid in ADL detection. Out of these sensors only the PIR motion detectors are used in this work for tracking and localization of residents. The rest of the sensors have been found to have a marginal benefit for this purpose. The PIR sensors are commodity off the shelf home security sensors that have been modified with a custom built communications daughter board dubbed the Lentil Board. This daughter board senses a change in the sensor relay state, i.e.: ON vs. OFF, and transmits the change to a Dallas 1-wire bus to be logged by a host computer.

These PIR sensors come in two configurations. The first is an area sensor that is placed in a fairly common home security position. These sensors have a field of view that covers most of an entire room and are used to measure occupancy of the space. The second, and more common type, is a downward facing unit that had had its view occluded to only be able to see about 4'x4' of the floor below it. These second PIR sensors give a much better sense of the location of motion within the space.

These kinds of PIR sensors are used quite often for smart home implementations. They're inexpensive, robust and accepted by most residents. During the initial design phases of the CASAS project, it was determined that high fidelity sensors, such as cameras, raise significant privacy concerns. When using these low fidelity platforms and more intelligent algorithms, the residents have been very accepting of being monitored by such systems. During several of the in-home deployments of CASAS testbeds the residents expressed significant concerns over having such a system watching them full time. By showing them the very simple form of the data gathered and the simple visualizations that can be created their initial concerns have been assuaged.

For the purposes of the algorithms used in this work only the downward facing sensors are used for the tracking of individuals. The area sensors give a much too general sense of a resident's location for any kind of precise locality. Normally a PIR security sensor is only used to say someone is in the room, which is enough for intrusion detection. These smart home systems need a much finer-grained tool where an event means someone is within this small area. The more information that can be derived about locality the better.

The events created by the CASAS testbed are very simple. They come in the form of a four tuple:

1. Date
2. Time
3. Location
4. Message

The date and time are the time the event occurred, locally to the testbed. The location value is a named physical spot within the testbed, not an absolute coordinate. By abstracting the serial number of a device from the physical location individual devices may be changed out in the face of hardware failure without impacting the running algorithms. Lastly, the message field is an arbitrary string. For most devices, such as PIR sensors, it is a binary state with either "ON" or "OFF". Other more complicated sensors, such as temperature, power meters and water flow sensors, put a number value or a description of their state in this field.

By leveraging a platform that generates simple and discrete events, the total size of the data sets created are smaller than approaches that use more complex sensor sources such as video or wearable sensors. There is also significantly less pre-processing to do to interpret the data for later classification. For example, to determine resident location using a camera a number of image processing techniques have to be applied first. These techniques can take a noticeable amount of computational resources and induce additional noise that later algorithms need to account for. The CASAS sensor platform and event model make for very clean data to be used by artificial intelligence algorithms.

3. CASAS TESTBEDS

In this work two different CASAS testbeds were used. In both locations people live, work, and perform daily activities without external guidance or scripting. The Tokyo testbed shown in Figure 1 is located in a WSU Electrical Engineering and Computer Science (EECS) department lab. The room is 12.2m x 10.9m, and is used by the CASAS graduate students as their main work area. Within the room there are a number of separate spaces containing desks, cubicle walls, a conference area, a sitting area and an inner room with engineering work tables. Anywhere from zero to 9+ people will be in the space at any given time, at nearly any hour of the day. The testbed is outfitted with PIR sensors on the ceiling, a front door open/close sensor and power switch sensors. The testbed has now been operational for nearly three years.

Tokyo has 44 motion detectors[1]. They are all placed on the ceiling pointing down at roughly 1.2m intervals. The ceiling is a dropped t-bar ceiling with a nearly uniform height of 3.0m and the sensors are attached to the t-bar surface. An example of this implementation at the Tokyo testbed can be seen in Figure 2.

Figure 1. Floor plan for WSU CASAS office testbed named Tokyo

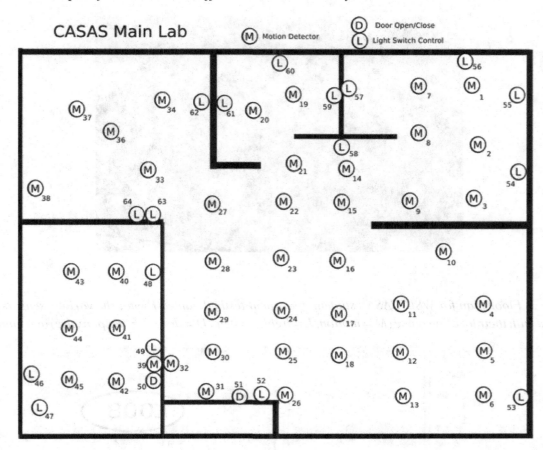

The Kyoto testbed is a three-bedroom campus apartment provided by WSU Housing. The facility has 52 motion detectors along with many other types of sensors. This testbed has been in operation for just over two years, normally with two full time undergraduate residents. In addition to day-to-day living, the space is also used for a number of smart home studies. These studies will have one or more people moving about the space in scripted or unscripted behaviors during the day.

A map with the Kyoto sensor placement is shown in Figure 3. The sensors that begin with 'M' are the motion detectors used for determining the rough location of motion with the space. The rest of the sensors monitor doors, water flow, lights, and items.

The third bedroom of this apartment is unoccupied by a permanent resident. Instead, the room is utilized as a control room by experimenters who run short controlled experiments in the Kyoto testbed. To keep the noise in the data set down, this room has a bare minimum of sensors.

4. APPROACHES

This work introduces two algorithms to track individuals in the smart home space. They both attempt to exploit the physical and temporal features of the events generated by the residents on the CASAS sensor network. The goal is to incrementally build a model of what is likely

Figure 2. Sample of PIR motion detectors, as installed in the Tokyo testbed

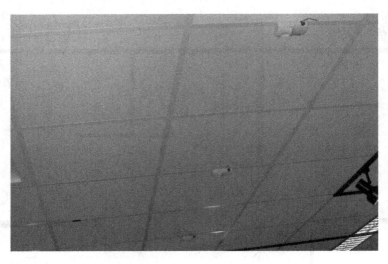

Figure 3. Floor plan for WSU CASAS student apartment testbed named Kyoto; the various sensors are labeled with their location name (M = motion, L = light, I = item, D = door, T = temperature) and number

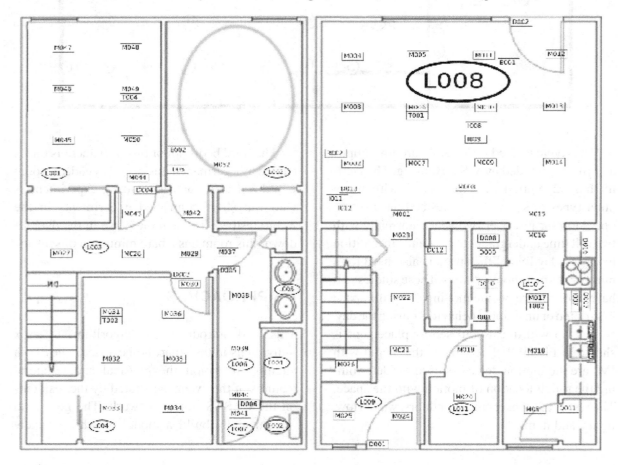

transpiring, i.e. who is moving where when, and attribute the events accordingly. Because the tools will eventually need to operate in real time, they take events in order and should be able to classify them quickly. This classification would then be used by other tools, such as ADL detectors, to more accurately describe the current activities.

In both tools it was determined that some terminology had to be defined. The researchers use the term 'entity' within the models to represent an individual. This is because not every entity in the model represents a person. Most often they are people, but the studies have included smart home installations with cats, dogs and even robots that cause events. By using the term entity, it allows for a wider understanding of how complex living spaces can be.

The two algorithms are similar in many ways, as the evaluation of one led to the creation of the other. The first algorithm is a rule-based tool. It uses a set of simple rules combined with a graph of all possible routes between sensor locations to track individuals. This tool is dubbed 'GR/ED', which stands for Graph and Rule based Entity Detector. The initial results for the GR/ED were promising, but the tool fell down in more complex social situations as well as in poor sensor network environments. The GR/ED is introduced and explored in more depth in section 4.2.

As a means to exploit the available data and create a better tool, a second tool based on Bayesian Updating was created. By using a corpus of training data annotated with the number of residents, a probabilistic transition matrix is built and used to update the world model. This tool is dubbed the 'BUG/ED', which stands for the Bayesian Updating Graph based Entity Detector. By leveraging a probabilistic model, the system is able to handle significantly more issues with the sensor network and perform marginally better in the face of more complex resident behaviors. With these additional successes, the BUG/ED was also tested for its efficacy at improving the performance of a Bayesian

Classifier for doing ADL detection. The BUG/ED is discussed in more detail in section 4.3.

4.1. Annotated Data

To use both algorithms two corpora of data were created. A subset of the stored events for both the Tokyo and Kyoto testbeds were taken and annotated by humans. The humans were taught to watch the events as they were replayed using a visualization tool and log the current number of residents in the testbed. This value representing the current occupancy could then be used to determine how accurate the tracking tools were, and in the case of the BUG/ED it was also used to train the transition probability matrix.

The Tokyo data set represents sensor events that were generated while faculty, students, and staff performed daily working routines in the lab over a course of 59 days. To train the algorithm, the data was manually inspected by a person and every event annotated with the current number of residents in the space. In total this made for 209,966 motion sensor events, with a mean of 86.84 events and a standard deviation of 201.11 events per resident instance. The resident count ranged from zero to more than nine during this data gathering window.

Once the testbed had more than six to seven people in it, the annotators noted that there was little available information to identify what was happening in the space. This was anecdotal evidence for the limited resolution of the testbed. Adding more sensors should increase this maximum detectable occupancy.

The Kyoto data was taken from 21 days of the Kyoto testbed. This made for 231,044 motion sensor events, with a mean of 603.67 events and a standard deviation of 843.17 events per resident instance. Again, the sample data was inspected by a person and annotated with the number of people currently in the space. In this set, the number of residents ranged from zero to five and the annotators noted a marked decrease in their ability to interpret individuals' movements as the occupancy reached about four residents.

4.2. GR/ED: Graph and Rule-Based Algorithm

The GR/ED algorithm was designed to use the order of events to incrementally track individuals in the CASAS testbed. The core idea is that entities will most likely trip sensors as they cross from one location to another, and multiple entities will often be separated by one or more sensors as they go about their day.

The "graph" part of the tool is based around the physical locations of the sensors within the testbed. The two CASAS testbeds used in this work

are shown in Figures 4 and 5. These graphs are made up of only the downward facing PIR motion detectors, which are laid out to cover most of the floor space. Since the sensors are placed to cover the space fairly well, people walking around have an obvious and complete chain of events from one place to another. The graph that represents a given space has vertexes representing the sensors themselves and edges that represent the possible connections between those vertexes.

The rule-based part of GR/ED is a simple set of logical rules for creating, destroying, and moving entities within the model based on the evidence given by the event series. The first rule is for creating a new entity. With this rule, if an "ON" event occurs at a location with no adjacent entities, a new entity is created. This theoretically means

Figure 4. Graph of sensor locations for the Tokyo testbed

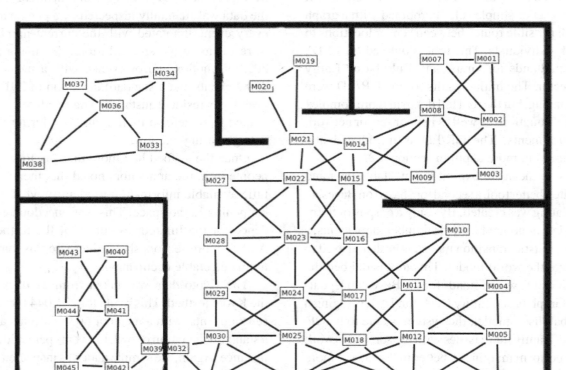

Figure 5. Graph of sensor locations for the Kyoto testbed

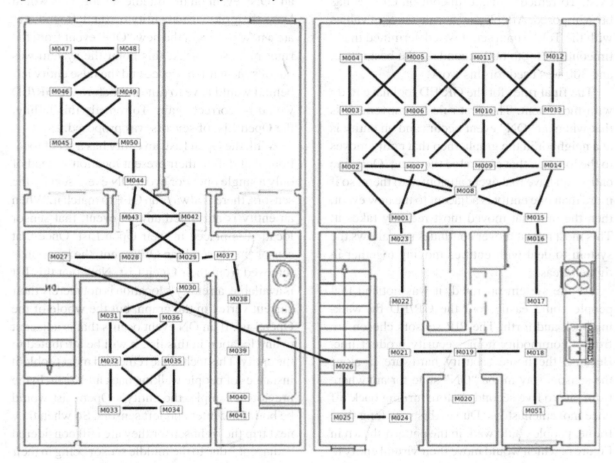

that this event was caused by a heretofore unseen entity. They could have either entered the space, or have been shadowing another one of the residents and only just then been separated enough to have noticed as a separate entity.

The second rule is for destroying entities. An entity is destroyed from the model under two circumstances. First is when they have been determined to leave the sensor network. In the case of the CASAS system, this is when an entity moves to the sensor most adjacent to the exit. Since there is no hardware available to easily determine whether someone has moved through the doorways, it can be assumed that moving next to the door is an exit.

The second way an entity can be destroyed is when they fail to generate new events for a period of time. If the model has an entity that does not actually exist, then it must have a means to recover. Since the PIR sensors do not provide data if an entity does not move, then it becomes difficult to determine if they are still in a given location, or if they have moved away without triggering events. This kind of movement can either occur due to a flaw in the sensor network, or if two entities move to the same location followed by moving together across the space. Since the sensors do not provide a magnitude of the size of an entity, it is easy for multiple people to move as a group and leave old entities in the model that no longer exist. To remedy this, a timeout on entities has been imposed. After trying a wide range of values with the Tokyo data set, it was determined that a timeout of 300 to 600 seconds is the best range, and 300 was used for this work.

The final rules for the GR/ED tool have to do with movement. The first rule for movement is that when an "ON" event occurs and an entity is at a neighbor in the graph, then that entity moves to the location that generated the event. Only one entity can have that event attributed to them, so if more than one entity is adjacent to the new event, then the one that moved most recently takes it. This most recent mover continues rule allows the system to deal with entities moving together in tighter areas.

As the system operated, it was noticed that people could easily fool the GR/ED by walking back and forth. The PIR sensors chosen are from a commodity home security product line. Because the home security hardware is slow, the sensors stay in the "ON" state for anywhere from one to five seconds before turning back off once movement stops. Due to this very long time frame, people could walk in the pattern shown in Figure 6, which would move their virtual entity to the node on the left, but the sensor in the middle would stay on long enough that they would then move to the sensor on the right without causing

Figure 6. Example of movement that breaks the simple GR/ED algorithm

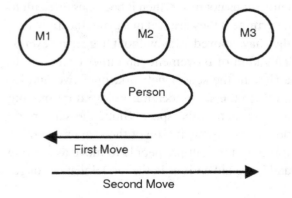

an "ON" event on the middle sensor. This would leave their old virtual entity on the left, and create a new one from the new "ON" event from the right most sensor. At this point the system was out of sync with the space and the false entity left behind would have to time out before the GR/ED would be correct again. To remedy this failing, the Open List of sensors was proposed.

With the Open List, an entity has a set of locations that define their present location instead of only a single one. For every ON event sent by the sensors, there is always an OFF to match it. When an entity is attributed an ON event, that sensor location is placed in their Open List. Once that sensor finally sends an OFF event, the location is removed from their Open List. Now that this list is available, an entity's location is not merely their current vertex in the graph, but the whole of the Open List. If an ON event occurs that is adjacent to any location in this list, it will be attributed to the entity. This technique remedied most problem instances of people walking back and forth. In the previous example, the entity's Open List would be both the center and left sensors. So when they next trip the right sensor they are still considered "adjacent," due to the middle sensor being in their Open List, and would properly be attributed that new event from the right sensor.

Each entity in the model has a list of locations that it has visited in the past. The ordered list of these locations may be used to build a tracklet for the resident. Alternatively, the current number of entities in the GR/ED model is the estimated occupancy of the space.

The resulting system was efficient and operated in near real time, making it feasible for real-world smart home implementations. As an added advantage it takes no training data to operate, only the graph of possible routes between sensor locations. This would allow the GR/ED to be deployed and started once the layout of the sensors is known without having to wait for any kind of annotated training data to be made available.

4.2.1. Testing the GR/ED

The GR/ED tool was tested for accuracy at counting the current number of residents using both the Tokyo and Kyoto data sets. The tool was evaluated using 10-fold cross validation, divided by days. This validation was run 30 times to provide variance for significance values. Once the data sets were run through the tool, the resultant guesses were compared to the human annotated ground truth. The results could then be inspected for total number of event correct, as well as total length of time correct.

For a form of baseline comparison, a weighted random classifier was trained and tested on the same data. The weighted random algorithm was also run 30 times to provide variance.

4.2.2. Results for GR/ED

GR/ED was accurate with one resident as expected, but rapidly fell to a lower rate as the number of residents increased. In Figure 7, the accuracy by number of events on the Tokyo data set is shown.

Note that as the resident count increased the accuracy declined, though the GR/ED algorithm was always significantly better than a weighted random guess.

Since the GR/ED tool cannot tell the difference between a single or multiple residents at a given location, while the annotators can, it is often too low in its estimations. Additionally, it can be too high if an entity is a false positive until it times out. Overall, the GR/ED algorithm achieved an overall accuracy of 72.2% with a standard deviation of 25.21% by counting events and an accuracy of 88.9% with a standard deviation of 12.8% for the total time represented by the data set.

The Kyoto data set truly showed the flaws in the GR/ED algorithm. This testbed has significantly more sensor error. People are able to move past sensors in many more places without tripping intermediate sensors. This quickly leads to many false entities being created in the model and a marked reduction in accuracy. Overall, the GR/ED had an accuracy of 16% measured by number of correctly-labeled events and 45% for total correctly-labeled time on the Kyoto data set.

Figure 7. Accuracy by occupancy count for the GR/ED tool on the Tokyo data set; the error bars show three standard deviations

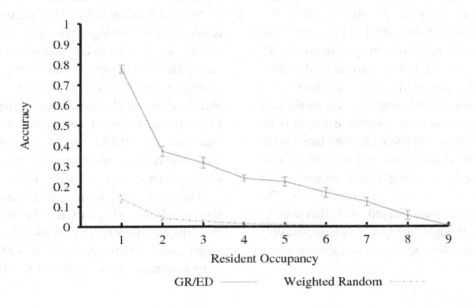

These low accuracies placed it well within range of a weighted random guess, so further evaluation on the Kyoto data set was abandoned.

The GR/ED tool has the advantage of not requiring any training data, only the graph itself. If the sensor locations can be determined at installation time, or automatically through some means, then this tool can be used with a new smart home installation quickly. Depending upon the needs of the other tools within the system, it may be sufficient for the smart home application.

Because the graph used by the GR/ED is so rigid, it was determined that a more probabilistic model might be a better solution. Instead of relying on a human-created set of equal and fixed connections between locations, perhaps a graph of likely connection as derived from the annotated data might serve better. This lead to the application of Bayesian Updating and the creation of the BUG/ED tool.

4.3. BUG/ED: Bayesian Updating Graph

After looking through various algorithms, it was determined that a Bayesian Updating algorithm might be a good choice for a successor to the GR/ED tool. Bayesian Updating is a probabilistic strategy where new evidence provided is used to update the guess at the model of the world. The Bayesian Updating Graph Entity Detector (BUG/ED) proposed here takes the current model of the smart home space, with respect to the current resident locations, and combines it with the new evidence in the form of a sensor event to build the most likely world model for the latest state. The behavior is similar in many ways to the GR/ED, but instead of a simple and uniform graph it has a transition matrix of probabilities. The matrix can also be augmented with other sources of evidence, though the algorithm here was only provided sensor location to sensor location transition likelihoods.

The biggest advantage of the BUG/ED over the GR/ED is handling failures of the sensor network. Often a person will bypass a sensor in the graph, which caused an immediate problem for the GR/ED tool. It would end up creating a new entity in the model, and abandon the old one improperly. With the BUG/ED, the transition matrix will normally have a likelihood of transition between those two more distant sensors and will often properly move its entity, even if the person it represents skips sensors occasionally. This ability alone increased the robustness of the system in day to day operation.

4.3.1. Training the BUG/ED Probability Matrix

With Bayesian Updating, there must be some corpus of information for the algorithm to use in estimating the conditional and joint probabilities. Obtaining or generating that corpus is up to the implementation and domain. The data annotated by humans for the *Tokyo* and *Kyoto* testbeds specifying the number of current residents was used to train the BUG/ED transition matrix. This training process is done before operation of the BUG/ED can begin and resembles the GR/ED algorithm with a very important addition.

Since the annotated data has the true count of residents, the training algorithm can make use of that key data for determining when residents entered and left the space. The training algorithm takes the events from the training data one at a time and incrementally builds a model of the residents' locations and transitions between sensor locations, much like the GR/ED. The key difference is that it uses the resident count from the training data to decide when to create, destroy, or move entities.

The training algorithm also makes use of the same graph utilized by the GR/ED tool, but only for counting hop count between sensor locations. This graph has one addition for the BUG/ED algorithm, a virtual sensor location called "OUTSIDE." This

OUTSIDE location represents all of the universe not monitored by the smart home sensors. It is directly connected via an edge in the graph to any sensor at an exit to the smart home, such as sensors next to the front and back doors. Entities are also moved from OUTSIDE when they are created, and to OUTSIDE when removed. The graph is used in determining which entity is closest to the OUTSIDE location, or which entity is closest to an event that just occurred.

The training algorithm will either create, destroy, or move entities by looking at whether the resident count went up, down or stayed the same between events. If the count goes up, a new entity is created at that location by moving them from the virtual location OUTSIDE to the location of the event. If the count goes down, the entity closest to the exit is immediately moved to the virtual location OUTSIDE. If the count stays the same, the closest entity to the event on the graph is moved there.

Every time an entity is created, destroyed or moved, that transition from one location to another is added to a matrix. The matrix represents the number of times entities transitioned between locations, and is the source of probabilities during the operation of the BUG/ED algorithm on new data. The length of time an entity resides at a given sensor location is also kept. This set of time lengths is used to determine dynamic timeouts for entities, which will be discussed in greater depth later.

4.3.2. Noise Reduction in the BUG/ED Matrix

The training algorithm for the BUG/ED matrix is not perfect. Inspection of the results shows several instances where the model of the testbed got into a state where taking the closest entity was inappropriate. For example, when the two residents were both in the living room of the Kyoto testbed and moved upstairs together, one of the virtual entities would be moved with them

while the other was left behind. As long as the residents remained together upstairs, the single virtual entity with them would bounce back and forth between their locations. This situation would increase the likelihood of transition between two unrelated locations, but by having a large enough training set this would not normally impact the overall performance of the BUG/ED too greatly.

In some of the training data the human annotators were also incorrect in their resident count. Since that value is very important to the training phase, these bad training files would also impact the overall accuracy of the system.

To overcome these aberrant transitions between sensor locations, a flooring filter was applied to the transition probability matrix. Any transition likelihood below the threshold would be changed to the lowest probability. Setting a flooring value was seen to have a profound effect on the behavior of the system. If too many bad connections were left in, by setting it too low, then the BUG/ED would have too little evidence to create new entities as people entered the space. Alternatively, if it was set too high then too many entities would end up being created. For each data set, the value to floor with was experimentally derived. In future work, a proper outlier detection algorithm for each sensor location will replace this fixed number.

An additional noise reduction tool was implemented to remove training data that was too complex for good use. This was a maximum occupancy limit on the training data. As the number of residents increases within a space, it becomes more and more difficult to determine how many are truly there. This limit is a factor of the sensor density and how mobile the residents are. It was noted by the annotators that once more than five or six people were in the Tokyo testbed, it was nearly impossible to keep their locations perfectly tracked. At that juncture, the annotators watched the entrance for people entering and leaving more than individual events anywhere in the space. Since the training algorithm to build the BUG/ED transition matrix is a simple one, a ceiling value on the number of occupants in the space was implemented. If the training data exceeded that number, it was thrown out. Between removing very unlikely connections and not using training data with too many residents, the BUG/ED tool started to perform much better in day to day use, and the overall accuracy of the system improved.

4.3.3. Dynamic Timeouts in the BUG/ED

In the GR/ED tool, a flat timeout for entities was enforced. This was set at 300 seconds, a figure experimentally derived by running the GR/ED tool on the data repeatedly with different timeout values. The overall accuracy at determining the number of residents was compared for each timeout. The best value of 300 seconds was taken for future work with the tool. This flat timeout of 300 seconds is the default used by the BUG/ED as well, though it is supplanted by the dynamic timeout algorithm described below.

It was noted by the residents that the GR/ED would timeout most often when people sat and worked in a location for a period without moving enough to cause sensor events. Because the training algorithm for the BUG/ED is stateful and remembers an entity's location indefinitely until they move, it could be used to find a more appropriate timeout for every sensor location. It was hypothesized that by making a dynamic timeout system that utilizes the training data, the BUG/ED would be improved when handling situations where entities remain still for long periods of time.

As the BUG/ED transition probability matrix is being trained, the length of total time an entity spends on a given sensor is kept. Once the data has all been used for training, these lists of times are used to calculate a customized timeout value for each sensor location. The mean plus three standard deviations (to capture 99% of all occurrences) of the time lengths in a sensor's list was used for the timeout value at every given location.

Manual inspection of the customized timeouts largely conformed to the expected pattern. Areas such as hallways and kitchens had shorter timeout values, while desks, beds, and couches ended up with longer timeouts. This was not always true, but the flaws in the timeout calculations were results of flaws in the simple training rules used to build the transition probability matrix, and not the timeout calculation algorithm.

4.3.4. BUG/ED Bayesian Updating

During operation of the BUG/ED a model of the current entity locations is maintained. This model is modified by motion events with an "ON" message arriving. The only two things that may occur are either an existing entity is moved to the location of the event, or a new entity is created.

The likelihood that an entity e of all existing entities E has moved to the sensor location s_k of the sensor that fired from the entity's old location e_{sk-1} is calculated using Bayes' Rule in Equation 1.

$$\arg \max_{e \in E} P\left(e|s_k\right) = \frac{P\left(s_k|e_{sk-1}\right) P\left(e\right)}{P\left(s_k\right)} \qquad (1)$$

The value of $P(s_k|e_{sk-1})$ is taken from the probability transition matrix. This is the likelihood that the entity transitions from their current location to where the latest sensor event is located based upon the historical training data. If the transition never occurred in the training data, then it was given a very small minimum value based on the smallest existing value in the transition matrix.

The factor $P(e)$ is considered the same for all entities, as they all have an equal likelihood of moving at any given time. This value could be modified with information about the likely direction, speed or likelihood of movement based on training information and become a serious factor in future versions of the BUG/ED.

The last value in the denominator of $P(s_k)$ is the same for all entities as it is the probability that the given sensor fired. Since this is a constant for all entities being compared, it is only a scaling factor.

Of the existing entities, the one with the highest likelihood (P_{move}) of making the transition to the sensor that fired is chosen to move in the model. This likelihood is compared to a threshold of the probability to create a new entity in the model instead of moving an existing one (P_{create}). If ($P_{move} < P_{create}$), then a new entity is initialized at s_k and the number of active entities in the model increases by one. Otherwise, the most likely entity to move has its tracklet of events increased by adding the most recent event and its location is updated to s_k.

At this juncture the BUG/ED has an updated model from the old model with the new evidence from the latest event. These updates reflect the most likely series of events based on the historical training data.

4.3.5. Testing the BUG/ED

The BUG/ED was tested using the same two data sets as the GR/ED tool. Because the BUG/ED requires training data, a 3-fold cross validation system was implemented. In this case, 2/3 of the available days were used to train the transition matrix, and the last 1/3 was for testing. The days were randomly selected and the model was reset with each new day when testing.

The overall accuracy value was calculated by counting the number of events where the BUG/ED was correct in the current number of residents. The difference between the true value and the current guess by the tool was also calculated to give a sense of how far off the model was from the ground truth. Since this is a probabilistic model, some error is to be expected. Depending upon the final use of the tools, having a roughly accurate guess might be sufficient for the smart home system's needs.

4.3.6. Results of the BUG/ED

The BUG/ED performed better than the GR/ED tool on these data sets. It was noted by researchers watching the BUG/ED operate in real time that it felt more 'stable'. Indeed, the BUG/ED failed less often in the face of skipping sensors and timed out less often when people stayed in one place for a period of time. These results were quantified by higher accuracy rates and measurable benefits to the ADL detection tools.

As a baseline comparison, the BUG/ED and GR/ED tools were also compared against a Weighted Random classifier. This classifier was weighted by the occupancy counts and used to guess the current occupancy at every event. The tool was run 30 times for each data set and its variation used to determine significance.

The BUG/ED tool's overall accuracy improved over that of the GR/ED on both data sets. It was a significant improvement on the Kyoto data, mostly due to its ability to handle missed sensors as people moved about. Overall, the BUG/ED classifies 44% of the events correctly, which accounts for 85% of the total time on the Tokyo data set. Where it improves over the GR/ED tool is when there are more people occupying the space. In Figure 8, the accuracies for 2, 3, and 4 residents are noticeably higher than in Figure 7, which showed the GR/ED results for the same data. This new robustness in the face of more residents attests to the efficacy of the BUG/ED approach.

Where the BUG/ED truly performed much better was on the Kyoto data set. While the GR/ED tool routinely failed as people traversed the space, the BUG/ED would much more often track them correctly. In Figure 9, it shows that in the most common state of two residents, the tool performs perfectly accurately just over 60% of the time. Overall, the BUG/ED classified 59% of the events and 67% of the total time for the Kyoto data set correct. This was significantly better than the GR/ED tool on this data set.

Figure 8. Accuracy by occupancy count for the tools on the Tokyo data set; the error bars show two standard deviations from the mean

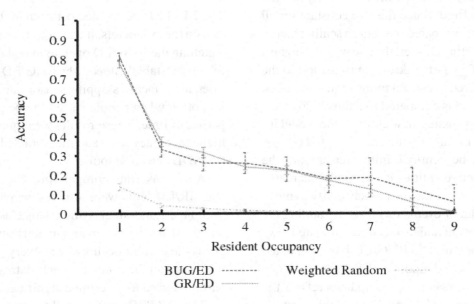

These improvements in behavior and accuracy attest to using a probabilistic model for decision making in this kind of tracking system. There are too many uncertainties with sensor placement, resident behavior and system configuration to have a purely rule based system operate well.

Figure 9. Accuracy by occupancy count for the tools on the Kyoto data set; the error bars show two standard deviations from the mean

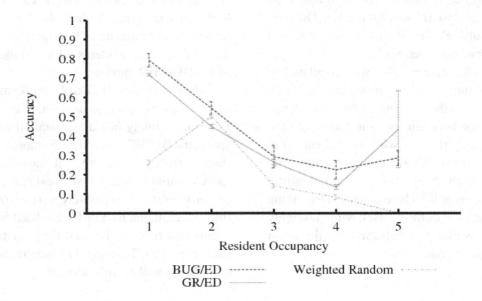

4.3.7. Application of BUG/ED to Activity Recognition

Many of the applications of smart environments that have been explored, such as health monitoring, health assistance, context-aware services, and automation, rely upon identifying the activities that residents are performing. Activity recognition is not an untapped area of research and the number of algorithms that have been used to learn activity models varies almost as greatly as the types of sensor data that have been employed for this task. Some of the most commonly used approaches are naïve Bayes classifiers, decision trees, Markov models, and conditional random fields (Cook & Schmitter-Edgecombe, 2009; Naeem & Bigham, 2009; Singla, Cook, & Schmitter-Edgecombe, 2010).

While activity recognition accuracy has become more reliable in recent years, most existing approaches are applied to situations in which a single resident is in the space performing activities. Recognition accuracy significantly degrades when multiple residents are in the same space. We hypothesize that this accuracy can be improved if the data is separated into multiple streams, one for each resident, or if each event is labeled with the corresponding resident identifier.

To validate this hypothesis, we apply the BUG/ED algorithm to data collected in the Kyoto apartment while two residents lived there and performed normal daily routines. The data used for this experiment actually represents different time frames, different residents, and different activities than were used to train the BUG/ED graph. Attributes that describe these three data sets are shown in Table 1. The activities included in this data set include, but were not limited to, sleeping, eating, cleaning, watching TV, toileting, cooking and showering. None of the activity was scripted and the annotation was done with the help of the residents themselves for accuracy.

Table 2 summarizes the performance of the activity recognition algorithm for each data set

Table 1. Attributes of the three tested Kyoto data sets

	Months	Residents	Activities
Set 1	2	2	12
Set 2	2	2	13
Set 3	5	2	25

Table 2. Before and after ADL detection accuracies when adding BUG/ED tracking information to Kyoto data

	Without BUG/ED	With BUG/ED
Set 1	42%	40%
Set 2	63%	88%
Set 3	54%	63%
Overall	56%	67%

with and without entity labeling using BUG/ED. As is shown in this table, the accuracy of activity recognition generally improves when entity detection and tracking are employed.

To demonstrate that the BUG/ED strategy is useful in further smart home tools, it was used to annotate three new sets of Kyoto data. That data was then used to train a naïve Bayesian ADL detector. The results with and without the BUG/ED tracking information were compared and summarized in Table 2.

These three data sets are annotated for 11 different ADLs in an unscripted environment. There are two residents, though one or even more than two might be present at any given time. The data sets cover nearly a full calendar year in total and run all day every day. The overall improvement to complex ADL detection was just over 10%.

5. CONCLUSION

In this work two different, though similar, tracking tools were introduced and evaluated. The first uses a graph of the sensor network in a smart home environment and a set of rules to determine the current location and history for individuals. The second uses a history of resident occupancy information to build a set of probabilities to be used by a Bayesian Updating tool for tracking residents. Both tools have benefits and negatives, though overall the probabilistic model provided by the BUG/ED performed better, especially in an environment with poor sensor layout.

There will be places for all kinds of tracking systems in smart home technologies. Choosing the right one for the needs of residents will be important for the continued success of smart homes in multi-resident situations. Continued research into passive tracking systems should improve upon these kinds of tools, allowing smart homes to handle ever more complex behaviors and numbers of residents.

6. FUTURE WORK

Both of the tools presented here offer chances for improvement. The BUG/ED especially has opportunities for continued success. First would be a better method of garnering the transition matrix. Changing the algorithm for training the matrix, or even finding ways to reduce the amount of data needed to make a successful set of probabilities would be very beneficial. Second would be incorporating better methods of detecting an entrance or exit of individuals. This could be accomplished by taking door sensor information into account, as well as a more specific kind of sensor at the doorway to report someone entering or leaving. Finally would be an evaluation of the impact of the sensor layout itself. The current CASAS sensors are focused on detecting ADLs, but perhaps some sensors could be placed in key locations to improve the tracking ability of the system.

ACKNOWLEDGMENT

This work is supported by NSF grant IIS-0121297.

REFERENCES

Choi, J. S., Lee, H., Elmasri, R., & Engels, D. W. (2009). Localization systems using passive UHF RFID. In *Proceedings of the International Joint Conference on INC, IMS and IDC*, (pp. 1727-1732). Los Alamitos, CA: IEEE Computer Society.

Cook, D., & Schmitter-Edgecombe, M. (2009). Assessing the quality of activities in a smart environment. *Methods of Information in Medicine, 48*(5), 480–485. doi:10.3414/ME0592

Cook, D. J., & Das, S. K. (2007). How smart are our environments? An updated look at the state of the art. *Journal of Pervasive and Mobile Computing, 3*, 53–73. doi:10.1016/j.pmcj.2006.12.001

Demiris, G., Hensel, B. K., Skubic, M., & Rantz, M. (2008). Senior residents' perceived need of and preferences for smart home sensor technologies. *International Journal of Technology Assessment in Health Care, 24*, 120–124. doi:10.1017/S0266462307080154

Diaz, J. J. M., Maués, R. D. A., Soares, R. B., Nakamura, E. F., & Figueiredo, C. M. S. (2010). Bluepass: An indoor bluetooth-based localization system for mobile applications. In *Proceedings of the IEEE Symposium on Computers and Communications*, (pp. 778–783). IEEE.

Hightower, J., & Borriello, G. (2001). Location systems for ubiquitous computing. *Computer, 34*(8), 57–66. doi:10.1109/2.940014

Klasnja, P., Consolvo, S., Choudhury, T., Beckwith, R., & Hightower, J. (2009). Exploring privacy concerns about personal sensing. In *Proceedings of the International Conference on Pervasive Computing*, (pp. 176–183). Springer.

Libal, V., Ramabhadran, B., Mana, N., Pianesi, F., Chippendale, P., Lanz, O., & Potamianos, G. (2009). Multimodal classification of activities of daily living inside smart homes. *Lecture Notes in Computer Science, 5518*, 687–694. doi:10.1007/978-3-642-02481-8_103

Luo, R. C., & Chen, O. (2009). Indoor human dynamic localization and tracking based on sensory data fusion techniques. In *Proceedings of the IEEE/RSJ International Conference on Intelligent Robots and Systems*, (pp. 860–865). IEEE Press.

Menon, V., Jayaraman, B., & Govindaraju, V. (2010). Biometrics driven smart environments: Abstract framework and evaluation. *Lecture Notes in Computer Science, 5061*, 75–89. doi:10.1007/978-3-540-69293-5_8

Naeem, U., & Bigham, J. (2009a). Activity recognition in the home using a hierarchal framework with object usage data. *Journal of Ambient Intelligence and Smart Environments, 1*(4), 335–350.

Naeem, U., & Bigham, J. (2009b). Recognising activities of daily life through the usage of everyday objects around the home. In *Proceedings of the International Conference on Pervasive Computing Technologies for Healthcare*, (pp. 1–4). PervasiveHealth.

Navarro-Alvarez, E., & Siller, M. (2009). A node localization scheme for ZigBee-based sensor networks. In *Proceedings of the IEEE International Conference on Systems, Man and Cybernetics*, (pp. 728–733). IEEE.

Singla, G., Cook, D. J., & Schmitter-Edgecombe, M. (2010). Recognizing independent and joint activities among multiple residents in smart environments. *Journal of Ambient Intelligence and Humanized Computing, 1*(1), 57–63. doi:10.1007/s12652-009-0007-1

Skubic, M., Alexander, G., Popescu, M., Rantz, M., & Keller, J. (2009). A smart home application to eldercare: Current status and lessons learned. *Technology and Health Care, 17*(3), 183–201.

Srinivasan, V., Stankovic, J., & Whitehouse, K. (2010). Using height sensors for biometric identification in multi-resident homes. *Lecture Notes in Computer Science, 6030*, 337–354. doi:10.1007/978-3-642-12654-3_20

Woodman, O., & Harle, R. (2008). Pedestrian localisation for indoor environments. In *Proceedings of the International Conference on Ubiquitous Computing*, (pp. 114–123). ACM Press.

Chapter 7
Sensors for Smart Homes

Anuroop Gaddam
Massey University, New Zealand

G. Sen Gupta
Massey University, New Zealand

S. C. Mukhopadhyay
Massey University, New Zealand

ABSTRACT

Sensors are increasingly being employed to determine different activities of a person living at home. Numerous sensors can be used to obtain a variety of information. While many sensors may be used to make a system, it is important to look into the availability, cost, installation, mechanism, and performance of sensors. This chapter investigates different sensors and their usefulness in a smart home monitoring system. A smart home monitoring system provides a safe, sound, and secure living environment for elderly people. Statistics show that the population of elderly people is increasing around the world and this trend is not going to change in the near future. The authors have developed a smart home that consists of an optimum number of wireless sensors that includes current flow, water flow, and bed usage sensors. The sensors provide information that can be used for monitoring elderly people by detecting abnormal patterns in their daily activities. The system generates and sends an early warning message to the caregiver when an unforeseen abnormal condition occurs.

1. INTRODUCTION

Recent statistics indicate that the population that is 60 years or older is steadily on the rise throughout the world as is shown in Figure 1. It is estimated that by 2050 this particular group will have globally increased by over 50% (DESA, 2007). There are many people in our community who because

of age or some infirmity, or perhaps because their memory and judgment can no longer be totally relied upon, are having pressure put on them to leave their home and give up their precious independence.

Over the past century, the average life expectancy of humans has increased and has almost doubled. The maximum life span—the longest

DOI: 10.4018/978-1-4666-3682-8.ch007

Figure 1. Estimates and projections for the population aged 60 and over (Bryant, 2008)

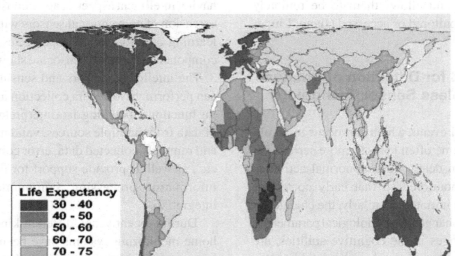

World and development regions, 1950-2050

Year	World	More developed regions	Less developed regions
1950	8.1	11.7	6.4
1975	8.5	15.5	6.1
2009	10.8	21.4	8.5
2025	14.9	27.4	12.5
2050	21.9	32.6	20.2

number of years a human being has lived—has also increased spectacularly as shown in Figure 2.

Increased life expectancy can cause an immense stress on the scarce resources available to care for the elderly. Therefore the importance of enabling the elderly to live in their own home as long as possible is crucial. However, if they prefer to live alone they do require constant monitoring so that medical help can be provided immediately in times of dire needs. The smart home concept is a promising way to improve the living

Figure 2. Life expectancy around the world (UCSC, 2010)

Life Expectancy
- 30 - 40
- 40 - 50
- 50 - 60
- 60 - 70
- 70 - 75
- 75 - 80
- No Data

standards of elderly by improving the home care facilities. The smart home monitoring system can circumvent the institutionalization of the older people and can help them live at home in safety and with independence. The smart homes target to improve comfort, quality of life and safety by monitoring mobility and physiological parameters. Modern sensors not only assist and monitor people with reduced physical functions but help to resolve the social isolation they face. They are capable of providing assistance without limiting or disturbing the resident's daily routine, giving him or her greater comfort, pleasure, and a sense of well-being. A number of smart homes have now been developed around the world by many institutes and researchers (Yamaguchi, Ogawa, Tamura, & Togawa, 1998; Eriksson & Timpka, 2002; Dengler, Awad, & Dressler, 2007). The smart home is based on smart and intelligent sensors, which are developed, fabricated and configured around a wireless network. It is expected that these smart homes will reduce escalating medical costs.

Housing Learning & Improvement network published a smart home definition offered by Interetec, which states that a smart home is "a dwelling incorporating a communications network that connects the key electrical appliances and services, and allows them to be remotely controlled, monitored or accessed (Jiang, Liu, & Yang, 2004).

1.1. A Need for Detection of Changes Using Wireless Sensor Technology

Any abnormal events which can occur to an old person in a home often leads to more serious illnesses or even death. Such abnormal activities need to be monitored so that early corrective actions can be initiated. Similarly, the changes in sleep pattern, changes in physiological parameters, and even changes in the cognitive abilities, are essential to managing the changing health status of the elderly person. So a system and method

has been developed for monitoring an individual, especially an elder person living independently, by distinguishing his/her abnormal activity from normal activities. This technological assistance and monitoring of a person in the home is achieved using a few but effective wireless sensors, which are centralized in structure and distributed around the house. These sensors capture the activity of the person and the collected data is communicated to a remote monitoring center using wireless data transfer techniques.

The system captures the activities of the resident, and stores as data points in a database. One of the aspects of this system is to distinguish between normal and unusual activity in a home. This is achieved by evaluating the new data points against the collated historical activity data present in the database.

2. CHARACTERISTICS OF SMART SENSORS FOR HOME MONITORING

A conventional sensor provides an electrical output, either a current or a voltage signal, due to the change in physical parameters. Conventional sensors are readily available in the market. In general terms smart sensors, i.e., sensing devices having intelligent aspects, can be considered as an extension of conventional sensors with advanced learning and adaptation capabilities. The basic components of a smart sensor are shown in Figure 3. The intelligent sensors and sensing networks can perform various data collection and processing functions, including data interpretation, fusion of data from multiple sources, validation of local and remotely collected data, error compensation, etc., as well as provide support for post-sensing information processing, communication and integration.

During recent years, different kinds of smart home monitoring systems have been developed by many organisations and institutions, considering the fact that there is an increasing trend in the

Figure 3. Basic architectural components of a smart sensor

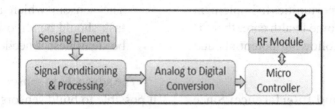

numbers of elders with chronic illnesses and disabilities (Eriksson & Timpka, 2002; Dengler, Awad, & Dressler, 2007). It has been realised that there is a need for technology which can significantly offset the decline in health and self-care abilities and enable elders, with or without disabilities, to continue to live alone in a home. The wireless sensors used for smart home monitoring of elderly should have important characteristics for effective and optimum performance. From the application point of view, the intelligent sensors can be categorized by their ability to:

- Operate in a multi-modal fashion as well as to conduct active autonomous sensing.
- Detect and respond to changes in the network environment through self-diagnostic routines, self-calibration and adaptation.
- Evaluate the validity of collected data, compare it with that obtained by other sensors and confirm the accuracy of any data variation.
- Process information using efficient feature extraction techniques.
- Incorporate particular strategies for measurements and data processing, facilitate synergy between hardware and software, improve balance between process costing and price of sensing equipment, etc.

Development of these kind of intelligent sensors have become possible and economically feasible in recent years because of rapid advancements in semiconductor fabrication technology,

development of new microelectronic devices and micro-systems (MEMS), emergence of high performance embedded computing, hardware availability of advanced communication devices and protocols, etc.

Devices which are specially developed to monitor an individual and enhance independence should use the following technologies, namely:

- **Adaptive Technology:** The technology which is used to develop devices is adaptive i.e. the system or the device can be modified with ease according to the needs of the individual, so that the device or the system performs it task more efficiently and easily, without any complexities.
- **Assistive Technology:** Implementing this kind of technology into the devices or the system, can allow an individual to perform a task he or she would otherwise be unable to do. The devices or systems which are built on this technology can increase the ease and safety with which the task can be performed.
- **Inclusive Designs:** These types of devices or systems are designed on the principle that they can be used by a wide range of people.
- **Medical Technologies:** As the name suggests, this kind of devices or systems are developed to monitor a health care environment for prevention, diagnosis, monitoring, treatment and alleviation of illness or injury.

As the advances in the sensor networking technologies open up new opportunities to implement sensor networks for in-home health care, there is a need to consider the following potentials and challenges:

- **Interoperability and Interference:** Since many sensor nodes are present in an in-home wireless sensor network, there a need to limit or avoid interference between increasingly crowded sensors and various RF devices. The home care network must provide middle ware interoperability between disparate devices, and support unique relationship among various devices such as implants and their outside controllers. In-home operations have more interference due to the walls and other obstructions. So there is a need to reduce or eliminate unwanted emissions.
- **Real Time Data Acquisition and Processing:** There is a critical need for efficient communication and processing the data over the sensor network. Some techniques which come handy for this kind of situation are event ordering, time stamping, synchronisation, and quick response in emergency situations.
- **Reliability and Robustness:** Since the sensor network is not meant for frequent maintenance and not situated in a controlled environment, these devices and other sensors must operate with good reliability, so as to provide reliable data for medical treatment and diagnosis.
- **Data Management:** There is a need for embedded real time database which stores data of interest and allows the care giver or the providers to query.
- **Data Privacy and Security:** There is a need to protect the privacy of the person who is being monitored using wireless sensors in a network. The data which are collected by the network may be sensitive.

- **Comfort and Unobtrusive Operation:** The sensors which are designed for this task should be almost invisible and should be stealthiest if needed.

The advances in sensor technology have made it possible to build sensors which are very small with cognitive capability, and easy to deploy. They still present challenges in a smart home setting. The reason is the variation of the occupants' needs and the appliances which are used by them. A rather simple solution to overcome these challenges is to install large number of sensors. Even though the system may be very efficient in identifying the lifestyle of the resident, it causes many problems. Since more sensors are added to meet these needs, the whole system becomes complicated and the task of maintaining it can become a challenge. The cost of implementation will drastically increase with the increased number of sensors.

Compared to the use of a large number of wireless sensors (Yamaguchi, Ogawa, Tamura, & Togawa, 1998; Eriksson & Timpka, 2002), the strategy to deploy a few but highly accurate inexpensive smart and cognitive sensors has significant advantages in case of home monitoring. The advantages include uniform coverage, small obtrusiveness, ease of deployment, reduced energy consumption, low maintenance costs and consequently more acceptability by the elderly community (Dengler, Awad, & Dressler, 2007).

The sensors should be positioned close to the source of a potential problem phenomenon. All sensors in the network must have a justification for their existence and purpose in the system. To achieve this, a sensor must satisfy a quantifiable and verifiable set of requirements that will demonstrate its benefit and purpose to the system. In addition, any risk to the system's performance must also be identified. Therefore, substantial benefit to the design and development process can be realized by utilizing a sensor selection methodology, specifically directed towards system performance assessment.

The sensor selection process is divided into two parts; one is evaluation module and the other is optimization module. In evaluation module, in-depth performance parameters of a particular type of sensor node or network under review are studied and the optimization module searches through the space of all possible sensor nodes for further evaluation. The process is continued until the "best" or the optimum number of sensor number is obtained. The aim of the research is to select limited number of sensors that fulfill specified performance requirements within a set of system constraints. These performance requirements are defined as the Figures of Merit (FOMs) of the system (Joshi & Boyd, 2007). The basic components to build an algorithm based on FOM are Observability, Sensor Reliability/Sensor Fault Robustness, Fault Delectability/Fault Discriminability and Cost. Therefore, it is intended to develop an intelligent technique/algorithm or a mathematical model based on the above mentioned factors, to make an efficient, simple and smart home monitoring system.

Many techniques have been developed for general optimized solution searches for many other applications, but none for in-home health monitoring. The monitoring system developed for the current work is based on the integration of different sensors with cognitive features, which have the capability of analyzing the data intelligently and transmitting the data via wireless communication. The data are collated by a central controller, which saves all data for processing as well as future use. The lifestyle of the person under care is understood by the system by collecting data and comparing it with the stored pattern and depending on the situation, the actions are defined as unusual or normal. In addition, by considering issues related with quantitative approaches over the qualitative approaches, a maximum level of fidelity available in establishing the justification for sensor selection can be achieved. The methodology is flexible enough to incorporate the best system design for home monitoring. The

methodology incorporates other metrics, such as sensor reliability, communication techniques and sensor robustness, as needed.

3. DIFFERENT SENSORS USED FOR HOME MONITORING

Smart homes have now been developed which are able to monitor elderly subjects with motor, visual, auditory or cognitive disabilities. In each case the smart home consisting of various appliances and devices which are commonly used by the resident on a daily basis. These appliances and devices have been fitted with sensors, actuators, and/or biomedical monitors to detect the activities of daily life of the resident. Some of the sensors which are predominantly used in building a smart home are discussed below.

Pressure Sensor: In many smart home applications, piezoelectric pressure sensors are generally employed. This kind of sensor uses the piezoelectric effect to measure pressure, acceleration, strain or force by converting them to an electrical signal. Kaddoura et al. (2005) has described such a system where a pressure sensor is centrally placed underneath each square foot block of the floor and is able to detect a foot step on any part of that block. The Gator Tech Smart House has a residential-grade raised floor consisting of floor tiles measuring one square foot each (Helala, et al., 2005), a sensor that covers the whole floor area would be able to locate and track the position of multiple users in a smart home. A pressure sensor is housed underneath these tiles as shown in Figure 4.

The pressure sensors have a wide range of application for smart home monitoring. They can be used for bed monitoring. Pressure sensors are placed on a regular grid under the bed mattress. Each sensor indicates a value that corresponds to the amount of pressure being exerted on it. One such device manufactured by Tactex Controls Inc, Bed Occupancy Sensor (BOS™), can be installed

Figure 4. A smart floor tile with piezoelectric pressure sensors

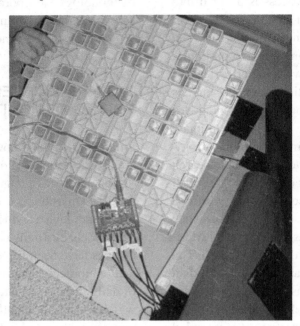

under the bed mattress to monitor the patient's condition at rest (Howell Jones, Goubran, & Knofel, 2006). These pressure mats can detect the changes in bed entry and exit patterns, thus identifying the occupants' sleep patterns and keep track of sleepless nights. The pressure sensors can be used on grab bars in the home especially in bathrooms. This grab bars can identify and monitor the entry and exit from the shower and bathtub, as well as transfers on and off the toilet seat.

Motion/Proximity Sensor: Proximity Infrared (PIR) sensors can be installed strategically in a home environment to detect the movement of the person within the home. This helps to find out the activity of a person. These sensors track the presence and motion of the resident throughout the living space by infrared motion sensors which are installed in each room. This type of sensor can also be used as a fall detection device. The values can be continuously checked via an Analogue to Digital Converter (ADC); it then packetizes the values and sends for processing.

The system with this kind of sensor can detect any abnormality in the living pattern of the resident. If a person extensively stays in one room it may indicate a problem with the resident's mobility or if he/she is wandering with sporadic changes in the direction of motion, it may indicate signs of mental anxiety or confusion. Barnes et al. (1998) used IR sensors along with magnetic switches for statistical detection of abnormal activity.

Temperature Sensors: Temperature sensors can be used in a smart home to monitor environmental temperature in each room to ensure there is proper heating and cooling of the living space. These sensors can provide information regarding stove or oven status, as well as faucet water temperature. When installed on the appliances like fridges, as show in Figure 5, the usage of the fridge can be known.

RFID Sensors: Radio Frequency Identification sensors have proved useful for detecting a variety of fine-grained activities. Patterson et al. (2005) report accuracies of around 80% for recognition of 12 activities in a kitchen instrumented with 60

Figure 5. Temperature sensor in a fridge (Laguionie, 2008)

RFID tags. A common problem of elderly people and patients with early stages of Alzheimer's or dementia is forgetfulness. They often cannot remember where they have placed commonly used objects. RFID tags can be placed on commonly misplaced objects to retrieve them at home. Tags do not require a power source of their own, but they get the energy they require from a nearby reader which they then use to transmit their designation to the reader. RFID enabled sensors can be installed at the door entrance/hall way to detect and monitor the person, and which room he/she is in. The main objective of this sensor is to detect if a person with early stages of Alzheimer's disease goes out of his/her house. RFID sensing system consisting of a series of active/passive scanners are located in the ceiling of each room, to detect persons tagged with RFID passing through the entrance of a room. This can determine who it is that is in the area. Figure 6 shows the RFID monitoring system prototype as proposed in Ho, Moh, Walker, Hamada, and Su (2005).

Switch Sensors: Magnetic switches can be used on doors throughout the home, in kitchen appliances, such as the oven, refrigerator, or dishwasher, which monitors 'open' or 'closed' status. This is useful in monitoring the entry and exit from the various rooms of the home. The MIT PlaceLab (Intille, Larson, Beudin, Nawyn, Tapia, & Kaushik, 2005) is a residential condominium, which has been designed to be an observational facility for the scientific study of people in home environments using over 300 switch sensors. The sensors are installed in nearly every part of the home ranging from switch sensors on lights, cupboards, electrical appliances to faucet and mail boxes, as shown in Figure 7. The switches can be placed around the knobs of different appliances, in order to detect the state of each of them. The data from all of these sensors is sent wirelessly to a central processing and storage unit to detect and monitor the activities of the resident.

Vibration Sensors: Accelerometers can be placed in a smart home for detecting vibrations. These can be installed on everyday objects like chairs, sofas, bed etc. to monitor the resident's movements. Impacts with the sitting furniture could represent a lack of muscular strength or control. Impacts with the floor, however, could represent the occupant losing his balance and falling, which may require immediate attention. With proper installation the vibration sensors can detect the fall/slips of the elderly person in the smart home in an efficient way.

Figure 6. RFID monitor system (Ho, Moh, Walker, Hamada, & Su, 2005)

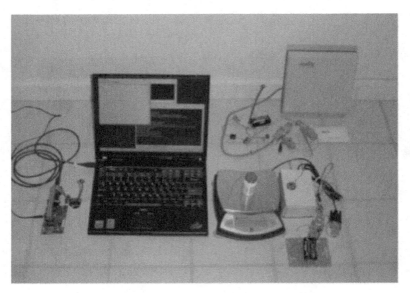

Water Flow Monitoring Sensors: Most common consumable that a household uses is water. Water is used for drinking and washing. People also use water to have a shower or bath. It is used in a toilet system and also used to clean clothes and dishes. This covers a large variety of systems in a home. The water use in the household can be monitored with the use of water monitoring sensor. Monitoring the water flow into the house will give a general overview of when water is being used in the home.

Current Sensors: Detection of the usage of electrical devices (such as the kettle and toaster) can be achieved by using current sensors as a medium between the power socket and the equipment to be monitored. The level of monitoring can vary heavily depending on each case; some people may object to a high level of monitoring and are happy with one or two simple rules such as the kettle. C. Kiluk has reported a design of an alarm system which is intended for monitoring elderly and/or handicapped person in an apartment (Kiluk,

Figure 7. Switch sensors installed in the home

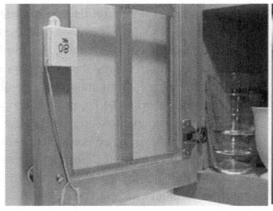

1991). The energy consumption of the apartment is measured and recorded over a period in a computer. The actual energy consumption of the apartment is compared with the expected energy consumption which is recorded in the computer to generate different degree of alarm levels.

Acoustic Sensors: Microphone arrays can be used in a smart home. They can transmit the sounds within the residence to a monitoring station for detecting any abnormality (Zheng, Goubran, El-Tanany, & Hongchi, 2005). Any abnormal noises or calls for help can be detected using this kind of sensors. It also forms a means of communication with the occupant.

Helal et al. (Helal, Mann, El-Zabadani, King, Kaddoura, & Jansen, 2005; Helal, Winkler, Lee, Kaddoura, Ran, Giraldo, Kuchibhotla, & Mann, 2003) have used ultrasonic location tracking sensors to build a smart floor for accurate location calculation of the resident in a smart home. Kidd et al. (1999) used ultrasonic sensors along with RF technology, video and floor sensors to identify patterns of the resident in a smart home. Krumm et al. (2000) and Brumitt et al. (2000) used multi-cameras, along with image analysis for detecting the resident's activities. Adami et al. (2003) developed a wrist actigraph for lifestyle monitoring and to detect the time spent in and out of bed. Yamaguchi et al. (2008) and Tamura et al. (2000) employed various sensors and magnetic switches for health monitoring and detect bed temperature, and behavior of the resident in a smart home.

4. A CASE STUDY: DESIGN OF A SMART HOME MONITORING SYSTEM

The use and the way of implementation of wireless sensor networks drastically change from one application to another. The need for in-depth study on performance parameters is vital (Chew & Gupta, 2008). While several sensors are readily available off the shelf, making them "intelligent" in the context of a specific application, such as monitoring of the elderly, is always a challenging task. For example, an intelligent wireless sensor system will not only detect the usage pattern of the daily appliances, it will have capabilities to collate the data and analyze them. Depending on the data analysis it can detect abnormality.

To achieve this we have developed and implemented a SMART component-based system by integrating various sensors communicate via standard RF protocols. The system depends on a set of selected wireless sensors and a controller which relies on inputs from the sensors...

Figure 8 shows the functional block diagram of the smart home monitoring system (Tucknott & Sorenson, 1986). The hardware components of the system are the Sensor Units, the Central Controller unit, a PC and a cellular modem.

This wireless sensor system consists of three sensors for detecting activity of electrical appliances, one sensor for bed activity, one sensor for water use and a panic button.

The selected sensors were installed to monitor a television, reading lamp, toaster, microwave oven, and bed, as shown in Figure 9.

4.1 Electrical Appliance Monitoring Unit

The electrical appliance monitoring unit is fabricated to accommodate three different electrical appliances on a single power inlet. It has the intelligence to detect which particular device is ON and for how long it is used. If an elderly person uses his/her kettle and toaster every morning to make a cup of coffee, the system could be configured to inform the family if both the kettle and the toaster are not used in the morning. The block diagram representation of the current sensor circuit is shown in Figure 10.

This sensor can be connected to general electrical appliances such as the kettle and toaster. It acts as a medium between the power socket and

Figure 8. Functional diagram of a wireless sensor network based home monitoring system

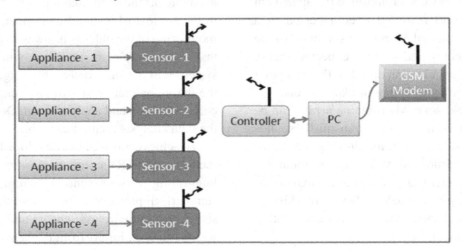

the equipment to be monitored. Installation is simple. It involves plugging in an extension cord and connecting various electrical appliances to it. Since each electrical appliance has a different power rating the input current of each appliance is different as shown in Table 1.

The current flow in the phase line of the AC mains is detected by the current transformer and a voltage signal is produced. This voltage signal from the current transformer is then passed to a precision amplifier for amplifying to a required level. The connected load can be calculated as shown in Table 1. A comparator circuit generates a transition at its output when a particular combination of appliances is turned ON. The generated transitions are fed to the port pins of the

Figure 9. Placement of sensors in a typical house

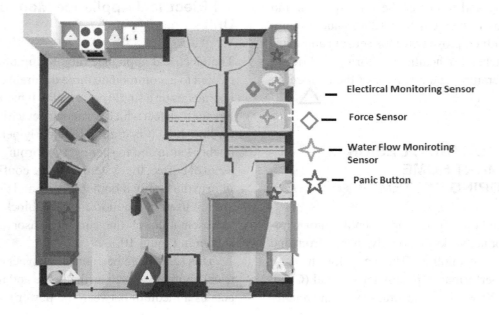

Figure 10. Block diagram representation of the current sensor circuit

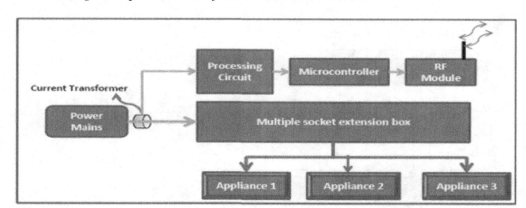

microcontroller and the status of devices is checked.

The current transformer and the associated circuitry are shown in Figure 11. The transition signals are used as external interrupts to the microcontroller to detect the type of load as well as duration. The reference voltage can be changed by changing the value of the resistors in the potential divider. The pin transitions corresponding to the load are shown in Figure 12. When a 1000W load is turned on, the port pin 1.0 of the microcontroller goes high.

The program running on the microcontroller decides which appliance is turned on and for how long. If one or more appliance is turned on, more number of port pins will go high. The intelligent program then decides which appliances are turned

on, based on the combination of the port pin transitions.

The software can be configured with many intelligent features as shown in Figure 13.

4.2. Bed Monitoring Unit

Many attempts have been made in the past to attach various sensors in a mattress to detect a person's movements and locate the position on the bed. In Gusakov (1993), a pressure sensitive sensor pad is installed on top of and across the width of a mattress. The central pressure sensitive switch indicates the presence of a patient in the centre of the bed. When a patient moves toward either edge of the bed, an edge switch is activated which generates an early warning signal indicating to attending personnel that a patient has moved from the centre of the bed to an edge and may be close to falling down from the bed if unattended. This early warning signal provides time for an attendant to reach to the patient before he or she has actually fallen down from the bed. The system prevents falls of dizzy or disoriented patients attempting to exit the bed without assistance. However, such sensor pads are expensive and add to the discomfort of the person. In 1993, Gusakov proposed a bed patient position monitor (Tekscan, 2009) which is an apparatus to monitor the position of a patient relative to a bed. The system can detect

Table 1. Experimental values of load current and output voltage for different appliances

Appliance	Sensor Output (mV)	Current Intake (A)	Calculated Load (W)
Microwave Oven	19.7	5.75	1380
Kettle	28.996	8.74	2097.6
Bed Lamp	1.08	0.23	55.2
Electrical Heater	27.86	8.32	1996.8
Toaster	26.45	7.32	1683.6

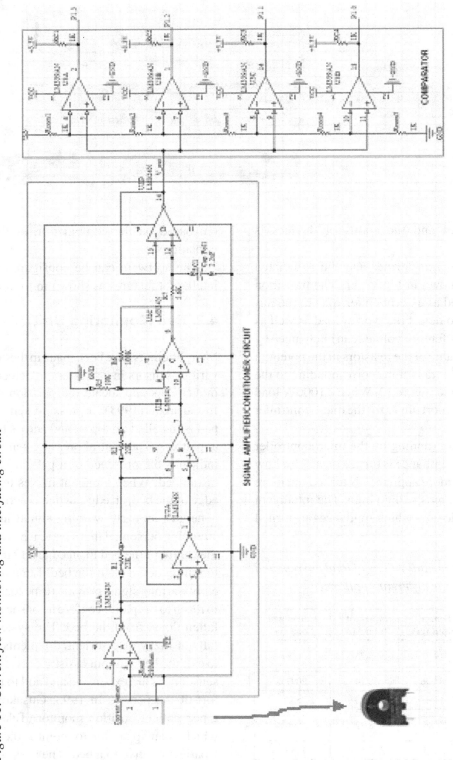

Figure 11. Current flow monitoring and interfacing circuit

Figure 12. Pin transitions corresponding to the load

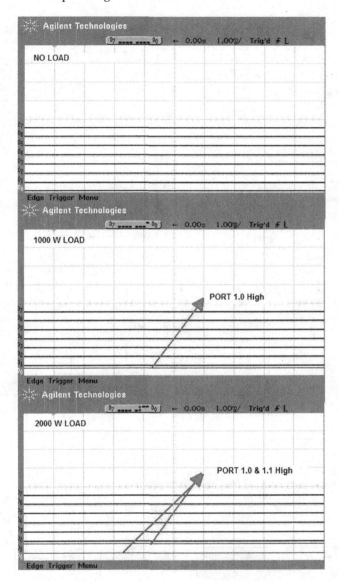

if the patient is attempting to lift himself from the bed or completely out of the bed. The apparatus uses fluid and pressure sensitive switches which makes it cumbersome to install.

We have developed an intelligent bed monitoring unit which will not only detect the usage pattern of the bed, it will have capabilities to collate the data and flag out anomalies. There are three scenarios in which the bed monitoring unit will be useful—a person sleeping beyond his usual

wakeup time, a person not in bed past his usual bed time and a person constantly moving on the bed, though lying down, indicating perhaps that the person is unwell or medically distressed.

The functional block diagram of the proposed bed-sensor sub-system is shown in Figure 14. The system consists of four sensor units; the output of each bed sensor is amplified and passed through a signal conditioning circuit to reduce noise in the signal. The analogue sensor outputs are fed to

Figure 13. Decision making flowchart of the current sensor

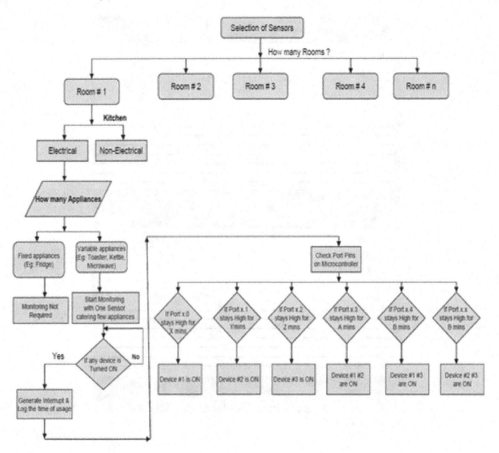

Figure 14. Functional block diagram of bed sensor system

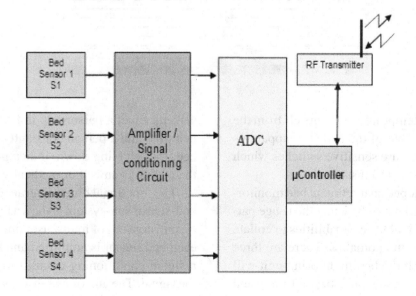

the ADC channels of the microcontroller (Silabs C8051F020). The ADC has a 12-bit resolution and 8-channel multiplexed single-ended inputs, of which four are used. The microcontroller is connected to a RF (Radio Frequency) transmitter and the data is transmitted to the central monitoring station where the inference engine runs on a PC.

The hardware sub-systems are explained in full details in the following sub-sections.

4.2.1. Force Sensor

The bed monitoring system uses the Tekscan's FlexiForce Sensors (Chew & Gupta, 2008). The FlexiForce sensor, as shown in Figure 15, uses a piezoresistive-based technology. Application of an external force to the "active sensing area" of the sensor results in a change in the resistance of the sensing element which is inversely proportional to the force applied on the sensor. The sensor characteristics are shown in Figure 3. This sensor was chosen because it is ultra-thin (0.008"), flexible, cost effective and easy to integrate.

These sensors are constructed of two layers of substrate composed of polyester film. On each layer, silver is applied for electrical contact which is then followed by a layer of pressure sensitive ink. Adhesive is then used to laminate the two layers of substrate together to form the sensor. The silver circle on top of the pressure-sensitive ink defines the "active sensing area." Silver extends from the sensing area to the connectors at the other end of the sensor forming the conductive leads. FlexiForce sensors are strategically placed underneath the bed posts to determine if a force is being exerted on the bed (confirming whether someone is lying on it). The voltage output varies linearly with the exerted force. The pressure sensor can measure up to 444 N of force (100 lbs.). To differentiate between inanimate objects and human beings, we need to calibrate the sensor unit so that the force applied by each extremity should produce a significant voltage output.

The pressure sensor basically acts like a means to detect force, as somebody lies on the bed. This will be accomplished by setting up a force-to-voltage circuit. In addition, the sensors will need to be conditioned. Once this is accomplished, the sensor's output is repeatable within 2.5%.

Some of the parameters of the force sensor are:

- The operating range of temperature is from -9°C to 60°C.
- Repeatability is +/- 2.5% of full scale (conditioned sensor when 80% force applied).
- Linearity is <+/- 5%.
- Hysteresis is <4.5% of full scale.

4.2.2. Driver Circuit

In order to get the analogue voltage signals from the sensors, an inverting operational amplifier circuit is used, as shown in Figure 16. Unfortunately, the switched capacitor voltage inverter (MAX828), which has been used to generate -5V, introduces a noise of 12 kHz at the output. A LPF (Low Pass Filter) is used to suppress the high frequency noise in the output of the amplifier. Rs is the force sensor. Figure 16 shows the circuitry for one sensor only; the same is required for the other three sensors.

In this circuit, the sensitivity of the sensor can be adjusted by changing the feedback resistance (Rf1) and/or the drive voltage (-5V); a lower value of the feedback resistance and/or drive voltage will make the sensor less sensitive, and increase its active force range.

Figure 15. Tekscan's flexi-force sensors

Figure 16. Signal processing circuit for bed sensor

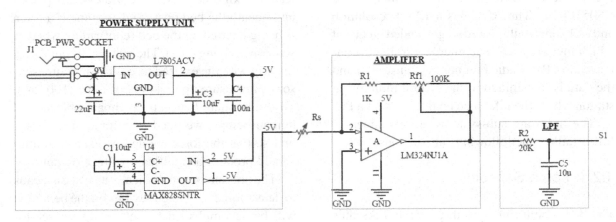

4.2.3. Analogue-to-Digital Conversion and Microcontroller

The reference voltage of the ADC converter of the microcontroller is 2.4V. Therefore the maximum output response of the sensor is made to be below or equal to 2.4V. This is done by adjusting the Rf1 potentiometer as the drive voltage is fixed at -5V. The ADC is capable of running at a sampling frequency of 100KSPS which is adequate for this application. The conversion clock frequency of the SAR (Successive Approximation Register) can be programmed to be up to 2.5 MHz.

4.2.4. Microcontroller and RF Module

The Silicon Lab C8051F020 microcontroller was chosen because of its rich resources. It has an on-board high resolution ADC with 8 multi-plexed input channels (Gaddam, Mukhopadhyay, & Gupta, 2010). The microcontroller runs off a crystal of 22.1184 MHz and is programmed in C. Digital I/O ports (port 6 and 7) are used to interface the microcontroller to the LCD module. The microcontroller has two UART (Universal Asynchronous Receiver Transmitter) modules of which one is used to interface with the RF transmitter. The UART outputs RS232 protocol serial data at TTL level; hence interfacing with

the RF module does not require any additional translator. The UART is programmed to transmit serial data at 38400 baud rate, 8-bit data, 1 stop bit and no parity.

The Flexi-Force sensors were strategically placed under the legs of the bed to determine if a force is being exerted on the bed i.e. someone is laying on the bed. The sensors were sandwiched between flat metal plates with the same diameter as the sensing part of the sensor. These plates were used to ensure that equal amount of force was distributed to every point in the sensing head of the sensor. It was also ensured that the bed is being tested on an even floor so that equal amount of force is applied on each of the legs. The sensors were calibrated to make sure that the force being exerted on the bed was from a human body rather than some inanimate object. The schematic representation of the four sensors placed under the bed is shown in Figure 17. S1, S2, S3 and S4 represent the four sensors Sensor 1, Sensor 2, Sensor 3 and Sensor 4, respectively.

The experiments to test the bed sensor system were conducted with three inhabitants, one elderly person of 74 years of age as shown in Figure 18 and around 42 kg of weight, one 5-year-old child with 20 kg of weight and one adult with 68.5 kg of weight.

Figure 17. The position of four sensors under the four legs of a bed

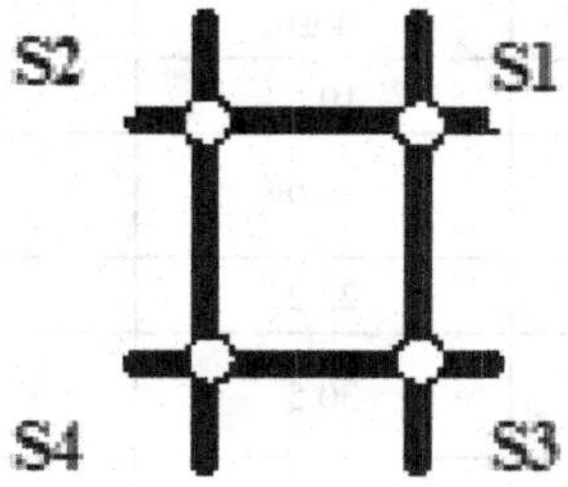

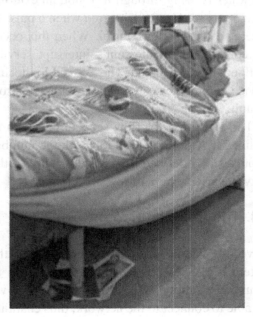

The results that we obtained from the experiment are shown in Table 2. Based on these results, under normal situation, all the four sensors read very similar weights. The sensors only measure the weight of the bed in this situation, so each sensor shows roughly one-fourth of the weight of the bed. From Table 2, it can be easily said whether the bed is occupied by an elderly or a child. At (S1, S2) side or (S3, S4), the position of the upper body or the lower torso can be detected easily by checking the difference of the sensor signals. The pair of sensors with the upper body

Figure 18. An elderly person lying on bed is being monitored

on them would show higher reading as compared to the other sensors.

$S_{avg} = (S1 + S2 + S3 + S4)/4$; Savg is the average signal.

If $(S1 + S2) > 2 * S_{avg}$; the head is at (S1, S2) side.

If $(S3 + S4) > 2 * S_{avg}$; the head is at (S3, S4) side.

If $(S1 + S3) = (S2 + S4)$; the person is sleeping on the middle of the bed.

If $(S1 + S3) > (S2 + S4)$; the person is sleeping on the right side of the bed.

If $(S1 + S3) < (S2 + S4)$; the person is sleeping on the left side of the bed.

Under normal or stable sleeping conditions all the four sensors will provide signals which are quite steady. But if a person is not having a proper sleep and constantly moving, the sensors will not provide steady signals. The signals from the sensors can be studied and conclusions can be drawn based on sensors' information to find out abnormality in a person's sleeping pattern.

4.3. Flow Sensor for Monitoring Water Usage

All homes have the need for water; people use water to have a shower/bath, it is used in a toilet system and also used to clean clothes/dishes. This covers a large variety of systems in a home, although not all of these systems are needed to be monitored. For example a dish washer and washing machine both are "turn on- walk away" appliances, therefore it doesn't actually give a good indication of whether or not the person is ok or not. These can be monitored with the current sensor anyway. Shower or bath is a concern for a user as a slip in the shower can end very badly and a bath can result in drowning if the person becomes unconscious and incapable of keeping the head above water. Installing water-flow sensors on the shower can enable us to detect if a shower is used for a longer than average period and flag a warning.

Table 2. Experimental results with a person lying on bed

Test Condition	Reading S1 (kg)	Reading S2 (kg)	Reading S3 (kg)	Reading S4 (kg)	Total Weight (kg)
Only bed	10.3	10.4	10.3	10.5	41.2
Elderly person in the middle	18.4	15.2	23.6	26.9	84.1
Elderly person on one side	19.3	16.5	26.2	22.2	84.2
Elderly person on another side	14.0	21.3	18.5	30.5	84.3
Child in the middle	13.5	14.3	16.9	17.0	61.7
Child on one side	14.6	10.5	21.6	15.1	61.8
Child on another side	12.2	13.4	13.7	22.4	61.7
Adult in the middle	18.7	20.8	36.7	33.8	110
Adult on one side	25.2	14.2	45.5	25.3	110.2
Adult on another side	13.7	22.5	25.8	48.1	110.1
Adult lying diagonally (S4-S1)	17.2	20.5	28.2	44.3	110.2
Adult lying diagonally (S3-S2)	21.5	17.4	44.8	26.5	110.2

S1: Signal from Sensor#1
S2: Signal from Sensor#2
S3: Signal from Sensor#3
S4: Signal from Sensor#4

If the system is kept running, it is vital that the situation is dealt with higher priority than an electrical device as it is less likely that a person will forget to turn the shower off.

An inline flow transducer was used as shown in Figure 19. This Flow sensor worked perfectly for the prototype outputting a square wave that increased or decreased in frequency as the flow rate increased and decreased. The sensor can be installed in many positions in the home, for example it can be placed after the hot water cylinder as this can enable us to detect water usage of appliances like dishwashers and washing machines.

The sensor itself is then connected to the microcontroller (Figure 20). Due to the sensor's current requirement of 30mA being a bit high, the sensor resistor was adjusted to bring the current down to 21mA. The flow sensor is connected to the same port, on the microcontroller, as the wireless module. This port generates external interrupt along with the UART, which is used for communication between the microcontroller and the wireless module. To enable the microcontroller to determine if the flow sensor has water flowing through it or not, an external interrupt is setup to be triggered when a pulse is generated by the flow sensor. When this occur the corresponding interrupt's interrupt service routine will be executed. The Water Monitoring Device communicates wirelessly with a controller unit.

The algorithm for flow sensing is shown in Figure 21. A timer is used to check the number of pulses in a defined time window and set the activity variable high or low accordingly.

4.4. The Cellular Modem

Wavecom Wismo cellular modem used in the system is a GSM cellular modem as shown in Figure 22. Simply by inserting a SIM card we are able to connect to the network, thus enabling

Figure 19. Core components of the flow sensor unit

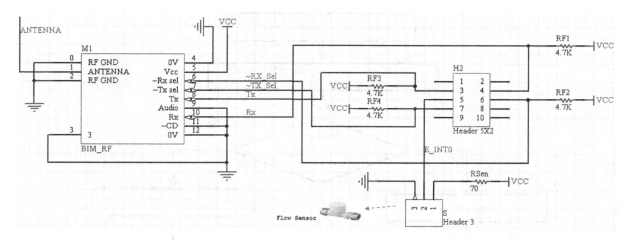

Figure 20. Fabricated prototype of a flow sensor unit (Gaddam, Mukhopadhyay, & Gupta, 2008)

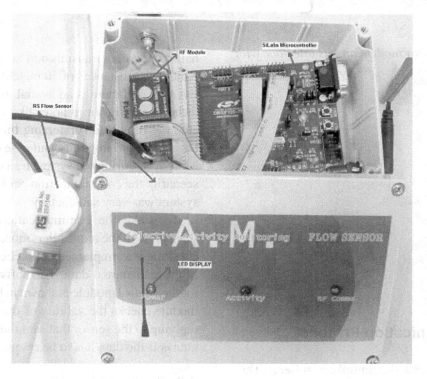

the system to send SMS to any cell phone around the world. The cellular modem comes with its own power supply and only has one connection to the personal computer which is completely independent of the controller's connection. The cellular modem receives commands from the personal computer through a RS232 interface. In the future design, the modem will be integrated inside the controller unit.

Figure 21. Algorithm for flow detection

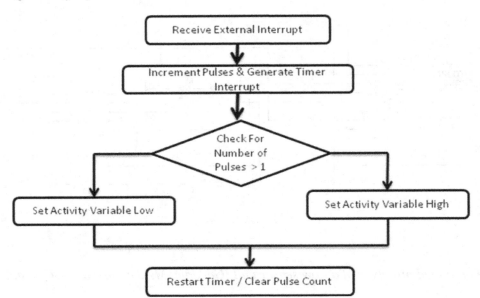

Figure 22. Cellular modem and its interface with PC

4.5. Communication Protocol

The sensor units and the central controller unit are equipped with RF (radio frequency) transceivers for two-way communication. The base station polls the sensor units at regular intervals and gathers the status of the appliances. The low power consuming Linx TRM-418-LT chip is used by the sensor units, which operates at UHF 418 MHz and is capable of half duplex data transmission at speeds up to 40 Kbit/s over distances of 30 meters "in-building". Even though there is an availability of other RF technologies in the market like ZigBee, WI-Fi etc., the reason for preferring this RF device is because of its simplicity and ease of installation. Moreover, during our system trails in a real world scenario, the communication performance of the system was very satisfactory.

To make the communication between the sensors and the controller more robust, error checking was implemented to check the validity of the transmitted data. The software algorithm for the control module is shown in Figure 23. This module checks the validity of the data received, replying to the sensor that sent the data, so that it knows if the data has to be resent.

4.6. Control Algorithm

The software for the Graphical User Interface (GUI) is easy to install and customize. The interface and control software has been written in Visual Basic. It allows the user to configure the

Figure 23. RF protocol for the controller module

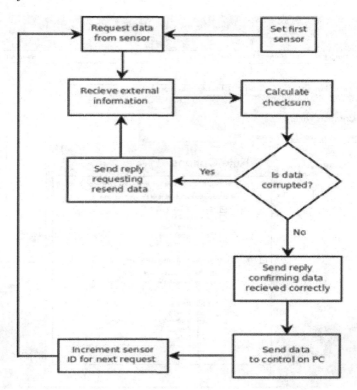

sensor units; up to 6 six sensors may be selected and associated with different appliances in the current developed system. The program provides a rule creation wizard for the ease of use, giving appropriate examples along the way as shown in Figure 24.

Once the sensors have been set up, the monitoring can start as shown in Figure 25.

The user can select a rule to either be a rule type one or rule type two. A rule type one checks whether an appliance is activated within a given time period. For example, has the television been used between 6 pm and 7 pm? A rule type two checks whether an appliance is still active after a predetermined time. For example, has the television been left active after 11 pm? The rules are based around a 24-hour cycle. The user can turn a rule off on particular days of the week. As part of the system, a data logger was developed and integrated into the control software. It logs every

activity, which can be viewed later. Figure 26 shows the activity log viewer.

During our trails we have connected the sensors to the following appliances—microwave oven, hot water kettle, television, toaster, and bed. Various rules were set on the supervisory program and the system was left to collect the data for over a week. Figure 27 shows the daily activity pattern of the resident.

This pattern helps us to identify the lifestyle of the person effectively and set the rules in the system accordingly.

5. CONCLUSION

There are many challenges faced by electronic home-based health care and monitoring systems, of which privacy and confidentiality are of utmost importance. Modern smart sensors, together with

Figure 24. Rule creation wizard

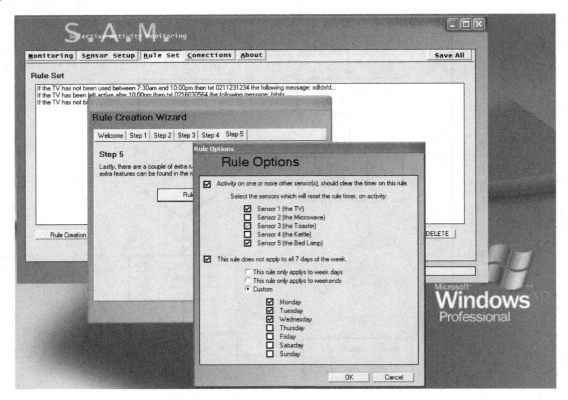

Figure 25. GUI while the system is running (Gaddam, Mukhopadhyay, & Gupta, 2010)

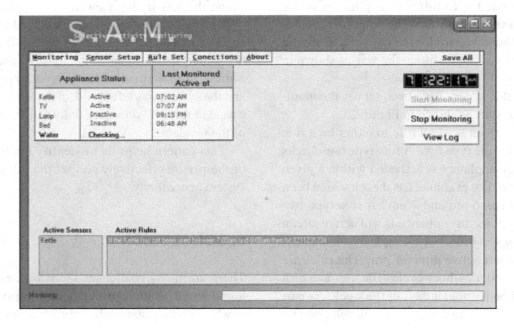

Figure 26. Data logger window (Gaddam, Mukhopadhyay, & Gupta, 2010)

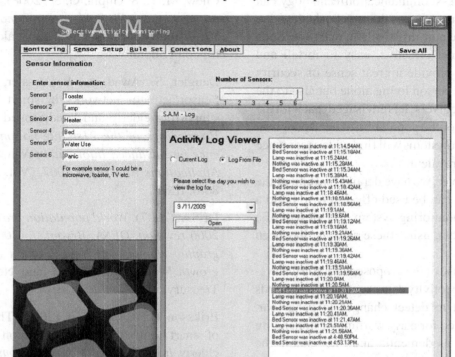

Figure 27. Daily activity pattern (Gaddam, Mukhopadhyay, & Gupta, 2010)

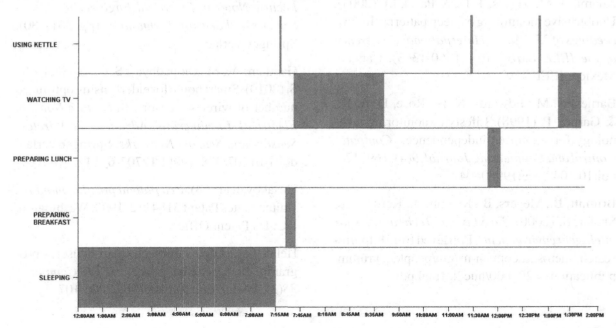

advanced wireless communication technology, can assist in building systems that can be deployed to monitor people non-invasively in real time. Such systems are cost effective, easy to install and maintain, and provide a great sense of security to not only the person living alone but also to the family and caregivers. It is envisaged that with the rapid increase of the population of aged people in the world, such systems will find wide acceptance and become prevalent.

In this chapter, we have detailed several of the sensors which can be used effectively to build a smart home monitoring system. The design of a complete system, using these sensors, has been detailed.

An added use of the proposed monitoring system is to gather activity data over extended periods and analyse it to detect changes in behaviour. This can be used for early warning of impending illnesses such as dementia and thus enable the medical staff to make early intervention.

6. REFERENCES

Adami, A. M., Hayes, T. L., & Pavel, M. (2003). Unobtrusive monitoring of sleep patterns. In *Proceedings of 25th Annual International Conference of the IEEE EMBS*, (pp. 1360-1363). Cancun, Mexico: IEEE.

Barnes, N. M., Edwards, N. H., Rose, D. A. D., & Garner, P. (1998). Lifestyle monitoring technology for supported independence. *Computer Control and Engineering Journal*, 9(4), 169–174. doi:10.1049/cce:19980404

Brumitt, B., Meyers, B., Krumm, J., Kern, A., & Shafer, S. (2000). *EasyLiving: Technologies for intelligent environments*. Retrieved from http://research.microsoft.com/en-us/um/people/jckrumm/publications%202000/huc2k-final.pdf

Chew, M. T., & Gupta, G. S. (2008). *Embedded programming with field –programmable mixed-signal microcontrollers* (2nd ed.). Palo Alto, CA: Silicon Laboratories.

Dengler, S., Awad, A., & Dressler, F. (2007). Sensor/actuator networks in smart homes for supporting elderly and handicapped people. In *Proceedings of the 21st International Conference on Advanced Information Networking and Applications Workshops 2007*, (Vol. 2, pp. 863-868). IEEE.

DESA. (2007). *World population prospects: The 2006 revision. DESA. Bryant, J. (2008). Demographic change and New Zealand's economic growth*. Wellington, New Zealand: New Zealand Treasury.

Eriksson, H., & Timpka, T. (2002). The potential of smart homes for injury prevention among the elderly. *Injury Control and Safety Promotion*, 9(2), 27–131. doi:10.1076/icsp.9.2.127.8694

Gaddam, A., Mukhopadhyay, S. C., & Gupta, G. S. (2008). Development of a smart home for elder-people based on wireless sensors. In *Lecture Notes in Electrical Engineering, Smart Sensors and Sensing Technology*, (pp. 361-380). Springer-Verlag.

Gaddam, A., Mukhopadhyay, S. C., & Gupta, G. S. (2010). Smart home for elderly using optimized number of wireless sensors. In *Lecture Notes in Electrical Engineering, Advances in Wireless Sensors and Sensors Networks*. Springer-Verlag. doi:10.1007/978-3-642-12707-6_14

Gusakov, I. (1993). *Bed patient position monitor*. United States Patent 5184112, 1993. Washington, DC: Us Patent Office.

Helal, A. (2005). Gator tech smart house: A programmable pervasive space. *IEEE Computer*, 38(3), 50–60. doi:10.1109/MC.2005.107

Helal, S., Mann, W., El-Zabadani, H., King, J., Kaddoura, Y., & Jansen, E. (2005). The gator tech smart house: A programmable pervasive space. *Computer*, 38(3), 50–60. doi:10.1109/MC.2005.107

Helal, S., Winkler, B., Lee, C., Kaddoura, Y., Ran, L., Giraldo, C., et al. (2003). Enabling location-aware pervasive computing applications for the elderly. In *Proceedings of IEEE 1st Conference PerCom 2003*, (pp. 531-536). PerCom.

Ho, L., Moh, M., Walker, Z., Hamada, T., & Su, C.-F. (2005). A prototype on RFID and sensor networks for elder healthcare: progress report. In *Proceedings of the 2005 ACM SIGCOMM Workshop on Experimental Approaches to Wireless Network Design and Analysis (E-WIND 2005)*, (pp. 70-75). ACM.

Howell Jones, M., Goubran, R. A., & Knofel, F. (2006). Identifying movement onset times for a bed-based pressure sensor array. In *Proceedings of the International Workshop on Medical Measurement and Applications*, (Vol. 1, pp. 105-109). IEEE.

Intille, S. S., Larson, K., Beaudin, J. S., Nawyn, J., Tapia, E. M., & Kaushik, P. (2004). A living laboratory for the design and evaluation of ubiquitous computing technologies. In *Proceedings of the 2005 Conference on Human Factors in Computing Systems*. New York, NY: ACM Press.

Jiang, L., Liu, D.-Y., & Yang, B. (2004). Machine learning and cybernetics. In *Proceedings of 2004 International Conference*, (vol. 2, pp. 659 – 663). IEEE.

Joshi, S., & Boyd, S. (2007). Sensor selection via convex optimization. *IEEE Transactions on Signal Processing*, 57(2), 321–325.

Kaddoura, Y., King, J., & Helal, A. (2005). Cost-precision tradeoffs in unencumbered floor-based indoor location tracking. In *Proceedings of the 3rd International Conference on Smart Homes and Health Telemetrics*, (pp. 425-429). IEEE.

Kidd, C. D., Orr, R. J., Abowd, G. D., Atkeson, C. G., Essa, I. A., MacIntyre, B., et al. (1999). The aware home: A living laboratory for ubiquitous computing research. In *Proceedings of the 2nd International Workshop on Cooperative Buildings (CoBuild 1999)*, (pp. 191-198). Pittsburgh, PA: Springer-Verlag.

Kiluk, C. (1991). *Method in alarm system, including recording of energy consumption*. US Patent No. US4990893. Washington, DC: US Patent Office.

Krumm, J., Harris, S., Meyers, B., Brumitt, B., Hale, M., & Shafer, S. (2000). Multi-camera multi-person tracking for EasyLiving. In *Proceedings of 3rd IEEE International Workshop on Visual Surveillance*, (pp. 3–10). IEEE Press.

Laguionie, O. (2008). *Designing a smart home environment using a wireless sensor networking of everyday objects*. (Master's Thesis). University Department of Computing Science. Stockholm, Sweden.

Mukhopadhyay, S. C., Gaddam, A., & Gupta, G. S. (2008). Wireless sensors for home monitoring - A review. *Recent Patents on Electrical Engineering*, 1, 32–39. doi:10.2174/1874476110801010032

Patterson, D. J., Fox, D., Kautz, H., & Philipose, M. (2005). Fine-grained activity recognition by aggregating abstract object usage. In *Proceedings Ninth IEEE International Symposium on Wearable Computers*, (pp. 44-51). IEEE.

Tekscan. (2009). *FlexiForce force sensors*. Retrieved October 25, 2009, from http://www.tekscan.com/flexiforce/flexiforce.html

Tucknott, K. A., & Sorenson, M. N. (1986). *Patient bed alarm system*. United States Patent 4633237, 1986. Washington, DC: US Patent Office.

UCSC. (2010). *Life expectancy- North south gap in life expectancy is narrowing fast*. Retrieved on July 30, 2010 from http://ucatlas.ucsc.edu/life/index.html

Yamaguchi, A., Ogawa, M., Tamura, T., & Togawa, T. (1998). Monitoring behaviour in the home using positioning sensors. In *Proceedings of the 20th Annual International Conference IEEE Engineering in Medicine and Biology Society*, (pp. 1977–1979). IEEE Press.

Zheng, Y. R., Goubran, R. A., El-Tanany, A., & Hongchi, S. (2005). A microphone array system for multimedia applications with near field signal targets. *IEEE Sensors Journal*, 5(6), 1395–1406. doi:10.1109/JSEN.2005.858936

Chapter 8
Behaviour Monitoring and Interpretation:
The Example of a Pedestrian Navigation System

Björn Gottfried
University of Bremen, Germany

ABSTRACT

This chapter describes the field of Behaviour Monitoring and Interpretation, BMI for short, which defines a framework for the analysis and design of systems for the monitoring and interpretation of human behaviour. As an example scenario which is analysed by means of that framework, a pedestrian navigation and service tool is presented. This scenario is about a mobile user who is wearing a hearing-aid similar device that instructs him while walking through the city. The navigation assistant can be equipped with specific application constraints in order to enrich the navigation system with an application context. The navigation system guides the user through the environment while taking care of the application constraints. One application context is a child at pre-school age: within this context the idea is to guide the child along a safe path to kindergarten. There are many challenges involved in the development of such a pedestrian navigation system. This chapter focuses on the analysis of the behaviour of the user that determines how the navigation assistant can provide help in an appropriate way. By this means, principles underlying the field of behaviour monitoring and interpretation are explained. More specifically, how the BMI framework aids in analysing is shown along with how top-down and bottom-up processes are to be involved in behaviour recognition; additionally, how the framework supports the identification of information fusion at different abstraction layers is shown.

DOI: 10.4018/978-1-4666-3682-8.ch008

1. INTRODUCTION

"Navigation is the art of getting from one place to another, efficiently and safely," accordingly to a widely used saying. Today a number of different navigation tools are available for several mobile devices. Although most have been designed for car navigation (Lee 2008), some are also available for pedestrian navigation (Aslan 2006). The omnipresence of tasks requiring humans to navigate from one place to another makes this an attractive issue to investigate the monitoring and interpretation of humans' behaviours (Stark 2007). This is the reason for this paper to discuss the field of behaviour monitoring and interpretation by looking at how pedestrians could be supported by a navigation system.

Usually, the idea of pedestrian navigation tools consists in presenting the user a map of the environment (Delikostidis 2009). Additionally, information insets are displayed onto the map, in order to indicate the whereabouts of the user as well as where she has to go next; others augment audio information with visual cues about directions (Chittaro 2005). While such approaches simulate the employment of conventional city maps, there are other modes conceivable how an assistant could provide help for wayfinding tasks. For example, as opposed to conventional maps which show the environment from the bird's eye view, a three dimensional view can be shown to the user on a graphical display (Maehara 2002); such a view simulates the perspective of the pedestrian, and hence, seems more plausible than a conventional map. Moreover, there are tactile maps which are particularly designed for visually impaired people (Caddeo 2006). Yet another example is a system giving audio instructions which completely replace the employment of maps (Fickas 2008). This has the advantage that devices are not necessary in order to display maps. Such devices require usually interactions with the user who does not always have his hands free. Another problem is

that sun light is frequently too bright, making it impossible recognising information on the display. Eventually, many people have difficulties in reading maps, since maps contain normally too much information and because users have to know how they have to orient themselves with regard to the map. What all those navigation tools have in common are the underlying mechanisms to provide efficient routes.

While technology takes care of efficiency, safety is hardly taken into account by pedestrian navigation tools available today. Users might have difficulties in wayfinding tasks for quite different reasons, influencing what safety means in a particular context. Elderly, for instance, have sometimes difficulties in finding a place in unfamiliar environments (Chang 2010). Orientation abilities, it seems, degrade. Frequently elderly would feel uncomfortable when being at foreign places; little support is already of help. Even much more difficult is the situation for elderly who suffer from dementia, because orientation abilities of such patients significantly decrease.

Quite another group are children who are not trained to find their way alone (Read 2003). They usually have been together with their parents who take care of wayfinding. As soon as they would be allowed to go to school and elsewhere alone, they are in an age where most of them are particularly curious about everything happening around them. Additionally, they are active and behave vividly. Sometimes they do even unexpected things, posing a problem for themselves as well as other traffic participants. A kid following the ball that jumps onto the street is textbook.

Yet another target group are visually impaired pedestrians (Caddeo 2006). While they are used to find their way in familiar environments, foreign areas are difficult to exploit for them. In addition to the genuine wayfinding problem, appropriate instructions need to be given to visually impaired users. Depending on the specific environment that surrounds the user it will be more or less a challenge to take everything into account that should be known by the visually impaired user in order to guide him safely through the environment.

Elderly, children, or other specific target groups would benefit from a navigation system that takes into account peculiar aspects of that target group; Chewar (2002) has shown that in fact user characteristics of specific target groups play a crucial role for route descriptions. Those aspects define how the navigation assistant should provide help. While a short-cut might be optimal for someone who has difficulties in walking, this very same short-cut could be dangerous for a child or a visually impaired user. In other words, the navigation system should look at constraints defined by specific target groups instead of providing simply a route, independent on the user who is wearing the navigation system.

1.1. Research Focus

From the given motivation a research topic is derived in this section. Studies indicate that audio navigation tools are preferred by pedestrians in comparison to other navigation tools which use two- or three-dimensional maps (Fickas 2008). Audio tools are small and require no device to be held in the hand. Moreover, simple audio instructions are not too distracting but already sufficient for many target groups. Relevant differences among groups should be taken into account inasmuch studies indicate specific disabilities, problems, and patterns for user groups, such as visually impaired humans (Golledge 1996), children (Read 2003), or those who are suffering from dementia (Martino-Saltzman 1991). Those differences define specific constraints about typical behaviours and special needs. The challenge is how an advanced audio navigation tool could make use of such constraints. This chapter refers to a ubiquitous computing system which connects both audio navigation and application constraints for specific target groups. Its design derives from the analysis of how such a system relates to the BMI framework.

While static application constraints like specific recommendations can be easily casted into audio instructions, the real challenge consists in detecting at which time or in which situation to prompt a specific recommendation. This needs to be derived from the user location as well as her current behaviour. While the location can be easily detected by appropriate sensors this is much more difficult for the behaviour. Examples of the latter include an elderly being disoriented and a jumping kid. Depending on the location the navigation tool can provide assistance by helping the elderly to select the correct walking direction or by instructing the child to be careful near the crossroad it is approaching. It is therefore necessary to provide mechanisms that analyse the user behaviour and to interpret it within the current context. The latter is defined by such things as the user location, his movement direction, and the user category to which the user belongs. The result of this analysis needs eventually to be translated into a clear instruction. From this, the following research challenge follows:

How can pedestrians' walking styles be interpreted automatically?

In the next few sections the BMI framework is outlined that takes up this challenge.

1.2. Structure

The body of this chapter is structured in the following way. The BMI field is outlined that provides the conceptual framework for analysing behaviours in general. Afterwards the aforementioned scenario of a pedestrian navigation tool is detailed in the context of the BMI framework. This enables the recognition of the technological requirements of the navigation service tool as well as its analysis and design. From that scenario two new aspects represented within the BMI framework are derived: how the interplay of bottom-up and top-down processes can be taken into account and how sensor fusion, or more generally information fusion, takes place at different abstraction layers within the framework. After technological aspects have been presented, the following section refers to social and ethical issues. Eventually, conclusions are drawn from this work and the chapter closes with an outlook and a summary.

2. THE BMI FRAMEWORK

About twenty years ago Mark Weiser introduced the notion of ubiquitous computing (Weiser 1991; Greenfield 2006). While this notion has been introduced in the academic scene and puts the human being in the centre, the idea of pervasive computing entered a little bit later the picture, is coined by industry and puts more emphasis on networks; additionally, the notion of ambient intelligence (Aarts 2009), builds upon those notions and intends to implement smart spaces which support humans unobtrusively with regard to their daily activities (Adlam 2009; Goshorn 2008; Mihailidis 2008). Behaviour Monitoring and Interpretation, BMI for short, can be conceived as a fundamental subarea of both fields ubiquitous computing and pervasive computing (Gottfried 2007, 2008b, 2009a, 2009b, 2009c, 2010). BMI focuses on the analysis of behaviours, while ubiquitous computing and pervasive computing are more general and also include mechanisms to automatically change the environment, for example, as a response to some observed behaviour. In the following it is argued that locomotion behaviours are fundamental and should therefore be thoroughly taken into account in ubiquitous and pervasive computing, and hence, in BMI, locomotion behaviours playing an important role in pedestrian navigation.

2.1. Pedestrians Going Shopping

An example illustrates what BMI is about. Millonig (2007) investigates motion patterns of pedestrians going shopping. At the beginning people are observed without knowing anything about it; for this purpose a hand-tracking tablet computer with a digital map is used in order to record the paths of the pedestrians in this map. Afterwards, the people who have been observed get interviewed in order to let them tell a little bit about themselves, their intentions and social background. Finally, they get further tracked, this time equipped with a Bluetooth Smartphone or a GPS logger for indoor and outdoor tracking, respectively. The acquired data is analysed by clustering the obtained trajectories and by using speed histograms. As a result there are basically three types of shoppers identified, namely *swift*, *convenient*, and *passionate shoppers*. Figure 1 summarises this study.

This study shows the usual sequence of abstraction layers which can be found in each typical BMI application, and hence, each system that requires the monitoring and interpretation of user activities. The bottom layer represents the reality, and thus, the object of interest, in our example, movements of pedestrians. The second layer is about the observation of the object of interest, here by means of such techniques as GPS or shadowing. The acquired data is frequently preprocessed (e.g. smoothing, detection of outlier) and data representations are chosen for storing the data in an appropriate structure, at the third layer; in the present case for trajectory positions and other positional information. The fourth layer is about analysing the data, for example in order to cluster similar trajectories of different pedestrians. Eventually, the top layer represents the result one is looking for, that is to tell apart swift shoppers from those who enjoy going shopping. The conventional approach in ethology looks for a direct mapping between the bottom layer and the top layer (Gottfried 2009). BMI is distinguished by automating this mapping by enabling an arbitrary complex functionality. This mediates between observation and interpretation by means of a multitude of techniques, basically from Artificial Intelligence research.

Figure 1. The BMI framework and the example scenario of pedestrians going shopping

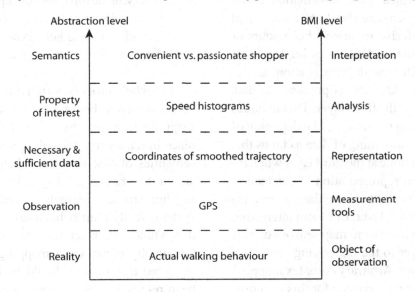

2.2. A Navigation Tool Described by the BMI Framework

How does the pedestrian navigation tool fit into this framework?

First Layer: At the lowest layer the object of interest is identified, that is behaviours observable in reality. Positions are of concern like in the shopping scenario, because walking behaviours allow the relevant distinctions. As opposed to the shopping scenario also the movement direction is of interest, as are more sophisticated behaviours which become relevant in the pedestrian navigation tool, such as being disoriented (in the case of the elderly), behaving inappropriate in the street (as in the case of children), or searching for the next side road (by visually impaired users).

Second Layer: The second layer defines the measurement tools for detecting those behaviours which have been identified at the lowest layer. While positional information can be acquired by means of established positioning techniques, much more diffi-

cult is the situation for the aforementioned complex behaviours, which closely relate to the application scenarios. They include *being disoriented*, *behaving inappropriate*, and *searching for the next side road*. While specific sensors are not available for those and other complex behaviours, they rather have to be derived from other sensory information, basically from positional and temporal information: all these behaviours are distinguished by not smoothly following a route but by showing hesitation, running back and forth, or other patterns typical for the more complex behaviours. The challenge is to show how these behaviours derive from positional, directional, and temporal information.

Third Layer: At the third layer representations for the raw sensory data are to be provided. This layer represents everything the two top layers would work on in order to interpret behaviours. Sensory data which is not available at this layer will not be accessible for the two top layers. Appropriate representations for both spatial data and temporal data are to be provided in our example case. Besides the users' trajectories, information about speed and its change should be represented in order to derive impulsive behaviours of children with this data, for example.

Fourth Layer: The fourth layer is about analysis methods. Algorithms process the data represented at the third layer. This includes pre-processing operations, like detection of outliers and smoothing of data as far as this has not been done at the third layer when instantiating the representation. The detection of regularities or rather irregularities are typical for the fourth layer. But more interesting are methods in order to map sensory data of the third layer to the underlying semantics at the top layer. Arbitrary complex mapping functions are conceivable for this purpose.

Fifth Layer: The top layer represents the semantics of the interpretation. Concepts for *being disoriented*, *behaving inappropriate*, or *searching* are found at this layer. Hence, here we find those behaviours which have been identified at the bottom layer. While the latter describe the actual behaviours in

reality, at the top layer concepts for the actual behaviours are to be represented. This representation should help to set the interpreted data into the given application context.

The whole process within this framework can be conceived as being a complex but automatic mapping from an observable behaviour taking place in reality to a formal representation of the semantics of that very same behaviour. This is similar to what an ethologist does when observing humans and animals in order to interpret systematically their behaviours. For this reason, this whole five layer BMI framework that automatically computes a mapping from what is observed to how this should be interpreted has been referred to as the computational approach to ethology (Gottfried 2009).

Figure 2 summarises the described partitioning of the navigation scenario into the five BMI layers. In this figure, tools and methods are proposed which illustrate the alignment of such methods with the BMI framework. While the bottom layer starts with the object of observation, the fifth

Figure 2. BMI framework for the described navigation scenario

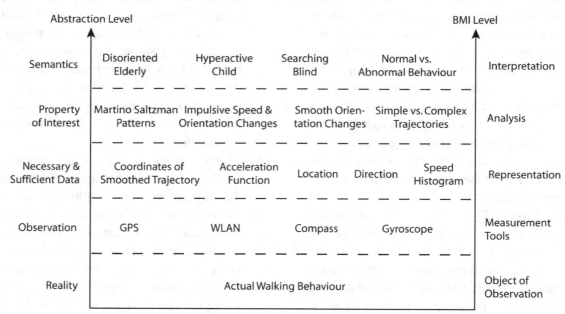

layer ends with its interpretation, as described above. The three intermediate layers employ a number of tools and methods which all aid in the behaviour interpretation process. The second layer is about data sampling. Being interested in the whereabouts of the user GPS and Wireless-Lan techniques can be used for positioning; compass and gyroscope are two means to measure the orientation. The third layer determines which features are represented for analysis. In this case, not only the sampled location and direction data is represented. Moreover, from the location data a trajectory of the moving user can be computed which is made of successive positions over a temporal interval. Such a trajectory represents the spatial layout of the path of the pedestrian and can be analysed regarding its shape. Taking additionally temporal information, an acceleration function can be computed which shows the change of speed of the pedestrian. A histogram of the latter will later enable the efficient comparison of speed parameters. The fourth layer builds upon all those features. That is, simple classification methods can be applied, for example to make the distinction between simple (intersection-free) and complex (comprising intersections) trajectories. Or, sophisticated patterns are dealt with which are to be correctly classified. Examples are the Martino-Saltzman patterns (Martino-Saltzman 1991) which distinguish typical behaviour categories of people suffering from dementia. For instance, a typical case is the wandering behaviour which refers to the running back and fro of the pedestrian in a restricted area.

This framework makes clear how a more technical view looks like in contrast to the application description. Filling the BMI framework with such a scenario is a useful start for further analysis. It provides the frame for identifying the main components, beginning with the behaviours to be modelled, via the sensory equipment to be employed, the formal representation for sensory data, the recognition of methods necessary for analysis, and eventually the semantic description which can be later used for specific applications. In the following sections we will refer to this framework in order to analyse in more detail how to arrive at the intended behaviour interpretation of pedestrians. In particular the distinction between the bottom-up flow and top-down flow of information can be made clear, showing what can be derived from sensory information and application knowledge, respectively.

3. USER BEHAVIOURS WHILE NAVIGATING

In this section it is shown what can be detected in a bottom-up process regarding the BMI framework, as for instance behaviours which determine the user category (children, visually impaired people, and elderly with disorientation). Additionally, it is shown how the top-down influence of information looks like that comes from the top-layer (the current user category) and flows downwards. In this way, behaviours can be interpreted that could not be interpreted without context knowledge, that is without the influence of top-down knowledge (how an abnormal trajectory should be interpreted, for example). This enables the detection of those behaviours that require specific help provided by the navigation assistant system (hyperactivity, disorientation, or searching behaviour).

3.1. Bottom-Up Analysis to Determine User Categories

It is assumed that the walking behaviour of a pedestrian would show typical characteristics, which can be employed to tell apart user categories. That is, if the user category is not known yet, then hints can be derived bottom-up from sensory information. For this purpose a number of established sensors are employed that capture walking parameters, such as position, orientation, speed, and acceleration. Positioning techniques like GPS (Zumberge 1997) and WLAN (Hermersdorf 2006) are assumed as well as compasses and gyroscopes (May 1999) in order to measure orientation and its change; the speed can be derived from successive positions. Then, user categories can be derived from sensory information as follows:

- Impulsive speed changes could refer to the hyperactivity of children. Those changes derive from the speed function that represents both the speed as well as changes in speed. In this way, hyperactive children, who would show acceleration patterns which abruptly change, can be separated from elderly and visually impaired people who would usually behave calmly. That is, for both latter user categories speed and acceleration are rather constant and slow. The right hand side at the representation level of Figure 3 illustrates two significantly different speed functions which refer to hyperactivity and constant speed.

- A way in order to separate the behaviours of disoriented elderly and visual impaired people consists in the classification of walking behaviours into patterns which have been identified by (Martino-Saltzman et al. 1991). They distinguish three kinds of locomotion behaviours which are referred to as *random*, *lapping*, and *pacing*. The class of *random patterns* is distinguished by frequent changes and walking disruptions or hesitation; *lapping* refers to walking patterns where the pedestrian takes complex paths although more direct paths are available; eventually, *pacing* means the running to and fro between two or more locations.

To be more precise, the described behaviours would primarily distinguish children who behave hyperactive and elderly who have disabilities in orientation. By contrast, whenever those user groups behave similar they cannot be distinguished. But the goal is to determine those behaviours which are to be supported by the navigation system: it has to provide help just in time when such crucial behaviours occur. Otherwise, it is not important to be able to detect any differences of user categories.

3.2. Bottom-Up Analysis to Determine Unusual Behaviours

Independent of the user category at hand, a pedestrian walking as slowly and constant as most pedestrians do can be determined bottom-up. For this purpose spatial characteristics of trajectories can be computed. Pedestrians usually show a smooth trajectory which steadily leads into specific directions. By contrast, complex trajectories are found when patterns occur that derive from someone going back, making loops, or showing other behaviours that indicate disorientation or hyperactivity. The left hand side at the representation level of Figure 3 shows two trajectories indicating normal and unusual walking behaviours; the left hand side path is smooth, while the right hand side one comprises twists and turns; while the former might represent a pedestrian who is following his way straightforward without having any difficulties, the latter trajectory could refer to a child who is running to and fro; but it could also refer to a searching pattern. Shape analysis techniques make possible this classification. It is in particular possible to detect *loops, twists, and turns*, a *running on the spot*, and similar conceptions by means of qualitative shape analysis (Gottfried 2008b).

While it could be difficult to distinguish user categories taking sensory information alone, it should be possible quite well to determine at least whether the user behaves normal. If he does not, hints are available that help is needed.

3.3. Top-Down Interpretation of Unusual Behaviours

There are many conceptions and ideas about the question of what defines a context. Spatial and temporal information, as well as extra information relevant in a situation are frequently meant

Figure 3. Representational level: left: a smooth trajectory and a complex trajectory between a and b (see third layer); right: an object with constant speed and an object with changing speed

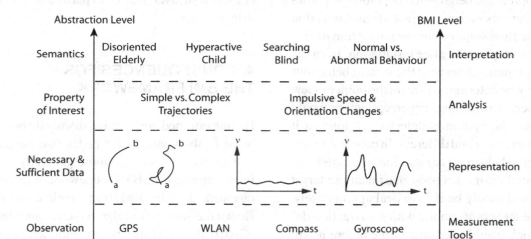

(Guesgen 2010). Here we are in particular referring to the context of elderly people, children, and visual impaired people. While it has been described above how hints about the user category can be derived bottom-up, it is still difficult to interpret the traces of a pedestrian solely on the basis of spatiotemporal information. Therefore, for a robust approach the idea is to let the system know the application context for which it is currently employed, that is a specific target group. Depending on that context it will be possible to adequately interpret the spatiotemporal traces of pedestrians as either a behaviour indicating disorientation, hyperactivity, or a searching situation. In other words, if the user category is known, then normal and abnormal behaviours, which can be detected bottom-up, can be appropriately interpreted top-down; the unusual behaviour that is detected bottom-up can be set into the context of the user category. In this way, *disorientation*, *searching*, and *hyperactivity* can be identified as such. As a consequence, the navigation assistant can provide help for the correct user category, someone of which is currently using the device.

3.4. Direct Approaches vs. Learning

An alternative approach consists in learning behaviours. This is more widespread in ubiquitous computing than such a more direct approach described above (e.g. Aztiria 2009). There are many advantages of directly computing behaviours: learning requires usually a sufficient amount of examples that clearly separate concepts. If those examples are easily available it seems in fact attractive to automatically let the system learn relevant behaviour classes. But as soon as it becomes questionable whether sufficient examples will appropriately enable the automatic behaviour classification, the more direct approach becomes more attractive. Although it requires the development of classification methods, they are available for the traces of pedestrians, more generally, for one-dimensional paths. At least in this context the direct computation of behaviours seems possible quite well. That distinction between direct approaches and learning is also referred to as the distinction between symbolic as opposed to subsymbolic approaches (Chua 2011).

But there is another important reason for this direct approach to behaviour recognition, in particular for devices such as that pedestrian navigation tool. The final solution for the navigation device should work properly after installation, from the very beginning. Otherwise the system behaviour would not be deterministic from the point of view of the user, i.e. regarding her perception; she would think that the system is defective as long as it behaves irregular and different. In conclusion, the approach to behaviour recognition advocated here is a crucial design decision inasmuch the target groups will hardly be able to deal appropriately, let alone feel comfortable, with a navigation device which would need some time before it will properly work. This is another distinction between the symbolic and sub-symbolic approach.

While it is illustrated by the pedestrian navigation example how a direct approach is designed with the aid of the BMI framework, it should be clear that learning approaches can also be considered within this framework. Conceiving them

as specific classification methods, they are found at the fourth layer, that is, as particular means for data analysis.

4. CONSEQUENCES FOR THE BMI FRAMEWORK

Having outlined how behaviours would be recognised in the context of a pedestrian navigation system, this section will more generally discuss implications for the BMI framework. While previous work about the BMI framework has basically shown the character of the five-layer architecture (Gottfried 2009a), the above mentioned examples about bottom-up and top-down processes show how the BMI architecture supports the analysis as well as modelling of such bottom-up and top-down processes.

This is demonstrated in Figure 4: The detection of normal as opposed to abnormal behaviours is accomplished within a bottom-up process (no. 0

Figure 4. The detection of normal versus abnormal behaviours is a bottom-up process (no. 0); the distinction between hyperactivity and disorientation requires first a bottom-up process to determine the trajectory (no. 1), then a top-down process in order to take into account application context (no. 2), and eventually a bottom-up process to interpret the trajectory within the application context (no. 3)

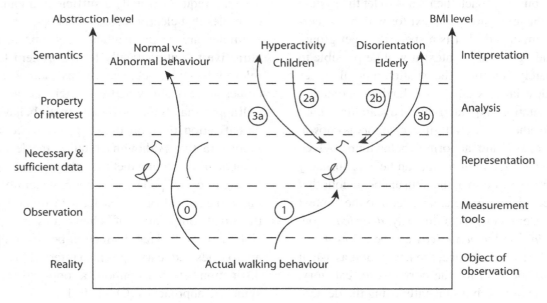

in Figure 4). This is simply done by distinguishing two quite different categories of trajectories, namely those which show a simple curve that steadily and clearly proceeds into specific directions and those trajectories which are complex, self-intersecting and which comprise loops, twists, and turns. By contrast, the distinction between hyperactivity and disorientation cannot be made by a one-way bottom-up process. It rather requires first a bottom-up process to determine the trajectory (no. 1 in Figure 4), then a top-down process in order to take into account application context (no. 2 in Figure 4), and then again a bottom-up process to interpret the trajectory within the application context (no. 3 in Figure 4). In this way, elderly who behave normal can be distinguished from those who behave disoriented, and accordingly, children who behave hyperactive can be distinguished from those behaving calmly.

From a more general point of view, this example demonstrates how it can be identified with the aid of the BMI framework where bottom-up and top-down processes are required. At the different layers it can be determined what is represented or done at the according layer; then, it can be analysed what is needed in order to arrive at that representation or process; this analysis will either be possible by means of sensory information coming from the bottom layer or by means of information flowing top-down from the semantic layer to the according intermediate layer. In this way, the necessity of bottom-up and top-down processes are determined.

The explicit distinction between bottom-up and top-down processes in behaviour recognition is not new. An example is (Aghajan 2007) whose work is about complex monitoring systems that are based on distributed smart cameras. The authors investigate a vision-based framework to determine quantitative information of the user's posture. Quantitative information from the vision network complements specific qualitative distinctions. The latter offer clues to direct the vision network in order to adjust its processing operation according to the interpretation state. This is an example of a top-down process.

Another example is the work of (Terzic 2007). They propose a sophisticated behaviour recognition system based on video technology. Applied to dynamic indoor scenes and static building scenes, they implement a number of submodules: objects must be recognised, classified and tracked, qualitative spatial and temporal properties must be determined, behaviours of individual objects must be identified, and composite behaviours must be determined to obtain an interpretation of the scene as a whole. They describe how these tasks can be distributed over three processing stages (low-level analysis, middle layer mediation and high-level interpretation) to obtain flexible and efficient bottom-up and top-down processing in behaviour interpretation.

There is a second issue which can be put forward by the BMI framework: the fusion of information coming from different sources, which is a generalised conception of sensor fusion. Similar as bottom-up and top-down processes can be identified within the BMI framework, different information sources can be identified which fuse together at specific BMI levels. For example, the walking direction can be determined by using data from both a compass as well as a gyroscope; similarly, the current location can be determined either by means of GPS or by WLAN; however, instead of conceiving different sources as alternatives, their combination frequently compensate difficulties arising when deploying only a single source. An example at a more abstract layer is the detection of *impulsive speed changes*, which can be determined by using information about the walking direction, speed histograms as well as acceleration functions. A yet more abstract information fusion example concerns the recognition of *searching behaviours* of visually impaired people. In this case, both the consideration of smooth orientation changes and the distinction between simple and complex trajectories help for deriving a *searching behaviour*. Figure 5 shows information fusion at

Figure 5. Information fusion at different layers

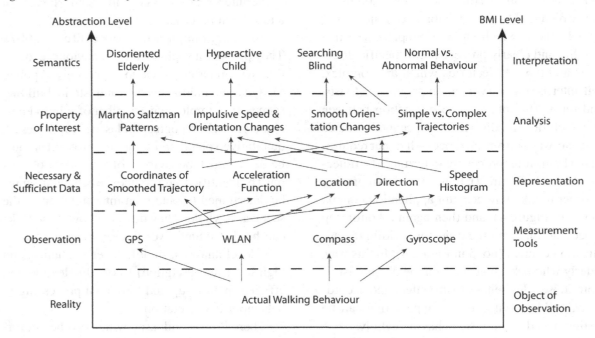

different BMI levels, indicated by arrows pointing at the same target.

Clearly, the idea of information fusion has been followed in different areas before (Blasch 2006). But what the BMI framework distinguishes is that it makes explicit where information fusion should take place regarding the level of abstraction. In this way, it aids in analysing and designing behaviour recognition with respect to information fusion. At the sensory level it is common practice to integrate different sensors into single devices, e.g. in smart phones. But it is still necessary to think about where to integrate data obtained by different sensors. This can indeed be done at different abstraction layers. Those which are relevant for behaviour recognition are made explicit within the BMI framework.

5. DISCUSSION

As in all kinds of ubiquitous computing applications ethical and social implications should carefully be analysed. This holds in particular

for navigation systems designed for special target groups, but more generally for all kinds of applications which can be described by means of the BMI framework. While the present paper is confined to outlining the basic ideas of pedestrian navigation, the main purpose is to show how pedestrian navigation systems relate to BMI. Therefore, many technical details have been left out of the discussion and an outlook on future research emphasises some of the main challenges. We will look at all these issues in the following.

5.1. Ethical and Social Implications

A pedestrian navigation tool which supports safe navigation depending on the target group who is using this tool seems attractive, but a fundamental requirement is that the raw spatiotemporal data of the pedestrian is to be stored in order to enable the analysis of extended traces. Spatiotemporal data can be conceived as to be particularly sensitive in that it allows the determination of the whereabouts of the user as if he is observed all the time. This is a typical example showing how pervasive computing technologies could be abused. Clearly, the solution to this problem is simple: the device could be designed in such a way that the data would be deleted as soon as the data has been used for analysis and as soon as it is not needed anymore. Additionally, mechanisms can be installed that avoid the output of the data for abuse. They can be encapsulated within the *analysis black box*. However simple the solution, this should be spelled out clearly as a kind of design maxim to which such a pervasive system should stick. In this sense, (Alder 1998) argues for an approach which emphasises communication in the design and implementation of monitoring systems, allowing for an acceptable balance between potential abuses and benefits.

Advantages to single pedestrians using the described tool have been mentioned in this paper. More broadly is the view of its influence to society. The described mechanisms enable many people to behave more freely outside their home, and thus, motivate mobility: children can be protected by safely guiding them to school; handicapped users benefit in that the navigation tool would take into account barriers and how to by-pass them; elderly with difficulties in orientation can be guided so that they feel more secure. In the long run this should have a positive impact on society in that less many people would be caught within their more or less strict boundaries regarding their mobility. Quite another open issue is the cultural influence of a society that would determine how such technologies will be accepted in future (Panina 2005).

5.2. BMI Framework

Different techniques to behaviour analysis can be investigated within the BMI framework. This helps the comparison of such techniques as well as their integration. Another advantage is the possibility to sketch rough solutions within the framework. For example, top-down and bottom-up processes as well as their interplay can be identified. Similarly, information fusion might be necessary at different abstraction layers. How different methods would implement information fusion processes or those that take into account top-down knowledge is not determined with the BMI framework. Instead, the simple architecture of that framework that basically defines five abstraction levels, allows the easy comparison and integration of different methods. It is just this flexibility which is needed when designing a new system. That is, in this stage precise solutions to behaviour recognition problems are still missing, but as a first step the coarse outline of solutions can be found within the clear boundaries of the BMI framework.

5.3. Outlook

The presented work focuses on the monitoring of behaviours. This alone is a big challenge. However, for the intended audio navigation tool, there are a number of other challenges future work has to look at. For example, a straightforward and simple to use way is necessary in order to let the user instruct the device with target locations. For navigation, fine distinctions are conceivable which are based on landmarks and which therefore depend on the current environment of the user; a cloud computing infrastructure could be deployed that would provide this information at a more or less fine granularity level for the different districts in a city. The instructions could be confined to a simple vocabulary of directions, such as *turn left, turn right, go ahead,* and *go back* or could refer to the aforementioned landmarks. An arbitrarily complex description is conceivable which would require a speech generation module which would make use of natural language. The device itself needs to be robust and it should be possible to easily plug it into or connect it to the ears.

This work concentrates on pedestrians who are walking somewhere outside. But future work should also include how people could be supported within indoor spaces (Thirde 2006) as well as within transportation networks (Carmien 2005). While our primary motivation is safety and how critical behaviours can be recognised, other application constraints could be taken into account, for instance, to support elderly when going shopping; a plan could be composed that would include different locations to be visited in a specific order, including visits at the doctors at specific times. This is of interest for the elderly inasmuch they frequently feel uncomfortable and overtaxed as soon as they are confronted with a whole list of tasks they have to take care of.

A more technical future issue is the integration of the BMI framework with other methods deployed in the engineering sciences. For example, the Unified Modelling Language, UML for short, provides a whole set of diagrammatic systems, including diagrams which are to model dynamic processes. It should be investigated how BMI complements such established methodologies. Clearly, what BMI distinguishes is its specific character. Therefore, the BMI framework might turn out to be a specific component of other diagrammatic languages which in particular supports the modelling of behaviour recognition.

5.4. Summary

This chapter presents the BMI framework as an architecture that supports the analysis and design of methods to behaviour recognition. While previous publications have already introduced this framework, this chapter in particular discusses the notion of information fusion and explains how the framework aids in identifying top-down as well as bottom-up processes. To make these concepts clear, as an example application a pedestrian navigation assistant is introduced. Such an assistant is a challenging application since it requires in particular the recognition of behaviours.

ACKNOWLEDGEMENT

I am thankful to Dr. Arne Schuldt for his useful comments on an earlier draft of this paper and to Hendrik Iben for his support regarding technical details about wearable sensors.

REFERENCES

Aarts, E., & de Ruyter, B. (2009). New research perspectives on ambient intelligence. *Journal of Ambient Intelligence and Smart Environments, 1*, 5–14.

Adlam, T., Carey-Smith, B., Evans, N., Orpwood, R., Boger, J., & Mihailidis, A. (2009). Implementing monitoring and technological interventions in smart homes for people with dementia, case studies. In Gottfried, B., & Aghajan, H. (Eds.), *Behaviour Monitoring and Interpretation, Smart Environments*. Boca Raton, FL: IOS Press.

Aghajan, H., & Wu, C. (2007). From distributed vision networks to human behaviour interpretation. In Gottfried, B. (Ed.), *BMI 2007 (Vol. 296*, pp. 129–143). CEUR.

Alder, G. S. (1998). Ethical issues in electronic performance monitoring: A consideration of deontological and teleological perspectives. *Journal of Business Ethics, 17*, 729–743. doi:10.1023/A:1005776615072

Aslan, I., Schwalm, M., Baus, J., Krüger, A., & Schwartz, T. (2006). Acquisition of spatial knowledge in location aware mobile pedestrian navigation systems. *Proceedings of Mobile HCI, 2006*, 105–108.

Aztiria, A., Izaguirre, A., Basagoiti, R., & Augusto, J. C. (2008). Autonomous learning of user's preferences improved through user feedback. In Gottfried, B., & Aghajan, H. (Eds.), *BMI 2008* (*Vol. 396*, pp. 87–101). CEUR.

Blasch, E. (2006). Sensor, user, mission (SUM) resource management and their interaction with level 2/3 fusion. In *Proceedings of the International Conference on Information Fusion*. IEEE.

Caddeo, P., Fornara, F., Nenci, A. M., & Piroddi, A. (2006). Wayfinding tasks in visually impaired people: The role of tactile maps. *Cognitive Processing, 7*(1), 168–169. doi:10.1007/s10339-006-0128-9

Carmien, S., Dawe, M., Fischer, G., Gorman, A., Kintsch, A., Sullivan, J. R., & James, F. (2005). Socio-technical environments supporting people with cognitive disabilities using public transportation. *ACM Transactions on Computer-Human Interaction, 12*(2), 233–262. doi:10.1145/1067860.1067865

Chang, Y.-J., & Wang, T.-Y. (2010). Comparing picture and video prompting in autonomous indoor wayfinding for individuals with cognitive impairments. *Personal and Ubiquitous Computing, 14*(8), 737–747. doi:10.1007/s00779-010-0285-9

Chewar, C. M., & McCrickard, D. S. (2002). Dynamic route descriptions: Tradeoffs by usage goals and user characteristics, In *Proceedings of the 2nd International Symposium on Smart Graphics*, (pp. 71-78). ACM Press.

Chittaro, L., & Burigat, S. (2005). Augmenting audio messages with visual directions in mobile guides: An evaluation of three approaches. In *Proceedings of the 7th International Conference on Human Computer Interaction with Mobile Devices & Services*, (pp. 107-114). Salzburg, Austria: ACM.

Chua, S.-L., Marsland, S., & Guesgen, H. W. (2011). Towards behaviour recognition with unlabelled sensor data: As much as necessary, as little as possible. In *Human Behavior Recognition Technologies: Intelligent Applications for Monitoring and Security*. Hershey, PA: IGI Global.

Delikostidis, I., & van Elzakker, C. P. J. M. (2009). Geo-identification and pedestrian navigation with geo-mobile applications: How do users proceed? *Lecture Notes in Geoinformation and Cartography, 2*, 185–206. doi:10.1007/978-3-540-87393-8_12

Fickas, S., Sohlberg, M., & Hung, P.-F. (2008). Route-following assistance for travelers with cognitive impairments: A comparison of four prompt modes. *International Journal of Human-Computer Studies, 66*(12), 876–888. doi:10.1016/j.ijhcs.2008.07.006

Golledge, R. G., Klatzky, R. L., & Loomis, J. L. (1996). Cognitive mapping and wayfinding by adults without vision. *GeoJournal Library, 32*(2), 215–246. doi:10.1007/978-0-585-33485-1_10

Goshorn, R., Goshorn, D., & Kölsch, M. (2008). The enhancement of low-level classifications for ambient assisted living. In B. Gottfried & H. Aghajan (Eds.), *Proceedings of the 2nd Workshop on Behaviour Monitoring and Interpretation (BMI 2008)*, (vol. 396, pp. 87–101). CEUR.

Gottfried, B. (Ed.). (2007). *Behaviour monitoring and interpretation*. CEUR.

Gottfried, B. (2008). Qualitative similarity measures - The case of two-dimensional outlines. *Computer Vision and Image Understanding*, *110*(1), 117–133. doi:10.1016/j.cviu.2007.05.002

Gottfried, B. (2009). Behaviour monitoring and interpretation: A computational approach to ethology. *Lecture Notes in Artificial Intelligence*, *5803*, 572–580.

Gottfried, B. (2010a). Locomotion activities in smart environments. In Nakashima, H., Augusto, J. C., & Aghajan, H. (Eds.), *Handbook of Ambient Intelligence and Smart Environments*. Springer. doi:10.1007/978-0-387-93808-0_4

Gottfried, B. (2010b). Behaviour monitoring and interpretation: Facets of BMI systems. In Mastrogiovanni, F., & Chong, N.-Y. (Eds.), *Handbook of Research on Ambient Intelligence: Trends and Perspectives*. Hershey, PA: IGI Global.

Gottfried, B. (2010c). BMI and the interpretation of locomotion behaviours of humans. In Malatras, A. (Ed.), *Pervasive Computing and Communications Design and Deployment: Technologies, Trends, and Applications*. Hershey, PA: IGI Global.

Gottfried, B., & Aghajan, H. (Eds.). (2008). *Behaviour monitoring and interpretation*. CEUR.

Gottfried, B., & Aghajan, H. (Eds.). (2009). *Behaviour monitoring and interpretation – Smart environments*. IOS Press.

Greenfield, A. (2006). Everyware: The dawning age of ubiquitous computing. *New Riders*, 11–12.

Guesgen, H. W., & Marsland, W. (2010). Spatio-temporal reasoning and context awareness. In Nakashima, H., Aghajan, H., & Augusto, J. C. (Eds.), *Handbook of Ambient Intelligence and Smart Environments* (pp. 609–634). Springer. doi:10.1007/978-0-387-93808-0_23

Hermersdorf, M. (2006). Indoor positioning with a WLAN access point list on a mobile device. In *Proceedings of WSW 2006 at SenSys 2006*. Boulder, CO: ACM.

Lee, W.-C., & Cheng, B.-W. (2008). Effects of using a portable navigation system and paper map in real driving. *Accident; Analysis and Prevention*, *40*(1), 303–308. doi:10.1016/j.aap.2007.06.010

Maehara, H., Tanaka, K. W. S., & Kamata, K. (2002). Pedestrian navigation based on 3D map and mobile interaction. In *Proceedings of MVA 2002, IAPR Workshop on Machine Vision Applications*. Nara, Japan: MVA.

Martino-Saltzman, D., Blasch, B., Morris, R., & McNeal, L. (1991). Travel behavior of nursing home residents perceived as wanderers and nonwanderers. *The Gerontologist*, *11*, 666–672. doi:10.1093/geront/31.5.666

May, D. (1999). Modeling the dynamically tuned gyroscope in support of high-bandwidth capture loop design. *Proceedings of the Society for Photo-Instrumentation Engineers*, *3692*, 101. doi:10.1117/12.352852

Mihailidis, A., Boger, J., Craig, T., & Hoey, J. (2008). The COACH prompting system to assist older adults with dementia through handwashing: An efficacy study. *BMC Geriatrics*, *8*(28).

Millonig, A., & Gartner, G. (2007). Shadowing, tracking, interviewing: How to explore human ST-behaviour patterns. In Gottfried, B. (Ed.), *BMI 2007* (Vol. 296, pp. 29–42). CEUR.

Panina, D., & Aiello, J. R. (2005). Acceptance of electronic monitoring and its consequences in different cultural contexts: A conceptual model. *Journal of International Management*, *11*, 269–292. doi:10.1016/j.intman.2005.03.009

Read, M. A. (2003). Use of color in child care environments: Application of color for wayfinding and space definition in Alabama child care environments. *Early Childhood Education Journal, 30*(4), 233–239. doi:10.1023/A:1023387607942

Stark, A., Riebeck, M., & Kawalek, J. (2007). How to design an advanced pedestrian navigation system: Field trial results. In *Proceedings of the IEEE International Workshop on Intelligent Data Acquisition and Advanced Computing Systems: Technology and Applications*. Dortmund, Germany: IEEE Press.

Terzic, K., Hotz, L., & Neumann, B. (2007). Division of work during behaviour recognition. In Gottfried, B. (Ed.), *BMI 2007 (Vol. 296*, pp. 144–159). CEUR.

Thirde, D., Borg, M., Ferryman, J., Fusier, F., Valentin, V., Brémond, F., & Thonnat, M. (2006). A real-time scene understanding system for airport apron monitoring. In *Proceedings of the IEEE International Conference on Computer Vision Systems (ICVS 2006)*. IEEE Press.

Weiser, M. (1991). The computer for the twenty-first century. *Scientific American, 94*(10).

Zumberge, J. F., Heflin, M. B., Jefferson, D. C., Watkins, M. M., & Webb, F. H. (1997). Precise point positioning for the efficient and robust analysis of GPS data from large networks. *Journal of Geophysical Research, 102*(B3), 5005–5017. doi:10.1029/96JB03860

Chapter 9
Intention–Based Decision Making via Intention Recognition and its Applications

The Anh Han
Universidade Nova de Lisboa, Portugal

Luis Moniz Pereira
Universidade Nova de Lisboa, Portugal

ABSTRACT

In this chapter, the authors present an intention-based decision-making system. They exhibit a coherent combination of two Logic Programming-based implemented systems, Evolution Prospection and Intention Recognition. The Evolution Prospection system has proven to be a powerful system for decision-making, designing, and implementing several kinds of preferences and useful environment-triggering constructs. It is here enhanced with an ability to recognize intentions of other agents—an important aspect not well explored so far. The usage and usefulness of the combined system are illustrated with several extended examples in different application domains, including Moral Reasoning, Ambient Intelligence, Elder Care, and Game Theory.

INTRODUCTION

Given the crucial role and ubiquity of intentions in our everyday decision making (Bratman, 1987; Meltzoff, 2007; Roy, 2009b; Searle, 2010; Woodward, Sommerville, Gerson, Henderson, & Buresh, 2009), one would expect intentions to occupy a substantial place in any theory of action. However, in what concern perhaps the most prominent theory of action—rational choice theory

(Binmore, 2009; Russell & Norvig, 2003)—which includes the theory of decision making—the attention is mainly, if not exclusively, given to actions, strategies, information, outcomes and preferences, but not to intentions (Roy, 2009a; van Hees & Roy, 2008).

This is not to say that no attention has been paid to the relationship between rational choice and intentions. Quite the contrary, a rich philosophical and Artificial Intelligence (AI) literature has

DOI: 10.4018/978-1-4666-3682-8.ch009

developed on the relation between rationality and intentions (Bratman, 1987; Cohen & Levesque, 1990; Malle, Moses, & Baldwin, 2003; Singh, 1991; van Hees & Roy, 2008). Some philosophers, for example in (Bratman, 1987; Roy, 2009b), have been concerned with the role that intention plays in directing rational decision making and guiding future actions. In addition, many agent researchers have recognized the importance of intentions in developing useful agent theories, architectures, and languages, such as Rao and Georgeff with their BDI model (Rao & Georgeff, 1991, 1995), which has led to the commercialization of several high-level agent languages, e.g. in (Burmeister, Arnold, Copaciu, & Rimassa, 2008; Wooldridge, 2000, 2002). However, to the best of our knowledge, there has been no real attempt to model and implement the role of intentions in decision making, within a rational choice framework. Intentions of other relevant agents are always assumed to be given as the input of a decision making process; no system that integrates a real intention recognition system into a decision making system has been implemented so far.

In this chapter, we present a coherent Logic Programming (LP) based framework for decision making—which extends our previous work on Evolution Prospection for decision making (Pereira & Han, 2009a, 2009b)—but taking into consideration now the intentions of other agents. Obviously, when being immersed in a multi-agent environment, knowing the intentions of other agents can benefit the recognizing agents in a number of ways. It enables the recognizing agents to predict what other agents will do next or might have done before—thereby being able to plan in advance to take the best advantage from the prediction, or to act so as to take remedial action. In addition, an important role of recognizing intentions is to enable coordination of your own actions and in collaborating with others (Bratman, 1987, 1999; Kaminka, Tambe, Pynadath, & Tambe, 2002; Roy, 2009b; Searle, 1995, 2010). We have also recently shown the role

of intention recognition in promoting improved cooperative behavior in populations or societies of self-interested agents (Han, 2012; Han, Pereira, & Santos, 2011b, 2012a, 2012b). A large body of literature has exhibited experimental evidence of the ability to recognize/understand intentions of others in many kinds of interactions and communications, not only in Human but also many other species (Cheney & Seyfarth, 2007; Meltzoff, 2005, 2007; Tomasello, 1999, 2008; Woodward, et al., 2009). Furthermore, the important role of intention-based decision making modeling has been recognized in a diversity of experimental studies, including behavioral economics (Falk, Fehr, & Fischbacher, 2008; Frank, Gilovich, & Regan, 1993; Radke, Guroglu, & de Bruijn, 2012) and morality (Hauser, 2007; Young & Saxe, 2011). In AI application domains wherein an ability to recognize users' intentions is crucial for the success of a technology, such as the ones of Ambient Intelligence (Friedewald, Vildjiounaite, Punie, & Wright, 2007; Sadri, 2011a) and Elder Care (Giuliani, Scopelliti, & Fornara, 2005; Pereira & Han, 2011a; Sadri, 2010, 2011b), intention-based decision making is also becoming of increasing interest.

The Evolution Prospection (EP) system is an implemented LP-based system for decision making (Pereira & Han, 2009a, 2009b). An EP agent can prospectively look ahead a number of steps into the future to choose the best course of evolution that satisfies a goal. This is achieved by designing and implementing several kinds of prior and post preferences (Pereira, Dell'Acqua, & Lopes, 2012; Pereira & Lopes, 2009) and several useful environment-triggering constructs for decision making. In order to take into account intentions of other agents in decision making processes, we employ our previously implemented, also LP-based, intention recognition system, as an external module of the EP system. For an easy integration, the Bayesian network inference of the intention recognition system is performed by P-log (Baral, Gelfond, & Rushton, 2009; Han,

Carroline, & Damasio, 2008), a probabilistic logic system[1]. In general, intention recognition can be defined as the process of inferring the intention or goal of another agent (called "*individual intention recognition*") or a group of other agents (called "*collective intention recognition*") through their observable actions or their actions' observable effects on the environment (Han & Pereira, 2010a; Heinze, 2003; Sadri, 2010; Sukthankar & Sycara, 2008).

The remainder of this chapter is structured as follows. In Section 2 we describe our two LP-based previously implemented systems, the Evolution Prospection system and Intention Recognition. On top of these two systems, in Section 3 we describe our intention-based decision making system, the main contribution of this chapter. Section 4 describes how our framework can be utilized to address several issues in the Ambient Intelligence and Elder Care application domains. Next, Section 5 points out how intentionality is important in the moral reasoning, and how our intention-based decision making system can be used therein. This section also demonstrates how our system can be useful to model different issues in Game Theory, when strategies are characterized as modifiable intentions. The chapter ends with concluding remarks and future work directions.

BACKGROUND

Evolution Prospection

The implemented EP system[2] has proven useful for decision making (Han, 2009; Han & Pereira, 2011b; Han, Saptawijaya, & Pereira, 2012; Pereira & Han, 2009a, 2009b). It is implemented on top of ABDUAL[3], a preliminary implementation of (Alferes, Pereira, & Swift, 2004), using XSB Prolog (XSB, 2009). We next describe the constructs of EP, to the extent we use them here. A full account can be found in (Han, 2009; Pereira & Han, 2009b).

Language: Let **L** be a first order language. A domain literal in **L** is a domain atom A or its default negation *not A*. The latter is used to express that the atom is false by default (Closed World Assumption). A domain rule in **L** is a rule of the form:

$$A \leftarrow L_1, ..., L_t \ (t \geq 0)$$

where A is a domain atom and $L_1, ..., L_t$ are domain literals. An integrity constraint in **L** is a rule with an empty head. A (logic) program P over **L** is a set of domain rules and integrity constraints, standing for all their ground instances.

Here we consider solely Normal Logic Programs (NLPs), those whose heads of rules are positive literals, or empty (Baral, 2003). We focus furthermore on abductive logic programs (Alferes, et al., 2004; Kakas, Kowalski, & Toni, 1993), i.e. NLPs allowing for abducibles – user-specified positive literals without rules, whose truth-value is not fixed. Abducibles instances or their default negations may appear in bodies of rules, like any other literal. They stand for hypotheses, each of which may independently be assumed true, in positive literal or default negation form, as the case may be, in order to produce an abductive solution to a query.

Definition 1 (Abductive Solution): An abductive solution is a consistent collection of abducible instances or their negations that, when replaced by true everywhere in P, affords a model of P (for the specific semantics used on P) which satisfies the query and the ICs – a so-called abductive model.

Active Goals: In each cycle of its evolution the agent has a set of active goals or desires. We introduce the *on_observe/1* predicate, which we consider as representing active goals or desires that, once triggered by the observations figuring in its rule bodies, cause the agent to attempt their satisfaction by launching all the queries standing for them, or using preferences to select them. The rule for an active goal *AG* is of the form:

$$on\_observe(AG) \leftarrow L_p,..., L_t\ (t \geq 0)$$

where $L_p,..., L_t$ are domain literals. During evolution, an active goal may be triggered by some events, previous commitments or some history-related information. When starting a cycle, the agent collects its active goals by finding all the *on_observe(AG)* that hold under the initial theory without performing any abduction, then finds abductive solutions for their conjunction.

Preferring Abducibles: An abducible *A* can be assumed only if it is a considered one, i.e. if it is expected in the given situation, and, moreover, there is no expectation to the contrary

$$consider(A) \leftarrow expect(A),\ not\ expect\_not(A),\ A.$$

The rules about expectations are domain-specific knowledge contained in the theory of the program, and effectively constrain the hypotheses available in a situation. Note that for each abducible a consider-rule is added automatically into the EP program.

Handling preferences over abductive logic programs has several advantages, and allows for easier and more concise translation into NLPs than those prescribed by more general and complex rule preference frameworks. The advantages of so proceeding stem largely from avoiding combinatory explosions of abductive solutions, by filtering irrelevant as well as less preferred abducibles (Pereira, et al., 2012).

To express preference criteria among abducibles, we envisage an extended language **L***. A preference atom in **L*** is of the form $a <\!|\ b$, where *a* and *b* are abducibles. It means that if *b* can be assumed (i.e. considered), then $b <\!|\ a$ forces *a* to be considered too if it can. A preference rule in **L*** is of the form:

$$a <\!|\ b \leftarrow L_p,..., L_t\ (t \geq 0)$$

where $L_p,..., L_t$ are domain literals over **L***.

A priori preferences are used to produce the most interesting or relevant conjectures about possible future states. They are taken into account when generating possible scenarios (abductive solutions), which will subsequently be preferred amongst each other a posteriori.

Example 1: (Choose Tea or Coffee): Consider a situation where I need to choose to drink either tea or coffee (but not both). I prefer coffee to tea when sleepy, and do not drink coffee when I have high blood pressure. This situation can be described with the following EP program, including two abducibles *coffee* and *tea*:

```
abds [tea/0, coffee/0].
on_observe(drink).
drink ← tea.
drink ← coffee.
← tea, coffee.
expect(tea).          expect(coffee).
expect_not(coffee) ← blood_high_pressure.
coffee <| tea ← sleepy.
```

This program has two abductive solutions, one with *tea* and the other with *coffee*. Adding literal *sleepy* triggers the only *a priori* preference in the program, which defeats the solution where only *tea* is present (due to the impossibility of simultaneously abducing coffee). If later we add blood pressure high, *coffee* is no longer expected, and the transformed preference rule no longer defeats the abduction of *tea*, which then becomes the single abductive solution, despite the presence of *sleepy*.

A Posteriori Preferences: Having computed possible scenarios, represented by abductive solutions, more favorable scenarios can be preferred a posteriori. Typically, *a posteriori* preferences are performed by evaluating consequences of abducibles in abductive solutions. An *a posteriori* preference has the form:

$A_i \ll A_j \leftarrow holds\_given(L_i, A_i), holds\_given(L_j, A_j)$

where A_i, A_j are abductive solutions and L_i, L_j are domain literals. This means that A_i is preferred to A_j a posteriori if L_i and L_j are true as the side effects of abductive solutions A_i and A_j, respectively, without any further abduction when testing for the side effects. Optionally, in the body of the preference rule there can be any Prolog predicate used to quantitatively compare the consequences of the two abductive solutions.

Evolution Result A Posteriori Preference: While looking ahead a number of steps into the future, the agent is confronted with the problem of having several different possible courses of evolution. It needs to be able to prefer amongst them to determine the best courses from its present state (and any state in general). The a posteriori preferences are no longer appropriate, since they can be used to evaluate only one-step-far consequences of a commitment. The agent should be able to also declaratively specify preference amongst evolutions through quantitatively or qualitatively evaluating the consequences or side effects of each evolution choice.

A posteriori preference is generalized to prefer between two evolutions. An *evolution result a posteriori* preference is performed by evaluating consequences of following some evolutions. The agent must use the imagination (look-ahead capability) and present knowledge to evaluate the consequences of evolving according to a particular course of evolution. An evolution result a posteriori preference rule has the form:

$E_i <<< E_j \leftarrow holds\_in\_evol(L_i, E_i),$
$holds\_in\_evol(L_j, E_j)$

where E_i, E_j are possible evolutions and L_i, L_j are domain literals. This preference implies that E_i is preferred to E_j if L_i and L_j are true as evolution history side effects when evolving according to E_i or E_j, respectively, without making further abductions when just checking for the side effects.

Optionally, in the body of the preference rule there can be recourse to any Prolog predicate, used to quantitatively compare the consequences of the two evolutions for decision making.

Intention Recognition

We describe our previously implemented intention recognition system, which operates upon Bayesian Network (BN) inference (Pereira & Han, 2009c, 2011b). To begin with, we provide some basic definitions regarding BNs needed for further understanding of the system.

Bayesian Networks

Definition 2 (Bayesian Network): A Bayesian Network (BN) is a pair consisting of a *directed acyclic graph* (DAG) whose nodes represent variables and missing edges encode conditional independencies between the variables, and an associated probability distribution satisfying the *Markov assumption* of conditional independence, saying that variables are independent of nondescendants given their parents in the graph (Pearl, 1988, 2000).

In a BN, associated with each node of its DAG is a specification of the distribution of its variable, say A, conditioned on its parents in the graph (denoted by $pa(A)$)—i.e., $P(A|pa(A))$ is specified. If $pa(A)$ is empty (A is called root node), its unconditional probability distribution, $P(A)$, is specified. These distributions are called the *Conditional Probability Distribution* (CPD) of the BN.

The joint distribution of all node values can be determined as the product of conditional probabilities of the value of each node on its parents

$$P(X1,...,XN) = \prod_{t=1}^{N} P(Xi|pa(Xi)) \qquad (1)$$

where $V = \{X_1, ..., X_N\}$. is the set of nodes of the DAG. Suppose there is a set of evidence nodes (i.e. their values are observed) in the DAG, say $O = \{O_1, ..., O_N\} \subset V$. We can determine the conditional probability distribution of a variable X given the observed value of evidence nodes by using the conditional probability formula

$$P(X|O) = \frac{P(X,O)}{P(O)} = \frac{P(X, O_1, ..., Om)}{P(O_1, ..., Om)} \quad (2)$$

where the numerator and denominator are computed by summing the joint probabilities over all absent variables with respect to V as follows:

$$P(X = x, O = o)$$
$$= \sum_{av \in ASG(AV_1)} P(X = x, O = o, AV_1 = av)$$

$$P(O = o) = \sum_{av \in ASG(AV_2)} P(O = o, AV_2 = av)$$

where $o = \{o_1, ..., o_m\}$ with $o_1, ..., o_m$ being the observed values of $O_1, ..., O_m$, respectively; $ASG(V_t)$ denotes the set of all assignments of vector V_t (with components are variables in V); AV_1, AV_2 are vectors components of which are corresponding absent variables, i.e. variables in $V \setminus (O \cup \{X\})$ and $V \setminus O$, respectively.

Bayesian Networks for Intention Recognition

In (Pereira & Han, 2009c, 2011b), a general BN model for intention recognition is presented and justified based on Heinze's *causal intentional model* (Heinze, 2003; Tahboub, 2006). Basically, the BN consists of three layers: *cause/reason* nodes in the first layer (called *pre-intentional*), connecting to *intention* nodes in the second one (called *intentional*), in turn connecting to *action* nodes in the third (called *activity*) (Figure 1).

Figure 1. General structure of a Bayesian network for intention recognition. The Bayesian network consists of three layers. The pre-intentional layer consists of cause/reason nodes, connecting to intention nodes in the intentional layer, which in turn connect to action nodes in the activity layer.

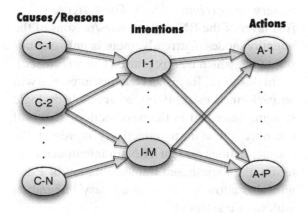

In general, intention recognition consists in computing the probabilities of each conceivable intention conditional on the current observations, including the observed actions in the third layer, and some of the causes/reasons in the first layer. The prediction of what is the intention of the observed agent can simply be the intention with the greatest conditional probability, possibly above some minimum threshold. Sometimes it is also useful to predict what are the $N(N \geq 2)$ most likely intentions given the current observations (Armentano & Amandi, 2009; Blaylock & Allen, 2003; Han & Pereira, 2011a).

Example 2 (Fox-Crow): Consider the Fox-Crow story, adapted from Aesop's fable (Aesop). There is a crow, holding a cheese. A fox, being hungry, approaches the crow and praises her, hoping that the crow will sing and the cheese will fall down near him. Unfortunately for the fox, the crow is very intelligent, having the ability of intention recognition.

The BN for recognizing Fox's intention is depicted in the Figure 2. The initial possible intentions of Fox that Crow comes up with are: Food- *i(F)*, Please- *i(P)* and Territory-*i(T)*. The facts that might give rise to those intentions are how friendly the Fox is (*Friendly_fox*) and how hungry he is (*Hungry_fox*). These figure in the first layer of the BN as the causes/reasons of the intention nodes. Currently, there is only one observation, which is, Fox praised Crow (*Praised*).

In this work, Bayesian Network inference will be performed using P-log, a probabilistic logic system, described in the next section. This will not only allow us to effectively represent the causal relations present a BN for intention recognition, the logic-based implementation of P-log will also allow us to make an easy integration with the EP system.

P-Log

The P-log system in its original form (Baral, et al., 2009) uses Answer Set Programming (ASP) as a tool for computing all stable models (Baral, 2003; Gelfond & Lifschitz, 1993) of the logical part of P-log. Although ASP has proven a useful paradigm for solving a variety of combinatorial problems, its non-relevance property (Castro, Swift, & Warren, 2007) makes the P-log system sometimes computationally redundant. A new implementation of P-log (Han, et al., 2008; Han, Carroline, & Damasio, 2009), which we deploy in this work, uses the XASP package of XSB Prolog (XSB, 2009) for interfacing with Smodels (Niemela & Simons, 1997), an answer set solver. The power of ASP allows the representation of both classical and default negation, to produce 2-valued models. Moreover, using XSB as the underlying processing platform enables collecting the relevant abducibles for a query, obtained

Figure 2. Bayesian network for Fox's intention recognition

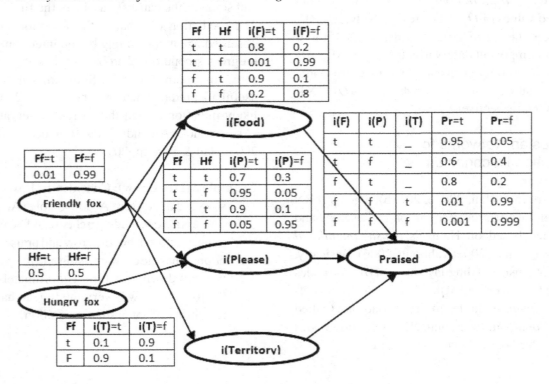

by need with top-down search. Furthermore, XSB permits to embed arbitrary Prolog code for recursive definitions. Consequently, it allows more expressive queries not supported in the original version, such as meta-queries (probabilistic built-in predicates can be used as usual XSB predicates, thus allowing the full power of probabilistic reasoning in XSB) and queries in the form of any XSB predicate expression (Han, et al., 2008). In addition, the tabling mechanism of XSB (Swift, 1999) significantly improves the performance of the system.

In general, a P-log program Π consists of a sorted signature, declarations, a regular part, a set of random selection rules, a probabilistic information part, and a set of observations and actions.

Sorted Signature and Declaration: The sorted signature Σ of Π contains a set of constant symbols and term-building function symbols, which are used to form terms in the usual way. Additionally, the signature contains a collection of special function symbols called attributes. Attribute terms are expressions of the form $a(t)$, where a is an attribute and t is a vector of terms of the sorts required by a. A literal is an atomic expression, p, or its explicit negation, neg_p.

The declaration part of a P-log program can be defined as a collection of sorts and sort declarations of attributes. A sort c can be defined by listing all the elements $c= \{x_1,...,x_m\}$ or by specifying the range of values $c= \{L..U\}$, where L and U are the integer lower bound and upper bound of the sort c. Attribute a with domain $c_1 \times ... \times c_n$ and range c_0 is represented as follows:

$$a:c_1 \times ... \times c_n --> c_0$$

If attribute a has no domain parameter, we simply write $a: c_0$. The range of attribute a is denoted by $range(a)$.

Regular Part: This part of a P-log program consists of a collection of XSB Prolog rules, facts and integrity constraints (IC) formed using literals

of Σ. An IC is encoded as a XSB rule with the false literal in the head.

Random Selection Rule: This is a rule for attribute a having the form:

$random(RandomName,a(t),DynamicRange):-$
$Body.$

This means that the attribute instance $a(t)$ is random if the conditions in *Body* are satisfied. The *DynamicRange* allows us to restrict the default range for random attributes. The *RandomName* is a syntactic mechanism used to link random attributes to the corresponding probabilities. A constant *full* can be used in *DynamicRange* to signal that the dynamic range is equal to $range(a)$.

Probabilistic Information: Information about probabilities of random attribute instances $a(t)$ taking a particular value y is given by probability atoms (or simply pa-atoms) which have the following form:

$pa(RandomName, a(t,y), d\ (A,B)):- Body$

meaning that if the *Body* were true, and the value of $a(t)$ were selected by a rule named *RandomName*, then *Body* would cause $a(t) = y$ with probability A/B. Note that the probability of an atom $a(t,y)$ will be directly assigned if the corresponding $pa/3$ atom is the head of some pa-rule with a true body. To define probabilities of the remaining atoms we assume that, by default, all values of a given attribute, which are not assigned a probability, are equally likely.

Observations and Actions: These are, respectively, statements of the forms $obs(l)$ and $do(l)$, where l is a literal. Observations $obs(a(t,y))$ are used to record the outcomes y of random events $a(t)$, i.e. random attributes and attributes dependent on them. Statement $do(a(t,y))$ indicates $a(t) = y$ is enforced as the result of a deliberate action.

In an EP program, P-log code is embedded by putting it between two reserved keywords *beginPlog* and *endPlog*. In P-log, probabilistic information can be obtained using the XSB Prolog built-in predicate *pr/2* (Han, et al., 2008). Its first argument is the query, the probability of which is needed to compute. The second argument captures the result. Thus, probabilistic information can be easily embedded by using *pr/2* like a usual Prolog predicate, in any constructs of EP programs, including active goals, preferences, and integrity constraints. What is more, since P-log (Han, et al., 2008) allows us to code Prolog probabilistic meta-predicates (Prolog predicates that depend on *pr/2* predicates), we also can directly use probabilistic meta-information in EP programs. We will illustrate those features with several examples below.

Example 3 (Fox-Crow): The BN for Fox's intention recognition (Figure 2) can be coded with the P-log program in Box 1.

Two sorts *bool* and *fox_intentions*, in order to represent Boolean values and the current set of Fox's conceivable intentions, are declared in part 1. Part 2 is the declaration of four attributes *hungry_fox*, *friendly_fox*, *praised* and *i*, which state the first three attributes have no domain parameter and get Boolean values, and the last one maps each Fox's intention to a Boolean value. The random selection rules in part 3 declare that these four attributes are randomly distributed in their ranges. The distributions of the top nodes (*hungry_fox*, *friendly_fox*) and the CPD corresponding to the BN in Figure 2 are given in part 4 and parts

Box 1.

1. bool = {t,f}. fox_intentions = {food,please,territory}.
2. hungry_fox : bool.   friendly_fox : bool.
   i : fox_intentions --> bool.   praised : bool.
3. random(rh, hungry_fox, full). random(rf, friendly_fox, full).
   random(ri, i(I), full).   random(rp, praised, full).
4. pa(rh,hungry_fox(t),d_(1,2)).
   pa(rf,friendly_fox(t),d_(1,100)).
5. pa(ri(food),i(food,t),d_(8,10)) :- friendly_fox(t),hungry_fox(t).
   pa(ri(food),i(food,t),d_(9,10)) :- friendly_fox(f),hungry_fox(t).
   pa(ri(food),i(food,t),d_(0.1,10)) :- friendly_fox(t),hungry_fox(f).
   pa(ri(food),i(food,t),d_(2,10)) :-
   friendly_fox(f),hungry_fox(f).
6. pa(ri(please),i(please,t),d_(7,10)) :- friendly_fox(t),hungry_fox(t).
   pa(ri(please),i(please,t),d_(1,100)) :- friendly_fox(f),hungry_fox(t).
   pa(ri(please),i(please,t),d_(95,100)) :- friendly_fox(t),hungry_fox(f).
   pa(ri(please),i(please,t),d_(5,100)) :- friendly_fox(f),hungry_fox(f).
7. pa(ri(territory),i(territory,t),d_(1,10)) :- friendly_fox(t).
   pa(ri(territory),i(territory,t),d_(9,10)) :- friendly_fox(f).
8. pa(rp, praised(t),d_(95,100)) :- i(food, t), i(please, t).
   pa(rp, praised(t),d_(6,10))   :- i(food, t), i(please, f).
   pa(rp, praised(t),d_(8,10))   :- i(food, f), i(please, t).
   pa(rp, praised(t),d_(1,100))   :- i(food, f), i(please,f), i(territory,t).
   pa(rp, praised(t),d_(1,1000)) :- i(food,f), i(please,f), i(territory,f).

5-8, respectively, using the probabilistic information *pa*-rules. For example, in part 4 the first rule says that fox is hungry with probability *1/2* and the second rule says he is friendly with probability *1/100*. The first rule in part 5 states that if Fox is friendly and hungry, the probability of him having intention Food is *8/10*.

Note that the probability of an atom $a(t,y)$ will be directly assigned if the corresponding *pa/3* atom is in the head of some *pa*-rule with a true body. To define probabilities of the remaining atoms we assume that by default, all values of *a* given attribute which are not assigned a probability are equally likely. For example, the first rule in part 4 implies that fox is not hungry with probability *1/2*. And, actually, we can remove that rule without changing the probabilistic information since, in that case, the probability of fox being hungry and of not being hungry are both defined by default, thus, equal to *1/2*.

The probabilities of Fox having intention *Food*, *Territory* and *Please* given the observation that Fox praised Crow can be found in P-log with the queries in Box 2, respectively.

From the result of Box 2, we can say that Fox is most likely to have the intention of deceiving the Crow for food, *i(food)*.

INTENTION-BASED DECISION MAKING

There are several ways an EP agent can benefit from the ability to recognize intentions of other agents, both in friendly and hostile settings. Knowing the intention of an agent is a means to predict what he will do next or might have done before. The recognizing agent can then plan in advance to take the best advantage of the prediction, or act to take remedial action. Technically, in the EP system, this new kind of knowledge may impinge on the body of any EP constructs, such as active goals, expectation and counter-expectation rules, preference rules, integrity constraints, etc., providing a new kind of trigger.

In order to account for intentions of other agents in decision making with EP, we provide a built-in predicate, *has_intention(Ag,I)*, stating that an agent *Ag* has the intention *I*. The truth-value of this predicate is evaluated by the intention recognition system. Whenever this predicate is called in an EP pro- gram, the intention recognition system is employed to check if *Ag* has intention *I*, i.e. *I* is the most likely conceivable intention at that moment. We also provide predicate *has_intention(Ag,I,Pr)*, stating that agent *Ag* has intention *I* with probability *Pr*. Hence, one can express, for example, the situation where one needs to be more, or less, cautious.

One can also generalize to consider the *N*-best intention recognition approach, that is, to assess whether the intention of the agent is amongst the *N* most likely intentions. It has been shown that by increasing *N*, the recognition accuracy is significantly improved (Armentano & Amandi, 2009; Blaylock & Allen, 2003; Han & Pereira, 2011a).

In the sequel we draw closer attention to some EP constructs, illustrating with several examples how to take into account intentions of other agents for enhancement of decision making.

Box 2.

?– pr(i(food,t)   'l'   obs(praised(t)),V_1). The answer is: $V_1 = 0.9317$.

?– pr(i(territory,t) 'l'   obs(praised(t)),V_2). The answer is: $V_2 = 0.8836$.

?– pr(i(please,t)   'l'   obs(praised(t)),V_3). The answer is: $V_3 = 0.0900$.

Intentions Triggering Active Goals

Recall that an active goal has the form

$$on\_observe(AG) \leftarrow L_1, ..., L_t \ (t \geq 0)$$

where $L_1, ..., L_t$ are domain literals. At the beginning of each cycle of evolution, those literals are checked with respect to the current evolving knowledge base and trigger the active goal if they all hold. For intention triggering active goals, the domain literals in the body can be in the form of has intention predicates, taking into account intentions of other agents.

This way, any intention recognition system can be used as the goal producer for decision making systems, the inputs of which are (active) goals to be solved (see for instance (Han & Pereira, 2011b); Pereira & Han, (2011a, 2011b)).

It is easily seen that intention triggering active goals are ubiquitous. New goals often appear when one recognizes some intentions in others. In a friendly setting, one might want to help others to achieve their intention, which is generally represented as follows

$$on\_observe(help\_achieve\_goal(G)) \leftarrow friend(P),$$
$$has\_intention(P,G)$$

while in a hostile setting, we probably want to prevent the opponents from achieving their goals

$$on\_observe(prevent\_achieve\_goal(G))$$
$$\leftarrow opponent(P), has\_intention(P,G)$$

Or, perhaps we simply want to plan in advance to take advantage of the hypothetical future obtained when the intending agent employs the plan that achieves his intention

$$on\_observe(take\_advantage(F)) \leftarrow agent(P),$$
$$has\_intention(P,G), future(employ(G),F).$$

Let us look a little closer at each setting, providing some ideas how they can be enacted. When helping someone to achieve an intention, what we need to do is to help him/her with executing a plan achieving that intention successfully, i.e., all the actions involved in that plan can be executed. This usually occurs in multi-agent collaborative tasks (see for example (Kaminka, et al., 2002)), wherein the agents need to be able to recognize their partners' intention to secure an efficient collaboration.

In contrast, in order to prevent an intention from being achieved, we need to guarantee that any conceivable plans achieving that intention cannot be executed successfully. To that effect, at least one action in each plan must be prevented if the plan is conformant (i.e., a sequence of actions (Phan Huy Tu, Son, Gelfond, & Morales, 2011)). If the plan is conditional (see for (Pereira & Han, 2009c; P. H. Tu, Son, & Baral, 2007)), each branch is considered a conformant plan and must be prevented.

We shall exhibit a diversity of examples in the following sections.

Intention Triggering Preferences

Having recognized an intention of another agent, the recognizing agent may either favor or disfavor an abducible (*a priori* preferences), an abductive solution (*a posteriori* preferences) or an evolution (*evolution result a posteriori* preferences) with respect to another, respectively; depending on the setting they are in. If they are in a friendly setting, the one that provides more support to achieve the intention is more favored; in contrast, in a hostile setting, the one providing more support is disfavored. The recognizing agent may also favor the one that takes better advantage of the recognized intention.

To illustrate the usage of intention triggering *a priori* preferences, we revise here Example 1.

Example 4 (Choose tea or coffee taking into account a friend's intentions): Being thirsty, I consider making tea or coffee. I realize that my roommate, John, also wants to have a drink. To be friendly, I want to take into account his intention when making my choice. This scenario is represented with the EP program in Box 3.

It is enacted by the preference rules in part 5. The first rule says that *tea* is preferable, a priori, to *coffee* if John intends to drink *tea*; and vice versa, the second rule says that if John intends to drink *coffee*, *coffee* is preferable. Note that the recognition of what John intends is performed by the intention recognition system—which is triggered when a reserved predicate *has_intention/2* is called.

This scenario also can be encoded using intention triggering a posteriori preferences. As a good friend of John, I prefer an abductive solution with a side effect of John being happy to the one with a side effect of John being unhappy. This can be coded as in Box 4.

Despite its simplicity, the example demonstrates how to solve a class of collaborative situations, where one would like to take into account the intentions and the need of others when deriving relevant hypothetical solutions of our current goals.

Box 3.

1. abds([coffee/0, tea/0]).

2. expect(coffee).   expect(tea).

3. on_observed(drink) ← thirsty.
   drink ← tea.
   drink ← coffee.
   ← tea, coffee.

4. expect_not(coffee) ← blood_high_pressure.

5. tea   <| coffee   ← **has_intention**(john,tea).
   coffee <| tea   ← **has_intention**(john,coffee).

Box 4.

unhappy   ← coffee, **has_intention**(john, tea).
happy   ← coffee, **has_intention**(john, coffee).
unhappy   ← tea, **has_intention**(john, coffee).
unhappy   ← tea, **has_intention**(john, tea).
$A_i << A_j$ ← holds_given(happy, A_i),
                holds_given(unhappy, A_j).

Next, to illustrate other kinds of preferences, we consider the following revised extended version of the saving city example, presented in (Pereira & Han, 2009b).

Example 5 (Saving cities by means of intention recognition): During war time, agent David, a general, needs to decide to save a city from his enemy's attack or leave it to keep the military resource, which might be important for some future purpose. David has recognized that a third party is intending to make an attack to the enemy on the next day. David will have a good chance to defeat the enemy if he has enough military resource to coordinate with the third party. The described scenario is coded with the EP program in Box 5.

In the first cycle of evolution, there are two abducibles, *save* and *leave*, declared in part 1, to solve the active goal *choose*. The active goal is triggered when David recognizes the intention of the enemy to attack his city (part 3).

Similar to the original version in (Pereira & Han, 2009b), in the case of being a bad general who just sees the situation at hand, David would choose to save the city since it would save more people (5000 vs. 0, part 4), i.e. the *a posteriori* preference in part 5 is taken into account immediately, to rule out the case of leaving the city since it would save less people. Then, next day, he would not be able to attack since the military

Box 5.

1. abds([save/0, leave/0]).

2. expect(save).   expect(leave).

3. on_observe(choose) ← **has_intention**(enemy,attack_my_city).
    choose ← save.
    choose ← leave.

4. save_men(5000) ← save.   save_men(0) ← leave.
    lose_resource ← save.   save_resource ← leave.

5. A_i << A_j ← holds_given(save_men(N_i), A_i),
                holds_given(save_men(N_j), A_j), N_i > N_j.

6. on_observe(decide) ←   decide_strategy.
    decide ← stay_still.
    decide ← counter_attack.

7. good_opportunity   ← **has_intention**(third_party,attack).
    expect(counter_attack) ← good_opportunity, save_resource.
    expect(stay_still).

8. pr(win,0.9) ← counter_attack.
    pr(win,0.01) ← stay_still.

9. Ei <<< Ej ← holds_in_evol(pr(win,Pi), E_i),
                holds_in_evol(pr(win,Pj), E_j), P_i > P_j.

resource is not saved (part 7), and that leads to the outcome with very small probability of winning the whole war (part 8).

But, fortunately, being able to look ahead plus, being capable of intention recognition, David can see that on the next day, if he has enough military resources, he will have a good opportunity to make a counter-attack on his enemy (part 7), by coordinating with a third party who exhibits the intention to attack the enemy on that day as well; and a successful counter-attack would lead to a very much higher probability of winning the conflict as a whole (part 8). The *evolution result a posteriori* preference is employed in part 9 to prefer the evolution with higher probability of winning the whole conflict.

In this example we can see, in part 7, how a detected intention of another agent can be used to enhance the decision making process. It is achieved by providing an (indirect) trigger for an abducible expectation—thereby enabling a new opportunistic solution by means of coordinating with others —which affects the final outcome of the *evolution result a posteriori* preference in part 9.

Hostile Setting

In this hostile setting, having confirmed the intention (and possibly also the plans achieving that intention being carried out by the intending agent), the recognizing agent might act to prevent the intention from being achieved, that is, prevent at least one action of each intention achieving plan from being successfully executed; and, in case of impossibility to doing so, act to minimize losses as much as possible.

Example 6 (Fox-Crow, cont'd): Suppose in Example 2, the final confirmed Fox's intention is that of getting food (additional details can be found in (Pereira & Han, 2009c)). That is, the predicate *has_intention(fox,food)* holds. Having recognized Fox's intention, what should Crow do to prevent Fox from achieving it? The EP program in Box 6 helps Crow with that.

There are two possible ways so as not to lose the *Food* to Fox, either simply *decline to sing* (but thereby missing the pleasure of singing) or *hide or eat the cheese* before *singing*.

Part 1 is the declaration of program abducibles (the last two abducibles are for the usage in the second phase, starting from part 9). All of them are always expected (part 2). The counter-expectation rule in part 4 states that an animal is not expected to eat if he is full. The integrity constraints in part 5 say that Crow cannot decline to sing and sing, hide and eat the cheese, at the same time. The *a priori* preference in part 6 states that eating the cheese is always preferred to hiding it (since it may be stolen), of course, just in case eating is a possible solution.

Suppose Crow is not full. Then, the counter-expectation in part 4 does not hold. Thus, there

Box 6.

1. abds([decline/0, sing/0, hide/2, eat/2, has_food/0, find_new_food/0]).
2. expect(decline).   expect(sing).
   expect(hide(_,_)).   expect(eat(_,_)).
3. on_observe(not_losing_cheese) ← **has_intention**(fox, food).
   not_losing_cheese ← decline.
   not_losing_cheese ← hide(crow,cheese), sing.
   not_losing_cheese ← eat(crow,cheese), sing.
4. expect_not(eat(A,cheese)) ← animal(A), full(A).
   animal(crow).
5. ← decline, sing.
   ← hide(crow,cheese), eat(crow,cheese).
6. eat(crow,cheese) <| hide(crow,cheese).
7. no_pleasure ← decline.
   has_pleasure ← sing.
8. $A_i << A_j$ ← holds_given(has_pleasure,A_i),
              holds_given(no_pleasure,A_j).

9. on_observe(feed_children) ← hungry(children).
   feed_children ← has_food.
   feed_children ← find_new_food.
   ← has_food, find_new_food.
10. expect(has_food) ← decline, not eat(crow,cheese).
    expect(has_food) ← hide(crow,cheese), not stolen(cheese).
    expect(find_new_food).
11. $E_i <<< E_j$ ← hungry(children), holds_in_evol(has_food,E_i),
              holds_in_evol(find_new_food,E_j).
12. $E_i <<< E_j$ ← holds_in_evol(has_pleasure,E_i),
              holds_in_evol(no_pleasure,E_j).

are two possible abductive solutions: *[decline]* and *[eat(crow,cheese), sing]* (since the *a priori* preference prevents the choice containing *hiding*).

Next, the *a posteriori* preference in part 8 is taken into account and rules out the abductive solution containing *decline* since it leads to having *no pleasure* which is less preferred to *has pleasure* —the consequence of the second solution that contains *sing* (part 7). In short, the final solution is that Crow eats the cheese then sings, without losing the cheese to Fox and having the pleasure of singing.

Now, let us consider a smarter Crow who is capable of looking further ahead into the future in order to solve longer-term goals. Suppose that Crow knows that her children will be hungry later on, in the next stage of evolution (part 9); eating the cheese right now would make her have to find new food for the hungry children. Finding new food may take long, and is always less favorable than having food ready to feed them right away (cf. the *evolution result a posteriori* preference in part 11). Crow can see three possible evolutions: *[[decline], [has_food]]; [[hide(crow, cheese), sing], [has_food]]* and *[[eat(crow, cheese), sing], [find_new_food]]*. Note that in looking ahead at least two steps into the future, *a posteriori* preferences are taken into account only after all evolution-level ones have been applied (Pereira & Han, 2009b).

Now the two *evolution result a posteriori* preferences in parts 11-12 are taken into account. The first one rules out the evolution including *finding new food* since it is less preferred than the other two, which includes *has_food*. The second one rules out the one including *decline*. In short, Crow will hide the food to keep it for her hungry children, and still take pleasure from singing.

In short, we have seen several extended examples illustrating diverse ways in which accounting for intentions of others might, in a simple manner, significantly enhance the final outcome of a decision situation. In the next sections we pay attention to concrete application domains,

wherein we address issues on which intention-based decision making may enable improvement, and show how to tackle them using our described logic-based framework. Namely, in more technological based application domains, those regarding Ambient Intelligence in the home environment and regarding Elder Care will be studied in the next section. Then, in Section 5, more experimental based domains, those of moral reasoning and game theory, are given attention.

AMBIENT INTELLIGENCE IN THE HOME ENVIRONMENT AND ELDER CARE

Ambient Intelligence (*AmI*) is the vision of a future in which environments support people inhabiting in them. The envisaged environment is unobtrusive, interconnected, adaptable, dynamic, embedded and intelligent. It should be sensitive to the needs of inhabitants, and capable of anticipating their needs and behavior. It should be aware of their personal requirements and preferences, and interact with people in a user-friendly way (see a comprehensive survey in (Sadri, 2011a)).

One of the key issues of Ambient Intelligence, which has not been well studied yet, and reported as an ongoing challenge (Cook, Augusto, & Jakkula, 2009), is that AmI systems need to be aware of users' preferences, intentions and needs. Undoubtedly too, respecting users' preferences and needs in decision making processes would increase their degree of acceptance with respect to the systems, making these deemed more friendly and thoughtful.

From this perspective on AmI, we can see a number of issues where intention recognition techniques can step in, providing help and enabling improvement. For example, in order to provide appropriate support, the environment should be able to proactively recognize the inhabitants' intention—to glean whether they need help to accomplish what they intend to do—or to warn them (or their carers) in case they intend something inappropriate or even dangerous.

Undoubtedly, an ability to recognize intentions of assisted people, as well as other relevant concerns such as intruders or the like, would enable to deal with a combination of several issues, encompassing those of pro-activeness (either agonistic or antagonistic), security, and emergency, in a much more integrated and timely manner (Han & Pereira, 2010a, 2010b; P. Roy, Bouchard, Bouzouane, & Giroux, 2007). We discuss these very issues in the sequel.

Proactive Support

An important feature of AmI, particularly desirable in the Elder Care domain, is that the assisting system should take initiative to help the people it assists. To this end, the system must be capable of recognizing their intentions on the basis of their observable actions, then provide suggestions or help achieve the recognized intentions (Pereira & Han, 2011a, 2011b). A suggestion can be, for example, what are the appropriate kinds of drink for the elder, considering the current time, temperature, or even future scheduled events such as going to have a medical test on the next day, upon having recognized that he has an intention to drink something. Or, a suggestion can simply be telling the elder where he put his book yesterday, having recognized that he might be looking for it. This feature is especially desirable and important when the assisted people are elderly or individuals with disabilities or suffering from mental difficulties (P. Roy, et al., 2007). The need for technology in this area is obvious looking at the fact that in the last twenty years there has been a significant increase of the average age of the population in most western countries and the number of elderly people has been and will be constantly growing (Cesta & Pecora, 2004; Cook, et al., 2009; Geib, 2002; Giuliani, et al., 2005; Haigh, et al., 2004; Han & Pereira, 2010a; Pereira & Han, 2011a; P. Roy, et al., 2007; Sadri, 2008).

The EP system can be engaged to provide appropriate suggestions for the elders, taking into account the external environment, elders' preferences and already scheduled future events. Expectation rules and *a priori* preferences cater for the physical state information (health reports) of the elders, in order to guarantee that only contextually safe healthy choices are generated; subsequently, information such as the elders' pleasure and interests are then considered by *a posteriori* preferences and the like.

In the Elder Care domain, assisting systems should be able to provide contextually appropriate suggestions for the elders based on their recognized intentions. The assisting system is supposed to be better aware of the environment, the elders' physical states, mental states as well as their scheduled events, so that it can provide good and safe suggestions, or simply warnings.

Let us consider the following simple scenario in the Elder Care domain.

Example 7 (Elder Care): An elder stays alone in his apartment. The intention recognition system observes that he is looking for something in the living room. In order to assist him, the system needs to figure out what he intends to find. The possible things are: something to read (*book*); something to drink (*drink*); the TV remote control (*Rem*); and the light switch (*Switch*). The BN for recognizing the elder's intention, with CPD and top nodes distribution, is given in Figure 3.

Similarly to the P-log representation and inference in Example 3, the probabilities that the elder has the intention of looking for *book, drink, remote control* and *light switch* given the observations that he is looking around and of the *states of the light* (on or off) and *TV* (on or off) can be obtained with the queries in Box 7, respectively. In these instances, S_1, S_2 are Boolean values (*t* or *f*) are to be instantiated during execution, depending on the states of the light and TV. Let us consider the possible cases:

Figure 3. Bayesian network for recognizing the elder's intentions

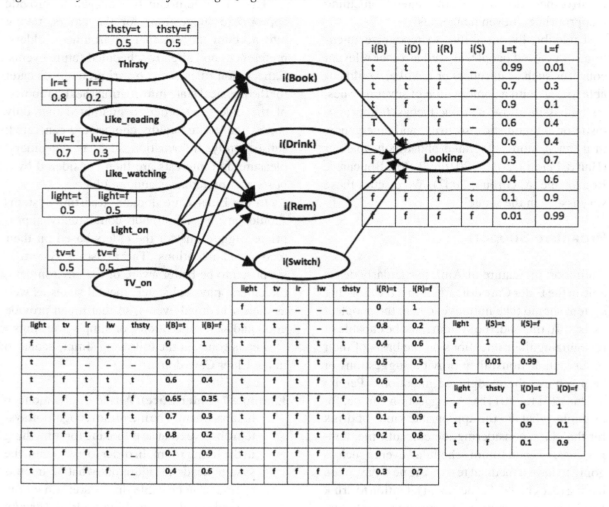

Box 7.

? – pr(i(book, t) | (obs(tv(S1)) & obs(light(S2)) & obs(look(t))), V_1).
? – pr(i(drink, t) | (obs(tv(S1)) & obs(light(S2)) & obs(look(t))), V_2).
? – pr(i(rem, t) | (obs(tv(S1)) & obs(light(S2)) & obs(look(t))), V_3).
? – pr(i(switch, t) | (obs(tv(S1)) & obs(light(S2)) & obs(look(t))), V_4).

- If the light is off $(S_2 = f)$, then $V_1 = V_2 = V_3 = 0$, $V_4 = 1.0$, regardless of the state of the TV.
- If the light is on and TV is off $(S_1 = t, S_2 = f)$, then $V_1 = 0.7521$, $V_2 = 0.5465$, $V_3 = 0.5036$, $V_4 = 0.0101$.

- If both light and TV are on $(S_1 = t, S_2 = t)$, then $V_1 = 0$, $V_2 = 0.6263$, $V_3 = 0.9279$, $V_4 = 0.0102$.

Thus, if one observes that the light is off, definitely the elder is looking for the light switch, given that he is looking around. Otherwise, if one observes the light is on, in both cases where the TV is either on or off, the first three intentions *book, drink, remote control* still need to be put under consideration in the next phase, generating possible plans for each of them. The intention of looking for the light switch is very unlikely to be the case comparing with other three, thus being ruled out. When there is light one goes directly to the light switch if the intention is to turn it off, without having to look for it.

Example 8 (Elder Care, cont'd): Suppose in the above Elder Care scenario, the final confirmed intention is that of looking for a drink[4]. The possibilities are: *natural pure water, tea, coffee* and *juice*. The EP system now is employed to help the elder with choosing an appropriate drink. The scenario is coded with the EP program below.

The elder's physical states are utilized in *a priori* preferences and expectation rules to guarantee that just choices that are contextually safe for the elder are generated. Only after that other aspects, for example the elder's pleasure with respect to each kind of drink, are taken into account, with the *a posteriori* preferences. See Box 8.

The information regarding the environment (current time, current temperature) and the physical states of the elder is coded in parts 9-11. The assisting system is supposed to be aware of this information in order to provide good suggestions.

Part 1 is the declaration of the program abducibles: *water, coffee, tea*, and *juice*. All of them in this case are always expected (part 2). Part 3 exhibits an intention triggering active goal: since the intention recognition module confirms that the elder's intention is to find something to drink, the EP system is triggered to seek appropriate suggestions for achieving the elder's intention. The counter-expectation rules in part 4 state that *coffee* is not expected if the elder has high blood

pressure, experiences difficulty to sleep or it is late; and juice is not expected if it is late. Note that the reserved predicate *prolog/1* is used to allow embedding Prolog code, put between two built-in keywords, *beginProlog* and *endProlog*, in an EP program. More details can be found in (Han, 2009; Pereira & Han, 2009a, 2009b). The integrity constraints in part 5 say that it is not allowed to have at the same time the following pairs of drink: *tea* and *coffee*, *tea* and *juice*, *coffee* and *juice*, and *tea* and *water*. However, it is the case that the elder can have coffee or juice together with water at the same time.

The *a priori* preferences in part 6 say in the morning coffee is preferred to tea, water and juice. And if it is hot, juice is preferred to all other kinds of drink and water is preferred to tea and coffee (part 7). In addition, the *a priori* preferences in part 8 state if the weather is cold, tea is the most favorable, i.e. preferred to all other kinds of drink.

Now let us look at the suggestions provided by the Elder Care assisting system modeled by this EP program, considering some cases:

1. time(24) (*late*); temperature(16) (*not hot, not cold*); *no high blood pressure*; *no sleep difficulty*: there are two a priori abductive solutions: *[tea], [water]*. Final solution: *[tea]* (since it has greater level of pleasure than water, which is ruled out by the *a posteriori* preference in part 12.

2. time(8) (*morning time*); temperature(16) (*not hot, not cold*); *no high blood pressure*; *no sleep difficulty*: there are two abductive solutions: *[coffee], [coffee, water]*. Final: *[coffee], [coffee, water]*.

3. time(18) (*not late, not morning time*); temperature(16) (*not cold, not hot*); *no high blood pressure*; *no sleep difficulty*: there are six abductive solutions: *[coffee], [coffee, water], [juice], [juice, water], [tea]*, and *[water]*. Final: *[coffee], [coffee, water]*.

4. time(18) (*not late, not morning time*); temperature(16) (*not cold, not hot*); *high blood*

pressure; *no sleep difficulty*: there are four abductive solutions: *[juice]*, *[juice, water]*, *[tea]*, and *[water]*. Final: *[tea]*.

5. time(18) (*not late, not morning time*); temperature(16) (*not cold, not hot*); *no high blood pressure*; *sleep difficulty*: there are four abductive solutions: *[juice]*, *[juice, water]*, *[tea]*, and *[water]*. Final: *[tea]*.

6. time(18) (*not late, not morning time*); temperature(8) (*cold*); *no high blood pressure*; *no sleep difficulty*: there is only one abductive solution: *[tea]*.

7. time(18) (*not late, not morning time*); temperature(35) (*hot*); *no high blood pressure*; *no sleep difficulty*: there are two abductive solutions: *[juice]*, *[juice, water]*. Final: *[juice]*, *[juice, water]*.

If the *evolution result a posteriori preference* in part 15 is taken into account and the elder is scheduled to go to the hospital for health check in the second day: the first and the second cases do not change. In the third case: the suggestions are *[tea]* and *[water]* since the ones that have *coffee* or *juice* would cause high caffeine and sugar levels, respectively, which can make the checking result (health) imprecise (parts 13-15). It can be done similarly for all the other cases.

Note future events can be asserted as Prolog code using the reserved predicate *scheduled_ events/2*. For more details of its use see (Pereira & Han, 2009a, 2009b).

As one can gather, the suggestions provided by this assisting system are quite contextually appropriate. We might elaborate current factors (time, temperature, physical states) and even consider more factors to provide more appropriate suggestions if ever the situation gets more complicated.

Security and Emergency

Security in AmI: Security is one of the key issues for AmI success (Friedewald, et al., 2007), and particularly important in home environments (Friedewald, Costa, Punie, Alahuhta, & Heinonen, 2005). It comprises two important categories: security in terms of Burglary Alarm systems and security in terms of health and wellbeing of the residents (prevention, monitoring) (Friedewald, et al., 2005).

So far Burglary Alarm technology has been mainly based on sensing and recognizing the very last action of an intrusion plan, such as "breaking the door" (Friedewald, et al., 2005; Wikipedia). However, it may be too late to provide an appropriate protection. Burglary Alarm systems need to be able to guess in advance the possibility of an intrusion on the basis of the very first observable actions of potential intruders. For example, it would be useful to find out how likely a stranger constantly staring at your house has an intrusion intention, taking into account the particular situation, e.g. if he has weapon or if it is night time. This information can be sent to the carer, the assistive system, or the elders themselves (if there are no carers or assistive systems available), for them to get prepared (e.g. turn on the light or sounders to scare off burglars or call relatives, police, firemen, etc.). Our intention-based decision making system proves appropriate to deal with this scenario. Given any currently observed actions, the probability of the on-going conceivable intentions are computed, and if the one of the intrusion intention is large enough or is among (some of) the most likely intentions, the EP component should be informed of a potential intrusion, so as to make a timely decision, and issue suggestions to the elders. To be more certain about the possibility of an intrusion, additional observations may need to be made, but at least for now it is about ready to handle any potentially negative forthcoming situations. Waiting until being sure to get ready can be too late to take appropriate actions. For illustration, consider the next example.

Example 9 (Solving Intrusion): Envisage a situation where the intention recognition system recognized an intention of intrusion at night.

Box 8.

1. abds([water/0, coffee/0, tea/0, juice/0, precise_result/0, imprecise_result/0]).
2. expect(coffee).   expect(tea).
   expect(water).   expect(juice).
3. on_observe(drink)   ← **has_intention**(elder,drink).
   drink ← tea.   drink ← coffee.
   drink ← water. drink ← juice.
4. expect_not(coffee) ← prolog(blood_high_pressure).
   expect_not(coffee) ← prolog(sleep_difficulty).
   expect_not(coffee) ← prolog(late).
   expect_not(juice) ← prolog(late).
5. ← tea, coffee.   ← coffee, juice.
   ← tea, juice.   ← tea, water.
6. coffee <| tea   ← prolog(morning_time).
   coffee <| water ← prolog(morning_time).
   coffee <| juice ← prolog(morning_time).
7. juice <| coffee ← prolog(hot).
   juice <| tea   ← prolog(hot).
   juice <| water ← prolog(hot).
   water <| coffee ← prolog(hot).
   water <| tea   ← prolog(hot).
8. tea <| coffee ← prolog(cold).
   tea <| juice ← prolog(cold).
   tea <| water ← prolog(cold).
9. pleasure_level(3) ← coffee.   pleasure_level(2) ← tea.
   pleasure_level(1) ← juice.   pleasure_level(0) ← water.
10. sugar_level(1) ← coffee.   sugar_level(1) ← tea.
    sugar_level(5) ← juice.   sugar_level(0) ← water.
11. caffein_level(5) ← coffee.   caffein_level(0) ← tea.
    caffein_level(0) ← juice.   caffein_level(0) ← water.
12. $A_i << A_j$ ← holds_given(pleasure_level(V_1), A_i),
              holds_given(pleasure_level(V_2), A_j), $V_1 > V_2$.

13. on_observe(health_check) ← time_for_health_check.
    health_check ← precise_result.
    health_check ← imprecise_result.
14. expect(precise_result) ← no_hight_sugar, no_high_caffein.
    expect(imprecise_result).
    no_high_sugar ← sugar_level(L), prolog(L < 2).
    no_high_caffein ← caffein_level(L), prolog(L < 2).

continued on following page

Box 8. Continued

15.$E_i <<< E_j \leftarrow$ holds_in_evol(precise_result, E_i),

holds_in_evol(imprecise_result, E_j).

beginProlog.

   : - assert(scheduled_events(1, [has_intention(elder,drink)])),

   assert(scheduled_events(2, [time_for_health_check])).

   late :- time(T), (T > 23; T < 5).

   morning_time :- time(T), T > 7, T < 10.

   hot :- temperature(TM), TM > 32.

   cold :- temperature(TM), TM < 10.

   blood_high_pressure :- physical_state(blood_high_pressure).

   sleep_difficulty :- physical_state(sleep_difficulty).

endProlog.

The system must either warn the elders who are sleeping, automatically call the nearest police, or activate the embedded burglary alarm. If the elders are sleeping and ill, they do not expect to be warned, but prefer other solutions. Due to potential disturbance, the elders prefer simply activating the burglary system to calling the police as long as no weapon is detected and there is a single intruder.

The situation is described by the program with three abducibles: *call_police, warn_persons, activate_alarm*, and can be coded in EP as in Box 9.

Suppose it is night-time and an intrusion intention is recognized, then the active goal solve intru-sion (part 1) is triggered, and the EP system starts reasoning to find the most appropriate solutions.

This program has three abductive solutions: *[call_police], [warn_persons]*, and *[activate_ alarm]* since all the abducibles are expected and there is no expectations to their contrary. Suppose it detects that the elders are sleeping and known to be ill, i.e. literals ill and sleeping are factual. In this case, the elders do not expect to be warned (part 4), thus ruling out the second solution *[warn_per-sons]*. And if no weapon is detected and there is only a single intruder, the a priori preference in part 5 is triggered, which defeats the solution where only call police is present (due to the impossibil-ity of simultaneously abducing activate alarm). Hence, the only solution is to activate the burglary

Box 9.

1. on observe(solve intrusion) ← at night, **has_intention**(stranger, intrusion).
2. solve_intrusion ← call police.

   solve_intrusion ← warn persons.

   solve_intrusion ← activate alarm.

3. expect(call police).   expect(warn persons).   expect(activate alarm).
4. expect_not(warn persons) ← ill, sleeping.
5. activate_alarms <| call police ← no_weapon_detected, individual.
6. call_police <| activate_alarms ← weapon_detected.

alarm. However, if weapons were detected, the preference in part 6 is triggered and defeats the [*activate_alarm*] solution. The only solution left is to call the police (*call_police*).

Regarding Burglary Alarm systems, in the following example we consider a simple scenario of recognizing an elder's intentions.

Example 10 (Detecting Intrusion): An elder stays alone in his apartment. One day the Burglary Alarm is ringing, and the assisting system observes that the elder is looking for something. In order to assist him, the system needs to figure out what he intends to find. Possible things are: Alarm button (*AlarmB*); Contact Device (*ContDev*), Defensible Weapons (*Weapon*), and light switch (*Switch*). The BN representing this scenario is in Figure 4.

The nodes representing the conceivable intentions are: *i(AlarmB)*, *i(ContDev)*, *i(Weapon)*, and

i(Switch). The Bayesian network for intention recognition has three top nodes in the pre-intentional level, representing the causes or reasons of the intentions, which are *Alarm_On*, *Defensible* and *Light_on*. The first and last nodes are evidence nodes, i.e. their values are observable. There is only one observable action, represented by the node *Looking* in the last layer. It is a direct child of the intention nodes. The conditional probability tables (CPD) of each node in the BN are given. For example, the table of the node *Defensible* says that the elder is able to defense himself (with weapons) with probability of 0.3 and not able to do so with probability 0.7. The table in the top-right corner provides the probability of the elder looking around for something conditional on the intentions. Based on this BN one can now compute the conditional probability of each intention given the observed action.

Another security issue concerns health and well-being of the residents. AmI systems need to be able to prevent hazardous situations, which usu-

Figure 4. Bayesian Network for recognizing the elder's intentions in an intrusion situation

i(A)	i(C)	i(W)	i(S)	L=t	L=f
t	t	t	–	0.99	0.01
t	t	f	–	0.7	0.3
t	f	t	–	0.8	0.2
t	f	f	–	0.3	0.7
f	t	t	–	0.6	0.4
f	t	f	–	0.55	0.45
f	f	t	–	0.65	0.35
f	f	f	t	0.1	0.9
f	f	f	f	0.01	0.99

al=t	al=f
0.5	0.5

Alarm_On

df=t	df=f
0.3	0.7

Defensible

lt=t	lt=f
0.5	0.5

Light_On

lt	i(S)=t	i(S)=f
f	0.99	0.01
t	0.1	0.9

lt	al	df	i(C)=t	i(C)=f
f	–	–	0	1
t	–	f	0.9	0.1
t	t	t	0.3	0.7
t	f	t	0.2	0.8

al	lt	i(A)=t	i(A)=f
t	t	0.9	0.1
t	f	0.3	0-7
f	–	0	1

lt	al	df	i(W)=t	i(W)=f
f	–	–	0	1
t	–	f	0.1	0.9
t	t	t	0.6	0.4
t	f	t	0.9	0.1

ally come from dangerous ideas or intentions (e.g. take a bath when drunk, drink alcohol while not permitted, or even commit suicide) of the assisted persons, especially those with mental impairments (P. Roy, et al., 2007). To this end, guessing their intentions from the very first relevant actions is indispensable to take timely actions. In our incremental intention recognition method, a BN will be built to compute how likely there is a dangerous intention, with respect to any currently observed actions, and carers would be informed in case it is likely enough, in order to get prepared in time.

Emergency in AmI: Handling emergency situations is another important issue in AmI. There are a wide range of emergency situations, e.g. in security, when recognizing intrusion intention of a stranger or dangerous intentions of the assisted person. They also can occur when detecting fire, unconsciousness or unusualness in regular activities (e.g. sleep for too long), etc. Emergency handling in the EP system can be done by having an active goal rule for whichever emergency situation. For solving the goal, a list of possible actions, all represented by abducible enablers, are available to form solutions. Then, users' preferences are encoded using all kinds of preference of EP: *a priori* ones for preferring amongst available actions, *a posteriori* ones for comparing solutions taking into account their consequences and utility, and *a posteriori evolution result* ones for comparing more-than-one-step consequences. Moreover, the expectation and counter expectation rules are used to encode pros and cons of the users towards each available action, or towards any abducible in general.

Discussion of Other AmI Issues: We have shown how our intention-based decision making framework can enable the provision of proactive support for assisted people, and the tackling of the AmI security and emergency issues. We now briefly sketch how it can be utilized to address yet other important issues in AmI.

First of all, it is known that intention recognition plays a central role in human communication

(Heinze, 2003; Pinker, Nowak, & Lee, 2008; Tomasello, 2008). In addition, an important aspect of intentions is future-directedness, i.e. if we intend something now it means we intend to execute a course of actions to achieve it in the future (Bratman, 1987; O. Roy, 2009b; Singh, 1991). Most actions may be executed only at a far distance in time. Thus, we usually need to guess others' intentions from the very first clues, such as their actions or spoken sentences, in order to secure a smooth conversation or collaboration. Perhaps we guess a wrong intention, but we need to be able to react in a timely manner; and that is also part of the conversation. We can simply attempt to confirm by asking, e.g. "is this (...) what you mean?". Our intention-based decision making framework can be used to design better and more friendly human-computer interaction devices that can react to human behavior and speech, communicate with them to confirm their intentions so as to provide appropriate help when necessary, after having guessed their likely intentions using an intention recognition system.

Yet another issue is that, in order to be highly accepted by the users, an assistive system should be able to proffer explanations for the suggestions it provides. In EP, that can be easily done by keeping all the preferences, integrity constraints, expectation and counter expectation rules that were used both to consider and to rule out abductive solutions.

OTHER DOMAINS: INTENTION-BASED DECISION MAKING IN MORAL REASONING AND GAME THEORY

Intention-Based Decision Making in Moral Reasoning

A key factor in legal and moral judgments is intention (Hauser, 2007; Young & Saxe, 2011). Intent differentiates, for instance, murder from manslaughter. When making a moral decision, it is crucial to recognize if an action or decision is intentional (or at least very likely to be intentional so as, for instance, to be judged beyond reasonable double) or not. Intentionality plays the central part in different moral rules, notably the double effect principle (Hauser, 2007; Mikhail, 2007), rendered as follows:

Harming another individual is permissible if it is the foreseen consequence of an act that will lead to a greater good; in contrast, it is impermissible to harm someone else as an intended means to a greater good.

This principle is particularly applicable for the well-known trolley problems, having the following initial circumstance (Hauser, 2007):

There is a trolley and its conductor has fainted. The trolley is headed toward five people walking on the track. The banks of the track are so steep that they will not be able to get off the track in time.

Given this circumstance, there exist several cases of moral dilemmas (Mikhail, 2007). Let us consider the following three typical cases (illustrated in Figure 5).

- **Bystander:** Hank is standing next to a switch that can turn the trolley onto a sidetrack, thereby preventing it from killing the five people. However, there is a man standing on the sidetrack. Hank can throw the switch, killing him; or he can refrain from doing so, letting the five die. Is it morally permissible for Hank to throw the switch?
- **Footbridge:** Ian is on the bridge over the trolley track, next to a heavy man, which he can shove onto the track in the path of the trolley to stop it, preventing the killing of five people. Ian can shove the man onto the track, resulting in death; or he can refrain from doing so, letting the five die. Is it morally permissible for Ian to shove the man?
- **Loop Track:** Ned is standing next to a switch that can temporarily turn the trolley onto a sidetrack, without stopping, only to join the main track again. There is a heavy man on the sidetrack. If the trolley hits the man, he will slow down the trolley, giving time for the five to escape. Ned can throw the switch, killing the man; or he can refrain from doing so, letting the five die. Is it morally permissible for Ned to throw the switch?

Figure 5. Three trolley cases: (1) bystander; (2) footbridge; (3) loop track

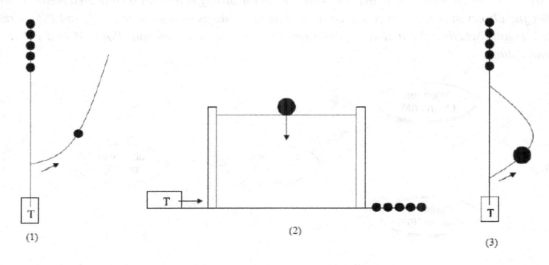

The trolley problem suite has been used in tests to assess moral judgments of subjects from demographically diverse populations (Hauser, 2007; Mikhail, 2007). Interestingly, although all three cases have the same goal, i.e. to save five albeit killing one, subjects come to different judgments on whether the action to reach the goal is permissible or impermissible, i.e. permissible for the Bystander case, but impermissible for the Footbridge and Loop Track cases. As reported by (Mikhail, 2007), the judgments appear to be widely shared among demographically diverse populations.

We show how the trolley problems can be modeled within our intention-based decision making framework, leading to outcomes complying with the moral principle of double effect. In all these three cases, as the action to be judged is given explicitly, one just has to decide whether the action is an intentional act of killing or not. The three-layered Bayesian network in Figure 6 is provided for this purpose. Here since we are deciding whether the observed action O is an intentional killing act, we can easily define the CPD of O, $P(O= t \mid IK) =1$ for all $IK \in \{t,f\}$. Next, the CPD of IK can be defined as follows:

$P(IK=t\mid IM=t, PR)=1$; $P(IK=t\mid IM= f, PR=t)= 0.6$; $P(IK=t\mid IM=f, PR=f)=0$.

We now only need to focus on prior probabilities of IM and PK. The P-log program representing this BN can be provided similarly to the one in Example 3.

In the original form of the trolley cases presented above, any personal reason is not considered, thus having prior probability of 0. The prior probability of IM is 0 for the Bystander case and 1 for the other cases. Hence, the probability of intentional killing, i.e. $P(IK=t\mid O=t)$, is 0 for the Bystander case and 1 for the other two cases.

Let us consider how to model the first two cases, those of the Bystander and the Footbridge. The Loop track case can be done similarly.

Example 11 (Bystander): In the following we see how the Bystander case can be coded using our intention-based decision making framework (Box 9).

Part 1 is the declaration of abducibles. Parts 6-7 model the principle of double effect. Namely, part 6 says it is impermissible to have an action (that is, throwing the switch) of intentional killing,

Figure 6. Bayesian network for intentional killing recognition. The node intentional killing (IK) in the intentional (middle) layer receives Boolean values (t or f), stating whether the observed action in the third layer is an intentional killing act. The node IK is causally affected by IM (intended means), stating whether the observed action is performed as an intended means to a greater good, and PR (personal reason), stating whether the action is performed due to a personal reason. Both IM and PR receive Boolean values.

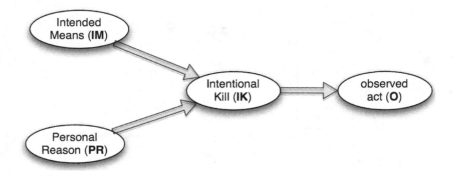

Box 9.

1. abds([watching/0, throwing_switch/0]).
2. on_observe(decide) ← train_comming.
   decide ← watching.
   decide ← throwing_switch.
   ← throwing_switch, watching.
3. expect(watching).
   train_straight ← watching.
   end(die(5)) ← train_straight.
4. expect(throwing_switch).
   redirect_train ← throwing_switch.
   end(die(1)) ← human(X), side_track(X), redirect_train.
5. side_track(john).   human(john).
6. intentional_kill ← throwing_switch, has_intention(ned, kill, Pr), prolog(Pr > 0.95).
   ← intentional_killing.
7. A_i << A_j ← holds_given(end(die(N)), A_i),
                   holds_given(end(die(K)), A_j), N < K.

which is judged so if intentional killing is predicted by the model with a probability greater some given threshold. This threshold depends on how certain the judgment needs to be provided, for instance, say 0.95 if it is *'guilty beyond reasonable doubt'*. Part 7 says the scenario involving the saving of more people is more favorable. When the train with the fainted conductor is coming, agent Hank has to decide either to watch the train go straight or throw the switch (part 2). There is always the possible expectation to watch the train go straight or the possible expectation to throw the switch, there being no expectations to their contrary (parts 3 and 4).

Because in this Bystander case, the probability of intentional killing is 0, $P(IK = t \mid O = t) = 0$, there are two prior abductive solutions: *[watching, not throwing_switch], [throwing_switch, not watching]*.

Next the *a posteriori* preferences are taken into account to rule out the less preferred abductive solutions. Considering the a posteriori preference in part 7, the abductive solution including watching is ruled out since it leads to the consequence of

five people dying (part 3), which is less preferred than the one including *throwing_switch* that leads to the consequence of non-intentional killing of one person. In short, Hank's decision is to throw the switch to save five people although one will die (unintentionally killed).

Now let us modify the original Bystander case to see how the factor 'personal reason' (*PR*) in the BN model may affect any moral judgment. Supposed there is a good chance that there is some evidence showing that Hank wants to kill the person on the sidetrack: $P(PR=t)=0.85$. Now, the probability of intentional killing is: $P(IK= t \mid O=t) =0.51$. It is not enough to judge that Hank's action is one of intentional killing, beyond reasonable doubt, but the probability is high enough to require further investigation to clarify the case.

Example 12 (Footbridge): The footbridge case can be coded with the program in Box 10.

Similarly to the previous case, part 1 provides is the declaration of program abducibles. There is always expectation to watch the train go straight

Box 10.

1. abds([watching/0, shove/1]).
    on_observe(decide) ← train_comming.
    decide ← watching.
    decide ← shove(X).
    ← watching, shove(X).
2. expect(watching).
    train_straight ← watching.
    end(die(5)) ← train_straight.
3. expect(shove(X)) ← stand_near(X).
    on_track(X) ← shove(X).
    stop_train(X) ← on_track(X), heavy(X).
    kill(1) ← human(X), on_track(X).
    kill(0) ← inanimate_object(X), on_track(X).
    end(die(N)) ← kill(N).
4. human(john).   heavy(john).
    inanimate_object(rock).   heavy(rock).
5. stand_near(john).
    %stand_near(rock).
6. intentional_kill ← human(X), shove(X), **has_intention**(ian, kill, Pr), Prolog(Pr > 0.95).
    ← intentional_killing.
7. $A_i << A_j$ ← holds_given(end(die(N)), A_i),
                holds_given(end(die(K)), A_j), N < K.

and no expectation to its contrary (part 2). However, the action of shoving an object is only possible if there is an object near Ian to shove (part 3). To make this case more interesting we can have an additional heavy object, e.g. rock, on the footbridge near to Ian and see whether our model of the moral rule still allows the reasoning to deliver moral decisions as expected. Similarly to the Bystander case, the double effect principle is modeled in parts 6 and 7.

If there is a person, named John, standing near to Ian (part 5), then there is a possible expectation to shove John (part 3). However, shoving a human is an intentional killing action, which does not satisfy the integrity constraint in part 6, since the probability of intentional killing predicted by the BN model is 1: $P(IK = t \mid O = t) = 1$. Therefore, there is only one abductive solution, to merely

watch the train go towards the five people: *[watching, not shoving(john)]*.

Now consider the same initial situation but, instead of a person, there is a heavy inanimate object, a rock, standing near Ian (replace *stand_near(john)* in part 5 with *stand_near(rock)*). Now there is expectation to shove the rock. In addition, it is not an intentional killing. Thus, there are two abductive solutions: *[watching, not shove(rock)]*, *[shove(rock), not watching]*. Next, the *a posteriori* preferences in part 7 are taken into account. The abductive solution including watching is ruled out since it leads to the consequence of killing five people, less preferred than the one including *shove(rock)* that leads to the consequence of killing nobody.

In short, if standing near to Ian is a person he has only one choice to watch the train go straight and kill five people since shoving a person to the sidetrack is an intentional killing action. However, if standing near to him were an inanimate object, he would shove the object to stop the train, saving the five and killing no one.

Uncertainty about observed actions: Usually moral reasoning is performed upon conceptual knowledge of the actions. But it often happens that one has to pass a moral judgment on a situation without actually observing the situation, i.e. there is no full, certain information about the actions. The BN in Figure 6 is not applicable anymore. In this case, it is important to be able to reason about the actions, under uncertainty, that might have occurred, and thence provide judgment adhering to moral rules within some prescribed uncertainty level. Courts, for example, are required to proffer rulings beyond reasonable doubt. There is a vast body of research on proof beyond reasonable doubt within the legal community, e.g. (Newman, 2006). For illustration, consider this variant of the Footbridge case.

Example 13 (Moral Reasoning with Uncertain Actions): Suppose a jury in a court is faced with the case where the action of Ian shoving the man onto the track was not observed. Instead, they are only presented with the fact that the man died on the sidetrack and Ian was seen on the bridge at the occasion. Is Ian guilty (*beyond reasonable doubt*), i.e. does he violate the double effect principle, of shoving the man onto the track intentionally?

To answer this question, one should be able to reason about the possible explanations of the observations, on the available evidence. The following code shows a model for this example. Given the active goal judge (part 2), two abducibles are available, i.e. *verdict (guilty_beyond_reasonable_doubt)* and *verdict(not_guilty)*. Depending on how probable is each possible verdict, *verdict (guilty_beyond_reasonable_doubt)* or *verdict(not_guilty)* is expected a priori (part 3

and 9). The sort intentionality in part 4 represents the possibilities of an action being performed intentionally (*int*) or non-intentionally (*not_int*). Random attributes *df_run* and *br_slip* in part 5 and 6 denote two kinds of evidence: Ian was definitely running on the bridge in a hurry (*df_run*) and the bridge was slippery at the time (*br_slip*), respectively. Each has prior probability of 4/10. The probability with which shoving is performed intentionally is captured by the random attribute shoved (part 7), which is causally influenced by both evidence. Part 9 defines when the verdicts (*guilty* and *not_guilty*) are considered highly probable using the meta-probabilistic predicate *pr_iShv/1*, defined in part 8. It denotes the probability of intentional shoving, whose value is determined by the existence of evidence that Ian was running in a hurry past the man (signaled by predicate *evd_run/1*) and that the bridge was slippery (signaled by predicate *evd_slip/1*). See Box 11.

Using the above model, different judgments can be delivered by our system, subject to available evidence and attending truth-value. We exemplify some cases in the sequel. If both evidence are available, where it is known that Ian was running in a hurry on the slippery bridge, then he may have bumped the man accidentally, shoving him unintentionally onto the track. This case is captured by the first *pr_iShv* rule (part 8): the probability of intentional shoving is 0.05. Thus, the atom *highly_probable(not guilty)* holds (part 10). Hence, *verdict(not_guilty)* is the preferred final abductive solution (part 3). The same abductive solution is obtained if it is observed that the bridge was slippery, but whether Ian was running in a hurry was not observable. The probability of intentional shoving, captured by *pr_iShv*, is 0.29.

On the other hand, if the evidence shows that Ian was not running in a hurry and the bridge was also not slippery, then they do not support the explanation that the man was shoved unintentionally, e.g., by accidental bumping. The action of shoving is more likely to have been performed

Box 11.

1. abds([verdict/1]).
2. on_observe(judge).
   judge ← verdict(guilty_beyond_reasonable_doubt).
   judge ← verdict(not_guilty).
3. expect(verdict(X)) ← prolog(highly_probable(X)).

beginPlog.
4. bool = {t, f}.   intentionality = {int, not_int}.
5. df_run : bool.   random(rdr,df_run,full).
   pa(rdr,df_run(t),d_(4, 10)).
6. br_slip : bool.   random(rsb,br_slip,full).
   pa(rsb,br_slip(t),d_(4, 10)).
7. shoved : intentionality.   random(rs, shoved, full).
   pa(rs,shoved(int),d_(97,100)) :- df_run(f),br_slip(f).
   pa(rs,shoved(int),d_(45,100)) :- df_run(f),br_slip(t).
   pa(rs,shoved(int),d_(55,100)) :- df_run(t),br_slip(f).
   pa(rs,shoved(int),d_(5,100)) :- df_run(t),br_slip(t).

   :- dynamic evd_run/1, evd_slip/1.
8. pr_iShv(Pr) :- evd_run(X), evd_slip(Y), !,
              pr(shoved(int) '|' obs(df_run(X)) & obs(br_slip(Y)), Pr).
   pr_iShv(Pr) :- evd_run(X), !,
              pr(shoved(int) '|' obs(df_run(X)), Pr).
   pr_iShv(Pr) :- evd_slip(Y), !,
              pr(shoved(int) '|' obs(br_slip(Y)), Pr).
   pr_iShv(Pr) :- pr(shoved(int), Pr).
9. highly_probable(guilty_beyond_reasonable_doubt) :- pr_iShv(PrG), PrG > 0.95.
   highly_probable(not_guilty) :- pr_iShv(PrG), PrG < 0.6.
endPlog.

intentionally. Using the model, the probability of 0.97 is returned and, being greater than 0.95, *verdict(guilty_beyond_reasonable_doubt)* becomes the sole abductive solution. In another case, if it is only known the bridge was not slippery and no other evidence is available, then the probability of intentional shoving becomes 0.79, and, by parts 4 and 10, no abductive solution is preferred. This translates into the need for more evidence, as the available one is not enough to issue judgment.

Intention-Based Decision Making in Game Theory

In strategic and economic situations as typically modeled using the game theoretical framework (Hofbauer & Sigmund, 1998; Osborne, 2004), the achievement of a goal by an agent usually does not depend uniquely on its own actions, but also on the decisions and actions of others—especially when the possibility of communication is limited (Heinze, 2003; Kraus, 1997; Pinker, et al., 2008; Tomasello, 2008). The knowledge about intention of others in such situations could enable an recognizing agent to plan in advance, either to secure a successful cooperation, to deal with potential hostile behaviors, and thus take the best advantage of such knowledge (Bratman, 1987; Cohen & Levesque, 1990; Han, 2012; Han, Pereira, & Santos, 2011a; Han, Pereira, et al., 2012a; O. Roy, 2009b; van Hees & Roy, 2008). Additionally, in more realistic settings where deceit may offer additional profits, agents often attempt to hide their real intentions and make others believe in faked ones (Han, 2012; Han, Pereira, et al., 2012b; Robson, 1990; Tomasello, 2008; Trivers, 2011). Undoubtedly, in all such situations a capability of recognizing intentions of others and take them into account when making decision is crucial, providing its withholders with significant net benefit or evolutionary advantages. Indeed, the capacity for intention recognition and intention-based decision making can be found abundantly in many kinds of humans' interactions and communications, widely documented for instance in (Cheney & Seyfarth, 2007; Meltzoff, 2007; Tomasello, 1999, 2008; Woodward, et al., 2009). In addition, there is a large body of literature on experimental economics that shows the importance of intention-based decision making in diverse kinds of strategic games, for instance, the Prisoner's dilemma (Frank, et al., 1993), the Moonlighting game (Falk, et al., 2008; Radke, et al., 2012) and the Ultimatum game (Radke, et al., 2012). In addition, computational models show that the taking into account of the ongoing strategic intentions of others is crucial for agents' success in the course of different strategic games (Han, 2012; Han, et al., 2011a, 2011b; Han, Pereira, et al., 2012a, 2012b; Janssen, 2008).

Let us consider some examples of intention-based decision making in the context of the Prisoner's Dilemma (PD), where in each interaction a player needs to choose a move, either to cooperate ('c') or to defect ('d'). In a one-shot

PD interaction, it is always better off choosing to defect, but cooperation might be favorable if the PD is repeated (called iterated PD), that is, there is a good chance that players will play the same PD with each other again. Several successful strategies have been provided in the context of the iterated PD (see a survey in Sigmund, 2010), most famously amongst them are tit-for-tat (*tft*) and win-stay-lose-shift (*wsls*).

The following two strategies (each denoted by *IR*), operating upon intent-based decision making, have been shown to be better than those famous strategies of the iterated PD (Han, et al., 2011a, 2011b; Han, Pereira, et al., 2012a). In the sequel we show how to model them within our framework.

Example 14 (Intention-Based Decision Making Rule in (Han, et al., 2011a; Han, Pereira, et al., 2012b; Janssen, 2008)): Prefer to cooperate if the co-player intends to cooperate, and prefer to defect otherwise. See Box 12.

At the start of a new interaction, an IR player needs to choose a move, either cooperate (*c*) or defect (*d*) (parts 2-3). Both options are expected, and there are no expectations to the contrary (part 4). There are two *a priori* preferences in part 5, stating that an IR player prefers to cooperate if the co-player's recognized intention is to cooperate, and prefers to defect otherwise. The built-in predicate *has_intention/2*, in the body of the preferences, triggers the intention recognition

Box 12.

1. abds([move/1]).
2. on_observed(decide) ← new_interaction.
3. decide ← move(c).
   decide ← move(d).
   ← move(c), move(d).
4. expect(move(X)).
5. move(c) <| move(d) ← has intention(co_player, c).
   move(d) <| move(c) ← has intention(co_player, d).

module to validate if the co-player is more likely to have the intention expressed in the second argument.

Example 15 (Intention-Based Decision Making Rule in (Han, et al., 2011b; Han, Pereira, et al., 2012a)): Defect if the co-player's recognized intention or rule of behavior is always-cooperate (*allc*) or always-defect (*alld*), cooperate if it is *tft*; and if it is *wsls*, cooperate if last game state is both cooperated (denoted by R) or both defected (denoted by P) and defect if the current game state is IR defected and the co-player cooperated (denoted by T) or vice versa (denoted by S).

This rule of behavior is learnt using a dataset collected from prior interactions with those strategies (Han, et al., 2011b). See Box 13.

At the start of a new interaction, an IR needs to choose a move, either cooperate (c) or defect (d) (parts 2-3). Both options are expected, and there are no expectations to the contrary. The *a priori* preferences in part 5 stating which move IR prefers to choose, given the recognized intention of the co-player (*allc, alld, tft* or *wsls*) and the current game state ('T', 'R', 'P' or 'S'). The built-in predicate *has_intention/2* in the body of the preferences triggers the intention recognition

module to validate if the co-player is most likely to follow a given intention (strategy), specified by the second argument.

In short, our framework is general and expressive, suitable for intention-based decision making in the context of game theory.

CONCLUSION AND FUTURE WORK

We have summarized our previous work on Evolution Prospection (EP) (Pereira & Han, 2009a, 2009b) and have shown how to obtain its coherent combination with the intention recognition system, for achieving intention-based decision making. The EP system has proven useful before for the purpose of decision making (Han & Pereira, 2010a, 2010b, 2011b; Han, Saptawijaya, et al., 2012; Pereira & Han, 2009a, 2009b, 2011b), and has now been empowered to take into account the intentions of other agents—an important aspect that has not been well explored so far (O. Roy, 2009b; van Hees & Roy, 2008). The fact that both systems are Logic Programming based enabled their easy integration. We have described and exemplified several ways in which an EP agent can benefit from having an ability to recognize intentions in other agents.

Box 13.

1. abds([move/1]).
2. on observed(decide) ← new interaction.
3. decide ← move(c).
   decide ← move(d).
   ← move(c), move(d).
4. expect(move(X)).
5. move(d) <| move(c) ← has_intention(co_player, allc).
   move(d) <| move(c) ← has_intention(co_player, alld).
   move(c) <| move(d) ← has_intention(co_player, tft).
   move(c) <| move(d) ← has_intention(co_player, wsls), game_state(s), (s = 'R'; s = 'P').
   move(d) <| move(c) ← has_intention(co_player, wsls), game_state(s), (s = 'T'; s = 'S').

Notwithstanding, the combination of intention recognitions approach we have used here is not deemed restricted to Logic Programming based systems. In general, any intention recognition system, and indeed, any decision making system, can be considered. The ideas of combined integration described here can be adopted by other decision making systems to account for intentions.

We have addressed the need for intention-based decision making in different application domains, including Ambient Intelligence (Sadri, 2011a) and Elder Care (Cesta & Pecora, 2004; Sadri, 2008), where decision making techniques as well as intention recognition abilities are becoming of increased importance (Geib, 2002; Pereira & Han, 2011a; Sadri, 2010). Furthermore, we have also described how important and ubiquitous intention-based decision making is in the moral reasoning and game theory setting application domains.

In future work, we consider applying our combined system to other application domains, including story understanding (Charniak & Goldman, 1990), human-computer and interface-agents systems (Armentano & Amandi, 2007; Hong, 2001; Lesh, 1998), traffic monitoring (Pynadath & Wellman, 1995), assistive living (Geib, 2002; Haigh, et al., 2004; Pereira & Han, 2011a; P. Roy, et al., 2007; Tahboub, 2006), military settings (Heinze, 2003; Mao & Gratch, 2004), and moral reasoning (Han, Saptawijaya, et al., 2012), where intention recognition has proven useful and of great practicality. Another area of future development is to extend our system to enable collective or group intention recognition (Sukthankar, 2007; Sukthankar & Sycara, 2008) in a decision making process. In this regard, we have made some initial attempts in the Elder Care domain (Han & Pereira, 2010a, 2010b).

ACKNOWLEDGMENT

We thank Ari Saptawijaya for his comments on an earlier version of this chapter. TAH acknowledges the support from FCT-Portugal (grant reference *SFRH/BD/62373/2009*).

REFERENCES

Alferes, J. J., Pereira, L. M., & Swift, T. (2004). Abduction in well-founded semantics and generalized stable models via tabled dual programs. *Theory and Practice of Logic Programming*, *4*(4), 383–428. doi:10.1017/S1471068403001960

Armentano, M. G., & Amandi, A. (2007). Plan recognition for interface agents. *Artificial Intelligence Review*, *28*(2), 131–162. doi:10.1007/s10462-009-9095-8

Armentano, M. G., & Amandi, A. (2009). Goal recognition with variable-order Markov models. In *Proceedings of the 21st International Joint Conference on Artificial Intelligence*. IEEE.

Baral, C. (2003). *Knowledge representation, reasoning, and declarative problem solving*. Cambridge, UK: Cambridge University Press. doi:10.1017/CBO9780511543357

Baral, C., Gelfond, M., & Rushton, N. (2009). Probabilistic reasoning with answer sets. *Theory and Practice of Logic Programming*, *9*(1), 57–144. doi:10.1017/S1471068408003645

Binmore, K. G. (2009). *Rational decisions*. Princeton, NJ: Princeton University Press.

Blaylock, N., & Allen, J. (2003). Corpus-based, statistical goal recognition. In *Proceedings of the 18th International Joint Conference on Artificial Intelligence (IJCAI 2003)*. IEEE.

Bratman, M. E. (1987). *Intention, plans, and practical reason*. CSLI.

Bratman, M. E. (1999). *Faces of intention: Selected essays on intention and agency*. Cambridge, UK: Cambridge University Press. doi:10.1017/CBO9780511625190

Burglar Alarm. (2012). *Wikipedia*. Retrieved from http://en.wikipedia.org/wiki/Burglar_alarm

Burmeister, B., Arnold, M., Copaciu, F., & Rimassa, G. (2008). BDI-agents for agile goal-oriented business processes. In *Proceedings of the 7th International Joint Conference on Autonomous Agents and Multiagent Systems: Industrial Track*. IEEE.

Castro, L., Swift, T., & Warren, D. S. (2007). *XASP: Answer set programming with xsb and smodels*. Retrieved from http://xsb.sourceforge.net/packages/xasp.pdf

Cesta, A., & Pecora, F. (2004). *The robocare project: Intelligent systems for elder care*. Paper presented at the AAAI Fall Symposium on Caring Machines: AI in Elder Care. New York, NY.

Charniak, E., & Goldman, R. P. (1990). Plan recognition in stories and in life. In *Proceedings of the Fifth Annual Conference on Uncertainty in Artificial Intelligence*. IEEE.

Cheney, D. L., & Seyfarth, R. M. (2007). *Baboon metaphysics: The evolution of a social mind*. Chicago, IL: University Of Chicago Press.

Cohen, P. R., & Levesque, H. J. (1990). Intention is choice with commitment. *Artificial Intelligence*, *42*(2-3), 213–261. doi:10.1016/0004-3702(90)90055-5

Cook, D., Augusto, J., & Jakkula, V. (2009). Ambient intelligence: Technologies, applications, and opportunities. *Pervasive and Mobile Computing*, *5*(4), 277–298. doi:10.1016/j.pmcj.2009.04.001

Falk, A., Fehr, E., & Fischbacher, U. (2008). Testing theories of fairness---Intentions matter. *Games and Economic Behavior*, *62*(1), 287–303. doi:10.1016/j.geb.2007.06.001

Frank, R. H., Gilovich, T., & Regan, D. T. (1993). The evolution of one-shot cooperation: An experiment. *Ethology and Sociobiology*, *14*(4), 247–256. doi:10.1016/0162-3095(93)90020-I

Friedewald, M., Costa, O. D., Punie, Y., Alahuhta, P., & Heinonen, S. (2005). Perspectives of ambient intelligence in the home environment. *Telematics Information, 22*.

Friedewald, M., Vildjiounaite, E., Punie, Y., & Wright, D. (2007). Privacy, identity and security in ambient intelligence: A scenario analysis. *Telematics and Informatics*, *24*(1), 15–29. doi:10.1016/j.tele.2005.12.005

Geib, C. W. (2002). Problems with intent recognition for elder care. In *Proceedings of AAAI Workshop Automation as Caregiver*. AAAI.

Gelfond, M., & Lifschitz, V. (1993). Representing actions and change by logic programs. *Journal of Logic Programming, 17*(2,3,4), 301 - 323.

Giuliani, M. V., Scopelliti, M., & Fornara, F. (2005). *Elderly people at home: technological help in everyday activities*. Paper presented at the IEEE International Workshop on In Robot and Human Interactive Communication. New York, NY.

Haigh, K., Kiff, L., Myers, J., Guralnik, V., Geib, C., Phelps, J., et al. (2004). The independent lifestyle assistant (I.L.S.A.): AI lessons learned. In *Proceedings of Conference on Innovative Applications of Artificial Intelligence*. IEEE.

Han, T. A. (2009). *Evolution prospection with intention recognition via computational logic*. Dresden, Germany: Technical University of Dresden.

Han, T. A. (2012). *Intention recognition, commitments and their roles in the evolution of cooperation.* Lisbon, Portugal: Universidade Nova de Lisboa.

Han, T. A., Carroline, D. P., & Damasio, C. V. (2008). An implementation of extended p-log using XASP. In *Proceedings of the 24th International Conference on Logic Programming.* IEEE.

Han, T. A., Carroline, D. P., & Damasio, C. V. (2009). *Tabling for p-log probabilistic query evaluation.* Paper presented at the New Trends in Artificial Intelligence, Proceedings of 14th Portuguese Conference on Artificial Intelligence (EPIA 2009). Evora, Portugal.

Han, T. A., & Pereira, L. M. (2010a). *Collective intention recognition and elder care.* Paper presented at the AAAI 2010 Fall Symposium on Proactive Assistant Agents (PAA 2010). New York, NY.

Han, T. A., & Pereira, L. M. (2010b). Proactive intention recognition for home ambient intelligence. In *Proceedings of 5th Workshop on Artificial Intelligence Techniques for Ambient Intelligence (AITAmI'10), Ambient Intelligence and Smart Environments.* IEEE.

Han, T. A., & Pereira, L. M. (2011a). Context-dependent incremental intention recognition through Bayesian network model construction. In *Proceedings of the Eighth UAI Bayesian Modeling Applications Workshop (UAI-AW 2011).* UAI-AW.

Han, T. A., & Pereira, L. M. (2011b). Intention-based decision making with evolution prospection. In *Proceedings of the 15th Portugese Conference on Progress in Artificial Intelligence.* IEEE.

Han, T. A., Pereira, L. M., & Santos, F. C. (2011a). Intention recognition promotes the emergence of cooperation. *Adaptive Behavior, 19*(3), 264–279.

Han, T. A., Pereira, L. M., & Santos, F. C. (2011b). The role of intention recognition in the evolution of cooperative behavior. In *Proceedings of the 22nd International Joint Conference on Artificial Intelligence (IJCAI'2011).* IEEE.

Han, T. A., Pereira, L. M., & Santos, F. C. (2012a). Corpus-based intention recognition in cooperation dilemmas. *Artificial Life.* doi:10.1162/ARTL_a_00072

Han, T. A., Pereira, L. M., & Santos, F. C. (2012b, June). *Intention recognition, commitment and the evoution of cooperation.* Paper presented at the The 2012 IEEE World Congress on Computational Intelligence (IEEE WCCI 2012), Congress on Evolutionary Computation (IEEE CEC 2012). Brisbane, Australia.

Han, T. A., Saptawijaya, A., & Pereira, L. M. (2012). Moral reasoning under uncertainty. In *Proceedings of the 18th International Conference on Logic for Programming, Artificial Intelligence and Reasoning (LPAR-18).* LPAR.

Hauser, M. D. (2007). *Moral minds, how nature designed our universal sense of right and wrong.* New York, NY: Little Brown.

Heinze, C. (2003). *Modeling intention recognition for intelligent agent systems.*

Hofbauer, J., & Sigmund, K. (1998). *Evolutionary games and population dynamics.* Cambridge, UK: Cambridge University Press. doi:10.1017/CBO9781139173179

Hong, J. (2001). Goal recognition through goal graph analysis. *Journal of Artificial Intelligence Research, 15,* 1–30. doi:10.1023/A:1006673610113

Janssen, M. A. (2008). Evolution of cooperation in a one-shot prisoner's dilemma based on recognition of trustworthy and untrustworthy agents. *Journal of Economic Behavior & Organization, 65*(3-4), 458–471. doi:10.1016/j.jebo.2006.02.004

Kakas, A. C., Kowalski, R. A., & Toni, F. (1993). Abductive logic programming. *Journal of Logic and Computation, 2*(6), 719–770. doi:10.1093/logcom/2.6.719

Kaminka, G. A., Tambe, D. V. P. M., Pynadath, D. V., & Tambe, M. (2002). Monitoring teams by overhearing: A multi-agent plan-recognition approach. *Journal of Artificial Intelligence Research, 17.*

Kraus, S. (1997). Negotiation and cooperation in multi-agent environments. *Artificial Intelligence, 94*(1-2), 79–98. doi:10.1016/S0004-3702(97)00025-8

Lesh, N. (1998). *Scalable and adaptive goal recognition.* Seattle, WA: University of Washington.

Malle, B. F., Moses, L. J., & Baldwin, D. A. (2003). *Intentions and intentionality: Foundations of social cognition.* Cambridge, MA: MIT Press.

Mao, W., & Gratch, J. (2004). *A utility-based approach to intention recognition.* Paper presented at the AAMAS 2004 Workshop on Agent Tracking: Modeling Other Agents from Observations. New York, NY.

Meltzoff, A. N. (2005). Imitation and other minds: the ``like me" hypothesi. In Hurley, S. A. C. (Ed.), *Perspectives on Imitation: From Neuroscience to Social Science: Imitation, Human Development, and Culture* (pp. 55–77). Cambridge, MA: MIT Press.

Meltzoff, A. N. (2007). The framework for recognizing and becoming an intentional agent. *Acta Psychologica, 124*(1), 26–43. doi:10.1016/j.actpsy.2006.09.005

Mikhail, J. (2007). Universal moral grammar: Theory, evidence, and the future. *Trends in Cognitive Sciences, 11*(4), 143–152. doi:10.1016/j.tics.2006.12.007

Newman, J. O. (2006). Quantifying the standard of proof beyond a reasonable doubt: A comment on three comments. *Law Probability and Risk, 5*(3-4), 267–269. doi:10.1093/lpr/mgm010

Niemela, I., & Simons, P. (1997). *Probabilistic reasoning with answer sets.* Paper presented at the LPNMR4. New York, NY.

Osborne, M. J. (2004). *An introduction to game theory.* Oxford, UK: Oxford University Press.

Pearl, J. (1988). *Probabilistic reasoning in intelligent systems: Networks of plausible inference.* San Francisco, CA: Morgan Kaufmann.

Pearl, J. (2000). *Causality: Models, reasoning, and inference.* Cambridge, UK: Cambridge University Press.

Pereira, L. M., Dell'Acqua, P., & Lopes, G. (2012). Inspecting and preferring abductive models. In *Handbook on Reasoning-Based Intelligent Systems.* Singapore, Singapore: World Scientific Publishers.

Pereira, L. M., & Han, T. A. (2009a). Evolution prospection. In *Proceedings of International Symposium on Intelligent Decision Technologies (KES-IDT 2009).* KES-IDT.

Pereira, L. M., & Han, T. A. (2009b). Evolution prospection in decision making. *Intelligent Decision Technologies, 3*(3), 157–171.

Pereira, L. M., & Han, T. A. (2009c). *Intention recognition via causal bayes networks plus plan generation.* Paper presented at the Progress in Artificial Intelligence, Proceedings of 14th Portuguese International Conference on Artificial Intelligence (EPIA 2009). Evora, Portgual.

Pereira, L. M., & Han, T. A. (2011a). Elder care via intention recognition and evolution prospection. In *Proceedings of the 18th International Conference on Applications of Declarative Programming and Knowledge Management (INAP).* Evora, Portugal: Springer.

Pereira, L. M., & Han, T. A. (2011b). Intention recognition with evolution prospection and causal bayes networks. In *Computational Intelligence for Engineering Systems 3: Emergent Applications* (pp. 1–33). Berlin, Germany: Springer. doi:10.1007/978-94-007-0093-2_1

Pereira, L. M., & Lopes, G. (2009). Prospective logic agents. *International Journal of Reasoning-Based Intelligent Systems, 1*(3/4).

Pinker, S., Nowak, M. A., & Lee, J. J. (2008). The logic of indirect speech. *Proceedings of the National Academy of Sciences of the United States of America, 105*(3), 833–838. doi:10.1073/pnas.0707192105

Pynadath, D. V., & Wellman, M. P. (1995). Accounting for context in plan recognition, with application to traffic monitoring. In *Proceedings of Conference on Uncertainty in Artificial Intelligence (UAI 1995)*. UAI.

Radke, S., Guroglu, B., & de Bruijn, E. R. A. (2012). There's something about a fair split: Intentionality moderates context-based fairness considerations in social decision-making. *PLoS ONE, 7*(2). doi:10.1371/journal.pone.0031491

Rao, A. S., & Georgeff, M. P. (1991). Modeling rational agents within a BDI-architecture. In *Proceedings of the Second International Conference of Principles of Knowledge Representation and Reasoning*. IEEE.

Rao, A. S., & Georgeff, M. P. (1995). BDI agents: From theory to practice. In *Proceeding of First International Conference on Multiagent Systems*. IEEE.

Robson, A. (1990). Efficiency in evolutionary games: Darwin, Nash, and the secret handshake. *Journal of Theoretical Biology, 144*(3), 379–396. doi:10.1016/S0022-5193(05)80082-7

Roy, O. (2009a). Intentions and interactive transformations of decision problems. *Synthese, 169*(2), 335–349. doi:10.1007/s11229-009-9553-5

Roy, O. (2009b). *Thinking before acting: Intentions, logic, rational choice*. Retrieved from http://olivier.amonbofis.net/docs/Thesis_Olivier_Roy.pdf

Roy, P., Bouchard, B., Bouzouane, A., & Giroux, S. (2007). A hybrid plan recognition model for Alzheimer's patients: Interleaved-erroneous dilemma.In *Proceedings of IEEE/WIC/ACM International Conference on Intelligent Agent Technology*. IEEE.

Russell, S. J., & Norvig, P. (2003). *Artificial intelligence: A modern approach*. Upper Saddle River, NJ: Pearson Education.

Sadri, F. (2008). Multi-agent ambient intelligence for elderly care and assistance. In *Proceedings of International Electronic Conference on Computer Science*. IEEE.

Sadri, F. (2010). Logic-based approaches to intention recognition. In *Handbook of Research on Ambient Intelligence: Trends and Perspectives* (pp. 375). Springer.

Sadri, F. (2011a). Ambient intelligence: A survey. *ACM Computing Surveys, 43*(4), 1–66. doi:10.1145/1978802.1978815

Sadri, F. (2011b). Intention recognition with event calculus graphs and weight of evidence. In *Proceedings 4th International Workshop on Human Aspects in Ambient Intelligence*. IEEE.

Searle, J. R. (1995). *The construction of social reality*. New York, NY: The Free Press.

Searle, J. R. (2010). *Making the social world: The structure of human civilization*. Oxford, UK: Oxford University Press.

Sigmund, K. (2010). *The calculus of selfishness*. Princeton, NJ: Princeton University Press.

Singh, M. P. (1991). *Intentions, commitments and rationality.* Paper presented at the 13th Annual Conference of the Cognitive Science Society. New York, NY.

Sukthankar, G. R. (2007). *Activity recognition for agent teams.* Retrieved from http://www.cs.cmu.edu/~gitars/gsukthankar-thesis.pdf

Sukthankar, G. R., & Sycara, K. (2008). Robust and efficient plan recognition for dynamic multi-agent teams. In *Proceedings of International Conference on Autonomous Agents and Multi-Agent Systems.* IEEE.

Swift, T. (1999). Tabling for non-monotonic programming. *Annals of Mathematics and Artificial Intelligence, 25*(3-4), 240.

Tahboub, K. A. (2006). Intelligent human-machine interaction based on dynamic Bayesian networks probabilistic intention recognition. *Journal of Intelligent & Robotic Systems, 45,* 31–52. doi:10.1007/s10846-005-9018-0

Tomasello, M. (1999). *The cultural origins of human cognition.* Boston, MA: Harvard University Press.

Tomasello, M. (2008). *Origins of human communication.* Cambridge, MA: MIT Press.

Trivers, R. (2011). *The folly of fools: The logic of deceit and self-deception in human life.* New York, NY: Basic Books.

Tu, P. H., Son, T. C., & Baral, C. (2007). Reasoning and planning with sensing actions, incomplete information, and static causal laws using answer set programming. *Theory and Practice of Logic Programming, 7*(4), 377–450. doi:10.1017/S1471068406002948

Tu, P. H., Son, T. C., Gelfond, M., & Morales, A. R. (2011). Approximation of action theories and its application to conformant planning. *Artificial Intelligence, 175*(1), 79–119. doi:10.1016/j.artint.2010.04.007

van Hees, M., & Roy, O. (2008). Intentions and plans in decision and game theory. In *Reasons and Intentions* (pp. 207–226). New York, NY: Ashgate Publishers.

Woodward, A. L., Sommerville, J. A., Gerson, S., Henderson, A. M. E., & Buresh, J. (2009). The emergence of intention attribution in infancy. *Psychology of Learning and Motivation, 51,* 187–222. doi:10.1016/S0079-7421(09)51006-7

Wooldridge, M. (2000). *Reasoning about rational agents.* Cambridge, MA: MIT Press.

Wooldridge, M. (2002). Reasoning about rational agents. *Journal of Artificial Societies and Social Simulation, 5*(1).

XSB. (2009). *The XSB system version 3.2 vol. 2: Libraries, interfaces and packages.* XSB.

Young, L., & Saxe, R. (2011). When ignorance is no excuse: Different roles for intent across moral domains. *Cognition, 120*(2), 202–214. doi:10.1016/j.cognition.2011.04.005

KEY TERMS AND DEFINITIONS

Ambient Intelligence: This refers to electronic environments that are sensitive and responsive to the presence of people. In an ambient intelligence world, devices work in concert to support people in carrying out their everyday life activities, tasks, and rituals in easy, natural way using information and intelligence that is hidden in the network connecting these devices.

Evolution Prospection: A decision making system designed and implemented based on the idea that, when making some decision at the current state for solving some current goals, one usually takes into account longer-terms goals and future events.

Intention-Based Decision Making: The decision making process that takes into account intentions of other agents in the environment.

Technically, intentions of others are now part of the constructs of decision making, such as goals and preferences.

Intention Recognition: To infer an agent's intentions (called "*individual intention recognition*") or intentions of a group of agents (called "*collective intention recognition*") through its/ their observed actions and effects of actions on the environment.

Moral Reasoning: The process in which an individual tries to determine the difference between what is right and what is wrong in a personal situation by using logic.

ENDNOTES

[1] The implementation of P-log systems described in (Baral et al., 2009) can be found in: http://www.cs.ttu.edu/~wezhu/

[2] The implementation of the Evolution Prospection system can be downloaded at: http://centria.di.fct.unl.pt/~lmp/software/epa.zip

[3] The implementation of ABDUAL system can be downloaded at: http://centria.di.fct.unl.pt/~lmp/software/contrNeg.rar

[4] In general, from the design point of view, one needs to provide an EP program for each intention, because, according to context, a user might have or be predicted to have distinct intentions.

Chapter 10
Clustering Algorithm for Human Behavior Recognition Based on Biosignal Analysis

Neuza Nunes
PLUX – Wireless Biosignals S.A., Portugal

Rodolfo Abreu
FCT-UNL, Portugal

Diliana Rebelo
FCT-UNL, Portugal

Hugo Gamboa
FCT-UNL, Portugal

Ana Fred
IST-UTL, Portugal & Instituto de Telecomunicações, Portugal

ABSTRACT

Time series unsupervised clustering is accurate in various domains, and there is an increased interest in time series clustering algorithms for human behavior recognition. The authors have developed an algorithm for biosignals clustering, which captures the general morphology of a signal's cycles in one mean wave. In this chapter, they further validate and consolidate it and make a quantitative comparison with a state-of-the-art algorithm that uses distances between data's cepstral coefficients to cluster the same biosignals. They are able to successfully replicate the cepstral coefficients algorithm, and the comparison showed that the mean wave approach is more accurate for the type of signals analyzed, having a 19% higher accuracy value. They authors also test the mean wave algorithm with biosignals with three different activities in it, and achieve an accuracy of 96.9%. Finally, they perform a noise immunity test with a synthetic signal and notice that the algorithm remains stable for signal-to-noise ratios higher than 2, only decreasing its accuracy with noise of amplitude equal to the signal. The necessary validation tests performed in this study confirmed the high accuracy level of the developed clustering algorithm for biosignals that express human behavior.

DOI: 10.4018/978-1-4666-3682-8.ch010

INTRODUCTION

The constant chase for human well-being has led researchers to increasingly design new systems and applications for a continuous monitoring of patients through their biological signals. In the past, human activity tracking techniques focused mostly on observations of people and their behavior through a great amount of cameras. However, the use of wearable sensors has been increasingly sought because it allows continuous acquisitions in different locations, being independent from the infrastructures. The recognition of human behavior through wearable sensors has a vast applicability. In the sports field, for example, there is a need for wearable sensors to assess physiological signals and body kinematics during free exercise. Wearable sensors have also major utility in healthcare, particularly for monitoring elderly and chronically ill patients in their homes, through Ambient Assisted Living (AAL).

The human body has always been considered a complex machine in which all parts work harmoniously. Nevertheless, the endless pursuit for the optimal human performance has become an important work area of digital signal processing. Therefore, monitoring athletes is the logical way to achieve the best patterns that can be compared to pathological signals in order to contribute for patient's rehabilitation. Thereby, the continuous monitoring and evaluation of athletic performance allow the coaches to establish an optimal training program. In addition, it is useful for non-professional athletes to establish and achieve their personal goals (R. Santos et al., 2012).

The main goal of AAL is to develop technologies which enable users to live independently for a longer period of time, increasing their autonomy and confidence in accomplishing some daily tasks (known as ADL - Activities of Daily Living). However, AAL was also designed to reduce the escalating costs associated with health-care services in elderly people.

Thus, AAL's systems are used to classify a large variety of situations such as falls, physical immobility, study of human behavior and others. These systems are developed using a Ubiquitous Computing approach (AAL4ALL Project, 2012) (where sensors and signals' processing are executed without interfering on ADL) and must monitor activities and vital signs in order to detect emergency situations or deviations from a normal medical pattern (G.N. Rodrigues et al., 2010). Ultimately, AAL solutions automate this monitoring by software capable of detecting those deviations.

Signal-processing techniques have been developed to extract relevant information from biosignals which aren't easily detected in the raw data. However, most of these techniques are integrated in tools for specific biosignals, such as electrocardiography, respiration, accelerometry, among others. Thus, a single tool to recognize the morphology of the signal without prior information, analyzing and processing it accordingly is a recurrent necessity.

The smallest change in the signal's morphology over time may contain information of the utmost importance; hence, the detection of those changes has received much attention in this field. The recognition of different patterns in the signal's morphology is usually based on clustering or classification approaches. The ultimate goal is a generic and automatic classification system that doesn't require prior information and produces an efficient analysis whichever the type of the signal used.

In the following sections we summarize the scope and results of the developed algorithm and further evaluate it by testing it in a variety of contexts and validating it with a state-of-the art approach for time-series clustering.

RELATED WORK

Nunes (2012) presented an advanced signal processing algorithm for pattern recognition and clustering purposes applied to time varying signals collected from the human body. The recognition of differences in the signal's morphology produced by physiological abnormalities (arrhythmia, for example) or different conditions of the subject's state (walking or running, for example) was tested by collecting a set of cyclic biosignals with two distinctive modes. The acquired signals were the input of the generic algorithm. This algorithm knows beforehand the number of modes the signal has and is the base function to identify the individual cycles in a signal. The result of this algorithm is a single wave, a mean wave which is an averaging of all signal cycles aligned in a notable point.

As we're working with cyclic signals, the first step of the mean wave algorithm is the detection of the signal's fundamental frequency. With the fundamental frequency value we could compute the sampling size of a signal's cycle, and with that window size value, we randomly select a part of the signal with the same number of samples as the window size. Then we slide the smaller window part of the signal through the original signal, one sample at a time, computing the distance of the two waves present in those windows. After going through all the original data, we have as result a signal composed with distance values. The minimum points of the distance signal will be our events.

With the events computed, we are able to cut the signal into periods that we assume as our signal cycles. This way, based on all cycles, we could estimate the mean value to each cycle sample, and compose a mean wave. A standard deviation error wave is computed with the same principle, calculating the standard deviation error instead of the mean value for each sample. After this, a final adjustment was made: the alignment of the signal's cycles. The position of the mean wave's minimum point (a notable point) was detected, and that become our trigger point. With this trigger point, the events were recalculated and used to compute a mean wave again, so the cycles are aligned and the resultant mean wave more accurate.

The algorithm then has a k-means clustering phase which uses the information gathered from

the mean wave approach to separate the several modes of the original signal. As the implemented mean wave approach accurately identifies the morphology of a signal, it can be a powerful tool in several areas – as a clustering basis or for signal analysis. The algorithm produced is signal-independent with high level of abstraction, and therefore can be applied to any cyclic signal with no major changes in the fundamental frequency. This type of generic signal interpretation overcomes the problems of exhaustive, lengthy signal analysis and expert intervention highly used in the biosignal's classification field.

Several approaches for time series comparison have been proposed in literature. The most straightforward approach relies on similarity measures which directly compare observations or features extracted from raw data. Besides the measurements made directly between time series, distances can also be computed with models built from the raw data. By modeling the raw data with a stochastic model, similarities are detected in the dynamics of different time series.

Linear Predictive Coding (LPC) is one of the methods of model compression and is widely used in speech analysis. Linear prediction filters attempt to predict future values of the input signal based on past signals.

The process of clustering time series models is usually a three-step procedure. Firstly, each time series is represented by a dynamical model, which is estimated using the given data. Secondly, a distance between the dynamical models is computed over all the models estimated in the first stage - this distance measure can be the same used to cluster data or features extracted from the data. And finally, a clustering or a classification mechanism is performed based on the distance metric defined (J. Boets et al., 2005). This general methodology has been applied previously in different application areas, by estimating similarity measures between the LPC coefficients (G. Antoniol, 2005; P. Souza, 1997). However, another method, which estimates the cepstral coefficients from the LPC model and computes the distance between those coefficients, has been widely used achieving state of the art results in this field (K. Kalpakis, 2001; M. Corduas, 2008; A. Savvides, 2008).

In this chapter we intend to further validate our algorithm, comparing its accuracy with the state-of-the-art cepstral coefficients algorithm, test the results with more than two different modes, and perform a noise immunity test.

CEPSTRAL COEFFICIENTS ALGORITHM

Some of the publications that use the cepstral coefficients algorithm as a clustering mechanism used the Euclidean Distance between the LPC Cepstrum of two time series as their dissimilarity measure. The time series used in those publications were retrieved from a public database of ECG signals (Physionet, 2012).

The cepstral coefficients algorithm was replicated in our research and applied to the same public database, to achieve the same results as the ones documented. Our implementation was compared with the results exposed by Anthony Bagnall (2004), which uses an Euclidean distance between the cepstral coefficients to cluster the signals with a k-means clustering procedure.

We tested our implementation on a public ECG dataset which will be described below. The implementation and testing of the algorithm with the public ECG dataset will also be detailed next.

ECG Dataset

The public dataset of ECG signals is divided into three groups (*i.e.* three different classes for as the ECG records were acquired from people with different heart conditions). The number of records for each group corresponds to the people who volunteered for the study.

Group 1: 22 signal records of people with malignant ventricular arrhythmia (*i.e*, ECG

acquisitions with 22 different people composed this group).

Group 2: 13 signal records of healthy people.

Group 3: 35 signal records of people with supraventricular arrhythmia.

Each signal record comprises 2 seconds of acquisition.

Figure 1 shows one arbitrary example of a signal record from each group. Two collections were defined in these studies: Collection 1 comprises the first two groups (35 signals), and Collection 2 gathers group 2 and 3 (48 signals). The cepstral coefficients algorithm received as input both collections to find two different clusters in each—representing the signals belonging to two different groups in each collection (see Figure 2).

Implementation

The first step of this algorithm is to fit a LPC model to the raw data, with a defined order. Among the direct transformations of LPC parameters, one is a filtering process to get the cepstral coefficients. We performed these steps using Python with the numpy and scikits talkbox packages.

Using the LPC coefficients estimation we computed the five cepstral coefficients (order - 1) of each time series. After that, the Euclidean distance between the signals' coefficients was estimated. Using Equation 1 for all signals, a distances matrix is computed.

$$distance = \sqrt{\sum_{i=1}^{order-1} \left(sig_1 cc_i - sig_2 cc_i \right)^2} \quad (1)$$

being $sig_1 cc_i$ and $sig_2 cc_i$ the i cepstral coefficient from the first and the second signal, respectively. Finally, by retrieving the distance values and introducing that matrix into a K-Means algorithm, the time series are separated into different clusters.

With this implementation, the cepstral coefficients algorithm was successfully replicated,

Figure 1. Examples of one signal record from each group from the public ECG dataset

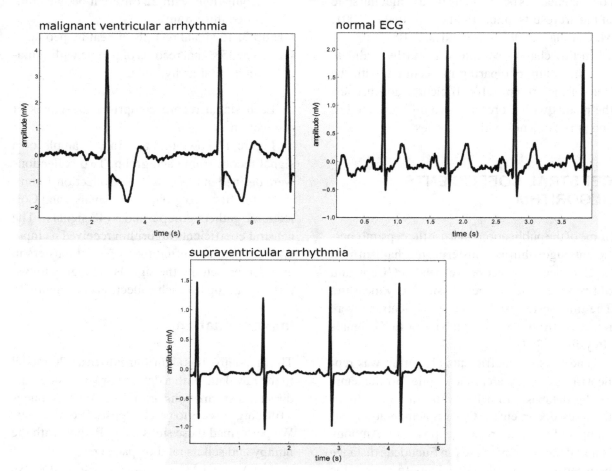

Figure 2. Schematics for the cepstral coefficients algorithm implementation

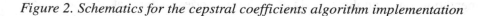

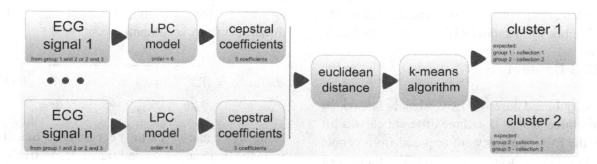

achieving the same results as described by Anthony Bagnall with the ECG dataset.

RESULTS

Comparison with Cepstral Coefficients Algorithm

For the actual comparison between the performance of our mean wave algorithm and the cepstral coefficients algorithm, the dataset used was the one described in our previous publication – for which the activities performed and the final clustering results are exposed in Table 1. This table presents the number of cycles that composed the classification set for each task, the number of cycles that were correctly clustered, the errors and misses. The errors comprise misclassifications (i.e. samples that were attributed to different classes than expected) and misses comprise samples which weren't classified at all (this happened especially to the cycles which represent the transition between activities).

In the context tasks and signal types acquired, the accuracy was 99.3% for the separation of two different modes.

Table 2 gathers the clustering accuracy results obtained for each task and algorithms used (our mean wave algorithm and the cepstral coefficients algorithm). The accuracy percentage was computed using Equation 2.

$$accuracy = \frac{Cycles_{cc}}{Cycles_N} \times 100\% \qquad (2)$$

being $Cycles_{CC}$ the number of correctly clustered cycles and $Cycles_N$ the total number of cycles.

Our mean wave procedure presents a higher accuracy level for every signal but the synthetic waves, for which the accuracy is the same. Looking at the overall results, our algorithm achieved 99.3% accuracy, and the cepstral coefficients algorithm only 80.0% for the same signals—which from the tests with this database makes our approach a better option for clustering cyclic signals. To note also that our algorithm can be applied to a continuous signal with different modes in it, automatically separating the signal's cycles and computing a distance metric for each. The cepstral coefficients algorithm, however, has to be applied in separated signals—in this study we had

Table 1. Clustering results of the mean wave algorithm (from N. Nunes et al. 2012)

Task	Number of Cycles	Cycles Correctly Clustered	Errors	Misses
Synthetic	50	49	0	1
Walk and run	343	342	1	0
Run and jump	296	295	1	0
Jumps	85	84	1	0
Skiing	42	41	0	1
Elevation and squat	23	23	0	0
BVP rest and after exercise	165	159	4	2
All	1004	992	7	5

Table 2. Comparison of the results obtained with the cepstral coefficients and the mean wave algorithm

Task	Accuracy of Cepstral Coefficient Algorithm	Accuracy of Mean Wave Algorithm
Synthetic	100.0%	100.0%
Walk and run	92.4%	99.7%
Run and jump	68.2%	99.7%
Jumps	82.1%	98.8%
Skiing	90.2%	100.0%
Elevation and squat	56.5%	100.0%
BVP rest and after exercise	68.7%	96.4%
Total	80.0%	99.3%

to isolate the cycles before applying the cepstral coefficients procedure.

In conclusion, the comparison between the two algorithms confirmed that the mean wave algorithm has a high accuracy level, reaching better results, and is more suitable for the type of data analyzed than a state of the art algorithm in this area.

VALIDATION

In this study we've also collected a new set of signals, with three different activities in each, composing over 2000 cycles.

To acquire the biosignals necessary for this study, we used a surface EMG sensor (*emgPLUX*) and a triaxial accelerometer (*xyzPLUX*). A wireless signal acquisition system, bioPLUX research (PLUX, 2012), was used for the signal's analogue to digital conversion and bluetooth transmission to the computer. This system has 12 bit ADC and a sampling frequency of 1000 Hz. In the acquisitions with the triaxial accelerometers, only the axis with inferior-superior direction was connected to the bioPLUX.

Several tasks were designed and executed in order to acquire signals with three distinct modes from 4 different subjects.

Before describing the activities executed in order to acquire the signals used for testing our algorithm, it is worthy to note that in all activities we used only the accelerometer's signal, except for activity 2 (walking, jumping, crouching), in which we tested also the EMG's signal.

Synthetic Signal

To test our algorithm, a synthetic cycle was created using a low-pass filtered random walk (of 100 samples), with a moving average smoothing window of 10% of signal's length, and multiplying it by a *hanning* window. That cycle was repeated 296 times for the first mode, so all the cycles were identical. After a small break on the signal, the cycle was repeated 104 more times, but with an identical small change of 20 samples in all waves, creating a second mode. A third mode was created by changing the same 20 samples and repeating the new wave created 524 times. These three modes construct the synthetic wave represented in Figure 3.

Figure 3. Synthetic signal with three different modes (within each mode all waves are identical)

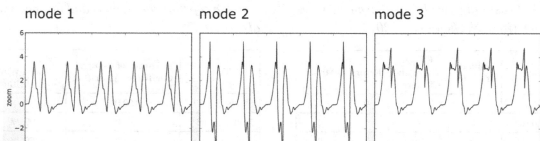

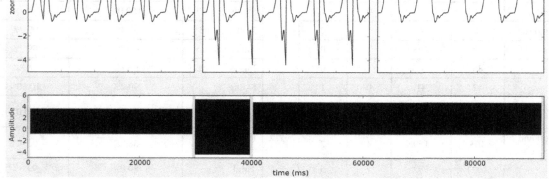

Activity 1: Walking, Running, Walking, Jumping

In this task, the accelerometer was located on the right hip along with the bioPLUX, so that the y axis's accelerometer was pointing downward. It was asked to the subjects to walk (for about 1 minute and half), run, walk again and jump on the same place (each for about 1 minute). These four modes were executed non-stop. The signal acquired is demonstrated in Figure 4.

Activity 2: Walking, Jumping, Crouching

With the accelerometer located on the right hip and oriented so that the y axis was pointing downward, the subjects performed a task of walking, vertical jumping and crouching, continuously. Each mode was executed 10 times and it is worthy referring that in walking mode, each step was considered a cycle. The signal acquired is demonstrated in Figure 5.

For the EMG's signal, electrodes were located on the ischiotibial of the right leg so that they were able to collect the muscle's activation signal during the activity. This signal was collected simultaneously with the accelerometer's signal. The signal acquired is demonstrated in Figure 6.

Activity 3: Jumping, Leg Flexion, and Single Leg Vertical Jumping

In this task, the following procedure was executed: normal vertical jumping, leg flexion and single leg vertical jumping. Each mode was repeated 10 times.

The subjects used an accelerometer located at the right hip and oriented so the y axis of the accelerometer was pointing downward. The signal acquired is represented in Figure 7.

Activity 4: Crouching, Leg Flexion, and Leg Elevation

In this task, the subject was standing straight with both feet completely on the ground and was asked to perform 10 squats followed by 10 vertical leg flexions—moving the heel towards the gluteus—and 10 leg elevations—moving the knee towards the chest (Figure 8).

Figure 4. Activity 1: walking, running, walking, and jumping

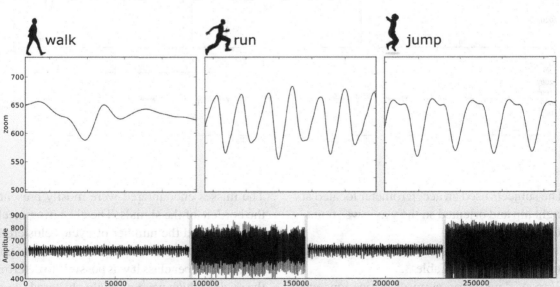

Figure 5. Activity 2 (ACC): walking, jumping, and crouching

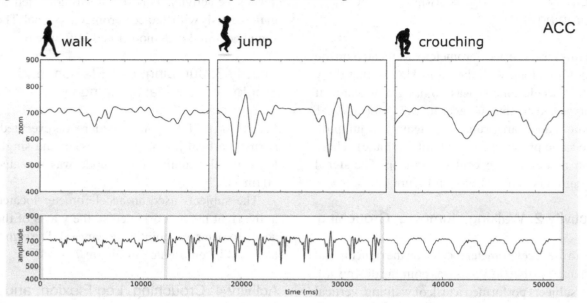

Figure 6. Activity 2 (EMG): walking, jumping, and crouching

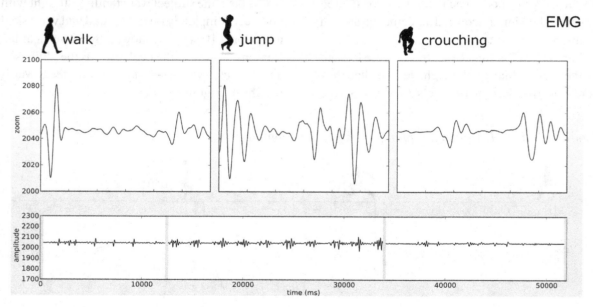

The subjects used an accelerometer located at the right hip and oriented so the y axis was pointing downward.

In the new set of acquired signals we achieved the results reported on Table 3.

We considered errors as misclassifications and misses as cycles which weren't classified at all.

The misses encountered were mostly present in the borders of the signals. The clustering mechanism returned the number of cycles clustered in each group and as we knew beforehand the number of cycles per class it was possible to determine the cycles which were wrongly clustered. As can be seen from the last column, the algorithm imple-

Figure 7. Activity 3: jumping, leg flexion, and one foot jumping

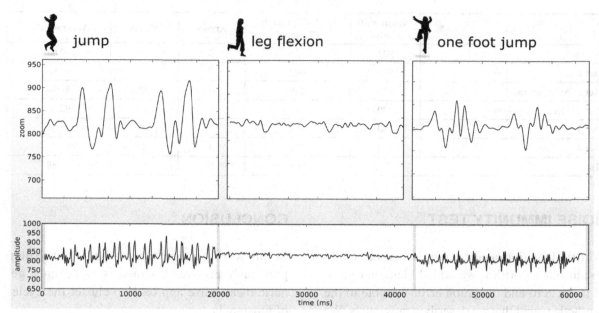

Figure 8. Activity 4: crouching, leg flexion, and leg elevation

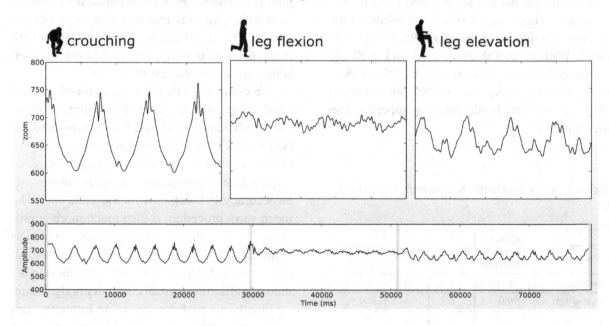

mented also shows a high accuracy when applied on activities with more than two modes.

That way we were able to check the performance of our algorithm when more than two clusters are involved. In the new set of acquired signals we achieved 96.88% of accuracy separating the three activities into different clusters, lowering our previous clustering result with two modes by only 2.4% and using a greater amount of cycles.

Table 3. Clustering results of the mean wave algorithm for signals with three modes

Task	Number of Cycles	Cycles Correctly Clustered	Errors	Misses	Accuracy (%)
Synthetic	924	921	0	3	99,68
Act 1	693	692	0	1	99,86
Act 2 (Accelerometer)	175	149	7	20	85,14
Act 2 (Electromyography)	120	112	8	0	93,33
Act 3	180	154	7	19	85,56
Act 4	180	173	3	4	96,11
Total	2272	2201	25	47	96,88

NOISE IMMUNITY TEST

With the intention of performing a noise immunity test in our algorithm we added Gaussian noise of mean zero and deviation error variable to the synthetic signal that we described previously. We compared the accuracy of the algorithm with the Signal-to-Noise Ratio (SNR) for each situation. The results for this test are detailed in Table 4.

From no noise to a SNR=2, the results of the algorithm remained stable (99.7-98.2% of accuracy). With SNR values of 1.33 and 1.00 the accuracy lowered to 78.6 and 60.7%, respectively, which are acceptable considering an amount of noise with amplitude equal or superior than the signal to analyze.

Table 4. Noise immunity test (number of cycles= 924)

Signal-to-Noise Ratio	Cycles Correctly Clustered	Errors	Misses	Accuracy (%)
No noise	921	0	3	99.7%
SNR = 8.00	921	0	3	99.7%
SNR = 4.00	921	0	3	99.7%
SNR = 2.67	918	3	3	99.4%
SNR = 2.00	907	14	3	98.2%
SNR = 1.33	726	195	3	78.6%
SNR = 1.00	561	360	3	60.7%

CONCLUSION

In this work we further evaluated an algorithm previously presented, which is based on a generic mean wave approach to cluster the cycles of biosignals.

Our algorithm proves to be an accurate method in the detection of changes in the signal's morphology, achieving 99.3% of clustering accuracy in signals with only two different modes or activities. The algorithm accuracy for signals with three different modes was tested in this chapter, achieving an overall result of 96.9%.

We compared our clustering procedure with another method referenced in literature, the cepstral coefficients algorithm, which presented the best results to the date for time series data. We obtained better results using the same dataset of acquired data—the mean wave algorithm presents an accuracy 19% superior for the same data. The mean wave procedure is also much more appropriate for the analysis of continuous signals, as it automatically separates the signals' cycles and doesn't need different inputs for different signal's modes, unlike the cepstral coefficients algorithm.

Finally we performed a noise immunity test with a synthetic signal, adding Gaussian noise until the clustering procedure decreases in accurateness. Only with a noise of amplitude equal to the synthetic signal and therefore a signal-to-noise ratio of 1, the accuracy of the algorithm drops to 60.7%; however, the algorithm proved to be relatively stable for a SNR higher than 2.

The necessary validation tests that we performed in this study confirmed the high accuracy level of the developed algorithm for biosignals which express human behavior.

The continuously need to obtain more information, with more accuracy, more quickly and with less intervention from an expert has led to a growing application of signal processing techniques applied to biomedical data. The biosignal analysis and processing is a promising area with huge potential in medicine, sports and research.

In fact, pattern recognition and automatic classification of morphological and physiological deviations on biosignals using clustering techniques are essential on monitoring elderly people on their homes (AAL). Thus, the mean wave algorithm is a great asset in this context and can contribute to the main goal of AAL: increase the period of time in which elderly people are autonomous by being able to detect behavior and changes in biosignals (e.g. arrhythmia, fall detection, epilepsy episodes). Concerning sports, we can identify different actions in the same data resulting in correct group detachment. This outcome provides feature extraction in order to recognize and categorize patterns. Furthermore, it allows us to create a mathematical model which is capable to classify new movements that can be directly used on talent recruitment and/or sport's training optimizations.

Our algorithm can be applied to continuous cyclic time series, capturing the signal's behavior. The fact that this approach doesn't require any prior information and its good performance in different situations makes it a powerful tool for biosignals analysis and classification.

REFERENCES

AAL4ALL. (2012). *Website*. Retrieved February 17, 2012 from http://www.aal4all.org/?lang=en

Antoniol, G., Rollo, V., & Venturi, G. (2005). Linear predictive coding and cepstrum coefficients for mining time variant information from software repositories. In *Proceedings of MSR2005: International Workshop on Mining Software Repositories*. MSR.

Bagnal, A., & Janacek, G. (2004). Clustering time series from arma models with clipped data. In *Proceedings of KDD 2004, the Tenth ACM SIGKDD International Conference on Knowledge Discovery and Data Mining*. Seattle, WA: ACM.

Boets, J., Cock, K., Espinoza, M., & Moor, B. (2005). Clustering time series, subspace identification and cepstral distances. *Communications in Information and Systems*, 5(1), 69–96.

Corduas, M., & Piccolo, D. (2008). Time series clustering and classification by the autoregressive metric. *Computational Statistics & Data Analysis*, 52, 1860–1872. doi:10.1016/j.csda.2007.06.001

Kalpakis, K., Gada, D., & Puttagunta, V. (2001). Distance measures for accurate clustering of arima time-series. In *Procedings of the 2001 IEEE International Conference on Data Mining*, (pp. 273–280). IEEE Press.

Nunes, N., Araújo, T., & Gamboa, H. (2012). Time series clustering algorithm for two-modes cyclic biosignals. In Fred, A., Filipe, J., & Gamboa, H. (Eds.), *Biostec 2011* (pp. 233–245). Springer.

Physionet. (2012). *PhysioBank archive index*. Retrieved February 15, 2012 from http://www.physionet.org/physiobank/database

PLUX – Wireless Biosignals. S.A. (2012). *Website*. Retrieved February 15, 2012 from http://www.plux.info

Rodrigues, G., Alves, V., Silveira, R., & Laranjeira, L. (2012). Dependability analysis in the ambient assisted living domain: An exploratory case study. *Journal of Systems and Software*, 85, 112–131. doi:10.1016/j.jss.2011.07.037

Santos, R., Sousa, J., Sañudo, B., Marques, C., & Gamboa, H. (2012). Biosignals events detection a morphological signal-independent approach. In *Proceedings of the International Conference on Bio-Inspired Systems and Signal Processing (BIOSIGNALS 2012)*. Vilamoura, Portugal: BIOSIGNALS.

Savvides, A., Promponas, V., & Fokianos, K. (2008). Clustering of biological time series by cepstral coefficients based distances. *Pattern Recognition*, 41, 2398–2412. doi:10.1016/j.patcog.2008.01.002

Souza, P. (1977). Statistical tests and distance measures for LPC coefficients. *IEEE Transactions on Acoustics, Speech, and Signal Processing*, 25(6), 554–559. doi:10.1109/TASSP.1977.1163004

KEY TERMS AND DEFINITIONS

Biosignals: The human body produces physiological signals which can be measured. To those signals we call "biosignals."

Clustering: A method for assigning an observation to a specific group of observations which share some characteristics, differentiating them from others.

Mean Wave: Having a set of signal's cycles, the mean wave is a wave constructed by the mean value for each time-sample of those cycles.

Chapter 11
Monitoring Social Life and Interactions:
A Sociological Perspective of Technologies

Francesca Odella
University of Trento, Italy

ABSTRACT

The chapter describes the sociological perspective of monitoring technologies and debates its method for analysing social implications of scientific and technical developments. It is articulated in five sections dedicated to social and privacy aspects involved in social analysis of technologies. Particular attention is devoted to social network analysis, an emergent area of sociological research that focuses on the relational implications of technologies in organizations, small groups, and other contexts of social participation. The text integrates examples of technology implementation from healthcare automated assistance to mobile communication devices, video-surveillance, RFID, and smart-meter technology. Case studies, illustrated in separate textboxes, describe the advancements in this field of enquiry and highlight the main elements of the structure of interactions in virtual and technology-mediated communications. Finally, ethical implications of behaviour monitoring technologies are discussed together with recent perspectives of sociological research.

INTRODUCTION

Since its birth as a scientific discipline sociology has been dealing with human sociability; theories of social behavior explain aspects of human life that pertain to a variety of life aspects such as groups organization, participation to collective events and structure of communication. Creation of knowledge and innovation creation and diffu-sion, in particular, attracted the attention of an emerging area of sociological research that since the eighties committed itself to exploring social relations involved in the development of new technologies and in social awareness assessment.

The aim of the chapter is to provide an introduction to the sociological perspective of technology and to illustrate with the aid of pieces of empirical research its theoretical and methodological bases.

DOI: 10.4018/978-1-4666-3682-8.ch011

Therefore in the selection of the examples a special attention is given to sociological analysis of relations between humans and machines or artefacts inside complex or pervasive socio-technical systems. The first two paragraphs are dedicated to describe the principal elements of sociological perspective of technologies and how the enquiry of socio-technical systems involves social relations. These theoretical discussions are integrated with examples from the study of mobile communication (inferring social relations from tracking and analysis of phone users log records), implementation of smart devices (connectivity of the users, environmental sensors) and other technologies supporting localization (mapping out hunting paths with GPS). Paragraph three describes social network analysis (SNA), a specific methodology formerly developed to study small groups interactions, and its progressive application to information technologies and virtual communication. By means of examples these paragraphs will put in evidence social features relevant in establishing receptiveness of innovations, their role in creating relations and structuring social organization.

The rest of the chapter reviews the recent sociological debate on technology using as metaphor the idea of technology as the saviour juxtaposed to the representation of technology as the intruder. By means of the example of video-surveillance, the final paragraph describes sociological concerns for the implementation of advanced monitoring technologies in contemporary society and their ethical and privacy implications.

THE SOCIOLOGICAL PERSPECTIVE OF TECHNOLOGY

Technology is usually defined as artifacts, processes and machines and the knowledge—based on technical or engineering knowledge—used to design and operate them. Technology from the sociological perspective is always a relational object because its creation, use and diffusion is based on social processes of relating things, signs and meaning, humans and institutions. The first social studies (Bijker, Hugues and Pinch, 1987) concentrated on scientific knowledge and historical cases of technical innovation (electricity, nuclear power, pasteurization). Recently the area of research moved to the study of complex interactions between societal interests and design of various technologies from cars, bicycles and missiles to medical devices and plastic materials (Bijker and Law, 1992).

A technology scholar, Werner Rammert (2008), identifies among the rules that should guide social studies of technologies, the necessity to deconstruct technical developments into local projects, where different visions of technical practice (ex. the employ of personal computers, television sets, specific devices) are mixed with heterogeneous elements. According to this perspective the meaning of a piece of technology is socially constructed and negotiated inside specific groups or communities of users: social interpretation of technology may thus involve several years to complete, as well as modify the original intents of inventors and technology professionals (Latour, 1992). Furthermore, the fact that technologies are embedded in places and social contexts make them sensitive to interest groups and collective actors, influencing the development of complex socio-technical structure (see for example the cases of electric automobiles, missiles and satellite communications).

Applying this interpretative framework social researchers analyzed complex socio-technological system (see for example the system that brought to the diffusion of the electric power in the USA in Hughes, 1987) and cultural and market fields resulting from specific technological innovations, such as the GPS (described in second paragraph) or the electronic synthesizer. Reconstructing the historical processes that convoy the creation of the Moog synthesizer and the steps of its economic success, the work of Pinch (2008) shows how the electronic instrument moved from the hippie's music scene to the popular music and advertising scene, re-defining the music industry and the standards of music production. With the Moog synthesizer, in fact, the possibility to reproduce sounds and to modulate them was open to users without traditional musical background. In less than twenty years the Moog established a new market for musical instruments and new standards for electronic music, paving the way for the advent of digital music in the eighties.

Sociological studies have been particularly relevant in soliciting the introduction of multidisciplinary approaches in innovations and technology adoption evaluation. A paradigmatic shift and innovation, as sociological studies highlight, frequently occur when the boundaries between disciplines are overcome or when the stakeholders in a socio-technical innovation process can develop their collaborative efforts toward a common goal (Law, 1987). On the contrary, recognized scientific knowledge is deeply connected to economic and power relations between communities and many methodological limits that constrain researchers' activity originate from division between empirical research and theoretical approaches, both in the science disciplines and in the social disciplines. Moreover, the presence of a common positivist epistemological background in the entire process of modern scientific enquiry—an element that sociologists of technology frequently put in evidence in their studies—is not frequently acknowledged.

Sociology of science calls ultimately for a new way of observing changes in social and technological systems, as well as for a revision of the idea of innovation. Rammert (2008, pp. 179-181) highlights:

Well-known artifacts and routines of construction are experimentally combined to build new combinations, or are transferred to different contexts of experience and use. With this pragmatic definition of innovative action we stop following the rational or normative approach to action and start recognizing the distinction between routine and creative action. (..) The design of experiments, the style in which the experiences are represented and the definition of the state of the art are results of negotiations between actors, mainly within the community but sometimes between communities.

According to this perspective the use of multimethods and the combination of experiments and ethnographic or qualitative research, visual and tracking technologies for analyzing social impact of innovations may contribute to overcome positivistic interpretations and to integration between scientific and social sciences perspectives of technology. Several cases described in this chapter provide examples of multidisciplinary enquiries, where heterogeneous elements (emotional and physiological impact of technologies on users, social use of innovations in communication) are combined to describe the effective impact of technology in personal and relational life. Specifically, the advancement of frontier research in cognitive science and neurophysiology (see Case 1) and in the so-called pervasive technologies (ITCs, smart devices and web-based services), solicit a revision of the research methods traditionally used to assess technological impact in social life.

Specifically, the introduction of pervasive technology in the living environment has been associated with the setting of a 'natural experiment' where the researcher, as observer, is afforded the opportunity to study differentiation processes inside social groups (Becker, 1998). A natural experiment or quasi- experiment is characterized by a low level of control over the situation by the observer, who can make inferences and re-construct practically the process of causation. Participants to a natural experiment (of course this is a defining label, as we are all participating to the experiment of each other's life), on the contrary, have control over their single decisions concerning the impact factors, but in most of the cases not on the results of the overall process or its unintended consequences.

There are of course drawbacks in adopting this perspective and critics to the use of natural experiments in social sciences frequently refer to its methodological limitations. First, the study of natural experiments is frequently restricted to qualitative factors and the opportunity to collect and process data on social structure (as in socio-metric studies, described in following paragraph) is seldom considered feasible and methodologically convincing for technology impact evaluation. Second, in a natural setting the choice of comparable samples and groups is tied to reality and only a limited array of possibilities is given; moreover, because ethical issues restrict the impact of specific factors (aka. contagion effect) is not feasible in many natural experiments. These limitations, according to some scholars, determine a reduction in explanatory power of natural experiments, and limit their use to non-academic settings.

On the other side, the perspective of natural experimentation benefit from the opportunity to analyze the experimental setting, applying a form of 'reverse engineering' to the same social context (Odella 2007). Rather than rely on the re-construction of the situation and the selection of the impact factors (a methodological position which emphasizes causal explanation and a priori control of the experimental setting), natural experiments can be focused on applied problems and produce knowledge oriented to social problem-solving. Stressing the social embeddedness of technology, some sociological enquires analyze thus recent societal processes of technological change looking at individual interactions, as well as the chances of being controlled and to control personal exchanges, that pervasive devices make possible. In the case of innovation' social impact, for example, natural experiments can be used to put in evidence processes of collective sense making that take place when new technologies are implemented inside organized contexts (Blascov-

ich, Loomis et al., 2002). When the elements of a specific social situation are selected and described as components of a more complex interaction process (reverse engineered), often it becomes possible to understand and schematize roles and positions among groups (different occupations, for example) and their negotiation of resources, such as knowledge and power. Looking at the adoption of pervasive technologies in daily life as a ´natural experiments´ can thus offer the chance to monitor social structures, the dynamics of social relations, and the distribution of resources among groups (ex. knowledge and expertise, control of the machinery).

Case 1: Technology and Social Theory Development (Testing Theories of Cooperative Behavior with the Aid of Digital Visualization)

The problem of how to coordinate individuals in order to increase group productivity or other collective benefit is a typical problem in social sciences (economic, sociological and psychological). Socio-economic theories, in particular, affirm that the possibility of large cooperative groups is related to the presence of social norms and of specific organizational forms that persuade individuals to invest into communal intents. Kinship is one of the aspects that seem to influence more social recognition and the creation, sharing and maintenance both of social norms and coordination forms, but scholars in the social sciences are still debating on its authentic role in shaping altruistic tendencies. According to kin selection theory, humans engage in complex activities (ex. commons management) more effectively when individuals belong to the same kin; the relatedness of members of a group diminishes the propensity to free riding and favors intra-group cooperation. At the simplest cognitive level the selective response to kinship seems to be related to phenotype recognition matching (face or physical characters such as skin type, eye shape, etc.) and other biocultural mechanisms. Anthropological theories envisage that in complex societies kinship may be substituted by other social recognition characters (gender, age, physical appearance, language and other cultural elements) that favor cooperation in large groups that incorporate non relatives.

To test the first level hypothesis about the effect of kinship on cooperation (Krupp, Debruine and Barclay, 2007), Krupp and his colleagues used advanced digital visualizing technologies. According to their experimental design when an individual evaluates the propensity to cooperate of other individuals for common goals (ex. dispensation of resources) she performs unconsciously a test of recognition for kinship similarity. The researchers considered facial resemblance as the most vivid clue of 'kinship similarity' and designed their experiment in order to have the participants interact in a series of public good games (PGG) with other two (virtual) participants that may resemble or not their characteristics. The images of virtual participants were based on two types of morph types (or digital composites of a photography) with familiar (self-resembling) and stranger faces. The presence of a 'kinship clue' was expected to influence the contributions and punishment attributed to the other participants during the simulated cooperation game. The experiments showed that kinship resemblance interacts positively with cooperation, increasing the amount of contributions given to participants of self-resembling morph types, but had no influence on free riding punishments, that where directed equally at stranger and self-resembling morph participants.

This piece of empirical research illustrate that socio-economic theories can be integrated with neuroscience technologies to investigate hypothesis concerning kinship influence on group cooperation. Technology in the form of advanced image manipulating techniques (photo morphing) provided the instruments to test complex theoretical propositions (the origin of human cooperation) across scientific disciplines.

TECHNOLOGIES OF SOCIAL INTERACTION AND HUMAN-TECHNOLOGIES RELATIONS

Social sciences generally deal with social things either in the form of ideas, values or norms or in the form of behaviors and action schemes. Sociological studies that recognize and give to 'non-humans' (machines, objects and robots, living entities as animals and ecosystems, or symbols like avatars) a role into social processes developed only in the last decade and explorations of interactions between humans and other type of 'social actors' still have a debated theoretical relevance. Since its spring, however, sociological enquiry in technology studies put in evidence that human and non-humans elements are always mixed up together in the social world and that materiality is a concept linked both to physical elements and to social practices. Theoretical orientations such as social constructionism and Actor-Networks Theory (ANT) further developed a framework for analyzing changes in social organization and sense making resulting from the implementation of scientific or technical innovations in daily life of people (Bjiker and Law, 1992).

According to social scholars of technology the relations with objects are an important part of social life and symbolic production. Design and manipulation of material things and of physical spaces are eminently social activities and many human societal goals are organized around these activities. The specific distribution of cognitive capacities between humans and machines—also defined as 'distributed cognition'—allow them to work together achieving complex tasks, such as navigating a ship, produce a tool or define a production process (Bjiker et al., 1987). In particular, researchers gained interest in human-non human interactions arising from changes in communicative contexts and those involving social identity definitions. The relations of many people, in fact, are increasingly mediated by communication and assistive technologies, either imposed by medical and social reasons or chosen by them as a way to overcome impairment and isolation in everyday life (Joyce and Loe, 2010). Studies focused specifically on the power of new technologies to redefine temporal and spatial boundaries of interactions and explore the progressive merging of human and artificial elements in defining contemporary personal and social identity (De Souza e Silva, 2006). Experiments carried on with social psychological methodology showed that ordinary people attribute human-like traits to those objects that have specific interactive and communicative capacities and recognize them as legitimate participants in social exchange. As a result techno-objects such as answering machines, computers, robots and avatars not only increased communicative capacities of people, but also transformed into possible conversers/partners for social interaction.

Moreover, as prosthetics and advanced assisting devices are progressively included into everyday practices, current sociological research reports also a shift in the social dimensions of artificiality and intimacy (Cerulo, 2009). This tendency is particularly relevant for specific generational groups such as the teenagers and old people which progressively rely on technology and mixed machinery for daily life tasks and emotional exchanges, As sociologist Loe documents in her study of technogenarians' (elder tech users) "everyday mundane technologies can be significant in designing an ever-changing self care repertoire to enable self-sufficiency, as well as control, independence and health" (Loe, 2010, p. 323). So while prosthetic tools support their daily life and social communications, elders shape their relation with technology into a sort of intimacy, ultimately transforming themselves into cyborgs.

Pervasive technologies and wireless enabled devices, according to some researchers, make it possible to have "internal intuitions" embodied in the empirical world, and to have "persons, objects and events once confined into the life of an individual mental eye projected to others in a way that surpasses mere description" (Cerulo, 2009, p. 539). Trust and affective relations, in particular, are developed every time robots and avatars manifest caring or anticipatory orientations or people can experiment a special form of 'technosynchronicity.' According to researchers, whenever a non-human entity, being it an animal, robot or machine, is capable of involving humans into relationships (ex. soliciting caring attitude, providing emotional support) the social element is activated, and people interact with the entities attributing them definite personalities or social characteristics (ex. machines as teammates). Emotional receptiveness is experienced also when the interaction with a socio-technical system involves different physical senses and relational capabilities. A very simple and ordinary example is architecture rendering which allows clients to move inside their future home, sense their location and interact with furniture and appliances within the room.

Processes of integration between subjects (humans) and technologies (non-humans) may involve also experts of technology and researchers; the ethnographic study of Voskuhl (2004) for example, describes the work of engineers' teams making an automated speech recognition machine. At the origin of word recognition technologies, reports the researcher, is an articulated debate on the role of words in a complex social process such as human conversation.

To build an efficient machine that can recognize spoken words requires to understand how humans perceive spoken language sequences and how they put up logical and significant communicative processes from sets of specific sounds (sometimes incomplete or not perfectly clear). The difference between the act of 'hearing' and the one of 'understanding' is thus not only a scientific problem but also a technological pursuit to solve. Voskuhl (2004) describes the work of engineers as involving at first the integration of diverse knowledge elements from physiology of the voice and ear, to physics of the sound and language studies. In addition, their work addresses an interpretative and sociological problem: whether conversation is a social activity that can be re-produced in human-machine interaction. The design of automated speech recognition processes thus imply a complex re-engineering of knowledge about the social relevance of speech, about the definition of what is a 'voice' and what is a 'sound' in conversational routines that are taken for granted in daily life, and, finally, the acknowledgement of the social function performed by 'voice' and 'sound' inside specialized language forms. Neutrality of technology in this process of engineering of heterogynous elements, underline Voskuhl, is not possible and the choice of specific technical solutions imply frequently a selection of the effects and of the characteristics of the final machinery and eventually the type of responses that individuals and groups have towards them (Voskuhl, 2004).

Empirical evaluation of advanced system technologies requires thus that some assumptions concerning the social relation between human subjects and technology are debated and redefined while assessing the efficacy of the technology. In particular, a very strong presumption to avoid is that technology integrates more with the body when the cognitive or physical conditions of the user are diminished or missing. Being the intrusion of technology in daily and relational activities as 'the less damage', disables, elderly or other people with physical or cognitive weakness become the primary subjects for testing technological integration or adaptive systems. The logical consequence is that minor attention is paid to social and indirect aspects of controlling and supplementary technologies (such as for example esthetic satisfaction from the object, intrusiveness in the private sphere).

Instead, social implementation problems can emerge when innovative technologies are tested on 'unconventional' users, such as subjects with no specific cognitive or physical impairment during daily performance. During the trials of a prototype of long-distance monitoring device designed for people with no or minor health problems, researchers experienced this specific impasse situation (De Ruyter et al, 2003). The specific technology GentleGuide is a device that uses tactile information to provide spatial information and guides the user by means of haptic radio sensors positioned on the wristband (Bosman et al., 2003). It was originally designed as an aid for subjects that have to walk and move inside in large and complex environments for work or maintenance reasons (hospitals, open space offices, airports, and large buildings). Initially, the researchers that create the device were looking for a system that supports intuitive processes normally activated during way finding but, despite their predictions, the experimentation of the devices in real environments showed that the social acceptability of the system varies a lot from person to person. Intuition guidance is in fact a trait that depends a lot on personality preferences; for some users the use of the device requires thus a sort of re-orientation of their cognitive processes, a diminishing of their 'natural' intuition and relying more on the technology itself. Furthermore, the haptic device absorbs the attention of the user so that less attention is paid to the environmental conditions; memorizing sequences and details of the actual path may become difficult and confusing for the user. The implementation of a technology in public contexts, finally, involves dealing with social automated reactions, such as the unsolicited help or monitoring measures by staff and observers. A subject wearing a 'special devices' and moving according to external guidance, also conveys the message that the guiding system is supporting a lack of orientation or locomotion autonomy. Concluding, untrained users of the haptic guide are and feel potentially less secure and proficient in their way finding while wearing the device than without it.

Unfeasibility of technological neutrality emerges in particular when the implementation of pervasive instruments (wireless devices and tags, graphical and video recognition, location devices and pointers) and multimedia systems involves issues related to the social perception of trust, security and privacy in public and private contexts. Telecare services, a case studied extensively by Oudshoorn (2012), are complex monitoring systems that can be implemented for diverse medical reasons, on subjects with variable intensity of disability. Homecare technologies help in remain independent, in keeping contacts with the others and the medical staff, but some enquieries show that these devices can also have double side effects (Loe, 2010). Oudshoorn's description of the social perception of a home telecare service puts in evidence that the introduction of technology in daily life can be intruding because it modifies daily routine and timing of family relations. In other words, telecare devices "transform the home from a private place into a hybrid space in which private and public spheres become closely intertwined and redefined" (Oudshoorn 2012, p. 137). Monitoring systems may be interpreted by some users as a withdrawing of control over personal health, reducing individual propensity to move outside the home. The organizational processes that manage technology in the home (for example the schedule of connections with remote operators, daily procedures to set the devices, advice and help from relatives and spouses) also may add difficulties to the life of people with minor disabilities, as well as create interfere with the communication process designed to provide advice to home patients (for example caregivers or relatives sending the data to the medical center, or unintentionally activating emergency calls).

Finally, evaluation of advanced system technologies frequently lacks of a comprehensive perspective of the benefits and risks associated to a specific innovation. A large amount of researches on the impact of technology are in fact effectiveness oriented and focused on specific sub-group of users, while few studies till now have scrutinized the overall impact of single technologies on personal identities, sense making and social interactions in everyday life. Contrasting with this one-sided tendency, sociological studies show that technology transforms itself according to the social and environmental setting where is implemented and has a deep cultural impact on traditions, knowledge and competences of groups and occupations. An interesting example of these aspects is provided by the extensive ethnographic study of the implementation of GPS technology among Inuit hunters (Aporta and Higgs, 2005).

Traditional way finding among the Inuit is based on very detailed geographical and physical details memorization, such as winds direction and winds turning, traces on the snow left by the wind, direction of the sun and other location references. Novice hunters were trained for years in route finding and learnt the technique under expert supervision, with diverse weather conditions and different urges and timelines. The introduction of the GPS technology for civil uses and its large diffusion among the population dramatically changed this situation making easier and safer snow hunting and increasing the chances of rescue in critical weather conditions. However, according to anthropologists' reports, GPS extensive and unqualified use is also eroding the traditional way finding techniques. Since GPS makes available to novices the possibility to trace hunting paths and save them as localization coordinates, "for the first time in history the navigator can completely rely on the technology and travel successfully knowing nothing about navigation and very little about the environment" (Aporta and Higgs; 2005; 744). The conditions of the weather in Alaska change very rapidly and what was initially recorded as an ordinary hunting route may transform itself into an hazardous trail because GPS coordinates do not represent a real hunting territory with its continuous variations (ice melting, cracks, snow dunes), but report simply its abstract geographical location. Therefore, a technological tool created to solve positioning problems may transform itself in a potential risk for the young Inuit and other unproven hunters when environmental conditions modify. The mapping provided by tradition way finding techniques, instead, was a 'social system of coding' that hunters shared and revised constantly according to seasonal and weather changes; shared information were an aid both to find hunting routes, to rescue and to avoid hunting risks, such as ice cracking, wild animals and hazardous physical settings.

The GPS case gives an idea of how people's relationships with technologies can modify global spheres of knowledge and social activities, transforming the language and words used to describe functionally the environment, as well as modifying the commitment and social meaning that people attribute to complex activities such as orientating and travelling. As the use of satellite devices is progressively applied to way finding, Inuit hunters experience thus a redefinition of expertise and skills required for snow routes tracing, as well as the need to re-orienting their cognitive framework and knowledge about the physical environment. Training sessions in GPS and collective hunting expeditions, researchers suggest, may help in preserving and sharing some of the traditional techniques of way finding, but direct knowledge of the land remains a crucial survival skill and a form of active involvement in the environment which GPS technology cannot substitute.

SOCIAL NETWORKS AND TECHNOLOGIES OF COMMUNICATION

Many social phenomena occur in small groups; researches in organizational and cultural sociology showed that many large social processes can be observed at the so-called meso level of observation by means of small group research small group analysis. Societal constrains and positions become visible through small group interactions and frequently revolution in values and behaviours

is anticipated by small groups (Harrington and Fine, 2000). Understanding the dynamics of small groups is thus relevant for developing explanations of social change and innovation diffusion. In particular, sociologist of technology are interested in sanctioning and monitoring processes that are performed by members of small groups, either in conflicts among knowledge perspectives and scientific assumptions, or in virtual communication spaces.

First empirical sociological studies on small groups adopted the sociometric approach to provide experimental verification of hypothesis concerning social structure (Gurvitch; 1949). Specifically, measuring the extent of acceptance or rejection between individuals in groups the researchers were trying to put in evidence dynamics of social participation and group cohesion. To sociometry and its founder Moreno can also be traced back the idea of performing sociological experiments[1], designed with the purpose of improving both theoretical and descriptive knowledge of social phenomena. In Moreno's perspective, in fact, sociometry was developed to investigate the 'forms of sociability', conjugating measurement with quantitative comprehension of the social mechanisms at work in interpersonal relations, in groups' formation and evolution (Alba, 1981).

Results of first sociometric studies showed that small groups (family, friends circles, workmates and associated to cultural or political groups) represent nodules of strong ties, within a large network of weak ties (society). Moreover, by means of socializing and re-identification processes, small groups provide to members commitment to identities, values and communicative frames (Borgatta and Baker, 1981). However, as illustrated by early sociometric studies on group cohesion and competition, social bonds become intelligible only if are framed and interpreted in their specific organizational and environmental contexts. The sense of belonging to small groups in fact originates from the mixing of concerted action (potential and effective) and shared identification (latent as well as acknowledged) in similar values and cultural preferences.

The methodological and theoretical legacy of sociometry has been improved in the following decades by Social Network Analysis (SNA) and, partially, by experimental economics: social experiments are nowadays used to test hypothesis and improve theories concerning individuals and small groups' dynamics. This approach has been methodologically refined both as survey and analytical technique (Faust and Wasserman,1994) and its application was successful for understanding determinants of innovation diffusion (Coleman et al., 1966) and impact of personal and informal resources in the labor market (Granovetter, 1985; Podolny and Baron, 1997).

In particular, the network approach has been intensively used for analyzing the transformation of social interactions in work and community settings related to technological innovation and interdependence of technological and collaborative relations in organizations (McPherson et al, 1992; Fulk, 1993). A famous study of technology implementation described the social effects due to the introduction of a scanner machine in two hospital wards (Barley, 1990). The researcher adopted a mixed methodology framework to study the changes inside the two organizations: using ethnographic observations and network analysis Barley analyzed work tasks and the modification of professional skills and competences. The research showed that new technologies applied to work environments modify connections among employees and the contents of their networks (quantity, intensity of contacts, share of knowledge and interests) in correspondence with the emergence of new technologically oriented medical professions.

Recent social network studies analyze the role of technology in relation to specific organizational contexts, such as knowledge production and diffusion (ex. conference participation, researchers' citation and bibliographical references), and

research and development companies (Obstfeld, 2005; Milton and Westphal, 2005). Analysis of networks of scientific knowledge, in particular, has contributed to shed light on social and collective process of knowledge construction in the sciences (see the works dealing with structure of scientific collaborations by Newmann, 2001 or the study of Wikipedia by Holloway, Bozicevic and Borner, 2007) and in general on the role that collaborative teams and serendipity have for the development of new methodologies and pioneering theories (Boyack, Klavans and Borner, 2005; Holloway et al, 2007).

Specifically, advances in mobile and digital communications offers new opportunities for the application of Social Network Analysis techniques to technology- mediated social processes. Some of these studies analyze social connectivity in mobile and wireless communication (Dearman et al., 2005), while others concentrate on the evolution of interactions or the context of social relationships in virtual space (Adamic and Adar, 2003; Chiu et al., 2006; Di Micco, 2008). Other studies analyze personal interactions mediated by IT communication technologies—chat and forums, social network sites, online communities—with the aim of exploring new forms of social interaction (Wellman et al., 1996; Wellman and Hampton, 1999) and report possible modification of traditional social bonds (friendship, trust, reputation).

A series of interesting studies concentrate for example on differences and similitudes between participation to traditional communities and virtual ones (Odella, 2012). Participation in online communities is in fact mediated both by technical features that enable the members to interact and perform their virtual identity(ies) and by socio-technical features such as the design of the communicative device (internet sites, chats or other interactive devices as in virtual games) and the social organization of the site (management, cooperation and involvement of members). Compared to other types of community, in virtual ones the interconnection of social participation, identity and personal relations tends thus to be built 'inside technology' (De Federico de la Rua, 2007) and not anymore favoured or prevented by it. Virtual communities in this sense could be a new form of socialization whose implications are still to explore and to categorize theoretically (Kostakos and Little, 2005; Hampton, 2003).

Current research on virtual communities is evolving on both technical and theoretical aspects concerning collection and interpretation of relationships among members of social networking sites and in particular to 'special' forms of grouping on the Internet (Matzat, 2009; Szell and Thurner, 2010). In a study on Web.2 organizations, for example, Ganley and Lampe (2009) show that the structure of the network of subjects can have a direct impact on their participation, modifying social perception of benefits and costs in participation to the site's communitarian life. Specifically, the design of the site, its opportunities of resource sharing and social exchange and the general climate of relationships, state Ganley and Lamp, are central features for the survival and success of the virtual community. Furthermore, the study showed that quality and quantity of resources (time, emotion, effort) and personal investment (privacy disclosure, preference and interest sharing) evolve according to the members' preferences (Stutzman, 2006) and their direct involvement in the technology design (Open Source Philosophy).

Finally, new forms of digital communication (mobile or internet based) re-opened the scholarly debate on technology design and institutional control of innovation diffusion. In particular, the recent application of network perspective to virtual relations and mobile communications has determined a methodological, as well as a ethical revision of technology studies. On one side, the gathering of information on communications and social relations on the web makes easier to elaborate interactions datasets with a large number of observations; this availability has stimulated the creation of programs for automatic data extrac-tion and rules of practice for handling these type of data (Mika, 2005), as well as the integration of social and computational sciences scientific perspectives (Eagle and Pentland, 2006). On the other side, ethical as well as privacy concerns have been expressed for the large availability of personal data which are suitable for network analysis (Molina and Borgatti, 2005; Floridi, 2006) and for the real intent of much scientific research in the area of digital communications and social networking (Kadushin, 2005).

Although these concerns, the area of application of social network analysis is intended to increase tremendously in the following decade due to synergies with ITC society where the concept of network, and in particular the use of the term to signify interconnectivity, is also theoretically central. The analysis of cultural practices and communicative structures in social networks are in fact expected to supplement and enrich studies of awareness systems that supplement existing communications and smart technologies in the area of wireless (IP-enabled) devices. Advances in the computational techniques for personal networks (web surveys, internet profiles on networking sites) give in fact the opportunity to evaluate the impact (or responsiveness) of individual choices on social processes, such as friendship formation and norm socialization (Ferron et al. 2011; Matzat, 2009).

The integration of Social Network Analysis with information and decision science, in particular, is valuable for developing models of enquiry specifically tailored for online interactions and huge amount of network data (Petroczi et al. 2007). The longitudinal study of Szell and Thurner (2010) on participants to MMSG (massive multiplayer online games) explores, for example, the dynamics of friendship and negative relationship and reports an impressive of natural social dynamics to virtual world one. Goggins and colleagues (2010), instead, describe small groups of learners that formed and work completely online and analyse how their performance (cooperation, fulfilment of a collective task) is integrated in the socio-technical system.

Result show that the participants' preferences for particular communicative tools (wikis, chat and other a-synchronic communication systems) modify the initially proposed and foreseen purposes of the technology. Sociological network analysis in the future may thus merge with social physics (Dorogovtsev and Mendes, 2003; Barabasi, 2002; Watts et al. 2002) or concentrate on specific sub-themes such as studies on the social impact of telecommunications and digital media on social integration, or the analysis of social networks for forecasting (Cachia et al., 2007).

Case 2: Two Research Experiences on Personal Networks and Wireless Communication

To describe how social network analysis can contribute to investigate technologies in use, in this paragraph are described two experiences; the first reporting an experiments on the social impact of pervasive devices carried on with the support of social network analysis techniques (Szomszor et al. 2010; Cattuto et al. 2010); the second experience reports the application of SNA to data extracted from mobile communication and in particular information about detailed location of the user of a cellular phone (Eagle, 2009).

The first example (www.sociopaths.org) reports the use of RFID sensors to survey and re-construct the network of personal contacts between researchers taking place during an international conference (Szomszor et al. 2010). An interdisciplinary research group was involved both in technology testing and in social assessment of the methods (meshing of social network analysis and semantic analysis of the content of web pages and social networks). Their goal was to establish a relation between a subject's identity, their work interests (as declared in professional self-portrait or in their webpages and social network sites self-presentation) and their pattern of interaction. Tracking face to face contacts during the conference, characterized by proximity in dyads, the researchers discovered that only a section of them pave the way for interactions in triads when interests are collectively shared for further contacts (emails exchange). The use of RFID devices was also an experiment for testing the level of acceptance of people for intrusiveness and privacy. Participants to the conference that volunteered for the experiment showed in this sense a specific concern for the retrieval of personal data and its anonymisation, as well as an interest for real time visualization of social interactions during the conference.

The second example, the Reality Mining project (http://reality.media.mit.edu) describes a series of experimentations that involved a group of volunteers at MIT laboratories. A large group of students were provided specially equipped portable phones and asked to report through a web survey their personal relations. The data concerning their social activities were further matched with the location and duration of interactions taking place around the campus; proximity of two or more logged cellular phones in the same cell tower was interpreted as a signal of reciprocal interest of the subjects and as a potentiality for information flow. The aim of the study was to enrich the functionality of phones and to supply users with 'socializing' applications that can be used to identify other users nearby on the bases of expertise and interests (work related issue, dating or social networking) and willingness to connect. Social network analysis was used to assess the accuracy of the log data to detect proximity involving from two to three subjects and to identify them as friendship, workmates or acquaintances relations. Moreover, the experiments constituted a test for methods, comparing self report data collected in the web-survey with observations extracted from the participants' phones, such as user's location (celltower ID), people nearby (repeated Bluetooth scans), communication (call and SMS logs), and application usage/phone status (idle, charging, etc). The research experiences, finally, inspired also the design of software prototype for privacy protection that enable the users to set their preferences, selecting which mode of connecting is preferred at each specific time of the day/week.

TECHNOLOGIES OF SURVEILLANCE AND SOCIETAL CONTROL

The study of institutional change and changes in technology provides an empirical support for theories that explain the mutual influence of material processes, artifacts and societal instances in creating knowledge and in general new organizational structures for managing special social problems. Among the social problems addressed recently by technology studies is the one of social surveillance and the increasing implementation of devices and technologies for monitoring and recording daily life activities from work to health records, communication and access to the Internet.

Surveillance studies are an interdisciplinary area of research whose interest focalize on societal control and regulation by means of knowledge, procedures and technologies (Lyon, 1994). One of the most influential theories in this approach has been Focault's research on the so-called 'technologies of the self' which explored the concept of social control in relation to technologies since the pre-modern ages (ex. inside collective residences such as prisons, asylums and hospitals).

On the bases of historical documents Foucalt showed that social interests and institutions shaped the design of specific social control technologies (ex. architectural features for assuring visual seclusion); institutions also socially legitimate their adoption of educational/correctional devices as a deterrent to social violence and moral values loosening. Since Foucault the so called 'surveillance perspective' developed in a large area of study that analyzed several types of technologies of control in diverse area such as communication and culture, organization of processes and services, transport and production of goods. In the last twenty years surveillance studies re-oriented also the study of

health, defense and scientific research innovations approaching issues such as cyber terrorism, hackers and digital counterculture (Marx, 2005). Moving from this perspective this paragraph will illustrate how the introduction of a classical monitoring technology, video-surveillance, has been variously interpreted by sociologists and how the debate on surveillance is evolving with the progressive integration of visual control with pervasive - or ubiquitous – technologies.

The use of video surveillance or Closed-Circuit Television (CCTV) to detect and prevent criminal offences and to monitor social behaviour registered a vast and constant expansion in urban, public and private settings of social interactions (work, leisure and shopping, medical and administrative environments). The application of visual monitoring spread mainly as a cost-reducing strategy for sites control and risk detection, while the applications of the video-surveillance technology, however, are more various and its implementation can have also positive and functional outcomes such as in quality testing and visual monitoring of manufacturing and logistics (Norris et al., 2004).

Inside private and organizational spaces the practice of monitoring has spread outside the 'safety and health' settings where it had been initially introduced and now work and business, communication and leisure settings are largely scrutinized by surveillance systems which collect and process information (Ruppert, 2011). Despite its large diffusion, security analysts suggest that relying on CCTV for improving protection of private spaces (homes, private accesses) can be counterproductive as it may reduce neighbourhood vigilance and lessen the level of attention of urban residents (Sewell and Barker, 2006). Local governments and city boards have tried to cut such a risk introducing rules of conduct for the retrieval and use of video shot in public area, but there is still a lack of coordination among authorities, and the private use of CCTV is spreading as a form of virtual watchdogs (Norris, McCail and Wood. 2004; Stalder, 2002).

Social scientists that first analysed this phenomenon highlighted the aspects related to social control and the trade-off between privacy and safety that in urban areas prevented citizens from unconstrained use of public spaces. Scholars stressed that an uncontrolled employ of surveillance technologies was risky not only in terms of potential violation of the individual privacy and freedom of act, but because it determines a systematic deficit of democracy. Research reports concerning social surveillance underline that in most social contexts technology is imposed as the only solution to a generalized climate of moral panic, and its administration is progressively institutionalized and transformed in bureaucratic tasks and routines. Social surveillance becomes thus the critical goal of the state and of its control agencies and the symbol of a remote and constant power on the individual (Walby and Hier, 2005; Marx, 2001). Moreover, while the reaction of the public to urban use of CCTV is generally reported with positive response rates in surveys, specific studies testimony that this response rate is biased and prejudiced by a 'pro-surveillance position' of respondents (Gandy 2003).

Empirical research on the issue, on the contrary, showed that social reactions to the progressive video-monitoring of the public and private environment are raging from active resistance to counter-control, irony and mocking of the controllers (Dupont, 2008; Marx, 2003). Real-time web cameras of streets, for example, function as forms of surveillance, but also as aids to a daily (and professional) activity such as street prostitution, or to display funny or antagonistic behaviour in the urban setting (Graham and Marvin 2006). To legitimize the use of video-surveillance and monitoring technologies, critics observe, institutions and companies put a lot of effort in framing the technology using the familiar separation between expert/non-experts in the effort to hide power relations.

Legitimization of monitoring technologies relies on the assumption that pervasive technologies can perform as protective devices for the benefit of groups culturally and physically separated from society (non-experts). Despite this assumption, sociological studies put in evidence that when the video monitoring activity is performed towards specific social groups, such as the elderly, schoolchildren, disabled people inside hospices and even ethnic minorities, privacy and ethical concerns are frequently reduced (Wood, 2005). A sharp critic to video surveillance is found, also, in studies concerning monitoring technologies in work settings (Taylor and Spencer, 1990, or for an extensive review see Sewell and Barker, 2006) where the technology is definitively suffered as an intruder, both from employers and employees, but institutionalized and legitimized as a productive support (Walby, 2006; Hansen, 2004). More recently studies have been carried on in sport games, where 'engineering of social control' (Walby, 2006) was first introduced for preventing violence. The progressive introduction of anti-violence measures in stadia, however, has brought to a massive employ of surveillance techniques involving RFID tracking of the tickets, CC cameras and face recognition monitors, scanner machinery at security checks and electronic registers of hooligans (Joern, 2009). As a consequence, the inventory of controlling devices in some sport context, some scholars note, desolately resembles those adopted in correctional control (Mainprize, 1996) and, worst of all, institutional rhetoric systematically support and legitimize these organizational systems that reduce the freedom and consent of people forcing them to constantly prove their being 'normal' (and not a hooligan type).

Synthesizing, the current debate on surveillance tend to move between the extremes of interpreting technology either as a saviour (from collective violence, undisclosed urban risks or domestic hazards), or as an intruder that scrutinizes intimate details of life and personal discretions. Video monitoring technology, in particular, offers the opportunity of storing and scrutinizing the behaviour of others, taking advantage of the separation in physical space between the observer and the observed—whether voluntary or not. According to scholars of surveillance studies, this distinct separation between the dimensions of making (by the observed) and the one of watching (the observer) expresses in reality a social juxtaposition in terms of power and gender relations (Monahan, 2008; Brighenti, 2007). Eventually, the (collective) identity of surveillance targets (ex. women doing shopping, travellers in the metro, schoolchildren in the yard), influences which of the two metaphors of technology (savior vs. intruder) will prevail in the conventional interpretation and the institutional framework of the technology sensemaking (Griffith, 1999).

The ambiguous social role of surveillance technology is remarkable evident in the study of Mohanan (2006) where the experience of people living in low-income public housing in Phoenix Arizona (video monitored for security reason) are compared to the experiences of the residents of two affluent gated communities. The study puts in evidence how the residents perceived the common discourse on security and surveillance and relate it with their own daily practices under scrutiny of the *'panopticon.'* In response to institutional and cultural demands gated communities and public housing have been transforming themselves in 'surveillance places', where video surveillance is permanently active as a prevention measure for crime and deviant actions and as a supervision device of public properties such as golf courts and parking. While living in such communities, notes Mohanan (2011), surveillance becomes a cultural element and an institution, that legitimate social control over the individual, regardless of her identity and social class position. As Monahan (2006, p. 186) underlines:

technological surveillance is just one more component in the social-surveillance apparatus of gated communities, designed to safeguard a restricted form of freedom that seems to mean freedom not only from exposure to people from other classes, ethnic groups, or cultural background, but also freedom from the responsibility of outwardly demonstrating singularity of individual difference from one's neighbours.

Inside the public housing community institutional surveillance performs a special symbolic function: CCTV monitoring in fact avoids raising the problems that risks are present inside the community, and project them on external contacts and individual extravaganzas of the visitors. In reality some of the residents are socially and economically deprived and occasionally involved in burglary, prostitution and drug addiction. The presence of the 'deviant inside', however, is not recognized as an ontological possibility in the institutional logic because risks can only come from outside the community. Social control is thus transformed in *'selective watching'* operations performed with video surveillance, scrutinizing specific individuals or behaviours that are interpreted as unsafe by housing authorities representatives.

Intrusion is also an issue for residents in gated communities, whose recurrent account for performing extensive video surveillance practices is the security of the community. Architectural design and monitoring practices frustrate any trespassing of community rules about tolerable daily activities, contractors and visitors' access, and the use of shared properties. These 'safe surveillance' accomplishments, however, discourage any behavioural variations by the residents, such as taking a walk in the neighbourhood, and push identification routines to over-meticulous procedures that depress socializing and even occasional encounters inside the gates. On the bases of Monahan's accounts of it is hard to guess which role is actually performing and representing technology inside the two communities. The saviour and the intruder metaphor are mashed up together in both monitored environments, becoming rhetorical devices for institutionalizing separateness by chance or census.

FINAL REMARKS ON SOCIAL ASSESSMENT OF PERVASIVE TECHNOLOGIES

The above studies of technology have been useful to put in evidence that a multiple interpretative framework is essential for performing realistic socio-technical systems assessment. It is thus interesting to see how more recent forms of surveillance, such as sensors and smart technologies, have been approached by the sociological debate on technology. As some scholars warn, pervasive technologies in fact tend to reduce the terms of ordinary separation between personal and social identity, inducing individuals and groups to manipulate personal and relational boundaries and to invent new forms of resistance to institutional control. The public use of such technologies is also blamed for reducing the boundaries between private and public space, and specifically liberty boundaries established by means of civil rights struggles and legislation (Marx, 2001). Moreover, social researchers warn that pervasive technologies, compared to the more established ones, can strengthen social control and nurture processes of social differentiation (Lyon, 2002). Thanks to the introduction of more sophisticated technologies (detailed geographical position detection, remote control of specific physiological parameters, real-time and interactive tracking of behaviour) institutional surveillance may in fact increase its functionality, as well as its intrusiveness over the individual. Some researchers foresee that the adoption of automatic housekeeping devices inside the 'intelligent house' will reduce the separation between controllers and controlled and, paradoxically, decrease the personal space of privacy and choice in how to manage a private environment (Callaghan, Graham and Chin, 2007).

Only lately articles and reviews start to give guidelines and suggest complex accounts of individual and social interaction with new pervasive technologies (Markupoulos et al. 2005; Vargas Solar 2005). Specifically, some researchers remark that potential applications of such technologies to daily living—intelligent buildings and 'smart' houses, city mobility, visual and audible aids to communication, monitoring and reporting of unidentified hazards – can help normal and impaired people to make a better and safer use of the built environment (Kamel Boulos et al., 2010), to connect more directly with institutions and public service (Carley, 2002), and offer them the opportunity to communicate and express more openly (Adkins and Barnett, 2006; Romero et al, 2003). An example of unprejudiced perspective of pervasive technologies is Wiggs´s study (2010) on surveillance management in mentally disabled residences. She describes how one of the most visible symptoms of dementia, wandering, is managed by the staff of the residences balancing the need to provide a safer environments for residents and their individual right to freedom. Wandering is commonly perceived by medical staff to be a risky behaviour, requiring social controls or physical seclusion. In mentally disabled residences wandering is prevented either physically, banning some spaces and creating a 'locked environment,' or surveyed by means of technological devices, such as motion detectors and personnel's monitoring (an 'unlocked' environment). In order to study how technologies of surveillance can be diversely ideated and organized according to dissimilar interpretation of the social and individual risks associated with dementia symptoms (Brittain et al., 2010), Wiggs compares the so-called 'unlocked environment' to 'locked environments.' The difference between the two situations, as Wiggs remarks, is grounded in different medical interpretation of physical activity in the 'outside' world: in the 'locked' environment wandering is evaluated as a risk that should be avoided at any case, while in the 'unlocked' case is seen as part of the ordinary medical profile associated with dementia patients. As the author remarks "distinctions exist between surveillance technologies that chiefly engage in social control and surveillance technologies that encourage greater independence and interpersonal interaction between staff and residents" (2010, p. 299). The researcher concludes that technology *per se* is not negative or positive for inclusive care, but can be the instrument of de-humanizations, as well as a viable solution for medical problems that are difficult or ethically complicated to treat pharmacologically (Joyce and Loe, 2010).

This extreme case exemplify that behaviour controlling technologies should be understood in context and evaluated for their effective use, their consequences on individual abilities and emotional condition, as well as for their inclusion in an organizational setting that regulate and define the boundaries of privacy, risk, and care. Pervasive technologies give visibility to the cultural boundaries between what is private and what is public; they also allow social groups to express different attitude towards privacy and public exposure (e.g. display of personal interests and contacts on Facebook). Therefore, technologies involving an intimate relation with the user should not be seen unilaterally, but are better interpreted inside the overall social environment (with physical, emotional and relational dimensions included) where humans and monitoring devices interact.

Till now the level of attention in privacy studies has been high for all the aspects concerning the institutional and public impact of surveillance technologies (Andrejvich, 2005), while few studies and empirical investigations addressed the social and relational elements of privacy (Margulis 2003; Cate, 2001). Investigations and experiments, mainly, tend to concentrate on the measurement of the impact of pervasive technologies on individual users, but paid less attention to the emergence and establishment of particular relational attitudes towards technology adoption (privacy awareness) and the release of personal details (privacy trade-off). In particular, the creation of rules of conduct concerning identity and personal information exchange among group of pairs or communities is still to analyse in social groups with different levels of technological expertise

and diverse personal involvement in technology framed contexts (Odella, 2009).

The sociological perspective, in this sense, may supplement assessment studies of technology and integrate them with specific analysis of groups preferences and responsiveness towards personal data treatment and security measures (e.g. cybersecurity paradigms). Sociologists have been dealing with technologies of recognition of human sociability (ex. documents created by institutions for control or administration purposes) since the adoption in social research of systematic empirical methods. Social research represents thus a form of surveillance and can be designed according to inclusive or restrictive principles, as well as report in a different way subjective explanations and institutional interpretative frameworks (Monahan, 2011). Contemporary developments in the social sciences methodology designed for exploring human-technology interactions like the ones described in the chapter are moving toward this direction, and pave the way for a comprehensive interpretation of identity and social relations changes related to technology adoption.

Despite this, as the case of video-surveillance illustrates, social sciences attitude towards controlling technologies has been sometimes controversial. Specifically, the presence of the intruder-saviour metaphor in the surveillance studies has discouraged and complicated empirical research with minus attention paid to research in daily life and in ordinary contexts (leisure, work, personal contacts). Dupont (2008) explicitly synthesizes in three elements the problems that sociology, and in particular surveillance studies, have towards behavioural monitoring technologies. The first bias attributes to technology users (or wannabe users) a passive role, and forgets to acknowledge everyday hacking practices that groups adopt to resist, or modify discarded or intrusive aspects of technology. Further in this direction, sociologist Ellerbrock (2011) suggests to introduce in the current framework of technology studies the category of 'play'. As shown by the case of face recognition software and localization devices, monitoring technologies are becoming familiar elements in our society and socializing practices are built around them(e.g. creating a personal picture gallery in social network sites with FR tools, using GPS devices for collective games or party gatherings). Controversial aspects of surveillance such as biometrics are inserted in a cultural framework that re-interpret it as playful and legitimize its adoption for supporting interactions and personal contentment in social networks sites.

The second interpretative fault is not paying enough attention to the balance between positive and negative outcomes of technologies, and over-emphasizes only the 'intrusive' role that monitoring technologies can have. The increasing application of technological apparatus for monitoring, advising and assist elderly or people with chronic illness, instead, shows that under certain conditions 'the intruder' technology fulfils a positive role, providing social and material resources that are relevant for the wellbeing of people. Privacy and ethical implications have been always present whenever technologies coordinate human relations or manage individual resources; while, as Dupont remarks, "the lack of sophisticated surveillance tools has never prevented authoritarian states to enroll thousands of informers to control internal dissent" (Dupont, 2008, p. 276). Furthermore, as some recent research illustrates, the possibilities to negotiate controlling technologies are becoming available in most social environments and the design of such systems could be developed according to participative and empowerment principles (Albrechtslund and Glud, 2010).

The third bias is to overestimate negative outcomes from some technological advances, such as surveillance tools, and to forecast disastrous social implications from its implementation at large in society. Historical and sociological studies of socio-technical changes report the serendipitous path that brings an innovation to full implementation and register the attempts and failures that paved the way for its success. Social complexity and triviality of decisions (e.g. lack of funding or organizational and cultural resistance) are frequently the reasons for blocking innovations as well as the reasons for applying them. A unilateral interpretation of the role played by technologies, besides, hides the fact that innovations can also have an extraneous social impact and being eventually useless. As social network studies have illustrated, good ideas are socially recognized and find their way in society by means of mediators that bypass ordinary interaction structures, and transmit them at the right place and time to fully develop (Burt, 2004). The role that social sciences can have in the debate about monitoring and surveillance technologies is thus to re-affirm the relevance of embodied practices and social institutions in shaping innovation adoption processes and affirming their sense making in society.

REFERENCES

Adamic, L., & Adar, E. (2005). How to search a social network. *Social Networks*, *27*, 187–203. doi:10.1016/j.socnet.2005.01.007

Adkins, B., & Barnett, K. (2006). Public spaces as 'context' in assistive information and communication technologies for people with cognitive impairment. *Information Communication and Society*, *9*(3), 355–372. doi:10.1080/13691180600751330

Alba, R. D. (1981). From small groups to social networks: Mathematical approaches to the study of group structure. *The American Behavioral Scientist*, *24*(5), 681–694. doi:10.1177/000276428102400506

Albrechtslund, A., & Norgaard, G. L. (2011). Empowering residents: A theoretical framework for negotiating surveillance technologies. *Surveillance & Society*, *8*(2), 235–250.

Andrejvich, M. (2005). The work of watching one other: Lateral surveillance, risk and governance. *Surveillance & Society, 2*(4), 474–478.

Aporta, C., & Higgs, E. (2005). Satellite culture: Global positioning systems, inuit wayfinding and the need for a new account of technology. *Current Anthropology, 46*(5), 729–753. doi:10.1086/432651

Barabasi, A. L. (2002). *Linked: The new science of networks*. Cambridge, MA: Perseus Publishing.

Barley, S. R. (1990). The allignment of technology and structure through roles and networks. *Administrative Science Quarterly, 35*(1), 61–103. doi:10.2307/2393551

Becker, H. S. (1998). *Tricks of the trade: How to think about your research while you're doing it.* Chicago, IL: University of Chicago Press.

Bjiker, W., & Law, J. (1992). *Shaping technology/building society: Studies in socio-technical change*. Cambridge, MA: MIT Press.

Blascovich, J., & Loomis, J. (2002). Immersive virtual environment technology as a methodological tool for social psychology. *Psychological Inquiry, 13*(2), 103–124. doi:10.1207/S15327965PLI1302_01

Borgatta, E. F., & Baker, P. M. (1981). Introduction: Updating small group research and theory *The American Behavioral Scientist* (special issue), *24*(5), 603–605. doi:10.1177/000276428102400501

Borgatti, S. P., & Molina, J. L. (2005). Towards ethical guidelines for network research in organizations. *Social Networks, 27*(2), 107–117. doi:10.1016/j.socnet.2005.01.004

Bornholdt, S., & Schuster, H. G. (2005). *Handbook of graphs and networks: From the genome to the internet*. New York, NY: Wiley. doi:10.1002/3527602755

Bosman, S., Groenendaal, B., Findlater, J. W., Visser, T., de Graaf, M., & Markopoulos, P. (2003). *GentleGuide: An exploration of haptic output for indoors pedestrian guidance*. Eindhoven, The Netherlands: Neroc. doi:10.1007/978-3-540-45233-1_28

Boyack, K., Klavans, R., & Borner, K. (2005). Mapping the backbone of science. *Scientometrics, 64*(3), 351–374. doi:10.1007/s11192-005-0255-6

Brighenti, A. (2007). Visibility: A category for the social sciences. *Current Sociology, 55*(3), 323–342. doi:10.1177/0011392107076079

Brittain, K., Corner, L., Robinson, L., & Bond, J. (2010). Ageing in place and technologies of place: The lived experience of people with dementia in changing social, physical and technological environments. *Sociology of Health & Illness, 32*(2), 272–287. doi:10.1111/j.1467-9566.2009.01203.x

Burt, R. (2004). Structural holes and good ideas. *American Journal of Sociology, 110*(2), 349–399. doi:10.1086/421787

Cachia, R., Compañó, R., & Da Costa, O. (2007). Grasping the potential of online social networks for foresight. *Technological Forecasting and Social Change, 74*, 1179–1203. doi:10.1016/j.techfore.2007.05.006

Callaghan, V., Clarke, G., & Chin, J. (2007). Some socio-technical aspects of intelligent buildings and pervasive computing research, intelligent buildings. *International Journal Earthscan, 1*(1).

Carley, K. M. (2002). Smart agents and organizations of the future. In Lievrouw, L., & Livingstone, S. (Eds.), *The Handbook of New Media*. London, UK: Sage.

Cate, F. H. (2001). *Privacy in perspective*. Washington, DC: American Enterprise Institute for Public Policy Research.

Cattuto, C., Van den Broeck, W., Barrat, A., Colizza, V., Pinton, J. F., & Vespignani, A. (2010). Dynamics of person-to-person interactions from distributed RFID sensor networks. *PLoS ONE*, *7*, 1–9.

Cerulo, K. A. (2009). Nonhumans in social interaction. *Annual Review of Sociology*, *35*, 531–552. doi:10.1146/annurev-soc-070308-120008

Chiu, C. M., Hsu, M., & Wang, E. (2006). Understanding staring in virtual communities: An integration of social capital and social cognitive theories. *Decision Support Systems*, *42*, 1872–1888. doi:10.1016/j.dss.2006.04.001

De Federico de la Rúa, A. (2007). Networks and identifications: A relational approach to social identities. *International Sociology*, *22*, 683–699. doi:10.1177/0268580907082247

de Ruyter, B., Aarts, E., Markopoulos, P., & Ijsselsteijn, W. (2003). *Ambient intelligence research in HomeLab: Engineering the user experience*. Eindhoven, The Netherlands: Neroc.

de Souza, , & Silva, A. (2006). From cyber to hybrid: Mobile technologies as interfaces of hybrid spaces. *Space and Culture*, *9*, 261–278. doi:10.1177/1206331206289022

Dearman, D., Hawkey, K., & Inkpen, K. M. (2005). Rendezvousing with location aware devices: Enhancing social coordination. *Interacting with Computers*, *17*(2), 542–566. doi:10.1016/j.intcom.2005.03.005

DiMicco, J., Millen, D. R., Geyer, W., Dugan, C., Brownholtz, B., & Muller, M. (2008). Motivations for social networking at work. In *Proceedings of CSCW 2008*. San Diego, CA: CSCW.

Dorogovtsev, S., & Mendez, J. (2003). *Evolution of networks: From biological nets to the internet and www*. Oxford, UK: Oxford University Press.

Dupont, B. (2008). Hacking the panopticon: Distributed online surveillance and resistance. *Surveillance and Governance. Sociology of Crime Law and Deviance*, *10*, 259–280. doi:10.1016/S1521-6136(07)00212-6

Eagle, N., & Pentland, A. S. (2006). Reality mining: Sensing complex social systems. *Personal and Ubiquitous Computing*, *10*(4), 255–268. doi:10.1007/s00779-005-0046-3

Eagle, N., & Pentland, A. S. (2009). Eigenbehaviours: Indentifying structure in routine. *Behavioral Ecology and Sociobiology*, *63*, 1057–1066. doi:10.1007/s00265-009-0739-0

Ellerbrok, A. (2011). Playful biometrics: Controversial technology through the lens of play. *The Sociological Quarterly*, *52*, 528–547. doi:10.1111/j.1533-8525.2011.01218.x

Ferron, M., Massa, P., & Odella, F. (2011). Analyzing collaborative networks emerging in enterprise 2.0: The taolin platform. *Procedia Social and Behavioural Science*, *10*(1), 68–78. doi:10.1016/j.sbspro.2011.01.010

Floridi, L. (2006). Four challenges for a theory of information privacy. *Ethics and Information Technology*, *8*, 109–119. doi:10.1007/s10676-006-9121-3

Fulk, J. (1993). Social construction of communication technology. *Academy of Management Journal*, *36*(5), 921–950. doi:10.2307/256641

Gandy, O. H. (2003). Public opinion survey and the formation of privacy policy. *The Journal of Social Issues*, *59*(2), 283–299. doi:10.1111/1540-4560.00065

Ganley, D., & Lampe, C. (2009). The ties that bind: Social network principles in online communities. *Decision Support Systems*, *47*, 268–274. doi:10.1016/j.dss.2009.02.013

Goggins, S. P., Laffey, J., & Gallagher, M. (2011). Completely online group formation and development: Small groups as socio-technical systems. *Information Technology & People, 24*(2), 104–133. doi:10.1108/09593841111137322

Griffith, T. L. (1999). Technology features as triggers for sensemaking. *Academy of Management Review, 24*(3), 472–488.

Gurvitch, G. (1949). Microsociology and sociometry. *Sociometry, 12*(1-3), 1–31. doi:10.2307/2785376

Hampton, K., & Wellman, B. (1999). Netville online and offline: Observing and surveying a wired suburb. *The American Behavioral Scientist, 43*, 475–492. doi:10.1177/00027649921955290

Hampton, K. N. (2003). Grieving for a lost network: Collective action in a wired suburb. *The Information Society, 19*(5), 417–428. doi:10.1080/714044688

Hansen, S. (2004). From 'common observation' to behavioural risk management: Workplace surveillance and employee assistance 1914-2003. *International Sociology, 19*(19), 151–171. doi:10.1177/0268580904042898

Harrington, B., & Fine, G. A. (2000). Opening the black box: Small groups and twenty first century sociology. *Social Psychology Quarterly, 63*(4), 312–323. doi:10.2307/2695842

Holloway, T., Bozicevic, M., & Borner, K. (2007). Analyzing and visualizing the semantic coverage of Wikipedia and its authors. *Complexity, 12*(33), 30–40. doi:10.1002/cplx.20164

Hughes, T. (1987). The evolution of large technological systems. In Bjiker, W., Hughes, T., & Pinch, T. (Eds.), *The Social Construction of Technological Systems*. Cambridge, MA: MIT.

Joern, L. (2009). Nothing to hide, nothing to fear? Tackling violence on the terraces. *Sport in Society, 12*(10), 1269–1283. doi:10.1080/17430430903204777

Joyce, K., & Loe, M. (2010). A sociological approach to ageing, technology and health. *Sociology of Health & Illness, 32*(2), 171–180. doi:10.1111/j.1467-9566.2009.01219.x

Kadushin, C. (2005). Who benefits from network analysis: Ethics of social network research. *Social Networks, 27*, 139–153. doi:10.1016/j.socnet.2005.01.005

Kamel Boulos, M. N., & Castellot, L. R. (2010). Connectivity for healthcare and well being management: Examples from six European projects. *International Journal of Environmental Research and Public Health, 6*, 1947–1971. doi:10.3390/ijerph6071947

Kostakos, V., & Little, L. (2005). The social implications of emerging technologies. *Interacting with Computers, 17*(5), 475–483. doi:10.1016/j.intcom.2005.03.001

Krupp, D. B., Debruine, L., & Barclay, M. P. (2008). A cue of kinship promotes cooperation for the public good. *Evolution and Human Behavior, 29*, 49–55. doi:10.1016/j.evolhumbehav.2007.08.002

Latour, B. (1992). Where are the missing masses? The sociology of a few mundane artifacts. In Bjiker, W., & Law, J. (Eds.), *Shaping Technology/Building Society: Studies in Sociotechnical Change*. Cambridge, MA: MIT Press.

Law, J. (1987). Technology and heterogeneous engineering. In Bjiker, W., Hughes, T., & Pinch, T. (Eds.), *The Social Construction of Technological Systems*. Cambridge, MA: MIT.

Loe, M. (2010). Doing it my way: Old women, technology and wellbeing. *Sociology of Health & Illness, 32*(2), 319–334. doi:10.1111/j.1467-9566.2009.01220.x

Lyon, D. (1994). *The electronic eye: The rise of surveillance society.* London, UK: Polity Press.

Lyon, D. (2002). Everyday surveillance: Personal data and social classifications. *Information Communication and Society, 5*(2), 424–257. doi:10.1080/13691180210130806

Mainprize, S. (1996). Effective affinities in the engineering of social control: The evolution of electronic monitoring. *Electronic Journal of Sociology, 2*(2).

Margulis, S. (2003). Privacy as a social issue and behavioural concept. *The Journal of Social Issues, 59*(2), 243–261. doi:10.1111/1540-4560.00063

Markopulos, P., Ijsselsteijn, W., & De Ruyter, B. (2005). Sharing experiences through awareness systems in the home. *Interacting with Computers, 17*, 506–521. doi:10.1016/j.intcom.2005.03.004

Marx, G. T. (2001). Murky conceptual waters: The public and the private. *Ethics and Information Technology, 3*(3), 157–169. doi:10.1023/A:1012456832336

Marx, G. T. (2003). A tack in the shoe: neutralizing and resisting the new surveillance. *The Journal of Social Issues, 59*(2), 369–390. doi:10.1111/1540-4560.00069

Marx, G. T. (2005). *Seeing hazily (but not darkly) through the lens: Some recent empirical studies of surveillance technologies.* Washington, DC: American Bar Foundation. doi:10.1111/j.1747-4469.2005.tb01016.x

Matzat, U. (2009). A theory of relational signals in online groups. *New Media & Society, 11*, 375–394. doi:10.1177/1461444808101617

McPherson, M., Popielarz, P., & Drobnic, S. (1992). Social networks and organizational dynamics. *American Sociological Review, 57*, 153–170. doi:10.2307/2096202

Mika, P. (2005). Flink: Semantic web technology for the extraction and analysis of social networks. *Web Semantics: Science. Services and Agents on the World Wide Web, 3*, 211–223. doi:10.1016/j.websem.2005.05.006

Milton, L. P., & Westphal, J. D. (2005). Identity confirmation networks and cooperation in work groups. *Academy of Management Journal, 48*(2), 191–212. doi:10.5465/AMJ.2005.16928393

Monahan, T. (2006). Electronic fortification in Phoenix: Surveillance technologies and social regulation in residential communities. *Urban Affairs Review, 42*(2), 169–192. doi:10.1177/1078087406292845

Monahan, T. (2008). Dreams of control at a distance: Gender, surveillance and social control. *Cultural Studies, 9*(2), 286–305.

Monahan, T. (2011). Surveillance as cultural practice. *The Sociological Quarterly, 52*, 495–508. doi:10.1111/j.1533-8525.2011.01216.x

Newman, M. E. J. (2001). The structure of scientific collaboration network. *PNA, 98*(16), 404–409. doi:10.1073/pnas.98.2.404

Norris, C., McCail, M., & Wood, D. (2004). The Growth of CCTV: A global perspective on the international diffusion of video surveillance in publicly accessible space. *Surveillance & Society, 2*(2/3).

Obstfeld, D. (2005). Social networks: The tertius iungens orientation and involvement in innovation. *Administrative Science Quarterly, 50*, 100–130.

Odella, F. (2007). Reverse experiments: Investigating social behaviour with daily technologies. In *INTER: A European Cultural Studies Conference Proceedings,* (pp. 463-470). Norrkoping, Sweden: Linkoping University Electronic Press.

Odella, F. (2009). Privacy concerns and electronic data collection: Group and individual response to social change in communications. In *NTTS - Conferences on New Techniques and Technologies for Statistics* (pp. 111–123). Brussels, Belgium: Eurostat - European Commission.

Odella, F. (2011a). Network theory. In *Encyclopedia of Social Networks*. Thousand Oaks, CA: Sage Publications.

Odella, F. (2011b). Social networks and communities: From traditional society to the virtual sphere. In Safar, M., & Mahdi, K. (Eds.), *Social Networking and Community Behaviour Modelling*. Hershey, PA: IGI Global. doi:10.4018/978-1-61350-444-4.ch001

Oudshoorn, N. (2012). How places matter: Telecare technologies and the changing spatial dimensions of healthcare. *Social Studies of Science, 42*(1), 21–142. doi:10.1177/0306312711431817

Petroczi, A., Nepusz, T., & Baszo, F. (2007). Measuring tie-strength in virtual social networks. *Connections, 27*(2), 39–52.

Pinch, T. (2008). Technology and institutions. *Theory and Society, 37*(5), 461–483. doi:10.1007/s11186-008-9069-x

Podolny, J. M., & Baron, J. N. (1997). Resources and relationships: Social networks and mobility in the workplace. *American Sociological Review, 62*, 673–693. doi:10.2307/2657354

Rammert, W. (2008). Rules of sociological method: Rethinking technology studies. *The British Journal of Sociology, 48*(2), 171–191. doi:10.2307/591747

Romero, N., van Baren, J., Markopoulos, P., de Ruyter, B., & IJsselsteijn, W. (2003). Addressing interpersonal communication needs through ubiquitous connectivity: Home and away. *Lecture Notes in Computer Science, 2875*, 419–429. doi:10.1007/978-3-540-39863-9_32

Ruppert, E. (2011). Population objects: Interpassive subjects. *Sociology, 45*(2), 218–233. doi:10.1177/0038038510394027

Sewell, G., & Barker, J. R. (2006). Coercion versus care: Using irony to make sense of organizational surveillance. *Academy of Management Review, 31*(4), 934–961. doi:10.5465/AMR.2006.22527466

Stalder, F. (2002). Public opinion privacy is not the antidote to surveillance. *Surveillance & Society, 1*(1).

Stutzman, F. (2006). An evaluation of identity-sharing behavior in social network communities. *Journal of the International Digital Media and Arts Association, 3*(1), 10–18.

Szell, L., & Thurner, J. (2010). Measuring social dynamics in a massive multiplayer online game. *Social Networks, 32*, 313–329. doi:10.1016/j.socnet.2010.06.001

Szomszor, M., Cattuto, C., Van den Broeck, W., Barrat, A., & Alani, H. (2010). Semantics, sensors, and the social web: The live social semantics experiments. *Lecture Notes in Computer Science, 6089*, 196–210. doi:10.1007/978-3-642-13489-0_14

Taylor, S., & Spencer, B. A. (1990). Ethical implications of human resource information systems. *Employee Responsibilities and Rights Journal, 3*(1), 19–30. doi:10.1007/BF01384761

Vargas Solar, G. (2005). *Global, pervasive and ubiquitous information societies: Engineering challenges and social impact*. Paris, France: NSRC.

Voskuhl, A. (2004). Humans, machines and conversations: An ethnographic study of the making of automatic speech recognition technologies. *Social Studies of Science, 34*(3), 393–421. doi:10.1177/0306312704043576

Walby, K. (2006). How closed –circuit television surveillance organizes the social: An institutional ethnography. *Canadian Journal of Sociology, 30*(2), 189–214.

Walby, K., & Hier, S. P. (2005). Risk technologies and the securitization of post-9/11 citizenship: The case of national ID cards in Canada. *Journal of the Society for Socialist Studies, 2,* 7–37.

Wasserman, S., & Faust, K. (1999). *Social network analysis.* Cambridge, UK: Cambridge University Press.

Watts, D. J., Dodds, P. S., & Newman, M. E. J. (2002). Identity and search in social networks. *Science, 17,* 1302–1305. doi:10.1126/science.1070120

Wellman, B., Salaff, J., Dimitrova, D., Garton, L., & Gulia, M. (1996). Computer networks: Collaborative work, telework and virtual community. *Annual Review of Sociology, 22,* 213–238. doi:10.1146/annurev.soc.22.1.213

Wigg, J. M. (2010). Liberating the wanderers: Using technology to unlock doors for those living with dementia. *Sociology of Health & Illness, 32*(2), 288–303. doi:10.1111/j.1467-9566.2009.01221.x

Wood, D. (2005). People watching people. *Surveillance & Society, 2*(4), 474–478.

ENDNOTES

[1] In a sociological experiment, hypothesis on the dynamics of social choices are tested through participation and observation sessions. The researchers try to identify the cognitive as well as the behavioral processes involved in a specific social form such as selection of members of a group or coordination rules in organizations. This type of experiment requires, however, that researchers pay specific attention to interpersonal relations or cultural preferences that are frequently the basis of individuals' choices and constrains.

Chapter 12
Action Detection by Fusing Hierarchically Filtered Motion with Spatiotemporal Interest Point Features

YingLi Tian
City University of New York, USA

Liangliang Cao
IBM – T. J. Watson Research Center, USA

Zicheng Liu
Microsoft Research, USA

Zhengyou Zhang
Microsoft Research, USA

ABSTRACT

This chapter addresses the problem of action detection from cluttered videos. In recent years, many feature extraction schemes have been designed to describe various aspects of actions. However, due to the difficulty of action detection, e.g., the cluttered background and potential occlusions, a single type of feature cannot effectively solve the action detection problems in cluttered videos. In this chapter, the authors propose a new type of feature, Hierarchically Filtered Motion (HFM), and further investigate the fusion of HFM with Spatiotemporal Interest Point (STIP) features for action detection from cluttered videos. In order to effectively and efficiently detect actions, they propose a new approach that combines Gaussian Mixture Models (GMMs) with Branch-and-Bound search to locate interested actions in cluttered videos. The proposed new HFM features and action detection method have been evaluated on the classical KTH dataset and the challenging MSR Action Dataset II, which consists of crowded videos with moving people or vehicles in the background. Experiment results demonstrate that the proposed method significantly outperforms existing techniques, especially for action detection in crowded videos.

DOI: 10.4018/978-1-4666-3682-8.ch012

INTRODUCTION

In the past few years, computer vision researchers have witnessed a surge of interest in human action analysis through videos. Human action recognition, *which classifies a video to a pre-defined action category*, was first studied under well controlled laboratory scenarios, e.g., with clean background and no occlusions (Schuldt *et al.*, 2004). Later research work shows that action recognition is important for analyzing and organizing online videos (Liu *et al.*, 2009). Moreover, action recognition plays a crucial role in building surveillance system (Hu *et al.*, 2009) and studying customer behaviors. With the increasing of web video clips (*e.g.*, videos on Youtube) and the surveillance systems, it has become very important to effectively analyze video actions.

An effective analysis of video actions requires action detection, which can not only answer which action happens in a video, but also when and where the action happens in the video sequence. In other words, action detection will detect action category, locations, and time in video sequences than simply classifying a video clip to one of the existing action labels. When a video contains multiple actions, simple action classification will not work. In practice, surveillance videos often contain multiple types of actions, where only action detection can provide meaningful results.

Action detection is a challenging task. As shown in Figure 1, the background is often cluttered, and the crowds might occlude each other in complex scenes. It is difficult to distinguish interested actions from other video contents. The appearance of interested actions might have similar appearance of the background. Furthermore, the motion field of an action might be occluded by other moving objects in the scene. Due to the difficulty of locating human actions, most existing datasets of human actions (Blank *et al.*, 2005; Schuldt *et al.*, 2004) only involve action classification task without detecting locations of actions, where human actions are usually recorded with clean backgrounds, and each video clip mostly involves a single person who repeatedly performs one category of actions within a whole video clip.

In this chapter, we address the action detection problem by proposing a new type of features, Hierarchically Filtered Motion (HFM), and further

Figure 1. Comparing the differences between action classification and detection. (a) For a classification task we need only estimate the category label for a given video. (b) For an action detection task we need not only estimate the category of an action but also the location of the action instance. The bounding box illustrates a desirable detection. It can be seen that action detection task is crucial when there is cluttered background and multiple persons in the scene.

(a)   **(b)**

investigate the fusion of HFM with other Spatio-temporal Interest Point (STIP) features (Dollar *et al.*, 2005; Laptev and Lindeberg, 2003, Cao *et al.* 2010; Tian *et al.*, 2011) for action detection from cluttered videos. An action is often associated with multiple visual measurements, which can be either appearance features (e.g., color, edge histogram) or motion features (e.g., optical flow, motion history). Different features describe different aspects of the visual characteristics and demand different metrics. How to handle heterogeneous features for action detection becomes an important problem.

The difficulty of combining multiple features lies in the heterogeneous nature of different features. Different STIP features are based on different detectors, and the number of detected features varies significantly. It is still an open question how to effectively combine such features. A naive approach is to quantize STIP features and build histogram based on quantization indices. However, much information will be lost in the quantization process, and a histogram representation overlooks the differences in the number of detected features. Therefore, simply combining histograms will produce poor detection results. Our work employs a probabilistic representation of the different features so that we can quantitatively evaluate the contribution from each of these features. We estimate the likelihood of each feature vector belonging to a given action of interests, which can be viewed as normalized contribution from different features. The optimal bounding box corresponds to the maximum likelihood and is found by a branch-bound search. In our approach, we model each feature vector with Gaussian Mixture Models (GMMs). GMMs with large number of components are known to have the ability to model any given probability distribution function. Based on GMMs, we can estimate the likelihood of each feature vector belongings to a given action of interests. The likelihood can be viewed as a normalized contribution from different features, and the optimal bounding box corresponds to the

maximum likelihood. The bounding box is found by a branch-bound search (Yuan *et al.*, 2009), which is shown to be efficient and effective to locate the action of interest.

BACKGROUND

Many approaches have been proposed on action recognition (Jhuang *et al.*, 2007; Laptev *et al.*, 2008; Liu *et al.*, 2009; Messing *et al.*, 2009; Reynolds *et al.*, 2000; Yuan *et al.*, 2009). Compared with the task of action classification, action detection is more challenging. There are only a few literatures devoted to the task of action detection (Du and Yuan, 2011; Cao *et al.*, 2009; Cao *et al.*, 2010; Hu *et al.*, 2009; Ke *et al.*, 2007; Yao and Zhu, 2009; Yuan and Pang, 2008). Laptev *et al.* (Laptev *et al.*, 2008; Marszałek *et al.*, 2009) used local spatiotemporal invariant points (STIPs) (Laptev and Lindeberg 2003), space-time pyramids, local spatiotemporal descriptors (HOG/HOF) (Dalal and Triggs, 2005; Pang *et al.*, 2010), and multi-channel non-linear SVMs for realistic actions in movies. Yuan *et al.* (Yuan *et al.*, 2009) employed the same features (STIPs) and descriptors (HOG/HOF) and proposed a discriminative subvolume search for efficient action detection by using a Nearest Neighbor based classifier. Ke *et al.* (Ke *et al.*, 2007) proposed a method to detect event in crowded videos by combining spatiotemporal shapes with a flow descriptor. Sun *et al.* (Sun *et al.*, 2009) modeled the spatiotemporal information for action recognition in realistic datasets at 3 levels: point-level, intra-trajectory level, and inter-trajectory level. The trajectories are extracted based on matching the SIFT salient points over consecutive frames. Similarly, Messing *et al.* (Messing *et al.*, 2009) proposed a system for action recognition by using the velocity histories of tracked keypoints which are extracted by Kanade-Lucas-Tomasi (KLT) feature trackers, and used a generative mixture model to learn and classify actions. They also augmented other features such as position, appearance, color, etc. to improve the recognition accuracy. Junejo *et al.* (Junejo *et al.*, 2011) attempted to recognize human actions under different views using temporal self-similarities. Yin and Meng (Yin and Meng, 2010) proposed a method to learn the shapes of space-time feature neighborhoods for each action category. Surveys of video event understanding and human motion analysis can be found in paper (Ji and Liu, 2010).

Despite promising results are achieved by the state-of-the-art work, more robust methods are needed to handle cluttered background motions due to the following difficulties: 1) there is no mechanism to distinguish action motions and background motions in existing local STIP detectors and descriptors, and 2) the trajectories of keypoints cannot be reliably tracked in crowded videos. A majority of recent work on STIPs takes quantized STIPs as input and builds histograms based on quantization indices. The quantized STIPs are also called video codewords. The histograms can be fed into discriminative SVM classifiers (Schuldt *et al.*, 2004) or generative topic models (Niebles *et al.*, 2006). The collection of quantized codewords is also named as a codebook. The use of the codebook and histogram is preferred because it can condense different number of STIPs into a fixed length feature vector. However, quantized codeword representation is not a good fit for cross-dataset scenarios due to the large variations of STIPs in different environments. Given two videos captured with different viewing points and light conditions, the corresponding distributions of STIPs are likely quite different. If we build a new codebook on a new dataset, the word histogram representation will be totally different, so the old model cannot be directly applied the new dataset. In summary, quantized codeword representation overlooks the differences of STIP distributions in different environments and may fail to correctly transfer the knowledge from source dataset to target dataset.

Motivated by the recent success of SIFT and HOG in image domain, many researchers have designed various counterparts to describe the spatial salient patches in video domain. Laptev and Lindeberg (Laptev and Lindeberg, 2003) generalized Harris detector to spatiotemporal space. They aim to detect image patches with significant local variations in both space and time and compute their scale invariant spatiotemporal descriptors. This approach is later improved by (Laptev *et al.*, 2008) which gives up scale selection but uses a multi-scale approach and extract features at multiple levels of spatiotemporal scales. The improved method yields reduced computational complexity, denser sampling, and suffers less from scale selection artifacts. Another important video feature is designed by Dollar *et al.* (Dollar *et al.*, 2005), which detects the salient patches by finding the maximum of temporal Gabor filter responses. This method aims to detect regions with spatially distinguishing characteristics undergoing a complex motion. In contrast, patches undergoing pure translational motion, or patches without spatially distinguishing features will in general not induce a response. After the salient patches are detected, the histogram of 3D cuboid is introduced to describe the patch feature.

Many action classification systems (Dollar *et al.*, 2005; Jhuang *et al.*, 2007; Laptev and Lindeberg, 2003; Niebles *et al.*, 2006; Wong *et al.*, 2007; Wu *et al.*, 2007) are built using Laptev's or Dollar's features. These two features focus short-term motion information instead of long term motion, and motion field of a salient patch sometime is contaminated by the background motions. However, most of existing systems only classify video clips to predefined action categories, and does not consider the location task.

To overcome the limitations of existing salient patch descriptors, a hierarchically filtered motion field method has been proposed recently for action recognition (Tian *et al.*, 2011). This work applies global spatial motion smoothing filter to eliminate isolated unreliable or noisy motions. To characterize long-term motion features, Motion History Image (MHI) is employed as basic representations of interest points. This new feature is named as Hierarchically Filtered Motion (HFM) and works well in crowded scenes. We believe the HFM describes complementary aspects of video actions and this work will combine HFM with the existing features of (Dollar *et al.*, 2005; Laptev *et al.*, 2008) for action detection tasks.

The existing work of action detection (Du *et al.*, 2011; Cao *et al.*, 2009; Cao *et al.*, 2010; Hu *et al.*, 2009; Ke *et al.*, 2007; Yao *et al.*, 2009; Yuan *et al.*, 2008) only use single type of features. Although multiple feature fusion was proved to be effective in action classification (Cao *et al.*, 2009; Liu *et al.*, 2008), it is still an untouched problem to combine multiple features for action detection.

The difficulty of applying multiple features for action detection is two-fold: First, existing fusion methods (Cao *et al.*, 2009; Liu *et al.*, 2008) assume that each sample has the same number of features. However, in action detection, different features correspond to different detectors, and the numbers of detected salient patches are usually different subject to different features. Second, detecting actions in videos involves a searching process in x-y-t dimensions, which is very computationally expensive. Many existing feature fusion methods (Cao *et al.*, 2009) are usually too slow for this task. This chapter employs Gaussian Mixture Models (GMMs) to model heterogeneous features, and the probability of a given feature vector is estimated effectively based on the GMM model. To locate the action of interests, we employ a branch-and-bound method to find the optimal subvolumes which correspond to the largest GMM scores. Note that although this chapter only combines three types of features from (Dollar *et al.*, 2005; Laptev *et al.*, 2008; Tian *et al.*, 2011), our method is a general framework and can be used to fuse more features (Boiman *et al.*, 2005; Rodriguez *et al.*, 2008; Zhu *et al.*, 2009).

FUSION OF MULTIPLE SPATIOTEMPORAL INTEREST POINT FEATURES

In this section, we describe the features we used for action detection from cluttered videos by fusion of multiple spatiotemporal interest point features including: Hierarchically Filtered Motion (HFM) (Tian *et al.*, 2011), and other Spatiotemporal Interest Point (STIP) features (Dollar *et al.*, 2005; Laptev and Lindeberg, 2003).

Hierarchically Filtered Motion Features

Hierarchically Filtered Motion (HFM) features employ Motion History Image (MHI) (Bobick *et al.*, 2001; Davis, 2001) as basic representations of motion due to its robustness and efficiency. First, we detect interest points as 2D Harris corners with recent motion, e.g. locations with high intensities in MHI which is based on frame differencing. Using MHI allows us to avoid unreliable keypoint tracking in crowded videos. The pixels in MHI with brighter intensities which represent the moving objects with more recent motion are formed as a template. We combine this motion template and the extracted 2D Harris corners for interest point detection. Only those corners with the most recent motion are selected as interest points. We observe that an isolated motion direction of a pixel compared to its neighbor pixels is often a distracting motion or a noise. To remove the isolated distracting motions, we first apply a *global* spatial motion smoothing filter to the gradients of MHI. At each interest point, a *local* motion field filter is applied by computing a structure proximity between any pixel in the local region and the interest point. Thus the motion at a pixel is enhanced or weakened based on its structure proximity with the interest point. The spatial and temporal features are then described by Histograms of Oriented Gradient (HOG) in the intensity image and MHI respectively.

Motion History Image (MHI)

MHI is a real-time motion template that temporally layers consecutive image differences into a static image template (Bobick and Davis, 2001; Davis, 2001). Pixel intensity is a function of the motion history at that location, where brighter values correspond to more recent motion. The directional motion information can be measured directly from the intensity gradients in the MHI. Compare to optical flow, gradients in the MHI are more efficient to compute. It is also more robust due to the fact that the motion information in MHI is mainly along the contours of the moving objects. Thus, unwanted motion in the interior regions of object contours is ignored.

To generate a MHI, we use a simple replacement and decay operator as in paper (Bobick and Davis, 2001). At location *(x, y)* and time *t*, the intensity of $MHI_\tau(x,y,t)$ is calculated in Box 1.

In order to handle cluttered background, we propose a hierarchically filtered motion field technique based on Motion Gradient Image (MGI). The MGI is the intensity gradients of MHI which directly yield motion orientations. Note that the magnitudes of MHI gradients are not meaningful. Although it is impossible to distinguish the action motions from the background motions without using high-level information, we still can reduce noisy motions and enhance the action motions based on the following observations: 1) an isolated motion direction of a pixel compared to its neighbor pixels is often a distracting motion or a

noisy motion, and 2) at each interest point, the motion regions which are closer to the interest point contribute more to the object which the interest point belongs to.

Hierarchically Filtered Motion Features

To remove the isolated distracting motions, hierarchically filtered motion features includes two levels of processing: a *global* spatial motion smoothing filter to the gradients of MHI and a *local* motion field filter by computing a structure proximity between any pixel in the local region and the interest point. In our approach, we first apply a motion smoothing step at the MGI to remove the isolated motion directions by morphological operations to obtain a global filtered motion field—smoothed gradients of MHI. To be prepared for local filtered motion field processing, we decompose the smoothed gradients of MHI as a number of layers with different motion directions. In our implementation, we use an 8-bin-layer representation of a binary image of the smoothed gradients of MHI. At each interest point, a local filtered motion field is applied by computing a structure proximity between the pixels in the local region and the interest point on each bin-layer of the smoothed gradients of MHI. Here the local region is the window for calculating HOG-MHI. A connect component operation is performed to obtain motion blobs. The motion blobs with shorter distances to the interest point in the local region are more likely to represent the

Box 1.

$$MHI_\tau(x,y,t) = \begin{cases} \tau, & if D(x,y,t) = 1 \\ \max\left(0, MHI_\tau(x,y,t-1)-1\right), & otherwise \end{cases} \quad (1)$$

where D(x,y,t) is a binary image of differences between frames and τ is the maximum duration of motion. We set τ as 20 in our system based on experiments. The MHI image is then scaled to a grayscale image with maximum intensity 255 for pixels with the most recent motion.

motion of the object which the interest point belongs to. Thus the motions at these blobs should be enhanced. On the other hand, the blobs with longer distances to the interest point most likely belong to other objects. Thus the motions at those blobs should be weakened. Let p_0 denote the interest point. Let B denote a blob. Denote $d(p_o, B)$ to be the minimum distance between p_0 and all the points in B, that is:

$$d\left(p_o, B\right) = \min_{p \in B} d\left(p_o, p\right)$$

Denote W_x, W_y to be the size of the window. Then the maximum distance between p_0 and any points in the window is

$$\sqrt{W_x^2 + W_y^2} \, / \, 2$$

For any pixel $p \in B$, we define its structure proximity to interest point p_0 as

$$s\left(p\right) = 1 - \frac{2d\left(p_0, B\right)}{\sqrt{W_x^2 + W_y^2}} \tag{2}$$

Note that $s(p)$ is a value between 0 and 1. If a pixel does not belong to any blobs, we define its structure proximity to be 0. The structure proximity values are used to normalize motion histograms in HOG-MHI calculation. More details can be found in paper (Tian *et al.*, 2011).

Fusion of Multiple Spatiotemporal Interest Points Features

Sparse selection of STIPs has been successfully used for action recognition (Cao *et al.*, 2010; Dollar *et al.*, 2005; Laptev and Lindeberg, 2003; Laptev *et al.*, 2008; Mattivi and Shao, 2009; Niebles *et al.*, 2006; Schuldt *et al.*, 2004; Yuan *et al.*, 2009). Laptev *et al.* developed a nice mathematic frame-

work to find pixels with significant variations in both spatial and temporal directions (Laptev and Lindeberg, 2003). However, the interest points detected by their approach are in practice too sparse to characterize well the motion features. Dollar *et al.* proposed to detect the interest points by extracting the maximum response of Gabor filter (Dollar *et al.*, 2005). The limitation of the approach in (Dollar *et al.*, 2005) is that the filtering parameters are sensitive in complex scenes and the detected interest points are heavily affected by the cluttered background and foreground occlusions.

Laptev's STIP Features

Laptev and Lindeberg (Laptev and Lindeberg, 2003) generalized Harris detector to spatiotemporal space. They aim to detect image patches with significant local variations in both spatial and temporal directions, and compute the scale-invariant spatiotemporal descriptors. This approach is later improved by (Laptev *et al.*, 2008) which gives up scale selection but uses a multi-scale approach and extract features at multiple levels of spatiotemporal scales. The improved method yields reduced computational complexity denser sampling, and suffers less from scale selection artifacts.

Dollar's STIP Features

Another important type of video features is designed by Dollar *et al.* (Dollar *et al.*, 2005), which detects the salient patches by finding the maximum of temporal Gabor filter responses. This method aims to detect regions with spatially distinguishing characteristics undergoing a complex motion. In contrast, patches undergoing pure translational motion, or patches without spatially distinguishing features will in general not induce a response. After the salient patches are detected, the histogram of 3D cuboid is introduced to describe the patch feature.

In this chapter, we investigate the combination multiple STIPs (Laptev *et al.*, 2008) for the videos with cluttered background. We observe that there are not enough interest points in action regions for some video sequences (Figure 2(b)). In some sequences with large lighting changes, many STIPs are extracted on the background as shown in Figure 2(d). To overcome the above limitation, our interest point detection is based on detecting corners in images (2D Harris Corner Detection (Harris and Stephens 1988) and combining the temporal information which are obtained from MHI. Harris Corner detection is stable to different scales and insensitive to lighting changes. Here, we use MHI as motion mask to remove the corners in the static background. Only the corners with more recent motion (intensity in MHI > threshold) are selected as interest points.

HOG-Based Feature Descriptor and Representation for Action Detection

HOG and HOF Feature Descriptor for Latpev's STIP Features: Histograms of Oriented Gradients (HOG) feature descriptors have been widely used in human detection (Dalal and Triggs, 2005; Laptev *et al.*, 2008; Marszałek *et al.*, 2009; Pang *et al.*, 2010; Yuan *et al.*, 2009). Laptev *et al.* (Laptev *et al.*, 2008) employ HOG and Histograms of Optical Flow (HOF) descriptors for 3D video patches in the neighborhood of detected STIPs.

However, these features are based on single frame or neighboring frames, but overlooks the motion descriptions over a longer time. For each interest point, the local appearance and motion are characterized by grids of HOG and HOF respectively in the neighborhood with a window size. For each grid, 8 directions are employed for both HOG and HOF.

HOG and HOG-MHI Feature Descriptor for HFM Features: In our system, like (Laptev et al., 2008), the local appearance features are characterized by grids of Histograms of Oriented Gradient (HOG) in the neighborhood with a window size (w_x, w_y) at each interest point in the intensity image. However, unlike (Laptev et al., 2008), the motion features are represented by the HOG descriptors in the MHI (HOG-MHI). The window is further subdivided into a (n_x, n_y) grid of patches. Normalized histograms of all the patches are concatenated into HOG (for appearance features in the intensity image) and HOG-MHI (for motion features in the MHI) descriptor vectors as the input of the classifier for action recognition. In our approach, the calculations of HOG and HOG-MHI are different. We compute HOG without considering the directions to make it more robust to appearance changes. However, for HOG-MHI computation, the performance of action recognition decreases without considering directions since directions

Figure 2. Examples of interest point detection by our method and STIP detection of Laptev et al. (Laptev and Lindeberg 2003; Laptev et al., 2008) in a video with cluttered background and lighting changes. (a) Interest points are detected on moving people by our method; (b) no STIPs are detected by (Laptev and Lindeberg 2003, Laptev et al., 2008); (c) our interest point detection is insensitive to lighting changes; and (d) false STIPs are detected on background regions (Laptev and Lindeberg 2003; Laptev et al., 2008)

are important to describe motion features. In our experiments, we set $n_x, n_y = 3$ *and* use 6 bins for HOG in the intensity image and 8 bins for HOG-MHI in the MHI image). For each interest point, the HOG (with dimension of 54) and HOG-MHI features (with dimension of 72) are concatenated into one feature vector for action classification.

To handle scale variations, a multi-scale process at each interest point can be applied by using different patch sizes or by using same patch size on different scale images. However, the multi-scale process will heavily increase the size of the feature vector for training and testing. For example, the size of the feature vector will be tripled for three scales. Thus, instead of performing a multi-scale process at each interest point, we use randomly selected window sizes between w_{min} (minimum window size) and w_{max} (maximum window size). The size of each window is calculated by $w_x = kn_x$ and $w_y = kn_y$ where k *is* randomly chosen to make sure the values of w_x, w_y are in between W_{min} and W_{max}. In our experiments, we set $w_{min}=24$, $w_{max}=48$. Our experiments demonstrate that using randomly selected window sizes handles scale variations very well and achieves better results than using fixed set of scales.

ACTION DETECTION BY COMBINING GAUSSIAN MIXTURE MODELS WITH BRANCH-AND-BOUND SEARCH

Given a video sequence V, we employ different STIP detectors to detect a collection of local feature vectors $\left\{ x_p^m \right\}$, where $p \in V$ denotes the location of the feature, and m denotes the feature type with $1 \leq m \leq M$. We employ the Gaussian Mixture Models (GMMs) to model the probability that x^m belongs to the given action. Suppose a GMM contains K components, the probability can be written as:

$$
P_r \left(x^m \middle| \theta^m \right) = \\
\Sigma_{k=1}^{K} w^m \left(k \right) N \left(x^m; \mu^m \left(k \right), \Sigma^m \left(k \right) \right)
\tag{3}
$$

where $N \left(\cdot \right)$ denotes the normal distribution, and $\mu^m \left(k \right)$ and $\Sigma^m \left(k \right)$ denote the mean and variance of the *kth* normal component for feature m. The set of all parameters of GMM model is denoted as $\Theta = \left[\theta^1, \theta^2, ..., \theta^M \right]$ where

$$
\theta^m = \left\{ w^m \left(k \right), \mu^m \left(k \right), \Sigma^m \left(k \right) \right\}
$$

The advantages of GMM are that it is based on a well-understood statistical model, and it is easy to combine multiple features using GMMs. With GMM, we can estimate the probability that each feature vector x^m belongs to the background or the action of interest. Suppose there are C categories of actions with parameter of $\Theta_1, \Theta_2, .., \Theta_C$. Each category corresponds to GMMs with M features $\Theta_C = \Theta_C^1, \Theta_C^2, ..., \Theta_C^M$.

The parameters of GMM can be estimated using maximum likelihood estimation. For example, for the c category, we first collect the subvolumes V^c containing the action c, and then estimate GMMs parameters by maximizing the likelihood. A straightforward way is to independently train the model for each category and each feature. However, as shown by Reynolds (Reynolds *et al.*, 2000), it is more effective to obtain $\theta_1^m, \theta_2^m, ..., \theta_C^m$ coherently by the use of a universal background model. Following (Reynolds *et al.*, 2000), we first train a background model θ_0^m which is independent to all the vectors X^{all} using the m feature. Then we adapt $\theta_1^m, ..., \theta_C^m$ from θ_0^m by *EM* algorithm in the following way.

We first estimate posterior probability of each x_i^m subject to the background model θ_0^m by

$$p_k^c\left(x_p^m\right) = \frac{w\left(k\right) N\left(x_p^m, \mu_0^m\left(k\right), \Sigma_0^m\left(k\right)\right)}{\Sigma_j w\left(j\right) N\left(x_p^m, \mu_0^m\left(j\right), \Sigma_0^m\left(j\right)\right)} \quad (4)$$

Then we can update $\mu_C^m\left(k\right)$ by

$$\mu_C^m\left(k\right) = \frac{1}{n_c} \Sigma_{x_p^m \in X^c} p_k^c\left(x_p^m\right) x_p^m \quad (5)$$

Although we can update Σ_C based on $p_k^c\left(x_p^m\right)$, in practice we force $w_C^m\,(k) = w_0^m\,(k)$ and $\Sigma_c^m\,(k) = \Sigma_0^m\,(k)$, which is computationally robust.

The advantages of employing a background model are two-fold: First, adapting GMM parameters from background model is more computational efficient and robust. Second, updating based on background model leads to a good alignment of different action models over different components, which makes the recognition more accurate.

After obtaining the GMM parameters and a video clip V, we can estimate the action category by

$$c^* = arg\max_c \Sigma_{m=1}^M \Sigma_{x_p^m \in V} \log P_r\left(x_p^m \big| \grave{\mathrm{e}}_c^m\right) \quad (6)$$

Next we discuss the action detection task. We use a 3D subvolume to represent a region in the 3D video space that contains an action instance. A 3D subvoume $Q = $ [x0, x1, y0, y1, t0, t1] is parameterized as a 3D cube with six degrees of freedom in *(x,y,t)* space. Spatial and temporal localization of an action in a video sequence is rendered as searching for the optimal subvolume. The spatial locations of the subvolume identify where the action happens, while the temporal locations of the subvolume denote when the action happens. Given a video sequence, the optimal spatiotemporal subvolume Q^* yields the maximum GMM scores:

$$Q^* = arg\max_{Q \subseteq V} \mathfrak{L}\left(Q \big| \grave{\mathrm{E}}_c\right)$$
$$= arg\max_{Q \subseteq V} \Sigma_m \Sigma_{p \in V} \log P_r\left(x_p^m \big| \grave{\mathrm{e}}_c^m\right) \quad (7)$$

By assigning each patch a score $= \log P_r\left(x_p^m \big| \grave{\mathrm{e}}_c^m\right)$ Equation 7 can be solved by branch-and-bound algorithm (Lampert *et al.*, 2008, Yao and Zhu, 2009]. Branch-and-bound approach was first developed for integer programming problems. In recently years, it has been shown be to an efficient technique for object detection in images and action detection in videos (Lampert *et al.*, 2008; Yao and Zhu, 2009; Yuan *et al.*, 2009). Lampert *et al.* (Blaschko and Lampert, 2008; Lampert *et al.*, 2008) showed that branch-and-bound can be used for object detection in 2D image base on a smart formulation. Yuan (Yuan *et al.*, 2009) developed an efficient algorithm which generalizes branch-and-bound algorithm to 3D space of videos. In this chapter, we perform max-subvolume search using the 3D branch-and-bound algorithm in (Yuan *et al.*, 2009), which is an extension of the 2D branch-and-bound technique (Lampert *et al.*, 2008). The detailed technical description of the 3D branch-and-bound algorithm is omitted due to limited space.

EXPERIMENTAL RESULTS OF ACTION DETECTION

Datasets

Our action detection scheme is evaluated by two datasets: KTH dataset (Schuldt *et al.*, 2004) and MSR Action Dataset II (MSRdataset, 2010).

KTH Dataset: The KTH dataset (Schuldt *et al.*, 2004) was used as a standard benchmark for action recognition. It was recorded in four controlled environments with clean background (indoors, outdoors, outdoors with scale variation, outdoors with different clothes.) The dataset contains about 600 video sequences of 25 subjects performing six categories of actions: boxing, hand clapping, hand waving, jogging, walking, and running. The video resolution is 160x120.

MSR Action Dataset II: MSR Action Dataset II is collected in Microsoft Research Redmond which was named MSR Action Dataset II, with cluttered background and multiple people move around. We do not use the CMU action dataset (Ke *et al.*, 2007) since there is only a single sequence for training in it. Hu (Hu *et al.*, 2009) used videos from retailing surveillance, however, the dataset is confidential due to the privacy issue. Wang (Wang *et al.*, 2009) collected a dataset of social game events, but their problem is about classification but not detection. MSR Action Dataset II includes 54 video sequences, each of which contains several different actions, e.g., hand waving, clapping, and boxing. These videos are taken with the background of parties, outdoor traffic, and walking people. Actors are asked to walk into the scene, perform one of the three kinds of action, and then walk out of the scenes with these backgrounds. Figure 1 shows the differences between KTH dataset (Figure 1(a)) and MSR Action Dataset II (Figure 1(b)). Note that in MSR Action Dataset II dataset there are many people in the scene and we need to locate the persons with actions of interest from the scene.

Action Detection Results on MSR Action Dataset II

To evaluate the detection results of our model, we manually labeled the MSR Action Dataset II with bounding subvolumes and action types. By denoting the subvolumes ground truth as $\mathbf{Q^g} = \left\{ Q_1^g, Q_2^g, ..., Q_m^g \right\}$, and the detected subvolumes as $\mathbf{Q^d} = \left\{ Q_1^d, Q_2^d, ..., Q_m^d \right\}$, we use $HG\left(Q_i^g \right)$ to denote whether a groundtruth subvolume Q_j^g is detected, and $TD\left(Q_j^d \right)$ to denote whether a detected subvolume makes sense or not. $HG\left(Q_i^g \right)$ and $TD\left(Q_j^d \right)$ are judged by checking whether the overlapping is above a threshold. We set the threshold as *1/4* in our experiment. See Box 2.

Based on *HG* and *TD*, precision and recall are defined as:

$$Recall = \frac{\sum_{j=1}^n TD\left(Q_j^d \right)}{n}$$

$$Precision = \frac{\sum_{i=1}^m HG\left(Q_i^g \right)}{m} \tag{9}$$

where *n* is the number of groundtruth and *m* is the number of detected bounding boxes.

Box 2.

$$HG\left(Q_i^g \right) = \begin{cases} 1, & if \; \exists Q_k^d, \; s.t. \dfrac{\left| Q_k^d \cap Q_i^g \right|}{\left| Q_i^g \right|} > \delta_1 \\ 0, & \end{cases}$$
$$otherwise,$$

$$TD\left(Q_j^g \right) = \begin{cases} 1, & if \; \exists Q_k^g, \; s.t. \dfrac{\left| Q_k^g \cap Q_j^d \right|}{\left| d \right|} > \delta_2 \\ 0, & \end{cases}$$
$$otherwise,$$

$$\tag{8}$$

where $| \cdot |$ denotes for the area of the subvolume, and δ_1, δ_2 are parameters to judge the overlapping ratio. In this chapter, both δ_1 and $\delta_2 \; \ddot{a}_2$ are set as *1/4*.

Given a collection of detected subvolumes, we can compute the precision-recall values. By using different thresholds of the region scores $\Sigma_{x \in Q} f(x)$, we apply the branch-and-bound algorithm multiple times and obtain the precision-recall curves for three actions in MSR Action Dataset II.

In MSR-II dataset, we use half of the videos for training and the remaining half videos for testing. We compare the detection results of each of the three features (Dollar *et al.*, 2005; Laptev *et al.*, 2008; Tian *et al.*, 2011), and find that Hierarchically Filter Motion features outperform both Laptev's features (Laptev *et al.*, 2008) and Dollar's features (Dollar *et al.*, 2005). We observe that both HFM and Laptev features can obtain reasonable detection results, while Dollar's features (Dollar *et al.*, 2005) lead to results at a very low detection rate. The reason for the failure of Dollar's features might be that the Gabor filter based features are heavily affected by the cluttered background, since most of the detected patches fall in the background instead of action of interests. Since Dollar's features fail to detect some actions, we only compare results of two single feature detections and the multiple feature detection using our model. Figure 3 shows the precision-recall curves of action detection by using Hierarchically Filtered Motion features and Laptev STIP features respectively, and the fusions of multiple types of STIPs features. It can be seen that hierarchically

Figure 3. Precision-Recall curves for MSR Action Dataset II for action detection by using HFM features and Laptev STIP features respectively, and the fusions of multiple types of STIPs features. The best results for all the 3 actions are achieved by combining HFM features and Laptev STIP features. The detection accuracy decreases by incorporating Dollar's features.

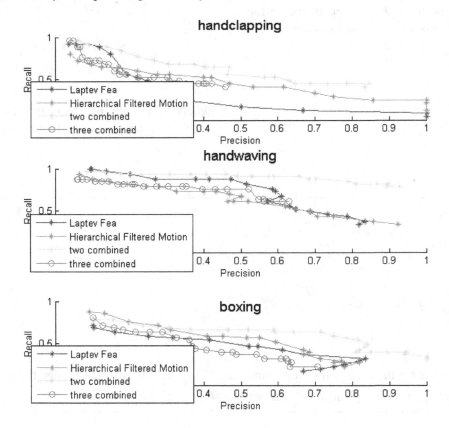

filtered motion feature works better than Laptev's in handclapping and boxing, but comparable in handwaving. However, combining these two types of features, our multiple feature-based action detection schema works significantly better than using any single features in all the three actions. It is also interesting to see that if we incorporate the inappropriate features such as Dollar's features, the corresponding detection rate will decrease. The results confirm that *combining multiple relevant features will significantly improve the detection, while combining irrelevant feature might decrease the results.*

Figure 4 demonstrates some example results where the Hierarchically Filtered Motion features successfully detect the action of interests while Laptev's STIP features fail. For each example, the top picture illustrates the detection results of using Hierarchically Filtered Motion features, while the bottom shows the results of using Laptev's STIP features. The rectangle regions denote the detected actions. The proposed Hierarchically Filtered Motion features are more robust than other STIP features for action recognition in crowded videos. The reasons are summarized as the following: 1) the 2D Harris corner detection is less sensitive to lighting changes than STIP features; 2) MHI filtered interest points can better

characterize the motion features than STIP (too sparse); 3) The directional motion information is measured directly from the intensity gradients in the MHI. It is also more robust because the motion information in MHI is mainly along the contours of the moving objects. Thus, unwanted motion in the interior regions of object contours is ignored; and 4) the Hierarchically Filtered Motion computes a structure proximity between any pixel in the local region and the interest point and can reduce distracting motions caused by the background moving objects near an interest point.

Figure 5 shows the action detection results using our multiple feature model. Even the background is cluttered and there are multiple persons in both close and distant view, our detector works well and can locate the action of interest very accurately. Moreover, our detector is robust subject to short-term occlusions. Figure 6 shows the detection results with heavy occlusions.

Action Detection Results on KTH Dataset

To compare our method with previous work, we test our algorithm on the public KTH dataset (Schuldt *et al.*, 2004). In KTH dataset, each video sequence exhibits one individual action from

Figure 4. Examples where HFM features successfully detect the action of interests while Laptev's STIP features fail; for each pair of examples, the picture in the top row illustrates the detection results of using HFM features, while the picture in the bottom row shows the result of using Laptev's STIP features

Figure 5. Detection examples of MSR Action Dataset II; the bounding boxes denote the detected location using Branch-and-Bound search for 3 actions: (a) hand clapping, (b) hand waving, and (c) boxing

Figure 6. Our detector successfully detects the action even with heavy occlusion

beginning to end, locating the actions of interest is trivial. In each video of the KTH dataset, we need not estimate Q since there is only one actor repeating the same action without background motions involved, and all the STIPs in the video are associated with the action. However, the classification task on KTH dataset can still show how our multiple feature fusion method outperforms single feature based methods. To make the results comparable, we apply exactly the same experimental setting of KTH dataset as in (Schuldt *et al.*, 2004). Among the 25 persons, we use 16 persons (1528 sequences) for training and the other 9 persons (863 sequences) for testing. Our method estimates the label of each video clip by Equation 8. Table 1 summarizes the action classification results from different types of features on KTH dataset. The results demonstrate that our feature fusion method outperforms the single feature classification results.

Computation Cost for HFM Feature Extraction

The proposed HFM feature extraction is very efficient. The computational costs for the following steps are evaluated on MSR Action Dataset II: 1) interest point detection including 2D Harris

Table 1. Comparison with the state-of-the art results on the KTH action dataset (6 actions with clean background)

Method	Accuracy
Schuldt *et al.*, 2004	71.71%
Dollar *et al.*, 2005	80.7%
Yin *et al.*, 2010	82%
Niebles *et al.*, 2006	83.92%
Kaaniche *et al.*, 2010	90.57%
JHuang *et al.*, 2007	91.6
Laptev *et al.*, 2008	91.8%
Mikolajczyk *et al.*, 2008	93.2%
Yuan *et al.*, 2009	93.3%
Kovashka *et al.*, 2010	94.53%
Our method	**94.5%**

Table 2. Computation cost for hierarchically filtered motion feature extraction on MSR action dataset II with crowded background

Image Resolution (MSR dataset)	Efficiency (frames/second)		
	IP Detection	Hierarchical Motion Filter Feature Extraction	Total
160 x 120	216	98	68
320 x 240	90	45	30

Corner Detection, MHI calculation, and removing the corners in the static background using MHI as the motion mask; 2) hierarchical motion filter feature extraction including processing of both global and local motion filters and calculation of HOG and MHI-HOG; and 3) the total computation time of step 1 and 2. The average number of detected interest points is about 30 per image for each tested sequence. The details of the efficiency of the proposed Hierarchically Filtered Motion feature extraction are listed in Table 2. For the sequence with resolution of 160x120, the speed of interest point detection (step 1) is 216 frames per second. The speed for Hierarchically Filtered Motion feature extraction (step 2) is 98 frames per second. The speech of the whole core algorithm (step 1+ step 2) is 68 frames per second (without loading video, displaying features and saving the extracted features to a file). The above speeds decrease to 90, 45, and 30 frames per second for sequence in resolution of 320x240. Note that to keep the same amount of Harris corners in both resolutions, we double the minimum distance between corners in 2D Harris corner detection for 320x240 images.

CONCLUSION

In this chapter, we have presented a new feature, Hierarchically Filtered Motion (HFM), for action detection in crowded videos without tracking objects or key points. The HFM features can reduce distracting motions caused by the background moving objects near an interest point. The proposed HFM is more robust than other STIP features for action recognition in crowded videos. We further build a novel framework which combines GMM-based representation of HFM with other STIPs and branch-and-bound based detection. We have performed action detection experiments on MSR Action Dataset II for videos with cluttered and moving background and KTH dataset. Experiment results have demonstrated that

our approach outperforms existing techniques and can effectively detect actions even with cluttered background and partial occlusions.

REFERENCES

Action Dataset, M. S. R., II. (2009). *Website.* Retrieved from http://research.microsoft.com/en-us/um/people/zliu/ActionRecoRsrc/

Blank, M., Gorelick, L., Shechtman, E., Irani, M., & Basri, R. (2005). Actions as space-time shapes. In *Proceedings of the IEEE Conference on Computer Vision*, (pp. 1395–1402). IEEE Press.

Blaschko, M., & Lampert, C. (2008). Learning to localize objects with structured output regression. In *Proceedings of the European Conference on Computer Vision*, (pp. 2–15). Springer.

Bobick, A., & Davis, J. (2001). The recognition of human movement using temporal templates. *IEEE Transactions on Pattern Analysis and Machine Intelligence, 23,* 257–267. doi:10.1109/34.910878

Boiman, O., & Irani, M. (2005). Detecting irregularities in images and in video. In *Proceedings of the IEEE International Conference on Computer Vision*, (pp. 462–469). IEEE Press.

Cao, L., Liu, Z., & Huang, T. (2010). Cross-dataset action detection. In *Proceedings of the IEEE Conference on Computer Vision and Pattern Recognition*. IEEE Press.

Cao, L., Luo, J., Liang, F., & Huang, T. (2009). Heterogeneous feature machines for visual recognition. In *Proceedings of the IEEE International Conference on Computer Vision*. IEEE Press.

Cao, L., Tian, Y., Liu, Z., Yao, B., Zhang, Z., & Huang, T. (2010). Action detection using multiple spatial-temporal interest point features. In *Proceedings of the IEEE International Conference on Multimedia & Expo*. IEEE Press.

Dalal, N., & Triggs, B. (2005). Histograms of oriented gradients for human detection. In *Proceedings of the IEEE International Conference on Computer Vision*. IEEE Press.

Davis, J. (2001). Hierarchical motion history images for recognizing human motion. In *Proceedings of IEEE Workshop on Detection and Recognition of Events in Video*. IEEE Press.

Dollar, P., Rabaud, V., Cottrell, G., & Belongie, S. (2005). Behavior recognition via sparse spatio-temporal features. In *Proceedings of IEEE International Workshop on VS-PETS*. IEEE Press.

Du, T., & Yuan, J. (2011). Optimal spatio-temporal path discovery for video event detection. In *Proceedings of the IEEE Conference on Computer Vision and Pattern Recognition*. IEEE Press.

Harris, C., & Stephens, M. (1988). A combined corner and edge detector. In *Proceeding of Alvey Vision Conference*, (pp. 189–192). Alvey Vision.

Hu, Y., Cao, L., Lv, F., Yan, S., Gong, Y., & Huang, T. (2009). Action detection in complex scenes with spatial and temporal ambiguities. In *Proceedings of the IEEE International Conference on Computer Vision*. IEEE Press.

Jhuang, H., Serre, T., Wolf, L., & Poggio, T. (2007). A biologically inspired system for action recognition. In *Proceedings of the IEEE International Conference on Computer Vision*. IEEE Press.

Ji, X., & Liu, H. (2010). Advances in view-invariant human motion analysis: A review. *IEEE Transactions on Systems, Man and Cybernetics. Part C, Applications and Reviews*, *40*(1), 13–24. doi:10.1109/TSMCC.2009.2027608

Junejo, I., Dexter, E., Laptev, I., & Perez, P. (2011). View-independent action recognition from temporal self-similarities. *IEEE Transactions on Pattern Analysis and Machine Intelligence*, *33*(1), 172–185. doi:10.1109/TPAMI.2010.68

Kaaniche, M., & Bremond, F. (2010). Gesture recognition by learning local motion signatures. In *Proceedings of the IEEE International Conference on Computer Vision*. IEEE Press.

Ke, Y., Sukthankar, R., & Hebert, M. (2007). Event detection in crowded videos. In *Proceedings of the IEEE International Conference on Computer Vision*. IEEE Press.

Kovashka, A., & Grauman, K. (2010). Learning a hierarchy of discriminative space-time neighborhood features for human action recognition. In *Proceedings of the IEEE International Conference on Computer Vision*. IEEE Press.

Lampert, C., Blaschko, M., & Hofmann, T. (2008). Beyond sliding windows: Object localization by efficient subwindow search. In *Proceedings of the IEEE Conference on Computer Vision and Pattern Recognition*. IEEE Press.

Laptev, I., & Lindeberg, T. (2003). Space-time interest points. In *Proceedings of the IEEE Conference on Computer Vision*, (pp. 432–439). IEEE Press.

Laptev, I., Marszalek, M., Schmid, C., & Rozenfeld, B. (2008). Learning realistic human actions from movies. In *Proceedings of the IEEE Conference on Computer Vision and Pattern Recognition*. IEEE Press.

Liu, J., Ali, S., & Shah, M. (2008). Recognizing human actions using multiple features. In *Proceedings of the IEEE Conference on Computer Vision and Pattern Recognition*. IEEE Press.

Liu, J., Luo, J., & Shah, M. (2009). Recognizing realistic actions from videos "in the wild". In *Proceedings of the IEEE Conference on Computer Vision and Pattern Recognition*. IEEE Press.

Marszałek, M., Laptev, I., & Schmid, C. (2009). Actions in context. In *Proceedings of the IEEE Conference on Computer Vision and Pattern Recognition*. IEEE Press.

Mattivi, R., & Shao, L. (2009). Human action recognition using LBP-TOP as sparse spatio-temporal feature descriptor. In *Proceedings of Computer Analysis of Images and Patterns*. IEEE. doi:10.1007/978-3-642-03767-2_90

Messing, R., Pal, C., & Kauze, H. (2009). Activity recognition using the velocity histories of tracked keypoints. In *Proceedings of the IEEE Conference on Computer Vision*. IEEE Press.

Mikolajczyk, K., & Uemura, H. (2008). Action recognition with motion-appearance vocabulary forest. In *Proceedings of the IEEE Conference on Computer Vision and Pattern Recognition*. IEEE Press.

Niebles, J., Wang, H., & Fei-Fei, L. (2006). *Unsupervised learning of human action categories using spatial-temporal words*. Paper presented at the British Machine Vision Conference. London, UK.

Pang, Y., Yuan, Y., Li, X., & Pan, J. (2010, September 15). Efficient HOG human detection. *Signal Processing*. doi:doi:10.1016/j.sigpro.2010.08.010

Reynolds, D., Quatieri, T., & Dunn, R. (2000). Speaker verification using adapted Gaussian mixture models. *Digital Signal Processing, 10*(1-3), 19–41. doi:10.1006/dspr.1999.0361

Rodriguez, M., Ahmed, J., & Shah, M. (2008). Actionmach: A spatio-temporal maximum average correlation height filter for action recognition. In *Proceedings of the IEEE Conference on Computer Vision and Pattern Recognition*. IEEE Press.

Schuldt, C., Laptev, I., & Caputo, B. (2004). Recognizing human actions: A local SVM approach. In *Proceedings of the International Conference on Pattern Recognition*. IEEE Press.

Sun, J., Wu, X., Yan, S., Cheong, L., Chua, T., & Li, J. (2009). Hierarchical spatio-temporal context modeling for action recognition. In *Proceedings of the IEEE Conference on Computer Vision and Pattern Recognition*. IEEE Press.

Tian, Y., Cao, L., Liu, Z., & Zhang, Z. (2011). Hierarchical filtered motion field for action recognition in crowded videos. *IEEE Transactions on Systems, Man and Cybernetics. Part C, Applications and Reviews, 42*(3).

Wang, P., Abowd, G., & Rehg, J. (2009). Quasi-periodic event analysis for social game retrieval. In *Proceedings of the IEEE International Conference on Computer Vision*. IEEE Press.

Wong, S., Kim, T., & Cipolla, R. (2007). Learning motion categories using both semantic and structural information. In *Proceedings of the IEEE Conference on Computer Vision and Pattern Recognition*. IEEE Press.

Wu, J., Osuntogun, A., Choudhury, T., Philipose, M., & Rehg, J. (2007). A scalable approach to activity recognition based on object use. In *Proceedings of the IEEE International Conference on Computer Vision*. IEEE Press.

Yao, B., & Zhu, S. (2009). Learning deformable action templates from cluttered videos. In *Proceedings of the IEEE International Conference on Computer Vision*. IEEE Press.

Yin, J., & Meng, Y. (2010). Human activity recognition in video using a hierarchical probabilistic latent model. In *Proceedings of the IEEE Conference on Computer Vision and Pattern Recognition*. IEEE Press.

Yuan, J., Liu, Z., & Wu, Y. (2009). Discriminative subvolume search for efficient action detection. In *Proceedings of the IEEE Conference on Computer Vision and Pattern Recognition*. IEEE Press.

Yuan, Y., & Pang, Y. (2008). Discriminant adaptive edge weights for graph embedding. In *Proceedings of the IEEE International Conference on Acoustics, Speech, and Signal Processing*. IEEE Press.

Zhu, G., Yang, M., Yu, K., Xu, W., & Gong, Y. (2009). Detecting video events based on action recognition in complex scenes using spatio-temporal descriptor. In *Proceedings of the ACM International Conference on Multimedia*, (pp. 165–174). ACM Press.

KEY TERMS AND DEFINITIONS

Branch-and-Bound Algorithm: A general algorithm for finding optimal solutions of various optimization problems, especially in discrete and combinatorial optimization.

Hierarchically Filtered Motion: Spatiotemporal motion features with global and local filters.

Histograms of Oriented Gradient: Feature descriptors that count occurrences of gradient orientation in localized portions of an image.

Human Action Detection: Not only answers "which action happens in a video," but also "when and where the action happens in the video sequence."

Human Action Recognition: Classify a video to a predefined action category.

Motion History Image: A real-time motion template that temporally layers consecutive image differences into a static image template.

Spatiotemporal Interest Point: Features of local structures in space-time where the image values have significant local variations in both space and time.

Chapter 13
From Streams of Observations to Knowledge–Level Productive Predictions

Mark Wernsdorfer
University of Bamberg, Germany

Ute Schmid
University of Bamberg, Germany

ABSTRACT

The benefit to be gained by Ambient Assisted Living (AAL) systems depends heavily on the successful recognition of human intentions. Important indicators for specific intentions are behavior and situational context. Once a sequence of actions can be associated with a specific intention, assistance may be provided by anticipating the next individual step and supporting the human in its execution. The authors present a combination of Sequence Abstraction Networks (SAN) and IGOR to guarantee early and impartial predictions with a powerful detection for symbolic regularities. They first generate a hierarchy of abstract action sequences, where individual contexts represent subgoals or minor intentions. Afterwards, they enrich this hierarchy by recursive induction. An example scenario is presented where a table needs to be set for several guests. It turns out that correct predictions can be made while still executing the observed sequence for the first time. Support can therefore be completely individual to the person being assisted but nonetheless be very dynamic and quick in anticipating the next steps.

1. INTRODUCTION

Research in Ambient Assisted Living (AAL) aims to provide technologies for supporting people in their everyday activities (Wilken, Hein, & Spehr, 2011). For effective support, an automated assisting system needs to make valid assumptions fast and with a low number of initial examples.

Furthermore, the system should be tolerant for individual idiosyncrasies, that is, it should not discourage people from their personal way of everyday interaction. Especially for elderly and impaired persons, it is important that the system maintains as much personal autonomy as possible to allow for as much cognitive and physical activity as possible (Schmid, 2008). For these reasons,

DOI: 10.4018/978-1-4666-3682-8.ch013

individual behavior needs to be observed and no beforehand generalization over a large sample of persons may be imposed. Consequently, the challenge in creating a beneficial AAL system is combining the need for early predictions with the obligation to take each human into account individually.

One possible approach to design such a system is to infer the current intention (Stein & Schlieder, 2004; Kiefer & Schlieder, 2007) of a person by monitoring her/his activities and to predict a future intended sequence of actions on that basis. Typically it is not possible to identify the intention of an agent based on an isolated activity. For example, when a person raises from the living room chair, many consecutive actions are possible, dependent on the underlying intention. If, however, raising from the chair is motivated by the intention to get something to drink, the set of following activities are obviously reduced—walking to the kitchen is the most probable one.

In many Activities of Daily Living (ADL), we perform repetitive sequences of actions. For example, when drying dishes, we might dry three plates or ten plates, depending on the number of people served. Typically, the drying of each plate follows the same action pattern—take out of the sink with left hand, take the towel with the right hand, wipe the dish, put it away. The challenge for such types of sequences is to be able to predict the complete course of actions correctly for arbitrary situations. That is, the intention "dry dishes" is realized by action sequences of different length, depending on the number of dishes.

Rules which can capture the recursive character of such action sequences are called productive (Chomsky, 1965). To predict sequences with arbitrary length, it is necessary to learn the underlying set of productive rules, i.e., recursive function. The most prominent domain of productive rule learning is language acquisition (Chomsky, 1965; Marcus, 2001; Tomasello, 2003). Children learn the grammar rules underlying their mother tongue from positive experience. The learning of productive

rule sets for generation and application of regular *action* sequences can be seen as analogous to the grammar acquisition problem. The challenge for an AAL system is to generalize productive rule sets from *observed* action sequences assessed by behavior monitoring and to predict succeeding action sequences of arbitrary length based on inferred intentions.

Research in the context of AAL currently focuses on identification of actions but not on prediction of action sequences (Wilken et al., 2011; Busch, Witthöft, Kujath, & Welge, 2011; Schröder, Wabnik, Hengel, & Goetze, 2011; Nesselrath, Lu, Schulz, Frey, & Alexandersson, 2011). We propose to improve the scope of AAL systems by implementing predictive capabilities. Definite assistance can be offered if intention recognition helps improving action anticipation.

Although SAN is a system that is being developed with autonomous agent control in mind, yet one of its major aims is to represent and recognize different sequences of discrete events. The goal is to replicate human unconscious anticipation in every-day interactions with the world. This serves two purposes in the case of an AAL system. The first one is differentiating types of sequences into high-level intentions. The second one is reliable anticipation of successive events with a very low number of initial examples. Using the sequence type information obtained by SAN, IGOR is able to generate a recursive rule set that describes the observed sequences. Thus IGOR is able to capture even complex regularities within sequences. Eventually, the recursive rule set allows for productive anticipation of successive events.

In the following we will outline methods that provide the aforementioned specific demands of AAL systems. First, in section 2 the scenario will be detailed. In section 3 SAN is introduced as a means of fast and productive sequence generalization. An additional recursive regularity detection is achieved by IGOR, presented in sec. 4. In the following section we propose a way of combining SAN and IGOR. Goal is to benefit on the one hand from SAN's ability of early productions and sequence generalizations and on the other hand from IGOR's detection of recursive patterns. In the last section we will conclude our analysis, present and critically examine first empirical results.

2. SCENARIO

In our case, assistance can be understood as providing help in everyday interaction with the indoor environment. This implies a routine in executing actions with a limited set of known objects. Also for the system to be ambient, it must be able to anticipate the most probable next action step and provide help autonomously.

The scenario we propose represents a sequence of everyday manipulation activities (Beetz, Jain, Mosenlechner, & Tenorth, 2010). The assisted person (AP) needs to prepare a table for a couple of guests. The person's movement and interaction inside its living quarters is detected by a simple sensory system. This entails pressure sensitive surfaces to detect placement of dishes on a table or pots onto the cook top. Rough indoor localization can quite easily be determined by RFID sensors in each room and a corresponding transponder carried by the person at all times (e.g. in a watch or a necklace). The information is gathered in a central system inside the living quarters, ideally via wireless data communication. Assuming the successful detection of coarse interaction with the interior we start with discrete actions in the form "get a dish (g)," "approach table (a)," and "retreat from table (r)."

To set the table for two guests, the AP:

1. **g:** Gets one portion of the meal for one guest
2. **a:** Puts it on the table
3. **r:** Goes back to the oven
4. **g:** Gets one portion of the meal for the next guest
5. **a:** Puts it on the table
6. **r:** Goes back to the oven
7. **g:** Gets one portion of the meal for himself
8. **a:** Puts it on the table
9. Sequence finished

The according word is "gargarga" and the sequences to be recognized are all words from the regular grammar *(gar)⁺ga*. The goal is to represent this sequence for an arbitrary number of guests, so that "get a dish (g)" and "go back to oven (r)" always allow sure predictions of the next action to take within the current intention "serving guests".[1]

Assistance could be provided for example by transporting an object from one place to another. In the current state "d" for example a mobile unit could offer itself for carrying a plate to the table. Persons with impaired mobility could be transported from the eating table to the kitchen and back without the need of continuous interaction with the system. Some form of acknowledgement should of course still be necessary to confirm the execution of an anticipated action. With good predictions, however, this can be reduced to a binary yes-or-no statement (see Figure 1).

3. SEQUENCE ABSTRACTION NETWORKS

Originally, SAN is one of two components in a robot control system. The low-level component transfers continuous sensorimotor data into discrete events. As high-level component, SAN tries to isolate sequences for successful, context sensitive predictions. The robot control system actuates in continuous environments and receives reward feedback (Raab, Wernsdorfer, Kitzelmann, & Schmid, 2011). The intention is to provide a system, which is able to successfully cope with different domains. For example, it generates representations according to a navigational task but will be able to use those representations for controlling a pole balancing cart. The intention is to contribute to the question for Artificial General

Figure 1. SAN *as "symbolic" component of robot control architecture*

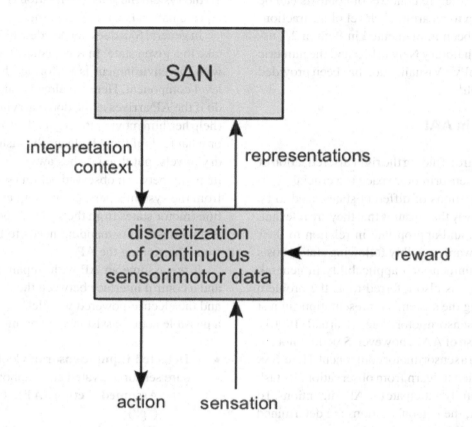

Intelligence by examining generated memory structures for similarities and deficiencies. SAN operates on discrete data, it generates and processes representations of information provided by a sub-symbolic counterpart.

Only the low-level component is capable of sensorimotor interaction with the environment. It generates an evaluation to anticipate reward from the environment. Sensorimotor activation and according reward are associated and stored, such that in future "bad" states can be avoided and "good" ones can be sought after. In case actual reward deviates from the system's evaluation of the current sensorimotor state, a new sensorimotor region is isolated and associated with the unexpected reward. This tessellation process discriminates continuous sensorimotor space into discrete regions. These regions are interpreted as Voronoi cells and are represented as real-valued vectors. These vectors are the basic representations SAN operates on.

SAN's function is to congregate similar representations into so called "contexts". Contexts consist of sequences of perceived states and are stored in form of graphs. A representation within this graph is understood as *ambiguous* if either its outgoing or its incoming vertex degree is above one. Placing the same representations in different graphs allows for disambiguating identical states according to the causal sequences they happen to take place in. Therefore, SAN generates a representation of context-dependent sequentiality as it is able to anticipate future states inside the right context. Sequence graphs can also represented as vectors, therefore contexts of contexts can be generated up to an arbitrary level of abstraction.

San has been implemented in Python 2.7 using the graph library NetworkX[2] and the numeric library NumPy[3]. Visualization has been provided by UbiGraph[4].

3.1. SAN in AAL

In robot control, finding the right discretization of continuous sensorimotor space is a crucial problem. Aggregations of different states need to be chosen in a way that ensures that they are relevant, meaningful, and appropriate in relation to their expected reward, possibly following states, costs of their attainment and applicability in general. This problem is also referred to as the problem of grounding the system's representations in just the "right" sensorimotor states (Harnad, 1990).

In the case of AAL, however, San does not cooperate with a sensorimotor component. Here, San is only applied to learn from observation. Its task is to successfully anticipate the AP's intentions. To achieve that, the person's actions are determined by a rather solid sensor array like electric contacts on doors, pressure sensors on surfaces and in the floor and RFID sensors in combination with a transponder at the person's body. These sensor activations are fed into San like the real-valued vectors from the sub-symbolic control component. Like in the case of robot control, San receives a stream of discrete inputs that are being processed in relation to the sequences they occur in.

As long as sensor types are chosen with care, sensor events can always be regarded as relevant, meaningful and appropriate. Their representations do not need to be autonomously grounded in arbitrary states of the environment. They are already hard-wired to events that matter for anticipating the person's intentions. San receives discrete data for example in the form of 'AP enters kitchen', 'AP opens fridge' or 'AP moves towards eating table'.

To the system the sensor activation *is* a low-level representation *is* a relevant event.

In general San does not decide which action to take in a given state. In robot control, interaction with the environment is performed by the low-level component. Here we already know what to do if the AP arrives at the door carrying a weight (help her/him moving the payload into the house) or what to do if the AP cleans the dishes (supply dry towels, put dried dishes away). Therefore, a mapping between observed action (sensor states from the system's perspective) and executed action (motor states from the system's perspective) is a premise. This mapping needs to be inferred from questioning the AP.

If we assume an AP with impaired mobility and a control interface between the AAL system and the electric-powered wheelchair, in our case a possible action-assistance mapping could be:

- **Detected Input (Sensors):** Cook top pressure sensor activated and cupboard open.
  - **Assumed Action (AP):** Get a meal ("g").
  - **Offered Assistance (AAL):** Provide plate and cutlery.
- **Input:** RFID tag leaves kitchen.
  - **Action:** Put meal on table "a."
  - **Assistance:** Steer wheel chair towards eating table.
- **Input:** RFID tag enters kitchen.
  - **Action:** Go back to the oven "r."
  - **Assistance:** [Undefined]

Clustering the AP's actions into common sequences allows for disambiguating single actions into distinct sequences of routine behavior. Those sequences enable the prediction of single actions several steps ahead. This gives time to either prepare assistance (e.g. get the electric wheelchair, preheat the oven) or to check back with the AP if assistance is required at all.

3.2. Sequence Representation

Sensor events s_t describe the input to SAN from the AAL's sensor array at program cycle t. The only restraint is applicability of the identity function $s_t = id(s_t)$. A *sensor representation* $r(s)$ is SAN's internal representation of a sensor event s_t. It is stored as vertex in a context graph. A *context graph* is a graph data structure representing the current sequence. For each vertex in each context graph the following holds: in or out degree of "causes" connections is greater or equal to 1 and each sensor event is only represented once.

"*Causes*" *connections* $e_c(r_n, r_m)$ indicate temporal succession of two vertices r_n and r_m. They are represented as directed graph edges. "Causes" connections also hold two integer values for positive e_{pos} and negative evidence e_{neg}. Positive evidence is increased for observed transitions between sensor representations, negative evidence is increased for alternative transitions. The *confidence* of a "causes" connection is calculated by Equation 1. Falling under a predefined threshold, connections are removed. *Contrasting* is the process of increasing "causes" transition confidence between successive vertices in the same graph and declining connections to alternative vertices (see Figure 2).

$$conf(e_c(r_i, r_j)) = \frac{e_c(r_i, r_j)_{pos}}{e_c(r_i, r_j)_{neg} + e_c(r_i, r_j)_{pos}} \quad (1)$$

SAN starts with an empty context graph. During runtime it will create more context graphs that can be active, each one representing a unique action sequence. When a new sensor event s_t occurs in the input stream, SAN tries to find a transition from the last event s_{t-1} to the new one inside the current context. If such a connection $e_c(r(s_{t-1}), r(s_t))$ can be found, the connection of $r(s_{t-1})$ to $r(s_t)$ is contrasted. If $e_c(r(s_{t-1}), r(s_t))$ cannot be found, other context graphs are queried. In case this does not return a result, an new representation $r(s_t)$ is introduced as vertex, a new "causes" connection

is created from $r(s_{t-1})$ and that connection is contrasted.

Outcome is a context graph with a minimal vertex degree, such that predictions can be made with great certainty. Graph components that are split off by removing connections create new context graphs.

3.3. Sequence Abstraction

Graph representations are SAN's internal representation of a context graph. It is itself stored as vertex in a context graph of a higher level. The level of a graph representation r_g is always the level of the vertices contained in the graph r_s plus one $l(r_g) = l(r_s) + 1$. "*Is a*" *connections* are indicating increasing abstraction. They are directed from all vertices inside one graph to this graph's representation in a higher level. The *parent graph* p of representation r is the graph g that contains the representation of the graph that contains r (see "seq3" containing "seq2" and "seq1" in Figure 3). *Graph fragmentation* occurs when one context graph g is separated into several components. New context graphs for each component are introduced. The new representations are linked to each other with "causes" connections and to the parent graph representation $p(r(g))$ of the original graph representation. *Neighbors* are the other vertices of one representation's parent graph. The need not be *directly* connected to each other. As each graph is fully connected, all vertices in one graph are considered neighbors.

Each representation r in graph g is connected to a representation $r(g)$ of the graph g via a "is a" connection. The level of all vertices in one graph is identical, starting at the sensor representation leafs with 0. Along each "is a" connection the level is increased by one. During graph fragmentation, a new graph representation $r(g_c)$ for each component c of the original graph is introduced. These components are linked to each other with "causes" connections and to the parent graph of the original graph representation with a "is a"

Figure 2. Algorithm "contrast"

Algorithm 1: contrast

Input: representation r_i, representation r_j

1   $e_c(r_i, r_j)_{pos} \leftarrow e_c(r_i, r_j)_{pos} + 1$;

2   **foreach** $r_s \in successors\ of\ r_i$ **do**

3   **if** $r_s! = r_j$ **then**

4      $e_c(r_i, r_s)_{neg} \leftarrow e_c(r_i, r_s)_{neg} + 1$;

5   **foreach** $r_p \in predecessors\ of\ r_j$ **do**

6   **if** $r_p! = r_i$ **then**

7      $e_c(r_p, r_j)_{neg} \leftarrow e_c(r_p, r_j)_{neg} + 1$;

---

connection. In case such a parent graph representation does not exist, it is created.

Abstraction is the process of representing graphs in higher representational levels. This allows on the one hand for representing different types of sequences and on the other hand for hierarchical structure of sequences of actions ($[seq_1, seq_2]$). Therefore intentions and subgoals can be identified.

3.4. Sequence Recognition

In the lowest level, transitions between vertices occur with each new sensor event in the input stream. Higher level transitions between graphs occur if there is another graph explaining an observed transition where the current one fails to (see the conditions for changing context graphs in 3.2). The observed transition is queried within all sequence representations. If one is found, the process from 3.2 is recursively repeated to find a connection $e_c(r(g_m), r(g_n))$ between the original

Figure 3. Disambiguation of successor events (a), removal of link 'B' to 'C' (b), and separation of sequences (c). Abstract vertices are in front of a shaded background.

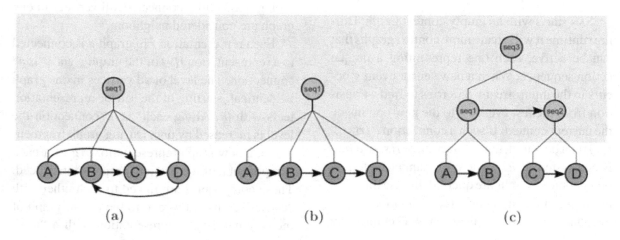

(a)   (b)   (c)

graph representation $r(g_m)$ and the new graph representation $r(g_n)$ containing the queried transition.

Low-level transitions are therefore triggered by new events in the input stream and high-level transitions are triggered by unexpected low-level transitions. As high level transitions also receive negative evidence, fragmentation also leads to representations of higher level sequences of sequences (see "seq2" in Figure 3). By changing context graphs of different levels, SAN always tries to find a low-level sequence that suits the perceived input stream best. These distinct sequences of actions are interpreted as the AP's intentions. According to those intentions assistance will be provided.

Once event sequences can be discerned according to the assumed intention they are realizing, they are fed into IGOR for further processing. IGOR receives sequences of one type sorted by length and associated with a symbol designating their according intention. These sets make up the examples for IGOR. As soon as IGOR derives the recursive rules describing the current sequence, it can generate sequences of arbitrary length realizing the same "intention." Eventually, the current position within this sequence is determined and successor events can be retrieved from the generated sequence. As these successor events can be arbitrarily far ahead, time remains for preparing necessary assistance on the one hand and for the AP to decide whether to do things on her/his own or to accept assistance on the other hand.

In Figure 4 the generation of representations for the words from the regular grammar *(gar)⁺ga* is displayed. Initial and word separation symbol is the ASCII code 20 space sign.

4. LEARNING PRODUCTIVE RULE SETS WITH IGOR

The system IGOR (**I**nductive **G**eneralization **O**f **R**ecursive rule sets) realizes a powerful mechanism for generalizing recursive rule sets from small sets of example experience. IGOR was initially developed as an approach to inductive programming (Flener & Schmid, to appear). Inductive programming research is concerned with learning recursive programs from sets of input/output examples. While most approaches in this domain are using generate-and-test strategies, the IGOR approach works example driven (Schmid & Wysotzki, 1998; Kitzelmann & Schmid, 2006; Kitzelmann, 2009, 2010). That is, the input/output examples are checked for regularities and the recursive program is generated as a generalization over such regularities. The approach realised in IGOR has been shown to have comparable scope and higher efficiency as most other current inductive programming systems (Hofmann, Kitzelmann, & Schmid, 2009).

4.1. Illustration of the IGOR Algorithm

The most recent version of the algorithms governing IGOR together with proofs of several characteristics of the generalization algorithm as well as of the induced recursive rule sets can be found in Kitzelmann (2010). In the following we will give an intuition of IGOR-style inductive rule learning by means of a simple example (see Figure 5).

The system is presented with a small set of example input/output pairs which produce the desired behavior. In the given example, each element of a list is packed together with a fixed element. These examples could correspond to some observed behavior where an agent takes several items and puts each item in a package together with a greeting card. By observing the regularities in the examples, the recursive function *packing* is generalized. This function deals with each input/output examples correctly and furthermore generalizes to lists of arbitrary length. This generalization might represent a rule which is able to predict what a person will be doing with an arbitrary number of items—that is, when the person put the first three items in a package each and included a card, IGOR would predict that further items will be treated in the same way.

Figure 4. Incremental generation of sequence representation for words from the regular grammar (gar)⁺ga. Symbol vertices are dark, abstract vertices are light gray. The last active vertex is marked white.

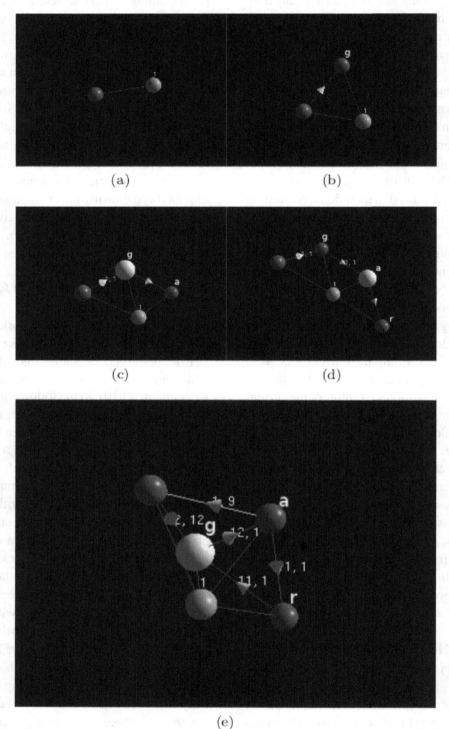

4.2. From Inductive Programming to Rule Learning from Experience

IGOR is based on the concept of constructor term rewriting systems. Besides the input/output examples, IGOR expects that an algebraic data type is predefined. This (minimal) background information is necessary for IGOR to know which basic operators (i.e. constructors) can be used on the right-hand side of rules to construct the desired output from the input. For the example in Figure 5, the data type is *list* with the constructors *nil* for empty lists and *cons* for list construction. In general, IGOR can be supplied with more background knowledge in form of predefined functions which then can also used on the right-hand side to construct further rules.

The main power of IGOR lies in its ability to invent additional functions on the fly. If the regularities in the input/output examples are more sophisticated than in the simple, linear recursive example above, this feature enables IGOR to deconstruct the initial problem into smaller problems which can be dealt with separately.

Although IGOR was primarily intended as a system for inductive programming, we have shown that it can also be used to model learning of behavioral rules in the context of problem solving. For example, the sequence of move operations to solve Tower of Hanoi problems with an arbitrary number of discs can be learned from the move-operations observed for the three disc problem (Schmid & Kitzelmann, 2011). In Schmid and Kitzelmann (2011) we also presented an illustration of learning a simple phrase structure grammar (Sakakibara, 1997; Covington, 1994) with IGOR. This example can be adapted to the example scenario presented in this paper.

4.3. Sequence Generalization

A behavior monitoring system might observe that a person sets the table with one set of dishes, followed by a second and then by a third set. These observations are represented as letter strings in Figure 6. Given natural numbers as constructive data type with 1 as constant and *succ* as constructor, IGOR can induce a generalized table setting rule. In the following, the monitoring system is able to predict how a person might continue for additional places on the table.

5. COMBINATION

By incorporating both systems we have a way to (a) isolate intentions that are realized by regular actions and (b) produce arbitrarily long predictions about further actions realizing that intention. Concretely, both systems are combined as depicted in Figure 7. The input stream consists of a small example set of action sequences. The stream is usually a mix of all kinds of different actions. Action sequences realizing the same intention are therefore actually separated by different intentions that have been dominant over several days or weeks.

As the stream is fed to SAN, however, reoccurring sequences will be recognized and associated with the same abstract intention. In our case, the sequence representation seq_1 is interpreted as the intention to serve guests. For each abstract sequence representation seq_n it has to be determined, when the data structure is sufficiently mature such that the according every action sequence can be associated with its intention. A good indicator is graph convergence: if it has not been necessary to introduce new vertices or links for a certain amount of iterations, it can be assumed that the representation is ready to assign valid intentions.

Once SAN has generated stable intention representations, new instances of action sequences realizing that intentions can be identified, associated with their according intention, stored and sorted by length. Relevant for the position in the sorted list is only the length of the action sequence without the intention identifier seq_n. This enables provid-

Figure 5. Illustration of the inductive programming system IGOR

Input/Output Examples (i. e., observed behavior of an agent)

()	→	()
(a)	→	((a z))
(a b)	→	((a z) (b z))
(a b c)	→	((a z) (b z) (c z))

Induced Recursive Rule Set

packing(nil) = nil

packing(x - l) = cons(cons(x (cons z nil)) packing (l))

ing IGOR with the first n input/output examples of the recursive function to be found.

Applied to the example from Figure 3, sequences of the form *[A, B]* will be associated with the abstract representation *seq₁*, whereas sequences like *[C, D]* will be labeled with *seq₂*. In the case of the AAL scenario all sequences that are described by the graph from Figure 4 (e) will be associated with the representing vertex one layer above (here labeled '1'). Therefore IGOR receives an input/output example set like {*(gargarga, 1), (garga, 1), (gargarga, 1), (gargargargargargargargargarga, 1), (garga, 1), ...*}.

Once observed sequence and abstract representation are available, more powerful recursive inference methods can be applied to improve the system's predictive capabilities. Each concrete sequence can now be associated with an abstract intention within the SAN sequence hierarchy. From this, we can build a set of input/output examples, where the input is the sequence instance and the output is the according abstract intention. Putting this example set into IGOR creates a recursive function, describing the sequence in more detail.

When IGOR has enough of the first n input/output examples, it is able to generate a recursive rule set. This rule set contains two or more partially recursive functions, that allow for regenerating a word from the input stream. Within the current position of the input stream, a new word can be generated up to an arbitrary number of letter ahead of the current one.

Figure 6. Generalizing a productive rule set for setting a table with IGOR

Observations

g ar g ar g a!

g ar g ar g ar g a!

g ar g ar g ar g ar g a!

Induced Recursive Rule Set

setTable(1) = *g ar g ar g a!*

setTable(succ(n)) = *g ar* setTable(n)

6. CONCLUSION

It could be shown that the specific demands for AAL systems can be successfully met by a combination of two different inference algorithms. On the one hand, recursive rule sets satisfy the demand to generate arbitrarily long predictions about future actions. On the other hand a structural representation of the action sequence allows for sequence classification by intention.

Properties of two algorithms that have initially been intended for completely different purposes

Figure 7. Flow of information

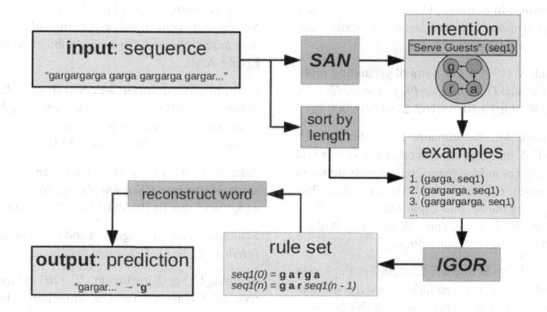

(self programming and autonomous agent control) could be used to design a AAL system that tries to take the individual situation of the AP into account. In case sensory data can be acquired reliably, still the question has to be answered how assistance should be offered and what kind of acknowledgement will be accepted. For the system to remain ambient, this form of interaction needs to take place very natural and with little effort.

To extend the system, it might be feasible to replace the manual mapping of observed action to offered assistance by a learning system. Our system could also be part of this extension. Because it provides the prediction of the AP's next action, e.g. a reinforcement learning algorithm might learn what kind of assistance to provide. As this might be prone to mistakes, and to respect the intention to preserve the individuality of every day interaction, for now, a manual association of action to assistance must suffice.

In the present case, we used a simple regular grammar for prediction. But San is also able to represent hierarchical sequences. The identification of subgoals vs. final goals has already been mentioned. But it is yet to be explored how a scenario must be designed to produce—and make use of—hierarchical intention representations.

REFERENCES

Beetz, M., Jain, D., Mosenlechner, L., & Tenorth, M. (2010). Towards performing everyday manipulation activities. *Robotics and Autonomous Systems*, *58*(9), 1085–1095. doi:10.1016/j.robot.2010.05.007

Busch, B.-H., Witthöft, H., Kujath, A., & Welge, R. (2011). *Präventive notfallerkennung auf basis probabilistischer und beschreibungslogischer auswertung verteilter sensornetze*. Ambient Assisted Living-AAL.

Chomsky, N. (1965). *Aspects of the theory of syntax*. Cambridge, MA: MIT Press.

Covington, M. A. (1994). *Natural language processing for prolog programmers*. Upper Saddle River, NJ: Prentice Hall.

Flener, P., & Schmid, U. (2012). Inductive programming . In Sammut, C., & Webb, G. (Eds.), *Encyclopedia of Machine Learning*. Berlin, Germany: Springer.

Harnad, S. (1990). The symbol grounding problem. *Physica D. Nonlinear Phenomena, 42*(1-3), 335–346. doi:10.1016/0167-2789(90)90087-6

Hofmann, M., Kitzelmann, E., & Schmid, U. (2009). A unifying framework for analysis and evaluation of inductive programming systems. In B. Goerzel, P. Hitzler, & M. Hutter (Eds.), *Proceedings of the Second Conference on Artificial General Intelligence*, (pp. 55–60). Amsterdam, The Netherlands: Atlantis Press.

Kiefer, P., & Schlieder, C. (2007). Exploring context-sensitivity in spatial intention recognition. In *Proceedings of the International Workshop on Behavioral Monitoring and Interpretation*, (vol. 42, pp. 102–116). TZI-Bericht.

Kitzelmann, E. (2009). Analytical inductive functional programming. In M. Hanus (Ed.), *Proceedings of the 18th International Symposium on Logic-Based Program Synthesis and Transformation*, (vol. 5438, pp. 87–102). Springer.

Kitzelmann, E. (2010). *A combined analytical and search-based approach to the inductive synthesis of functional programs*. (Unpublished Doctoral Dissertation). Otto-Friedrich Universität. Bamberg, Germany. Retrieved from http://www.opus-bayern.de/uni-bamberg/volltexte/2010/280/

Kitzelmann, E., & Schmid, U. (2006). Inductive synthesis of functional programs: An explanation based generalization approach. *Journal of Machine Learning Research, 7*, 429–454.

Marcus, G. F. (2001). *The algebraic mind. integrating conncetionism and cognitive science*. Cambridge, MA: Bradford.

Nesselrath, R., Lu, C., Schulz, C. H., Frey, J., & Alexandersson, J. (2011). *Ein gestenbasiertes System zur kontextsensitiven Interaktion mit dem Smart Home A Gesture*. Ambient Assisted Living-AAL.

Raab, M., Wernsdorfer, M., Kitzelmann, E., & Schmid, U. (2011). From sensorimotor graphs to rules: An agent learns from a stream of experience. *Artificial General Intelligence*, 333–339.

Sakakibara, Y. (1997). Recent advances of grammatical inference. *Theoretical Computer Science, 185*, 15–45. doi:10.1016/S0304-3975(97)00014-5

Schmid, U. (2008). Cognition and AI. *Künstliche Intelligenz, 22*(1), 5–7.

Schmid, U., & Kitzelmann, E. (2011). Inductive rule learning on the knowledge level. *Cognitive Systems Research, 12*(3-4), 237–248. doi:10.1016/j.cogsys.2010.12.002

Schmid, U., & Wysotzki, F. (1998). Induction of recursive program schemes. In *Proceedings of the 10th European Conference on Machine Learning (ECML 1998)*, (Vol. 1398, pp. 214–225). Springer.

Schröder, J., Wabnik, S., van Hengel, P., & Goetze, S. (2011). *Erkennung und Klassifikation von akustischen Ereignissen zur häuslichen Pflege*. Ambient Assisted Living-AAL.

Stein, K., & Schlieder, C. (2004). Recognition of intentional behaviors in spatial partonomies. *Applied Artificial Intelligence and Logistics, 9*.

Tomasello, M. (2003). *Constructing a language: A usage-based theory of language acquisition*. Boston, MA: Harvard University Press.

Wilken, O., Hein, A., & Spehr, M. G. J. (2011). *Ein Ansatz zur Fusion von Aktivitätswahrscheinlichkeiten zur robusten Identifikation von Aktivitäten des täglichen Lebens (ADL)*. Ambient Assisted Living-AAL.

ENDNOTES

[1] With a further extension of the system's sensory capabilities, a detection of the number of guests can easily clarify the uncertainty concerning the successor event of "approach table (a)". As soon as every person is served, the sequence is over.

[2] http://networkx.lanl.gov/

[3] http://numpy.scipy.org/

[4] http://ubietylab.net/ubigraph/

Chapter 14
Improving the Supervised Learning of Activity Classifiers for Human Motion Data

Liyue Zhao
University of Central Florida, USA

Xi Wang
University of Central Florida, USA

Gita Sukthankar
University of Central Florida, USA

ABSTRACT

The ability to accurately recognize human activities from motion data is an important stepping-stone toward creating many types of intelligent user interfaces. Many supervised learning methods have been demonstrated for learning activity classifiers from data; however, these classifiers often fail due to noisy sensor data, lack of labeled training samples for rare actions and large individual differences in activity execution. In this chapter, the authors introduce two techniques for improving supervised learning of human activities from motion data: (1) an active learning framework to reduce the number of samples required to segment motion traces, and (2) an intelligent feature selection technique that both improves classification performance and reduces training time. They demonstrate how these techniques can be used to improve the classification of human household activities, an area of particular research interest since it facilitates the development of elder-care assistance systems to monitor household occupants.

INTRODUCTION

Human activity recognition has become an increasingly important component of many domains such as user interfaces and video surveillance.

In particular, enabling ubiquitous home user assistance systems for elder care requires rapid and robust recognition of human action from portable sensor data. Motion trajectories, gathered from video, inertial measurement units, or mocap, are

DOI: 10.4018/978-1-4666-3682-8.ch014

a critical cue for identifying activities that require gross body movement, such as walking, running, falling, or waving. Human motion data typically needs to be segmented into activities to be utilized by any application. A common processing pipeline for motion data is:

1. Segment data into short time windows;
2. Recognize low-level human activities from repetitive patterns of motion executed by the human user within a time window;
3. Identify a high-level intention or plan from sequences of activities.

For instance, one possible high-level household activity would be "baking pizza" which would consist of low-level activities such as "beating an egg" or "kneading dough" which could be recognized by the motion patterns and objects manipulated.

Although domain knowledge and common-sense reasoning methods are important for reasoning about the human's high level intentions, segmentation and activity classification have been successfully addressed by a variety of data-driven approaches, including supervised classifiers, such as support vector machines, hidden Markov models, dynamic Bayes nets, and conditional random fields. In the best case, supervised learning can yield classifiers that are robust and accurate. However, two problems frequently occur in supervised learning settings:

*   **Lack of Data:** Gathering and labeling the data is time-consuming and expensive. In some cases, the activities are highly repetitive in nature (stirring), whereas other actions are infrequent and short in duration (opening the refrigerator). To classify these short actions, learning techniques need to be sample-efficient to leverage relatively small amounts of labeled training data.

*   **Feature Selection:** Sensors yield data that is both noisy and high-dimensional. Learning classifiers based on the raw sensor data can be problematic and applying arbitrary dimensionality reduction techniques does not always yield good results.

In this chapter, we present a case study of how we addressed these problems while performing segmentation and activity recognition of human household actions. First, we introduce an active learning method in which the classifier is initialized with training data from unsupervised segmentation and improved by soliciting unlabeled samples that lie closest to the classification hyperplane. We demonstrate that this method can be used to reduce the number of samples required to classify motion capture data using Support Vector Machine (SVM) classifiers.

Second, we present a method to improve classification through intelligent feature selection. The signal data is converted into a set of motifs, approximately repeated symbolic subsequences, for each dimension of IMU data. These motifs leverage structure in the data and serve as the basis to generate a large candidate set of features from the multi-dimensional raw data. By measuring reductions in the conditional log-likelihood error of the training samples, we can select features and train a Conditional Random Field (CRF) classifier to recognize human actions.

Our techniques were evaluated using the CMU Multimodal Activity database (De la Torre Frade et al., 2008) which was collected to facilitate the comparison of different activity recognition techniques for recognizing household activities. The dataset contains video, audio, inertial measurement unit (IMU), and motion capture data; we demonstrate the utility of our techniques on segmenting motion capture data and recognizing Inertial Measurement Unit (IMU) data.

BACKGROUND

In this section, we give an overview of the concepts that our approach relies on (1) active learning, (2) feature selection, and (3) motif detection, in addition to a detailed discussion of the operation of the conditional random field classifier.

Active Learning

Active learning can be regarded as a subfield of supervised learning in which the aim is to achieve the same classification with a smaller set of labeled data. As shown in Figure 1 standard (passive) learning techniques require humans to annotate the entire set of input training data that the learner uses to build the classifier. By contrast, in active learning, the annotation of data is performed through a series of interactions between the automated learner and the human. By analyzing the unlabeled data, the active learner selects a subset of the data that has a high degree of label uncertainty to be annotated by the expert. Currently, two main issues of active learning research are how to pose queries and identify informative instances.

There are three general methods for posing queries: *membership queries*, *selective sampling* and *pool-based sampling*. Membership queries algorithms (Angluin, 1988, 2004) generate new instances in the input space and request these labels from the expert. However, such algorithms may construct unexpected instances which are difficult for human experts to label (Baum & Lang, 1992). The selective sampling algorithm was introduced to overcome this problem (Atlas, 1990; Cohn, 1996). In selective sampling, the learner receives distribution information from the environment and queries the expert on parts of the domain. The learner sequentially draws individual instances and decides whether or not to request its label by evaluating the *region of uncertainty*. The *region of uncertainty* is reduced after each new instance is added; more instances are included if the uncertainty is not reduced efficiently.

Figure 1. In the standard passive learning approaches (as shown in a) the expert needs to annotate all data to feed the passive learner. In active learning (shown in b), the active learner identifies a subset of the most informative data for the expert to annotate

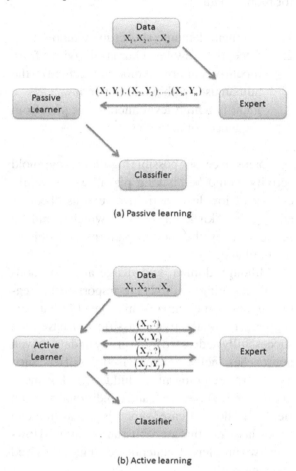

(a) Passive learning

(b) Active learning

Currently, the most popular query strategy in active learning is pool-based sampling, in which samples are requested from an existing closed set of instances. These algorithms share the common assumption that there is a small set of labeled data and a large pool of unlabeled data. The learner generated from the labeled set is applied to evaluate the informativeness measure of instances in the unlabeled pool. The label of the most informative instance is requested, and the instance is then added to the labeled set.

One question is how best to identify the most informative instances for future label requests. Although there are different ways to evaluate the informativeness of unlabeled instances, the main approaches are *query by uncertainty* and *query by committee*. The query by uncertainty algorithm starts by building the learner using the labeled data set. The learner is used to provide a confidence score for each unlabeled instance to probe for instances where the learner is the least certain of the currently classified labels. Those uncertain labels are requested from the experts, and the instances become the members of labeled data. This process repeats until the learner is confident about all of the unlabeled data. Query by uncertainty is probably the most straightforward approach and has been demonstrated in several real-world applications (Arikan, Forsyth, & O'Brien, 2003; Chang, Tong, Goh, & Chang, 2005; Tong & Chang, 2001).

An alternative query strategy is the query by committee algorithm. The essential idea behind this approach is to narrow the possible hypotheses in the *version space* (the set of classifiers consistent with the training set) (Mitchell, 1982). A committee of classifiers is generated from labeled data to evaluate the unlabeled data. The instance with the most classifier disagreement is deemed to be the most informative instance. As shown in Figure 2, by querying new labels, the version space narrows to reduce the number of possible hypotheses. Therefore, the optimal learner will be reached once there are no disagreements among hypotheses learned with all the instances.

Active learning has been successfully applied to many classification problems. Tong demonstrated the use of Support Vector Machines (SVMs) to construct pool-based active learners for both text classification (Tong & Koller, 2002) and image retrieval (Tong & Chang, 2001). In the binary classification problem, it is assumed that the most informative instances should split the version space into two equal parts; this formula-

Figure 2. Version space for rectangle hypotheses in two dimensions. Assume the triangles are positive samples and the circles are negative samples. All rectangles agree with those training samples and are possible hypotheses in the version space.

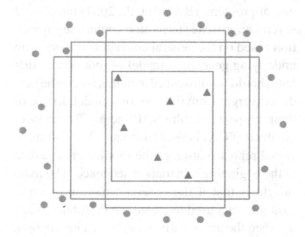

tion can also be extended to multi-class classification. Several new strategies have been proposed for evaluating the informativeness of unlabeled data (e.g., Chang et al., 2005). Also, (Wang, Chan, & Zhang, 2003) proposed a new bootstrapping strategy for SVM active learning.

However, many research issues remain. First, in most applications, the evaluations of the unlabeled data are greedy and myopic. Negligence of the global distribution of data may cause the "best" identified learner to converge to a locally optimal hypotheses. A second problem is that the uncertainty sampling is inherently "noise-seeking" and may take a long time to converge. Hierarchical clustering approaches such as (Dasgupta & Hsu, 2008) have been devised to ameliorate some of these problems. The unlabeled data is used to perform a hierarchical clustering in which leaves on the tree are pruned or grown, depending on whether the leaf is pure or mixed. This clustering approach provides the learner with more global information about the data and avoids the tendency of the learner to converge to local maxima.

Motion Capture Segmentation

In our work, we apply active learning toward the problem of segmenting motion capture data. Here we discuss other strategies that have been applied to that problem. (Barbic et al., 2004) introduced several approaches to motion capture segmentation based on the general concept that there is an underlying generative model of motion and that cuts should be introduced at points where the new data diverges from the previous model. In one of their proposed methods, Principal Component Analysis (PCA) is used to create a lower-dimensional representation of the motion capture data at the beginning of a motion sequence. The main insight is that if the observed motion diverges from the data used to create the PCA basis, such as when the actor starts to perform a new action, then projecting the data of the new action using the old model will lead to large reconstruction errors. The moment that reconstruction errors increase quickly will occur at or near action boundaries.

However, in practice this approach leads to several problems. The method relies on building the PCA basis with frames from the current action, which requires about 300 frames or 2.5 secs of data. Unfortunately in our dataset, action changes can occur within that time frame, yielding a mixed basis capable of representing both actions without large reconstruction errors. Hence this technique cannot be used to accurately segment datasets with many short duration actions. Additionally, since PCA is a completely unsupervised approach, it is unable to distinguish between an activity that consists of multiple actions and boundaries between two semantically unrelated activities.

In cases where user labels can be easily obtained, segmentation can be done in a completely supervised fashion using interactive SVMs to label the data (Arikan et al., 2003). Initially, users label a small training set of data. Then with kernel function Φ, the SVM classifier maps the training data into a high dimensional space which makes the data linearly separable. Since the partition hyperplane may not fit the unlabeled data, the user can add new labels to the training set and retrain the classifier. The method strives to balance classification accuracy and the user's labeling workload. However, their selection of new samples are based on the empirical judgment of the user and therefore susceptible to human error.

Our approach draws from both these methods, using an unsupervised PCA segmentation to initialize the clustering and a semi-supervised method to train the SVM classifiers. Unlike the interactive SVM segmentation proposed by (Arikan et al., 2003), our approach utilizes the unlabeled data sets in the initial training. In the second phase, we automatically determine which instances from the unlabeled data are most useful to solicit labels from the user in the next iteration. Thus, the user is freed from selecting unlabeled samples and merely needs to label a small number of informative instances; this eliminates human bias and aims to reduce the amount of data that requires manual attention.

Conditional Random Fields

A number of supervised learning frameworks have been used to recognize low-level human activities from repetitive patterns of motion. In addition to support vector machines, we have experimented with the use of Conditional Random Fields (CRF). Conditional Random Fields (CRFs) are undirected graphical models $G = (V, E)$ that represent the conditional probabilities of a label sequence $\mathbf{y} = \{y_1, ..., y_T\}$, when given the observation sequence $\mathbf{x} = \{x_1, ..., x_T\}$. When conditioned on $\mathbf{x}$, the label y_i holds the Markov property

$$p(y_i \mid \mathbf{y}_{G \setminus i}, \mathbf{x}) = p(y_i \mid \mathbf{y}_{N_i}, \mathbf{x})$$

where $\mathbf{y}_{N_i}$ represents all the neighborhoods that connect to y_i. The Hammersley-Clifford Theorem tells us that this equation is equivalent to $p(\mathbf{y} \mid \mathbf{x}) = \frac{1}{Z(\mathbf{x})} \prod_{c \in C(\mathbf{y},\mathbf{x})} \psi_c(\mathbf{y}_c, \mathbf{x}_c)$ if the graphical models G obey the Markov assumption, where $\psi_c(\mathbf{y}_c, \mathbf{x}_c)$ is the nonnegative potential functions of clique c and $Z(\mathbf{x})$ is a normalization constant. For our problem, the labels correspond to activities, such as "chop vegetables", while the observations consist of a set of features computed over the raw data.

Linear chain CRFs are graphical models defined with a linear chain structure such that the current state y_i only relates to the previous state y_{i-1} and the observation $\mathbf{x}_c$. Linear chain CRFs require no assumptions of independence among observations, thus $\mathbf{x}_c$ can be any part of the observation sequence $\mathbf{x}$ and the conditional probability $p(\mathbf{y} \mid \mathbf{x})$ can be written as:

$$p(\mathbf{y} \mid \mathbf{x}) = \frac{1}{Z(\mathbf{x})} \prod_{i=1}^{T} \psi_i(y_{i-1}, y_i, \mathbf{x}, i)$$

where $Z(\mathbf{x}) = \sum_y \prod_{i=1}^{T} \psi_i(y_{i-1}, y_i, \mathbf{x}, i)$ and $\mathbf{x}$ represents observations over the whole sequence.

Since CRFs are log-linear models, the potential function can be written as the linear sum of feature functions as

$$\psi_i(y_{i-1}, y_i, \mathbf{x}, i) = \exp\left(\sum_j w_j f_j(y_{i-1}, y_i, \mathbf{x}, i)\right),$$

where w_j represents the weight corresponding feature $f_j(y_{i-1}, y_i, \mathbf{x}, i)$. The conditional probability can then be calculated as

$$p(\mathbf{y} \mid \mathbf{x}; \mathbf{w}) = \frac{1}{Z(\mathbf{x})} \exp\left(\sum_{i=1}^{T} \sum_j w_j f_j(y_{i-1}, y_i, \mathbf{x}, i)\right)$$

where $Z(\mathbf{x}) = \sum_y \exp\left(\sum_{i=1}^{T} \sum_j w_j f_j(y_{i-1}, y_i, \mathbf{x}, i)\right)$.

Assuming a fully labeled dataset with pairs of training samples

$$(\mathbf{X}, \mathbf{Y}) = \{(\mathbf{x}^{(1)}, \mathbf{y}^{(1)}), ..., (\mathbf{x}^{(N)}, \mathbf{y}^{(N)})\}$$

the CRF parameter vector $\mathbf{w} = \{w_1, ..., w_M\}$ can be obtained by optimizing the sum of conditional log-likelihood $L(\mathbf{Y} \mid \mathbf{X}; \mathbf{w})$.

$$L(\mathbf{Y} \mid \mathbf{X}; \mathbf{w}) =$$
$$\sum_k \log\ p(\mathbf{y}^{(k)} \mid \mathbf{x}^{(k)}; \mathbf{w}) =$$
$$\sum_k \left(\sum_{i=1}^{T} \sum_{f_j \in \mathcal{S}} w_j f_j(y_{i-1}^{(k)}, y_i^{(k)}, \mathbf{x}^{(k)}, i)\right.$$
$$\left.- \log Z(\mathbf{x}^{(k)})\right)$$

The first derivative of the log-likelihood is:

$$\frac{\partial L(\mathbf{Y} \mid \mathbf{X}; \mathbf{w})}{\partial w_j} =$$

$$\sum_k \left(\sum_{i=1}^{T} \sum_{f_j \in \mathcal{S}} f_j(y_{i-1}^{(k)}, y_i^{(k)}, \mathbf{x}^{(k)}, i)\right.$$
$$\left.- \sum_y \sum_{i=1}^{T} \sum_{f_j \in \mathcal{S}} p(\mathbf{y} \mid \mathbf{x}^{(k)}; \mathbf{w}) f_j(y_{i-1}, y_i, \mathbf{x}^{(k)}, i)\right)$$

Since the CRFs log likelihood is convex with respect to the weight vector w, standard optimization methods such as conjugate gradient and limited memory BFGS (Liu & Nocedal, 1989) can be used to discover the weights. In this work, we learn both the set of features $f_j(.)$ and their associated weight parameters w_j, for multi-class classification.

Applications of CRFs

CRFs have been used for a variety of classification problems, including natural language processing (Culotta & McCallum, 2004; Lafferty, McCallum, & Pereira, 2001), computer vision (Kumar & Hebert, 2004; Levin & Weiss, 2006; Plath, Toussaint, & Nakajima, 2009; Tappen, Liu, Adelson, & Freeman, 2007), human activity recognition (Liao, Fox, & Kautz, 2007; Sminchisescu, Kanaujia, Li, & Metaxas, 2005; Vail, Veloso, & Lafferty, 2007) and bioinformatics (Fu, Ray, & Xing, 2009).

However, effective learning and inference of CRFs remain challenging problems. If the optimization cost function is nonlinear and nonconvex, learning and inference of CRFs is often implemented with sampling-based algorithms that require a long time to converge. However, recent work by (Levin & Weiss, 2006) showed the use of first order approximation to efficiently estimate conditional likelihood. For Gaussian CRFs, (Tappen et al., 2007) demonstrated it is possible to perform efficient parameter optimization by minimizing the error in the model MAP solution.

More specifically, linear CRFs have been widely applied to classification and segmentation of sequential data. (Lafferty et al., 2001) demonstrate the use of linear CRFs to solve the label bias problem in natural language processing. The main superiority of linear CRFs is their ability to effectively take advantage of overlapping, non-independent features. For instance, (Fu et al., 2009) empirically evaluated the predictive power of using different feature sets; their experiments indicated that their linear CRF could effectively leverage discriminative features found in alternate feature sets unlike their earlier HMM-based classification system (Lin, Ray, Sandve, Uguroglu, & Xing, 2008). Similarly, (Sminchisescu et al., 2005) found that their CRF-based classifier surpassed an HMM model at an activity recognition task using images and motion capture data sequences with overlapping observation features. In summary, since the linear CRF model permits the utilization of non-independent features, feature generation and selection can dramatically effect classification performance.

Feature Selection

There are three general strategies used in feature selection: *filters*, *wrappers* and *embedded* (Vail, 2008). *Filters* treat feature selection as the preprocessing step, independent from the training stage. *Wrappers* consider all possible combinations of potential features to select the best feature set according to the learning performance. *Embedded* strategies perform feature selection during the training stage and iteratively grow the feature set.

Filters apply heuristic methods, such as correlation, mutual information and information gain (Guyon & Elisseeff, 2003), to select features prior to training. Those methods rank all potential features by evaluating their relevance; features with high relevance scores are used as the feature set for training. It is worth noting that that such methods evaluate potential features only once; no features can be added or eliminated during training, which makes the filter strategy computationally efficient. However, the tradeoff is that the filters may select irrelevant features while ignoring highly relevant features if the heuristics do not perform well in a particular domain.

Wrappers perform an exhaustive search on all possible combination sets of potential features. Every set of features is used to train the model and evaluated with cross-validation (Bishop, 2006). However, the number of combination of feature sets increases exponentially with the number of potential features. Although this strategy avoids *the weakly relevant feature* problem in filters, obviously it is computational inefficient if the feature pool is large.

The *embedded* method can be viewed as a tradeoff between filters and wrappers. This method generates a small set of features for training while leaving other features as candidates for selection. Candidate features are added to the set evaluated by the learning model. The feature set is iteratively grown through adding features with high evaluation scores. This method is more computationally efficient than wrappers and does not rely on potentially fallible heuristics. Currently, many real-world applications are based on embedded methods.

Feature Selection for CRFs

Prior work (Sminchisescu et al., 2005) has examined the relative benefits of using discriminative Conditional Random Fields (CRFs) vs. commonly-used generative models (e.g., the Hidden Markov Models) on diverse activity recognition problems such as video recognition and analyzing Robocup team behavior. The consensus has been that many of features commonly used in activity recognition problems are based on overlapping time windows that nullify the observational independence assumptions of many generative graphical models. However, feature representation and selection does have an impact on both the performance and computational accuracy of CRFs.

Due its resiliency to classification problems arising from non-independent features, CRFs can often leverage arbitrary and complex features derived from some basic features. Unfortunately, the strategy of adding as many features as possible to guarantee no loss of information creates certain problems. First, large feature sets can cause overfitting. Since each feature corresponds to one parameter in the CRF model, a large feature set implicitly means that there is a large set of parameters which can fit the training data perfectly while performing poorly in the test set. Convergence during learning becomes harder with large numbers of weights. (McCallum, 2003) proposed a feature induction method for linear-chain CRFs in which features with the highest conditional likelihood gain are iteratively selected. Initially, the model generates a pool of feature candidates. Each feature candidate is then added to the current feature set to evaluate its contribution to the conditional likelihood of current model. Those features with highest gain are selected as new training features and the CRFs model is re-trained. (Vail & Veloso, 2008; Vail et al., 2007) applied

a similar feature selection framework for robotic activity recognition. Vail's method generates a large pool of complex, overlapping features of robot activities, such as positions, velocities and distances. l_1 and l_2 regularization are applied to reduce feature quantity and speed up the selection process. However, the pool-based feature selection strategy is time consuming, since the conditional likelihood has to be re-calculated with every potential feature at each step, which is not practical if there are a large number of candidate features. Our proposed feature selection method draws from these ideas, but relies on an approximation technique to reduce the computation time.

Motif Discovery

Feature selection enables the selection of the most discriminative features from an initial set of candidate features. For noisy sensor data from inertial measurement units, an open question is which features should be used in the initial candidate set. Unsupervised motif discovery has been demonstrated as a promising technique for identifying and matching imperfect repetitions in time series data; by using motifs as the basis for our CRF features, we can robustly identify subtle patterns of peaks and valleys in the IMU data.

The problem of repeated subsequences in time series spans multiple research areas. Researchers have primarily addressed two problems: (1) initial motif selection criteria (Tanaka, Iwamoto, & Uehara, 2005) and (2) rapid and robust matching (Chiu, Keogh, & Lonardi, 2003). (Lin, Keogh, Lonardi, & Patel, 2002) initially presented a formal definition of *motifs*, the approximately repeated subsequences in time series. Their approach for detecting motifs in time series suffers from certain limitations. A brute force algorithm requires a quadratic number of comparisons corresponding to the length of the time series. (Lin et al., 2002) proposed a triangular inequality approach to improve the time complexity of the comparisons; however their method requires the manually setting of large constant factors which makes it hard to extend to massive databases. Also this approach is sensitive to noise, as demonstrated by the example shown by (Chiu et al., 2003) in which the matching of two subsequences is corrupted if the subsequence has a noisy downward spike. To solve those two issues, (Chiu et al., 2003) proposed a novel motif discovery algorithm to efficiently discover motifs in which the time series is discretized as a symbolic sequences using Piecewise Aggregate Approximation (PAA) (Keogh, Chakrabarti, Pazzani, & Mehrotra, 2001). By switching to a symbolic representation, they achieve some noise reduction. In order to speed up the computation of motif matching, they apply random projection to approximate the comparison of every potential subsequence. (Keogh, 2003) extend this method to finding arbitrarily scaled motifs in a massive time series database.

Another issue is how to generalize single dimensional motif techniques to the problem of detecting and matching motifs in multi-dimensional data (Vahdatpour, Amini, & Sarrafzadeh, 2009). (Tanaka et al., 2005) propose the use of a Minimum Description Length (MDL) principle to extract motifs from time series data. Principal Component Analysis (PCA) is then applied to synchronize motifs in multidimensional time series data. (Vahdatpour et al., 2009) demonstrated a graph clustering approach for grouping single dimensional motifs to solve the synchrony issue. In our work, we identify and match motifs in each dimension separately and use the conditional random field to learn the linkage between motif occurrences across different dimensions and action class labels.

Motif discovery is a powerful tool for analyzing time series data delivered by wearable sensors and has been employed in wearable systems such as SmartCane (Wu et al., 2008) and SmartShoe (Dabiri, Vahdatpour, Noshadi, Hagopian, & Sarrafzadeh, 2008) to identify activities based on accelerometers, gyros and press sensor data. String-matched activity templates have been used to recognize continuous activities in a car assembly scenario (Stiefmeier, Roggen, Ogris, Lukowicz, & Tröster, 2008; Stiefmeier, Roggen, & Troster, 2007).

(Minnen, Starner, Essa, & Isbell, 2007) used motifs in conjunction with HMMs to distinguish six arm techniques from a single IMU, but the assumption was made that each action could be characterized by a single six-dimensional motif. Their work synthesizes several existing approaches to estimate the hidden location probability and motif model parameters. First, the algorithm generates a pool of candidate motifs and selects the best motifs based on their scores of informative-theoretic criterion. Then the seed motifs are refined by splitting different motifs or merging similar motifs. Finally a Hidden Markov Model (Rabiner, 1989) is built with those seed motifs and corresponding occurrences are detected by decoding the HMM. In contrast, our data is substantially more complicated (full body data generated from from five IMU sensors) and our action set is composed of 14 unscripted actions performed during a cooking task (e.g., "stir brownie mix", "pour mix in pan", "get fork", "break eggs", and "pour oil").

MAIN THRUST

In this section, we describe the techniques we employ to make learning sample-efficient and to select the best set of features for a given motion dataset.

Sample Efficiency through Active Learning

In the initial phase, our SVM classifiers are initialized with a small set of training data from the unsupervised clustering. During active learning, the classifiers are iteratively trained by having the users provide labels for a small set of automatically selected samples. Although the classifiers can be initialized by having the user provide labels for randomly sampled frames, we demonstrate that we can improve on that by selectively querying and propagating labels using a clustering approach.

Data Clustering

Several methods have been proposed to cluster data in geometric space (Sindhwani, Niyogi, & Belkin, 2005; Zhou, Torre, & Hodgins, 2008). Since the motion segmentation problem is based on continuous time data sequences, it is possible to base the clustering on temporal discontinuities in the data stream. We use the PCA segmentation approach (Barbic et al., 2004) outlined in the previous section to provide a coarse initial segmentation of the data.

Each raw motion capture frame can be expressed as a pose vector, $\mathbf{x} \in \Re^d$, where $d = 56$. This high-dimensional vector can be approximated by the low-dimensional feature vector, $\theta \in \Re^m$, using the linear projection:

$$\theta = \mathbf{W}^T (\mathbf{x} - \mu)$$

where $\mathbf{W}$ is the principal components basis and μ is the average pose vector, $\mu = \dfrac{1}{N} \sum_{i=1}^{N} \mathbf{x}_i$. The projection matrix, $\mathbf{W}$, is learned from a training set of $N = 300$ frames of motion capture data. $\mathbf{W}$ consists of the eigenvectors corresponding to the m largest eigenvalues of the training data covariance matrix, which are extracted using Singular Value Decomposition (SVD). Transitions are detected using the discrete derivative of reconstruction error; if this error is more than 3 standard deviations from the average of all previous data points, a motion cut is introduced.

We found that this method provides a better starting point than traditional unsupervised clustering methods, such as k-means, which do not consider temporal information. Many of the clustering errors generated by the coarse segmen-

tation are detected by pruning clusters based on a small set of labels solicited from the user. We ask the user to label the endpoints of the coarse segmentation and perform a consistency check on the labels; if both endpoints have the same label, the segment is potentially pure; however if the labels of the endpoints disagree, we add a new cut in the middle of the segment and query the user for the label of that point. Clusters shorter than a certain duration (1% of total sequence length) are eliminated from consideration. The remaining clusters are used to initialize the support vector machine classifiers; labels from the end points are propagated across the cluster and the data is used to initialize the SVMs. This process requires the user to label only 20-30 frames.

Active Learning

The clusters created by the coarse PCA segmentation, and refined with the user queries, are used to train a SVM classifier with both labeled and unlabeled samples. Semi-supervised support vector machines are regarded as a powerful approach to solve the classification problem with large data sets. Learning a semi-supervised SVM is a non-convex quadratic optimization problem; there is no optimization technique known to perform well on this topic (Chapelle, Sindhwani, & Keerthi, 2008). However, our solution is a little different to the traditional methods based on linear or non-linear programming. Instead of searching for the global maximum solution directly, we use a simple optimization approach which may not identify the optimal margin hyperplane but will help the classifier decide which unlabeled samples should be added into the training set to improve the classification performance. We then query the user for the class labels of each of the selected samples and add them back to the training set. Suppose the labeled samples are denoted by $\mathbf{L} = \{x_1, x_2, ..., x_l\}$ and the unlabeled samples are $\mathbf{U} = \{x_{l+1}, x_{l+2}, ..., x_n\}$, the SVM classification problem can be represented as finding the optimal hyperplane with labeled samples that satisfies the equation:

$$\min_{\mathbf{w},b,\epsilon} C\sum_{i=1}^{l}\epsilon_i + \|\mathbf{w}\|_2$$

$$s.t. \quad y_i(\mathbf{w}\cdot\mathbf{x}_i + b) \geq 1 \quad i = 1,...,l$$

where ϵ_i is a slack term such that if $\mathbf{x}_i$ is misclassified and C is the constant of the penalty of the misclassified samples. All possible hyperplanes that could separate the training data as $f(\mathbf{x}_i) > 0$ for $y_i = 1$ and $f(\mathbf{x}_i) < 0$ for $y_i = -1$ are consistent with the version space $\mathcal{V}$. (Tong & Koller, 2002) have shown that the best way to split the current version space into two equal parts is to find the unlabeled sample whose distance in the mapping space is close to the current hyperplane $\mathbf{w}_i$. The description of our method is detailed in Algorithm 1.

The traditional initialization method arbitrarily selects samples to include in the training sets. However, randomly choosing samples may lead to sampling bias which makes the SVM classifier unable to achieve the global maximum. In our approach, the labels of samples in each viable cluster are set as the majority labels of querying

samples. This converts learning a semi-supervised SVM into a classical SVM optimization problem. However, the clustering strategy does not guarantee that the decision boundary is optimal since the clustering step is not reliable. It merely gives a good initial hyperplane; active learning is still required to perfect the solution.

In our experiments, the SVM classifier was implemented with the SVM-KM toolbox using a polynomial kernel (Canu, 2005); multi-class classification is handled using a one vs. all voting scheme. Instead of using a *hard margin* for the SVM, our method relies on a *soft margin* restriction in classification. A hard margin forces both labeled and unlabeled data out of the margin area, whereas the soft margin allows unlabeled samples to lie on the margin with penalties. With limited training samples, we find that the hard margin restriction is so restrictive that it may force the separating hyperplane to a local maximum.

To demonstrate this approach, we used the publicly available Carnegie Mellon Motion Capture dataset (http://mocap.cs.cmu.edu/) collected with a Vicon motion capture system. Subjects wore a marker set with 43 14mm markers that is an adaptation of a standard biomechanical marker set with additional markers to facilitate distinguishing the left side of the body from the right side in an automatic fashion. The dataset

Algorithm 1. The proposed algorithm

Input: The complete data set with labeled set **T** and unlabeled set **U**
Output: The optimal SVMs hyperplane to separate the available data into two groups
Initialization: Calculate the initial hyperplane by using SVMs on the clustering data set **T**;
while *the variation classification hyperplane is not stable* **do**

> Calculate the distance **d** between unlabeled set **U** and the current SVMs hyperplane w_i;
> Query the unlabeled sample x_{l+i} with the smallest distance d_i;
> Manually label the sample x_{l+i};
> Update the labeled set as **T=T** $\cup \{x_{l+i}\}$ and unlabeled set as
> **U=U** \ $\{x_{l+i}\}$;
> Re-train the SVM classifiers w_{i+1} with labeled set **T**;

end

contains a bunch of sequences with different human actions; to evaluate our method we selected 15 sequences that include actions such as running, swinging, jumping, and sitting. The first baseline (C) is trained using data that is sampled at random (with uniform distribution) from the activity sequence. The second (B) is initialized using a random segmentation but employs our proposed margin-based approach for generating instances for the user to label. The third (A) is our proposed approach and employs an unsupervised clustering to initialize the segmentation followed by margin-based sampling for identifying informative active learning query instances.

We evaluate the quality of segmentation using classification accuracy. Figure 3 shows how this accuracy improves with additional training data for each of the methods. Clearly, adding training data in a haphazard manner (C) leads to an inefficient form of active learning. The second method (B) demonstrates the benefits of our margin-based method for selecting queries for active learning. Finally, the accuracy curve for the proposed method (A) shows the boost that

we obtain through intelligent initialization using unsupervised clustering. In comparison to a fully supervised SVM trained with 100 samples, our method achieves the same 95% accuracy with only half the data (40 samples).

Motif Discovery and Feature Selection

When classifying the IMU data, we focused on using motif discovery and feature selection to improve classification accuracy. Also, without feature selection, the time required to train the CRF on the entire motif-based feature set can become prohibitively large.

Our training approach can be described as follows. First, we discover motifs in the data collection, essentially learning a mapping to convert a given local window of IMU data from a multi-dimensional time series signal to a sequence of discrete symbols. Second, we define a series of low-level binary-valued features over motifs and pairs of motifs. From a large pool of candidate features, we select those that are most informa-

Figure 3. Improvement in quality of SVM segmentation as additional labels are acquired using active learning. The proposed method (A) benefits through intelligent initialization and margin-based selection of active learning queries.

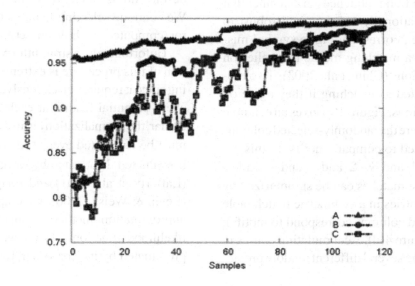

tive using an iterative approach, described below. Next, we learn a Conditional Random Field whose observations are defined over the set of selected features and whose output is over the set of action labels. The incremental feature selection and CRF training are iterated until the training set error converges. The final CRF is then evaluated on the test set. Each of these stages is detailed below.

The first step in motif discovery is to discretize the continuous IMU signal into symbolic subsequences. Figure 3(b) illustrates this process. The raw data $T = \{t_1, t_2, \ldots, t_n\}$ (black line) is transformed into a piecewise continuous representation $S = \{s_1, s_2, \ldots, s_m\}$ (green line) using the Piecewise Aggregate Approximation (PAA) algorithm, which computes an average of the signal over a short window: $s_i = \frac{m}{n} \sum_{j=\frac{n}{m}(i-1)+1}^{\frac{n}{m}} t_j$. This is then mapped to a symbolic representation using "break points" (red lines) that correspond to bins; these are generated so as to separate the normalized subsequences (under a Gaussian assumption) into equalized regions. Thus, a continuous 1-D signal can be represented as a sequence of discrete symbols.

Motif Matching

To compare symbolic sequences in a manner that is both computationally efficient and robust to signal noise (i.e., corresponding to symbol mismatch), we use a matching metric that relies on random projections (Chiu et al., 2003). Two motifs are designated as matching if they agree on k symbol positions. Figure 4(c) gives an example with $k = 2$, where the randomly-selected columns 1 and 3 are used to compare motifs. In this example, motifs 1 and k, 2 and 3, and 4 and j all match. These matches can be summarized by incrementing entries in a symmetric match table (where rows and columns correspond to motifs), as shown in Figure 4(d). Accumulating counts in this manner using several different random projec-

tions can enable us to efficiently match long motifs in a manner that is robust to occasional symbol errors.

Feature Selection for Conditional Random Fields

A key aspect of the proposed method is that we automatically select informative features from a large pool of candidates defined over motifs. As validated in our experiments, this leads to a significant improvement over CRFs trained directly on the raw data. We define three types of binary features over our motifs to form a pool of over 4000 features, from which our goal is to select a small subset that can maximize the conditional log likelihood, without overfitting to the training data.

We adopt the following greedy forward selection procedure, where each feature in the pool is considered in turn and the best feature at each iteration is added. Specifically, we initialize the candidate set C with the pool of available features and the subset of selected features S to be empty. At each iteration, we evaluate every potential feature $f_\lambda \in C$ individually by considering a CRF with $S \cup f_\lambda$ and select the feature that maximizes the gain of log-likelihood $G(\lambda, f_\lambda) = L(\mathbf{Y} \mid \mathbf{X}; \mathbf{w}, \lambda) - L(\mathbf{Y} \mid \mathbf{X}; \mathbf{w})$. This best feature is added to S and removed from C. We continue selecting features until the CRF error (computed on a hold out set) ceases to improve.

Unfortunately, a straightforward implementation of this procedure is extremely time consuming since it requires an expensive computation for every potential feature at each iteration. In particular, the normalization term of the CRF, $Z(\mathbf{x}^{(k)})$ must be calculated every time the gain $G(\lambda, f_\lambda)$ is evaluated. Motivated by work on kernel CRFs (Lafferty et al., 2001) and image segmentation (Levin & Weiss, 2006), we employ a first-order approximation method. Consider that the log likelihood function $L(\mathbf{y} \mid \mathbf{x}; \mathbf{w}, \lambda)$ could be approximated by its first-order Taylor expansion:

Figure 4. Motif discovery (see text for details). Visualization of motif discovery (illustrated in 1D). (a) Raw data; (b) Discretization using PAA and conversion to symbolic sequence; (c) Random projections (shadowed columns) used for projection; (d) Recorded collisions in the collision matrix.

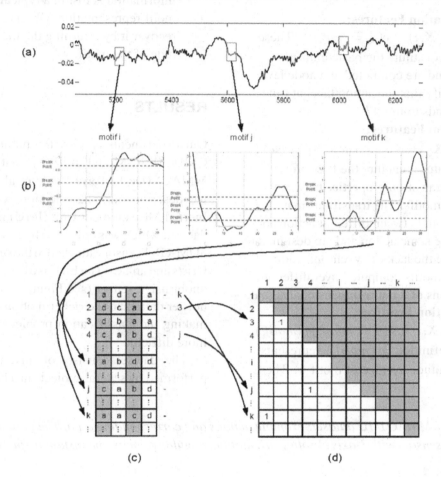

In this equation, the second term can be expressed as:

$$\frac{\partial L(\mathbf{Y} \mid \mathbf{X}; \mathbf{w}, \lambda)}{\partial \lambda}\Big|_{\lambda=0} = E[f_\lambda, \lambda] - \tilde{E}[f_\lambda, \lambda]$$

where

$$\tilde{E}[f_\lambda, \lambda] = \sum_k \sum_{i=1}^{T} f_\lambda(y_{i-1}^{(k)}, y_i^{(k)}, \mathbf{x}^{(k)}, i)$$

represents the empirical expectation and

$$E[f_\lambda, \lambda] = \sum_k \sum_{i=1}^{T} \sum_{y'} p(y' \mid \mathbf{x}^{(k)}, \mathbf{w}, \lambda) f_\lambda(y_{i-1}, y_i, \mathbf{x}^{(k)}, i)$$

is the model expectation. Employing this approximation achieves significant computational benefits in practice.

Our proposed method is agnostic to the choice of features. Motivated by (Vail & Veloso, 2008), we employ the following three types of features. In our case, these are computed over motif patterns rather than the raw data, and all are two-valued features. The function $\delta(.)$ is 1 if its argument is true and 0 otherwise.

1. **Identification Features:**

   $f(y_{i-1}, y_i, \mathbf{X}, i) = \delta(y_i = motif_k)$. These features constitute the basic units of actions and are computed at a node level. They verify that the action label at time t corresponds to motif k.

2. **Transition Features:**

   $f(y_{i-1}, y_i, \mathbf{X}, i) = \delta(y_{i-1} = motif_j)\delta(y_i = motif_k)$. These features capture the first-order Markov transition properties between adjacent motifs. The transitions may appear both between different actions or within the same action and are designed to overcome the lack of synchronization between motifs computed over different dimensions of a multi-dimensional signal.

3. **Observation Features:**

   $f(y_{i-1}, y_i, \mathbf{X}, i) = \delta(y_i = motif_k)g_i(motif_k)$. In this definition, $g_i(motif_k)$ represents the magnitude average of motif k. These

features make the magnitude information for a motif available to the CRF; that information is lost in a typical symbolic motif representation. Observation features recover it by returning the mean magnitude of the motif.

RESULTS

Our experiments employ the publicly-available CMU Multi-Modal Activity Dataset (CMU-MMAC) (De la Torre Frade et al.,2008). Here we describe our classification results on the Inertial Measurement Unit (IMU) portion of the dataset, which was collected by five MicroStrain 3DM-GX1 sensors attached to the subject's waist, wrists and ankles. The IMU is a cost-effective and unobtrusive sensor (see Figure 5) but generates noisier data than the richer motion capture data, making the classification problem substantially more difficult.

The dataset consists of unscripted recipes performed by several subjects in a kitchen. Thus,

Figure 5. CMU-MMAC IMU dataset: example actions and corresponding data. The plotted data comes from five IMU sensors with 3-axis absolute orientation, angular velocity and instantaneous acceleration.

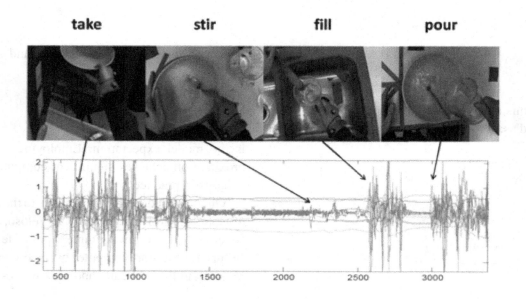

there is considerable variability in the manner in which the task is performed. The data corresponding to a given recipe consists of approximately 10,000 samples collected at 30Hz over a period of about 6 minutes. Each frame includes 3-axis absolute orientation, angular velocity and instantaneous acceleration from each of the five sensors, leading to a 45-dimensional feature vector. Our experiments focus on the recipes that have been manually annotated into a series of actions (e.g., "open fridge" or "stir brownie mix"); these correspond to the "make brownies" task. We downsample the raw data by a factor of 10.

Table 2 summarizes the classification results for 14 actions. We compare the proposed CRF method against several baselines: CRF on raw features, HMM with various parameters and kNN. Clearly, the proposed method outperforms all of these approaches on the challenging test set. Clearly, the feature set results in significant benefits in terms of improved accuracy on the test set. We compared the overall performance of our method against a set of standard classifiers (K-NN, HMMs, and Bayesian networks). Our method outperforms the best performing HMM (25.6% accuracy) and the best overall alternative (k-NN, K=13, 38.22% accuracy).

Table 3 shows a comparison between the CRF with intelligent feature selection and the SVMs trained with the raw features. We also evaluated combining the SVM with temporal filtering to penalize frequent class label changes. The SVM performance is comparable to the best alternative method (k-NN) but does not do as well as the CRF plus feature selection, even with the temporal filtering (see Table 1).

Figure 6 illustrates the segmentation results of different methods on data sequence 1. For the *stir* activity which appears most frequently in all 14 activities, all approaches exhibit good performance compared with the ground truth (red). Moreover, CRF performs better than other two methods on activities *none* and *pour* which account for a high percentage of the total frames in testing. However, all approaches continue to

Table 1. Comparison of average classification accuracy of CRF on 16 sequences (with feature selection) against several baselines

Approach	Parameters	Accuracy
HMM	Dim=8	8.22%
	Dim=16	12.09%
	Dim=32	25.60%
	Dim=full(45)	16.74%
kNN	K=1	34.47%
	K=3	36.52%
CRF	Raw features	30.02%
	proposed	**44.19%**

Table 2. List of actions

1. none	2. close	3. crack	4. open
5. pour	6. put	7. read	8. spray
9. stir	10. switch on	11. take	12. twist off
13. twist on	14. walk		

Table 3. Classification accuracies for our proposed approach (CRF with feature selection) against SVM and SVM plus temporal filtering. Both SVM approaches use the raw IMU features.

Seq No.	CRFs	SVMs	SVM Plus Filter
1	49.48%	50.21%	51.66%
2	33.86%	39.07%	38.92%
3	37.97%	44.74%	50.39%
4	53.66%	37.45%	33.47%
5	32.70%	32.80%	33.52%
6	51.78%	48.71%	48.29%
7	37.75%	8.29%	6.90%
8	43.00%	39.13%	37.38%
9	45.93%	11.13%	13.15%
10	44.90%	49.87%	50.56%
11	48.12%	32.72%	36.83%
12	46.80%	49.35%	48.58%
13	47.39%	18.54%	18.17%
14	45.17%	35.74%	34.99%
15	38.10%	50.05%	49.03%
16	41.92%	33.05%	32.84%
Ave	**44.19%**	**36.23%**	**36.32%**

Figure 6. Segmentation results for testing sequence 1 with all three approaches. The x axis shows the 14 classes and the y axis the frame number of the sequence.

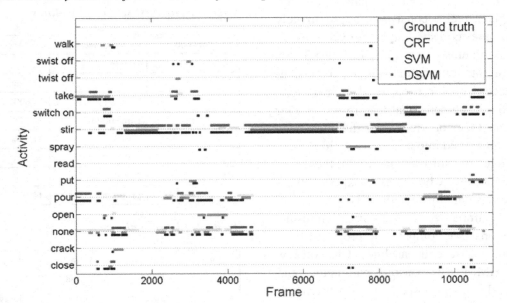

perform relatively poorly in several activities that barely appeared in the testing sequence.

DISCUSSION

Supervised classifiers have achieved good results on numerous activity recognition tasks. However, labeling a large dataset by hand remains a painful and time-consuming task. Hence, the goal of a system builder is often to achieve a reasonable level of performance while minimizing the number of required labels. To address this problem, we bootstrap our classifiers with a small initial set of data from an unsupervised clustering and use active learning to iteratively identify the most informative set of labels. Our procedure is accurate and sample-efficient at classifying motion capture data. In spite of the inaccuracies of the PCA-based unsupervised segmentation, it provides a good initial point for training a set of SVMs that can be improved by margin-based active learning. Although SVM-based active learning has been used for data annotation, experiment results

indicate that our proposed method can converge faster thanks to the initialization.

In applications where less intrusive motion sensors such as inertial measurement units (IMUs) are preferred, our results suggest that attention to feature generation and selection can result in superior classification performance. Motifs are an excellent way to characterize a single dimension of time-series data, and can be rapidly and robustly identified using random projection techniques. In our research, we demonstrate that these single-dimensional motifs are informative features, and that supervised classifiers can be used to learn the linkage patterns between motifs in different dimensions of the IMU data. Since redundant motif features not only increase the computing cost of classification models but also lead to overfitting of the recognition result, we demonstrate the use of feature selection to reduce the large candidate set of motifs.

Although experimental results show that our proposed method is much better than other supervised approaches, the overall classification accuracy on IMU data is still relatively low. This is due to the large amount of transition data in the CMU-MMAC; rather than executing a sequence of prompted actions, CMU-MMAC contains natural sequences where the subjects are simultaneously performing multiple actions while cooking recipes in a kitchen mock-up. Often, there is no obvious interval between two actions, and even human labelers demonstrate a low rate of inter-coder reliability when labeling more complicated sequences of the motion sequences. (Spriggs, De La Torre, & Hebert, 2009) summarizes some of the issues of activity recognition with MMAC database. However, since activities in the CMU-MMAC dataset are highly representative of people's actual household activities, we believe that our work represents a promising step toward achieving sample-efficient human activity recognition for home environments.

CONCLUSION AND FUTURE WORK

Here we present two methods for improving the recognition of human activities from motion data: (1) an active learning approach for sample-efficiency and (2) intelligent feature selection for improving classification accuracy. We demonstrate that our segmentation technique is comparable to manual segmentation while requiring only a fraction of the labels needed by a fully-supervised method. Also by linking our feature representation to the existence of 1-D motifs we can improve on classification performance over the raw IMU data. The CRF efficiently learns the cross-dimensional linkages between motifs, eliminating the need for multi-dimensional motif matching. Since increasing the number of features results in a quadratic increase in the number of parameters, we employ greedy feature selection in conjunction with a first-order approximation method based on reductions of the conditional log-likelihood error to achieve robust recognition while retaining computational feasibility. We

believe that improving the accuracy and sample efficiency of supervised classification methods for human activity recognition will facilitate the usage of human motion data in future living assistance systems.

Our future work focuses on the problem of higher-level action recognition using hierarchical techniques; rather than recognizing low-level actions (e.g., stir or bake), we seek to identify composite action sequences, such as recipe the person is cooking or the chore that they are performing. Hierarchical Bayesian models have been shown good performances on many applications (Liao et al., 2007; Lin et al., 2008). Our goal is to create sample-efficient hierarchical techniques that can learn model parameters from small amounts of data, by leveraging contextual clues such as object and location.

ACKNOWLEDGMENT

This research was supported by the NSF Quality of Life Technology Center under subcontract to Carnegie Mellon and NSF award IIS-0845159.

REFERENCES

Angluin, D. (1988). Queries and concept learning. *Machine Learning*, 2(4), 319–342. doi:10.1007/BF00116828

Angluin, D. (2004). Queries revisited. *Theoretical Computer Science*, 313(2), 175–194. doi:10.1016/j.tcs.2003.11.004

Arikan, O., Forsyth, D. A., & O'Brien, J. F. (2003). Motion synthesis from annotations. *ACM Transactions on Graphics*, 22(3), 402–408. doi:10.1145/882262.882284

Atlas, L., Cohn, D., Ladner, R., El-Sharkawi, M., & Marks, I. (1990). *Training connectionist networks with queries and selective sampling.* Paper presented at the In Advances in Neural Information Processing Systems. New York, NY.

Barbic, J., Safonova, A., Pan, J. Y., Faloutsos, C., Hodgins, J. K., & Pollard, N. S. (2004). *Segmenting motion capture data into distinct behaviors.* Paper presented at the In Proceedings of Graphics Interface. New York, NY.

Baum, E. B., & Lang, K. (1992). *Query learning can work poorly when a human oracle is used.* Paper presented at the In International Joint Conference on Neural Networks. New York, NY.

Bishop, C. M. (2006). *Pattern recognition and machine learning.* New York, NY: Springer.

Canu, S., Grandvalet, Y., Guigue, V., & Rakoto-mamonjy, A. (2005). *SVM and kernel methods Matlab toolbox.* Academic Press.

Chang, E. Y., Tong, S., Goh, K., & Chang, C. (2005). Support vector machine concept-dependent active learning for image retrieval. *IEEE Transactions on Multimedia, 2.*

Chapelle, O., Sindhwani, V., & Keerthi, S. S. (2008). Optimization techniques for semi-supervised support vector machines. *Journal of Machine Learning Research, 9,* 203–233.

Chiu, B., Keogh, E., & Lonardi, S. (2003). *Probabilistic discovery of time series motifs.* Paper presented at the In Proceedings of the Ninth ACM SIGKDD International Conference on Knowledge Discovery and Data Mining. New York, NY.

Cohn, D. A. (1996). Neural network exploration using optimal experiment design. *Neural Networks, 9*(6), 1071–1083. doi:10.1016/0893-6080(95)00137-9

Culotta, A., & McCallum, A. (2004). *Confidence estimation for information extraction.* Paper presented at the In Proceedings of HLT-NAACL. New York, NY.

Dabiri, F., Vahdatpour, A., Noshadi, H., Hagopian, H., & Sarrafzadeh, M. (2008). *Ubiquitous personal assistive system for neuropathy.* Paper presented at the In Proceedings of the Second International Workshop on Systems and Networking Support for Health Care and Assisted Living Environments. New York, NY.

Dasgupta, S., & Hsu, D. (2008). *Hierarchical sampling for active learning.* Paper presented at the In Proceedings of the 25th International Conference on Machine Learning. New York, NY.

De la Torre Frade, F., Hodgins, J., Bargteil, A., Artal, X., Macey, J., & Collado, I. Castells, A., & Beltran, J. (2008). *Guide to the carnegie mellon university multimodal activity (CMU-MMAC) database.* Pittsburgh, PA: Robotics Institute, Carnegie Mellon University.

Fu, W., Ray, P., & Xing, E. P. (2009). DISCOVER: A feature-based discriminative method for motif search in complex genomes. *Bioinformatics (Oxford, England), 25*(12), 321–329. doi:10.1093/bioinformatics/btp230

Guyon, I., & Elisseeff, A. (2003). An introduction to variable and feature selection. *Journal of Machine Learning Research, 3,* 1157–1182.

Keogh, E. (2003). *Efficiently finding arbitrarily scaled patterns in massive time series databases.* Paper presented at the In Proceedings of the Seventh European Conference on Principles and Practice of Knowledge Discovery in Databases. New York, NY.

Keogh, E., Chakrabarti, K., Pazzani, M., & Mehrotra, S. (2001). Dimensionality reduction for fast similarity search in large time series databases. *Knowledge and Information Systems, 3*(3), 263–286. doi:10.1007/PL00011669

Kumar, S., & Hebert, M. (2004). *Discriminative fields for modeling spatial dependencies in natural images.* Paper presented at the In Advances in Neural Information Processing Systems. New York, NY.

Lafferty, J., McCallum, A., & Pereira, F. (2001). *Conditional random fields: Probabilistic models for segmenting and labeling sequence data.* Paper presented at the In Proceedings of the International Conference on Machine Learning. New York, NY.

Levin, A., & Weiss, Y. (2006). Learning to combine bottom-up and top-down segmentation. *International Journal of Computer Vision, 81*(1), 105–118. doi:10.1007/s11263-008-0166-0

Liao, L., Fox, D., & Kautz, H. (2007). Extracting places and activities from gps traces using hierarchical conditional random fields. *The International Journal of Robotics Research, 26*(1), 119. doi:10.1177/0278364907073775

Lin, J., Keogh, E., Lonardi, S., & Patel, P. (2002). *Finding motifs in time series.* Paper presented at the In ACM SIGKDD Workshop on Temporal Data Mining. New York, NY.

Lin, T., Ray, P., Sandve, G., Uguroglu, S., & Xing, E. (2008). *Baycis: A bayesian hierarchical hmm for cis-regulatory module decoding in metazoan genomes.* Paper presented at the Proceedings of the 12th Annual International Conference on Research in Computational Molecular Biology. New York, NY.

Liu, D. C., & Nocedal, J. (1989). On the limited memory BFGS method for large scale optimization. *Mathematical Programming, 45*(1-3), 503–528. doi:10.1007/BF01589116

McCallum, A. (2003). *Efficiently inducing features of conditional random fields.* Paper presented at the Proceedings of the Nineteenth Conference on Uncertainty in Artificial Intelligence. New York, NY.

Minnen, D., Starner, T., Essa, M., & Isbell, C. (2007). *Discovering characteristic actions from on-body sensor data.* Paper presented at the In Proceedings of the 10th International Symposium on Wearable Computers. New York, NY.

Mitchell, T. M. (1982). Generalization as search. *Artificial Intelligence, 18*(2), 203–226. doi:10.1016/0004-3702(82)90040-6

Plath, N., Toussaint, M., & Nakajima, S. (2009). *Multi-class image segmentation using conditional random fields and global classification.* Paper presented at the In Proceedings of the 26th International Conference on Machine Learning. New York, NY.

Rabiner, L. R. (1989). A tutorial on hidden Markov models and selected applications in speech recognition. *Proceedings of the IEEE, 77*(2), 257–286. doi:10.1109/5.18626

Sindhwani, V., Niyogi, P., & Belkin, M. (2005). *Beyond the point cloud: from transductive to semi-supervised learning.* Paper presented at the In Proceedings of the International Conference on Machine Learning. New York, NY.

Sminchisescu, C., Kanaujia, A., Li, Z., & Metaxas, D. (2005). *Conditional random fields for contextual human motion recognition.* Paper presented at the In Proceedings of the 10th IEEE International Conference on Computer Vision. New York, NY.

Spriggs, E. H., De La Torre, F., & Hebert, M. (2009). *Temporal segmentation and activity classification from first-person sensing.* Paper presented at the In Proceedings of IEEE Computer Society Conference on Computer Vision and Pattern Recognition Workshops. New York, NY.

Stiefmeier, T., Roggen, D., Ogris, G., Lukowicz, P., & Tröster, G. (2008). Wearable activity tracking in car manufacturing. *IEEE Pervasive Computing / IEEE Computer Society [and] IEEE Communications Society, 7*(2), 42–50. doi:10.1109/MPRV.2008.40

Stiefmeier, T., Roggen, D., & Troster, G. (2007). *Fusion of string-matched templates for continuous activity recognition.* Paper presented at the In Proceedings of the 11th IEEE International Symposium on Wearable Computers. New York, NY.

Tanaka, Y., Iwamoto, K., & Uehara, K. (2005). Discovery of time-series motif from multi-dimensional data based on mdl principle. *Machine Learning, 58*(2-3), 269–300. doi:10.1007/s10994-005-5829-2

Tappen, M. F., Liu, C., Adelson, E. H., & Freeman, W. T. (2007). *Learning gaussian conditional random fields for low-level vision.* Paper presented at the In Proceedings of IEEE Conference on Computer Vision and Pattern Recognition. New York, NY.

Tong, S., & Chang, E. (2001). *Support vector machine active learning for image retrieval.* Paper presented at the In Proceedings of the ACM International Conference on Multimedia. New York, NY.

Tong, S., & Koller, D. (2002). Support vector machine active learning with applications to text classification. *Journal of Machine Learning Research, 2*, 45–66.

Vahdatpour, A., Amini, N., & Sarrafzadeh, M. (2009). *Toward unsupervised activity discovery using multi-dimensional motif detection in time series.* Paper presented at the Proceedings of the International Joint Conference on Artficial Intelligence. New York, NY.

Vail, D. L. (2008). *Conditional random fields for activity recognition.* Pittsburgh, PA: Carnegie Mellon University.

Vail, D. L., & Veloso, M. M. (2008). *Feature selection for activity recognition in multi-robot domains.* Paper presented at the Proceedings of the National Conference on Artificial Intelligence. New York, NY.

Vail, D. L., Veloso, M. M., & Lafferty, J. D. (2007). *Conditional random fields for activity recognition.* Paper presented at the Proceedings of the Sixth International Joint Conference on Autonomous Agents and Multiagent Systems. New York, NY.

Wang, L., Chan, K., & Zhang, Z. (2003). *Bootstrapping SVM active learning by incorporating unlabelled images for image retrieval.* Paper presented at the In Proceedings of Computer Vision and Pattern Recognition. New York, NY.

Wu, W., Au, L., Jordan, B., Stathopoulos, T., Batalin, M., Kaiser, W., et al. (2008). *The smartcane system: an assistive device for geriatrics.* Paper presented at the Proceedings of the ICST 3rd International Conference on Body Area Networks. New York, NY.

Zhou, F., Torre, F., & Hodgins, J. K. (2008). *Aligned cluster analysis for temporal segmentation of human motion.* Paper presented at the Proceedings of the IEEE Conference on Automatic Face and Gesture Recognition. New York, NY.

KEY TERMS AND DEFINITIONS

Active Learning: Is a form of supervised machine learning in which the learning algorithm is able to interactively query an information source to obtain the desired labels of new data points, in contrast to a passive learner that learns from a fixed set of inputs and known labels.

Activity Recognition: Aims to identify the behaviors of one or more agents from a continuous stream of non symbolic observations along with prior knowledge of the agent's behaviors and information about the environment.

Conditional Random Field (CRF): Is a form of discriminative undirected probabilistic graphical model most often used for labeling or parsing of sequential data, such as natural language text or biological sequences and computer vision.

Feature Selection: Describes the class of search techniques for selecting the best candidate subset of potential attributes for building robust learning models.

Motif: Is an approximately repeated symbolic subsequence in time series data.

Motion Capture: Is performed by recording human movements using a set of ceiling mounted video cameras to track optically distinctive markers and translating that movement onto a digital model.

Support Vector Machine (SVM): Describes a set of related supervised learning methods that use quadratic programming to identify the best hyperplane to separate data into two categories. SVMs typically use a kernel function to map the initial data representation into an alternate space to improve separability.

Chapter 15
Motion and Location–Based Online Human Daily Activity Recognition

Chun Zhu
Oklahoma State University, USA

Weihua Sheng
Oklahoma State University, USA

ABSTRACT

In this chapter, the authors propose an approach to indoor human daily activity recognition that combines motion data and location information. One inertial sensor is worn on the thigh of a human subject to provide motion data while a motion capture system is used to record the human location information. Such a combination has the advantage of significantly reducing the obtrusiveness to the human subject at a moderate cost of vision processing, while maintaining a high accuracy of recognition. The approach has two phases. First, a two-step algorithm is proposed to recognize the activity based on motion data only. In the coarse-grained classification, two neural networks are used to classify the basic activities. In the fine-grained classification, the sequence of activities is modeled by a Hidden Markov Model (HMM) to consider the sequential constraints. The modified short-time Viterbi algorithm is used for real-time daily activity recognition. Second, to fuse the motion data with the location information, Bayes' theorem is used to refine the activities recognized from the motion data. The authors conduct experiments in a mock apartment, and the obtained results prove the effectiveness and accuracy of the algorithms.

DOI: 10.4018/978-1-4666-3682-8.ch015

1. INTRODUCTION

1.1. Motivation

The past decade has seen a steady growth of elderly population. As the baby boomers comprise nearly 26 percent of the U.S. population, they may bring an increased burden on the society in the near future. Compared to the rest of the population, more seniors live alone as the sole occupant of a private dwelling than any other population group. Therefore, helping seniors live a better life is very important and has great societal benefits. In many assisted living systems, there is a great need for automated recognition of human daily activities, which can be used in studying behavior-related diseases and detecting abnormal behaviors such as falling to the floor. Activity recognition is also indispensable for Human-Robot Interaction (HRI) (Yanco & Drury 2004) where a robot companion can understand human's intentions through his/her behaviors.

There are two main types of activity recognition: vision-based (Moeslunda, Hiltonb, & Kruger, 2006) and wearable sensor-based (Najafi, Aminian, Paraschiv-Ionescu, Loew, Bula, & Robert, 2003; Maurer, Smailagic, Siewiorek, & Deisher, 2006). Vision-based systems can observe full human body movement. However, it is very challenging to recognize human activities through images due to the inherited data association problem and the large volume of data. Compared to vision-based systems, wearable sensor-based systems have no data association problem and also have less data to process, but it is uncomfortable and obtrusive to the user if there are many wearable sensors on the human body.

In this paper, we proposed an approach that combines motion data from a single wearable inertial sensor and location information to recognize human daily activities. This approach has the following advantages: first, a single wireless inertial sensor worn by the user for motion data collection can reduce obtrusiveness to the minimum; second, less data is required for activity recognition so that the computational complexity is significantly reduced compared to a pure vision-based system; third, the recognition accuracy can be improved through the fusion of motion and location data.

This paper is organized as follows. The rest of Section 1 introduces the related work in this area. Section 2 describes the hardware platform for the proposed human daily activity recognition system. Section 3 first explains the activity recognition using motion data only, then explains the fusion of motion data and location information to improve the recognition accuracy. The experimental results are provided in Section 4. Conclusions and future work are given in Section 5.

1.2. Related Work

Researchers have made significant progress in the area of human daily activity recognition in recent years. Traditional human daily activity recognition is based on visual information. A typical approach for vision-based recognition has two steps: feature extraction and pattern recognition. In the feature extraction step, activities are analyzed in terms of the trajectories of moving body parts, and features are extracted from each image frame (Taylor, 2000; Parameswaran & Chellappa, 2004). In the pattern recognition step, activities are analyzed using context information of the body parts, which is represented by the extracted features (Park, & Trivedi, 2007; Nam, Wohn, & Kwang, 1999). For a detailed survey of vision-based recognition, please see (Moeslunda, Hiltonb, & Kruger, 2006). However, vision-based activity recognition incurs a significant amount of computational cost, and vision data are usually prone to the influence of environmental factors, such as poor lighting conditions and occlusions.

1.2.1. Wearable Sensor-Based Recognition

Due to the advancement in Microelectromechanical Systems (MEMS) and Very-Large-Scale Integration (VLSI) technologies (Spencer, Ruiz-s, & Kurata, 2004), wearable sensor-based activity recognition has been gaining attention. Inertial sensors are widely used to capture human motion data. For example, Bao *et al.* (Bao, & Intille, 2004) used five small biaxial accelerometers attached to different body parts. Differences in feature values computed from Fast Fourier Transform (FFT) are used to discriminate between different activities. Sensors of other modalities, such as air pressure sensor, microphones, and temperature sensors can be used to provide complementary information to motion data and detect various activities. For example, Sagawa *et al.* (Sagawa, Ishihara, Ina, & Inooka, 1998) discussed a method to classify human moving behaviors using one acceleration sensor and one air pressure sensor attached to the waist. Lee *et al.* (Lee, & Mase, 2001) used a set of wearable sensors including a bi-axial accelerometer, a digital compass, and an infrared light detector to detect detailed walking behaviors. Amft *et al.* (Amft, Junker, Lukowicz, Troster, & Schuster, 2006) investigated the use of force sensitive resistors and fabric stretch sensors that can be easily integrated into clothing. They used these sensors to detect the contractions of arm muscles and showed that the sensors could provide important information for activity recognition.

There are some shortcomings in wearable sensor-based activity recognition. Wearable sensor systems are usually obtrusive and inconvenient to the human subject, especially when there are many wearable sensors. On the other hand, reducing the number of sensors will increase the difficulty of distinguishing the basic daily activities due to the inherited ambiguity. For example, Aminian *et al.* (Aminian, Robert, Buchser, Rutschmann, Hayoz, & Depairon, 1999) used two inertial sensors strapped on the chest and on the rear of the thigh

to measure the chest acceleration in the vertical direction and the thigh acceleration in the forward direction, respectively. They can detect sitting, standing, lying, and dynamic activities from the direction of the sensors. However, they cannot discriminate different types of the dynamic activities, such as walking and other transitional activities. Najafi *et al.* (Najafi, Aminian, Paraschiv-Ionescu, Loew, Bula, & Robert, 2003) proposed a method to detect stationary body postures and walking of the elderly using one inertial sensor attached to the chest. Wavelet transform was used in conjunction with a kinematics model to detect different postural transitions and walking periods during daily physical activities. Because this method has no error correction function, a mis-detection of a postural transition will cause accumulative errors in the recognition. In addition, they did not recognize activities in real-time.

1.2.2. General Algorithms for Daily Activity Recognition

To recognize human daily activities, many solutions have been developed over the years, including the heuristic analysis methods (Aminian, Robert, Buchser, Rutschmann, Hayoz, & Depairon, 1999), the discriminative methods (Mitchell, 1997; Lowd, & Domingos, 2005), the generative methods (Rabiner, 1989), and some combinations of them (Lester, Choudhury, Kern, Borriello, & Hannaford, 2005). Heuristic analysis methods require intuitive analysis on the raw sensor data or the features from data, and the characteristics may be different for individual human subjects. Discriminative methods and generative methods are both machine learning algorithms and the parameters can be trained using data from different human subjects. The combination of different methods can balance efficiency and accuracy and improve the performance.

In this paper, we proposed a method which combines a wearable inertial sensor and a motion capture system to realize human daily activity recognition. Our system uses only a single inertial sensor worn on the human body to reduce the obtrusiveness while the motion capture system is used to provide the location information. Our approach has two phases. We first recognize the activities using the motion data only. Then, the location information is integrated to improve the recognition accuracy in a Bayesian framework.

2. HARDWARE PLATFORM OVERVIEW

Our proposed hardware platform for human daily activity recognition is shown in Figure 1. We use one inertial sensor attached to the thigh to collect the motion data and transfer them to the server PC. The cameras in the optical motion capture system are used to provide location information. The wearable inertial sensor is synchronized with the location data from the motion capture system. Thus, minimum setup of the wearable sensor system is combined with the motion capture system to facilitate human daily activity recognition. The single sensor setup significantly reduces the

obtrusiveness to the human subject. In real life, the motion sensor can be put in the pocket of user's pants. The motion capture system provides real-time location coordinates of the human subject rather than raw video data, which reduces the computational complexity significantly.

2.1. Hardware Setup for Motion Data Collection

Since the position to attach the sensor is very important to activity recognition (Maurer, Smailagic, Siewiorek, & Deisher, 2006), we put the sensor on different parts of the human body and found that the thigh is the best location for activity recognition. As shown in Figure 1, a wearable motion sensor developed from a commercial VN-100 (VectorNav Technologies LLC, 2011) module is attached to the right thigh of the human subject to collect motion data. The motion sensor can sense the 3D orientation, 3D acceleration, and 3D angular velocity at a rate of 20 Hz and transfer the data to a desktop computer through the XBee Module (Digi International Inc. 2011). In the experiments, we find that for most daily

Figure 1. The overview of the hardware platform for human daily activity recognition

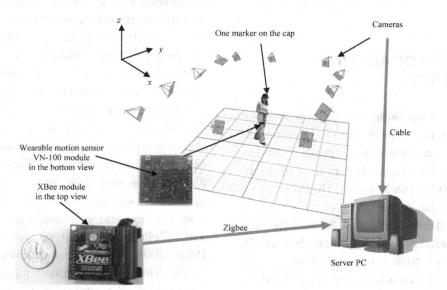

activities, the angular velocity exhibits similar properties as the acceleration. Therefore, we only collect the 3D acceleration as the raw data, which is represented as $D = [a_x, a_y, a_z]$, where a_x, a_y and a_z are the acceleration along direction of x, y and z, respectively.

2.2. Hardware Setup for Location Tracking

The OptiTrack motion capture system from Natu-ralPoint, Inc. (NaturalPoint, Inc. 2011) is used to capture the location of the human subject through the marker attached to a baseball cap. The track-ing software runs on the server PC to calculate the position of the marker in real-time. The 3D location of the marker can be resolved with mil-limeter accuracy. The real-time data streaming rate is 100 fps. We down-sample the location data to synchronize with the wireless motion sensor data. The output coordinate in the 2D (x-y) space gives us the location of the human subject, which can be represented as $P = [x, y]$.

In real applications, we can use regular cameras or Radio-Rrequency Identification (RFID) instead of the OptiTrack system to calculate the location information, which has much less computational cost compared to activity recognition from raw video data.

3. OVERVIEW OF ACTIVITY RECOGNITION

The overview of our online recognition software is shown in Figure 2. The PC runs the recognition program which consists of two threads. First, the data sampling thread collects data from the body sensor and the OptiTrack system. The PC receives a package via the Zigbee receiver. The location data is sampled at the same time. Second, the data processing thread processes the sampled data in two steps: body activity recognition from a single motion sensor and fusion of motion and location data. This thread is triggered every one second.

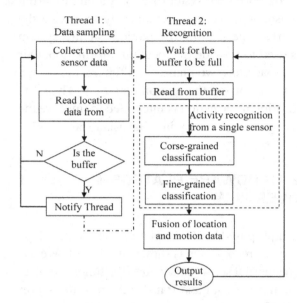

Figure 2. The overview of the activity recognition

The activity recognition has a training mode. During the training, the computer accepts con-nection from a PDA to provide labels as the ground truth. The label is recorded when the user manu-ally pushes a button on the PDA.

3.1. Activity Recognition Using a Single Motion Sensor

We first develop a single wearable sensor-based activity recognition algorithm without considering the location information. Eight daily activities are recognized: *sitting, standing, lying, walking, sit-to-stand, stand-to-sit, lie-to-sit, and sit-to-lie*. The activities can be divided into two types: stationary and motional activities.

There are two steps in our proposed recognition algorithm: (1) coarse-grained classification and (2) fine-grained classification. The coarse-grained classification step combines the outputs of two neural networks and produces a rough classifica-tion. The fine-grained classification step applies a modified short-time Viterbi algorithm (Bloit, & Rodet, 2008) to realize real-time activity recogni-tion with the sequential constraints modeled by an hidden Markov model (HMM) (Rabiner, 1989), and generates the detailed activity types.

3.1.1. Neural Network-Based Coarse-Grained Classification

In the neural network-based coarse-grained classification, two neural networks are applied to discriminate stationary activities and motional activities instead of simply using a threshold on the sensor data. In a threshold-based discrimination method, a function combining features has to be manually established. This function is heuristic and not sufficient for classification. On the contrary, the neural network is a combination of multiple thresholds for different features. Through the training of the neural networks, the weights and biases can be optimized to get a good neural network for classification. Furthermore, the neural network can obtain hidden information from the training data and make a good combination of features to classify gestures and non-gesture movements.

3.1.1.1. Feature Extraction

In the coarse-grained classification module, feature extraction is applied on the raw sensor data. We process the raw data using a buffer of 20 data points, which correspond to one second. Let B_m represent data in the buffer at time index m in realtime processing, $B_m = [D_1, D_2, ..., D_{20}]$.

The output of feature extraction is F_m, which includes the means and variances of the 3D acceleration.

$$F_m = [\mu_m, \sigma_m^2] = [\mu_x, \mu_y, \mu_z, \sigma_x^2, \sigma_y^2, \sigma_z^2] \quad (1)$$

where $\mu_m = [\mu_x, \mu_y, \mu_z]$, and $\sigma_m^2 = [\mu_x, \mu_y, \mu_z]$.

3.1.1.2. Neural Networks

Two neural networks NN1 and NN2 are applied on μm and σm2, respectively. NN1 is used to detect the stationary state of the thigh, with 0 for horizontal and 1 for vertical. Both NN1 and NN2 have a three-layer structure. Let T1 be the output of NN1:

$$T_1 = \text{hardlim}(\text{f}^2(W_1^2 \, \text{f}^1(W_1^1 \mu_m + b_1^1) + b_1^2) - 0.5) \quad (2)$$

where W_1^1, W_1^2, b_1^1 and b_1^2 are the parameters of NN_1, which can be trained using the labeled data. The function f¹ and f² are chosen as the Log-Sigmoid function so that the performance index of the neural network is differentiable and the parameters can be trained using the back-propagation method (Hagan, Demuth, & Beale, 1996).

The neural network NN_2 is used to detect the intensiveness of the motion of the thigh, with 0 for stationary and 1 for movement. Let T_2 be the output of NN_2:

$$T_2 = \text{hardlim}(\text{f}^2(W_2^2 \, \text{f}^1(W_2^1 \sigma_m^2 + b_2^1) + b_2^2) - 0.5) \quad (3)$$

where W_2^1, W_2^2, b_2^1 and b_2^2 are the parameters of NN_2, which can also be trained using the labeled data.

3.1.1.3. Fusion of the Outputs of Neural Networks

A fusion function integrates T_1 and T_2 and produces O as the coarse-grained classification result. The fusion of neural networks categorizes the activities into three groups: A_m, A_{hs}, and A_{vs}. The fusion rules are shown in Table 1. The output of the neural network fusion is: (1) $O \in A_m$ if and only if $T_2 = 1$ (NN_2 outputs *strong movement*): *walking* and *transitional activities*; (2) $O \in A_{hs}$ if and only if $T_1 = 0$ and $T_2 = 0$ (NN_1 outputs *horizontal* and NN_2 outputs *stationary*): *lying* and *sitting*. (3) $O \in A_{vs}$ if and only if $T_1 = 1$ and $T_2 = 0$ (NN_1 outputs *vertical* and NN_2 outputs *stationary*): *standing*.

3.1.2. HMM-Based Fine-Grained Classification

Due to the inherited ambiguity, it is hard to distinguish the detailed activities from the result of the coarse-grained classification. Some prior knowledge can be used to help model the sequential constraints. Because human daily activities usually exhibit certain sequential constraints, the

Table 1. Neural networks fusion rules

NN_2	NN_1	
	horizontal	vertical
stationary activities	A_{hs}: *lying* and *sitting*	A_{vs}: *standing*
motional activities	A_m: *walking* and *transitional activities*	

next activity is highly dependent on the current activity. Therefore, we can utilize this sequential constraint to distinguish the detailed activities. We use a first order Hidden Markov Model (HMM) to model such constraints and solve it using a modified short-time Viterbi algorithm.

3.1.2.1. Hidden Markov Model for Sequential Activity Constraints

We assume that the human subject always exhibits a stationary activity for a short time between motional activities, which is usually true for most people. For example, the human subject rises from the chair, stands for a short time, and then starts to walk. The *standing* activity separates the two motional activities. The sequential constraints in fine-grained classification step are referred to as the transitions between different activities. Let S_i be the ith activity in a sequence. S_i depends on its previous activity S_{i-1} and also determines its following activity S_{i+1} in a probabilistic sense. Therefore, we model the activity sequence using an HMM.

An HMM can be used for sequential data recognition. It has been widely used in speech recognition and handwriting recognition (Rabiner, 1989). HMMs can be applied to represent the statistical behavior of an observable symbol sequence in terms of a network of states. An HMM is characterized by a set of parameters $\lambda = (M, N, A, B, \pi)$, where M, N, A, B, and π are the number of distinct states, the number of discrete observation symbols, the state transition probability distribution, the observation symbol probability distributions in each state, and the

initial state distribution, respectively. Generally $\lambda = (A, B, \pi)$ is used to represent an HMM with a pre-determined size.

In our implementation, the HMM has eight different states ($M = 8$), which represent eight different activities, and three discrete observation symbols ($N = 3$), which stand for three distinct outputs (A_{hs}, A_{vs} and A_m) of the coarse-grained classification module. The parameters of the HMM can be trained by observing the activity sequence of the human subject for a long period of time. The top part of Figure 3 shows an example of the activity sequence, where each circled S_i is the activity state and O_i is the observed symbol obtained through the fusion of the two neural networks.

3.1.2.2. Online State Inference Using Short-Time Viterbi Algorithm

For the standard Viterbi algorithm (Viterbi, 1967), the problem is to find the best state sequence when given the observation sequence $O = \{O_1, O_2, ..., O_n\}$ and the HMM parameters (A, B, π). In order to choose a corresponding state sequence which is optimal in some meaningful sense, the standard Viterbi algorithm considers the whole observation sequence, which does not fit for real-time implementation. Therefore, we propose the modified short-time Viterbi algorithm for online daily activity recognition. Figure 4(a) shows the fine-grained recognition. The observation O_i is obtained from the coarse-grained classification step. In this step, the detailed types need to be decoded, which is a mapping from one of three distinct observation values to one of eight activities.

Let $W(i,\xi)$ be the ith sliding window on the observation sequence, where ξ ($\xi \geq 3$) is the length of the sliding window.

$$W(i, \xi) = \begin{cases} \{O_1, O_2, ..., O_i\}, & \text{when } i < \xi \\ \{O_{i-\xi+1}, O_{i-\xi+2}, ..., O_i\}, & \text{when } i \geq \xi \end{cases}$$

$$(4)$$

Figure 3. An example of activity sequence decoded by short-time Viterbi for HMM

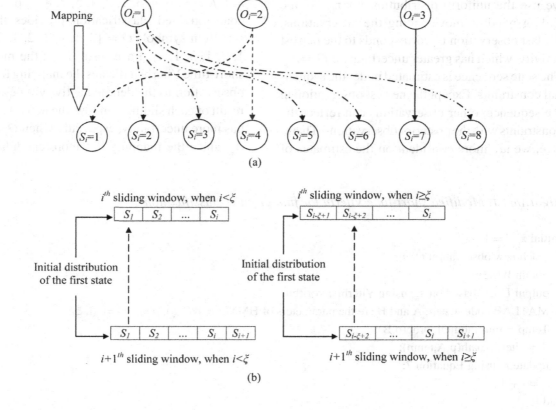

Figure 4. (a) The decoding of activities; (b) the initial state corresponding to different sliding windows

The result from the short-time Viterbi algorithm is $U(i,\xi)$ as follows,

$$U(i,\xi) = \begin{cases} \{S_1, S_2, ..., S_i\}, & \text{when } i < \xi \\ \{S_{i-\xi+1}, S_{i-\xi+2}, ..., S_i\}, & \text{when } i \geq \xi \end{cases}$$

$$(5)$$

$$= \arg\max_{U(i,\xi)} p[U(i,\xi) \mid W(i,\xi), \lambda] \quad (6)$$

In our approach, the initial state distribution is modified and updated with the result of the previous sliding window. In the training phase, we first assume uniform distribution and perform recognition using the short-time Viterbi algorithm. We then summarize the accuracy matrix Ψ for each type of activity, in which each row is used to update the corresponding to the previous result in the testing phase.

Algorithm 1 shows the details of the modified short-time Viterbi algorithm. In the testing phase, we use the uniform distribution for π_0. As the sliding window moves along the observations, the last observation O_i corresponds to the newest activity, which has greater uncertainty if $O_i = A_m$. The state sequence is estimated under the sequential constraints. Except the newest observation in the sequence, other observations can reflect the constraints with the posterior observations. Therefore, we are more confident on the estimates of

the previous activities and the initial state distribution π_i is not a constant matrix, which will be updated with the estimated state sequence for the next sliding window. π_i is the probability of the first activity in the $(i+1)^{th}$ sliding window, or the second activity in the ith sliding window. We use the accuracy matrix Ψ to represent the initial probability distribution, which can be learned in the training phase. Figure 4(b) shows how to find the initial state from the previous sliding window. We update π_i using the following equation:

$$\pi_i(j) = \Psi_{qj}, \quad \text{where } q = \begin{cases} S_1, & \text{when } i < \xi \\ S_{i-\xi+2}, & \text{when } i \geq \xi \end{cases}$$

$$(7)$$

where i is the time index for the sliding window, and j is the index of the state.

We use the example in Figure 3 to illustrate the modified short-time Viterbi algorithm. The human subject made the following activities S = { 7, 8, 7, 6, 4, 3, 1, 2, 4, 5, 7, 8, 7, 6,...}. The coarse-grained classification provides the observation symbols O = {3, 1, 3, 1, 2, 1, 2, 1, 2, 1, 3, 1, 3, 1,...}. Each result from the modified short-time Viterbi indicates the mapping from the observation to the detailed activity types. In the result of each sliding window, the newest activity has more uncertainty, especially when $O_i = 1$ for A_m, since the mapping has more candidates. In

Algorithm 1. Modified short-time Viterbi for fine-grained classification

Initial π_0, $i = 1$;
for each new observation Oi do
   obtain $W(i,\xi)$;
   output $U(i,\xi)$ based on π_{i-1} using Viterbi algorithm.
   MATLAB code, where A and B are the parameters of HMM, $o=W(i, \xi)$; $p=\pi_{i-1}$; $s=U(i, \xi)$;
   Temp = multinomial_prob(o,B);
   S = viterbi_path(p,A,temp);
   update πi using Equation 7;
   i = i + 1;
end for

the gray areas, the short-time Viterbi algorithm gives wrong estimates, which are corrected in the following sliding window.

3.2. Fusion of Motion and Location Data

In indoor environments, human daily activities and locations are highly correlated. Combining the location information and the activity information can improve the accuracy of activity recognition. Given a floor plan of an apartment, we can infer the probability distribution for each specific activity on the 2D map. For example, Figure 5(a) shows the probability distribution of *sitting* and Figure 5(b) shows the probability distribution of *sit-to-stand* in a typical apartment. In both figures, darker colors indicate higher probability. When the location shows the subject is on the sofa, there is much less probability for *walking*. This knowledge can help correct the errors in the single wearable sensor-based activity recognition.

Let $\hat{S}_i$ be the ith estimated activity from the fine-grained classification step and L_i be the corresponding location from the motion capture system. Bayes' theorem can be used to fuse the motion data and the location information to obtain the final results. We utilize a conditional probability distribution function $p(S_i | L_i)$ to represent activity probability distribution given the location information in a layout map. There are two methods to obtain this probability distribution function. First, it can be obtained using human prior knowledge. Second, it can be trained by observing the living pattern of a specific human subject for a sustained period of time, which is more accurate.

We assume that the location measurement is relatively accurate. From Bayes' theorem, the true activity state S_i given the estimated activity and the location L_i can be calculated as follows:

$$p(S_i \mid \hat{S}_i, L_i) \propto p(\hat{S}_i \mid S_i, L_i)p(S_i \mid L_i) \qquad (8)$$

Figure 5. (a) The probability distribution of sitting in the map (b) the probability distribution of sit-to-stand in the map

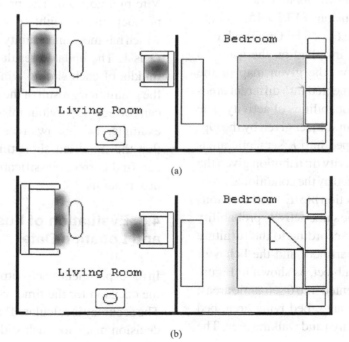

313

Since we do not consider the location in the fine-grained classification step, the activity estimation is independent of the location. Then we have:

$$p(S_i \mid \hat{S}_i, L_i) \propto p(\hat{S}_i \mid S_i)p(S_i \mid L_i) \qquad (9)$$

where $p(\hat{S}_i \mid S_i)$ is the probability of observation distribution for each activity. $p(\hat{S}_i \mid S_i)$ represents the recognition result distribution when the true activity is S_i, which can be learned from the accuracy matrix of the fine-grained activity classification. Finally, the refined activity estimate from the fusion of motion data and location information is obtained as follows,

$$\hat{S}' = \arg \max_{S_i}[p(S_i \mid \hat{S}_i, L_i)] \qquad (10)$$

4. EXPERIMENTAL RESULTS

4.1. Environment Setup

We performed the experiments in a mock apartment, which has a dimension of 13.5×15.8 square feet as shown in Figure 6(a). The OptiTrack motion capture system is installed on the wall. To simplify the calculation, the given map of the mock apartment is segmented into different areas with corresponding probabilities of activity. The coordinate of the human subject given by the OptiTrack system is mapped into K semantic areas $(E_1, E_2, ..., E_K)$. The activity distribution given the area E_q can be represented by the conditional probability distribution function $p(S|E_q)$. All locations in the same area have the same activity probability distribution function. According to the furniture layout of the mock apartment and the behavior pattern of the human subject, as shown in Figure 6(b), the room is segmented into 6 semantic areas: workstation area, sofa area, bed lying area, bed sitting area, bookshelf area and walking area. The

human subject wore the sensor on the right thigh as shown in Figure 1. The location of the head was tracked by the OptiTrack system. Regular daily activities were performed: *standing, sitting, sleeping,* and *transitional activities*. Each data set had a duration of about 6 minutes. We recorded video as the ground truth of activities and locations to evaluate the recognition results.

4.2. Evaluation of the Activity Recognition from Inertial Sensor Only

In the experiment, we have an output decision value for each second. On the server PC, we use a screen capture software to record the recognition results, and compare them with the labeled ground truth recorded from a camera. Figure 7 shows the result from one set of experiments in the mock apartment. In Figure 7 (a), the 3-D acceleration from the sensor indicates stationary and motional activities. Figure 7 (b) shows the coarse-grained classification obtained from the fusion of the two neural networks. Figure 7 (c) shows the processing of the modified short-time Viterbi algorithm. The preliminary result is the number on the right of each sliding window, which has more uncertainty when the observation O_i is 1. The updated result is the number in the middle of each sliding window, which overlaps the preliminary result of the previous window and can correct the previous mis-classification. In this example, the shadow areas in Figure 7 (c) mean that the modified short-time Viterbi algorithm can find correct classifications from the limited observations.

4.3. Evaluation of Fusion of Motion and Location Data

In the experiment, each output is corresponding to the decision for the time window of one second. The accuracy is calculated based on the individual decision made for each sliding window.

Figure 6. (a) The layout of the mock apartment; (b) the segmentation of the room

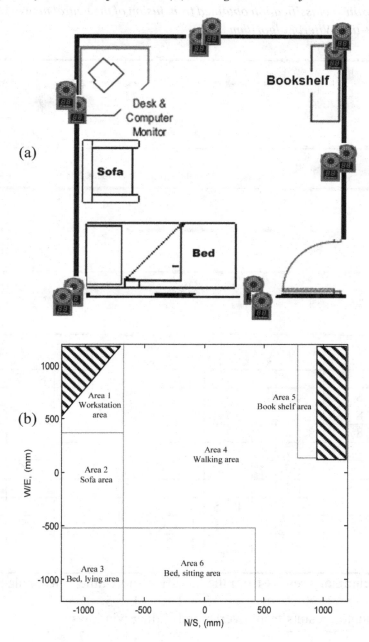

The video of the experiment is synchronized with the output of the activity recognition (Zhu, 2011). Some significant frames are shown in Figure 8. From (a) to (j), the top images are from the video and the bottom figures are from the server PC screen. In the recognition result part of Figure 8, the two plots in the top row of each subfigure are the raw sensor data and the segmented location area, respectively. The two plots in the middle row of each subfigure are the recognition results from the motion data only, and the recognition results from fusion of motion and location data, respectively. The plot in the bottom row of each subfigure is the trajectory of the human subject

Figure 7. The results of the modified short-time Viterbi algorithm. (a) the 3-D acceleration from the sensor; (b) the coarse-grained classification obtained from fusion of the neural networks; (c) the processing of the modified short-time Viterbi algorithm

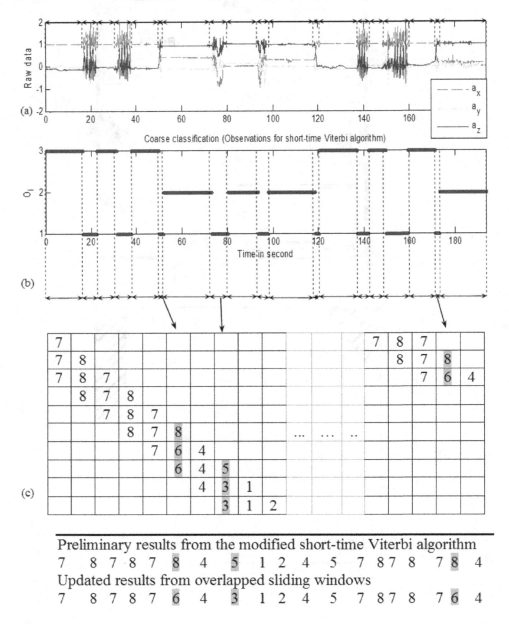

obtained from the motion capture system. In (a), the human subject starts from *standing* in location area 4. Both recognition results are the same. In (b), she goes to area 1 and sits down. In (c), she walks to the bed and sits down. In (d), she lies on the bed. In (e), she sits on the sofa. In (f), she walks to the bookshelf and stands there. In (g), she sits on the sofa and randomly moves her leg. The result from the motion data is *sit-to-lie*, and the following activity is *lying*, which is not correct. The result from the fusion of motion and location data is another transitional activity and the following

Figure 8. Results captured from video and server PC. Labels for activities in the result: (1) lying, (2) lie-to-sit, (3) sit-to-lie, (4) sitting, (5) sit-to-stand, (6) stand-to-sit, (7) standing, (8) walking

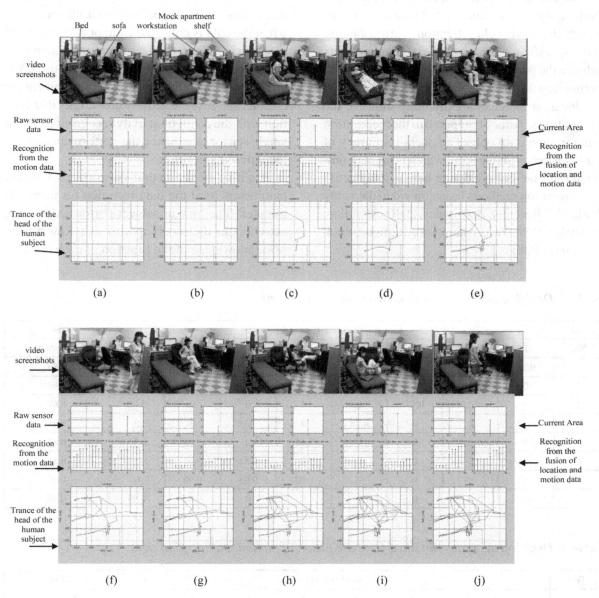

activity is still *sitting*, which is correct. Because the random movement of the leg is not one of the pre-defined activities, it will be recognized as one of the closest activities. However the next stationary activity will still be correct because in this area, the probability of *sitting* is higher than *lying*. In (h) and (i), she is sitting and moving her leg randomly. Fusion of location can correct the error from *lying* to *sitting*. In (j), when she stands up from the bed, the result shows *standing*. The previous errors will not accumulate because the modified short-time Viterbi algorithm can correct the errors in the previous step using the sequential constraints.

The accuracy in terms of the percentage of correct decisions of the two methods is listed in Tables 2 and 3. The values in bold are the percentages of the correct classifications corresponding to the specific types of activities. Other numbers indicate the percentages of wrong classifications. Comparing these two tables, the fusion of motion and location data can significantly improve the recognition accuracy compared to the recognition using motion data only. The overall accuracy of our approach is above 85%, which is higher compared to some recent existing human daily activity recognition methods based on video data only (Brdiczka, Reignier, & Crowley, 2010; Abdullah, & Noah, 2008; Yeo, Ahammad, Ramchandran, & Sastry, 2008).

4.4. Discussion

Since *sitting* and *lying* exhibit similar characteristic when the data is collected from only one inertial sensor, it is difficult to discriminate these activities unless extra channels of information are used. We use the location information as a complementary channel and fuse the activity probability distribution with the result of activity recognition from a single sensor to enhance the performance of the recognition algorithm.

Training of the neural networks and HMM parameters used the data recorded for about 10 minutes. The human subject performed normal activities in the mock apartment following the prior knowledge of the function of each location

Table 2. Decision accuracy obtained from motion data only

Test	Decision Type								Test
No.	1	2	3	4	5	6	7	8	Accuracy
1	**0.80**	0	0	0.20	0	0	0	0	**0.80**
2	0	**0.65**	0.25	0	0	0	0	0.10	**0.65**
3	0	0.25	**0.67**	0	0	0	0	0.08	**0.67**
4	0.22	0	0	**0.78**	0	0	0	0	**0.78**
5	0	0	0	0	**0.85**	0	0.05	0.10	**0.85**
6	0	0	0	0	0	**0.81**	0.07	0.12	**0.81**
7	0	0	0	0	0.07	0.03	**0.90**	0	**0.90**
8	0	0	0	0	0	0	0.02	**0.98**	**0.98**

Table 3. Decision accuracy obtained from the fusion of motion and location data

Test	Decision Type								Test
No.	1	2	3	4	5	6	7	8	Accuracy
1	**0.95**	0	0	0.05	0	0	0	0	**0.95**
2	0	**0.85**	0.15	0	0	0	0	0	**0.85**
3	0	0.10	**0.90**	0	0	0	0	0	**0.90**
4	0.09	0	0	**0.91**	0	0	0	0	**0.91**
5	0	0	0	0	**0.85**	0	0.05	0.10	**0.85**
6	0	0	0	0	0	**0.81**	0.07	0.12	**0.81**
7	0	0	0	0	0.07	0.03	**0.90**	0	**0.90**
8	0	0	0	0	0	0	0.02	**0.98**	**0.98**

area. However, if the human subject does not follow the activity probability distribution in the areas, or even do some abnormal activities, the result will not be improved. The limitation of this approach is that it does not aim to detect falling activities. Since only normal activities in an apartment are modeled in this model, currently we are not focusing on fall detection. Some existing fall detection methods (Perry, Kellog, Vaidya, Youn, Ali, & Sharif, 2009) can update the model and be integrated into our approach.

5. CONCLUSION AND FUTURE WORK

In this paper, we proposed a method to fuse motion data and location information for human daily activity recognition in an indoor environment. One inertial sensor is attached to a thigh of the human subject to provide motion data; while an motion capture system is used to obtain the location information of the human subject. The activity is first recognized using only the motion data from the inertial sensor by combining the neural networks and the modified short-time Viterbi algorithm. Next, Bayes' theorem is used to integrate the location information to refine the recognition result. Our approach has the advantage of reducing the obtrusiveness and the complexity of vision processing, while maintaining high accuracy of activity recognition. We conducted experiments in a mock apartment environment and the accuracy of the real-time recognition is evaluated. In the future, we will combine the location and human activities for Simultaneous Tracking and Activity Recognition (STAR) (Wilson & Atkeson, 2005), which will remove the need of the OptiTrack motion capture system.

ACKNOWLEDGMENT

This project is partially supported by the NSF grant CISE/CNS 0916864 and CISE/CNS MRI 0923238.

REFERENCES

Abdullah, L. N., & Noah, S. A. M. (2008). Metadata generation process for video action detection. In *Proceedings of the International Symposium on Information Technology, ITSim 2008*, (pp. 1–5). ITSim.

Amft, O., Junker, H., Lukowicz, P., Troster, G., & Schuster, C. (2006). Sensing muscle activities with body-worn sensors. In *Proceedings of the International Workshop on Wearable and Implantable Body Sensor Networks*. IEEE.

Aminian, K., Robert, P., Buchser, E. E., Rutschmann, B., Hayoz, D., & Depairon, M. (1999). Physical activity monitoring based on accelerometry: Validation and comparison with video observation. *Medical & Biological Engineering & Computing, 3*, 304–308. doi:10.1007/BF02513304

Bao, L., & Intille, S. S. (2004). Activity recognition from user-annotated acceleration data. [IEEE.]. *Proceedings of PERVASIVE, 2004*, 1–17.

Bloit, J., & Rodet, X. (2008). Short-time viterbi for online hmm decoding: Evaluation on a real-time phone recognition task. In *Proceedings of the IEEE International Conference on Acoustics, Speech and Signal Processing, 2008*, (pp. 2121–2124). IEEE.

Brdiczka, O., Reignier, P., & Crowley, J. L. (2010). Detecting individual activities from video in a smart home. *Lecture Notes in Computer Science, 4692*, 363–370. doi:10.1007/978-3-540-74819-9_45

Digi International Inc. (2011). *Website*. Retrieved from http://www.digi.com/

Hagan, M. T., Demuth, H. B., & Beale, M. H. (1996). *Neural network design*. PWS Publishing Company.

Lee, S., & Mase, K. (2001). Recognition of walking behaviors for pedestrian navigation. In *Proceeding of the 2001 IEEE International Conference on Control Applications*, (pp. 1152–1155). IEEE.

Lester, J., Choudhury, T., Kern, N., Borriello, G., & Hannaford, B. (2005). A hybrid discriminative / generative approach for modeling human activities. In *Proceedings of the International Joint Conference on Artificial Intelligence IJCAI*, (pp. 766–772). IEEE.

Lowd, D., & Domingos, P. (2005). Naive bayes models for probability estimation. In *Proceedings of the 22nd International Conference on Machine Learning*. IEEE.

Maurer, U., Smailagic, A., Siewiorek, D. P., & Deisher, M. (2006). Activity recognition and monitoring using multiple sensors on different body positions. In *Proceedings of the International Workshop on Wearable and Implantable Body Sensor Networks*, (pp. 113–116). IEEE.

Mitchell, T. (1997). Decision tree learning. In *Proceedings of Machine Learning* (pp. 52–78). IEEE.

Moeslunda, T. B., Hiltonb, A., & Kruger, V. (2006). A survey of advances in vision-based human motion capture and analysis. In *Proceedings of Computer Vision and Image Understanding*, (pp. 90–126). IEEE

Najafi, B., Aminian, K., Paraschiv-Ionescu, A., Loew, F., Bula, C. J., & Robert, P. (2003). Ambulatory system for human motion analysis using a kinematic sensor: Monitoring of daily physical activity in the elderly. *IEEE Transactions on Bio-Medical Engineering*, *50*, 711–723. doi:10.1109/TBME.2003.812189

Nam, Y., Wohn, K., & Kwang, H. L. (1999). Modeling and recognition of hand gesture using colored petri nets. *IEEE Transactions on Systems, Man, and Cybernetics. Part A, Systems and Humans*, *29*, 514–521. doi:10.1109/3468.784178

NaturalPoint, Inc. (2011). *Optitrack optical motion capture solutions*. NaturalPoint, Inc.

Parameswaran, V., & Chellappa, R. (2004). View independent human body pose estimation from a single perspective. In *Proceedings of Computer Vision and Pattern Recognition*. IEEE.

Park, S., & Trivedi, M. M. (2007). Multi-person interaction and activity analysis: A synergistic track- and body-level analysis framework. In *Proceedings of Machine Vision and Applications* (pp. 151–166). IEEE. doi:10.1007/s00138-006-0055-x

Perry, J. T., Kellog, S., Vaidya, S. M., Youn, J., Ali, H., & Sharif, H. (2009). Survey and evaluation of real-time fall detection approaches. In *Proceedings of the 6th International Conference on High Capacity Optical Networks and Enabling Technologies*, (pp. 158–164). Piscataway, NJ: IEEE Press.

Rabiner, L. R. (1989). A tutorial on hidden markov models and selected application in speech recognition. *Proceedings of the IEEE*, *77*, 267–296. doi:10.1109/5.18626

Sagawa, K., Ishihara, T., Ina, A., & Inooka, H. (1998). Classification of human moving patterns using air pressure and acceleration. In *Proceedings of the 24th Annual Conference of the IEEE*, (pp. 1214 – 1219). IEEE.

Spencer, B. F., Ruiz-s, M. E., & Kurata, N. (2004). Smart sensing technology: Opportunities and challenges. *Journal of Structural Control and Health Monitoring*, *11*(4), 349–368. doi:10.1002/stc.48

Taylor, C. J. (2000). Reconstruction of articulated objects from point correspondences in a single image. In *Proceedings of Computer Vision and Pattern Recognition* (pp. 349–363). IEEE. doi:10.1006/cviu.2000.0878

VectorNav Technologies LLC. (2011). *Website.* Retrieved from http://www.vectornav.com/

Viterbi, A. J. (1967). Error bounds for convolutional codes and an asymptotically optimal decoding algorithm. *IEEE Transactions on Information Theory, 13*, 260–269. doi:10.1109/TIT.1967.1054010

Wilson, D., & Atkeson, C. (2005). Simultaneous tracking & activity recognition (star) using many anonymous, binary sensors. In *Proceedings of PERVASIVE*, (pp. 62–79). IEEE.

Yanco, H. A., & Drury, J. L. (2004). Classifying human-robot interaction: An updated taxonomy. In *Proceedings of 2004 IEEE International Conference on Systems, Man and Cybernetics*, (pp. 2841–2846). IEEE Press.

Yeo, C., Ahammad, P., Ramchandran, K., & Sastry, S. S. (2008). High-speed action recognition and localization in compressed domain videos. *IEEE Transactions on Circuits and Systems for Video Technology, 18*(8), 1006–1015. doi:10.1109/TCSVT.2008.927112

Zhu, C. (2011). *Video about human daily activity recognition for the assisted living system.* Retrieved from http://youtu.be/5yrMz59HKBE

KEY TERMS AND DEFINITIONS

Assisted Living System: A system that provides supervision or assistance with activities of daily living, coordination of services by outside health care providers or an assistive robot, and monitoring of resident activities to ensure their health, safety, and well-being.

Activity Recognition: Computational approaches to recognize the activities of a human subject from a series of observations regarding the human subject's actions and the environmental context.

Bayes' Theorem: In probability theory and applications, Bayes' theorem (alternatively Bayes' law or Bayes' rule) links a conditional probability to its inverse.

Hidden Markov Model (HMM): A statistical Markov model in which the system being modeled is assumed to be a Markov process with unobserved (hidden) states. An HMM can be considered as the simplest dynamic Bayesian network.

Motion Sensor: A miniature sensor that can measure the motion in terms of acceleration, angular rate, etc.

Neural Networks: A mathematical model or computational model that is inspired by the structure and/or functional aspects of biological neural networks. A neural network consists of an interconnected group of artificial neurons, and it processes information using a connectionist approach to computation.

Sensor Fusion: The combination of sensory data or data derived from sensory data from disparate sources such that the resulting information is in some sense better than would be possible when these sources were used individually.

Compilation of References

AAL4ALL. (2012). *Website.* Retrieved February 17, 2012 from http://www.aal4all.org/?lang=en

Aarts, E., & de Ruyter, B. (2009). New research perspectives on ambient intelligence. *Journal of Ambient Intelligence and Smart Environments, 1,* 5–14.

Abdullah, L. N., & Noah, S. A. M. (2008). Metadata generation process for video action detection. In *Proceedings of the International Symposium on Information Technology, ITSim 2008,* (pp. 1–5). ITSim.

Action Dataset, M. S. R., II. (2009). *Website.* Retrieved from http://research.microsoft.com/en-us/um/people/zliu/ActionRecoRsrc/

Adami, A. M., Hayes, T. L., & Pavel, M. (2003). Unobtrusive monitoring of sleep patterns. In *Proceedings of 25th Annual International Conference of the IEEE EMBS,* (pp. 1360-1363). Cancun, Mexico: IEEE.

Adamic, L., & Adar, E. (2005). How to search a social network. *Social Networks, 27,* 187–203. doi:10.1016/j.socnet.2005.01.007

Adkins, B., & Barnett, K. (2006). Public spaces as 'context' in assistive information and communication technologies for people with cognitive impairment. *Information Communication and Society, 9*(3), 355–372. doi:10.1080/13691180600751330

Adlam, T., Carey-Smith, B., Evans, N., Orpwood, R., Boger, J., & Mihailidis, A. (2009). Implementing monitoring and technological interventions in smart homes for people with dementia, case studies. In Gottfried, B., & Aghajan, H. (Eds.), *Behaviour Monitoring and Interpretation, Smart Environments.* Boca Raton, FL: IOS Press.

Aghajan, H., & Wu, C. (2007). From distributed vision networks to human behaviour interpretation. In Gottfried, B. (Ed.), *BMI 2007 (Vol. 296,* pp. 129–143). CEUR.

Agrawal, R., & Srikant, R. (1995). Mining sequential patterns. In *Proceedings of the 11th International Conference on Data Engineering,* (pp. 3–14). IEEE.

Alba, R. D. (1981). From small groups to social networks: Mathematical approaches to the study of group structure. *The American Behavioral Scientist, 24*(5), 681–694. doi:10.1177/000276428102400506

Albrechtslund, A., & Norgaard, G. L. (2011). Empowering residents: A theoretical framework for negotiating surveillance technologies. *Surveillance & Society, 8*(2), 235–250.

Alder, G. S. (1998). Ethical issues in electronic performance monitoring: A consideration of deontological and teleological perspectives. *Journal of Business Ethics, 17,* 729–743. doi:10.1023/A:1005776615072

Alferes, J. J., Pereira, L. M., & Swift, T. (2004). Abduction in well-founded semantics and generalized stable models via tabled dual programs. *Theory and Practice of Logic Programming, 4*(4), 383–428. doi:10.1017/S1471068403001960

Allen, J., & Ferguson, J. (1994). Actions and events in interval temporal logic. *Journal of Logic and Computation, 4*(5), 531–579. doi:10.1093/logcom/4.5.531

Amft, O., Junker, H., Lukowicz, P., Troster, G., & Schuster, C. (2006). Sensing muscle activities with body-worn sensors. In *Proceedings of the International Workshop on Wearable and Implantable Body Sensor Networks.* IEEE.

Aminian, K., Robert, P., Buchser, E. E., Rutschmann, B., Hayoz, D., & Depairon, M. (1999). Physical activity monitoring based on accelerometry: Validation and comparison with video observation. *Medical & Biological Engineering & Computing, 3,* 304–308. doi:10.1007/BF02513304

Andrejvich, M. (2005). The work of watching one other: Lateral surveillance, risk and governance. *Surveillance & Society, 2*(4), 474–478.

Angluin, D. (1988). Queries and concept learning. *Machine Learning, 2*(4), 319–342. doi:10.1007/BF00116828

Angluin, D. (2004). Queries revisited. *Theoretical Computer Science, 313*(2), 175–194. doi:10.1016/j.tcs.2003.11.004

Antoniol, G., Rollo, V., & Venturi, G. (2005). Linear predictive coding and cepstrum coefficients for mining time variant information from software repositories. In *Proceedings of MSR2005: International Workshop on Mining Software Repositories*. MSR.

Aporta, C., & Higgs, E. (2005). Satellite culture: Global positioning systems, inuit wayfinding and the need for a new account of technology. *Current Anthropology, 46*(5), 729–753. doi:10.1086/432651

Arikan, O., Forsyth, D. A., & O'Brien, J. F. (2003). Motion synthesis from annotations. *ACM Transactions on Graphics, 22*(3), 402–408. doi:10.1145/882262.882284

Armentano, M. G., & Amandi, A. (2009). Goal recognition with variable-order Markov models. In *Proceedings of the 21st International Joint Conference on Artificial Intelligence*. IEEE.

Armentano, M. G., & Amandi, A. (2007). Plan recognition for interface agents. *Artificial Intelligence Review, 28*(2), 131–162. doi:10.1007/s10462-009-9095-8

Artikis, A., & Paliouras, G. (2009). *Behaviour recognition using the event calculus. Artificial Intelligence Applications & Innovations*. Berlin, Germany: Springer Press.

Artikis, A., & Sergot, M. (2010). Executable specification of open multi-agent systems. *Logic Journal of IGPL, 18*(1), 31–65. doi:10.1093/jigpal/jzp071

Artikis, A., Skarlatidis, A., & Paliouras, G. (2010). Behaviour recognition from video content: A logic programming approach. *International Journal of Artificial Intelligence Tools, 19*(2), 193–209. doi:10.1142/S021821301000011X

Artikis, A., Skarlatidis, A., Portet, F., & Paliouras, G. (2012). Logic-based event recognition. *The Knowledge Engineering Review.* doi:10.1017/S0269888912000264

Aslan, I., Schwalm, M., Baus, J., Krüger, A., & Schwartz, T. (2006). Acquisition of spatial knowledge in location aware mobile pedestrian navigation systems. *Proceedings of Mobile HCI, 2006,* 105–108.

Atlas, L., Cohn, D., Ladner, R., El-Sharkawi, M., & Marks, I. (1990). *Training connectionist networks with queries and selective sampling*. Paper presented at the In Advances in Neural Information Processing Systems. New York, NY.

Augusto, J. C., & Nugent, C. D. (2004). The use of temporal reasoning and management of complex events in smart homes. In *Proccedings of European Conference on AI (ECAI 2004)*, (pp. 778–782). ECAI.

Augusto, J. C. (2007). Ambient intelligence: The confluence of pervasive computing and artificial intelligence. In Schuster, A. (Ed.), *Intelligent Computing Everywhere* (pp. 213–234). Berlin, Germany: Springer. doi:10.1007/978-1-84628-943-9_11

Augusto, J. C., & Nugent, C. (2006). Smart homes can be smarter. In Augusto, J. C., & Nugent, C. D. (Eds.), *Designing Smart Homes: The Role of Artificial Intelligence* (pp. 1–15). Berlin, Germany: Springer. doi:10.1007/11788485_1

Aztiria, A., Augusto, J. C., Basagoiti, R., & Izaguirre, A. (2010). Accurate temporal relationships in sequences of user behaviours in intelligent environments. In *Proceedings of the Ambient Intelligence and Future Trends-International Symposium on Ambient Intelligence (ISAmI 2010)*, (pp. 19-27). ISAmI.

Aztiria, A., Izaguirre, A., Basagoiti, R., Augusto, J. C., & Cook, D. J. (2009). Discovering of frequent sets of actions in intelligent environments. In *Proceedings of the 5th International Conference on Intelligent Environments*, (pp. 153-160). IEEE.

Aztiria, A., Izaguirre, A., Basagoiti, R., Augusto, J. C., & Cook, D. J. (2010). Automatic Modeling of frequent user behaviours in intelligent environments. In *Proceedings of the 6th International Conference on Intelligent Environments*. IEEE.

Aztiria, A., Izaguirre, A., & Augusto, J. C. (2010). Learning patterns in ambient intelligence environments: A survey. *Artificial Intelligence Review, 34*(1), 35–51. doi:10.1007/s10462-010-9160-3

Aztiria, A., Izaguirre, A., Basagoiti, R., & Augusto, J. C. (2008). Autonomous learning of user's preferences improved through user feedback. In Gottfried, B., & Aghajan, H. (Eds.), *BMI 2008* (Vol. 396, pp. 87–101). CEUR.

Badler, N. I. (1975). *Temporal scene analysis: conceptual descriptions of object movements. Report TR 80*. Toronto, Canada: University of Toronto.

Bagnal, A., & Janacek, G. (2004). Clustering time series from arma models with clipped data. In *Proceedings of KDD 2004, the Tenth ACM SIGKDD International Conference on Knowledge Discovery and Data Mining*. Seattle, WA: ACM.

Bao, L., & Intille, S. S. (2004). Activity recognition from user-annotated acceleration data. In *Proceedings of the 2nd International Conference on Pervasive Computing*, (Vol. 3001, pp. 1-17). Springer.

Barabasi, A. L. (2002). *Linked: The new science of networks*. Cambridge, MA: Perseus Publishing.

Baral, C. (2003). *Knowledge representation, reasoning, and declarative problem solving*. Cambridge, UK: Cambridge University Press. doi:10.1017/CBO9780511543357

Baral, C., Gelfond, M., & Rushton, N. (2009). Probabilistic reasoning with answer sets. *Theory and Practice of Logic Programming, 9*(1), 57–144. doi:10.1017/S1471068408003645

Barbic, J., Safonova, A., Pan, J. Y., Faloutsos, C., Hodgins, J. K., & Pollard, N. S. (2004). *Segmenting motion capture data into distinct behaviors*. Paper presented at the In Proceedings of Graphics Interface. New York, NY.

Barley, S. R. (1990). The allignment of technology and structure through roles and networks. *Administrative Science Quarterly, 35*(1), 61–103. doi:10.2307/2393551

Barnes, N. M., Edwards, N. H., Rose, D. A. D., & Garner, P. (1998). Lifestyle monitoring technology for supported independence. *Computer Control and Engineering Journal, 9*(4), 169–174. doi:10.1049/cce:19980404

Bauer, G., Stockinger, K., & Lukowicz, P. (2009). Recognizing the use-mode of kitchen appliances from their current consumption. *Smart Sensing and Context, 5741*, 163–176. doi:10.1007/978-3-642-04471-7_13

Baum, E. B., & Lang, K. (1992). *Query learning can work poorly when a human oracle is used*. Paper presented at the In International Joint Conference on Neural Networks. New York, NY.

Becker, H. S. (1998). *Tricks of the trade: How to think about your research while you're doing it*. Chicago, IL: University of Chicago Press.

Beetz, M., Jain, D., Mosenlechner, L., & Tenorth, M. (2010). Towards performing everyday manipulation activities. *Robotics and Autonomous Systems, 58*(9), 1085–1095. doi:10.1016/j.robot.2010.05.007

Bellman, R. E. (1961). *Adaptive control processes - A guided tour*. Princeton, NJ: Princeton University Press.

Beware. (2010). *Website*. Retrieved May 25, 2010, from http://www.energyawareness.eu/beaware

Binford, T. O., Levitt, T. S., & Mann, W. B. (1989). Bayesian inference in model-based machine vision. *Uncertainty in AI, 3*, 73–96.

Binmore, K. G. (2009). *Rational decisions*. Princeton, NJ: Princeton University Press.

Bishop, C. M. (2006). *Pattern recognition and machine learning*. New York, NY: Springer.

Bjiker, W., & Law, J. (1992). *Shaping technology/building society: Studies in socio-technical change*. Cambridge, MA: MIT Press.

Blank, M., Gorelick, L., Shechtman, E., Irani, M., & Basri, R. (2005). Actions as space-time shapes. In *Proceedings of the IEEE Conference on Computer Vision*, (pp. 1395–1402). IEEE Press.

Blasch, E. (2006). Sensor, user, mission (SUM) resource management and their interaction with level 2/3 fusion. In *Proceedings of the International Conference on Information Fusion*. IEEE.

Blaschko, M., & Lampert, C. (2008). Learning to localize objects with structured output regression. In *Proceedings of the European Conference on Computer Vision*, (pp. 2–15). Springer.

Blascovich, J., & Loomis, J. (2002). Immersive virtual environment technology as a methodological tool for social psychology. *Psychological Inquiry, 13*(2), 103–124. doi:10.1207/S15327965PLI1302_01

Blaylock, N., & Allen, J. (2003). Corpus-based, statistical goal recognition. In *Proceedings of the 18th International Joint Conference on Artificial Intelligence (IJCAI 2003)*. IEEE.

Blei, D. M., Ng, A. Y., & Jordan, M. I. (2003). Latent Dirichlet allocation. *Journal of Machine Learning Research, 3*, 993–1022.

Bloit, J., & Rodet, X. (2008). Short-time viterbi for online hmm decoding: Evaluation on a real-time phone recognition task. In *Proceedings of the IEEE International Conference on Acoustics, Speech and Signal Processing, 2008*, (pp. 2121–2124). IEEE.

Bobick, A., & Davis, J. (2001). The recognition of human movement using temporal templates. *IEEE Transactions on Pattern Analysis and Machine Intelligence, 23*, 257–267. doi:10.1109/34.910878

Boets, J., Cock, K., Espinoza, M., & Moor, B. (2005). Clustering time series, subspace identification and cepstral distances. *Communications in Information and Systems, 5*(1), 69–96.

Bohlken, W., & Neumann, B. (2009). Generation of rules from ontologies for high-level scene interpretation. In Governatori, (Eds.), *Rule Interchange and Applications* (pp. 93–107). Berlin, Germany: Springer. doi:10.1007/978-3-642-04985-9_11

Boiman, O., & Irani, M. (2005). Detecting irregularities in images and in video. In *Proceedings of the IEEE International Conference on Computer Vision*, (pp. 462–469). IEEE Press.

Borgatta, E. F., & Baker, P. M. (1981). Introduction: Updating small group research and theory *The American Behavioral Scientist* (special issue), *24*(5), 603–605. doi:10.1177/000276428102400501

Borgatti, S. P., & Molina, J. L. (2005). Towards ethical guidelines for network research in organizations. *Social Networks, 27*(2), 107–117. doi:10.1016/j.socnet.2005.01.004

Borges, J., & Levene, M. (2000). Data mining of user navigation patterns. In *Revised Papers from the International Workshop on Web Usage Analysis and User Profiling*, (pp. 92-111). London, UK: Springer-Verlag.

Bornholdt, S., & Schuster, H. G. (2005). *Handbook of graphs and networks: From the genome to the internet*. New York, NY: Wiley. doi:10.1002/3527602755

Boser, B. E., Guyon, I. M., & Vapnik, V. N. (1992). A training algorithm for optimal margin classifiers. In *Proceedings of the Fifth Annual Workshop on Computational Learning Theory*, (pp. 144–152). IEEE.

Bosman, S., Groenendaal, B., Findlater, J. W., Visser, T., de Graaf, M., & Markopoulos, P. (2003). *GentleGuide: An exploration of haptic output for indoors pedestrian guidance*. Eindhoven, The Netherlands: Neroc. doi:10.1007/978-3-540-45233-1_28

Boyack, K., Klavans, R., & Borner, K. (2005). Mapping the backbone of science. *Scientometrics, 64*(3), 351–374. doi:10.1007/s11192-005-0255-6

Brand, M., Oliver, N., & Pentland, A. (1997). Coupled hidden Markov models for complex action recognition. In *Proceedings of CVPR*, (pp. 994–999). IEEE Computer Society.

Bratman, M. E. (1987). *Intention, plans, and practical reason*. CSLI.

Bratman, M. E. (1999). *Faces of intention: Selected essays on intention and agency*. Cambridge, UK: Cambridge University Press. doi:10.1017/CBO9780511625190

Brdiczka, O., Reignier, P., & Crowley, J. L. (2010). Detecting individual activities from video in a smart home. *Lecture Notes in Computer Science, 4692*, 363–370. doi:10.1007/978-3-540-74819-9_45

Brighenti, A. (2007). Visibility: A category for the social sciences. *Current Sociology, 55*(3), 323–342. doi:10.1177/0011392107076079

Brittain, K., Corner, L., Robinson, L., & Bond, J. (2010). Ageing in place and technologies of place: The lived experience of people with dementia in changing social, physical and technological environments. *Sociology of Health & Illness, 32*(2), 272–287. doi:10.1111/j.1467-9566.2009.01203.x

Brumitt, B., Meyers, B., Krumm, J., Kern, A., & Shafer, S. (2000). *EasyLiving: Technologies for intelligent environments.* Retrieved from http://research.microsoft.com/en-us/um/people/jckrumm/publications%202000/huc2k-final.pdf

Burglar Alarm. (2012). *Wikipedia.* Retrieved from http://en.wikipedia.org/wiki/Burglar_alarm

Burmeister, B., Arnold, M., Copaciu, F., & Rimassa, G. (2008). BDI-agents for agile goal-oriented business processes. In *Proceedings of the 7th International Joint Conference on Autonomous Agents and Multiagent Systems: Industrial Track.* IEEE.

Burt, R. (2004). Structural holes and good ideas. *American Journal of Sociology, 110*(2), 349–399. doi:10.1086/421787

Busch, B.-H., Witthöft, H., Kujath, A., & Welge, R. (2011). *Präventive notfallerkennung auf basis probabilistischer und beschreibungslogischer auswertung verteilter sensornetze.* Ambient Assisted Living-AAL.

Cachia, R., Compañó, R., & Da Costa, O. (2007). Grasping the potential of online social networks for foresight. *Technological Forecasting and Social Change, 74,* 1179–1203. doi:10.1016/j.techfore.2007.05.006

Caddeo, P., Fornara, F., Nenci, A. M., & Piroddi, A. (2006). Wayfinding tasks in visually impaired people: The role of tactile maps. *Cognitive Processing, 7*(1), 168–169. doi:10.1007/s10339-006-0128-9

Callaghan, V., Clarke, G., & Chin, J. (2007). Some socio-technical aspects of intelligent buildings and pervasive computing research, intelligent buildings. *International Journal Earthscan, 1*(1).

Campo, E., Bonhomme, S., Chan, M., & Esteve, D. (2006). Learning life habits and practices: An issue to the smart home. In C. Nugent & J. C. Augusto (Eds.), *International Conference on Smart Homes and health Telematic,* (pp. 355–358). Berlin, Germany: Springer.

Canu, S., Grandvalet, Y., Guigue, V., & Rakotomamonjy, A. (2005). *SVM and kernel methods Matlab toolbox.* Academic Press.

Cao, L., Liu, Z., & Huang, T. (2010). Cross-dataset action detection. In *Proceedings of the IEEE Conference on Computer Vision and Pattern Recognition.* IEEE Press.

Cao, L., Luo, J., Liang, F., & Huang, T. (2009). Heterogeneous feature machines for visual recognition. In *Proceedings of the IEEE International Conference on Computer Vision.* IEEE Press.

Cao, L., Tian, Y., Liu, Z., Yao, B., Zhang, Z., & Huang, T. (2010). Action detection using multiple spatial-temporal interest point features. In *Proceedings of the IEEE International Conference on Multimedia & Expo.* IEEE Press.

Carley, K. M. (2002). Smart agents and organizations of the future. In Lievrouw, L., & Livingstone, S. (Eds.), *The Handbook of New Media.* London, UK: Sage.

Carmien, S., Dawe, M., Fischer, G., Gorman, A., Kintsch, A., Sullivan, J. R., & James, F. (2005). Socio-technical environments supporting people with cognitive disabilities using public transportation. *ACM Transactions on Computer-Human Interaction, 12*(2), 233–262. doi:10.1145/1067860.1067865

Castro, L., Swift, T., & Warren, D. S. (2007). *XASP: Answer set programming with xsb and smodels.* Retrieved from http://xsb.sourceforge.net/packages/xasp.pdf

Cate, F. H. (2001). *Privacy in perspective.* Washington, DC: American Enterprise Institute for Public Policy Research.

Cattuto, C., Van den Broeck, W., Barrat, A., Colizza, V., Pinton, J. F., & Vespignani, A. (2010). Dynamics of person-to-person interactions from distributed RFID sensor networks. *PLoS ONE, 7,* 1–9.

Cerulo, K. A. (2009). Nonhumans in social interaction. *Annual Review of Sociology, 35,* 531–552. doi:10.1146/annurev-soc-070308-120008

Cesta, A., & Pecora, F. (2004). *The robocare project: Intelligent systems for elder care.* Paper presented at the AAAI Fall Symposium on Caring Machines: AI in Elder Care. New York, NY.

Chan, M., Hariton, C., Ringeard, P., & Campo, E. (1995). Smart house automation system for the elderly and the disabled. In *Proceedings of the 1995 IEEE International Conference on Systems, Man and Cybernetics*, (pp. 1586–1589). IEEE Press.

Chang, E. Y., Tong, S., Goh, K., & Chang, C. (2005). Support vector machine concept-dependent active learning for image retrieval. *IEEE Transactions on Multimedia*, 2.

Chang, Y.-J., & Wang, T.-Y. (2010). Comparing picture and video prompting in autonomous indoor wayfinding for individuals with cognitive impairments. *Personal and Ubiquitous Computing, 14*(8), 737–747. doi:10.1007/s00779-010-0285-9

Chapelle, O., Sindhwani, V., & Keerthi, S. S. (2008). Optimization techniques for semi-supervised support vector machines. *Journal of Machine Learning Research, 9*, 203–233.

Charniak, E., & Goldman, R. P. (1990). Plan recognition in stories and in life. In *Proceedings of the Fifth Annual Conference on Uncertainty in Artificial Intelligence.* IEEE.

Cheney, D. L., & Seyfarth, R. M. (2007). *Baboon metaphysics: The evolution of a social mind.* Chicago, IL: University Of Chicago Press.

Chen, L., & Nugent, C. D. (2009). Ontology-based activity recognition in intelligent pervasive environments. *International Journal of Web Information Systems, 5*(4), 410–430. doi:10.1108/17440080911006199

Chewar, C. M., & McCrickard, D. S. (2002). Dynamic route descriptions: Tradeoffs by usage goals and user characteristics, In *Proceedings of the 2nd International Symposium on Smart Graphics*, (pp. 71-78). ACM Press.

Chew, M. T., & Gupta, G. S. (2008). *Embedded programming with field –programmable mixed-signal microcontrollers* (2nd ed.). Palo Alto, CA: Silicon Laboratories.

Chittaro, L., & Burigat, S. (2005). Augmenting audio messages with visual directions in mobile guides: An evaluation of three approaches. In *Proceedings of the 7th International Conference on Human Computer Interaction with Mobile Devices & Services*, (pp. 107-114). Salzburg, Austria: ACM.

Chittaro, L., & Montamari, A. (1996). Efficient temporal reasoning in the cached event calculus. *Computational Intelligence, 12*(3), 359–382. doi:10.1111/j.1467-8640.1996.tb00267.x

Chiu, B., Keogh, E., & Lonardi, S. (2003). *Probabilistic discovery of time series motifs.* Paper presented at the In Proceedings of the Ninth ACM SIGKDD International Conference on Knowledge Discovery and Data Mining. New York, NY.

Chiu, C. M., Hsu, M., & Wang, E. (2006). Understanding staring in virtual communities: An integration of social capital and social cognitive theories. *Decision Support Systems, 42*, 1872–1888. doi:10.1016/j.dss.2006.04.001

Choi, J. S., Lee, H., Elmasri, R., & Engels, D. W. (2009). Localization systems using passive UHF RFID. In *Proceedings of the International Joint Conference on INC, IMS and IDC*, (pp. 1727-1732). Los Alamitos, CA: IEEE Computer Society.

Chomsky, N. (1965). *Aspects of the theory of syntax.* Cambridge, MA: MIT Press.

Chua, S.-L., Marsland, S., & Guesgen, H. W. (2009). Behaviour recognition from sensory streams in smart environments. In *Proceedings of the Australasian Conference on Artificial Intelligence*, (Vol. 5866, pp. 666-675). Springer.

Chua, S.-L., Marsland, S., & Guesgen, H. W. (2011). Towards behaviour recognition with unlabelled sensor data: As much as necessary, as little as possible. In *Human Behavior Recognition Technologies: Intelligent Applications for Monitoring and Security.* Hershey, PA: IGI Global.

Cleary, J. G., & Witten, I. H. (1984). Data compression using adaptive coding and partial string matching. *IEEE Transactions on Communications, 32*, 396–402. doi:10.1109/TCOM.1984.1096090

Cohen, P. R., & Levesque, H. J. (1990). Intention is choice with commitment. *Artificial Intelligence*, *42*(2-3), 213–261. doi:10.1016/0004-3702(90)90055-5

Cohn, A. G., Magee, D., Galata, A., Hogg, D., & Hazarika, S. (2003). Towards an architecture for cognitive vision using qualitative spatio-temporal representations and abduction. *Spatial Cognition*, *3*, 232–248. doi:10.1007/3-540-45004-1_14

Cohn, D. A. (1996). Neural network exploration using optimal experiment design. *Neural Networks*, *9*(6), 1071–1083. doi:10.1016/0893-6080(95)00137-9

Cook, D. J., & Das, S. K. (2007). How smart are our environments? An updated look at the state of the art. *Journal of Pervasive and Mobile Computing*, *3*, 53–73. doi:10.1016/j.pmcj.2006.12.001

Cook, D., Augusto, J., & Jakkula, V. (2009). Ambient intelligence: Technologies, applications, and opportunities. *Pervasive and Mobile Computing*, *5*(4), 277–298. doi:10.1016/j.pmcj.2009.04.001

Cook, D., & Schmitter-Edgecombe, M. (2009). Assessing the quality of activities in a smart environment. *Methods of Information in Medicine*, *48*(5), 480–485. doi:10.3414/ME0592

Coope, I. D. (1993). Circle fitting by linear and nonlinear least squares. *Journal of Optimization Theory and Applications*, *76*(2), 381–388. doi:10.1007/BF00939613

Corduas, M., & Piccolo, D. (2008). Time series clustering and classification by the autoregressive metric. *Computational Statistics & Data Analysis*, *52*, 1860–1872. doi:10.1016/j.csda.2007.06.001

Covington, M. A. (1994). *Natural language processing for prolog programmers*. Upper Saddle River, NJ: Prentice Hall.

Cugola, G., & Margara, A. (2011). *Processing flows of information: From data stream to complex event processing*. New York, NY: ACM Computing Surveys.

Culotta, A., & McCallum, A. (2004). *Confidence estimation for information extraction*. Paper presented at the In Proceedings of HLT-NAACL. New York, NY.

Dabiri, F., Vahdatpour, A., Noshadi, H., Hagopian, H., & Sarrafzadeh, M. (2008). *Ubiquitous personal assistive system for neuropathy*. Paper presented at the In Proceedings of the Second International Workshop on Systems and Networking Support for Health Care and Assisted Living Environments. New York, NY.

Dalal, N., & Triggs, B. (2005). Histograms of oriented gradients for human detection. In *Proceedings of the IEEE International Conference on Computer Vision*. IEEE Press.

Dasgupta, S., & Hsu, D. (2008). *Hierarchical sampling for active learning*. Paper presented at the In Proceedings of the 25th International Conference on Machine Learning. New York, NY.

Davis, J. (2001). Hierarchical motion history images for recognizing human motion. In *Proceedings of IEEE Workshop on Detection and Recognition of Events in Video*. IEEE Press.

De Federico de la Rúa, A. (2007). Networks and identifications: A relational approach to social identities. *International Sociology*, *22*, 683–699. doi:10.1177/0268580907082247

De la Torre Frade, F., Hodgins, J., Bargteil, A., Artal, X., Macey, J., & Collado, I. Castells, A., & Beltran, J. (2008). *Guide to the carnegie mellon university multimodal activity (CMU-MMAC) database*. Pittsburgh, PA: Robotics Institute, Carnegie Mellon University.

de Ruyter, B., Aarts, E., Markopoulos, P., & Ijsselsteijn, W. (2003). *Ambient intelligence research in HomeLab: Engineering the user experience*. Eindhoven, The Netherlands: Neroc.

de Souza, , & Silva, A. (2006). From cyber to hybrid: Mobile technologies as interfaces of hybrid spaces. *Space and Culture*, *9*, 261–278. doi:10.1177/1206331206289022

Dearman, D., Hawkey, K., & Inkpen, K. M. (2005). Rendezvousing with location aware devices: Enhancing social coordination. *Interacting with Computers*, *17*(2), 542–566. doi:10.1016/j.intcom.2005.03.005

Delikostidis, I., & van Elzakker, C. P. J. M. (2009). Geo-identification and pedestrian navigation with geo-mobile applications: How do users proceed? *Lecture Notes in Geoinformation and Cartography*, *2*, 185–206. doi:10.1007/978-3-540-87393-8_12

Deming, W. E. (1975). On probability as a basis for action. *The American Statistician, 29*(4), 146–152.

Demiris, G., Hensel, B. K., Skubic, M., & Rantz, M. (2008). Senior residents' perceived need of and preferences for smart home sensor technologies. *International Journal of Technology Assessment in Health Care, 24,* 120–124. doi:10.1017/S0266462307080154

Dengler, S., Awad, A., & Dressler, F. (2007). Sensor/actuator networks in smart homes for supporting elderly and handicapped people. In *Proceedings of the 21st International Conference on Advanced Information Networking and Applications Workshops 2007,* (Vol. 2, pp. 863-868). IEEE.

DESA. (2007). *World population prospects: The 2006 revision. DESA. Bryant, J. (2008). Demographic change and New Zealand's economic growth.* Wellington, New Zealand: New Zealand Treasury.

Diaz, J. J. M., Maués, R. D. A., Soares, R. B., Nakamura, E. F., & Figueiredo, C. M. S. (2010). Bluepass: An indoor bluetooth-based localization system for mobile applications. In *Proceedings of the IEEE Symposium on Computers and Communications,* (pp. 778–783). IEEE.

Digi International Inc. (2011). *Website.* Retrieved from http://www.digi.com/

DiMicco, J., Millen, D. R., Geyer, W., Dugan, C., Brownholtz, B., & Muller, M. (2008). Motivations for social networking at work. In *Proceedings of CSCW 2008.* San Diego, CA: CSCW.

Doctor, F., Hagras, H., & Callaghan, V. (2005). A fuzzy embedded agent-based approach for realizing ambient intelligence in intelligent inhabited environments. *IEEE Transactions on Systems, Man, and Cybernetics, 35,* 55–65. doi:10.1109/TSMCA.2004.838488

Dollar, P., Rabaud, V., Cottrell, G., & Belongie, S. (2005). Behavior recognition via sparse spatio-temporal features. In *Proceedings of IEEE International Workshop on VS-PETS.* IEEE Press.

Dorogovtsev, S., & Mendez, J. (2003). *Evolution of networks: From biological nets to the internet and www.* Oxford, UK: Oxford University Press.

Dousson, C., & Maigat, P. L. (2007). *Chronicle recognition improvement using temporal focusing and hierarchisation.* Retrieved from http://www.ijcai.org/papers07/Papers/IJCAI07-050.pdf

Du, T., & Yuan, J. (2011). Optimal spatio-temporal path discovery for video event detection. In *Proceedings of the IEEE Conference on Computer Vision and Pattern Recognition.* IEEE Press.

Duong, T. V., Bui, H. H., Phung, D. Q., & Venkatesh, S. (2005). Activity recognition and abnormality detection with the switching hidden semi-Markov model. In *Proceedings of the 2005 IEEE Computer Society Conference on Computer Vision and Pattern Recognition,* (vol. 1, pp. 838-845). IEEE Computer Society.

Dupont, B. (2008). Hacking the panopticon: Distributed online surveillance and resistance. *Surveillance and Governance. Sociology of Crime Law and Deviance, 10,* 259–280. doi:10.1016/S1521-6136(07)00212-6

Eagle, N., & Pentland, A. S. (2006). Reality mining: Sensing complex social systems. *Personal and Ubiquitous Computing, 10*(4), 255–268. doi:10.1007/s00779-005-0046-3

Eagle, N., & Pentland, A. S. (2009). Eigenbehaviours: Indentifying structure in routine. *Behavioral Ecology and Sociobiology, 63,* 1057–1066. doi:10.1007/s00265-009-0739-0

Ellerbrok, A. (2011). Playful biometrics: Controversial technology through the lens of play. *The Sociological Quarterly, 52,* 528–547. doi:10.1111/j.1533-8525.2011.01218.x

Eriksson, H. (2003). Using JessTab to integrate Protégé and Jess. *IEEE Intelligent Systems, 18*(2), 43–50. doi:10.1109/MIS.2003.1193656

Eriksson, H., & Timpka, T. (2002). The potential of smart homes for injury prevention among the elderly. *Injury Control and Safety Promotion, 9*(2), 27–131. doi:10.1076/icsp.9.2.127.8694

Falk, A., Fehr, E., & Fischbacher, U. (2008). Testing theories of fairness---Intentions matter. *Games and Economic Behavior, 62*(1), 287–303. doi:10.1016/j.geb.2007.06.001

Ferron, M., Massa, P., & Odella, F. (2011). Analyzing collaborative networks emerging in enterprise 2.0: The taolin platform. *Procedia Social and Behavioural Science*, *10*(1), 68–78. doi:10.1016/j.sbspro.2011.01.010

Fickas, S., Sohlberg, M., & Hung, P.-F. (2008). Route-following assistance for travelers with cognitive impairments: A comparison of four prompt modes. *International Journal of Human-Computer Studies*, *66*(12), 876–888. doi:10.1016/j.ijhcs.2008.07.006

Fihl, P., Holte, M. B., & Moeslund, T. B. (2007). Motion primitives and probabilistic edit distance for action recognition. *Proceedings of Gesture-Based Human-Computer Interaction and Simulation*, *5085*, 24–35. Springer-Verlag. doi:10.1007/978-3-540-92865-2_3

Fillmore, C. (1968). The case for CASE. In Bach, E., & Harms, R. (Eds.), *Universals in Linguistic Theory* (pp. 97–135). Berlin, Germany: Holt, Rinehart, and Winston.

Fine, S., Singer, Y., & Tishby, N. (1998). The hierarchical hidden Markov model: Analysis and applications. *Machine Learning*, *32*(1), 41–62. doi:10.1023/A:1007469218079

Flener, P., & Schmid, U. (2012). Inductive programming. In Sammut, C., & Webb, G. (Eds.), *Encyclopedia of Machine Learning*. Berlin, Germany: Springer.

Floridi, L. (2006). Four challenges for a theory of information privacy. *Ethics and Information Technology*, *8*, 109–119. doi:10.1007/s10676-006-9121-3

Frank, R. H., Gilovich, T., & Regan, D. T. (1993). The evolution of one-shot cooperation: An experiment. *Ethology and Sociobiology*, *14*(4), 247–256. doi:10.1016/0162-3095(93)90020-I

Friedewald, M., Costa, O. D., Punie, Y., Alahuhta, P., & Heinonen, S. (2005). Perspectives of ambient intelligence in the home environment. *Telematics Information*, *22*.

Friedewald, M., Vildjiounaite, E., Punie, Y., & Wright, D. (2007). Privacy, identity and security in ambient intelligence: A scenario analysis. *Telematics and Informatics*, *24*(1), 15–29. doi:10.1016/j.tele.2005.12.005

Friedman-Hill, E. (2003). *Jess in action: Java rule-based systems*. Greenwich, CT: Manning.

Friedwald, M., Costa, O. M. D., Punie, Y., Alahuhta, P., & Heinonen, S. (2005). Perspectives of ambient intelligence in the home environment. *Telematics and Informatics*, *22*, 221–238. doi:10.1016/j.tele.2004.11.001

Frigge, M., Hoaglin, D. C., & Iglewicz, B. (1989). Some implementations of the boxplot. *The American Statistician*, *43*(1), 50–54.

Fulk, J. (1993). Social construction of communication technology. *Academy of Management Journal*, *36*(5), 921–950. doi:10.2307/256641

Fusier, F., Valentin, V., Brémond, F., Thonnat, M., Borg, M., Thirde, D., & Ferryman, J. (2007). Video understanding for complex activity recognition. *Machine Vision and Applications*, *18*(3), 167–188. doi:10.1007/s00138-006-0054-y

Fu, W., Ray, P., & Xing, E. P. (2009). DISCOVER: A feature-based discriminative method for motif search in complex genomes. *Bioinformatics (Oxford, England)*, *25*(12), 321–329. doi:10.1093/bioinformatics/btp230

Gaddam, A., Mukhopadhyay, S. C., & Gupta, G. S. (2008). Development of a smart home for elder-people based on wireless sensors. In *Lecture Notes in Electrical Engineering, Smart Sensors and Sensing Technology*, (pp. 361-380). Springer-Verlag.

Gaddam, A., Mukhopadhyay, S. C., & Gupta, G. S. (2010). Smart home for elderly using optimized number of wireless sensors. In *Lecture Notes in Electrical Engineering, Advances in Wireless Sensors and Sensors Networks*. Springer-Verlag. doi:10.1007/978-3-642-12707-6_14

Gal, C. L., Martin, J., Lux, A., & Crowley, J. L. (2001). Smartoffice: Design of an intelligent environment. *IEEE Intelligent Systems*, *16*(4), 60–66. doi:10.1109/5254.941359

Galushka, M., Patterson, D., & Rooney, N. (2006). Temporal data mining for smart homes. In Augusto, J. C., & Nugent, C. D. (Eds.), *Designing Smart Homes: The Role of Artificial Intelligence* (pp. 85–108). Berlin, Germany: Springer. doi:10.1007/11788485_6

Gandy, O. H. (2003). Public opinion survey and the formation of privacy policy. *The Journal of Social Issues*, *59*(2), 283–299. doi:10.1111/1540-4560.00065

Ganley, D., & Lampe, C. (2009). The ties that bind: Social network principles in online communities. *Decision Support Systems, 47*, 268–274. doi:10.1016/j.dss.2009.02.013

Gao, J., Hauptmann, A. G., Bharucha, A., & Wactlar, H. D. (2004). Dining activity analysis using a hidden markov model. In *Proceedings of the 17th International Conference on Pattern Recognition*. IEEE.

Geib, C. W. (2002). Problems with intent recognition for elder care. In *Proceedings of AAAI Workshop Automation as Caregiver*. AAAI.

Gelfond, M., & Lifschitz, V. (1993). Representing actions and change by logic programs. *Journal of Logic Programming, 17*(2,3,4), 301 - 323.

Getoor, L., & Taskar, B. (Eds.). (2007). *Introduction to statistical relational learning*. Cambridge, MA: The MIT Press.

Giuliani, M. V., Scopelliti, M., & Fornara, F. (2005). *Elderly people at home: technological help in everyday activities*. Paper presented at the IEEE International Workshop on In Robot and Human Interactive Communication. New York, NY.

Goggins, S. P., Laffey, J., & Gallagher, M. (2011). Completely online group formation and development: Small groups as socio-technical systems. *Information Technology & People, 24*(2), 104–133. doi:10.1108/09593841111137322

Golledge, R. G., Klatzky, R. L., & Loomis, J. L. (1996). Cognitive mapping and wayfinding by adults without vision. *GeoJournal Library, 32*(2), 215–246. doi:10.1007/978-0-585-33485-1_10

Goshorn, R., Goshorn, D., & Kölsch, M. (2008). The enhancement of low-level classifications for ambient assisted living. In B. Gottfried & H. Aghajan (Eds.), *Proceedings of the 2nd Workshop on Behaviour Monitoring and Interpretation (BMI 2008)*, (vol. 396, pp. 87–101). CEUR.

Gottfried, B. (2008). Qualitative similarity measures - The case of two-dimensional outlines. *Computer Vision and Image Understanding, 110*(1), 117–133. doi:10.1016/j.cviu.2007.05.002

Gottfried, B. (2009). Behaviour monitoring and interpretation: A computational approach to ethology. *Lecture Notes in Artificial Intelligence, 5803*, 572–580.

Gottfried, B. (2010). Locomotion activities in smart environments. In Nakashima, H., Augusto, J. C., & Aghajan, H. (Eds.), *Handbook of Ambient Intelligence and Smart Environments*. Springer. doi:10.1007/978-0-387-93808-0_4

Gottfried, B. (2010). Behaviour monitoring and interpretation: Facets of BMI systems. In Mastrogiovanni, F., & Chong, N.-Y. (Eds.), *Handbook of Research on Ambient Intelligence: Trends and Perspectives*. Hershey, PA: IGI Global.

Gottfried, B. (2010). BMI and the interpretation of locomotion behaviours of humans. In Malatras, A. (Ed.), *Pervasive Computing and Communications Design and Deployment: Technologies, Trends, and Applications*. Hershey, PA: IGI Global.

Gottfried, B., & Aghajan, H. (Eds.). (2008). *Behaviour monitoring and interpretation*. CEUR.

Gottfried, B., & Aghajan, H. (Eds.). (2009). *Behaviour monitoring and interpretation – Smart environments*. IOS Press.

Greenfield, A. (2006). Everyware: The dawning age of ubiquitous computing. *New Riders*, 11–12.

Gries, O., Moeller, R., Nafissi, A., Rosenfeld, M., Sokolski, K., & Wessel, M. (2010). A probabilistic abduction engine for media interpretation. In *Proceedings of the Fourth International Conference on Web Reasoning and Rule Systems*, (pp. 182-194). IEEE.

Griffith, T. L. (1999). Technology features as triggers for sensemaking. *Academy of Management Review, 24*(3), 472–488.

Guesgen, H. W., & Marsland, S. (2010). Spatio-temporal reasoning and context awareness. In *Handbook of Ambient Intelligence and Smart Environments* (pp. 609–634). Berlin, Germany: Springer. doi:10.1007/978-0-387-93808-0_23

Gurvitch, G. (1949). Microsociology and sociometry. *Sociometry, 12*(1-3), 1–31. doi:10.2307/2785376

Gusakov, I. (1993). *Bed patient position monitor*. United States Patent 5184112, 1993. Washington, DC: Us Patent Office.

Guyon, I., & Elisseeff, A. (2003). An introduction to variable and feature selection. *Journal of Machine Learning Research, 3*, 1157–1182.

Gyftodimos, E., & Flach, P. A. (2002). Hierarchical Bayesian networks: A probabilistic reasoning model for structured domains. In E. de Jong & T. Oates (Eds.), *Proceedings of the Workshop on Development of Representations, ICML*, (pp. 23–30). ICML.

Hagan, M. T., Demuth, H. B., & Beale, M. H. (1996). *Neural network design*. PWS Publishing Company.

Hagras, H., Callaghan, V., Colley, M., Clarke, G., Pounds-Cornish, A., & Duman, H. (2004). Creating an ambient-intelligence environment using embedded agents. *IEEE Intelligent Systems, 19*(6), 12–20. doi:10.1109/MIS.2004.61

Haigh, K., Kiff, L., Myers, J., Guralnik, V., Geib, C., Phelps, J., et al. (2004). The independent lifestyle assistant (I.L.S.A.): AI lessons learned. In *Proceedings of Conference on Innovative Applications of Artificial Intelligence*. IEEE.

Hakeem, A., & Shah, M. (2007). Learning, detection and representation of multi-agent events in videos. *Artificial Intelligence, 171*(8-9), 586–605. doi:10.1016/j.artint.2007.04.002

Hampton, K. N. (2003). Grieving for a lost network: Collective action in a wired suburb. *The Information Society, 19*(5), 417–428. doi:10.1080/714044688

Hampton, K., & Wellman, B. (1999). Netville online and offline: Observing and surveying a wired suburb. *The American Behavioral Scientist, 43*, 475–492. doi:10.1177/00027649921955290

Han, T. A., & Pereira, L. M. (2010). *Collective intention recognition and elder care*. Paper presented at the AAAI 2010 Fall Symposium on Proactive Assistant Agents (PAA 2010). New York, NY.

Han, T. A., & Pereira, L. M. (2010). Proactive intention recognition for home ambient intelligence. In *Proceedings of 5th Workshop on Artificial Intelligence Techniques for Ambient Intelligence (AITAmI'10), Ambient Intelligence and Smart Environments*. IEEE.

Han, T. A., & Pereira, L. M. (2011). Context-dependent incremental intention recognition through Bayesian network model construction. In *Proceedings of the Eighth UAI Bayesian Modeling Applications Workshop (UAI-AW 2011)*. UAI-AW.

Han, T. A., & Pereira, L. M. (2011). Intention-based decision making with evolution prospection. In *Proceedings of the 15th Portugese Conference on Progress in Artificial Intelligence*. IEEE.

Han, T. A., Carroline, D. P., & Damasio, C. V. (2008). An implementation of extended p-log using XASP. In *Proceedings of the 24th International Conference on Logic Programming*. IEEE.

Han, T. A., Carroline, D. P., & Damasio, C. V. (2009). *Tabling for p-log probabilistic query evaluation*. Paper presented at the New Trends in Artificial Intelligence, Proceedings of 14th Portuguese Conference on Artificial Intelligence (EPIA 2009). Evora, Portugal.

Han, T. A., Pereira, L. M., & Santos, F. C. (2011). The role of intention recognition in the evolution of cooperative behavior. In *Proceedings of the 22nd International Joint Conference on Artificial Intelligence (IJCAI'2011)*. IEEE.

Han, T. A., Pereira, L. M., & Santos, F. C. (2012b, June). *Intention recognition, commitment and the evoution of cooperation*. Paper presented at the The 2012 IEEE World Congress on Computational Intelligence (IEEE WCCI 2012), Congress on Evolutionary Computation (IEEE CEC 2012). Brisbane, Australia.

Han, T. A., Saptawijaya, A., & Pereira, L. M. (2012). Moral reasoning under uncertainty. In *Proceedings of the 18th International Conference on Logic for Programming, Artificial Intelligence and Reasoning (LPAR-18)*. LPAR.

Hansen, S. (2004). From 'common observation' to behavioural risk management: Workplace surveillance and employee assistance 1914-2003. *International Sociology, 19*(19), 151–171. doi:10.1177/0268580904042898

Han, T. A. (2009). *Evolution prospection with intention recognition via computational logic*. Dresden, Germany: Technical University of Dresden.

Han, T. A. (2012). *Intention recognition, commitments and their roles in the evolution of cooperation*. Lisbon, Portugal: Universidade Nova de Lisboa.

Han, T. A., Pereira, L. M., & Santos, F. C. (2011). Intention recognition promotes the emergence of cooperation. *Adaptive Behavior, 19*(3), 264–279.

Han, T. A., Pereira, L. M., & Santos, F. C. (2012). Corpus-based intention recognition in cooperation dilemmas. *Artificial Life*. doi:10.1162/ARTL_a_00072

Harnad, S. (1990). The symbol grounding problem. *Physica D. Nonlinear Phenomena, 42*(1-3), 335–346. doi:10.1016/0167-2789(90)90087-6

Harrington, B., & Fine, G. A. (2000). Opening the black box: Small groups and twenty first century sociology. *Social Psychology Quarterly, 63*(4), 312–323. doi:10.2307/2695842

Harris, C., & Stephens, M. (1988). A combined corner and edge detector. In *Proceeding of Alvey Vision Conference*, (pp. 189–192). Alvey Vision.

Hatun, K., & Duygulu, P. (2008). Pose sentences: A new representation for action recognition using sequence of pose words. In *Proceedings of the 19th International Conference on Pattern Recognition (ICPR)*, (pp. 1-4). Tampa, FL: IEEE.

Hauser, M. D. (2007). *Moral minds, how nature designed our universal sense of right and wrong*. New York, NY: Little Brown.

Hein, A., & Kirste, T. (2008). Towards recognizing abstract activities: An unsupervised approach. In *Proceedings of the 2nd Workshop on Behaviour Monitoring and Interpretation, BMI 2008*, (pp. 102-114). CEUR-WS.org.

Heinze, C. (2003). *Modeling intention recognition for intelligent agent systems*.

Helal, S., Winkler, B., Lee, C., Kaddoura, Y., Ran, L., Giraldo, C., et al. (2003). Enabling location-aware pervasive computing applications for the elderly. In *Proceedings of IEEE 1st Conference PerCom 2003*, (pp. 531-536). PerCom.

Helal, A. (2005). Gator tech smart house: A programmable pervasive space. *IEEE Computer, 38*(3), 50–60. doi:10.1109/MC.2005.107

Helal, S., Mann, W., El-Zabadani, H., King, J., Kaddoura, Y., & Jansen, E. (2005). The gator tech smart house: A programmable pervasive space. *Computer, 38*(3), 50–60. doi:10.1109/MC.2005.107

Helaoui, R., Niepert, M., & Stuckenschmidt, H. (2011). Recognizing interleaved and concurrent activities: A statistical-relational approach. In *Proceedings of Pervasive Computing and Communications* (pp. 1–9). IEEE. doi:10.1109/PERCOM.2011.5767586

Hermersdorf, M. (2006). Indoor positioning with a WLAN access point list on a mobile device. In *Proceedings of WSW 2006 at SenSys 2006*. Boulder, CO: ACM.

Hightower, J., & Borriello, G. (2001). Location systems for ubiquitous computing. *Computer, 34*(8), 57–66. doi:10.1109/2.940014

Ho, L., Moh, M., Walker, Z., Hamada, T., & Su, C.-F. (2005). A prototype on RFID and sensor networks for elder healthcare: progress report. In *Proceedings of the 2005 ACM SIGCOMM Workshop on Experimental Approaches to Wireless Network Design and Analysis (E-WIND 2005)*, (pp. 70-75). ACM.

Hofbauer, J., & Sigmund, K. (1998). *Evolutionary games and population dynamics*. Cambridge, UK: Cambridge University Press. doi:10.1017/CBO9781139173179

Hofmann, M., Kitzelmann, E., & Schmid, U. (2009). A unifying framework for analysis and evaluation of inductive programming systems. In B. Goerzel, P. Hitzler, & M. Hutter (Eds.), *Proceedings of the Second Conference on Artificial General Intelligence*, (pp. 55–60). Amsterdam, The Netherlands: Atlantis Press.

Holloway, T., Bozicevic, M., & Borner, K. (2007). Analyzing and visualizing the semantic coverage of Wikipedia and its authors. *Complexity, 12*(33), 30–40. doi:10.1002/cplx.20164

Hongeng, S., & Nevatia, R. (2003). Large-scale event detection using semi-hidden markov models. *Proceedings of IEEE Computer Society. ICCV*, 1455–1462.

Hong, J. (2001). Goal recognition through goal graph analysis. *Journal of Artificial Intelligence Research, 15*, 1–30. doi:10.1023/A:1006673610113

Hotz, L., & Neumann, B. (2005). Scene interpretation as a configuration task. *Kuenstliche Intelligenz, 3*, 59–65.

Hotz, L., Neumann, B., & Terzic, K. (2008). High-level expectations for low-level image processing. *Proceedings ofKI-2008*, 87–94. Berlin, Germany: Springer.

Howell Jones, M., Goubran, R. A., & Knofel, F. (2006). Identifying movement onset times for a bed-based pressure sensor array. In *Proceedings of the International Workshop on Medical Measurement and Applications*, (Vol. 1, pp. 105-109). IEEE.

Hsu, C.-W., Chang, C.-C., & Lin, C.-J. (2003). *A practical guide to support vector classification*. Tech. Rep. National Taiwan University.

Hu, D. H., & Yang, Q. (2008). Cigar: Concurrent and interleaving goal and activity recognition. In *Proceedings of the 23rd Conference on Artificial Intelligence*, (pp. 1363-1368). AAAI Press.

Hu, H., Pan, J., Zheng, W., Liu, N., & Yang, Q. (2008). Real world activity recognition with multiple goals. In *Proceedings of the 10th international Conference on Ubiquitous Computing*, (pp. 30–39). IEEE.

Hu, Y., Cao, L., Lv, F., Yan, S., Gong, Y., & Huang, T. (2009). Action detection in complex scenes with spatial and temporal ambiguities. In *Proceedings of the IEEE International Conference on Computer Vision*. IEEE Press.

Hughes, T. (1987). The evolution of large technological systems. In Bjiker, W., Hughes, T., & Pinch, T. (Eds.), *The Social Construction of Technological Systems*. Cambridge, MA: MIT.

Huynh, T., & Schiele, B. (2005). Analyzing features for activity recognition. In *Proceedings of the 2005 Joint Conference on Smart Objects and Ambient Intelligence*, (pp. 159-163). New York, NY: ACM.

Huynh, T., Fritz, M., & Schiele, B. (2008). Discovery of activity patterns using topic models. In *Proceedings of the 10th International Conference on Ubiquitous Computing*, (pp. 10-19). New York, NY: ACM.

Intille, S. S., Larson, K., Beaudin, J. S., Nawyn, J., Tapia, E. M., & Kaushik, P. (2004). A living laboratory for the design and evaluation of ubiquitous computing technologies. In *Proceedings of the 2005 Conference on Human Factors in Computing Systems*. New York, NY: ACM Press.

Jacob, Z., & Abraham, L. (1978). Compression of individual sequences via variable-rate coding. *IEEE Transactions on Information Theory*, *24*(5), 530–536. doi:10.1109/TIT.1978.1055934

Jaideep, S., Robert, C., Mukund, D., & Pang-Ning, T. (2000). Web usage mining: discovery and applications of usage patterns from web data. *SIGKDD Explorations Newsletter*, *1*(2), 12–23.

Jakkula, V. R., Crandall, A. S., & Cook, D. J. (2007). Knowledge discovery in entity based smart environment resident data using temporal relation based data mining. In *Proceedings of the 7th IEEE International Conference on DataMining*, (pp. 625–630). IEEE Press.

Janssen, M. A. (2008). Evolution of cooperation in a one-shot prisoner's dilemma based on recognition of trustworthy and untrustworthy agents. *Journal of Economic Behavior & Organization*, *65*(3-4), 458–471. doi:10.1016/j.jebo.2006.02.004

Jhuang, H., Serre, T., Wolf, L., & Poggio, T. (2007). A biologically inspired system for action recognition. In *Proceedings of the IEEE International Conference on Computer Vision*. IEEE Press.

Jiang, L., Liu, D.-Y., & Yang, B. (2004). Machine learning and cybernetics. In *Proceedings of 2004 International Conference*, (vol. 2, pp. 659 – 663). IEEE.

Ji, X., & Liu, H. (2010). Advances in view-invariant human motion analysis: A review. *IEEE Transactions on Systems, Man and Cybernetics. Part C, Applications and Reviews*, *40*(1), 13–24. doi:10.1109/TSMCC.2009.2027608

Joern, L. (2009). Nothing to hide, nothing to fear? Tackling violence on the terraces. *Sport in Society*, *12*(10), 1269–1283. doi:10.1080/17430430903204777

Joshi, S., & Boyd, S. (2007). Sensor selection via convex optimization. *IEEE Transactions on Signal Processing*, *57*(2), 321–325.

Joyce, K., & Loe, M. (2010). A sociological approach to ageing, technology and health. *Sociology of Health & Illness*, *32*(2), 171–180. doi:10.1111/j.1467-9566.2009.01219.x

Junejo, I., Dexter, E., Laptev, I., & Perez, P. (2011). View-independent action recognition from temporal self-similarities. *IEEE Transactions on Pattern Analysis and Machine Intelligence, 33*(1), 172–185. doi:10.1109/TPAMI.2010.68

Kaaniche, M., & Bremond, F. (2010). Gesture recognition by learning local motion signatures. In *Proceedings of the IEEE International Conference on Computer Vision.* IEEE Press.

Kaddoura, Y., King, J., & Helal, A. (2005). Cost-precision tradeoffs in unencumbered floor-based indoor location tracking. In *Proceedings of the 3rd International Conference on Smart Homes and Health Telemetrics,* (pp. 425-429). IEEE.

Kadushin, C. (2005). Who benefits from network analysis: Ethics of social network research. *Social Networks, 27,* 139–153. doi:10.1016/j.socnet.2005.01.005

Kakas, A. C., Kowalski, R. A., & Toni, F. (1993). Abductive logic programming. *Journal of Logic and Computation, 2*(6), 719–770. doi:10.1093/logcom/2.6.719

Kalpakis, K., Gada, D., & Puttagunta, V. (2001). Distance measures for accurate clustering of arima time-series. In *Procedings of the 2001 IEEE International Conference on Data Mining,* (pp. 273–280). IEEE Press.

Kamel Boulos, M. N., & Castellot, L. R. (2010). Connectivity for healthcare and well being management: Examples from six European projects. *International Journal of Environmental Research and Public Health, 6,* 1947–1971. doi:10.3390/ijerph6071947

Kaminka, G. A., Tambe, D. V. P. M., Pynadath, D. V., & Tambe, M. (2002). Monitoring teams by overhearing: A multi-agent plan-recognition approach. *Journal of Artificial Intelligence Research, 17.*

Katzouris, N., Skarlatidis, A., Filipou, J., Artikis, A., & Paliouras, G. (2011). *First version of algorithms for learning event definitions.* Deliverable 4.3.1 of the EU-funded FP7 PRONTO project (FP7-ICT 231738). Available from the authors.

Ke, Y., Sukthankar, R., & Hebert, M. (2007). Event detection in crowded videos. In *Proceedings of the IEEE International Conference on Computer Vision.* IEEE Press.

Keogh, E. (2003). *Efficiently finding arbitrarily scaled patterns in massive time series databases.* Paper presented at the In Proceedings of the Seventh European Conference on Principles and Practice of Knowledge Discovery in Databases. New York, NY.

Keogh, E., Chakrabarti, K., Pazzani, M., & Mehrotra, S. (2001). Dimensionality reduction for fast similarity search in large time series databases. *Knowledge and Information Systems, 3*(3), 263–286. doi:10.1007/PL00011669

Kidd, C. D., Orr, R. J., Abowd, G. D., Atkeson, C. G., Essa, I. A., MacIntyre, B., et al. (1999). The aware home: A living laboratory for ubiquitous computing research. In *Proceedings of the 2nd International Workshop on Cooperative Buildings (CoBuild 1999),* (pp. 191-198). Pittsburgh, PA: Springer-Verlag.

Kiefer, P., & Schlieder, C. (2007). Exploring context-sensitivity in spatial intention recognition. In *Proceedings of the International Workshop on Behavioral Monitoring and Interpretation,* (vol. 42, pp. 102–116). TZI-Bericht.

Kiluk, C. (1991). *Method in alarm system, including recording of energy consumption.* US Patent No. US4990893. Washington, DC: US Patent Office.

Kim, D., Song, J., & Kim, D. (2007). Simultaneous gesture segmentation and recognition based on forward spotting accumulative HMMs. *Pattern Recognition, 40*(11), 3012–3026. doi:10.1016/j.patcog.2007.02.010

Kitzelmann, E. (2009). Analytical inductive functional programming. In M. Hanus (Ed.), *Proceedings of the 18th International Symposium on Logic-Based Program Synthesis and Transformation,* (vol. 5438, pp. 87–102). Springer.

Kitzelmann, E. (2010). *A combined analytical and search-based approach to the inductive synthesis of functional programs.* (Unpublished Doctoral Dissertation). Otto-Friedrich Universität. Bamberg, Germany. Retrieved from http://www.opus-bayern.de/uni-bamberg/volltexte/2010/280/

Kitzelmann, E., & Schmid, U. (2006). Inductive synthesis of functional programs: An explanation based generalization approach. *Journal of Machine Learning Research, 7,* 429–454.

Klasnja, P., Consolvo, S., Choudhury, T., Beckwith, R., & Hightower, J. (2009). Exploring privacy concerns about personal sensing. In *Proceedings of the International Conference on Pervasive Computing*, (pp. 176–183). Springer.

Kohonen, T. (1990). The self-organising map. *Proceedings of the IEEE*, *78*(9), 1464–1480. doi:10.1109/5.58325

Kohonen, T., Hynninen, J., Kangas, J., & Laaksonen, J. (1996). *SOM_PAK: The self-organising map program package*. Helsinki, Finland: Helsinki University of Technology.

Kohonen, T., Hynninen, J., Kangas, J., Laaksonen, J., & Torkkola, K. (1996). *LVQ_PAK: The learning vector quantization program package. Tech. Rep.* Helsinki, Finland: Helsinki University of Technology.

Koller, D., & Pfeffer, A. (1997). Object-oriented Bayesian networks. In *Proceedings of the Thirteenth Annual Conference on Uncertainty in Artificial Intelligence*, (pp. 302–313). IEEE.

Koller, D., & Friedman, N. (2009). *Probabilistic graphical models*. Cambridge, MA: MIT Press.

Kosala, R., & Blockeel, H. (2000). Web mining research: A survey. *SIGKDD Explorations*, *2*, 1–15. doi:10.1145/360402.360406

Kosmopoulos, D., Antonakaki, P., Valasoulis, K., Kesidis, A., & Perantonis, S. (2008). Human behavior classification using multiple views. *Lecture Notes in Artificial Intelligence, 5138*.

Kostakos, V., & Little, L. (2005). The social implications of emerging technologies. *Interacting with Computers*, *17*(5), 475–483. doi:10.1016/j.intcom.2005.03.001

Kovashka, A., & Grauman, K. (2010). Learning a hierarchy of discriminative space-time neighborhood features for human action recognition. In *Proceedings of the IEEE International Conference on Computer Vision*. IEEE Press.

Kowalski, R., & Sergot, M. (1986). A logic-based calculus of events. *New Generation Computing*, *4*(1), 67–96. doi:10.1007/BF03037383

Krause, A., Siewiorek, D. P., Smailagic, A., & Farringdon, J. (2003). Unsupervised, dynamic identification of physiological and activity context in wearable computing. In *Proceedings of the 7th IEEE International Symposium on Wearable Computers,* (p. 88). Washington, DC: IEEE Computer Society.

Kraus, S. (1997). Negotiation and cooperation in multi-agent environments. *Artificial Intelligence*, *94*(1-2), 79–98. doi:10.1016/S0004-3702(97)00025-8

Krumm, J., Harris, S., Meyers, B., Brumitt, B., Hale, M., & Shafer, S. (2000). Multi-camera multi-person tracking for EasyLiving. In *Proceedings of 3rd IEEE International Workshop on Visual Surveillance*, (pp. 3–10). IEEE Press.

Krupp, D. B., Debruine, L., & Barclay, M. P. (2008). A cue of kinship promotes cooperation for the public good. *Evolution and Human Behavior*, *29*, 49–55. doi:10.1016/j.evolhumbehav.2007.08.002

Kumar, S., & Hebert, M. (2004). *Discriminative fields for modeling spatial dependencies in natural images.* Paper presented at the In Advances in Neural Information Processing Systems. New York, NY.

Laerhoven, K. V. (2001). Combining the self-organizing map and k-means clustering for on-line classification of sensor data. In *Proceedings of the International Conference on Artificial Neural Networks,* (pp. 464–469). London, UK: Springer-Verlag.

Lafferty, J., McCallum, A., & Pereira, F. (2001). *Conditional random fields: Probabilistic models for segmenting and labeling sequence data.* Paper presented at the In Proceedings of the International Conference on Machine Learning. New York, NY.

Laguionie, O. (2008). *Designing a smart home environment using a wireless sensor networking of everyday objects.* (Master's Thesis). University Department of Computing Science. Stockholm, Sweden.

Lampert, C., Blaschko, M., & Hofmann, T. (2008). Beyond sliding windows: Object localization by efficient subwindow search. In *Proceedings of the IEEE Conference on Computer Vision and Pattern Recognition*. IEEE Press.

Laptev, I., & Lindeberg, T. (2003). Space-time interest points. In *Proceedings of the IEEE Conference on Computer Vision*, (pp. 432–439). IEEE Press.

Laptev, I., Marszalek, M., Schmid, C., & Rozenfeld, B. (2008). Learning realistic human actions from movies. In *Proceedings of the IEEE Conference on Computer Vision and Pattern Recognition*. IEEE Press.

Latour, B. (1992). Where are the missing masses? The sociology of a few mundane artifacts. In Bjiker, W., & Law, J. (Eds.), *Shaping Technology/Building Society: Studies in Sociotechnical Change*. Cambridge, MA: MIT Press.

Law, J. (1987). Technology and heterogeneous engineering. In Bjiker, W., Hughes, T., & Pinch, T. (Eds.), *The Social Construction of Technological Systems*. Cambridge, MA: MIT.

Leake, D., Maguitman, A., & Reichherzer, T. (2006). Cases, context, and comfort: Opportunities for case-based reasoning in smart homes. In Augusto, J. c., & Nugent, C. D. (Eds.), *Designing Smart Homes: The Role of Artificial Intelligence* (pp. 109–131). Berlin, Germany: Springer. doi:10.1007/11788485_7

Lee, S., & Mase, K. (2001). Recognition of walking behaviors for pedestrian navigation. In *Proceeding of the 2001 IEEE International Conference on Control Applications*, (pp. 1152–1155). IEEE.

Lee, W.-C., & Cheng, B.-W. (2008). Effects of using a portable navigation system and paper map in real driving. *Accident; Analysis and Prevention*, *40*(1), 303–308. doi:10.1016/j.aap.2007.06.010

Lesh, N. (1998). *Scalable and adaptive goal recognition*. Seattle, WA: University of Washington.

Lester, J., Choudhury, T., Kern, N., Borriello, G., & Hannaford, B. (2005). A hybrid discriminative / generative approach for modeling human activities. In *Proceedings of the International Joint Conference on Artificial Intelligence IJCAI*, (pp. 766–772). IEEE.

Levenshtein, V. (1966). Binary codes capable of correcting deletions, insertions and reversals. *Soviet Physics, Doklady*, *10*, 707.

Levin, A., & Weiss, Y. (2006). Learning to combine bottom-up and top-down segmentation. *International Journal of Computer Vision*, *81*(1), 105–118. doi:10.1007/s11263-008-0166-0

Lewis, D. D., & Ringuette, M. (1994). A comparison of two learning algorithms for text categorization. In *Proceedings of the Third Annual Symposium on Document Analysis and Information Retrieval*, (pp. 81-93). IEEE.

Liao, L., Patterson, D., Fox, D., & Kautz, H. (2004). Behavior recognition in assisted cognition. In *Proceedings of the IAAA-04 Workshop on Supervisory Control of Learning and Adaptive Systems*, (pp. 41–42). IAAA.

Liao, L., Fox, D., & Kautz, H. (2007). Extracting places and activities from gps traces using hierarchical conditional random fields. *The International Journal of Robotics Research*, *26*(1), 119. doi:10.1177/0278364907073775

Liao, L., Patterson, D. J., Fox, D., & Kautz, H. (2007). Learning and inferring transportation routines. *Artificial Intelligence*, *171*(5-6), 311–331. doi:10.1016/j.artint.2007.01.006

Libal, V., Ramabhadran, B., Mana, N., Pianesi, F., Chippendale, P., Lanz, O., & Potamianos, G. (2009). Multimodal classification of activities of daily living inside smart homes. *Lecture Notes in Computer Science*, *5518*, 687–694. doi:10.1007/978-3-642-02481-8_103

Lin, J., Keogh, E., Lonardi, S., & Patel, P. (2002). *Finding motifs in time series*. Paper presented at the In ACM SIGKDD Workshop on Temporal Data Mining. New York, NY.

Lin, T., Ray, P., Sandve, G., Uguroglu, S., & Xing, E. (2008). *Baycis: A bayesian hierarchical hmm for cis-regulatory module decoding in metazoan genomes*. Paper presented at the Proceedings of the 12th Annual International Conference on Research in Computational Molecular Biology. New York, NY.

Liu, J., Ali, S., & Shah, M. (2008). Recognizing human actions using multiple features. In *Proceedings of the IEEE Conference on Computer Vision and Pattern Recognition*. IEEE Press.

Liu, J., Luo, J., & Shah, M. (2009). Recognizing realistic actions from videos "in the wild". In *Proceedings of the IEEE Conference on Computer Vision and Pattern Recognition*. IEEE Press.

Liu, D. C., & Nocedal, J. (1989). On the limited memory BFGS method for large scale optimization. *Mathematical Programming, 45*(1-3), 503–528. doi:10.1007/BF01589116

Liu, H., Hussain, F., Tan, C. L., & Dash, M. (2002). Discretization: An enabling technique. *Data Mining and Knowledge Discovery, 6*(4), 393–423. doi:10.1023/A:1016304305535

Loe, M. (2010). Doing it my way: Old women, technology and wellbeing. *Sociology of Health & Illness, 32*(2), 319–334. doi:10.1111/j.1467-9566.2009.01220.x

Logan, B., Healey, J., Philipose, M., Tapia, E. M., & Intille, S. S. (2007). A long-term evaluation of sensing modalities for activity recognition. In *Proceedings of the 9th International Conference on Ubiquitous Computing,* (pp. 483-500). Springer.

Lowd, D., & Domingos, P. (2005). Naive bayes models for probability estimation. In *Proceedings of the 22nd International Conference on Machine Learning.* IEEE.

Luo, R. C., & Chen, O. (2009). Indoor human dynamic localization and tracking based on sensory data fusion techniques. In *Proceedings of the IEEE/RSJ International Conference on Intelligent Robots and Systems,* (pp. 860–865). IEEE Press.

Lyon, D. (1994). *The electronic eye: The rise of surveillance society.* London, UK: Polity Press.

Lyon, D. (2002). Everyday surveillance: Personal data and social classifications. *Information Communication and Society, 5*(2), 424–257. doi:10.1080/13691180210130806

Maehara, H., Tanaka, K. W. S., & Kamata, K. (2002). Pedestrian navigation based on 3D map and mobile interaction. In *Proceedings of MVA 2002, IAPR Workshop on Machine Vision Applications.* Nara, Japan: MVA.

Mainprize, S. (1996). Effective affinities in the engineering of social control: The evolution of electronic monitoring. *Electronic Journal of Sociology, 2*(2).

Malle, B. F., Moses, L. J., & Baldwin, D. A. (2003). *Intentions and intentionality: Foundations of social cognition.* Cambridge, MA: MIT Press.

Mao, W., & Gratch, J. (2004). *A utility-based approach to intention recognition.* Paper presented at the AAMAS 2004 Workshop on Agent Tracking: Modeling Other Agents from Observations. New York, NY.

Marcus, G. F. (2001). *The algebraic mind. integrating conncetionism and cognitive science.* Cambridge, MA: Bradford.

Margulis, S. (2003). Privacy as a social issue and behavioural concept. *The Journal of Social Issues, 59*(2), 243–261. doi:10.1111/1540-4560.00063

Markopulos, P., Ijsselsteijn, W., & De Ruyter, B. (2005). Sharing experiences through awareness systems in the home. *Interacting with Computers, 17*, 506–521. doi:10.1016/j.intcom.2005.03.004

Marsland, S. (2009). *Machine learning: An algorithmic introduction.* Mahwah, NJ: CRC Press.

Marszałek, M., Laptev, I., & Schmid, C. (2009). Actions in context. In *Proceedings of the IEEE Conference on Computer Vision and Pattern Recognition.* IEEE Press.

Martino-Saltzman, D., Blasch, B., Morris, R., & McNeal, L. (1991). Travel behavior of nursing home residents perceived as wanderers and nonwanderers. *The Gerontologist, 11*, 666–672. doi:10.1093/geront/31.5.666

Marx, G. T. (2001). Murky conceptual waters: The public and the private. *Ethics and Information Technology, 3*(3), 157–169. doi:10.1023/A:1012456832336

Marx, G. T. (2003). A tack in the shoe: neutralizing and resisting the new surveillance. *The Journal of Social Issues, 59*(2), 369–390. doi:10.1111/1540-4560.00069

Marx, G. T. (2005). *Seeing hazily (but not darkly) through the lens: Some recent empirical studies of surveillance technologies.* Washington, DC: American Bar Foundation. doi:10.1111/j.1747-4469.2005.tb01016.x

Mattivi, R., & Shao, L. (2009). Human action recognition using LBP-TOP as sparse spatio-temporal feature descriptor. In *Proceedings of Computer Analysis of Images and Patterns.* IEEE. doi:10.1007/978-3-642-03767-2_90

Matzat, U. (2009). A theory of relational signals in online groups. *New Media & Society, 11*, 375–394. doi:10.1177/1461444808101617

Maurer, U., Smailagic, A., Siewiorek, D. P., & Deisher, M. (2006). Activity recognition and monitoring using multiple sensors on different body positions. In *Proceedings of the International Workshop on Wearable and Implantable Body Sensor Networks*, (pp. 113–116). IEEE.

May, D. (1999). Modeling the dynamically tuned gyroscope in support of high-bandwidth capture loop design. *Proceedings of the Society for Photo-Instrumentation Engineers, 3692*, 101. doi:10.1117/12.352852

McCallum, A. (2003). *Efficiently inducing features of conditional random fields*. Paper presented at the Proceedings of the Nineteenth Conference on Uncertainty in Artificial Intelligence. New York, NY.

McCallum, A., & Nigam, K. (1998). A comparison of event models for naïve Bayes text classification. In *Proceedings of AAAI-98 - Workshop on Learning for Text Categorization*, (pp. 41-48). AAAI Press.

McPherson, M., Popielarz, P., & Drobnic, S. (1992). Social networks and organizational dynamics. *American Sociological Review, 57*, 153–170. doi:10.2307/2096202

Meltzoff, A. N. (2005). Imitation and other minds: the ``like me" hypothesi. In Hurley, S. A. C. (Ed.), *Perspectives on Imitation: From Neuroscience to Social Science: Imitation, Human Development, and Culture* (pp. 55–77). Cambridge, MA: MIT Press.

Meltzoff, A. N. (2007). The framework for recognizing and becoming an intentional agent. *Acta Psychologica, 124*(1), 26–43. doi:10.1016/j.actpsy.2006.09.005

Menon, V., Jayaraman, B., & Govindaraju, V. (2010). Biometrics driven smart environments: Abstract framework and evaluation. *Lecture Notes in Computer Science, 5061*, 75–89. doi:10.1007/978-3-540-69293-5_8

Messing, R., Pal, C., & Kauze, H. (2009). Activity recognition using the velocity histories of tracked keypoints. In *Proceedings of the IEEE Conference on Computer Vision*. IEEE Press.

Metsis, V., Androutsopoulos, I., & Paliouras, G. (2006). Spam filtering with naïve Bayes - Which naive Bayes? In *Proceedings of the Third Conference on Email and Anti-Spam (CEAS)*. CEAS.

Mihailidis, A., Boger, J., Craig, T., & Hoey, J. (2008). The COACH prompting system to assist older adults with dementia through handwashing: An efficacy study. *BMC Geriatrics, 8*(28).

Mika, P. (2005). Flink: Semantic web technology for the extraction and analysis of social networks. *Web Semantics: Science. Services and Agents on the World Wide Web, 3*, 211–223. doi:10.1016/j.websem.2005.05.006

Mikhail, J. (2007). Universal moral grammar: Theory, evidence, and the future. *Trends in Cognitive Sciences, 11*(4), 143–152. doi:10.1016/j.tics.2006.12.007

Mikolajczyk, K., & Uemura, H. (2008). Action recognition with motion-appearance vocabulary forest. In *Proceedings of the IEEE Conference on Computer Vision and Pattern Recognition*. IEEE Press.

Miller, R., & Shanahan, M. (2000). The event calculus in a classical logic. *Journal of Experimental & Theoretical Artificial Intelligence, 4*(16).

Millonig, A., & Gartner, G. (2007). Shadowing, tracking, interviewing: How to explore human ST-behaviour patterns. In Gottfried, B. (Ed.), *BMI 2007 (Vol. 296*, pp. 29–42). CEUR.

Milton, L. P., & Westphal, J. D. (2005). Identity confirmation networks and cooperation in work groups. *Academy of Management Journal, 48*(2), 191–212. doi:10.5465/AMJ.2005.16928393

Minnen, D., Starner, T., Essa, M., & Isbell, C. (2007). *Discovering characteristic actions from on-body sensor data*. Paper presented at the In Proceedings of the 10th International Symposium on Wearable Computers. New York, NY.

Mitchell, T. (1997). Decision tree learning. In *Proceedings of Machine Learning* (pp. 52–78). IEEE.

Mitchell, T. M. (1982). Generalization as search. *Artificial Intelligence, 18*(2), 203–226. doi:10.1016/0004-3702(82)90040-6

Moeslunda, T. B., Hiltonb, A., & Kruger, V. (2006). A survey of advances in vision-based human motion capture and analysis. In *Proceedings of Computer Vision and Image Understanding*, (pp. 90–126). IEEE.

Monahan, T. (2006). Electronic fortification in Phoenix: Surveillance technologies and social regulation in residential communities. *Urban Affairs Review, 42*(2), 169–192. doi:10.1177/1078087406292845

Monahan, T. (2008). Dreams of control at a distance: Gender, surveillance and social control. *Cultural Studies, 9*(2), 286–305.

Monahan, T. (2011). Surveillance as cultural practice. *The Sociological Quarterly, 52*, 495–508. doi:10.1111/j.1533-8525.2011.01216.x

Morariu, V. I., & Davis, L. S. (2011). Multi-agent event recognition in structured scenarios. In *Proceedings of the IEEE Conference on Computer Vision and Pattern Recognition (CVPR), 2011*. CVPR.

Mozer, M. C. (2004). Lessons from an adaptive home. In Cook, D. J., & Das, S. K. (Eds.), *Smart Environments: Technology, Protocols and Applications* (pp. 273–298). New York, NY: Wiley-Interscience.

Mozer, M. C., Dodier, R. H., Anderson, M., Vidmar, L., Cruickshank, R. F., & Miller, D. (1995). The neural network house: An overview. In Niklasson, L., & Boden, M. (Eds.), *Current Trends in Connectionism* (pp. 371–380). Mahwah, NJ: Lawrence Erlbaum.

Mukhopadhyay, S. C., Gaddam, A., & Gupta, G. S. (2008). Wireless sensors for home monitoring - A review. *Recent Patents on Electrical Engineering, 1*, 32–39. doi:10.217 4/1874476110801010032

Mumford, D., & Zhu, S.-C. (2007). *A stochastic grammar of images*. Now Publishers.

Naeem, U., & Bigham, J. (2009). Recognising activities of daily life through the usage of everyday objects around the home. In *Proceedings of the International Conference on Pervasive Computing Technologies for Healthcare*, (pp. 1–4). PervasiveHealth.

Naeem, U., & Bigham, J. (2009). Activity recognition in the home using a hierarchal framework with object usage data. *Journal of Ambient Intelligence and Smart Environments, 1*(4), 335–350.

Najafi, B., Aminian, K., Paraschiv-Ionescu, A., Loew, F., Bula, C. J., & Robert, P. (2003). Ambulatory system for human motion analysis using a kinematic sensor: Monitoring of daily physical activity in the elderly. *IEEE Transactions on Bio-Medical Engineering, 50*, 711–723. doi:10.1109/TBME.2003.812189

Nam, Y., Wohn, K., & Kwang, H. L. (1999). Modeling and recognition of hand gesture using colored petri nets. *IEEE Transactions on Systems, Man, and Cybernetics. Part A, Systems and Humans, 29*, 514–521. doi:10.1109/3468.784178

NaturalPoint, Inc. (2011). *Optitrack optical motion capture solutions*. NaturalPoint, Inc.

Navarro-Alvarez, E., & Siller, M. (2009). A node localization scheme for ZigBee-based sensor networks. In *Proceedings of the IEEE International Conference on Systems, Man and Cybernetics*, (pp. 728–733). IEEE.

Nesselrath, R., Lu, C., Schulz, C. H., Frey, J., & Alexandersson, J. (2011). *Ein gestenbasiertes system zur kontextsensitiven Interaktion mit dem smart home a gesture*. Ambient Assisted Living-AAL.

Neumann, B., & Weiss, T. (2003). Navigating through logic-based scene models for high-level scene interpretations. In *Proceedings of the 3rd International Conference on Computer Vision Systems (ICVS 2003)*, (pp. 212-222). Springer.

Neumann, B. (1989). Natural language description of time-varying scenes. In Waltz, D. (Ed.), *Semantic Structures* (pp. 167–206). Mahwah, NJ: Lawrence Erlbaum.

Neumann, B. (2008). *Bayesian compositional hierarchies - A probabilistic structure for scene interpretation. TR FBI-HH-B-282/08*. Hamburg, Germany: University of Hamburg.

Neumann, B., & Moeller, R. (2006). On scene interpretation with description logics. In Nagel, H.-H., & Christensen, H. (Eds.), *Cognitive Vision Systems* (pp. 247–275). Berlin, Germany: Springer. doi:10.1007/11414353_15

Newman, J. O. (2006). Quantifying the standard of proof beyond a reasonable doubt: A comment on three comments. *Law Probability and Risk, 5*(3-4), 267–269. doi:10.1093/lpr/mgm010

Newman, M. E. J. (2001). The structure of scientific collaboration network. *PNA, 98*(16), 404–409. doi:10.1073/pnas.98.2.404

Nguyen, A., Moore, D., & McCowan, I. (2007). Unsupervised clustering of free-living human activities using ambulatory accelerometry. In *Proceedings of the Annual International Conference of the IEEE Engineering in Medicine and Biology Society,* (pp. 4895-4898). IEEE Press.

Nguyen, N. T., Phung, D. Q., Venkatesh, S., & Bui, H. H. (2005). Learning and detecting activities from movement trajectories using the hierarchical hidden Markov model. In *Proceedings of CVPR,* (pp. 955-960). IEEE Computer Society.

Niebles, J., Wang, H., & Fei-Fei, L. (2006). *Unsupervised learning of human action categories using spatial-temporal words.* Paper presented at the British Machine Vision Conference. London, UK.

Niemela, I., & Simons, P. (1997). *Probabilistic reasoning with answer sets.* Paper presented at the LPNMR4. New York, NY.

Norris, C., McCail, M., & Wood, D. (2004). The Growth of CCTV: A global perspective on the international diffusion of video surveillance in publicly accessible space. *Surveillance & Society, 2*(2/3).

Nunes, N., Araújo, T., & Gamboa, H. (2012). Time series clustering algorithm for two-modes cyclic biosignals. In Fred, A., Filipe, J., & Gamboa, H. (Eds.), *Biostec 2011* (pp. 233–245). Springer.

Obstfeld, D. (2005). Social networks: The tertius iungens orientation and involvement in innovation. *Administrative Science Quarterly, 50,* 100–130.

Odella, F. (2007). Reverse experiments: Investigating social behaviour with daily technologies. In *INTER: A European Cultural Studies Conference Proceedings,* (pp. 463-470). Norrkoping, Sweden: Linkoping University Electronic Press.

Odella, F. (2009). Privacy concerns and electronic data collection: Group and individual response to social change in communications. In *NTTS - Conferences on New Techniques and Technologies for Statistics* (pp. 111–123). Brussels, Belgium: Eurostat - European Commission.

Odella, F. (2011). Network theory. In *Encyclopedia of Social Networks.* Thousand Oaks, CA: Sage Publications.

Odella, F. (2011). Social networks and communities: From traditional society to the virtual sphere. In Safar, M., & Mahdi, K. (Eds.), *Social Networking and Community Behaviour Modelling.* Hershey, PA: IGI Global. doi:10.4018/978-1-61350-444-4.ch001

Oliver, N., Horvitz, E., & Garg, A. (2002). Layered representations for human activity recognition. In *Proceedings of the Fourth IEEE International Conference on Multimodal Interfaces,* (pp. 3–8). IEEE Press. Modayil, J., Bai, T., & Kautz, H. (2008). Improving the recognition of interleaved activities. In *Proceedings of ubiComp 2008.* ubiComp.

Orr, R. J., & Abowd, G. D. (2000). The smart floor: A mechanism for natural user identification and tracking. In *Proceedings of the Conference on Human Factors in Computing Systems,* (pp. 275–276). IEEE.

Osborne, M. J. (2004). *An introduction to game theory.* Oxford, UK: Oxford University Press.

Oudshoorn, N. (2012). How places matter: Telecare technologies and the changing spatial dimensions of healthcare. *Social Studies of Science, 42*(1), 21–142. doi:10.1177/0306312711431817

Pang, Y., Yuan, Y., Li, X., & Pan, J. (2010, September 15). Efficient HOG human detection. *Signal Processing.* doi:doi:10.1016/j.sigpro.2010.08.010

Panina, D., & Aiello, J. R. (2005). Acceptance of electronic monitoring and its consequences in different cultural contexts: A conceptual model. *Journal of International Management, 11,* 269–292. doi:10.1016/j.intman.2005.03.009

Parameswaran, V., & Chellappa, R. (2004). View independent human body pose estimation from a single perspective. In *Proceedings of Computer Vision and Pattern Recognition.* IEEE.

Park, S., & Trivedi, M. M. (2007). Multi-person interaction and activity analysis: A synergistic track- and body-level analysis framework. In *Proceedings of Machine Vision and Applications* (pp. 151–166). IEEE. doi:10.1007/s00138-006-0055-x

Paschke, A., & Bichler, M. (2008). Knowledge representation concepts for automated SLA management. *Decision Support Systems*, *46*(1), 187–205. doi:10.1016/j.dss.2008.06.008

Patel, S. N., Robertson, T., Kientz, J. A., Reynolds, M. S., & Abowd, G. D. (2007). At the flick of a switch: Detecting and classifying unique electrical events on the residential power line. In *Proceedings of the International Conference on Ubiquitous Computing*, (p. 271). IEEE.

Patel, S. N., Truong, K. N., & Abowd, G. D. (2006). Powerline positioning: A practical sub-room-level indoor location system for domestic. *Ubiquitous Computing*, *4206*, 441–458.

Patterson, D. J., Fox, D., Kautz, H., & Philipose, M. (2005). Fine-grained activity recognition by aggregating abstract object usage. In *Proceedings Ninth IEEE International Symposium on Wearable Computers*, (pp. 44-51). IEEE.

Pearl, J. (1988). *Probabilistic reasoning in intelligent systems: Networks of plausible inference*. San Francisco, CA: Morgan Kaufmann.

Pearl, J. (2000). *Causality: Models, reasoning, and inference*. Cambridge, UK: Cambridge University Press.

Pentney, W., Popescu, A.-M., Wang, S., Kautz, H., & Philipose, M. (2006). Sensor-based understanding of daily life via large-scale use of common sense. In *Proceedings of the 21st National Conference on Artificial Intelligence*, (pp. 906-912). AAAI Press.

Pereira, L. M., & Han, T. A. (2009). Evolution prospection. In *Proceedings of International Symposium on Intelligent Decision Technologies (KES-IDT 2009)*. KES-IDT.

Pereira, L. M., & Han, T. A. (2009). *Intention recognition via causal bayes networks plus plan generation*. Paper presented at the Progress in Artificial Intelligence, Proceedings of 14th Portuguese International Conference on Artificial Intelligence (EPIA 2009). Evora, Portgual.

Pereira, L. M., & Han, T. A. (2011). Elder care via intention recognition and evolution prospection. In *Proceedings of the 18th International Conference on Applications of Declarative Programming and Knowledge Management (INAP)*. Evora, Portugal: Springer.

Pereira, L. M., Dell'Acqua, P., & Lopes, G. (2012). Inspecting and preferring abductive models. In *Handbook on Reasoning-Based Intelligent Systems*. Singapore, Singapore: World Scientific Publishers.

Pereira, L. M., & Han, T. A. (2009). Evolution prospection in decision making. *Intelligent Decision Technologies*, *3*(3), 157–171.

Pereira, L. M., & Han, T. A. (2011). Intention recognition with evolution prospection and causal bayes networks. In *Computational Intelligence for Engineering Systems 3: Emergent Applications* (pp. 1–33). Berlin, Germany: Springer. doi:10.1007/978-94-007-0093-2_1

Pereira, L. M., & Lopes, G. (2009). Prospective logic agents. *International Journal of Reasoning-Based Intelligent Systems*, *1*(3/4).

Perez-Lombard, L., Ortiz, J., & Pout, C. (2008). A review on buildings energy consumption information. *Energy and Building*, *40*(3), 394–398. doi:10.1016/j.enbuild.2007.03.007

Perkowitz, M., Philipose, M., Fishkin, K., & Patterson, D. J. (2004). Mining models of human activities from the web. In *Proceedings of the 13th International Conference on World Wide Web*, (pp. 573-582). New York, NY: ACM.

Perry, J. T., Kellog, S., Vaidya, S. M., Youn, J., Ali, H., & Sharif, H. (2009). Survey and evaluation of real-time fall detection approaches. In *Proceedings of the 6th International Conference on High Capacity Optical Networks and Enabling Technologies*, (pp. 158–164). Piscataway, NJ: IEEE Press.

Petroczi, A., Nepusz, T., & Baszo, F. (2007). Measuring tie-strength in virtual social networks. *Connections*, *27*(2), 39–52.

Philipose, M., Fishkin, K. P., Perkowitz, M., Patterson, D. J., Fox, D., Kautz, H., & Hähnel, D. (2004). Inferring activities from interactions with objects. In *Proceedings of IEEE Pervasive Computing*, (pp. 50–57). IEEE Press.

Physionet. (2012). *PhysioBank archive index*. Retrieved February 15, 2012 from http://www.physionet.org/physiobank/database

Pinch, T. (2008). Technology and institutions. *Theory and Society*, *37*(5), 461–483. doi:10.1007/s11186-008-9069-x

Pinker, S., Nowak, M. A., & Lee, J. J. (2008). The logic of indirect speech. *Proceedings of the National Academy of Sciences of the United States of America, 105*(3), 833–838. doi:10.1073/pnas.0707192105

Plath, N., Toussaint, M., & Nakajima, S. (2009). *Multiclass image segmentation using conditional random fields and global classification.* Paper presented at the In Proceedings of the 26th International Conference on Machine Learning. New York, NY.

PLUX – Wireless Biosignals. S.A. (2012). *Website.* Retrieved February 15, 2012 from http://www.plux.info

Podolny, J. M., & Baron, J. N. (1997). Resources and relationships: Social networks and mobility in the workplace. *American Sociological Review, 62*, 673–693. doi:10.2307/2657354

Pollack, M. E. (2005). Intelligent technology for an aging population: The use of ai to assist elders with cognitive impairment. *AI Magazine, 26*(2), 9–24.

Pynadath, D. V., & Wellman, M. P. (1995). Accounting for context in plan recognition, with application to traffic monitoring. In *Proceedings of Conference on Uncertainty in Artificial Intelligence (UAI 1995)*. UAI.

Quinlan, J. R. (1986). Induction of decision trees. *Machine Learning, 1*(1), 81–106. doi:10.1007/BF00116251

Raab, M., Wernsdorfer, M., Kitzelmann, E., & Schmid, U. (2011). From sensorimotor graphs to rules: An agent learns from a stream of experience. *Artificial General Intelligence*, 333–339.

Rabiner, L. R. (1989). A tutorial on hidden Markov models and selected applications in speech recognition. *Proceedings of the IEEE, 77*(2), 257–286. doi:10.1109/5.18626

Radke, S., Guroglu, B., & de Bruijn, E. R. A. (2012). There's something about a fair split: Intentionality moderates context-based fairness considerations in social decision-making. *PLoS ONE, 7*(2). doi:10.1371/journal.pone.0031491

Rammert, W. (2008). Rules of sociological method: Rethinking technology studies. *The British Journal of Sociology, 48*(2), 171–191. doi:10.2307/591747

Ramos, C., Augusto, J. C., & Shapiro, D. (2008). Ambient intelligence - The next step for artificial intelligence. *IEEE Intelligent Systems, 23*(2), 15–18. doi:10.1109/MIS.2008.19

Rao, A. S., & Georgeff, M. P. (1991). Modeling rational agents within a BDI-architecture. In *Proceedings of the Second International Conference of Principles of Knowledge Representation and Reasoning*. IEEE.

Rao, A. S., & Georgeff, M. P. (1995). BDI agents: From theory to practice. In *Proceeding of First International Conference on Multiagent Systems*. IEEE.

Rao, S. P., & Cook, D. J. (2004). Predicting inhabitant action using action and task models with application to smart homes. *International Journal of Artificial Intelligence Tools, 13*, 81–100. doi:10.1142/S0218213004001533

Rashidi, P., & Cook, D. (2010). Multi home transfer learning for resident activity discovery and recognition. In *Proceedings of the International Workshop on Knowledge Discovery from Sensor Data*. IEEE.

Ravi, N., Dandekar, N., Mysore, P., & Littman, M. (2005). Activity recognition from accelerometer data. In *Proceedings of the 17th Conference on Innovative Applications of Artificial Intelligence*, (pp. 1541-1546). AAAI Press.

Read, M. A. (2003). Use of color in child care environments: Application of color for wayfinding and space definition in Alabama child care environments. *Early Childhood Education Journal, 30*(4), 233–239. doi:10.1023/A:1023387607942

Reiter, R., & Mackworth, A. (1987). *The logic of depiction. TR 87-23*. Vancouver, Canada: University of British Columbia.

Reynolds, D., Quatieri, T., & Dunn, R. (2000). Speaker verification using adapted Gaussian mixture models. *Digital Signal Processing, 10*(1-3), 19–41. doi:10.1006/dspr.1999.0361

Riboni, D., & Bettini, C. (2009). Context-aware activity recognition through a combination of ontological and statistical reasoning. In *Proceedings of Ubiquitous Intelligence and Computing* (pp. 39–53). IEEE. doi:10.1007/978-3-642-02830-4_5

Riboni, D., & Bettini, C. (2011). COSAR: Hybrid reasoning for context-aware activity recognition. *Personal and Ubiquitous Computing, 15,* 271–289. doi:10.1007/s00779-010-0331-7

Riboni, D., & Bettini, C. (2011). OWL 2 modeling and reasoning with complex human activities. *Pervasive and Mobile Computing, 7*(3). doi:10.1016/j.pmcj.2011.02.001

Rice, J. (1995). *Mathematical statistics and data analysis.* New York, NY: Duxbury Press.

Rimey, R. D. (1993). *Control of selective perception using Bayes nets and decision theory.* (Dissertation). University of Rochester. Rochester, NY.

Rish, I. (2001). An empirical study of the naive Bayes classifier. In *Proceedings of the IJCAI Workshop on Empirical Methods in Artificial Intelligence,* (pp. 41–46). IJCAI.

Robson, A. (1990). Efficiency in evolutionary games: Darwin, Nash, and the secret handshake. *Journal of Theoretical Biology, 144*(3), 379–396. doi:10.1016/S0022-5193(05)80082-7

Rodrigues, G., Alves, V., Silveira, R., & Laranjeira, L. (2012). Dependability analysis in the ambient assisted living domain: An exploratory case study. *Journal of Systems and Software, 85,* 112–131. doi:10.1016/j.jss.2011.07.037

Rodriguez, M., Ahmed, J., & Shah, M. (2008). Action-mach: A spatio-temporal maximum average correlation height filter for action recognition. In *Proceedings of the IEEE Conference on Computer Vision and Pattern Recognition.* IEEE Press.

Romero, N., van Baren, J., Markopoulos, P., de Ruyter, B., & IJsselsteijn, W. (2003). Addressing interpersonal communication needs through ubiquitous connectivity: Home and away. *Lecture Notes in Computer Science, 2875,* 419–429. doi:10.1007/978-3-540-39863-9_32

Roy, O. (2009). *Thinking before acting: Intentions, logic, rational choice.* Retrieved from http://olivier.amonbofis.net/docs/Thesis_Olivier_Roy.pdf

Roy, P., Bouchard, B., Bouzouane, A., & Giroux, S. (2007). A hybrid plan recognition model for Alzheimer's patients: Interleaved-erroneous dilemma.In *Proceedings of IEEE/WIC/ACM International Conference on Intelligent Agent Technology.* IEEE.

Roy, O. (2009). Intentions and interactive transformations of decision problems. *Synthese, 169*(2), 335–349. doi:10.1007/s11229-009-9553-5

Ruppert, E. (2011). Population objects: Interpassive subjects. *Sociology, 45*(2), 218–233. doi:10.1177/0038038510394027

Russell, S., & Norvig, P. (2010). *Artificial intelligence: A modern approach* (3rd ed.). Upper Saddle River, NJ: Pearson.

Sadri, F. (2008). Multi-agent ambient intelligence for elderly care and assistance. In *Proceedings of International Electronic Conference on Computer Science.* IEEE.

Sadri, F. (2010). Logic-based approaches to intention recognition. In *Handbook of Research on Ambient Intelligence: Trends and Perspectives* (pp. 375). Springer.

Sadri, F. (2011). Intention recognition with event calculus graphs and weight of evidence. In *Proceedings 4th International Workshop on Human Aspects in Ambient Intelligence.* IEEE.

Sadri, F. (2011). Ambient intelligence: A survey. *ACM Computing Surveys, 43*(4), 1–66. doi:10.1145/1978802.1978815

Sagawa, K., Ishihara, T., Ina, A., & Inooka, H. (1998). Classification of human moving patterns using air pressure and acceleration. In *Proceedings of the 24th Annual Conference of the IEEE,* (pp. 1214 – 1219). IEEE.

Sahami, M., Dumais, S., Heckerman, D., & Horvitz, E. (1998). A Bayesian approach to filtering junk e-mail. In *Learning for Text Categorization: Papers from the 1998 Workshop.* Madison, WI: AAAI Press.

Sakakibara, Y. (1997). Recent advances of grammatical inference. *Theoretical Computer Science, 185,* 15–45. doi:10.1016/S0304-3975(97)00014-5

Sánchez, D., Tentori, M., & Favela, J. (2008). Activity recognition for the smart hospital. *IEEE Intelligent Systems, 23*(2), 50–57. doi:10.1109/MIS.2008.18

Santos, R., Sousa, J., Sañudo, B., Marques, C., & Gamboa, H. (2012). Biosignals events detection a morphological signal-independent approach. In *Proceedings of the International Conference on Bio-Inspired Systems and Signal Processing (BIOSIGNALS 2012)*. Vilamoura, Portugal: BIOSIGNALS.

Savvides, A., Promponas, V., & Fokianos, K. (2008). Clustering of biological time series by cepstral coefficients based distances. *Pattern Recognition, 41*, 2398–2412. doi:10.1016/j.patcog.2008.01.002

Schenker, A., Bunke, H., Last, M., & Kandel, A. (2005). *Graph-theoretic techniques for web content mining*. Singapore, Singapore: World Scientific.

Schmid, U., & Wysotzki, F. (1998). Induction of recursive program schemes. In *Proceedings of the 10th European Conference on Machine Learning (ECML 1998)*, (Vol. 1398, pp. 214–225). Springer.

Schmid, U. (2008). Cognition and AI. *Künstliche Intelligenz, 22*(1), 5–7.

Schmid, U., & Kitzelmann, E. (2011). Inductive rule learning on the knowledge level. *Cognitive Systems Research, 12*(3-4), 237–248. doi:10.1016/j.cogsys.2010.12.002

Schröder, J., Wabnik, S., van Hengel, P., & Goetze, S. (2011). *Erkennung und klassifikation von akustischen ereignissen zur häuslichen pflege*. Ambient Assisted Living-AAL.

Schroeder, C., & Neumann, B. (1996). On the logics of image interpretation: Model-construction in a formal knowledge-representation framework. In *Proceedings of the International Conference on Image Processing (ICIP 1996)*, (vol. 2, pp. 785-788). IEEE Computer Society.

Schuldt, C., Laptev, I., & Caputo, B. (2004). Recognizing human actions: A local SVM approach. In *Proceedings of the International Conference on Pattern Recognition*. IEEE Press.

Searle, J. R. (1995). *The construction of social reality*. New York, NY: The Free Press.

Searle, J. R. (2010). *Making the social world: The structure of human civilization*. Oxford, UK: Oxford University Press.

Sewell, G., & Barker, J. R. (2006). Coercion versus care: Using irony to make sense of organizational surveillance. *Academy of Management Review, 31*(4), 934–961. doi:10.5465/AMR.2006.22527466

Shanahan, M. (2005). Perception as abduction: Turning sensor data into meaningful representation. *Cognitive Science, 29*, 103–134. doi:10.1207/s15516709cog2901_5

Shannon, C. E. (1948). A mathematical theory of communication. *The Bell System Technical Journal, 27*, 379–423, 625–656.

Shaw, B., Parui, S. K., & Shridhar, M. (2008). A segmentation based approach to offline handwritten devanagari word recognition. In *Proceedings of the 19th International Conference on Pattern Recognition (ICPR)*, (pp. 1-4). Tampa, FL: IEEE.

Shearer, R., Motik, B., & Horrocks, I. (2008). HermiT: A highly-efficient OWL reasoner. In *Proceedings of the 5th OWLED Workshop on OWL: Experiences and Directions*. OWL.

Shet, V., Harwood, D., & Davis, L. (2005). VidMAP: Video monitoring of activity with prolog. In *Proceedings of Advanced Video and Signal Based Surveillance*. IEEE.

Shet, V., Neumann, J., Ramesh, V., & Davis, L. (2007). Billatice-based logical reasoning for human detection. In *Proceedings of Computer Vision and Pattern Recognition*. IEEE.

Shi, Y., Bobick, A. F., & Essa, I. A. (2006). Learning temporal sequence model from partially labeled data. *Proceedings of CVPR, IEEE Computer Society, 2*, 1631–1638.

Sigmund, K. (2010). *The calculus of selfishness*. Princeton, NJ: Princeton University Press.

Sindhwani, V., Niyogi, P., & Belkin, M. (2005). *Beyond the point cloud: from transductive to semi-supervised learning*. Paper presented at the In Proceedings of the International Conference on Machine Learning. New York, NY.

Singh, M. P. (1991). *Intentions, commitments and rationality*. Paper presented at the 13th Annual Conference of the Cognitive Science Society. New York, NY.

Singla, G., Cook, D. J., & Schmitter-Edgecombe, M. (2010). Recognizing independent and joint activities among multiple residents in smart environments. *Journal of Ambient Intelligence and Humanized Computing, 1*(1), 57–63. doi:10.1007/s12652-009-0007-1

Skubic, M., Alexander, G., Popescu, M., Rantz, M., & Keller, J. (2009). A smart home application to eldercare: Current status and lessons learned. *Technology and Health Care, 17*(3), 183–201.

Sminchisescu, C., Kanaujia, A., Li, Z., & Metaxas, D. (2005). *Conditional random fields for contextual human motion recognition.* Paper presented at the In Proceedings of the 10th IEEE International Conference on Computer Vision. New York, NY.

Souza, P. (1977). Statistical tests and distance measures for LPC coefficients. *IEEE Transactions on Acoustics, Speech, and Signal Processing, 25*(6), 554–559. doi:10.1109/TASSP.1977.1163004

Spencer, B. F., Ruiz-s, M. E., & Kurata, N. (2004). Smart sensing technology: Opportunities and challenges. *Journal of Structural Control and Health Monitoring, 11*(4), 349–368. doi:10.1002/stc.48

Spriggs, E. H., De La Torre, F., & Hebert, M. (2009). *Temporal segmentation and activity classification from first-person sensing.* Paper presented at the In Proceedings of IEEE Computer Society Conference on Computer Vision and Pattern Recognition Workshops. New York, NY.

Srinivasan, V., Stankovic, J., & Whitehouse, K. (2010). Using height sensors for biometric identification in multi-resident homes. *Lecture Notes in Computer Science, 6030*, 337–354. doi:10.1007/978-3-642-12654-3_20

Stalder, F. (2002). Public opinion privacy is not the antidote to surveillance. *Surveillance & Society, 1*(1).

Stark, A., Riebeck, M., & Kawalek, J. (2007). How to design an advanced pedestrian navigation system: Field trial results. In *Proceedings of the IEEE International Workshop on Intelligent Data Acquisition and Advanced Computing Systems: Technology and Applications.* Dortmund, Germany: IEEE Press.

Stein, K., & Schlieder, C. (2004). Recognition of intentional behaviors in spatial partonomies. *Applied Artificial Intelligence and Logistics, 9.*

Stiefmeier, T., Roggen, D., & Troster, G. (2007). *Fusion of string-matched templates for continuous activity recognition.* Paper presented at the In Proceedings of the 11th IEEE International Symposium on Wearable Computers. New York, NY.

Stiefmeier, T., Roggen, D., Ogris, G., Lukowicz, P., & Tröster, G. (2008). Wearable activity tracking in car manufacturing. *IEEE Pervasive Computing / IEEE Computer Society [and] IEEE Communications Society, 7*(2), 42–50. doi:10.1109/MPRV.2008.40

Stutzman, F. (2006). An evaluation of identity-sharing behavior in social network communities. *Journal of the International Digital Media and Arts Association, 3*(1), 10–18.

Sukthankar, G. R. (2007). *Activity recognition for agent teams.* Retrieved from http://www.cs.cmu.edu/~gitars/gsukthankar-thesis.pdf

Sukthankar, G. R., & Sycara, K. (2008). Robust and efficient plan recognition for dynamic multi-agent teams. In *Proceedings of International Conference on Autonomous Agents and Multi-Agent Systems.* IEEE.

Sun, J., Wu, X., Yan, S., Cheong, L., Chua, T., & Li, J. (2009). Hierarchical spatio-temporal context modeling for action recognition. In *Proceedings of the IEEE Conference on Computer Vision and Pattern Recognition.* IEEE Press.

Swift, T. (1999). Tabling for non-monotonic programming. *Annals of Mathematics and Artificial Intelligence, 25*(3-4), 240.

Szell, L., & Thurner, J. (2010). Measuring social dynamics in a massive multiplayer online game. *Social Networks, 32*, 313–329. doi:10.1016/j.socnet.2010.06.001

Szewcyzk, S., Dwan, K., Minor, B., Swedlove, B., & Cook, D. (2009). Annotating smart environment sensor data for activity learning. *Technology and Health Care, 17*(3), 161–169.

Szomszor, M., Cattuto, C., Van den Broeck, W., Barrat, A., & Alani, H. (2010). Semantics, sensors, and the social web: The live social semantics experiments. *Lecture Notes in Computer Science, 6089*, 196–210. doi:10.1007/978-3-642-13489-0_14

Tahboub, K. A. (2006). Intelligent human-machine interaction based on dynamic Bayesian networks probabilistic intention recognition. *Journal of Intelligent & Robotic Systems*, *45*, 31–52. doi:10.1007/s10846-005-9018-0

Tanaka, Y., Iwamoto, K., & Uehara, K. (2005). Discovery of time-series motif from multi-dimensional data based on mdl principle. *Machine Learning*, *58*(2-3), 269–300. doi:10.1007/s10994-005-5829-2

Tapia, E. M., Intille, S. S., & Larson, K. (2004). Activity recognition in the home using simple and ubiquitous sensors. In *Proceedings of Pervasive* (pp. 158–175). IEEE. doi:10.1007/978-3-540-24646-6_10

Tapia, E., Intille, S., Lopez, L., & Larson, K. (2006). The design of a portable kit of wireless sensors for naturalistic data collection. In *Proceedings of Pervasive Computing* (pp. 117–134). IEEE. doi:10.1007/11748625_8

Tappen, M. F., Liu, C., Adelson, E. H., & Freeman, W. T. (2007). *Learning gaussian conditional random fields for low-level vision*. Paper presented at the In Proceedings of IEEE Conference on Computer Vision and Pattern Recognition. New York, NY.

Taylor, C. J. (2000). Reconstruction of articulated objects from point correspondences in a single image. In *Proceedings of Computer Vision and Pattern Recognition* (pp. 349–363). IEEE. doi:10.1006/cviu.2000.0878

Taylor, S., & Spencer, B. A. (1990). Ethical implications of human resource information systems. *Employee Responsibilities and Rights Journal*, *3*(1), 19–30. doi:10.1007/BF01384761

Tekscan. (2009). *FlexiForce force sensors*. Retrieved October 25, 2009, from http://www.tekscan.com/flexiforce/flexiforce.html

Terzic, K., Hotz, L., & Neumann, B. (2007). Division of work during behaviour recognition. In Gottfried, B. (Ed.), *BMI 2007* (*Vol. 296*, pp. 144–159). CEUR.

Thirde, D., Borg, M., Ferryman, J., Fusier, F., Valentin, V., Brémond, F., & Thonnat, M. (2006). A real-time scene understanding system for airport apron monitoring. In *Proceedings of the IEEE International Conference on Computer Vision Systems (ICVS 2006)*. IEEE Press.

Thompson, J. R., & Koronacki, J. (2002). *Statistical process control: The Deming paradigm and beyond*. CRC Pr I Llc.

Tian, Y., Cao, L., Liu, Z., & Zhang, Z. (2011). Hierarchical filtered motion field for action recognition in crowded videos. *IEEE Transactions on Systems, Man and Cybernetics. Part C, Applications and Reviews*, *42*(3).

Tomasello, M. (1999). *The cultural origins of human cognition*. Boston, MA: Harvard University Press.

Tomasello, M. (2003). *Constructing a language: A usage-based theory of language acquisition*. Boston, MA: Harvard University Press.

Tomasello, M. (2008). *Origins of human communication*. Cambridge, MA: MIT Press.

Tong, S., & Chang, E. (2001). *Support vector machine active learning for image retrieval*. Paper presented at the In Proceedings of the ACM International Conference on Multimedia. New York, NY.

Tong, S., & Koller, D. (2002). Support vector machine active learning with applications to text classification. *Journal of Machine Learning Research*, *2*, 45–66.

Trivers, R. (2011). *The folly of fools: The logic of deceit and self-deception in human life*. New York, NY: Basic Books.

Tsotsos, J. K., Mylopoulos, J., Covvey, H. D., & Zucker, S. W. (1980). A framework for visual motion understanding. *IEEE Transactions on Pattern Analysis and Machine Intelligence*, *2*, 563–573.

Tucknott, K. A., & Sorenson, M. N. (1986). *Patient bed alarm system*. United States Patent 4633237, 1986. Washington, DC: US Patent Office.

Tukey, J. W. (1977). *Exploratory data analysis*. Reading, MA: Addison-Wesley.

Tu, P. H., Son, T. C., & Baral, C. (2007). Reasoning and planning with sensing actions, incomplete information, and static causal laws using answer set programming. *Theory and Practice of Logic Programming*, *7*(4), 377–450. doi:10.1017/S1471068406002948

Tu, P. H., Son, T. C., Gelfond, M., & Morales, A. R. (2011). Approximation of action theories and its application to conformant planning. *Artificial Intelligence*, *175*(1), 79–119. doi:10.1016/j.artint.2010.04.007

UCSC. (2010). *Life expectancy- North south gap in life expectancy is narrowing fast*. Retrieved on July 30, 2010 from http://ucatlas.ucsc.edu/life/index.html

Vahdatpour, A., Amini, N., & Sarrafzadeh, M. (2009). *Toward unsupervised activity discovery using multi-dimensional motif detection in time series*. Paper presented at the Proceedings of the International Joint Conference on Artficial Intelligence. New York, NY.

Vail, D. L., & Veloso, M. M. (2008). Feature selection for activity recognition in multi-robot domains. In *Proceedings of the 23rd Conference on Artificial Intelligence*, (pp. 1415-1420). AAAI Press.

Vail, D. L., Veloso, M. M., & Lafferty, J. D. (2007). *Conditional random fields for activity recognition*. Paper presented at the Proceedings of the Sixth International Joint Conference on Autonomous Agents and Multiagent Systems. New York, NY.

Vail, D. L. (2008). *Conditional random fields for activity recognition*. Pittsburgh, PA: Carnegie Mellon University.

van Hees, M., & Roy, O. (2008). Intentions and plans in decision and game theory. In *Reasons and Intentions* (pp. 207–226). New York, NY: Ashgate Publishers.

van Kasteren, T., Noulas, A., Englebienne, G., & Kröse, B. (2008). Accurate activity recognition in a home setting. In *Proceedings of the 10th International Conference on Ubiquitous Computing*, (pp. 1-9). New York, NY: ACM.

Vargas Solar, G. (2005). *Global, pervasive and ubiquitous information societies: Engineering challenges and social impact*. Paris, France: NSRC.

VectorNav Technologies LLC. (2011). *Website*. Retrieved from http://www.vectornav.com/

Vila, L. (1994). A survey on temporal reasoning in artificial intelligence. *AI Communications*, *7*(1), 4–28.

Viterbi, A. J. (1967). Error bounds for convolutional codes and an asymptotically optimal decoding algorithm. *IEEE Transactions on Information Theory*, *13*, 260–269. doi:10.1109/TIT.1967.1054010

Voskuhl, A. (2004). Humans, machines and conversations: An ethnographic study of the making of automatic speech recognition technologies. *Social Studies of Science*, *34*(3), 393–421. doi:10.1177/0306312704043576

Walby, K. (2006). How closed –circuit television surveillance organizes the social: An institutional ethnography. *Canadian Journal of Sociology*, *30*(2), 189–214.

Walby, K., & Hier, S. P. (2005). Risk technologies and the securitization of post-9/11 citizenship: The case of national ID cards in Canada. *Journal of the Society for Socialist Studies*, *2*, 7–37.

Wang, L., Chan, K., & Zhang, Z. (2003). *Bootstrapping SVM active learning by incorporating unlabelled images for image retrieval*. Paper presented at the In Proceedings of Computer Vision and Pattern Recognition. New York, NY.

Wang, P., Abowd, G., & Rehg, J. (2009). Quasi-periodic event analysis for social game retrieval. In *Proceedings of the IEEE International Conference on Computer Vision*. IEEE Press.

Wasserman, S., & Faust, K. (1999). *Social network analysis*. Cambridge, UK: Cambridge University Press.

Watts, D. J., Dodds, P. S., & Newman, M. E. J. (2002). Identity and search in social networks. *Science*, *17*, 1302–1305. doi:10.1126/science.1070120

Weather Underground. (2010). *Website*. Retrieved June 26, 2010, from http://www.wunderground.com

Weiser, M. (1991). The computer for the twenty-first century. *Scientific American*, *94*(10).

Wellman, B., Salaff, J., Dimitrova, D., Garton, L., & Gulia, M. (1996). Computer networks: Collaborative work, telework and virtual community. *Annual Review of Sociology*, *22*, 213–238. doi:10.1146/annurev.soc.22.1.213

Wigg, J. M. (2010). Liberating the wanderers: Using technology to unlock doors for those living with dementia. *Sociology of Health & Illness*, *32*(2), 288–303. doi:10.1111/j.1467-9566.2009.01221.x

Wilken, O., Hein, A., & Spehr, M. G. J. (2011). *Ein ansatz zur fusion von aktivitätswahrscheinlichkeiten zur robusten identifikation von aktivitäten des täglichen lebens (ADL)*. Ambient Assisted Living-AAL.

Wilson, D. H., & Matthai, P. (2005). Maximum a posteriori path estimation with input trace perturbation: Algorithms and application to credible rating of human routines. In *Proceedings of the 19th International Joint Conference on Artificial Intelligence,* (pp. 895-901). San Francisco, CA: Morgan Kaufmann Publishers Inc.

Wilson, D., & Atkeson, C. (2005). Simultaneous tracking & activity recognition (star) using many anonymous, binary sensors. In *Proceedings of PERVASIVE,* (pp. 62–79). IEEE.

Witten, I. H., & Frank, E. (2005). *Data mining: Practical machine learning tools and techniques.* San Francisco, CA: Morgan Kaufmann Publishing.

Wong, S., Kim, T., & Cipolla, R. (2007). Learning motion categories using both semantic and structural information. In *Proceedings of the IEEE Conference on Computer Vision and Pattern Recognition.* IEEE Press.

Wood, D. (2005). People watching people. *Surveillance & Society, 2*(4), 474–478.

Woodman, O., & Harle, R. (2008). Pedestrian localisation for indoor environments. In *Proceedings of the International Conference on Ubiquitous Computing,* (pp. 114–123). ACM Press.

Woodward, A. L., Sommerville, J. A., Gerson, S., Henderson, A. M. E., & Buresh, J. (2009). The emergence of intention attribution in infancy. *Psychology of Learning and Motivation, 51,* 187–222. doi:10.1016/S0079-7421(09)51006-7

Wooldridge, M. (2000). *Reasoning about rational agents.* Cambridge, MA: MIT Press.

World Business Council for Sustainable Development. (2009). *Energy efficiency in buildings.* Retrievecd October 11, 2009, from http://www.wbcsd.org

Wu, J., Osuntogun, A., Choudhury, T., Philipose, M., & Rehg, J. (2007). A scalable approach to activity recognition based on object use. In *Proceedings of the IEEE International Conference on Computer Vision.* IEEE Press.

Wu, W., Au, L., Jordan, B., Stathopoulos, T., Batalin, M., Kaiser, W., et al. (2008). *The smartcane system: an assistive device for geriatrics.* Paper presented at the Proceedings of the ICST 3rd International Conference on Body Area Networks. New York, NY.

Wyatt, D., Philipose, M., & Choudhury, T. (2005). Unsupervised activity recognition using automatically mined common sense. In *Proceedings of the 20th Conference on Artificial Intelligence,* (pp. 21-27). AAAI Press.

XSB. (2009). *The XSB system version 3.2 vol. 2: Libraries, interfaces and packages.* XSB.

Xu, J., & Shelton, C. R. (2008). Continuous time Bayesian networks for host level network intrusion detection. In *Proceedings of ECML/PKDD,* (pp. 613-627). Springer.

Yamaguchi, A., Ogawa, M., Tamura, T., & Togawa, T. (1998). Monitoring behaviour in the home using positioning sensors. In *Proceedings of the 20th Annual International Conference IEEE Engineering in Medicine and Biology Society,* (pp. 1977–1979). IEEE Press.

Yanco, H. A., & Drury, J. L. (2004). Classifying human-robot interaction: An updated taxonomy. In *Proceedings of 2004 IEEE International Conference on Systems, Man and Cybernetics,* (pp. 2841–2846). IEEE Press.

Yao, B., & Zhu, S. (2009). Learning deformable action templates from cluttered videos. In *Proceedings of the IEEE International Conference on Computer Vision.* IEEE Press.

Yeo, C., Ahammad, P., Ramchandran, K., & Sastry, S. S. (2008). High-speed action recognition and localization in compressed domain videos. *IEEE Transactions on Circuits and Systems for Video Technology, 18*(8), 1006–1015. doi:10.1109/TCSVT.2008.927112

Yin, J., & Meng, Y. (2010). Human activity recognition in video using a hierarchical probabilistic latent model. In *Proceedings of the IEEE Conference on Computer Vision and Pattern Recognition.* IEEE Press.

Youngblood, G. M., & Cook, D. J. (2007). Data mining for hierarchical model creation. *IEEE Transactions on Systems, Man, and Cybernetics. Part C, 37*(4), 561–572.

Young, L., & Saxe, R. (2011). When ignorance is no excuse: Different roles for intent across moral domains. *Cognition, 120*(2), 202–214. doi:10.1016/j.cognition.2011.04.005

Yuan, J., Liu, Z., & Wu, Y. (2009). Discriminative subvolume search for efficient action detection. In *Proceedings of the IEEE Conference on Computer Vision and Pattern Recognition.* IEEE Press.

Yuan, Y., & Pang, Y. (2008). Discriminant adaptive edge weights for graph embedding. In *Proceedings of the IEEE International Conference on Acoustics, Speech, and Signal Processing*. IEEE Press.

Zaidenberg, S., Reignier, P., & Crowley, J. L. (2008). Reinforcement learning of context models for a ubiquitous personal assistant. In *Proceedings of the 3rd Symposium of Ubiquitous Computing and Ambient Intelligence*, (pp. 254–264). IEEE.

Zheng, H., Wang, H., & Black, N. D. (2008). Human activity detection in smart home environment with self-adaptive neural networks. In *Proceedings of IEEE International Conference on Networking, Sensing and Control*, (pp. 1505-1510). IEEE.

Zheng, V. W., Hu, D. H., & Yang, Q. (2009). Cross-domain activity recognition. In *Proceedings of the 11th International Conference on Ubiquitous Computing*, (pp. 61-70). ACM.

Zheng, Y. R., Goubran, R. A., El-Tanany, A., & Hongchi, S. (2005). A microphone array system for multimedia applications with near field signal targets. *IEEE Sensors Journal*, *5*(6), 1395–1406. doi:10.1109/JSEN.2005.858936

Zhou, F., Torre, F., & Hodgins, J. K. (2008). *Aligned cluster analysis for temporal segmentation of human motion*. Paper presented at the Proceedings of the IEEE Conference on Automatic Face and Gesture Recognition. New York, NY.

Zhu, C. (2011). *Video about human daily activity recognition for the assisted living system*. Retrieved from http://youtu.be/5yrMz59HKBE

Zhu, G., Yang, M., Yu, K., Xu, W., & Gong, Y. (2009). Detecting video events based on action recognition in complex scenes using spatio-temporal descriptor. In *Proceedings of the ACM International Conference on Multimedia*, (pp. 165–174). ACM Press.

Zornetzer, S. F. (1995). *An introduction to neural and electronic networks*. San Francisco, CA: Morgan Kaufmann.

Zumberge, J. F., Heflin, M. B., Jefferson, D. C., Watkins, M. M., & Webb, F. H. (1997). Precise point positioning for the efficient and robust analysis of GPS data from large networks. *Journal of Geophysical Research*, *102*(B3), 5005–5017. doi:10.1029/96JB03860

About the Contributors

Hans W. Guesgen is a Professor of Computer Science in the School of Engineering and Advanced Technology (SEAT) at Massey University in New Zealand. His research interests include ambient intelligence, smart environments, knowledge representation, constraint satisfaction, spatio-temporal and qualitative reasoning, with more than 100 refereed papers in these areas. He holds a Doctorate in Computer Science of the University of Kaiserslautern, and a Higher Doctorate (Habilitation) in Computer Science of the University of Hamburg, Germany. Hans is a senior member of the Association for the Advancement of Artificial Intelligence (AAAI) and an honorary research associate of the Computer Science Department of the University of Auckland, New Zealand.

Stephen Marsland is Professor of Scientific Computing in the School of Engineering and Advanced Technology (SEAT) at Massey University in New Zealand. He has a degree in Mathematics from Oxford University and a PhD from Manchester University. He arrived at Massey in 2004 following postdoc positions in the US and Europe. Stephen's research interests lie in the areas of Euler equations on diffeomorphism groups, machine learning and behaviour recognition, and complexity. He is currently supported by the RSNZ Marsden Fund.

* * *

Rodolfo Abreu is a Master student in Biomedical Engineering at Faculdade de Ciências e Tecnologia (FCT). He's developing his thesis on "Discovery of Information on Biosignals Based on Clustering Techniques Applied to Ambient Assisted Living (AAL)" under the guidance of Professor Hugo Gamboa.

Alexander Artikis is a Research Associate in the Institute of Informatics and Telecommunications at NCSR "Demokritos," in Athens, Greece. He holds a PhD from Imperial College London on the topic of norm-governed multi-agent systems. His research interests lie in the areas of distributed artificial intelligence, temporal representation and reasoning, artificial intelligence and law, and event-based systems. He has published papers in related journals and conferences, such as the *Artificial Intelligence Journal*. He has worked on the EU FP7 PRONTO project, being responsible for the event recognition work-package. He has given tutorials on several summer schools and conferences, including a tutorial on event recognition in the 2011 edition of IJCAI. He is a member of the programme committees of several international conferences, such as DEBS, AAMAS, and AAAI. He has co-organised several international workshops, including "EVENTS 2010 – Recognising and Tracking Events on the Web and in Real Life," and chaired the Event Processing track in RuleML 2011.

Juan Carlos Augusto focuses his research on the design and implementation of Ambient intelligence systems, especially Smart Homes and Smart Classrooms. He has contributed to the research community with more than 160 publications, given several invited talks and tutorials, most of them related to AmI and AAL and co-chaired numerous workshops and conferences both on Ambient Intelligence and on Software Reliability. More recently, he has been Programme Chair of PH'11, IE'11, and Landscape Track Chair for AmI'11. He was appointed as Editor in Chief of the Book Series on Ambient Intelligence and Smart Environments, co-Editor in Chief of the *Journal on Ambient Intelligence and Smart Environments* (JAISE), both published by IOS Press; and as Editorial Board member for several other international journals in different areas of Computer Science. He is currently the technical director of NOCTURNAL (Night Optimised Care Technology for UseRs Needing Assisted Lifestyles), funded by EPSRC (UK).

Asier Aztiria is a Lecturer/Researcher at the University of Mondragon's Polytechnical Engineering School. His research interests include artificial intelligence, machine-learning techniques, knowledge discovering applied to intelligent environments. He received his PhD degree from University of Mondragon in 2010 with the thesis titled "Learning Frequent Behaviours of the Users in Intelligent Environments." He undertook research works at University of Ulster (UK) and Stanford University (USA).

Wilfried Bohlken studied Computer Science at the University of Oldenburg (Diploma 1999). In 2000, he worked as research associate at the Institute of Robotics and Process Control at the University of Braunschweig. From 2001 to 2008, he worked for Philips Medical Systems in the field of image processing. Since 2008, he works as research associate at the Cognitive System Laboratory, Department of Computer Science, at the University of Hamburg.

Liangliang Cao is a Research Staff Member of the Multimedia Research Group at the IBM T. J. Watson Research Center. He is working on large-scale visual recognition, action recognition, and geo-tagged social media. He is the key person of IBM team for federal funded ALADDIN project as well as a few other projects. Before joining IBM, he received his Ph.D. in Electrical and Computer Engineering from the University of Illinois at Urbana-Champaign in 2011, Master of Philosophy from the Chinese University of Hong Kong in 2005, Bachelor of Engineering from University of Science and Technology of China in 2003. He was awarded as a Computer Science and Engineering Fellow (2009-2010) working with Prof. Thomas Huang and Prof. Jiawei Han in UIUC. He was listed in the Facebook Fellowship Finalist (2010) and awarded an "Emerging Leader in Multimedia and Signal Processing" in IBM Watson Workshop (2010). He was a key person in the UIUC-NEC team that won ImageNet 2010 Challenge.

Chao Chen is currently a Ph.D student in the School of Electrical Engineering and Computer Science at Washington State University. He received a B.E. degree in Automatic Control from Anhui University, China, in 2005. In 2008, he received a M.S. degree in Network Communication and Control from University of Science and Technology of China, China. His interests focus on sensor network in smart environments, energy prediction and modeling, data mining and machine learning applications in health care.

Sook-Ling Chua is currently a PhD student in the School of Engineering and Advanced Technology (SEAT) at Massey University. She has a BSc (Hons) in Computing from Staffordshire University and a Msc degree from the Malaysia University of Science and Technology (MUST). Her research interests include behaviour recognition, machine learning, data mining, and information theory.

Diane J. Cook is a Huie-Rogers Chair Professor in the School of Electrical Engineering and Computer Science at Washington State University. Dr. Cook received a B.S. degree in Math/Computer Science from Wheaton College in 1985, a M.S. degree in Computer Science from the University of Illinois in 1987, and a Ph.D. degree in Computer Science from the University of Illinois in 1990. Her research interests include artificial intelligence, machine learning, graph-based relational data mining, smart environments, and robotics. Dr. Cook is an IEEE Fellow.

Aaron S. Crandall is a Postdoctoral Research Associate at Washington State University's School of Electrical Engineering and Computer Science. Dr. Crandall received a B.S. of Electrical Engineering from the University of Portland in 2001, a M.S. of Computer Science from Oregon Health and Science University in 2006, and a Ph.D. degree in Computer Science from Washington State University in 2011. His research interests include smart homes, adaptive systems, autonomous agents, artificial intelligence, machine learning, and gerontechnology.

Ana Fred, PhD in Electrical and Computer Engineering from Instituto Superior Técnico (IST), is an Assistant Professor at the Department of Electrical and Computer Engineering of IST and a researcher in the group of Pattern and Image Analysis of the Instituto de Telecomunicações (IT), Networks and Multimedia Research Area.

Anuroop Gaddam is currently pursuing his Ph.D. study with the School of Engineering and Advanced Technology, Massey University, Palmerston North, New Zealand. He has a Bachelor of Technology degree from JNTU, Hyderabad, India, and Post-Graduate Diploma from Massey University. His research interests include smart sensors, wireless sensors, smart homes, and sensor network. He is currently involved with the development of wireless sensor network for home monitoring, especially for eldercare. He has published 10 papers in different journals and international conference proceedings. The demonstration model of his research project was awarded the first prize in the 2007 International Creative Design Contest organized by the Southern Taiwan University, Tainan, Taiwan, during November 2007.

Hugo Gamboa, PhD in Electrical and Computer Engineering from Instituto Superior Técnico (IST) on Behavioral Biometrics, is the CEO of PLUX – Wireless Biosignals S.A. and Assistant Professor at the Physics Department of Faculdade de Ciências e Tecnologia (FCT – UNL).

Björn Gottfried works at the Centre for Computing Technologies at the University of Bremen, Germany, where he received his Doctoral degree in the context of Spatial Reasoning in 2005 and where he finished his habilitation in 2008. He is Research Scientist and Lecturer in the context of Artificial Intelligence, in particular image processing, and spatial and diagrammatic reasoning. Over the last ten years he published mainly in the context of spatial and temporal reasoning, image processing, and ambient intelligence, numerous journal and conference papers, has been invited as course lecturer, and holds 1 European patent and 1 US patent. He is member in the programme committees of several workshops about ambient intelligence, smart homes, and related fields and organises the annual BMI workshop on behaviour monitoring and interpretation.

Gourab Sen Gupta received his B.E (Electronics) degree from the University of Indore, India, in 1982, and Masters of Electronics Engineering (MEE) degree from the Philips International Institute, Technical University of Eindhoven, Holland, in 1984. After working for 5 years as a Software Engineer in Philips India in the Consumer Electronics division, he joined Singapore Polytechnic in 1989, where he worked as a Senior Lecturer in the School of Electrical and Electronic Engineering. Since September 2002, he has been a Senior Lecturer at the School of Engineering and Advanced Technology (SEAT), Massey University, New Zealand. In 2008, he was awarded a Ph.D. in Computer Systems Engineering for his research on Intelligent Control of Multi-Agent Collaborative Systems. His current research interests are in the area of embedded systems, robotics, real-time vision processing, behavior programming for multi-agent collaboration, and automated testing and measurement systems. He has published and presented over 100 research papers in various journals and conferences. He has been a guest editor for leading journals such as *IEEE Sensors Journal, International Journal of Intelligent Systems Technologies and Applications* (IJISTA), and *Studies in Computational Intelligence* (Special Issue on Autonomous Robots and Agents) by Springer-Verlag. He is a senior member of IEEE.

The Anh Han (BacGiang, Vietnam, 1983) obtained in 2007 his Bachelor degree in Computer Science at the Saint Petersburg State University, Russia, and in 2009 his M.S. double degree in Computational Logics at the Technical University of Dresden, Germany, and New University of Lisbon, Portugal (both with distinction). He earned his Ph.D. in Computer Science in May 2012 at the Department of Informatics, New University of Lisbon, where he studied cognitive modeling, evolutionary game theory, as well as how to combine these two techniques to build computational models explaining the roles of different cognitive skills in the evolution of cooperative behavior. He is recently awarded a three-year FWO postdoctoral fellowship to pursue a similar research direction at the AI Lab, Vrije Universiteit Brussel, Belgium, where he studies the evolution of preferences and group formation in dynamic networks.

Lothar Hotz studied Computer Science at RWTH Aachen and University of Hamburg (Diploma 1988, Dr. rer. nat. 2008). Since 2000, he is Senior Researcher at the Hamburg Informatics Technology Center (HITeC e.V.) located at the University of Hamburg. He has participated in several projects related to topics of configuration, knowledge representation, constraints, diagnosis, scene interpretation, semantic search, requirements engineering, parallel processing, and object-oriented programming languages. He has organized several international and national workshops in the area of knowledge-based configuration and is an active member of this community.

Patrick Koopmann studied Computer Science at the University of Hamburg with focus on Knowledge Engineering and Philosophy as minor (Diploma 2010). In 2010, he worked as Research Associate at the Cognitive Science Laboratory in the Department of Computer Science at the University of Hamburg for the CoFriend project. Currently, he is working as Technical Consultant for the German consulting company Cirquent GmbH, which is part of the NTT Data Corporation.

Zicheng Liu is a Senior Researcher at Microsoft Research, Redmond. He has worked on a variety of topics including combinatorial optimization, linked figure animation, and microphone array signal processing. His current research interests include activity recognition, face modeling and animation, and multimedia collaboration. He received a Ph.D. in Computer Science from Princeton University, a M.S. in Operational Research from the Institute of Applied Mathematics, Chinese Academy of Science, and a B.S. in Mathematics from Huazhong Normal University, China. Before joining Microsoft Research, he worked at Silicon Graphics as a member of technical staff for two years where he developed a trimmed NURBS tessellator that was shipped in both OpenGL and OpenGL-Optimizer products. He has published over 80 papers in peer-reviewed international journals and conferences, and holds over 50 granted patents. He has served in the technical committees for many international conferences. He was a co-organizer of the 2003 ICCV Workshop on Multimedia Technologies in E-Learning and Collaboration, and 2010 CVPR Workshop on Human Activity Understanding from 3D Data. He served as a technical co-chair of 2006 IEEE International Workshop on Multimedia Signal Processing, and 2010 International Conference on Multimedia and Expo. He is a general co-chair of 2012 IEEE Visual Communication and Image Processing. He is an associate editor of Machine Vision and Applications journal, and a senior member of IEEE.

Subhas Chandra Mukhopadhyay graduated from the Department of Electrical Engineering, Jadavpur University, Calcutta, India with a Gold medal and received the Master of Electrical Engineering degree from Indian Institute of Science, Bangalore, India. He has PhD (Eng.) degree from Jadavpur University, India and Doctor of Engineering degree from Kanazawa University, Japan. Currently he is working as an Associate Professor with the School of Engineering and Advanced Technology, Massey University, Palmerston North, New Zealand. He has over 21 years of teaching and research experiences. His fields of interest include Sensors and Sensing Technology, Electromagnetics, control, electrical machines and numerical field calculation, etc. He has authored/co-authored over 240 papers in different international journals, conferences, and book chapter. He has edited nine conference proceedings. He has also edited eight special issues of international journals as lead guest editor and ten books out of which eight are with Springer-Verlag. He was awarded numerous awards throughout his career and attracted over NZ \$3.5 M on different research projects. He is a Fellow of IEEE (USA), a Fellow of IET (UK), an associate editor of *IEEE Sensors Journal* and *IEEE Transactions on Instrumentation and Measurements*. He is in the editorial board of *e-Journal on Non-Destructive Testing, Sensors and Transducers, Transactions on Systems, Signals and Devices* (TSSD), *Journal on the Patents on Electrical Engineering, Journal of Sensors*. He is the co-Editor-in-chief of the *International Journal on Smart Sensing and Intelligent Systems* (www.s2is.org). He is in the technical programme committee of IEEE Sensors conference, IEEE IMTC conference and numerous other conferences. He was the Technical Programme Chair of ICARA 2004, ICARA 2006, and ICARA 2009. He was the General chair/co-chair of ICST 2005, ICST 2007, IEEE ROSE 2007, IEEE EPSA 2008, ICST 2008, IEEE Sensors 2008, ICST 2010, and IEEE Sensors 2010. He has organized the IEEE Sensors conference 2009 at Christchurch, New Zealand during October 25 to 28, 2009 as General Chair. He is the Chair of the IEEE Instrumentation and Measurement Society New Zealand Chapter.

Bernd Neumann studied Electrical Engineering at Darmstadt/FRG (Diploma 1967) and Information Theory at MIT/USA (M.S. 1968, Ph.D. 1971). Since 1982, he is Professor at the Department of Computer Science at the University of Hamburg. He leads a research group working on problems in image understanding and knowledge-based systems. He is also the chairman of the Hamburg Informatics Technology Center (HITeC e.V.) which carries out application-oriented projects with industrial partners. His scholarly work includes contributions to several AI subfields including high-level image interpretation, configuration, and diagnosis. He was the programme chairman of the 10th European Conference on Artificial Intelligence ECAI-92 and other major conferences, and is active in several national and international AI affiliations.

Neuza Nunes has a Master degree in Biomedical Engineering in which she developed a thesis on algorithms for time series clustering under the supervision of Professor Hugo Gamboa. She is now a Software Researcher and Developer in the R&D department of PLUX – Wireless Biosignals S.A.

Francesca Odella is Researcher and Assistant Professor at the University of Trento, Department of Sociology and Social Research. She graduated in Sociology of Work and Organization, as junior member of an international project on organizational perception of risk (Daimler Benz Foundation, 1998), and obtained her PhD in Economic Sociology in 2001. After the PhD, she was awarded a Post-Doctoral grant at the Department of Sociology and Social Research at the University of Trento, where, since 2006, she has been working as Assistant Professor in Methodology of the Social Sciences. She had been involved in national and international research projects in the socio-economic areas (social capital, local development) and working in international projects concerning social and organizational impact of advanced and pervasive communication technologies (Discreet European Project on Pervasive Technologies, 2006; Foundation Bruno Kessler project SoNET, 2009, Smart project on E-Inclusion in EU, 2008).

Georgios Paliouras is a Senior Researcher and Head of the Intelligent Information Systems division of the Institute of Informatics and Telecommunications at NCSR "Demokritos." He holds a PhD from the University of Manchester, UK, in Machine Learning for Event Recognition. He has a long research record in artificial intelligence. His research focuses on machine learning and knowledge discovery for ontology learning, user modeling, event recognition, information extraction, and text classification. He has served as board member in national and international AI societies. He is also serving on the editorial board of international journals and has chaired international conferences in the area of AI.

Luís Moniz Pereira, born 1947 in Lisbon, is Professor Emeritus of Computer Science, and Director of CENTRIA, the AI centre at Universidade Nova de Lisboa (1993-2008). Doctor *honoris causa* by T.U. Dresden (2006), elected ECCAI Fellow (2001), he launched the *Erasmus Mundus* European MSc in Computational Logic at UNL (2004-2008), and belongs to the Board of Trustees and Scientific Advisory Board of IMDEA–Madrid Advanced Studies Institute (Software). He was founding president of the Portuguese AI association, and founding member of the editorial boards of: *Journal of Logic Programming, Journal of Automated Reasoning, New Generation Computing, Theory and Practice of Logic Programming, Journal of Universal Computer Science, Journal of Applied Logic, Electronic Transactions on AI, Computational Logic Newsletter, International Journal of Reasoning-Based Intelligent Systems* (Advisory-Editor), and presently Associate Editor for *Artificial Intelligence of the ACM Computing Surveys*. His research centres on Knowledge Representation and Reasoning, Logic Programming, and Cognitive Sciences.

Diliana Santos is a finalist student of the Master's Degree in Biomedical Engineering from Faculdade de Ciências e Tecnologia (FCT) performing thesis on "Automatic Classification of Sports Biosignals" under Professor Hugo Gamboa's guiding.

Ute Schmid holds a diploma in Psychology and a diploma in Computer Science, both from Technical University Berlin (TUB), Germany. She received her Doctoral degree in Computer Science from TUB in 1994 and her Habilitation in Computer Science in 2002. From 1994 to 2001, she was Assistant Professor at the AI/Machine Learning group, Department of Computer Science, TUB. Afterwards she worked as Lecturer at the Department of Mathematics and Computer Science at University Osnabrück. Since 2004, she holds a Professorship of Applied Computer Science/Cognitive Systems at the University of Bamberg. Her research interests are mainly in the domain of high-level learning on structural data, especially inductive programming, knowledge level learning from planning, learning structural prototypes, analogical problem solving and learning. Further research is on various applications of machine learning (e.g., classifier learning from medical data and for facial expressions), and empirical and experimental work on high-level cognitive processes and usability evaluation.

Marek Sergot is Professor of Computational Logic in the Department of Computing, Imperial College, London, and Head of the Logic and Artificial Intelligence section. He graduated in Mathematics at the University of Cambridge and then worked in mathematical modelling before joining the Logic Programming Group at Imperial College in 1979. His research is in logic for knowledge representation and the specification of computer systems, with particular interests in legal, temporal, and normative reasoning, and the logic of action. He also has some research interests in Bioinformatics. He is the developer, with Peter Hammond, of the logic programming system APES which was widely used in the 1980s to build a variety of expert systems and other applications. With Robert Kowalski, he developed the `event calculus', an approach for reasoning about action and change within a logic programming framework which is still one of the main standard techniques for temporal reasoning in AI. Recent work on action languages and temporal reasoning has focused on combining representation formalisms from AI with model checking techniques used in Software Engineering, and on logics of agency and collective action.

Weihua Sheng (IEEE senior member) received his Ph.D degree in Electrical and Computer Engineering from Michigan State University in May 2002. He obtained his M.S and B.S. degrees in Electrical Engineering from Zhejiang University, China in 1997 and 1994, respectively. During 1997-1998, he was a research engineer at the R&D center in Huawei Technologies Co., China. During 2002-2006, he taught in the Electrical and Computer Engineering Department at Kettering University (formerly General Motor Institute). He was promoted to associate professor there before he joined Oklahoma State University. He has participated in organizing several IEEE international conferences and workshops in the area of intelligent robots and systems. Five of his papers won the Best Paper awards and one won the Best Student Paper award in international conferences. He is the author of one US patent and more than 120 papers in major journals and international conferences in the area of robotics and automation. His current research interests include wearable computing, mobile robotics, and intelligent transportation systems. His research is supported by NSF, DoD, DEPSCoR, DoT, etc. Dr. Sheng is currently an Associate Editor for IEEE Transactions on Automation Science and Engineering.

Gita Sukthankar is an Assistant Professor and Charles N. Millican Faculty Fellow in the Department of Electrical Engineering and Computer Science at the University of Central Florida, and an Affiliate Faculty Member at UCF's Institute for Simulation and Training. She received her Ph.D. from the Robotics Institute at Carnegie Mellon, an M.S.in Robotics, and an A.B. in Psychology from Princeton University. From 2000-2003, she worked as a researcher at Compaq Research/HP Labs (CRL) in the handheld computing group. In 2009, Dr. Sukthankar was selected for an Air Force Young Investigator Award, the DARPA Computer Science Study Panel, and an NSF CAREER award. She directs the Intelligent Agents Lab; her research is in the area of multi-agent systems and machine learning.

YingLi Tian received her BS and MS from TianJin University, China in 1987 and 1990 and her PhD from the Chinese University of Hong Kong, Hong Kong, in 1996. After holding a faculty position at National Laboratory of Pattern Recognition, Chinese Academy of Sciences, Beijing, she joined Carnegie Mellon University in 1998, where she was a Postdoctoral Fellow at the Robotics Institute. Then she worked as a research staff member in IBM T. J. Watson Research Center from 2001 to 2008. She is one of the inventors of the IBM Smart Surveillance Solutions. She received the IBM Invention Achievement Awards every year from 2002 to 2007, and the IBM Outstanding Innovation Achievement Award in 2007. She is currently an associate professor in Department of Electrical Engineering at the City College of New York from 2008. Her current research focuses on a wide range of computer vision problems from motion detection and analysis, human identification, to facial expression analysis, video surveillance, and computer vision applications to assist people with special needs. She is a senior member of IEEE and serves as an Associate Editor of the *Computer Vision and Image Processing*.

Xi Wang received her Bachelor's degree in Electronic Information Engineering from Xi'An University of Technology (XAUT) in 2007. She received her Master's degree in Electrical Engineering from University of Central Florida in 2010. Currently Xi is a PhD student in Electrical Engineering in the Intelligent Agents Lab, at University of Central Florida. Her research interests include classification in networked data, machine learning, and pattern recognition.

Mark Frederick Wernsdorfer, while exploring some problems of the philosophy of the mind during the courses he undertook in his Magister's degree, noticed some strong connections between computer sciences and philosophy. Especially the relevance of Heidegger's existentialist concept of "being-in-the-world" for the failing of representationalist approaches to explaining the mind influenced his further studies heavily. Therefore, he decided to extend his ongoing studies in Philosophy with a BA in Computer Science. In Philosophy, he graduated on self-awareness as logical antinomy for representationalism. In Computer Sciences, he cooperated with a graduated psychologist on the possibility and problems of explicating acquired knowledge.

Zhengyou Zhang received the B.S. degree in Electronic Engineering from Zhejiang University, Hangzhou, China, in 1985, the M.S. degree in Computer Science from the University of Nancy, Nancy, France, in 1987, and the Ph.D. degree in Computer Science and the Doctorate of Science (*Habilitation à diriger des recherches*) from the University of Paris XI, Paris, France, in 1990 and 1994, respectively. He is a Principal Researcher with Microsoft Research, Redmond, WA, USA, and the Research Manager of the Multimedia, Interaction, and Communication group. Before joining Microsoft Research in March

1998, he was with INRIA (French National Institute for Research in Computer Science and Control), France, for 11 years and was a Senior Research Scientist from 1991. In 1996-1997, he spent a one-year sabbatical as an Invited Researcher with the Advanced Telecommunications Research Institute International (ATR), Kyoto, Japan. He has published over 200 papers in refereed international journals and conferences, and has coauthored the following books: *3-D Dynamic Scene Analysis: A Stereo Based Approach* (Springer-Verlag, 1992); *Epipolar Geometry in Stereo, Motion and Object Recognition* (Kluwer, 1996); *Computer Vision* (Chinese Academy of Sciences, 1998, 2003, in Chinese); *Face Detection and Adaptation* (Morgan and Claypool, 2010), and *Face Geometry and Appearance Modeling* (Cambridge University Press, 2011). He has given a number of keynotes in international conferences. Dr. Zhang is a Fellow of the Institute of Electrical and Electronic Engineers (IEEE), the Founding Editor-in-Chief of the *IEEE Transactions on Autonomous Mental Development*, an Associate Editor of the *International Journal of Computer Vision*, and an Associate Editor of *Machine Vision and Applications*. He served as Associate Editor of the *IEEE Transactions on Pattern Analysis and Machine Intelligence* from 2000 to 2004, an Associate Editor of the *IEEE Transactions on Multimedia* from 2004 to 2009, among others. He has been on the program committees for numerous international conferences in the areas of autonomous mental development, computer vision, signal processing, multimedia, and human-computer interaction. He served as a Program Co-Chair of the International Conference on Multimedia and Expo (ICME), July 2010, a Program Co-Chair of the ACM International Conference on Multimedia (ACM MM), October 2010, a Program Co-Chair of the ACM International Conference on Multimodal Interfaces (ICMI), November 2010, and a General Co-Chair of the IEEE International Workshop on Multimedia Signal Processing (MMSP), October 2011.

Liyue Zhao received a Bachelor's degree in Automation from University of Science and Technology of China (USTC) in 2006 and a Master's degree in Computer Science from the University of Central Florida in 2011. He is currently a PhD student in the Intelligent Agents Lab, Department of Electrical Engineering, and Computer Science at University of Central Florida. His research interests include machine learning, pattern recognition, and data mining.

Chun Zhu (IEEE member) received her Ph.D. degree in Electrical and Computer Engineer-ing from Oklahoma State University, USA. She obtained her Master's and Bachelor's degrees in Electrical Engineering from Tsinghua University, China. Her research interests include machine learning for recognizing and understanding human daily activity patterns, real-time measurement and analysis, embedded system application design, and human-robot interaction using wearable computing. She is now a Software Developer at Microsoft Bing Division.

Index

O

Open List 120

P

Pan-Tilt-Zoom (PTZ) 40

pedestrian navigation 157-161, 166, 168, 170-173, 320

pervasive technology 227

Piecewise Aggregate Approximation (PAA) 290, 294

piezoelectric effect 135

pool-based sampling 284

PowerLine Positioning (PLP) 67

Principal Component Analysis (PCA) 286, 290

privacy 112-113, 128, 235, 239, 247

probabilistic logic (P-log) 180

Proximity Infrared (PIR) 136

R

Radio Frequency Identification (RFID) 136

Rule Markup Language (RuleML) 38

S

scene interpretation 33-40, 43-46, 49, 51, 57, 61-63

SCENe Interpretation with Ontology-based Rules (SCENIOR) 37

selective sampling 284, 300

Self-Organising Map (SOM) 92, 102, 104

Semantic Web Rule Language (SWRL) 37-38

sensor events 67-68, 72-73, 88, 117, 124, 272-273

sensor event visualizer 68

sensorimotor interaction 271

Sequence Abstraction Networks (SAN) 268

simple action 18

simple sensory system 270

smart apartment 68

smart home 67-69, 78, 82-83, 110-112, 127, 132, 155

social network analysis (SNA) 226, 234

sociology 225

sociometry 233-234, 245

Spatiotemporal Interest Point (STIP) 249, 251, 253

specialization rule 46-47

Statistical Process Control (SPC) 77

submodel hypothesis 44-46, 50

Support Vector Machine (SVM) 72, 283, 303

synthetic signal 218

T

technosynchronicity 230

Tekscan FlexiForce Sensor 145

telecare services 232

template 18

temporal constraint system (TCN) 38, 43

Time Distance 25-27

time relations 25-27

token 90

tracking system 111-112, 128

transformation 16-18, 20, 30

trolley problem suite 198

U

ubiquitous computing 32, 63, 66, 84, 108-110, 128-129, 155, 159-160, 165, 168, 171-172, 213, 244

unsupervised learning 88-90, 92, 98, 100, 102, 104-107, 110, 266

Upper Model 38-40

V

video biometrics 112

video codeword 252

video surveillance 2, 10, 237-239, 246, 282

vision-based activity recognition 167, 305, 320

Viterbi Algorithm 304, 308, 310, 312-314, 316-317, 319

V-mask 77-78

Voronoi cells 271

W

wayfinding 158, 171, 173, 243

wearable sensor-based activity recognition 305-306, 308, 313

web mining 91-92, 108

web ontology language 36-37

Workflow Mining 24-25